FRANK
SINATRA

AN AMERICAN LEGEND

FRANK SINATRA

AN AMERICAN LEGEND

BY NANCY SINATRA

Publisher: W. Quay Hays
Editor: Peter Hoffman
Art Director: Susan Anson
Contributing Editor: Murray Fisher
Production Director: Nadeen Torio
Color and Pre-press Director: Gaston Moraga
Copy Editors: Dianne Woo, Carolyn Wendt, Colby Allerton
Production Assistants: Tom Archibeque, Dave Chadderdon, Bill Neary
Discographical Research: Will Friedwald, Chuck Granata, Ric Ross and Eliot Scott

The Publisher wishes to especially thank Charlie Raab and Frank Military, without whom this book would not exist. Also, sincere thanks for their generous help goes to Nancy Sinatra Sr., Tina Sinatra, Frank Sinatra Jr., Barbara Sinatra, Amanda Lambert, A.J. Lambert, Robert Finkelstein, Chuck Granata, Ellen Alperstein, Ann Fisher and Pamela Leven. Most of all, the publisher is forever indebted to Francis Albert Sinatra for living such an inspiring life and sharing it with the world.

This special edition published by Reader's Digest Association, Inc., Pleasantville, NY

Library of Congress Cataloging-in-Publication Data:

Sinatra, Nancy.
    Frank Sinatra : an American legend / by Nancy Sinatra.
        p.   cm.
    Includes index.
    Discography:
    Filmography:
    ISBN 0-7621-0134-2
    1. Sinatra, Frank, 1915-   --Chronology. I. Title.
ML420.S565S63   1998b
782.42164'092--dc21
                                                            98-37800
                                                            CIP
                                                            MN

Printed in the USA
10 9 8 7 6 5 4 3 2 1

CONTENTS

THANKS TO YOU

There is no way I can thank Peter Hoffman enough. He deserves most of the credit for this book. He devoted almost four months of his life to me with tireless energy. He kept up with my constant attempts to tell the truth and make things right, taking my requests to the other members of the editorial team. He fought battles for me. He was astounded by the amount of negative material he saw in the preliminary research. It was an overwhelming case against my father and it would have been easy for him, as it was for other people, to accept it as fact. It was my job to show Peter the other side of the story. As I began to reveal the real Frank Sinatra to him, he became a champion of my father's civil rights. I grew to respect Peter. He is an extremely talented writer and editor and, I'm proud to say, a good friend. My thanks to you, Peter, and to all the talented and generous people listed below, who gave us wings…

General Publishing Group
Publisher: Quay Hays. This book is a result of his vision.
Editor: Peter Hoffman. He took Quay's vision and made it a book.
Art Director: Susan Anson
Contributing Editor: Murray Fisher
Publicist: Sharon Hays
Sales and Marketing: Brian Hays, Rachelle Whetmore, Julianne Nachtrab
Production Director: Nadeen Torio
Color and Pre-press Director: Gaston Moraga
Production Assistants: Catherine Bailey, Michael Lira, Brad Slepack, Tom Archibeque, Alan Peak
Researcher: Marvin Wolf
Assistant to the Publisher: Dana Stibor
Copy Editors: Dianne Woo, Carolyn Wendt, Colby Allerton
Intern: Vanessa Osborne

*Though some were only echoes or whispers that softly guided my thoughts,
I am eternally grateful to all of the voices in this book.*

Family, Friends, Assistants

Eleanor Roth Grasso	Deborah Paull	Barbara Sinatra	*Extra special thanks*
Brad Benedict	Bill Moynihan	Eliot Weisman	Dorothy Uhlemann
Orlando Ramirez	DeDe Merrill	Tony Oppedisano	Frank Military
Bernie Abramson	John Dubuque	Susan Reynolds	Chuck Granata
Rosanne Letterese	Hal Lifson	Lori Thompson	
Ric Ross	Roni Spitzer		
	Chata Hermosilla	Amanda Lambert	
Jack Haley Jr.		A.J. Lambert	
Mark Davis	Sonny Golden	Tina Sinatra	
Tracey Davis	Robert Finkelstein	Frank Sinatra Jr.	
Kelly Brandt		Nancy Sinatra Sr.	

*All the composers, lyricists and musicians
and, of course, Frank Sinatra*

INTRODUCTION

This book represents a forty-year dream. Although Frank Sinatra has to be the most documented entertainer in history—there is no end of information available on him—no one, including the best biographer, could possibly tell the whole story of his life. It is too great in scope. To tell this tale as my father lives his life is simply not possible. I am still amazed at what he is able to accomplish on any given day.

With the feeling that no book has been able to present a true portrait of my father, I have been working, on and off, for twenty years, collecting memories, letters, photographs, and above all, talking with him and those close to him in order to capture as much as I can of his incredible life. The results, which you hold in your hands, have been enlightening, frustrating, rapturous, surprising and ultimately satisfying.

The process itself was challenging. Just as outside sources are unable to agree on the exact nature of the events in his life, so even among family and friends and business associates, there has been conflict over dates, names, places and what actually took place. When possible I have used double and triple sources to corroborate stories, and sometimes I have given the edge to eyewitnesses other than Sinatra. Rest assured, the people who were there and the man himself are the main sources for this book.

I have wanted to answer the untruths and false charges against Frank Sinatra almost all of my life. These allegations have been going on for most of that time. Often what began as an accusation or rumor—and what was printed and reprinted and broadcast as speculation and conjecture—would end up reported as fact. My job was to separate the true facts from the false facts.

My father is the first to point out that he has received a square deal from most of the Fourth Estate throughout his life, but there have been a handful of irresponsible journalists who, because of their own self-serving agendas, chose to use him (and abuse him) as a tool, a scapegoat. They made him guilty by association, and this is a very dangerous practice. Unfortunately they were able to, and did, use and hide behind our beloved First Amendment. One writer actually waged a campaign to discredit Sinatra with the help of the FBI, and we have the FBI files to prove it. When the *New York Times* versus Sullivan precedent was set in the mid 1960s, it sealed the fate of people who had chosen and will choose a life in the public view. I learned at an early age to be very careful about believing everything that appears in print.

The Sinatra I know is a patriarch, a friend, a patriot, a musician, a businessman, a saloon singer and much more. He is a man with a public image built partly on fact but mostly on myth. He is a man who embraces consistency yet embodies contradiction. A man who treats the room to caviar and champagne and himself to a sandwich and a Coke. A man who is strong in a crisis and dissolves behind closed doors when it ends. Who likes to be alone as long as he knows someone is near. Who is publicly the quintessential swinger and privately old-fashioned, uncomfortable with "living together," secure with marriage.

To some Frank Sinatra epitomizes a Dead End kid never grown up, yet to others he evokes elegance and gentility. He is a perfectionist who is impatient with the process of perfecting. A compassionate friend and a fierce foe. A musical genius who doesn't really read music. A maverick who lives by rigid codes. A winner who feels connected to losers. The complexities run deep.

"…The nightingale pierces his bosom with a thorn when he sings his song…"

The music of Frank Sinatra sings our joys, our sorrows and our silences. He sings of love and loneliness, of exultant life and of still, small hours of sadness, and in some very profound way the Holy Spirit moves and abides in him, I think. He sings as he operates, with spirit not fear; with energy not ennui. In his soul, way down deep, is a force that motivates him, guides him and separates him from himself, making him and his work bigger than his life. It is this force that enables him to find a measure of eternity before his body tires of the journey.

Sinatra has received much. This is, in part, because he has given much. And also because he has driven so hard, so far and so fast. He is a little crazy because, as it is said, "The overly concerned and sincere drive themselves crazy." He has been driven by ambition, by ego, by inextinguishable talent and by gentleness, a force that can be almost violent, a love that is surpassing.

He is timely and timeless. His passions are greater and so is his pain. Seeing him hurt is devastating for me because he suffers as violently as he loves. Outside the grin remains, the sudden flash of that keyboard smile. The façade. The jokes.

As I attempt to put feelings on paper, the words don't seem quite right. They seem so inadequate. If we cannot, in the end, understand him, perhaps he is a phenomenon of life, a force of nature to be respected more than understood.

If I could have one wish, it would be that you the reader accept the information here as the truth. I know this is not necessarily what will happen; as Pop said just last week, "You can't force people to believe what they don't want to believe, no matter what you say or how hard you try."

My father and I are still as close as can be, and yet we have lived our lives in the relentless presence of the end of things. It is said that the way to love anyone is to realize he could be lost to you. That is a painful way to love but it is how I love my father. When he is gone, when it is "done and done," I'll still carry his blood in my veins, his life's music in my heart and see his immortal soul in the bright, loving eyes of my children.

Nancy Sinatra
July 20, 1995

For Mom and Dad

Chicken—a thought,

Strange, but I feel the world we live in demands that we be turned out in a pattern which resembles, in fact, is, a facsimile of itself, and those of us who roll with the punches, who grin, who dare to wear foolish clown faces, who defy the system—well, we do it, and bully for us!

Of course, there are those who do not. And the reason I think is that (and I say this with some sadness) those uptight, locked-in people who resent and despise us, who fear us and are bewildered by us, will one day come to realize that we possess rare and magical secrets. And more—love.

Therefore, I am beginning to think that a few (I hope many) are wondering if maybe there might be value to a firefly, or an instant-long Roman candle.

Keep the faith,

Dad

1915-1939

ALL OR NOTHING AT ALL

Born and brought up in Agrigento, Sicily, my great-grandparents John and Rosa Sinatra were married young. Soon after the birth of their son Anthony Martin, they took a long look at their prospects among the hardscrabble grape growers of rural Catania and decided to take their chances in America. Joining waves of landless immigrants who were leaving their homelands in Italy, Ireland and Germany around the turn of the century, they sailed to New York and settled among the other urban poor in a working-class neighborhood of Hoboken, New Jersey—the American Liverpool—a grimy one-square-mile industrial port across the Hudson River from the spires of lower Manhattan. John got a job as a boilermaker and then worked at the American Pencil Company for eleven dollars a week. He inhaled the dust there for 17 years until his lungs gave out, but he was never able to do any better because there was nobody to teach him English. Rosa opened a little grocery store, and young "Marty"—who could neither read nor write—found work as an apprentice in a cobbler's shop to help pay the bills.

Eventually, he took up prizefighting. He fought under the name "Marty O'Brien" because, in a town of ethnic tensions controlled by the Irish politicians, it was better to have an Irish name than an Italian one. He also did some extra work in the very early movies and labored as a boilermaker in a shipyard. As a kid, Marty had met and fallen for Natalie Catherine "Dolly" Garavente, the daughter of a well-educated lithographer who had emigrated with his family from Genoa. Because of class differences, her parents opposed the romance, but my grandmother was a determined, strong-minded girl who did what she wanted to do. One night, she disguised herself as a boy—women were barred from prizefights in those days—and sneaked out of the house with her brother Dominic (Champ), who was to fight her boyfriend Marty in the ring. There was no limit to the rounds back then—you fought until somebody dropped. In that particular match-up, Marty and Champ seemed to fight forever. Nobody fell down. And until the day my grandfather died, they argued over who had won that night.

When Dolly announced her intention to marry Marty, her family refused to host a wedding, so the couple eloped. They were married at City Hall in Jersey City on Valentine's Day, 1913. Only later, when their families acquiesced, did they have a second ceremony. They set up housekeeping in a four-story, eight-family tenement at 415 Monroe Street in the heart of Hoboken and began their life together. Even though they were complete opposites—Marty was quiet and gentle, Dolly was aggressive and outgoing—it was to be a long and happy marriage. And nearly three years later, in their bedroom at home, their first and only child was born.

Marty and Dolly at their second wedding ceremony, which was attended by both families.

Frank: "My mother had the photographer take this picture from the right because the wounds on the other side of my face and neck were still healing."

DECEMBER 12, 1915: My father almost died the day he was born. The doctor had trouble getting the huge 13½-pound baby out of his tiny mother, a woman less than five feet tall. Using forceps, the doctor tugged away, ripping and scarring the baby's ear, cheek and neck, and puncturing his eardrum. But the baby wasn't breathing, so his grandmother Rose, an experienced midwife, grabbed him from the doctor and held him under cold running water until he gasped his first breath and cried out. Francis Albert Sinatra entered the world fighting for his life—and he won.

APRIL 2, 1916: Three and a half months later, after his birth wounds had healed, little Frank was finally baptized at Hoboken's St. Francis Church. The baby was named for his godfather, Frank Garrick, a politically well connected Irish newspaperman who was one of Marty's closest friends and his teammate on an amateur baseball club.

In his parents' cold-water flat that day, that experience, I believe, became a prevailing influence, a deeply personal tie to that invisible margin between being alive—or not. The new baby, in unthinkable pain, disconnected suddenly from his mother, desperate for breath. The struggle of the infant would shape the character and conduct of the boy and remain a motivating force in the man. Perhaps in those few moments lie some of the forces behind the impatience, the steamroller ambition, his exhausting pace, his extravagant style.

1917-21: My grandfather was too old to join the American forces setting sail for France to fight in World War I, so he scratched out a living between prize-fights as a dock laborer and running a bar. But most of his working years were with the Hoboken Fire Department, where he was always first to arrive at a fire. He also did the cooking at the firehouse. As quiet and reserved as he was, he was also known for his wicked sense of humor. The owner of a saloon owed Grandpa money for a long time. Finally, instead of giving him the money, the man tried to pay him off with a horse. A horse not in the best of health. Dying, in fact. He delivered the horse to Grandpa and took off, leaving the animal to die. Later, in the dark, Marty walked the horse to the guy's saloon. He put the horse in the doorway and shot it. By the time the saloonkeeper arrived to open up, rigor mortis had set in. Business was off for a while, with a stiff horse blocking the doorway.

When Frankie was three, Dolly had a dream job. She worked as a chocolate dipper, covering the candies with chocolate and decorating them with identifying letters: V for vanilla cream and M for maple. "I remember my first visit to the candy store. She had a bucket of ice water and a vat of hot, fudgy chocolate," he recalled. "She dunked her hand in the icy water and then the hot chocolate, which stuck to her fingers. She then wrote the correct letter with the drippings from her fingertips. She gave me three pieces of chocolate. It was wonderful."

1921-26: From when Frankie was six to twelve, his parents were so consumed with work that their only child spent much of his time either by himself or in the care of his grandmother Rose, his aunt Mary or Dolly's sister Rosalie. Dolly worked at various jobs including midwifery. Later, she became a commit-

Frank Who?

Frank Sinatra's birth certificate, filed five days after his birth, was filled out by a non-Italian clerk who not only recorded both family names incorrectly—as "Sinestro" and "Garaventi"—but listed Marty's country of birth as USA, not Italy. Ironically, when he and Dolly got around to correcting that misinformation 23 years later—changing the first name to Francis, and adding the middle initial "A" for Albert—the recording clerk again misspelled the name, this time as "Sinastre." It was the last time anyone would fail to recognize the name of Francis Albert Sinatra.

It seems clear that Dolly was not a lady to be trifled with. When she heard that Marty's sisters had made up a story about her having another boyfriend, she confronted them in their grocery store, knocking over olive barrels and pulling cans off the counter.

teewoman for the Democratic party and, as she developed political clout, her personality grew even more domineering. She once even planned to run for mayor of Hoboken, prompting Grandpa to pull Dad aside and say, "Listen, you've got to do something. Stop her. She's impossible to live with now." But her influence helped Grandpa become a captain in the Fire Department, and her additional income allowed them to move from the tenement house to an apartment on Hoboken's Park Avenue in a better part of town. Still, Dad grew up a loner, often finding nothing to eat when he came home from school, not because they didn't have money, but because his mother was always off doing something else. "Aunt Dolly was always busy and I think Frankie was always underfoot a bit," recalled cousin John Tredy. "We used to go around the firehouse to see Frankie's father, and he'd throw us a nickel or dime. They didn't have too much time for Frankie. He was always alone. He was warm, he wanted friendship. And that's why he always came around to our different homes. Frankie was a really soft kind of boy. You know, like his father, Marty. Marty was a pussycat, a real nice guy. He used to talk loud and rough, but he had a heart of gold. Frank's got a lot of character like his mother. And he's got the other side like his father. When he was little, Frankie was the quietest boy of everybody. He and I used to sit in the corner and listen to the grown-ups. We never interfered." Not long after my first child was born—my daughter A.J.—Dad told me, "I hope you'll consider having another baby. It was very lonely for me. Very lonely."

1926: Little Frankie got small scars on his face that came as a result of his walking home through the "wrong" neighborhood: A kid went into an ethnically dif-

FRANK
ON HIS MOTHER:

My mother was a devout Democrat. To tease her, my father and I would drop the word Republican. And she wouldn't cook. Fortunately, my father was a great cook, so we would eat. She was the force!

FRANK
ON A FORMAL WETTING:

One of my father's sisters, Dora, was married in an elaborate church event—a monsignor, a priest, a High Mass. I was the ring boy. The ceremony was long…very long…and I kept signaling my mother. But she wouldn't pay attention. So I wet my pants there at the altar.

My dad, seen here in his first Holy Communion portrait, did not always like what he heard when the grown-ups were talking. As a boy his passion for what came to be known as civil rights was triggered, he told me, by name-calling; kids in his neighborhood "calling each other ethnic names: nigger, wop, kike, sheenie, dago and all that kind of stuff. Something rubbed me the wrong way."

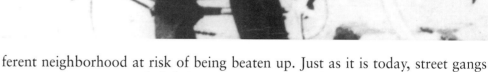

Above: Marty, Frank's father, displaying the injuries he received as a Hoboken fireman. Right: Frank, sporting the T-shirt of his street gang, the Turks. Just like they do today, street gangs protected their territory.

ferent neighborhood at risk of being beaten up. Just as it is today, street gangs guarded their turf. At one point, the neighborhood kids were calling him "Scarface" because of the scars from his birth injury. "Mom kept physically fit chasing me and whacking me around now and then. But my mother wasn't tough; the neighborhood was tough," he recalled. "She wanted me to be safe, to be a gentleman. She would have had me wear velvet pants, I think, except that, when we lived on Monroe Street, I would have gotten killed. The funny thing about the Park Avenue neighborhood was that the guys there were worse than the guys downtown. They were brighter, more insidious; well mannered, with good clothes—and deadly."

1928: At David E. Rue Junior High School, Frank, the budding performer, annoyed his teachers by doing imitations of popular movie stars and radio comics. Not much of a student, he was popular with the other kids.

1930: As a student at A.J. Demarest High School, he tried out his voice and people responded. He liked the feeling and the applause.

1931: His high school years were not very productive. "To my crowd," he recalled, "school was very uninteresting, and homework was something we never bothered with. The few times we attended class, we were rowdy. So it isn't surprising that a bunch of us were expelled." Cousin John Tredy remembered: "He played hooky for a whole year before Aunt Dolly ever knew that he was out of school." Fed up with school anyway, he left Demarest in his senior year, and his formal education ended with a semester at the Drake Business School to satisfy state minimum educational requirements for children under 16. My grandmother was crushed. She had had her heart set on seeing her son become the family's first college graduate—and she threw up her hands when he said he'd like to try his luck as a singer. But, finally she resigned herself: "If he wants to go into music, that's where he should go." "At one point," he remembers, "I said I wanted to

The first, and only, diploma Frank Sinatra would ever receive. He never graduated from high school. He later recalled: "There are things I think I would have done if I had a chance again. I would have been a little more patient about getting out into the world, had more formal education."

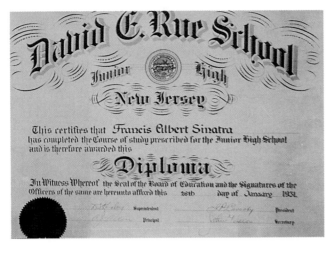

be an engineer, to go to Stevens Institute in Hoboken, number two after MIT when I was a boy—a great school—because I love the idea of bridges, tunnels and highways. It was my great desire until I got mixed up in vocalizing." Marty, who never said much in the best of times, finally spoke up: "Do you want to get a regular job? Or do you wanna be a bum?" It was OK to leave school, Marty said, but Frank had to get a real job—no music business.

I love this picture of my father. I can see why my mother fell in love with him.

1932: It was time for the Sinatras to move up in the world again, and they left their Park Avenue apartment for a house they couldn't really afford at 841 Garden Street, a roomy place with three stories, four bedrooms and a real dining room. Frank even had his own room on the top floor. It was Dolly's showplace, with a gold birdbath outside the front door, a baby grand piano in the living room and a gold-and-white French telephone on a pedestal in her bedroom. As my mother later recalled, "It was lovely, beautifully furnished, beautifully kept. Always."

EARLY 1932: One of Dad's uncles got him a job in the Teijent and Lang shipyards. For three days, he caught white-hot rivets hanging over a four-story shaft until he swayed a little too far out and a rivet came down, barely missing his shoulder. It crashed at the bottom of the shaft. "It scared me so much I couldn't handle it. I had acrophobia and didn't know it. And I was hanging on to that rope and that burning hot rivet went by me like a bullet, singeing my shoulder. I got a different job." He began unloading crates of books for Lyons and Carnahan on 16th Street in New York City. The repetitiveness of that job got the better of Frank and one day he said to his co-worker, "You know, this job is stupid." He insisted there were better jobs. And he got one back on the ships, working for the United Fruit Lines. He had to crawl inside and unscrew tubes in the condenser units so they could be pulled out and cleaned. Then he'd screw them back in again. It was winter and there was ice on the water, and the snowflakes were as big as quarters. Some of the work was on the night shift. "We were so cold that we would sneak around to the big coffeepot for some hot coffee to get warm. We got caught once by the guy above us. He had a Southern accent and he said to the snapper, or foreman, 'Ah don't lak what's goin' on around heah with you an' those dagos.' And, whack, the foreman knocked him right in the river. Somebody dragged the guy out and defrosted him." When he quit the docks again, my exasperated grandfather finally threw him out of the house, and he was forced to take a room in New York. "I remember the moment. We were having breakfast. I was supposed to get up that morning and

Prohibition and Racketeering Come to Hoboken

In 1917, when American troops began arriving to board ships bound for France in World War I, President Woodrow Wilson closed hundreds of waterfront bars, bringing Prohibition to Hoboken years before it came to the rest of the country. But local authorities refused to enforce the laws against tavernkeepers, and northern New Jersey became an unofficial sanctuary for the leaders of New York's Prohibition-era rackets. The Sinatras, like virtually everyone in their community, had little choice but to rub elbows with the enterprising uomini respettati—Men of Respect—who imported, manufactured or distributed alcoholic beverages—and defended their territories any way they could. Among them was Sicilian-born "Waxey Gordon," boss of the territory in which Dolly and Marty lived. In a turf war, a small-time hood was once shot down in front of Dolly's sister Josie Monaco's Hoboken home.

FRANK

ON BEING HONEST:

You find that there are just as many angles to figure in being honest as there are in being crooked. If what you do is honest and you make it, you're a hero. If what you do is crooked and you make it, you're a bum. Me—I grabbed a song.

Most of 19-year-old Frank's time was spent pursuing an elusive goal—making it as a popular singer.

look for a job because I had decided that I didn't want to go to college. And he wanted me to go to college in the worst way. He was a man who could never read or write his name and his big point was education. He got a little fed up with me because I just wasn't going out looking for work. And on this particular morning he said to me, 'Why don't you just get out of the house and go out on your own?' My mother was nearly in tears, but we agreed that it may be a good thing. And then I packed up a small case and I came to New York." Discouraged by his inability to find steady work, he soon returned home.

LATE 1932: It was the Great Depression, and millions of Americans were out of work. Through family connections, my father had jobs available to him, but he just didn't seem to be cut out for manual labor. Gradually the idea came to Frank that he might want to sing for a living. He made money wherever he could, at whatever jobs he could get, but singing remained his central passion, even if it had to be relegated to the periphery of his day. "At night I was working with little combinations, singing with the bands," he recalled. "I was making nothing, but it was a great experience. I was using a megaphone like Rudy Vallee, and guys would throw pennies and try to get them into my mouth. But I used to move a great deal so they couldn't hit it. It was great fun." He borrowed $65 from his parents and purchased a portable sound system in a rhinestone-studded case along with sheet music arrangements. This gave him a distinct edge over other vocalists competing for one-nighters with local bands. He sang at nightclubs, roadhouses, Democratic Party meetings and gatherings of the Hoboken Sicilian Cultural League, usually on weekends or evenings after his workday was over. Frank worked hard for bookings, and he was developing a style.

SUMMER 1934: At 19, while spending the summer at his aunt Josie's house in Long Branch on the Jersey Shore, my father met my mother, Nancy Rose Barbato, 17, who was vacationing across the road in a big house with her father, Mike (a plastering contractor), his brother Ralph, his sister Kate and their families. Nancy was giving herself a manicure on the front porch when Frank came over with his ukulele and began to serenade her. One thing led to another, and they started going together.

EARLY 1935: Still trying to earn a living, Frank and Nancy's brother, Bart, plastered walls for "The Chief," as they called Grandpa Mike, but their work always had to be redone. According to my mother, though, my father did eventually improve, and her father didn't have to undo it *all*. And Frank was always falling asleep on the job after staying up late the night before on singing gigs. My grandfather wouldn't fire him, and Dad desperately wanted to quit, but Grandpa Mike said, "No job, no Nancy." It had become increasingly obvious that Frank wasn't cut out to be a working stiff—but his music career didn't seem to be going anywhere either. Once he finally quit his job working for Nancy's father, he and Nancy continued to see each other on the sly, and he spent all his spare time singing anywhere he could find an audience—even competing in amateur contests. "I sang at social clubs and at roadhouses," Dad recalled, "sometimes for nothing or for a sandwich or cigarettes—all night for three packs. But I worked on one basic theory: Stay alive, get as much practice as you can."

SUMMER 1935: On a fateful evening together, Frank took Nancy to see his idol Bing Crosby in a performance at Loew's Journal Square, an old vaudeville theater in downtown Jersey City. It was a night that changed his life forever. "I was a big fan of Bing's," he recalled. "He was the first real troubadour that any of us

Seventeen-year-old Nancy Barbato became Frank's first serious girlfriend and was one of the few who believed in his dream.

Frank's Early Heroes: The Crooners

After radio networks were born in the last rush of the Roaring Twenties—NBC in 1927 and CBS the next year—it was possible for a singer to become a star not only in his own hometown but from coast to coast. Among the first were Gene Austin, whose "My Blue Heaven" sold a million phonograph disks, and Will Osborne, who, like Rudy Vallee, crooned through a megaphone. But it wasn't until the early thirties, in the wake of the stock market's jarring crash of 1929, that romantic crooners like Bing Crosby and Russ Columbo— singing with big dance bands—began to seize the American imagination on the low-fidelity radios and Victrolas of that era. Columbo, a former violinist with the looks and sensual presence of a Rudolph Valentino, formed his own band with such jazz-oriented musicians as drummer Gene Krupa. Columbo's untimely death in a shooting accident in 1934 shocked and saddened Sinatra. After Crosby's record 700 performances at New York's Paramount Theatre, and his smash 1933 movie musical The Big Broadcast, *it seemed that everyone in America was humming his hits "Just One More Chance" and "I've Found a Million-Dollar Baby (in a Five-and-Ten Cent Store)." The clean-cut, low-key king of the crooners became Sinatra's personal idol.*

Bing Crosby

Russ Columbo

Nancy Sr.

ON DATING FRANK:

We wound up spending a lot of time together that summer. We walked along the boardwalk and went on the rides. We went to dances at the casino and had picnics at the beach. It was lovely and romantic. Labor Day, everybody goes back to school, and I figured that would be the end of our little summer fling, forgetting that Hoboken is only a few miles away from Jersey City, where I lived. He called me and we continued going out. He would take buses to come to see me. When I was working and he wasn't, I would give him the fare. We would either go out to a show or sit home with my family and listen to opera on their record player. That's when Frank heard Caruso for the first time, and I think that's when he fell in love with opera.

had heard. After seeing him that night, I knew I had to be a singer. But I never wanted to sing like him, because every kid on the block was boo-boo-booing like Crosby. My voice was up higher, and I said, 'That's not for me. I want to be a different kind of singer.'"

SEPTEMBER 8, 1935: Frank Sinatra's first big break came when he and a local trio who called themselves the Three Flashes auditioned separately for an appearance on *Major Bowes and His Original Amateur Hour,* a popular radio show broadcast nationwide on NBC from the stage of the Capitol Theater in New York. "They won and I won," said my father, "and when I was accepted, the old man said, 'They're going to be on the show a week from Sunday. Why don't we put you on together and we'll call it the Hoboken Four.'" The brash 19-year-old declared on the air, "I'm Frank, Major. We're looking for jobs. How about it? Everyone that's ever heard us, liked us. We think we're pretty good." They sang the Mills Brothers song "Shine"—and racked up the biggest vote in the history of the show, with 40,000 people calling in. Bowes was so impressed that he brought them back several weeks in a row.

OCTOBER 1935: Frank appeared with the rest of the Hoboken Four in two movie shorts for Major Bowes: *The Night Club* and *The Big Minstrel Act,* shot at Biograph Studios in the Bronx and later shown briefly at Radio City Music Hall. In the first he played a waiter, in the second a member of a blackface singing troupe.

My father wrote this poem to my mother when he was courting her.

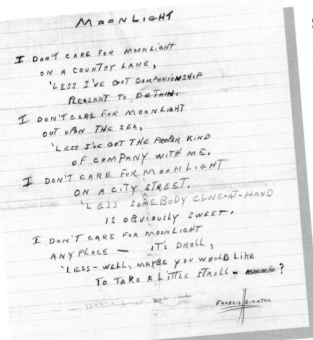

LATE 1935: The Hoboken Four toured the country with one of several Major Bowes amateur companies—performing in front of a full band at local theaters for radio audiences out on the town—at a salary of $50 apiece per week plus meals. Wherever they stayed overnight, a white banner announcing their presence was hung from the hotel: MAJOR BOWES' AMATEURS STOPPING HERE. But of course, they really were no longer amateurs. They began their tour in the West, playing San Francisco and Los Angeles and a succession of smallish, out-of-the-way cities. Frank remembered, "The radio program was such a hit that people wanted to see what we looked like, like animals in a cage. But one of the niceties was that people came backstage with cakes and homemade food, and women would say, 'You must miss your mother's cooking' and all that kind of jazz, and they'd give us food like we were starving. It was sweet."

SPRING 1936: Frank was getting more attention from audiences on the road—particularly from young women—than the other three members of the Hoboken Four. Acting out their petty jealousies, they began to bully their partner. But he stood up to them. Nonetheless, he was lonely for home and after three months elected to leave the tour. "It was the first time I had ever been away from home. I missed my girl and I missed my family. I also felt I was going nowhere. I had auditioned as a solo and now I was part of a quartet, and I was thinking solo."

> ## FRANK
> **ON MUSIC LESSONS:**
> *I could have had piano lessons when I was a kid, but I was too impatient. Sit on a piano stool for an hour every day? Nothing doing! I had time to study then, but I wouldn't. I could kick myself when I remember.*

Nancy Sr.

ON THE NIGHT FRANK DECIDED

TO BECOME A SINGER:

It was a very exciting evening for both of us, but for Frank it was the biggest moment of his life. Bing had always been his hero, and he had listened to all his records, but watching him perform in person seemed to make it all come alive for him. I mean, he loved to sing; he'd sing at parties, he sang for me all the time, and he used to take me along on some of his appearances around town. But I don't think he really believed it, I don't think he believed it would ever really happen for him, until that night. "Someday," he told me on the way home, "that's gonna be me up there."

Major Bowes' Original Amateur Hour

Broadcasting from the stage of New York's Capitol Theater, Major Bowes and His Original Amateur Hour *was a Depression-era phenomenon that capitalized on America's hunger for entertainment. Bowes sifted through legions of aspiring singers and entertainers in tryouts, gonging lame or overlong acts off the stage and singling out the best for his NBC show. "Round and round she goes," the Major would intone, "and where she stops, nobody knows." The "she" was the wheel of fortune, and one of those acts, on September 8, 1935, was the Hoboken Four, Bowes' own name for a singing group that included Sinatra, Pat Principe, James Petrozelli and Fred Tamburro (right), who proceeded to bring down the house—and run up the biggest score on the applause meter in the history of the show.*

Bowes cast the foursome in a short film called The Big Minstrel Act, *featuring Frank as a blackface chorus boy (below, fourth from right). Then Bowes took his amateurs on the road for a succession of one-night stands across the country (left).*

These performances in blackface were done in total innocence. I asked my father if he thought white men like Al Jolson performing in blackface was an insult to black performers of the day and he responded sadly, "We didn't realize that we were hurting anybody at the time, until the mid-forties when the NAACP made us all aware. We were insensitive."

Frank's First Road Trip

Dad's road trip with the Major Bowes Amateurs was the first time he had been away from home. He was excited, but life on the road was a grind. He missed his family and his girlfriend. To ease his homesickness, he would send Mom photos with messages written on the back. It was a ritual they would maintain for many years to come whenever Dad was touring.

This is an imitation of a star returning from Europe; after a long vacation.
S.S. Princess Charlotte.
Wednesday November 6th 1935

Regardless of the gloomy day, I'm in a jovial mood On board S.S. Princess Charlotte Wednesday November 6th 1935 On route from Seattle to Victoria B.C.

Mo – I'm not asleep standing up. I was caught resting my eyes from the wind, and "Regina" ("Gypsy Troubador") the rat! He snapped it. On board the S.S. Princess Charlotte Wednesday, November 6th 1935

Freddie and I
Chicago, Ill.

Me - one of Stauffer twins and Patty
train stop - Newton Kansas

(m.c.)
me Julio Vittolo, Bob Oakley and Skelly
Pueblo, Colo.

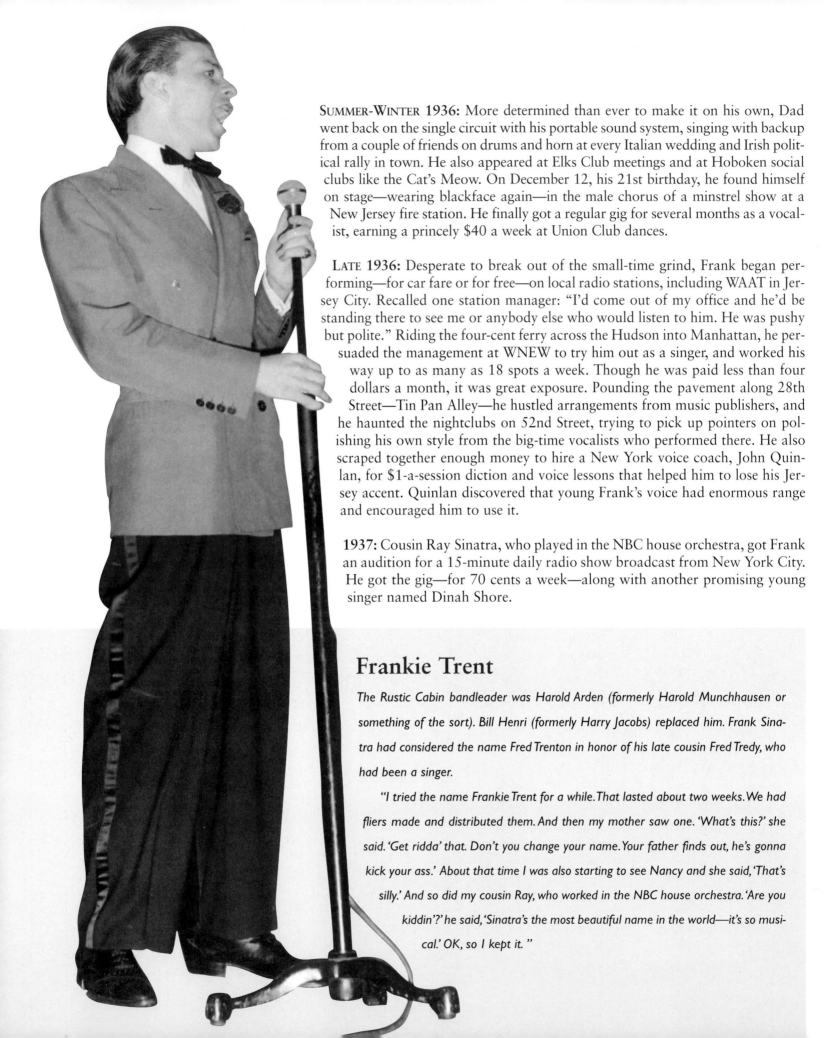

SUMMER-WINTER 1936: More determined than ever to make it on his own, Dad went back on the single circuit with his portable sound system, singing with backup from a couple of friends on drums and horn at every Italian wedding and Irish political rally in town. He also appeared at Elks Club meetings and at Hoboken social clubs like the Cat's Meow. On December 12, his 21st birthday, he found himself on stage—wearing blackface again—in the male chorus of a minstrel show at a New Jersey fire station. He finally got a regular gig for several months as a vocalist, earning a princely $40 a week at Union Club dances.

LATE 1936: Desperate to break out of the small-time grind, Frank began performing—for car fare or for free—on local radio stations, including WAAT in Jersey City. Recalled one station manager: "I'd come out of my office and he'd be standing there to see me or anybody else who would listen to him. He was pushy but polite." Riding the four-cent ferry across the Hudson into Manhattan, he persuaded the management at WNEW to try him out as a singer, and worked his way up to as many as 18 spots a week. Though he was paid less than four dollars a month, it was great exposure. Pounding the pavement along 28th Street—Tin Pan Alley—he hustled arrangements from music publishers, and he haunted the nightclubs on 52nd Street, trying to pick up pointers on polishing his own style from the big-time vocalists who performed there. He also scraped together enough money to hire a New York voice coach, John Quinlan, for $1-a-session diction and voice lessons that helped him to lose his Jersey accent. Quinlan discovered that young Frank's voice had enormous range and encouraged him to use it.

1937: Cousin Ray Sinatra, who played in the NBC house orchestra, got Frank an audition for a 15-minute daily radio show broadcast from New York City. He got the gig—for 70 cents a week—along with another promising young singer named Dinah Shore.

Frankie Trent

The Rustic Cabin bandleader was Harold Arden (formerly Harold Munchhausen or something of the sort). Bill Henri (formerly Harry Jacobs) replaced him. Frank Sinatra had considered the name Fred Trenton in honor of his late cousin Fred Tredy, who had been a singer.

"I tried the name Frankie Trent for a while. That lasted about two weeks. We had fliers made and distributed them. And then my mother saw one. 'What's this?' she said. 'Get ridda' that. Don't you change your name. Your father finds out, he's gonna kick your ass.' About that time I was also starting to see Nancy and she said, 'That's silly.' And so did my cousin Ray, who worked in the NBC house orchestra. 'Are you kiddin'?' he said, 'Sinatra's the most beautiful name in the world—it's so musical.' OK, so I kept it."

MAY 12, 1937: As the vocalist and ukelele player for Frank Sinatra and the Sharps, he performed on *Town Hall Tonight*, an amateur show that was hosted by comedian Fred Allen.

1938: Still living at home with his parents, Frank heard about an opening at the Rustic Cabin, a roadhouse on Route 9W near Alpine, New Jersey, where they needed a singing waiter who could act as master of ceremonies. "Saxophonist Harry Schuchman said, 'I hear they're going to have auditions at the Rustic Cabin where I'm working,'" Dad recalled. "I asked him to intercede, and I went up and sang a few songs and got the job. The piano player and I performed from table to table between sets. I would push his little half piano around. He'd play and I'd sing. We had a little dish on the piano and people would drop in coins. I earned about 15 clams a week. I did a little bit of everything. I never stopped. I showed people to tables, I sang with the band, I sang in between sets. But I didn't mind. Because I was learning. And we were on the air every night. *The WNEW Dance Parade*. That's what I wanted; I wanted to be heard. By people. No salary—they just picked up the orchestra. And people at home apparently danced to it. There were about 15 clubs all around the area, each hooked up. It was great."

NOVEMBER 26, 1938: After his closing set at the Rustic Cabin, Frank was arrested by two constables from Hackensack, New Jersey, and taken to the county courthouse, where he was released after posting $1,500 bail. The charge was breach of promise. According to FBI files later released under the Freedom of Information Act, the claim read: "On the second and ninth days of November, 1938, under

Nancy Sr.: "He was always striving to be better. Learning. Hoping to get on with a bigger band. He knew the Rustic Cabin was only a stepping-stone."

Harry Schuchman
ON FRANK'S SEX APPEAL:

I played the saxophone at the Rustic Cabin when Frank was singing there, and he had more broads around than you ever saw. I used to sit there and watch the gals with him and I'd think to myself, What do they see in him? He's such a skinny little guy. But when he opened his mouth, you knew. He had that charisma that went right out to every gal in the room.

Mr. and Mrs. Michael Barbato
request the honor of your presence
at the marriage of their daughter
Nancy Rose
to
Mr. Francis A. Sinatra
on Saturday the fourth of February
nineteen hundred and thirty nine
at four thirty o'clock
at the Church of Our Lady of Sorrows
Claremont Avenue
Jersey City, N. J.

the promise of marriage, Frank Sinatra had a sexual relationship with a single female of good repute named Antoinette Della Penta." The complaint was quickly dropped when it was learned that Della Penta was in fact already married to a man named Edward Franke. She filed a new complaint on December 22, this time charging Frank with "committing adultery." He posted a bond of $500 and the case was sent to a jury.

JANUARY 24, 1939: The complaint charging adultery was dismissed in open court. Nancy, outraged, asked, "Was she the first?" Frank's reply: "No, but she's the last." Years later the incident would return to haunt him once again.

FEBRUARY 4, 1939: With his problems behind him for the moment, Frank Sinatra married Nancy Barbato at Our Lady of Sorrows Church in Jersey City, with both families attending. As a wedding present, he gave her the record of a song—dedicated to her—that he had recorded privately the day before: "Our Love." After a reception at the Barbato home, they honeymooned in their three-room, third-floor walkup on Garfield Avenue—for $42 a month—and Dad resumed his gig at the Rustic Cabin, where he had just received a raise to $25 a week. And he landed a nightly gig in Manhattan on *The WNEW Dance Parade* and partnered with guitarist Tony Mottola on a 15-minute, five-day-weekly radio show, *Blue Moon.* Nancy, meanwhile, went to work as a secretary for $25 a week at American Type Founders in Elizabeth, New Jersey. During Dad's rare moments at home, she said, "He was handy around the house, putting up towel racks and hanging curtains for me. We really had fun in our first home." And Dad recalls, "In Nancy I found beauty, warmth and understanding; being with her was my only escape from what seemed to be a grim world."

FEBRUARY 1939: A 24-year-old unknown, Frank had been planning to sign on with a band run by Bob Chester—bandleader of one of the groups that played at the Rustic Cabin. Frank said, "In those days, working with a big band was the end of the rainbow for any singer who wanted to make it." My mother got a 15-dollar advance on her salary so Dad could have publicity pictures taken to give to trumpeter Harry James, who had just left Benny Goodman, the "King of

Nancy Sr.
ON THE WEDDING:

We'd been going together for four and a half years, and we were ready to get married. Frank gave me his own sentimental little wedding present—a bag of jellybeans with a diamond watch inside. When the big day finally came, there were maybe 50 members of the family on each side of the aisle. They had all given us furniture for our new apartment. Frank was in a cutaway tuxedo. I was wearing my sister's wedding dress, and the ring—a gold band with a cluster of diamonds—had been his mother's. I don't think I'd ever seen Frank so happy in his whole life.

Frank: "You know, if it's possible, Harry was thinner than I was. He really was a rail." (Frank is standing in the rear with the coffee cup, James is seated directly to his right.)

Swing," to start a band of his own. Harry Schuchman said: "I remember that day. He had the pictures taken but he couldn't get to Harry James. So he got someone to put them on Harry's desk." Soon afterward James happened to hear Dad on the radio. Already knowing what Frank looked like from the pictures, James then went to see him live at the Rustic Cabin. When James showed up, Frank sang "Begin the Beguine." James said later that he "liked Frank's way of talking a lyric" and signed him up as male vocalist with his newly formed band—a two-year contract at $75 a week.

JUNE 30, 1939: James wanted to call him "Frankie Satin," but my father had had it with name-changing and said he would take his chances as Sinatra from then on. Appearing with the band on their first tour stop at the Hippodrome Theatre in Baltimore, he sang "Wishing" and "My

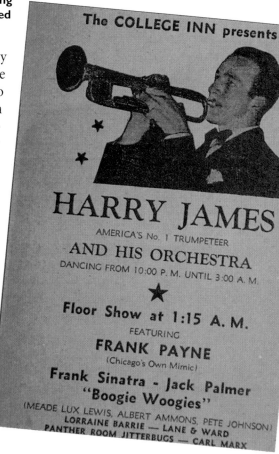

The COLLEGE INN presents

HARRY JAMES
AMERICA'S No. 1 TRUMPETEER
AND HIS ORCHESTRA
DANCING FROM 10:00 P. M. UNTIL 3:00 A. M.

★

Floor Show at 1:15 A. M.
FEATURING
FRANK PAYNE
(Chicago's Own Mimic)

Frank Sinatra - Jack Palmer
"Boogie Woogies"
(MEADE LUX LEWIS, ALBERT AMMONS, PETE JOHNSON)
LORRAINE BARRIE — LANE & WARD
PANTHER ROOM JITTERBUGS — CARL MARX

Love for You." They spent most of the summer touring the East and playing at the Roseland Ballroom in midtown Manhattan, where a one-line review in *Metronome* by George Simon complimented "the very pleasing vocals of Frank Sinatra, whose easy phrasing is especially commendable."

JULY 13, 1939: Frank Sinatra cut his first record with James, "From the Bottom of My Heart" (backed with "Melancholy Mood") on the Brunswick label. Recorded at 78 rpm, neither song hit the charts.

AUGUST 31, 1939: For Columbia, Frank recorded a song that was destined to become one of his first big hits: "All or Nothing at All."

FALL 1939: Still a newlywed, my mother went along on tour with the band. It was a rough life, and money ran short, but she recalled those days as the happiest of her married life.

LATE FALL 1939: Harry James recalled when the band played to a nearly empty room at Victor Hugo's in Beverly Hills. "They didn't care for us and refused to pay us." As the band scrambled to find some paying work, money ran short. One day, according to Harry, "The whole band chipped in to buy spaghetti and the makings for your mom to cook for us. Spaghetti never tasted so good. The only bright spot in that seemingly desperate time was the happy news from your mother

Frank Sinatra received his first important reviews in the summer of 1939—his first year with the James band—when they played at Manhattan's legendary Roseland Ballroom.

Life on the Road

NANCY SR.:

We were together 24 hours a day—driving from one show to another in our new car—and he was doing what he loved. It was wonderful. But after a couple of months we started getting worried, because I was pregnant and we had to make payments on the car—they were about to take it away from us—and we didn't want to write to the family about it and worry them. Somebody always came up with a few dollars. But for a long time I was living on fried-onion sandwiches.

FRANK:

I'll never forget the time some legal proceeding temporarily blocked the band members' salaries. We were in California, we had no savings, knew nobody there and you were on the way. Your mother had developed an appetite for ham sandwiches and apple pie, and asked for them one night when I hadn't a cent in my pocket. I gathered up all the empty pop bottles in the building and when I returned them and collected the deposits, I got just enough change to buy her that meal. Luckily, the legal business was settled, we signed for another show and everybody was OK in the pocketbook department once more. And I was no longer singing on an empty stomach.

With Harry James and the Music Makers at the Fountain Lake Bandshell, August 22, 1939. It's his first big break, his first big band. FS: "This is the New York World's Fair, one of the early jobs I played. A matinee job; we played in the afternoons, not at night. The singer was named Marge, an Italian girl from Newark." In very short order, Marge would be replaced by Connie Haines.

that you were on the way." "In looking back at that period of panic," Dad recalled, "I can truthfully say it was full of happiness—in spite of the trouble and hardships we had. It's one of the things I can't forget—and besides, I wouldn't want to anyway."

NOVEMBER 8, 1939: For Columbia, Frank recorded his last two songs with the James band: "Ciribiribin," a vocal version of James' theme song, and "Every Day of My Life."

DECEMBER 1939: The James band had dropped to number 12 on the Downbeat poll of the top dance bands, but Frank Sinatra had no intention of sinking with them. When Dad found out that Tommy Dorsey—number-one big-band leader in the country—was planning to catch a show at the Rustic Cabin, he arranged to be there that night as guest singer. Before signing with James, my father had considered signing with Bob Chester and his band. They'd even rehearsed together. "The rumor came through the grapevine," according to Harry Schuchman, who had joined the Chester band which was appearing that night at the Rustic Cabin, "that Frank was going to come by that night and sing with us. The reason was that Tommy Dorsey, a friend of Bob Chester's, was going to be at the show. Frank showed up and was sitting at a table with your mother and my wife, Helen, when Tommy walked in. Frank whispered to Nancy and Helen, 'Listen to this, Tom,' then got up from the table, went to the bandstand and told Bob what song to play. It was an audition for Tommy, whether or not Tommy knew it. Frank knew where

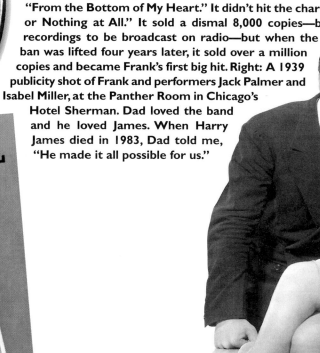

Frank emerged as a performer of star stature on his very first record with James: 1939's "From the Bottom of My Heart." It didn't hit the charts, but six weeks later came "All or Nothing at All." It sold a dismal 8,000 copies—because ASCAP wouldn't allow recordings to be broadcast on radio—but when the ban was lifted four years later, it sold over a million copies and became Frank's first big hit. Right: A 1939 publicity shot of Frank and performers Jack Palmer and Isabel Miller, at the Panther Room in Chicago's Hotel Sherman. Dad loved the band and he loved James. When Harry James died in 1983, Dad told me, "He made it all possible for us."

he was going and where he wanted to go." Dorsey liked Frank, and after a split-up with his vocalist Jack Leonard, he offered Dad the job, and Dad accepted. "I was so excited that I called Nancy at home in New Jersey," he remembered, "and told her what had happened. And she said that means you'll be getting more money and I said, 'Money?' I never even talked money. She said what did you mean you didn't talk money? I said, 'I don't know. I was just so happy to get the job.'" Well, as it turned out, it was a hundred dollars a week on a long-term contract. Just how long, and how binding, my dad would discover later. Harry James, ever the gentleman, tore up Frank's contract and said, "I think that's what you want. And just be sure he's paying you a lot more than I'm paying." But at that moment Frank didn't care, because at 24, after struggling day and night for seven years to make it, it seemed to him that all his dreams were finally beginning to come true.

FRANK

ON HIS AMBITION TO SING WITH TOMMY DORSEY:

Once in my life I saw something that might happen and I tried to plant it. And that was to sing with the Tommy Dorsey Orchestra. I wanted to do it in the worst way. I watched all of the orchestras, and in those days one band was as good as another, but they had different styles. And there were fine singers with all of the bands. Jack Leonard was with Tommy in those days. I used to watch them if they did a one-nighter in Roseland. I'd stand in front of the bandstand and watch how Tommy handled the singers with such finesse. He would set a singer up so that the singer would sing the first chorus, the orchestra would play a small piece of music, a turn around, and the singer would finish it. The singer was featured and Tommy was simpatico about vocalizing. Because the instrument that he played had the same physical qualities as the human voice.

*"Night and day
     under the hide of me
There's an oh such a hungry yearning
     burning inside of me..."*

Street Of Dreams

In the early 1940s, big-band music in America defined and dominated pop culture. To be a singer in the most popular big band of the era was a dream come true for Frank Sinatra from Hoboken. He was at center stage during one of the most exciting times in modern music: the glory days of swing.

The music business was given a boost by the mass public acceptance of two mighty technological forces: the radio and the phonograph. They were fast becoming an indispensable accoutrement in more and more homes. Exposure through these powerful media meant unprecedented access to millions of Americans—especially teenagers. Swing music became the rallying point of a generation.

But nothing took the place of live performances. Touring the nation, pressing records, doing movie cameos, singing with Tommy Dorsey in nationwide radio "remotes," my father was a huge success even before he left the band after two years to make it on his own. From the moment he appeared solo on stage at New York's Paramount Theatre on December 30, 1942, he walked into the annals of show business. "The sound that greeted me," he recalled, "was absolutely deafening, a tremendous roar." The 5,000 bobby-soxers who packed the theater were yelling, screaming, applauding—even fainting in ecstasy—before he opened his mouth to sing. By the end of his first run at the Paramount, this skinny 27-year-old baritone was a household name from coast to coast.

It was more than just the splendid purity of that sweet young voice, more than the seamless phrasing and heartfelt reading of the lyrics that became his trademark. For those who watched him on the bandstand, even in his earliest days with Dorsey, it was the shock of those blue eyes and the longing and loneliness behind their twinkle. The stance, the lean body, the quivering lower lip. The expressive hands. The soft speaking voice. The shyness. The vulnerability. That needy, hungry quality. With their boyfriends off at war, teenage girls wanted to feed him, take care of him—make love to him.

As clucking critics and uncomprehending parents recoiled in disbelief, the hysterical adoration of his fans kept building from show to show and from week to week. Frank Sinatra had become a superstar. Neither he nor American music would ever be the same.

The Tommy Dorsey Band put in so much overtime making *Las Vegas Nights* that the studio, as a form of compensation, made a portrait of each of the members of the band. Never one to miss an opportunity, Tommy said, "Let's have a composite done for publicity."

TOMMY DORSEY   And His Orchestra

JANUARY 1940: After playing his last gig with the Harry James Band and Connie Haines at Buffalo's Shea Theatre—billed along with acrobat Burt Lancaster and comic Red Skelton, both struggling to break into show business themselves—Dad "was going home to spend some time with Nancy. The band was going to Hartford and I stood in the snow with my two bags and the bus was pulling away and I had lived with those guys and they were fun and I stood there like a schmuck and I'm in tears as I see the red lights going away. And I figure to myself I ain't never gonna make it, and I'll never get home and it'll be terrible, I'm going to die up here in the Buffalo snow." He joined the Dorsey band on tour. The band manager sent a ticket. "I took the train from Grand Central Station to Chicago and then one to Rockford, Illinois where the band was playing."

FEBRUARY 1, 1940: At the RCA studios in Chicago, Dad recorded his first two songs with the Dorsey band, "The Sky Fell Down" and "Too Romantic."

FEBRUARY 2-8, 1940: When the Dorsey band opened at the Lyric Theatre in Indianapolis, the theater's ad in the *Indianapolis Star* listed Tommy's name in inch-high letters. At the bottom, in 1/8-inch type, was a listing for "Frank Sinatra, Romantic Virtuoso."

FEBRUARY 9, 1940: Still on the road, the band played a college date at the University of Michigan.

Dorsey conducts Dad and the Pied Pipers. Tommy's tough standards became my father's tough standards—and his work ethic. Harry James taught him the compassion, Dorsey the discipline.

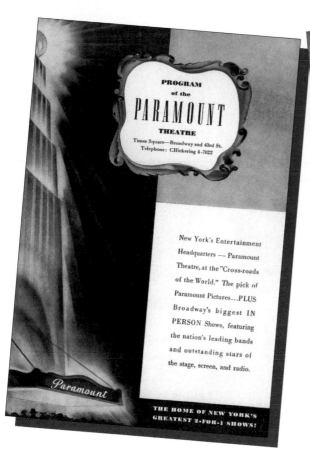

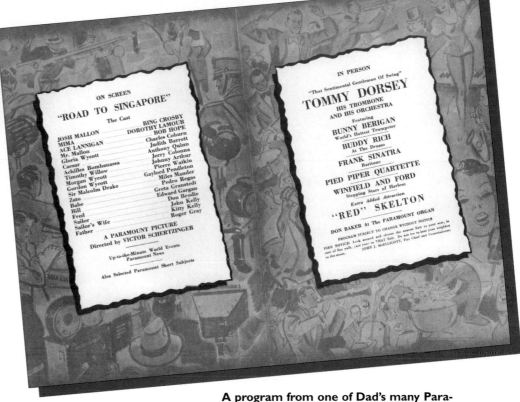

A program from one of Dad's many Paramount appearances. Decades later, when this landmark theater was reduced to rubble along with all of its history, he said to me sadly, "Gee, you'd think they'd have at least given me the dressing room door-knob or something."

FEBRUARY 20-MARCH 11, 1940: The band played a three-week engagement at the Meadowbrook nightclub in Cedar Grove, New Jersey.

MARCH 13-APRIL 9, 1940: Debuting at New York's Paramount Theatre, the premier big-band venue in the country, Dad sang to his largest crowds yet with the Dorsey band.

MAY 23, 1940: After an unsuccessful pressing in April, Frank, the Pied Pipers and Dorsey recorded their first big hit, "I'll Never Smile Again," a beautiful, poignant song written by the widowed Ruth Lowe about her late husband. Frank would record an amazing 40 more singles with the band for RCA before the end of the year.

Jo Stafford

ON MEETING SINATRA:

We were all sort of sitting back— like, "Oh, yeah, who are you?" Then he began to sing. After four bars, I thought, Wow! This is an absolutely new, unique sound. In those days, most male singers tried to sound as much like Bing as possible. Well, he didn't sound anything like Bing. He didn't sound like anybody else that I had ever heard.

JUNE 8, 1940: Dad was in Hollywood with the band when I was born at Margaret Hague Hospital in Jersey City. Already I was being prepared for having to share him with the rest of the world. It was the start of one of the themes of my life: a father who was always going away. But as Jo Stafford recalled, "He was so excited that all he did all night was talk about his new baby girl."

One of the snapshots my mother sent to my father on the road. It was one of the themes of my life: My father was always going away!

JUNE 1940: Throughout the month, Dad performed with the band on Saturday nights at New York's Astor Hotel in live NBC radio "remotes."

JUNE 25, 1940: NBC booked the band to fill in for Bob Hope on a summer-replacement variety show.

JULY 2–SEPTEMBER 24, 1940: Impressed with the band's ratings on its Bob Hope replacement show, NBC signed Dorsey to a musical program called *Summer Pastime*—broadcast on Tuesday nights from New York—that began to elevate Frank Sinatra to a new level of national exposure.

OCTOBER 17, 1940: With Dorsey, Dad began a weekly radio show, *Fame and Fortune*—which was sponsored by Lewis Home Company and was broadcast on NBC for six months from 8:30 to 9 p.m.—that gave amateur songwriters a chance to compete for a $100 prize and the right to see their work published by NBC Music, a company in which Dorsey had an interest. It was also a great clinic for the young singer to hone his craft, challenging him to learn and perform new and different material every week.

FRANK

ON DEVELOPING HIS OWN STYLE AS A SINGER:

It was in 1940 that I really began developing a style of my own. Tommy didn't work much with me. He devoted his time to the musicians and the arrangements, so that left me on my own to experiment. The thing that influenced me most was the way Tommy played his trombone. He would take a musical phrase and play it all the way through seemingly without breathing for 8, 10, maybe 16 bars. How in the hell did he do it? I used to sit behind him on the bandstand and watch, trying to see him sneak a breath. But I never saw the bellows move in his back. His jacket didn't even move. So I edged my chair around to the side a little and peeked around to watch him. Finally, after a while, I discovered that he had a "sneak pinhole" in the corner of his mouth—not an actual hole, but a tiny place he left open where he was breathing. In the middle of a phrase, while the tone was still being carried through the trombone, he'd go "shhhhh" and take a quick breath and play another four bars with that breath.

Fascinated, I began listening to other soloists. I bought every Jascha Heifetz record I could find and listened to his constant bowing, where you never heard a break, carrying the melody line straight on through, just like Dorsey's trombone. Why couldn't a singer do that too? I decided to make my voice work in the same way as a trombone or violin—not sounding like them, but "playing" the voice like those instruments. The first thing I needed was extraordinary breath control, so I began swimming in public pools, taking laps under water and thinking song lyrics to myself as I swam, holding my breath. Over six months or so, I began to develop and delineate a method of long phraseology. Instead of singing only two bars or four bars at a time—like most of the other guys around—I was able to sing six bars, and in some songs eight bars, without taking a visible or audible breath. That gave the melody a flowing, unbroken quality, and that's what made me sound different. When I started singing that way, people began taking notice.

Jo Stafford

ON THE BACK OF THE BUS:

We traveled a lot by bus and, well, a band bus is arranged like a bandstand. On a bandstand, if you have strings, the strings are in front, and they're fairly calm people who behave themselves. Next are the saxophones, who get a little rowdy—but not too much. Next come the trombones, who get pretty raunchy, and then the trumpet players, who are out of control. And that's exactly the way the bus worked. Starting in front it's fairly calm, but as you worked your way back, you came to your sax players, then the trombone players, then the trumpet section. All the way in back was the rhythm section. They were the worst; they were real evil. That's where Frank usually sat. So did I.

OCTOBER 1940: After returning to Hollywood with the Dorsey band to open the Palladium, an opulent new dance club, Dad made his first feature-length movie, Paramount's *Las Vegas Nights*, performing for an extra's wages—$15 a day. Meanwhile, his song with the Pied Pipers, "I'll Never Smile Again," became the first Dorsey/Sinatra record to reach number one on the charts.

DECEMBER 18, 1940-JANUARY 14, 1941: Frank Sinatra returned to New York with the band for a second big run at the Paramount.

JANUARY 20, 1941: Sinatra's rendition of "Without a Song," recorded with the Dorsey band, was released by RCA. It was the first of 29 singles he would record with Tommy and arrangers Sy Oliver and Axel Stordahl on that label in 1941.

FEBRUARY 11, 1941: Still in New York—continuing on the *Fame and Fortune* show every Thursday night on NBC radio—the band made a second sold-out appearance at the Meadowbrook.

MARCH 24, 1941: *Las Vegas Nights* was released nationally.

SPRING 1941: After a one-nighter at Ricker Gardens in Portland, Maine, the band was having dinner at a Howard Johnson's when a 17-year-old high school student

The Dorsey Band playing, with the Pied Pipers singing, for a ballroom full of dancers. My father is the guy in the back on the far right, trading jokes with the great piano man Joe Bushkin. Buddy Rich is on drums. Dad told me: "I used to sit up at the back. Not down front. I didn't like sitting with the singers."

The entire Tommy Dorsey congregation in full throttle: Leader: Tommy Dorsey; Trumpets: Ziggy Elman, Jimmy Zito, Jim Blake, Ray Linn; Trombones: George Arus, Dave Jacobs, Jim Skiles; Saxes: Fred Stulce, Heinie Beau, Done Lodice, Vince Yocum, Harry Schuchman; Drums: Buddy Rich; Guitar: Clark Yocum; Piano: Milton Raskin; Harp: Ruth Hill; Bass: Phil Stephens; Violins: Lenny Posner, Raoul Paliaken, Bill Ehrenkrantz, Al Beller, Cy Miroff, Bernie Linterow; Violas: Sam Ross, Lenny Atkins; Cello: George Ricci; Vocalists: Chuck Lowry, Jo Stafford, John Huddleston—and Frank Sinatra.

named Paul Keyes—later a presidential speechwriter and television producer—approached Dorsey at his table with an autograph book in hand. He didn't know he was violating the privacy of a section of the restaurant Dorsey had ordered closed off to everybody except band members, and Tommy had him physically removed from the premises. As Paul Keyes recalls, "A few minutes after Dorsey threw me out, I saw Frank Sinatra leave the private room and followed him to the men's room to get his autograph. He was very friendly. 'What's your name, kid?' he asked, signing my book to me personally. I mentioned that I wanted to get the autographs of the rest of the orchestra but that Mr. Dorsey had had me thrown out of the room. Frank took me back and introduced me warmly to Ziggy Elman, Jo Stafford, Buddy Rich and all the others. They all signed my book. Then he took me over to Tommy and said, 'This is my friend Paul, and I want you to write something nice in his book. He's a good kid.' Mr. Dorsey, recognizing me but not batting an eye, did as Frank requested and signed my book. Frank then invited me to pull up a chair and have a bite with the band."

MAY 1941: Frank Sinatra seemed to be everywhere: on radio, on record, on stage and in the movies. In 15 months, he had become the hottest new singing star in the country— especially among teenagers—and *Billboard* named him top male vocalist of the year. "You could almost feel the excitement coming up out of the crowds when that kid stood up to sing," Dorsey told a reporter. "Remember, he was no matinee idol. He was just a skinny kid with big ears. I used to stand there so amazed that

Dad huddles with Hank Sanicola, his longtime friend, manager and co-composer.

Army Croons Melody in 1-A To Sinatra

Sinatra Taps Out 4F On Muffled Eardrum

Sinatra Rejected In Draft Physical

I'd almost forget to take my own solos." With bobby-soxers swooning in front of the bandstand, the musicians would stop playing and "swoon" right back at them. But Dorsey began to feel upstaged.

MAY 28, 1941: In his first venture as a songwriter, Dad co-authored the lyrics for "This Love of Mine," with music by Sol Parker and friend Hank Sanicola for RCA. He recorded the song with the Dorsey band.

AUGUST 27-SEPTEMBER 16, 1941: After a Midwestern swing, Dorsey returned East for a third sold-out run at the Paramount in New York. By now Dad was the band's big draw, and he was beginning to think about going solo.

NOVEMBER 1941: Back in Hollywood with the band, Dad made a second screen appearance with two songs in MGM's *Ship Ahoy:* "The Last Call for Love" and "Poor You." It would be his last film with Dorsey. Emmanuel "Manie" Sacks, head of Columbia Records—"one of the nicest people God ever made in this world," according to my father—heard him singing with the band and told him he liked what he heard. "Would you record me as a soloist?" Frank asked. "Anytime you're ready," said Sacks. Dad was more than ready, but he was still tied to RCA through his contract with Dorsey, so Manie and Columbia had to wait. But not for long.

DECEMBER 7, 1941: When the Japanese attack on Pearl Harbor precipitated America's entry into World War II, Dad was drafted almost immediately, but because of the punctured eardrum resulting from his birth injury, he was turned down and classified 4-F. He tried in vain to enlist for the next several years.

JANUARY 19, 1942: Restless for the recognition he felt he deserved, Frank began recording solo in Hollywood for the Bluebird label, a lesser subsidiary of RCA. It was thought that since RCA was Dorsey's label, a recording on Bluebird would be less upsetting to the bandleader. With arranger Axel Stordahl as his conductor—and a lush string section playing behind him to weave a romantic mood—he recorded poetic renditions of "Night and Day," "The Lamplighter's Serenade," "The Night We Called It a Day" and "The Song Is You." The next day, listening to what they had recorded, he said, "I've got to go out on my own."

APRIL 1-28, 1942: Back in New York after a series of one-nighters in the Midwest, the band returned for a blockbuster month at the Paramount.

MAY 18, 1942: Frank Sinatra and the band began recording a series of 10 singles to stockpile in anticipation of a strike by the American Federation of Musicians that would shut down RCA Victor and several other labels for the next two and a half years. They would be the last records he would make with Tommy or with RCA.

MAY 1942: As reports about Nazi atrocities against Jews began to filter back from Europe—many of them reported in the *New York Times*—Dad felt he had to do something about racial and ethnic discrimination, so he had 100 copies of a special medallion made. On one side was a St. Christopher medal, on the other a Star of David. Wearing one himself, he gave others to friends.

JUNE 16-SEPTEMBER 8, 1942: Following one-nighters at the Forum in Montreal and the Hotel Astor in New York, Frank and the band were booked by CBS as the summer replacement for Red Skelton's popular 30-minute radio show.

JULY-AUGUST 1942: Between their weekly radio shows, Dad and the band rolled through the Midwest and the East with a series of standing-room-only (SRO) appearances in Detroit, Philadelphia, Baltimore, Washington and Akron. It was his last tour with the band.

AUGUST 28, 1942: Dad's departure from the band was announced on stage during a performance at the Circle Theater in Indianapolis, and he introduced his successor: crooner Dick Haymes.

SEPTEMBER 8, 1942: Dad left the band for good. He had asked Dorsey to let him out of his contract, but Tommy had refused. So he had to ask for help from some influential friends. Over the years, all sorts of outrageous accounts have been told of how he extricated himself from the punitive Dorsey deal—and the stories are as punishing and unfair as that ridiculous contract, which my dad described as a "ratty piece of paper. It called for me to pay him one third of my earnings for as long as I was in the entertainment business."

Below: FS and Dorsey promoting their latest release with radio host Paul Brenner on New Jersey's WAAT radio. Right: This shot of my father shows that his early fashion savvy made him cool before anybody knew what cool was!

Breaking the Dorsey Contract

While the band was performing in Washington, D.C., Dad went into Dorsey's dressing room and told him he wanted to leave. Dorsey smiled. "What for?" he asked. "You're doing great with the band and we've got a lot of arrangements for you." Dad said he appreciated all the things Dorsey had done for him, but now he wanted to get on with his career. "I don't think so," said Dorsey, citing the terms of their contract: 43 percent of his professional income for life. Dad replied, "I had a contract with Harry [James], but he took the contract and tore it up and wished me luck." But even when Dad offered to give his boss a year's notice, Dorsey stood firm.

"I loved and admired the guy," said Dad. "He was a taskmaster and a brilliant musician, and I liked the way he made everybody toe the line. But he was also a man who detested the idea that a member of his orchestra would leave. He wanted the band to be set. I could understand that, because the orchestra was drilled like a platoon and when new men arrived, it meant rehearsing and getting the guy to fit in. But I was earning $150 a week and saw no future."

To Dorsey's dismay, Dad began going out as a single on weekend gigs. Then Columbia's Manie Sacks helped find him a few bookings. That brought angry letters from Dorsey's attorneys, demanding their share of his earnings as specified in the contract. What happened then has been the subject of rumor and innuendo ever since. "According to legend," says Dad, "I secured my release from Tommy when three men told him out of the sides of their mouths to 'sign or else.' What actually happened was I hired a couple of lawyers to get me out of it." Manie Sacks took Frank to Henry Jaffe, an entertainment attorney whose clients included the American Federation of Radio Artists. Dorsey's manager refused even to discuss the contract with Jaffe until FS had paid him the share called for under their original contract.

"Do you like broadcasting on NBC?" Jaffe asked Dorsey, referring to the many shows the band had aired on that network.

"I like it a lot," said Dorsey. "Well, then," said Jaffe, "how about we talk about Frank Sinatra and we'll see what kind of deal we can make—that is, if you want to continue on radio." When Dorsey still refused to cancel the contract, Jaffe went to Jules Stein, head of MCA, the talent agency, and offered to let them represent Dad, who was then handled by Rockwell-O'Keefe. Jaffe said he'd get the other agency to release Dad if MCA could get Dorsey to make a deal. So Stein had a heart-to-heart chat with Dorsey. After a series of phone calls from Radio Artists officials and recording executives who took Jaffe's threats very seriously, Dorsey was finally persuaded to take $75,000 and some additional bookings through MCA in exchange for letting Frank go. "My end of it cost me something like $25,000," my father recalled. "I hope you fall on your ass," said Dorsey in a parting shot. But Dad's powerful new agents, Sonny Werblin and Norman Weiss, didn't get to be partners in MCA by betting on the wrong client.

Jack Benny

ON FRANK'S FIRST NIGHT AT THE PARAMOUNT:

Theater manager Bob Weitman asked if I could come over to the Paramount for the debut of Frank Sinatra. I said, "Who the hell is Frank Sinatra?" He said to me, "You mean you never heard of Frank Sinatra? He's the hottest thing in the country right now." I said, "I'm sorry. I've never heard of him, but I'll do this for you and Benny Goodman, and Sinatra too if it's any help." So they introduce me to this skinny little kid called Frank Sinatra. I shook hands with him and said hello, and he said, "Hello, Mr. Benny." Now it's time for the introductions, and first Benny Goodman went on and did his act. And then he says, "Now, ladies and gentlemen, to introduce our honored guest, we have Jack Benny." I certainly didn't think Sinatra would get much of anything 'cause I never heard of him. So I did two or three jokes, and they laughed, and then I realized there were a lot of young people out there, and they were probably just waiting for Sinatra. So I introduced him as if he were one of my closest friends. And then I said, "Well, anyway, ladies and gentlemen, here he is, Frank Sinatra." And I thought the god-damned building was going to cave in. I never heard such a commotion, with people running down to the stage screaming and nearly knocking me off the ramp. All this for a fellow I never heard of.

OCTOBER 1, 1942: While rehearsing his new act as a soloist—for a debut appearance that would make show-business history—Frank headlined *Reflections*, a twice-weekly unsponsored, or sustaining, 15-minute CBS radio show on Tuesdays and Thursdays from New York.

Mom kept a copy of the program for Dad's first historic appearance at the Paramount.

DECEMBER 30, 1942: With tremendous fanfare, Frank Sinatra was about to create the first generation gap. He opened with Benny Goodman, the "King of Swing," at New York's Paramount Theatre and—with wife Nancy watching from the audience in disbelief—literally brought down the house. In the weeks that followed, SRO audiences of teenagers stomped and swooned as thousands more waited in line outside chanting, "Frankie, Frankie!" His original two-week engagement at the Paramount was extended for eight additional weeks, shattering Bing Crosby's 15-year-old record. Within a month

Sinatra's fans were mostly young girls. In acknowledgment of the ankle-high socks they wore, usually with saddle shoes, they were labeled bobby-soxers. The ones who fainted away at the sound or sight of Sinatra were called swooners.

George Evans

George Evans (shown over Frank's right shoulder) was the brilliant press agent Dad hired when he began his solo career. According to Bob Weitman, manager of the Paramount Theatre, Evans hired some teenage girls to swoon and faint. He thought it would make a good story for the press. But it turned out to be an unnecessary publicity stunt. The fire had ignited quite well on its own and the girls needed no provocation. The understandably frightened faces of the young people and the police show how group admiration can turn into unintended mob violence. Jack Entratter is the large man to Frank's left.

Sinatra fan club coordinator Marjorie Diven

ON THE TYPICAL FAN:

She's a 14-year-old girl living in a small town. She never gets to see anybody except her family—who haven't much money—and her schoolmates. She's lonely. On the way home from school, she stops at the drugstore for an ice cream soda and picks up a movie magazine. She reads about Frank's life and it sounds wonderful. She writes him a letter. She imagines he gets about six or seven letters a day, and she visualizes him at his breakfast table with her letter propped against the toaster. She calculates how long it will take for his answer to come to her. When the time arrives and she hears the postman coming, she runs down the lane to her mailbox, one of those wobbly rural boxes. She's kept this up for three weeks, while her family makes fun of her. It's the thought of that 14-year-old girl running down that lane to that wobbly mailbox that makes me sympathetic to the fans.

Dad's salary leaped from $750 a week to $25,000, and he was being called "The Voice"—a national phenomenon and the hottest new singing star in show-business history.

"Bob Weitman called and asked if I wanted to play along with a Crosby movie and the Benny Goodman Orchestra," my father recalled. "When I came around the corner in a taxi and saw the marquee with my name on it I was knocked out. The sound that greeted me was absolutely deafening, a tremendous roar. Five thousand kids, stamping, yelling, screaming, applauding. They let out a yell and I thought the roof would come off. I was scared stiff. I couldn't move a muscle. Benny Goodman froze too. He turned around, looked at the audience and said, 'What the hell is that?' I burst out laughing." But the schedule at the Paramount was grueling. "We had rehearsal at 7:00 a.m. and did six or seven performances a day, eleven on Saturdays, the movie ran in between each show. It was hard, but we were young and we were strong and we liked it." Bob Weitman remembers that "there were about 5,000 people in the theater. And all 5,000 were of one voice, 'F-R-A-N-K-I-E-E-E-E-E-!' As they danced in the aisles and on the stage, the loge and the balcony swayed. One of the managers came over to me and said, 'The balcony is rocking. What do we do?' We struck up the National Anthem."

My mother made the soft, floppy bow ties that he wore. They were becoming a trademark. "I had a terrible time keeping him in ties. Fans would yank them off of him for souvenirs. I made them by the dozens." Until his press agent's office took over, Mom was in charge of his fan mail. "I sent out hundreds of pictures. I would sign his name, then copy his signature because he didn't have time for that. My sisters would help in addressing the envelopes. We'd do it a couple hours a night." As she remembered, "It was exciting and it was a lot of work. It was constant work. Frank worked very, very hard. He'd come home so tired, he'd just flop. And I'd think, 'Whatever happens, it's going to be worth it because he's giving his all.'"

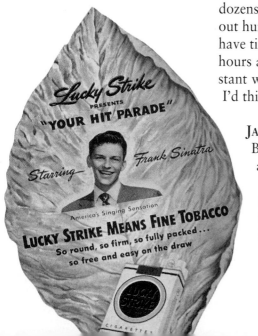

JANUARY 27, 1943: Moving on to other commitments after a month at the Paramount, Benny Goodman and his band were replaced by Johnny Long and his orchestra for an unprecedented second record-breaking month behind Sinatra.

Richie Lisella, Dorsey's former band boy and Dad's assistant road manager, remembered the Paramount run: "He'd come on stage and he'd recognize some of the same faces in the audience. He'd say, 'I know you kids are out of school, you're here six shows.' So he'd send me out to get a lot of sandwiches for them—30, 40

Swooners

From the very first show, Sinatramania took on a life of its own. Trying to keep crowds thronging the streets outside the Paramount to a minimum, Bob Weitman, the theater manager, went to extraordinary efforts to clear the house between performances. Booking the worst movies he could find to show between stage performances, he required patrons to leave box lunches at a checkstand. But this didn't prevent thousands from smuggling sandwiches, fruit and candy in their clothing so they could stay in their seats.

Newspapers of the time reported on the extreme devotion of many of his fans. Some were soon signing letters to friends "Frankly yours" and writing F.S. instead of P.S. for postscript. Members of fan clubs like the Slaves of Sinatra pinned club buttons over their hearts and on their socks and wrote his name on their coats and sweaters. One even inscribed the titles of 200 Sinatra songs on the back of her jacket; another did her hair in twin braids, labeling one "Frankie" and the other "Sinatra." And one girl, after accidentally being brushed by Dad's arm, covered the spot with a bandage which she refused to remove for weeks. Some begged him to autograph their bras, and others bribed hotel chambermaids for a brief opportunity to enter his empty room and lie between the sheets of his bed, finish the remains of his morning cornflakes and even fish a cigarette butt from an ashtray.

Dad's fame was equally hard on his wardrobe, which included 50 suits, 25 sport jackets, 100 pairs of slacks and 60 pairs of shoes. Not only did fans regularly tear his sleeves, lapels and buttons, they zeroed in on his trademark floppy bow ties—handmade by my mother—which became a prized souvenir. After a tussle with some of these schoolgirls, one of Dad's bodyguards, who had previously trained heavyweight boxers, said that prizefighters "fought cleaner" than these teenage girls.

According to E.J. Kahn Jr., a New Yorker writer who penned a 1946 book about Dad, most of his young fans were dazzled by Dad's lifestyle and yearned to share in it. With an estimated 40 million fans around the country, he was deluged with as many as 5,000 letters a week, including one in lipstick that said, "I love you so bad it hurts. Do you think I should see a doctor?" Even the family was deluged with as many as 2,000 letters a week.

Kahn also noted that "girls have plucked hairs from his head and collected clippings of his hair from barber shops. One Sinatra fan carries around, in a locket, what she insists is a Sinatra hangnail. 'I shiver all the way up and down my spine when you sing,' a girl wrote Sinatra, 'just like I did when I had scarlet fever.' As a rule, any public appearance by Sinatra is a guarantee of at least a modest riot. When he was to appear in a Boston armory, the management had the seats bolted to the floor..."

"The Paramount is the shrine of their disorder. Many of his fans literally consider the theater their home and spend the day in it, occupying a seat through a half a dozen shows for the price of one ticket. An admirer of Sinatra had to be taken to the hospital after her roommate, a Crosby fan, stabbed her with an ice pick during a debate."

Dad's most loyal fans never tried to speak to him or even ask for an autograph; they were content to merely stare. The winner of a 1946 "Why I Like Frank Sinatra" essay contest sponsored by a Detroit radio station spoke for all of them when she wrote, "He is one of the greatest things that ever happened to Teen Age America. We were kids that never got much attention, but he made us feel like we were worth something."

Frank Meets Franklin

Just after being introduced to the President of the United States, Franklin Delano Roosevelt, who was in a wheelchair due to polio, FDR summoned Dad—"Psst, Frank"—to stoop down. He leaned over, put his ear close to the President's face, and FDR whispered in his ear: "I promise not to tell anyone. What's number one this Saturday?" On another occasion, the President invited my father to the White House for tea. Roosevelt remarked, teasing, "You know, fainting, which was once so prevalent, has become a lost art among the ladies. I'm glad you have revived it." My father found it all more impressive than funny. He thought, after their first meeting, There's the greatest guy alive today—and here's a little guy from Hoboken, shaking his hand.

Nancy Sr.

ON THE FACES IN THE WINDOW:

We had moved from the apartment on Bergen Street to a seven-room brick house at 220 Lawrence Avenue in Hasbrouck Heights, New Jersey, and fans began to invade our home. There was no wall around the property, and I'd look out my bedroom window and there would be somebody's face in the window. They'd sit out there on the lawn for hours. We tried asking them to go home, but they wouldn't leave. It scared me, but finally I'd feel so sorry for them I'd send out doughnuts and something for them to drink.

At our comfortable new home in Hasbrouck Heights, New Jersey, Dad tried patiently to teach me a few chords on another new acquisition: an upright piano.

sandwiches at a time. Outside the Paramount, the lines started at 11 o'clock at night for a show at 11 o'clock in the morning. They'd be there all night. And when they saw him they'd go wild. I saw fans run under the horses of mounted policemen. I saw them turn over a car."

FEBRUARY 4, 1943: Columbia Pictures' *Reveille with Beverly*, Dad's first film without the Dorsey band, was released. Though it was only a cameo part—singing "Night and Day"—the timing couldn't have been more perfect to spread the word from coast to coast about America's teenage idol.

FEBRUARY 13, 1943: By the time he made his second sold-out appearance at the Paramount, Dad had left his *Reflections* series and joined the cast of CBS' *Your Hit Parade*, sponsored by Lucky Strike, a musical countdown of the top hits and Saturday night's most popular weekly radio show. Working with research, which included sales of records, sheet music and the number of times records were played on jukeboxes, the *Hit Parade* disclosed and ranked the most popular songs in the country. With even the cast and crew sworn to keep the results secret until airtime, all week people waited eagerly for the countdown, during which they'd learn of the ratings and hear the songs sung by the top talent in America. *Your Hit Parade* producers had long viewed vocalists as incidental to the orchestra, but Frank's effect on the show was immediate and emphatic: The vocalist became the star.

MARCH 1943: Finally freed legally from his contract with Dorsey and RCA, Frank signed with Columbia Records. Manie Sacks wanted him to debut with a rerecording of "All or Nothing at All," but since the musicians' union was still out on strike, Columbia rereleased the 1939 version Frank recorded with Harry James. It became Dad's first million seller—and a Sinatra classic.

MARCH 11, 1943: In search of a more sophisticated audience, Dad opened at the Rio Bamba club, a watering hole for Manhattan socialites. It was uptown and upscale from the bobby-soxer set who thronged the Paramount, but since the place was in financial difficulties, he took a mere $800 a week in salary. By the end of his first week, it was standing room only, and *Life* magazine ran a major story on his appearance.

SPRING 1943: *Downbeat* magazine reported that as he was leaving a Manhattan broadcast studio, Frank Sinatra noticed a 12-year-old girl who became so excited by his presence that she caught her hand in a door. He then sent Hank Sanicola back to find out if she was badly hurt. She wasn't, so he treated her to ice cream at the Hotel Astor's chic restaurant.

MAY 14, 1943: Still going strong on *Your Hit Parade*, he debuted on *Broadway Band Box*, a classy half-hour Friday night radio series that showcased his talents not only as a vocalist singing his own selections, but also as a casual host to musical giants such as Benny Goodman and Duke Ellington.

MAY 16, 1943: Appearing on stage with other stars on "I Am an American Day," a World War II bond rally in New York's Central Park, Dad stopped the show with his heartfelt rendition of "God Bless America."

MAY 18, 1943: He gave another benefit performance, this time on behalf of Greek war relief, at Madison Square Garden.

MAY 26, 1943: He was back again at the Paramount for a third sold-out month of daily shows.

JUNE 7, 1943: In his first sessions at the Columbia studios in New York, Dad recorded a series of songs with the Bobby Tucker Singers. Since the musicians' strike was still in effect, they could not use a live orchestra and had to record a cappella. Recorded were songs such as "You'll Never Know," "Close to You" and "People Will Say We're in Love."

An increasingly familiar scene wherever he appeared in public: Dad wading through his fans.

Crooning on the Airwaves

During World War II, with 10 million men and women in uniform, tens of millions more involved in the war effort and some of the big bands traveling overseas, network radio began to overshadow the impact of recorded music on malt-shop jukeboxes and home phonographs around the country. New radio personalities emerged—mostly comedians like Bob Hope, Edgar Bergen, Fred Allen and Fibber McGee and Molly. Vocalists like Frank Sinatra became popular with big bands in live radio "remotes" from theater and nightclub stages. As the importance of radio in promoting music became evident, networks like NBC/RCA began expanding their own record labels.

A moment for the memory books: his debut at the Hollywood Bowl.

ONE NIGHT ONLY
SAT. AUG. 14 9:00 P.M.
FRANK SINATRA
with the L. A. Philharmonic Orchestra
HOLLYWOOD ★ BOWL ★
ONE NIGHT ONLY
SAT. AUG. 14 9:00 P.M.

Gen. Adm. 75c → Reserved $1.10, 1.65, 2.20 Tax Included
HQ. 3151 or So. Calif. Music Co., 737 So. Hill St., TU. 1141 and All Mutual Agencies

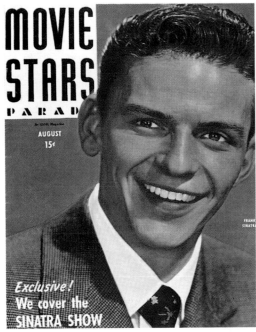

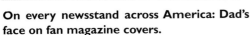
On every newsstand across America: Dad's face on fan magazine covers.

JUNE 17, 1943: To entertain the men and women of the armed forces, Frank appeared at a Stage Door Canteen show on ABC radio in New York.

JULY 14, 1943: In his first appearance with a classical orchestra, he performed with the Cleveland Philharmonic.

AUGUST 3, 1943: Appearing with the Philadelphia Philharmonic at Lewisohn Stadium, Dad sang to a turnout of 5,000 classical-music fans. According to *Life* magazine, music critics felt he was out of his league, but couldn't find fault with his voice.

AUGUST 11, 1943: Traveling by train to Los Angeles, Dad tried to avoid the waiting crowds by deboarding in Pasadena, but it was no use: A huge throng of bobbysoxers mobbed the station, and he was rushed by police to the safety of a nearby garage. "They converged on our car and practically picked it up," Dad recalls. "There must have been 5,000 kids mashed against the car. It was exciting, but it scares the wits out of you, too."

AUGUST 14, 1943: Ending weeks of public controversy over whether or not to showcase Frank in a venue previously reserved exclusively for highbrow music, the directors of the all-but-bankrupt Hollywood Bowl reluctantly agreed to book him. He played to a packed house of 10,000, wiping out the Bowl's debt in a single stroke. The first half of the program, featuring such lighter classical numbers as Mussorgsky's "Night on Bald Mountain" and Rimsky-Korsakov's "Flight of the Bumblebee," was conducted by Constantin Bakaleinikoff. Then my father, billed only as a "baritone soloist," walked on stage in a white dinner jacket to begin his own program with "Dancing in the Dark," followed by "Night and Day," "You'll Never Know" and "The Song Is You." Before singing Jerome Kern's "Ol' Man River," he told the audience, "I'm not going to sing it like Paul Robeson—I'm not in his class. Yet." He concluded with "All or Nothing at All" and left to a standing ovation. He was awed and humbled by the reaction of the fans. Frank Sinatra had conquered a new arena.

FS establishing a beachhead with the upscale audience at uptown nightspots like the Waldorf's Wedgwood Room.

Producer
Norman Corwin

ON SINATRA'S EARLY POLITICS:

It took great courage for Frank Sinatra to stand up for his political beliefs the way he did. You may think that's just something you do every time you vote and pay taxes. But it's different with an artist whose fortune depends on his appeal to the public. During FDR's re-election campaign in 1944, a famous comedian had agreed to appear on a big election-eve broadcast I was producing on behalf of the President, but the star's advisers warned that he might alienate millions of voters and risk losing half his income, so he canceled out at the last minute. Frank, on the other hand, fought tooth and nail for the candidate of his choice. He electioneered for FDR all over the country. He made speeches and sang, and never worried for a minute whether any of his fans differed with his politics. It would have been easy for him to rest on his laurels, use his fame strictly as a source of income. But above all else he is a citizen. And a patriot.

Left: Orson Welles, Quentin Reynolds and Toots Shor hoist Frank in the air to celebrate Roosevelt's victory.

President Roosevelt, for whom he was a major campaign contributor. On his way out, reporters asked him what he thought of Roosevelt's prospects for winning an unprecedented fourth term. "You might say I'm in favor of it," Dad replied.

FALL 1944: Along with Bing Crosby, Bob Hope and Harpo Marx, Dad did his bit for the war effort by promoting the purchase of war bonds in a U.S. Treasury short subject, *The All-Star Bond Rally.* He sang "Saturday Night (Is the Loneliest Night of the Week)" with the Harry James Band.

OCTOBER 11, 1944: With 5,000 teenage fans screaming, stamping their feet and running up the aisles to the stage, Dad opened another historic engagement at New York's Paramount. When many of the bobby-soxers refused to leave the theater at noon after his first performance, the 30,000 fans waiting outside—many there since the night before—stampeded in rage, and it took the police until late that night to quell what became known as the Columbus Day Riot. New York's *Sunday News* compared the mass hysteria attending Sinatra's appearance with such historic events as the mob scene at silent-screen star Rudolph Valentino's funeral and the Children's Crusade of Europe's Dark Ages.

NOVEMBER-DECEMBER 1944: At the end of the musicians' strike, after a year-long hiatus in recording, Dad recorded 19 songs with Alex Stordahl in four amazingly productive marathon sessions at the Columbia studios in New York. Among them: "Saturday Night (Is the Loneliest Night of the Week)," "White Christmas," "Ol' Man River," "Stormy Weather," "Embraceable You," "Nancy" and "She's Funny That Way."

Above: A huge crowd of Sinatra fans outside New York's Paramount stampeded in rage after being turned away when many of the 5,000 screaming teenagers inside refused to leave after Dad's previous performance. It took the police hours to quell what became known as the Columbus Day Riot on October 11, 1944. Even Mayor LaGuardia was affected by the hysteria. He gave his annual speech to a smaller crowd than Frank Sinatra had waiting in line at the Paramount.

FS with conductor-arranger Axel Stordahl at one of their many Columbia recording sessions in 1945.

DECEMBER 30, 1944: When his two-year contract with *Your Hit Parade* came up for a one-year option renewal, producer George Washington Hill balked when Frank asked for a raise, so my father proposed a 13-week layoff instead. Hill wouldn't agree to that either, or to moving the whole show to the West Coast, so Frank ended his relationship with the program and was replaced by Metropolitan Opera star Lawrence Tibbett—at $3,500 a week.

JANUARY 3, 1945: *The Frank Sinatra Show*, sponsored by Max Factor, returned to the air on CBS.

JANUARY 29, 1945: Dad kicked off his most prolific year yet in the recording studio with an outpouring of huge hits for Columbia. Among them were the "Soliloquy" from *Carousel*, "She's Funny That Way," "Someone to Watch over Me," "Embraceable You," "The House I Live In," "Nancy" and Ruth Lowe's "Put Your Dreams Away," which became his theme song—43 in all, four of them Top Ten, all of them singles in the old 78 rpm format.

SHE'S FUNNY THAT WAY

Words by
RICHARD A. WHITING

Music by
NEIL MORÉT

Featured by
FRANK SINATRA

ROBBINS MUSIC CORPORATION

My father sang this song for my mother— recorded it for her and addressed it to her when she was in the audience. I still think of them when I hear it. It remains one of his favorite songs.

SPRING 1945: Hollywood was Dad's oyster, and he was befriending a wide circle of the famous: Bing Crosby, Jack Benny, Phil Silvers and the town's most famous couple, Lauren Bacall and Humphrey Bogart, who took a liking to Dad from the time they met him at Players Restaurant on the Sunset Strip. As Lauren Bacall wrote in her memoirs, when Bogart was introduced to Frank, he said, "They tell me you have a voice that makes girls faint. Make me faint." FS grinned and said he was taking the week off. Bogart laughed, and the two became fast friends.

Bogie liked Dad's cockiness and his irreverence toward the Hollywood establishment. Both would become increasingly evident as FS ignored the advice of publicist George Evans and movie-industry bigwigs to be more discreet about conducting his personal life in public. During this heady period of newfound stardom, he was allegedly seen around town squiring starlet Marilyn Maxwell and "sweater girl" Lana Turner, among other women. It would be only a matter of time until the gossip columnists would begin to report on his "extracurricular activities."

APRIL 12, 1945: "The President is dead," said the radio announcer. I was only four, but there was no misunderstanding those four words. My dad had lost a hero. The times were changing. Harry Truman, FDR's Vice President, stepped into the Oval Office. Looming on the horizon were Hiroshima and Nagasaki. The bobby-soxers were growing up, but Frank Sinatra was still on top.

APRIL 1945: On a social evening out with friends at the Mocambo, a Sunset Strip nightclub, Dad met a sultry siren named Ava Gardner, who was about to become the hottest female star in town. There was chemistry between them, but the 22-year-old North Carolinean was married to Mickey Rooney. Recalled Ava years later in her autobiography: "He gave me the big grin and said, 'Hey, why didn't I meet you before Mickey? Then I could have married you myself.'" Frank was an engaging flirt, but nothing happened because she knew he was a married man with children.

JUNE 1945: For the duration of the war, my father wanted to entertain the troops overseas. But the FBI had denied him a visa because of the alleged Communist charges in the Hearst newspapers. Finally cleared, he was permitted to visit America's front lines only after V-E Day, touring North Africa and Italy and entertaining the troops with his friend Phil Silvers.

AUGUST 15, 1945: *Anchors Aweigh* opened to rave reviews and big box office around the country, and Frank Sinatra became a major movie star.

SEPTEMBER 11, 1945: Putting his convictions on the line, Dad played himself, preaching tolerance to a group of boys in *The House I Live In,* a 10-minute short for RKO—his last project with that studio—on the theme of racial tolerance: "Look, fellas, religion makes no difference except to a Nazi or somebody as stupid. Why, people

Declared 4-F, physically ineligible for military service despite his efforts to enlist, Dad supported the war effort by touring North Africa and Italy, entertaining the troops with his friend Phil Silvers.

all over the world worship God in different ways. This wonderful country is made up of a hundred different kinds of people, and a hundred different ways of talking, and a hundred different ways of going to church. But they're all American ways. My dad came from Italy, but I'm an American. Should I hate your father 'cause he came from Ireland or France or Russia? Wouldn't I be a first-class fathead?" The film was written by Albert Maltz, produced by Frank Ross and directed by Mervyn LeRoy, but it was Dad's baby from start to finish: It was his idea, he persuaded every-one involved to donate their time and, because he was the star, its message of tol-erance was communicated to a lot of people who might not have been inclined to listen otherwise. The proceeds were donated to various charities, and the film won a special Oscar from the Academy of Motion Picture Arts and Sciences.

SEPTEMBER 12, 1945: *The Frank Sinatra Show* was revived on CBS radio, this time as a half-hour program with guest stars sponsored by Old Gold cigarettes. It would remain on the air for almost two years.

LATE SEPTEMBER 1945: Broke, out of work and sharing a two-dollar-a-night hotel room with his dad and uncle, young hoofer Sammy Davis Jr. waited at the KFWB stage door in Hollywood for Dad to finish signing autographs. Reminded that they appeared on the same bill with Tommy Dorsey in Detroit five years earlier, Dad left a pass allowing Sammy to watch the next week's broadcast from the studio

Above: A staged shot with the cast of the film *The House I Live In*. Left: Gathering in the Oscar for *The House I Live In*, FS shares the stage with the actor (later senator) who pre-sented it, George Murphy, and the young actress Peggy Ann Garner. He could not have known how long it would be before he'd hold another Oscar or how important the next one would be to his life, career and spirits.

audience. After the show, he invited Sammy to stop by his dressing room. It was the start of a beautiful friendship.

NOVEMBER 1, 1945: Impressed by the impact of *The House I Live In*—and the passion of Dad's involvement in civil rights—William Paley of CBS arranged for him to do a lecture tour on racial tolerance at campuses around the country. In Gary, Indiana, Dad happened to appear at Froebel High School at the height of a strike by white students protesting the "pro-Negro" policies of a new principal who allowed some 270 black children to share classrooms and other facilities with 1,000 whites. Facing them down in the school auditorium, he actually defused the situation.

Armed Forces Radio drew its complement of stars, including some of Hollywood's most famous and talented children. Back Row: Gary Crosby, Peggy Ann Garner, Elizabeth Taylor, Roddy McDowall, FS. Front Row: Lindsay Crosby, Margaret O'Brien, Nancy Sinatra, Dennis Crosby, Philip Crosby.

Sinatra defuses a racial confrontation:

"Frank walked out on stage and stood dead center," recalled publicist Jack Keller, who accompanied Dad to Gary, Indiana, "while all these rough, tough steel workers and their kids started catcalling and whistling and stamping their feet. Frank folded his arms, looked down at them and stared for a full two minutes, until there was dead silence in the room. 'I can lick any son of a bitch in this joint!' he said without the trace of a smile." Cheering and screaming, the kids went crazy. In that instant, he had shown that he was one of them, and captured their hearts. "I implore you to return to school," he said. "This is a bad deal, kids. It's not good for you and it's not good for the city of Gary, which has done so much to help with the war for freedom the world over. Believe me, I know something about the business of racial intolerance. At eleven I was called 'a dirty wop' back home in New Jersey. We've all done it. We've all used the words nigger or kike or mick or polack or dago. Cut it out, kids. Go back to school." He left to thunderous applause. That didn't end the strike, but his effort was nevertheless honored by New York's Bureau of Intercultural Education, the National Conference of Christians and Jews, the Newspaper Guild, and the Catholic Youth Organization of Chicago, among several other organizations. This kind of commitment to equality prompted the conservative press to continue its insinuations that Dad was a Communist.

ONE WEEK ONLY

FRANK SINATRA in Person

Marquee, Golden Gate Theatre, San Francisco, March, 1946

IN PERSON **FRANK SINATRA** IN PERSON

THE PIED PIPERS
AXEL STORDAHL
AND HIS AUGMENTED RADIO ORCH.

SINGING HIS LATEST COLUMBIA RECORDING HITS

ON THE STAGE

FRANK SINATRA

"This is our Frank Sinatra ward"

NOVEMBER 7-DECEMBER 17, 1945: Back in New York, Dad ran the gamut of audiences from teenage America to high society with three weeks at the Paramount, followed by two more in the Wedgwood Room of the Waldorf-Astoria.

FEBRUARY-MARCH 1946: Beginning with this first session at the Columbia studio in Hollywood, Dad began the busiest year in his recording history, logging 57 songs. Many were memorable—"That Old Black Magic," "They Say It's Wonderful," "The Girl That I Marry," "September Song" and "Begin the Beguine."

MARCH 4, 1946: Frank released his 78 rpm album "The Voice."

MARCH 20-26, 1946: Embarking on a cross-country tour of extended engagements around the country, he appeared for a week at the Golden Gate Theater in San Francisco and went on to Philadelphia in April, Detroit in May, New York's Madison Square Garden and Chicago Stadium in June and the Hollywood Bowl in July and August.

SEPTEMBER 9, 1946: When Phil Silvers signed to star at the Copacabana in New York, he planned to appear with Rags Ragland, his buddy and best friend from their early days in burlesque. Sadly, Rags died two weeks before opening night, and Phil was about to go on alone, grieving and distraught, when there came a knock on his dressing room door an hour before curtain time. It was his friend Frank Sinatra, who had worked with him on Rags' routines while they were entertaining the troops in Europe. "Hi," he said, "what do we open with?"

An Unforgettable Fourth

My parents invited everyone who lived around the lake to sit outside at sunset for our fireworks show. My brother and I, who had never seen fireworks, were in charge of the music: a record player with marching band records. Mom did the decorating—lots of red, white and blue. And Dad, of course, did the fireworks. He had two big cartons of them out on the raft. And on the newly erected flagpole, he nailed the pinwheels. He had on his white pants, his blue-and-white-striped French Navy T-shirt, his yachting hat and his brand-new wristwatch. All the neighbors were out with their blankets and picnic baskets, and the people whose homes were around the bend rowed their boats nearby so they could see. At dusk, Dad pushed the raft away from our dock and dropped anchor halfway across the lake. He pointed to Frankie and me on our grassy hill (that was our signal to start "The Star-Spangled Banner") and he raised the flag. The National Anthem played and the people stood up and saluted and Dad opened up the cartons of fireworks. We were breathless, Frankie and I, hands over hearts, mouths and eyes wide open as we watched Dad set a match to the first pinwheel... It started to whistle and spin, and the bright sparks went flying around, and some of them set the next whistling pinwheel off, and some of them landed in one of the boxes of fireworks... BOOM! Suddenly everything exploded. All at once Roman candles shot up and rockets flew and everything got smoky. Our father disappeared to the strains of "The Stars and Stripes Forever." Frankie and I ran down the hill screaming, "Daddy, Daddy!" He finally reappeared, pulling himself out of the water, still wearing his hat and his brand-new, not-very-waterproof watch, as the people in the boats put the fire out with lake water.

Phil Silvers

ON OPENING NIGHT AT THE COPA WITH SINATRA:

Frank was in the middle of making a picture in Hollywood, but there he was standing in the doorway. I know Frank—you don't say, "Gee, you came." You play it cool. So I said, "Well, I'll do a few minutes first, and when I touch my tie you appear and we'll do our routines. You know them all." I can't tell you the reaction when he came out and I looked at him and said, "Scram, kid, I work alone." And then the standard jokes like, "I know there's a food shortage, but this is ridiculous," and "The blood bank is two blocks up the street," etc. We proceeded to do an hour and three quarters of material, and at our conclusion received an ovation. But gratitude embarrassed Frank. I looked for him to thank him for this expression of love and friendship, and he was gone—back to Hollywood, where he had caused a two-day delay because of this gesture. But that's Sinatra. You don't thank him. You just lean back and accept it.

OCTOBER 1, 1946: Dad performed at a star-studded tribute to Al Jolson in New York.

DECEMBER 1946: Along with a galaxy of MGM stars, Dad made a cameo appearance in *Till the Clouds Roll By*, a lavishly mounted biopic on the life and music of Jerome Kern. But he sang his powerfully moving rendition of "Ol' Man River."

DECEMBER 21, 1946: In a taste of what was in store for him throughout the next decade—despite his countless unreported acts of kindness and consideration—Frank won in a landslide as the Hollywood Women's Press Club voted him "Least Cooperative Star" of 1946 because of his standoffishness with the press. His attitude was misconstrued because many fans and even responsible journalists never saw the sleazy columns attacking him. He had no forum to respond to these false allegations and attacks.

DECEMBER 31, 1946: My mother discovered a diamond bracelet in the glove compartment of the new Cadillac convertible that Dad was teaching her to drive. Figuring it was a gift for her, she said nothing. But that night at the family New Year's Eve party, she spied actress Marilyn Maxwell wearing the bracelet. Outraged, she ordered Maxwell out of the house and then confronted her husband: "How dare you shame me in my own home? My father fooled around on my mother, but I won't stand for it!" Contrite, Dad protested later, "But she doesn't mean anything to me. No one could compare to you." Glaring at him, she said, "Go to hell." But she forgave him and they made up—for the moment. It wasn't a promising way to end the year.

*"I'm not much to look at
nothin' to see
Just glad I'm livin'
and lucky to be
I got a woman crazy for me
she's funny that way."*

Just One Of Those Things

World War II was over, and as people everywhere began the healing process, everything had changed. Before and during the war, Frank Sinatra was the king of crooners. But now, the bobby-soxers who had listened to his radio shows, watched his movies, bought his records and lined up for his concerts were growing older, and the national interest in swing was waning. The big-band era was in its final hurrah, and radio was taking a back seat to the new household phenomenon—television. All this made it appear that the skyrocketing career of Frank Sinatra was leveling off.

The next few years were to test Dad's mettle and significantly shape the man he eventually became. It was a time in which he experienced excruciating trauma in his personal life with a divorce from Mom and a tempestuous courtship and marriage to Ava Gardner. Although he was constantly working, this was definitely a low point in his career. Even some of his "good friends" abandoned him. It was a time of heartache and frustration—a time he continues to this day to refer to as the darkest years.

But Dad never gave up, and though he found himself broke at various times, he was still able to pay the bills. With dogged persistence and some serious soul searching, he was able to come back stronger than before. With a new singing style, a new record label, a new agent and a jaunty new attitude, he once again became a man of the times.

It was one of the most dramatic comebacks in show-business history, and the public loved him for it.

Looking out from our new dining room on Toluca Lake in the San Fernando Valley, North Hollywood. We also spent time at the Lone Palm Hotel in Palm Springs while our new house there—designed by my mother and father—was being built.

Writer/Producer Dore Schary, Melvyn Douglas, Danny Kaye and Frank Sinatra flank Eleanor Roosevelt at a Democratic fundraiser.

JANUARY 9, 1947: In the new year's opening session at Columbia studios in New York, Frank recorded the first of an incredibly prolific 71 songs he would turn out in 1947. Among them were "Always," "I Concentrate on You" and "My Love for You." The year also produced "Almost Like Being in Love," "Have Yourself a Merry Little Christmas," "The Nearness of You," "But Beautiful," "All of Me," "Laura," "None but the Lonely Heart," "Fools Rush In," "Body and Soul" and "Autumn in New York."

FEBRUARY 1947: FS was continuing his radio show *Songs by Sinatra*—sponsored by Old Gold cigarettes—in New York on Wednesday nights.

FEBRUARY 8, 1947: He gave a "Command Performance" show for the armed forces in Miami.

FEBRUARY 11, 1947: En route to Mexico City for a vacation with Mom, Dad stopped off for two days to gamble in Havana. Deplaning from a Pan-American clipper, he was allegedly photographed with Rocco and Joe Fischetti, former childhood acquaintances from Hoboken. After a day spent at a casino and the racetrack, friends of the Fischettis invited him to join a group in the dining room of the Hotel

Nacional. Later that evening, another photographer allegedly took Dad's picture with several other friends of the Fischettis. One of them was Charles "Lucky" Luciano, deported boss of the Cosa Nostra crime syndicate. In a series of articles, Lee Mortimer of the Hearst syndicate accused my father of being a sidekick of mobsters, which only exacerbated the continuing FBI investigation. Publicist George Evans had to fly to Havana to discuss these charges with Dad, telling him that his career was in jeopardy and he had better return home. My father followed Evans' advice. Unfortunately, this story—which would later be blown completely out of proportion—wouldn't go away.

FEBRUARY 1947: With Harry Truman elevated to the presidency by the death of FDR, Republicans launched an early campaign to oust the lame-duck president and regain the White House by smearing prominent Democratic campaign contributors—including, once again, my father. In the right-wing Hearst and Scripps-Howard papers, columnist Robert Ruark and Dad's nemesis Lee Mortimer accused Frank of sinister motives for being in Cuba with Luciano and the Fischetti brothers. They even printed a ludicrous story that he carried $2,000,000 in small bills on a plane from Miami to Havana and was to deliver it personally to Luciano. And columnist Westbrook Pegler—who Dad later described as "a man with clout"—soon revived the old charges that Frank Sinatra was a Communist "fellow traveler."

Frank on Louis B. Mayer and MGM

I was sitting in the makeup chair at RKO when Joe Nolan, a nice guy who was in charge of production, came in and said to me, "You'd better get your bag packed. You've been traded." I said, "What is this, a ball club or something?" He said that Mayer wanted me and he had me. I went from $25,000 a picture to $130,000 a picture. Now if you were at Metro, they signed you and you got paid every week. But it was almost like the rule of the NFL: If you didn't do a picture you were on suspension until the end of the picture. Then they'd give you another script and if you took it, fine, and if you didn't take it, they didn't kick you out, you just didn't get paid for a time. But you didn't want for anything. Instead of chintzy little dressing rooms, theirs were beautiful, made of cedar, with settees and coffeemakers and a record player. But no telephone, because it could spoil a scene if the phone started ringing in the middle of it. But I said I had to have a phone. I love the telephone. I don't love it when it rings and rings and nobody answers, but I needed one because I was beginning to get into businesses too. So we came up with an idea of how to solve it. We silenced the bell and put on a light. I did a lot of other things, and usually the minute I said I'd like something, bang, it was done. I was Mayer's boy until I made a wisecrack later on, but for a long time there was nothing better. It was almost like a womb. Everything was done for you. If an actor was signed and had to move out from the east, and he wanted to buy a house for his family, they would lay out the money and deduct a little each week. It was warm and happy and I miss it today. There is no such thing anymore. Mayer was a genius. I don't think he knew the front of a camera from the back, but he knew people, and when he booked people I don't think he ever missed. They became major stars. He had good people working under him and the best of everything around him.

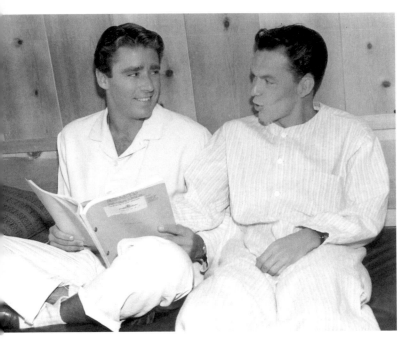

Peter Lawford and FS running their lines on the set of *It Happened in Brooklyn*.

In internal memos to and from FBI Associate Director Clyde Tolson during this same period—released many years later under the Freedom of Information Act—it became clear that unofficial "cooperation" had been offered privately to Mortimer by the FBI, and that much of its own file on Sinatra, in turn, was based on unsupported accusations and innuendos passed along to the agency by Mortimer without any corroboration. Most of the charges, however, came from "leaks" by Harry Anslinger of the National Narcotics Bureau, who had denounced my father as a dangerous "pinko" because of his vocal support for civil rights, his roots in the Sicilian community and his many friendships with "dope-smoking" musicians. So began another myth.

MARCH 1947: MGM's Louis B. Mayer told my father's agents at MCA that he was distressed by the negative publicity. At MGM, Frank's relationship with Mayer had always been an odd one. Mayer had been so taken with Dad's singing—at the benefit for the Jewish Home for the Aged back in 1944—that he sort of adopted him. He really loved him, and the feeling was mutual.

MARCH 11, 1947: FS recorded "Stella by Starlight" and "Mam'selle," which became a top ten single.

MARCH 14, 1947: Dad co-starred with Kathryn Grayson, Jimmy Durante and Peter Lawford in MGM's *It Happened in Brooklyn*, which began filming in Los Angeles. Dad won critical praise for his performance as an ex-soldier returning home to civilian life after World War II, and he sang seven songs. Among them: "Time After Time." According to *Newsweek*, "Sinatra becomes a smoother performer every time out."

MARCH 27, 1947: He played the San Francisco Paramount with Bob Hope and Jack Benny in a benefit for the Damon Runyon Cancer Fund.

APRIL 8, 1947: At Ciro's in West Hollywood, Dad heard that reporter Lee Mortimer, dining at a nearby table, had just called him "a dago son of a bitch," and after an angry altercation, proceeded to punch him out. Arrested for assault, Frank was bailed out, and the sheriff revoked his gun permit. The bad blood between him and Mortimer ran deep—after all, this was the guy who began the 50-year smear that cost Dad some important jobs and caused the family so much heartache—and the case wasn't settled until the day he was scheduled to go to trial: Frank paid him $9,000 and was ordered by the court to give a public apology. The story made headlines around the country, and though some applauded my father for teaching Mortimer a lesson he deserved, it was also a field day for his critics in the press, who were becoming increasingly numerous.

APRIL 13, 1947: At the Waldorf-Astoria in New York, Dad received the Thomas Jefferson Award for his fight against intolerance. That same day, he was interviewed by Walter Winchell and Louella Parsons on their radio shows.

Lee Mortimer (standing behind Frank in the courthouse) was not the first journalist to abuse his responsibilities and then hide behind the First Amendment.

A personal note of gratitude

In a remarkable open letter written on MGM studio letterhead in the late spring of 1947, Frank Sinatra spoke candidly about his recent troubles and thanked his fans and friends for believing in him.

Dear Friends,

This is a letter of heartfelt gratitude to all of you everywhere. I've been told that there are a thousand different ways to say "Thank you." I just wish I knew how to thank you in all the languages spoken on this Earth. But besides a little Italian, I know only English, and that will have to do.

Lately I've been in a little trouble. Certain unscrupulous newspapermen were enjoying a field day in print. They belted my name and my reputation around, called me a "red" and the intimate chum of Lucky Luciano.

Not a word of that happens to be true. Some people, I suppose, wondered why I didn't defend myself. The extraordinary thing about it is that I wasn't given a chance.

It wasn't necessary. Too many people, many of them friends I didn't even know I had, rushed to my aid. Their messages expressing complete and unqualified faith in me came by telephone, wire and letter, an overwhelming, spontaneous vote of confidence from people in all walks of life, and of all ages.

Most of the better-known columnists came to bat for me in a hurry. Fellows like Walter Winchell, Ed Sullivan and Erskine Johnson. In fact, the vast majority of Broadway and Hollywood writers unhesitatingly announced in print that they were on my side.

Many refused to wait even to hear the evidence against me, if any. They wrote that they knew me too well and too long to doubt my integrity or patriotism.

What happened here on the MGM lot is also something I will always remember with humility and gratitude. As soon as a certain little newspaperman from New York announced he was filing suit against me, the attitude of every employee in the studio seemed to change.

I'd always got along well, I think, with my fellow workers. But this was different. Finding me under fire, everyone from messengers and prop men to the biggest MGM stars took the trouble to stop me on the studio's streets, on the sound stages and in the commissary to shake my hand. They all said the same thing.

"If it means anything, Frankie, count me on your side."

If it means anything!

It meant everything, a great comfort, a great incentive. The finest thing that ever happened in my whole lucky life. The wallops in the press began to seem like love taps. The slashing, scandalous lies that had hurt me so deeply at first became less than pin pricks. But the most thrilling surprise of all came in your reaction. You, my fans and my friends, rushed to defend me like some vast avenging army.

From the beginning of my career, I have always been aware that whatever I am and whatever I hope to be depended and depends on you. Most of you have never spoken to me or even seen me in person. You only know me as a voice on the air and a shadow on the screen.

Apparently, that was enough.

Newspapers are business enterprises, too, and if too many people refuse to buy them, they go bankrupt. And thousands of you, in every city and town where these cowardly attacks on my character were published, threatened to quit reading these newspapers unless they played fair with me. Thanks to you, the attacks ceased.

The one thing I can do in return is try to live in such a way, both as a performer and a human being, as to merit your confidence, respect and affection. Please, all of you, believe me when I say you have given me an experience that I'll always remember, an inspiration few men have been fortunate enough to enjoy.

Gratefully yours,
Frank Sinatra

Frank Sinatra and the talented musician Skitch Henderson. The two performed together countless times over three decades.

APRIL 20, 1947: He performed in an afternoon concert at Carnegie Hall with an orchestra conducted by Skitch Henderson.

APRIL 21, 1947: Dad starred with Lucille Ball and Bob Hope in the Screen Guild Theater radio production of *Too Many Husbands*.

APRIL 28, 1947: He appeared in Galveston, Texas, with Jack Benny, Alice Faye, Phil Silvers and Gene Autry in a benefit for victims of the Texas City petroleum explosion.

MAY 1947: Returning to the scene of his early triumph with Major Bowes in 1935, Dad headlined at New York's Capitol Theater. As the opening act, theater manager Sidney Fairmont wanted the Nicholas Brothers—the hottest dance act in the business—but Dad said he'd rather book an up-and-coming trio he'd heard about. "It's a dancing act," he said. "The kid in it works with his dad and his uncle. I don't know the name." So Fairmont hired Will Mastin, his brother Sammy Davis Sr. and Sammy's talented young son for $1,250 a week, far more money than they'd ever earned before. "Frank was giving us twelve hundred and fifty dollars a week!" Sammy recalled. "We had never seen that much money in our lives." "You can imagine what I had to go through to get you here," Sid told young Sammy, "because Frank didn't want any of the leading dance acts, he wanted you."

MAY 6, 1947: Dad guest-starred on NBC's *The Bob Hope Show*.

JUNE 4, 1947: He closed the season on *The Frank Sinatra Show*. It was the final show of the series.

JUNE 1947: The cast of *It Happened in Brooklyn* moved to New York for location shooting.

Sammy Davis Jr.

ON MEETING SINATRA:

Our first rehearsal, in walks Frank with the coat over his shoulder. He said, "Good afternoon, everybody." And he walked over to me and said, "My name is Frank Sinatra." I said, "I know. I was the kid in the Army who used to go see you do your radio show." He said, "Wait a minute! Are you the one that I used to give tickets to in Hollywood? You had on an Army uniform. You used to come and catch The Old Gold Show?" I said, "Yessir, I am." So in the show, Frank himself does the opening. He comes out, sings a couple of songs, then he says, "Ladies and gentlemen, now I'm going to get the show started. Here's some cats that dance up a storm. Keep your eye on the little guy in the middle— personal friend of mine." Well, that's all!

How many friends like him does a man find in a lifetime? I not only idolized him, I carefully studied his style as a performer. It got to where I sounded so much like him that I had no real style of my own. Even with this, Frank proved a friend. He talked to me about it and helped me to develop my own style or I would never have made it as a singer. Of course he was right. A selfish star would have let me continue, knowing full well that imitations only benefit the original.

JUNE 27, 1947: FS performed in a *Stars in the Spotlight* show on the Armed Forces Radio Service.

AUGUST 1, 1947: He filled in for vacationing sportscaster Bill Stern, telling sports anecdotes in a 15-minute radio show.

SEPTEMBER 6, 1947: After a two-and-a-half-year hiatus, Dad returned to NBC's *Your Hit Parade,* this time with Doris Day as a co-star.

SEPTEMBER 10-30, 1947: Hearst columnist Westbrook Pegler, fueled by Lee Mortimer and the FBI, resumed his attacks on my father, this time raking up the 1938 morals charge of "seducing a woman of good repute," never mentioning that the woman was discredited and the charges dismissed. In addition, Pegler attempted unsuccessfully to link Frank to a rogues' gallery of gangsters that included not only Lucky Luciano but Frank Costello, Joe Adonis, Longie Zwillman, Bugsy Siegel, Meyer Lansky and Willie Moretti, reputed Mob chief of Bergen County, New Jersey.

SUMMER-FALL 1947: On weekends in Los Angeles, Dad led a softball team, the Swooners, in games against other celebrity teams at various locations such as the Hollywood Bowl Field and Gilmore Field (now home to CBS Television City). He played second base in a lineup that included manager Hank Sanicola, actors Anthony Quinn and Barry Sullivan and songwriters Sammy Cahn and Jule Styne. They even had their own cheerleaders: Virginia Mayo, Marilyn Maxwell, Shelley Winters and Ava Gardner.

"Doris is so cute," said FS. "She has something wonderful about her style. It kind of bubbles. I love working with her." Doris remembered, "Frank is a wonderful guy to work with. I really owe him so much. Just watching him and working with him is a lot of help to any singer. He's so relaxed, he gave me confidence. He's just the sweetest person I've ever known in the business."

Over the course of his long run on *Your Hit Parade,* Frank shared the mike with some wonderful co-stars: Eileen Barton, Beryl Davis, Joan Edwards, Marjorie Hughes, Carol Richards, Bea Wayne, Bonnie Lou Williams and Eileen Wilson.

OCTOBER 30, 1947: Hoboken celebrated "Frank Sinatra Day," and he was there with Dolly and Marty and my mother (who was pregnant again) to receive a key to the city from the mayor and the chief of police.

As his parents looked on proudly, Frank Sinatra received a key inscribed: FROM THE HEARTS OF THE CITIZENS OF THE CITY OF HOBOKEN, NEW JERSEY. "SINATRA DAY" OCTOBER 30, 1947. In the same year, an ABC radio poll named Frank Sinatra "The Second Most Popular Living Person." (Bing Crosby was first, Pope Pius XII was third.)

*"The leaves began to fade like promises we made
How could a love that seemed so right go wrong?
The things we did last summer
I'll remember all winter long..."*

NOVEMBER 19, 1948: Back at MGM, my father was miscast—opposite Kathryn Grayson—in *The Kissing Bandit*, which opened to dismal reviews that roasted his performance in the starring role. The songs, though, were wonderful.

DECEMBER 2, 1948: Dad staged a return engagement on *Spotlight Review*.

DECEMBER 1948: FS confided in Manie Sacks, his friend and mentor at Columbia Records, that so many things were going wrong that he felt like he was all washed up. Sacks replied that life is cyclical, and that he was too talented not to bounce back. "In a few years," he said, "you'll be on top again."

JANUARY 1949: The *Downbeat* poll listed Frank Sinatra as number five among male singers—his first rating below the top three spots since the thirties.

JANUARY 4, 1949: Dad recorded 27 songs for Columbia—among them "Some Enchanted Evening" and "Just a Kiss Apart." In this Hollywood recording session, he sang "Kisses and Tears"—this version was unreleased—and "If You Stub Your Toe on the Moon."

the Sinatras

"It wasn't a very happy Christmas in 1948," my mother recalled, "but it was the cutest card I'd ever seen." My father's third LP, *Christmas Songs by Sinatra*, was Top Ten that year.

JANUARY 1949: In her book, Ava Gardner recalled running into my father on the way to MGM for the studio's famous 25th anniversary group portrait of its stars. "A car sped past me, swung in front and slowed down so much I had to pass it. Then it overtook me again and repeated the process. After this happened about three times, the driver pulled alongside me, raised his hat and sped away to the same photo session. That was Frank. He could even flirt in a car."

FEBRUARY 1949: Dad's version of "Some Enchanted Evening" was panned by *Downbeat* for a lack of intimacy and "a few off-pitch" notes. And his next release, "Bali Ha'i," fared even worse: "For all his talent," wrote the *Downbeat* reviewer, "it very seldom comes to life."

FEBRUARY 1949: Ava wrote about running into Frank again at a party in Palm Springs. This time the sparks really began to fly. "I suppose we were rushing things a little the last time we met," he said. "*You* were rushing things," she replied. "Let's start again," he suggested. "What are you doing now?" "That night we did not kiss or make a date," remembered Ava. "But we knew, and I think it must have frightened both of us."

I remember visiting my father on the set of *The Kissing Bandit*. He wore the most beautiful costume, beaded and embroidered. I thought he was the handsomest man in the whole world. He may make jokes about this movie and equate sitting through it to a sadistic form of torture, but I think it's adorable.

A classic group portrait: MGM's roster of stars at the Silver Jubilee, 1949. Left to right, top row: Alexis Smith, Ann Sothern, J. Carroll Naish, Dean Stockwell, Lewis Stone, Clinton Sundberg, Robert Taylor, Audrey Totter, Spencer Tracy, Esther Williams, Keenan Wynn. Second row: Peter Lawford, Ann Miller, Ricardo Montalban, Jules Munshin, George Murphy, Reginald Owen, Walter Pidgeon, Jane Powell, Ginger Rogers, Frank Sinatra, Red Skelton. Third row: Katharine Hepburn, John Hodiak, Claude Jarman, Jr., Van Johnson, Jennifer Jones, Louis Jourdan, Howard Keel, Gene Kelly,

Christopher Kent (Alf Kjellin), Angela Lansbury, Mario Lanza, Janet Leigh. Fourth row: Gloria DeHaven, Tom Drake, Jimmy Durante, Vera Ellen, Errol Flynn, Clark Gable, Ava Gardner, Judy Garland, Betty Garrett, Edmund Gwenn, Kathryn Grayson, Van Heflin. Bottom row: Lionel Barrymore, June Allyson, Leon Ames, Fred Astaire, Edward Arnold, Mary Astor, Ethel Barrymore, Spring Byington, James Craig, Arlene Dahl—and Lassie.

The cast of *Take Me Out to the Ball Game,* directed by the great Busby Berkeley.

Back in Hollywood, they went on another date. "We went to a little yellow house in Nichols Canyon and made love. And, oh, God, it was magic. We became lovers eternally," she said years later. I believe Ava truly loved my father. She never married again!

MARCH 10, 1949: MGM released *Take Me Out to the Ball Game,* a romantic comedy reteaming my Dad with Gene Kelly, and casting Esther Williams as Kelly's love interest. Gene told me how shocked he was during the filming by my skinny father's idea of a good lunch: a Coca-Cola and a Mars bar!

APRIL 10, 1949: Dad recorded his top ten single "The Huckle Buck" at CBS Studio on Vine Street in Los Angeles. "It's not a bad record," recalled producer George Siravo. "In fact, it's quite an entertaining package with a chorus and a characteristically kicking contribution from saxophonist Herbie Hamer. I'll never forget that session, because that's the last time I or anybody else saw Herbie. That night after the date, he got killed crossing the street."

Yankee Stadium, 1949: DiMaggio and Sinatra in the Yankees' locker room.

SPRING 1949: Hedda Hopper, Louella Parsons, Sheilah Graham and other nationally syndicated columnists began berating my father for a host of alleged extramarital affairs. His press agent, George Evans, warned that his performances were suffering from too many distractions. One of the few people in the inner circle who could tell him unpleasant truths, Evans said it was time to go home to Nancy, cut down on the booz-ing—and stay away from people with under-world connections.

MAY 28, 1949: Dad's long run on *Your Hit Parade* finally ended.

SUMMER 1949: To be nearer his work so that he could spend more time at home, Dad moved us from Toluca Lake to a $250,000 mansion at 320 Carolwood Drive in West Los Angeles, where we lived almost next door to Loretta Young, Walt Disney and Robert Ryan.

JUNE 1949: Fanning a red scare, vitriolic demagogue Senator Joseph McCarthy of Wisconsin revved up the House Un-American Activities Committee and its California counterpart. Targeting Hollywood, the state committee named Frank Sinatra—a well-known supporter of both civil rights and the Democratic Party—as one of several prominent figures who had "followed or appeased some of the Communist Party line program over a period of time." Dad was angry and hurt and felt it was unfair, but he knew it was just red-baiting. They were just fishing for Communists, and nothing came of the subsequent investigation. Yet he saw the lives of many of his friends completely destroyed.

JULY 10, 1949: FS appeared on a radio show entitled *Citizens of the World*.

JULY 15, 1949: He emceed *Sports Newsreel* for NBC radio.

SEPTEMBER 5, 1949: Dad co-starred opposite an unlikely partner, operatic soprano Dorothy Kirsten, on *Light Up Time*, a new 15-minute musical variety show sponsored by Lucky Strike cigarettes and broadcast on NBC five nights a week.

OCTOBER 30, 1949: Dad returned once again to the *Jack Benny Show.*

NOVEMBER 6, 1949: He performed on *Guest Star*, a radio show for the U.S. Treasury Department.

DECEMBER 8, 1949: Ava remembered when their relationship finally began to turn serious. She wrote in her book that he told her: "All my life, being a singer was the most important thing in the world. Now you're all I want." They turned up together in New York to attend the premiere of *Gentlemen Prefer Blondes*, and gossip columnists reported spotting them at the Hampshire House hotel, where Manie Sacks had a suite.

Bomber Shapiro, Frankie and I were the only kids on Carolwood Drive. Tina was a baby. It was our territory and we took full advantage of it. Our favorite thing was tormenting the neighbors.

Frank and his *Light Up Time* partner, Dorothy Kirsten.

"Here at MGM I was in a sailor suit," Dad recalled. **"I was never out of a sailor suit."**

The wire services picked up the story, and their romance, despite proforma denials, made headlines. George Evans advised Dad to stay away from Ava as long as he was still married to Nancy. And he warned that Louis B. Mayer at MGM was threatening to terminate both their contracts if there was more adverse publicity about them. It was about this time that Evans announced his resignation.

DECEMBER 12, 1949: *On the Town*, third in MGM's trio of co-starring roles for Dad and Gene Kelly, put them back in sailor suits with co-star Jules Munshin for a film version of the Broadway hit, with Gene and Stanley Donen directing, songs by Betty Comden and Adolph Green and an incidental score by Leonard Bernstein. Three sailors on shore leave in New York meet three pretty girls: What else does a movie musical need? "New York, New York, a wonderful town. The Bronx is up and the Battery's down..." Dad and Betty Garrett do one of the niftiest duets ever, "Come Up to My Place." I love this movie. So do my kids, by the way—and so does half the world, I think. In rehearsal, Gene taught Dad to "really dance." Gene recalled: "I took Frank's hands off the mike, so to speak, and taught him a few simple steps. He was a quick study." FS also came to admire co-stars Ann Miller, Betty Garrett and Vera-Ellen: "Those girls could move, and they gave us a lot of ooomph." Cast and crew shot musical numbers on city streets—a difficult technical achievement and an MGM first. It was another hit.

DECEMBER 26, 1949: Dad guest-starred on the radio mystery series, *Inner Sanctum*.

JANUARY 1950: Dad's most steadfast ally in the recording world, Manie Sacks, resigned from Columbia Records. The new boss, Mitch Miller, would have trouble matching the commercial songs of the day with the voice and persona of Frank Sinatra. Miller had more success with Frankie Laine, Tony Bennett and Johnny Ray, and he began a pattern of pairing Frank with songs unsuitable for his style and voice.

JANUARY 12, 1950: In Frank's first concert in two years, in Hartford, Connecticut, *Variety* announced that the take was his biggest ever: $18,267 for two days.

JANUARY 27, 1950: George Evans died at age 48 of a massive coronary. Deeply grieved, Dad flew to New York for the funeral.

JANUARY 28, 1950: Straight from Evans' funeral, Dad flew to Houston for the grand opening of the luxurious new Shamrock Hotel. Ava Gardner surprised him there. When they were spotted together in Vincento's Sorrentino restaurant by a pushy photographer, Dad's temper exploded and the scene was reported in the papers. "The trouble started when the mayor of Houston invited us to dinner at one of the city's best Italian restaurants," Ava recalled. "In the middle of the meal, a photographer from the *Houston Post* arrived to commemorate the occasion. Frank reacted as if he'd found a live cobra in his salad. No punches were exchanged, only a few angry words, before the owner calmed everybody down. But within 24 hours the news that Frank Sinatra and Ava Gardner were honoring the new hotel with their presence made headlines. A press storm of major proportions broke over our heads, dooming forever the 'just good friends' line we'd been successful with so far."

Dad dancing with lucky fan Dolores Browning during a 1950 appearance at the Shamrock Hotel in Beaumont, Texas.

FEBRUARY 14, 1950: Humiliated by press accounts of her husband in Houston with Ava, Mom announced that they were splitting up—on Valentine's Day. As a Catholic, she couldn't divorce him, so she filed for a legal separation, which would grant Dad his freedom. Press reaction was swift and harsh, with him depicted as a heel and Ava as a homewrecker. One day while I was playing dress-up in Mom's dressing room, I climbed up on a chair to get a shoebox off a shelf and knocked to the floor a stack of magazines that Mom had hidden in her closet. They were movie magazines—*Modern Screen, Photoplay* and so forth—and they were filled with pictures of Dad and a pretty lady

Ava Gardner
ON THE MORALS OF THE FIFTIES:

When Nancy said, "My married life with Frank has become unhappy and almost unbearable," the shit really hit the fan. In the next few weeks, I received scores of letters accusing me of being a scarlet woman and worse. One correspondent addressed me as "Bitch-Jezebel-Gardner," the Legion of Decency threatened to ban my movies, and Catholic priests found the time to write me accusatory letters. I even read where the Sisters of Mary and Joseph asked their students at St. Paul the Apostle School in Los Angeles to pray for Frank's poor wife. I didn't understand then and still don't why there should be this prurient mass hysteria about a male and a female climbing into bed and doing what comes naturally.

Tina

ON THE SPLIT-UP:

When he left home, I was a baby, so I wasn't accustomed to a man in the house. I didn't feel the wrench; I didn't know him. Conversely, I had to deal with this very nice man coming through our lives from time to time. It was always—certainly—a special occasion. But there was a point where you realized that everything had to be just so. You know, we had to get cleaned and washed and combed and groomed and it wasn't comfortable. And he would come and go and come and go. And I didn't know where to find him. But I think I've gotten off a lot easier than others. I never had the feelings of what I'm told all children go through, where the child feels as much to blame—he's left me, not you, Mommy. What I did feel was that when he was around, I was different. I couldn't figure out why. Who is "he" that I should change? I used to feel nervous when I was going to see him. I had anxiety.

named Ava Gardner, and Mom and Frankie and Baby Tina and me. There were also pictures of Dad with other ladies. I remember Marilyn Maxwell and Lana Turner. I was devastated—just like Mom. He had left me, too. I knew then that this trip was different. This was the long goodbye we had rehearsed so often, but the one I could never completely accept. My brother was to suffer, too. And my infant sister and her father said goodbye before she could even say hello.

Eventually, inevitably, I would meet this other woman. The first time we met, there was no preparation. It was meant to be matter-of-fact. They were living in a house in Coldwater Canyon. My father picked me up and said, "I want to show you my house." When we went in, there was a woman upstairs at her dressing table, brushing her shoulder-length hair. Daddy said, "Chicken, this is Ava." I said, "Hi, how do you do?" or whatever, just as I had been taught, and that was that. Except that instead of feeling pain or resentment or anger, what I saw helped me understand what my father felt. And he was clearly swept away. My heart melted just looking at her. I was only a kid. I didn't know about beauty—that awesome kind of beauty that takes your breath away. She was just the most beautiful creature I had ever seen in my life. I couldn't stop staring at her. At last, in my pre-teenage wisdom, I had some understanding of why Daddy left us. In 1984, I asked him if, given the choice again, he would have left us, and he said, "No."

FEBRUARY 26, 1950: FS appeared in a fund-raising gala at the Biltmore Bowl on behalf of the Jewish Home for the Aged.

MARCH 1950: Amid stories about his torrid affair with Ava, Frank opened at the Copacabana in New York, his first nightclub appearance in five years. After 10 nights in the audience, Ava left for Europe to make *Pandora and the Flying Dutchman*.

APRIL 26, 1950: Dad's voice was faltering, and he finally lost it entirely, canceling the last two days of his engagement at the Copacabana because of a vocal-cord hemorrhage. He was coughing up blood, and doctors ordered him to remain completely silent for at least a week. He did as he was told.

I was doing three shows a night at the Copa, five radio shows a week, benefit performances and recording at the same time. And then I opened at the Capitol Theatre in the daytime towards the end of the engagement. I went out to do the third show at about half past two or a quarter to three in the morning, and I went for a note, and nothing came out...absolutely nothing. Just dust. I was never so panic-stricken in my whole life. I remember looking at the audience, there was a blizzard outside, about 70 people in the place—and they knew something serious had happened. There was absolute silence—stunning, absolute silence. I looked at them, and they looked at me, and I looked at Skitch Henderson, who was playing the piano. His face was ghastly white. Finally I whispered to the audience, "Good night," and walked off the floor.

APRIL 27, 1950: Even though his personal and professional reputation was in a nosedive, and his draw among the new generation of teenage moviegoers was in decline, L.B. Mayer kept Dad on at MGM because he cared for him so much, and would have continued to do so. Ironically, it was a careless remark about Mayer's mistress that precipitated Frank's dismissal from the studio. "So?" L.B. said, "I hear you been making jokes about my lady friend." A mortified Frank responded, "Yeah, I wish I could take that back. I'm so sorry. I wish I'd never said anything so stupid." He would never intentionally hurt this lovely man. And L.B. said, "That's not a very nice thing to do. I want you to leave here, and I don't ever want you to come back again." His relationship with MCA, his talent agency, had also deteriorated. And by this time his records weren't selling well because the music business was changing.

MAY 10, 1950: Still recovering physically and emotionally from the stresses of the last few months, Dad canceled his performance at the Chez Paree in Chicago, where he was scheduled to open on May 12, and headed to Spain's Tossa del Mar on the Mediterranean to see Ava on location, where the press was buzzing with rumors that she was dating a bullfighter named Mario Cabre.

Mitch Miller

ON THE CHANGE IN FRANK'S RECORDING CAREER:

Frank did very few rhythm songs. I thought he should do more. I thought he did them so remarkably that we should do a whole album of them. But when he came to do these records, Frank's voice was in terrible shape. Frank would be in an isolation booth, and he'd sing a beautiful phrase, and then on the next phrase his voice would crack. But you couldn't edit! So you'd have to throw the whole thing out. I can say this now—I could have been kicked out of the Musicians Union, because tracking was not allowed. There were a lot of musicians involved. So what I did to save the session, I just shut off his mike, and got good background tracks. Didn't even tell him. Then after it was over, I said, "When your voice is back..." We'd come in crazy hours, in a locked building, so no union representative could come in. Then when Frank came in, say, at midnight, we would play the disc, he would put earphones on and he would sing, just the way they do now. And we would remix it. He did them very well after that, and the whole orchestra was perfect on it.

Frank and Dorothy Kirsten on a promotional tour of the Lucky Strike plant in Richmond, Virginia.

MAY 27, 1950: Back from Spain, Dad made his first TV appearance on Bob Hope's show *Star Spangled Revue*. Guesting with Peggy Lee and Beatrice Lillie, he sang "Come Rain or Come Shine" and joined in a couple of comedy skits, including one in which he played Bing Crosby.

MAY 29-JUNE 2, 1950: Frank returned to the *Light Up Time* radio series opposite Dorothy Kirsten. But his contract had expired, and this was to be his last week on the show.

JUNE 28, 1950: In New York, Dad recorded "Goodnight Irene," backed with "Dear Little Boy of Mine." Side one rose to Number Five on the charts.

JULY 10-23, 1950: The *Daily Graphic* reported that he appeared in an SRO engagement at the Palladium in London, where the public still loved him. On opening night he arrived to pandemonium and barely escaped with his clothes. According to the newspaper, he said, "Two tall redheaded girls nearly got my tie. One was actually pulling it off my neck. I pulled back." Sipping tea on stage between songs, he began with "Bewitched," "Embraceable You" and "I Fall in Love Too Easily." When he started singing "I've Got a Crush on You," the screaming started. Saying "Steady now," he changed the mood with "Ol' Man River," followed by a parody, "Old Man Crosby, He Just Keeps Singing Along," that brought down the house. The *Daily Graphic* reported that Ava Gardner was in the audience that night but slipped out of the theatre before the end of his act.

AUGUST 1950: Frank and his band played Atlantic City. Recalled drummer Johnny Blowers, "It was so mobbed. They had a feature film, a short subject and then

Ava

ON A NEW YORK INTERLUDE WITH FRANK:

We never had any trouble inventing reasons to be at each other's throats. Restaurants were frequently where our quarrels began, and I confess I started a lot of them, sometimes before the appetizer arrived. A pretty girl would pass and recognize Frank. She'd smile. He'd nod and smile back. I'd say something sweet and ladylike, such as "I suppose you're sleeping with all these broads," and we'd be off to the races.

The quarrel started along those lines that night. One second I was there and the next I'd scooped up my handbag and was outside hailing a taxi. When I got back to the three-room Hampshire House suite I shared with Frank, I needed to talk about my problems with someone. So I phoned [ex-husband] Artie Shaw at his apartment and he invited me to come over for a nightcap with him and his girlfriend. After a few minutes, I made my way back to Hampshire House. Then the phone rang. It was Frank in the next room. He said, "I can't stand it any longer. I'm going to kill myself—now!" Then there was a tremendous bang in my ear, and I knew it was a revolver shot. My whole mind sort of exploded in a great wave of panic, terror and shocked disbelief. I threw the phone down and raced into Frank's room and there was a body lying on the bed.

The goddamn revolver was still smoking in his hand. He had fired through a pillow and into the mattress, thinking that would muffle the sound and I would be the only one startled by the noise. He hadn't realized that half of New York would be sitting up, pencils poised, waiting to include this moment in their memoirs. When the call about the shot came from the desk clerk, Frank's denials could have won him an Oscar. We had to get rid of the evidence, so we called Hank Sanicola, and he was in the room in seconds with the mattress and bedding from his own room. He grabbed Frank's mattress and bedding and made a run for the back stairs. When the police arrived, Frank was in his robe, and his innocence was very convincing. I was trembling like jelly inside, but I was probably convincing, too.

Sinatra. It was a madhouse. So they took out the feature. They just had the short and then Sinatra. We didn't even leave the theater! God almighty, I think we must have done 25 shows. The crowd kept demanding 'Goodnight Irene.' I don't think Frank liked it too much, but it was a big hit for him. I used to think to myself, How in the world did Mitch ever get him to do this? But anyway, he did it and it was big. It went over."

SEPTEMBER 1950: With Mom and Dad legally separated, she was granted $50,000 and a small percentage of his income for the rest of her life, plus custody of the children, her 1950 Cadillac and their home in Holmby Hills. The separation was, of course, roughest on my mother. I would see her faint into her plate at dinner from the stress. Sometimes it was heart palpitations, sometimes a cold, sometimes fatigue. Until then, she had never been sick. I used to think it was the food. Maybe she wasn't eating right. She was in pain. And though I wasn't aware of it, her pain was exacerbated by the scandal. She was deeply in love and terribly hurt. I would hear her crying quietly at night while I was going to sleep. She would never show it in front of us, never, but my room was next to hers and I would tiptoe out and I'd listen at the door and she'd be crying. Sometimes I would go in to her and just put my arms around her. And sometimes I would just go away, thinking, "Mind your own business. Daddy's just on the road again," and cry myself to sleep.

OCTOBER 7, 1950: FS headlined *The Frank Sinatra Show* on CBS television from 9 to 10 p.m. on Saturday nights. With the star singing and joining in comedy routines, the one-hour variety program rated well enough—opposite NBC's powerhouse *Your Show of Shows*—to stay on the air for the next two years with a guest list that included Sarah Vaughan, Jackie Gleason, Phil Silvers, Rudy Vallee, Louis Armstrong, the Three Stooges, Buster Keaton, Jack Benny and Dad's protégé, Sammy Davis Jr. Dad's detractors in the press gleefully predicted that this low period in his life was the end of the road for Frank Sinatra, but they were wrong as usual. His career was at a low point compared to the crooner-swooner era. But he never stopped working.

OCTOBER 29, 1950: Concurrent with his new TV series on Saturdays, Dad debuted on *Meet Frank Sinatra*, a weekly CBS radio show on Sundays in the late afternoon.

NOVEMBER 26, 1950: He did another guest shot on *The Bob Hope Show*, which was a holiday special.

NOVEMBER 28, 1950: He appeared with Milton Berle on the hugely popular *Texaco Star Theatre*.

DECEMBER 1950: Joseph Nellis, one of the lawyers for Senator Estes Kefauver's Special Committee to Investigate Crime in Interstate Commerce, questioned my father about his alleged "underworld associations." And the FBI continued to maintain a file on him. At the meeting, conducted at 4 a.m. in Nellis' Rockefeller Center law offices, Dad denied knowing any of them except to say hello or goodbye, and he wasn't called to testify before the committee.

Frank Jr.
ON THE "BAD TIMES":

Pop's old friend Manie Sacks had been lured away from Columbia and was now the head of RCA Victor. Manie called a meeting with his entire staff, the whole A&R Department, the Marketing Department, the Distribution Department, everybody at RCA Victor, New York. He said, "We want to sign Sinatra. What can you do with him?" Three days later the staff reported back, "Manie, we can't do it. There's nothing we can do with Sinatra." Manie, in turn, reported this to Dad. Manie said it was the hardest thing he ever had to tell him. "The guys don't think they can move you. Not interested. I could force it and get you on the label with us, but I'd rather you went somewhere else than have you come on with these guys who think, in all honesty, they can't do it." Pop assured Manie that he understood.

Ava

ON LIVING IN A FISHBOWL:

Nothing we did was too inconsequential for the ever-present swarm of reporters and photographers to feed on like bees at a honeypot. It's very easy to say that we should have accepted this as the price of fame, but that turns out to be a hell of a tall order to live up to when you practically can't go to the bathroom without finding yourself in the paper. We decided to go away for a desperately needed vacation in Mexico. We thought we could sneak in a little bit of peace and quiet. Not a chance. The chaos started at the Los Angeles Airport when reporters and photographers filled the tarmac and even crowded onto the steps of the plane, treating our departure like a goddamn presidential visit. Things were quieter in Mexico City, but the press made the four days we spent at Acapulco unpleasant. A Mexican friend of Frank's offered us the use of his private plane for the journey back to L.A. Since a car could be driven right onto the runway in those days, we hoped to avoid the press and just drive home. Talk about naive!

It was dark when we arrived, but a horde of photographers were gathered, eager to pounce, and flashbulbs were popping as we scrambled into the waiting car. Frank took the wheel, and given that there was a crowd, he drove quite slowly. Our windows were closed, and the chances of getting a decent shot through the glass were negligible. One of the photographers was quick-witted enough to realize that no photos meant no story. And as we drove past him, he leaned across the fender and hood on my side, deliberately sliding along it and throwing himself off. I was so indignant I rolled down the window and shouted, "I saw that, Buster."

JANUARY 16, 1951: He returned to the *Texaco Star Theatre* for another go-round with Uncle Miltie.

MARCH 27, 1951: Recording what one writer called "his intensely moving and despairing version" of "I'm a Fool to Want You," Frank was "so overcome with grief that he bolted from the studio in tears" according to Will Friedwald in a Columbia Records retrospective. My father co-wrote the song with Jack Wolf and Joel Herron. As Herron later recalled, "Frank changed part of the lyric, and made it say what he felt when he was doing it. We said, 'He's gotta be on this song!' and we invited him in as co-writer." It was one of 14 songs he'd record for Columbia that year.

APRIL 25-MAY 8, 1951: He returned to New York's Paramount for a two-week engagement with the Joe Bushkin Orchestra.

MAY 10, 1951: At the urging of Columbia's Mitch Miller, Frank recorded a novelty song called "Mama Will Bark." Dad recalled, "I growled and barked on the record. The only good business it did was with dogs."

SUMMER 1951: It took one year for a divorce decree to become final in California, and Dad was afraid he would lose Ava if he couldn't marry her before then. Mom didn't want to stand in his way, so she gave him permission to get a quickie divorce in Mexico. "I refused for a long time because I thought he would come back to his home," she told Louella Parsons, a close friend and a fellow Catholic. "I am now convinced that a divorce is the only way for my happiness as well as Frank's. I think it's better for the children, too." After the split, many of the people who professed to be my mother's friends disappeared. Mom tried to keep us stable during the months of scandal. The teasing from the kids at school...the pieces in the paper. Mores were different then. People were supposed to stay married. But after a time, I think she felt she was destroying Dad's life by not giving him his free-

I'M A FOOL TO WANT YOU

Words and Music by JACK WOLF, JOEL HERRON and FRANK SINATRA

FRANK SINATRA

BARTON MUSIC CORP.
1619 BROADWAY, NEW YORK, N. Y.

40¢

dom, and that this thing with Ava was more than just another casual affair. She also had her pride. And although, in her heart, as a good Catholic, she knew she would always be his wife, she let Dad go and get a divorce. Nancy Barbato Sinatra survived the pain and the notoriety and surfaced with her dignity intact.

JUNE 3-9, 1951: Still in New York, Frank moved to the smaller and more exclusive venue of the Latin Quarter for a one-week engagement.

JUNE 9, 1951: He did the final *Frank Sinatra Show* of the season on CBS television.

SUMMER 1951: Ava recalled going to Hoboken to meet the Sinatra clan and how my father became furious when Dolly started dragging out albums full of his baby photos: "Sweet little pictures of Frank dressed up in all kinds of little outfits, the kinds of shots mothers treasure and sons would like to stick up the chimney."

JULY 22, 1951: After nine months on CBS radio, *Meet Frank Sinatra* ended.

AUGUST 4, 1951: Frank flew to Acapulco for a brief stay with Ava, and a few days after his return, he announced their engagement.

AUGUST 11-24, 1951: He headlined at Reno's Riverside Inn and Casino. It was his very first appearance at a casino in the state of Nevada.

AUGUST 30, 1951: Dad denied a widely publicized story that after another fight with Ava, he attempted suicide at Lake Tahoe with an overdose of sleeping pills.

SEPTEMBER 1951: FS made his first appearance in Las Vegas—at the Desert Inn.

OCTOBER 1951: He began the second season of *The Frank Sinatra Show*, sponsored by Ekco Housewares and the Bulova Watch Company, on Tuesday evenings from 8 to 9 p.m. on CBS.

SINATRA
TO THE PRESS ON HIS "SUICIDE ATTEMPT":

The following quote from my father appeared in Time *magazine: "Ava and I, my manager Henry Sanicola and Mrs. Sanicola went to the Christmas Tree restaurant for dinner. Ava was planning to return to Hollywood that night. I didn't feel so good, so I took two sleeping pills. Ava left by auto for Reno and the plane trip to Hollywood. By now it was very early in the morning. I guess I wasn't thinking, because I'm very allergic to sleeping pills and always have been. I had drunk two or three brandies and I broke out in a rash. Hank called the doctor and he came right over. He gave me a glass of water with some salts in it, trying to get those pills off my stomach. That's all there was to it."*

Ava
ON THE LAKE TAHOE INCIDENT:

We were desperately in love and tried so hard to make each other happy. But Frank's deep depression at being in a career low, and the realization that people he'd once thought of as friends were pretty good at kicking him when he was down there, was not good for us. And we both had a terrible tendency to needle each other's weaknesses, a habit that led to fallings out like the one that Labor Day weekend.

It started with a phone call from Frank saying he'd rented a house on Lake Tahoe and why didn't I come by. A few nights later, when we had both drunk too much, Frank made an offhand remark that hurt me so deeply that I decided to go back to Los Angeles.

As I reached my house in Pacific Palisades, I was exhausted, hung over and miserable. The telephone rang; it was Hank saying, "Oh, my God, Ava. Hurry back! Frank's taken an overdose!" I have been exasperated with Francis Albert Sinatra many times, but never more so than on the morning when I rushed to his bedside back at Lake Tahoe. I ran into his bedroom and looked down at him and he turned his sad blue eyes to look at me. "I thought you'd gone," he said weakly. He'd had a fine rest, doctors watching over him, feeling his pulse, and they didn't even have to pump his stomach; he hadn't taken enough phenobarbitol for that. Everybody had been up all night except Frank. I could have killed him. Instead I forgave him in about 25 seconds.

Sinatra and Vegas

It had begun in 1946 when a flashy resort hotel named the Flamingo opened to crowds of Hollywood high rollers in the middle of the Nevada desert. It was the grandiose pipe dream of a visionary West Coast mobster named Benjamin "Bugsy" Siegel, who envisioned Las Vegas as a new gambler's mecca to rival the syndicate-owned casinos of Fulgencio Battista's Havana. Siegel never lived to see his dream come true, but even he would have been stunned by the scale of the city that began to spring up in the boomtown years that followed. By the time my father made his first appearance at the Desert Inn, there were only four other hotels on the Vegas "Strip," but big business soon joined the bandwagon and a parade of high-rise resorts soon lined the boulevard. The Sands, best of them all in those early days, would become Dad's new home away from home. So would Vegas, as he would make it his own, helping to reshape the entertainment landscape as a pioneer performer in the world's spectacular new capital of live entertainment. With Dean Martin, Jerry Lewis, Sammy Davis Jr., Red Skelton, Danny Thomas and others joining him as the biggest headliners in a town of superstars, he imbued this anything-goes oasis with his own high-living personality, turned it into a glitzy movie set for one of his own films, transformed it into a giant sandbox for grown-ups—and invited everybody in the world to come and play.

OCTOBER 1951: On page one in papers from coast to coast were headline stories alleging that Frank Sinatra intentionally ran over photographer William Eccles with Ava Gardner in his car at Los Angeles Airport, then threatened to kill him. FS swore it was a setup, and Ava backed up his story.

OCTOBER 30, 1951: Mom won an interlocutory divorce decree in Santa Monica, California. It would be recognized as final after one year.

Dad with Groucho Marx in a scene from *Double Dynamite.*

NOVEMBER 1, 1951: Two days later, after establishing state residency with a five-week stay in Las Vegas, Dad got a Nevada divorce and freed himself to marry Ava.

NOVEMBER 2, 1951: Frank and Ava applied for a marriage license in Manie Sacks' hometown, Philadelphia, where they hoped to avoid media attention.

NOVEMBER 7, 1951: Dad married Ava at the suburban Philadelphia home of Lester Sacks, Manie's brother, with Axel Stordahl as his best man. It was Ava's third marriage; her first two were to actor Mickey Rooney and bandleader Artie Shaw.

NOVEMBER 1951: In RKO's *Double Dynamite*—his first film in almost two years, after being dropped by MGM—Dad might have been a bit overshadowed by co-stars Jane Russell and Groucho Marx and, according to one critic, wound up "looking like an uninvited guest." It was a happy little movie but it didn't do well.

Frank Sinatra and Ava Gardner on their wedding day. They were married in Pennsylvania at a friend's house on November 7, 1951.

DECEMBER 6, 1951: Both the *Los Angeles Examiner* and the *Los Angeles Times* reported that after a group of Los Angeles ministers complained to authorities about widespread bigamy in connection with Nevada divorces, the Nevada Bar Association agreed to hear a complaint that Sinatra perjured himself to obtain his divorce. Las Vegas attorney William G. Ruymann filed the charge, noting that Sinatra swore under oath on November 1 that he was a resident of Nevada and the next day, on his Pennsylvania marriage license application, claimed to be a resident of Beverly Hills, California. The story made headlines everywhere for days, but eventually the matter fizzled when writers began to point out that thousands of divorces and marriages occurred under near-identical circumstances.

DECEMBER 1951: Dad appeared at the London Coliseum in a command performance before Prince Philip and Princess Elizabeth to benefit the Duke of Edinburgh's favorite charity, the Playing Fields Association. He and Ava stayed at London's swank Washington Hotel, where their suite was burglarized. The thief got almost $17,000 worth of loot, said an article in the *Hollywood Citizen News*, including Ava's dazzling diamond necklace—her favorite piece of jewelry—along with his cameo cufflinks and a platinum-and-sapphire ring.

DECEMBER 25, 1951: He guested on Bob Hope's NBC Christmas show.

JANUARY 7, 1952: In the first of only four recording sessions for Columbia this year, Dad sang "I Hear a Rhapsody," "I Could Write a Book" and "Walkin' in the Sunshine," the first two with the Jeff Alexander Choir.

JANUARY 18, 1952: FS appeared as a guest on the Martin and Lewis television show.

WINTER 1952: Ava went off to Kenya to shoot *The Snows of Kilimanjaro*, leaving Frank in New York with a sore throat. Recalled Ava: "His agents were having difficulty booking him into top night spots and he

> ## Sammy Davis Jr.
> ### ON FRANK'S DECLINING FORTUNES:
>
> *Around 1952, Frank's career took a nosedive. His radio and television shows were off the air and his record sales began dropping. The Will Mastin Trio, in the meantime, was going great. We were a hit in Hollywood. One day I got a cablegram:* THE REVIEWS WERE GREAT. KEEP IT UP. FRANK. *Here was a guy with his whole world falling down around him, taking the time to send me his congratulations.*

Frank, Ava, Dolly and Marty attend the premiere of *Meet Danny Wilson*. "It was the first role I could sink my teeth into," Dad recalled.

"Meet DANNY WILSON"

Starring

Frank SINATRA

Shelley WINTERS

Alex NICOL

with RAYMOND BURR

was having to play saloons and dates that were way beneath him, and feeling that way, it was really important to him that his wife be by his side." Ava persuaded Darryl Zanuck and director Henry King to rearrange the shooting schedule so that her scenes could be shot in 10 days. The last day, when thousands of extras were required, there were production problems and she had to stay 24 hours longer than anticipated. "I knew Frank would give me holy hell about it, and he did," wrote Ava.

FEBRUARY 8, 1952: Dad's latest film, *Meet Danny Wilson*—in which he starred as a brash but likable young crooner—premiered at the Orpheum Theater in San Francisco, and he attended the opening. There were some great songs in this one, including "I've Got a Crush on You," "She's Funny That Way," "You're a Sweetheart" and "All of Me." The *Los Angeles Times* observed that Danny Wilson's rise to fame and fortune as a bobby-soxer idol was "so much like Frankie's that the parallel is inescapable." The film didn't fare well at the box office.

MARCH 6, 1952: He guest-starred on NBC television's *The Dinah Shore Show.*

MARCH 26-APRIL 8, 1952: Dad returned once again to the stage of New York's Paramount, this time with Buddy Rich, comedian Frank Fontaine and former Pied Piper June Hutton, who was married to Axel Stordahl. But the big-band era was over, the bobby-soxers who had lionized him had grown up.

Frank Jr.

ON THE DECLINE OF SINATRA'S RECORDING CAREER:

Pop's old-style records—Sinatra singing good music with good arrangements—wasn't working anymore. Meantime, the power structure in the record business was changing, too. Dad's experience was that if you were a bandleader or a solo singer, you had control over what you recorded. Now the word was, "Butt out." The A&R—Artists and Repertoire—man was in charge. At Columbia, that was Mitch Miller. He told Pop to record a song using a washboard. Pop said, "Mitch, really? A washboard?" The song was "Tennessee Newsboy." Pop recorded it.

APRIL 1, 1952: Ratings for *The Frank Sinatra Show* on CBS television, never hefty, declined as the show was pitted against the popular Milton Berle. After two years on the air, the series was canceled.

APRIL 1952: Dad went to Hawaii for a series of concerts, including a sparsely attended performance at the rustic Kauai County Fair. But he delivered one of the greatest performances of his life, and it marked a turning point not only in his career but in his personal life.

JUNE 21, 1952: FS performed with Hope and Crosby in a telethon for the U.S. Olympic Committee.

JUNE 1952: Frank Sinatra was dropped by Columbia Records and his talent agency, MCA. His latest movies hadn't done well. And his records weren't selling well either. He no longer had the security of his three remaining contracts. He didn't have a movie studio, an agent or a record label.

JULY 1952: Hearst's *American Weekly* magazine, a Sunday newspaper supplement, ran a two-part series, "bylined" by my father, explaining his breakup from my mother and his relationship with Ava, and apologizing for previous disagreements with the press and refuting accusations about his supposed "pinko" political attitudes and "links" to the Mafia. When I recently asked Dad whether he wrote it, he said succinctly, "It's C-R-A-P. They made the whole thing up." I knew Dad would never have discussed his personal life in print. Never!

SUMMER 1952: On a second peacemaking pilgrimage to Hoboken, Ava visited

Dorothy Manners
(assistant to Louella Parsons)
ON THE PRESSURES FACING SINATRA:

The thing that worried him the most was his family out at the house in Holmby Hills. His main thing was to pay that mortgage. It was a big load for him to carry because that was a big house and a lot of property. I think the only thing that would have done him in would have been if his family had been forced to move out of that house. He was dead set and determined to do it. And he did!

Buck Buchwach, reporter, *Honolulu Advertiser* (a Honolulu newspaperman who spent time with him in Hawaii)

ON SINATRA'S COMEBACK CONCERT:

It was raining at the Kauai County Fair and the dilapidated tent was leaking. "For just one second," Frank told me, "I wondered if the show really did have to go on. Then I peeked out at the audience. There were a few hundred, tops. They weren't wearing fancy clothes or expensive jewelry. They wore aloha shirts, jeans, muumuus and such. Homey. And their warmth and friendliness smacked me in the face. And when two brown-skinned young girls gave me a couple of handmade leis and little kisses, I almost broke down." Well, Frank went on and sang, song after song, hit after hit, maybe twenty. I was stunned. It was fantastic; it was one thousand percent for several hundred small-town ticket holders with big hearts and hands that grew red from clapping. Afterward, Frank had tears in his eyes. "Buck," he told me, "I sang the best I know how. Those people deserved it. It's a night I'll never forget. Tonight marks the first night on the way back. I can feel it in every bone." From that moment, everything seemed to go right for him.

mother-in-law Dolly Sinatra, and heads turned as they strolled the streets arm-in-arm. But the conflicts between Dad and Ava were too deep to heal, and later this year another painful split-up with Ava brought him to the brink of suicide, this time for real. At Manie Sacks' apartment in New York, Dad was revived after inhaling gas from the kitchen stove. He credited Jackie Gleason, Manie Sacks and Jimmy Van Heusen with getting him through those dark days.

SEPTEMBER 17, 1952: In New York, Dad recorded "Why Try to Change Me Now?" with Percy Faith. This was the last song he would sing for Columbia Records before ending his 10-year releationship with the company.

OCTOBER 17, 1952: He gave a memorable interview to columnist Hy Gardner on Gardner's nationally broadcast radio show.

OCTOBER 18, 1952: Frank made an appearance on *Jimmy Durante's All Star Revue*.

OCTOBER 27, 1952: In a campaign appearance for Democratic presidential candidate Adlai Stevenson at the Hollywood Palladium, Frank sang "The House I Live In" and "The Birth of the Blues."

NOVEMBER 1952: While FS was away, Ava discovered that she was pregnant. She recalled later: "I had the strongest feelings about bringing a child into the world. I felt that unless you were prepared to devote practically all your time to your child in its early years, it was unfair to the baby. If a child is unwanted—and somehow they know that—it is handicapped from the time it's born." Ava said she was also mindful that MGM had written penalty clauses into her contract. If she carried the baby to term, the studio would cut off her salary. With my father's career in decline, she couldn't take the chance, so she flew to England and had a legal abortion—without even telling him she was pregnant.

EARLY NOVEMBER 1952: After reading the James Jones novel *From Here to Eternity*, FS decided he was born to play the meaty role of Angelo Maggio, a feisty underdog from the streets of Brooklyn, in a forthcoming film version of the

Jackie Gleason and Frank Sinatra were friends since the forties when they drove Toots Shor nuts signing his name to tabs, adding tips as big as endowments. Later, they did bits on each other's TV shows, "rehearsing" by phone, working from a few cues. Gleason once saw Sinatra in the shower and told him he looked like a "tuning fork."

best-selling book. "For the first time in my life," Dad recalled, "I was reading something I really had to do. I just felt it—I just knew I could do it. I just couldn't get it out of my head." But the prospect seemed distant: Few in Hollywood believed Sinatra could carry an important dramatic role—or even attract moviegoers to theaters.

NOVEMBER 1952: Artist Paul Clemens, a close friend of Ava's, was living in a guest house on Harry and Joan Cohn's estate. Harry, the head of Columbia Pictures, asked Paul if he would invite Ava for dinner. As Paul recalled, "Ava knew that what producer Buddy Adler and Cohn were working on was the script for *From Here to Eternity*. And at the Cohns' that night Ava said, 'You know who's right for that part of Maggio, don't you? That sonofabitch of a husband of mine. He's perfect for it.' And Joan said, 'My God, you're right!'" Ava had to leave for Africa to begin filming *Mogambo*. Dad went with her. Joan carried the ball. A week later Frank Sinatra received a telegram from his new agent, Bert Allenberg of the William Morris Agency, telling him to come home. He did his screen test for Maggio in Hollywood. Joan Cohn said, "Harry called me at home one day and told me to come to the Columbia lot. He sat me down—just the two of us—in a projection room and he ran Eli Wallach's and Frank Sinatra's screen tests. Not once, not twice, but three times. Then Harry turned to me and I said, 'Well, you've got a nice Jewish boy and you've got a nice Italian boy, Harry. What's your problem?'" Harry made the ethnically accurate choice. Frank got the role—$1,000 a week—co-starring with Burt Lancaster, Montgomery Clift, Deborah Kerr and Donna Reed.

DECEMBER 1952: Dad spent a few weeks with Ava in Africa before *From Here to Eternity* began production. Before he went home, she was pregnant again. "This time," she wrote, "he knew about it, and he was delighted. Right on the spot, for the first and only time in our relationship, Frank decided to sing to me." But she felt she had "no right to produce a child unless you had a sane, solid lifestyle. Frank and I had no such thing. We didn't even possess the ability to live together like any normal married couple." So she "checked into a small nursing home near Wimbledon" and terminated the pregnancy. "I'll never forget waking up after the operation," she wrote, "and seeing Frank sitting next to the bed with tears in his eyes."

JANUARY 20-31, 1953: Dad returned from Africa for an engagement at the Latin Quarter nightclub in Boston.

Frank going along for the ride to Africa with Ava and the cast of *Mogambo*: Donald Sinden, Grace Kelly and Clark Gable.

JANUARY 26-27, 1953: Before leaving Boston, FS spent two days as a guest DJ subbing for Norm Prescott on WORL. He did a four-hour show each day, talking about music and playing songs he had recorded with arranger George Siravo.

FEBRUARY 6-15, 1953: During his appearance with the Bob Harrington Orchestra at the Chez Paree in Montreal, Dad forged a warm working relationship with pianist Bill Miller that continues today.

APRIL 1953: Frank Sinatra signed with Capitol Records. With his crooner-swooner period behind him, a "new" Sinatra emerged with confidence, maturity, cockiness and a renewed pride in his voice. These were among his finest years as a recording artist. At Capitol, producer Voyle Gilmore took Frank under his wing. In addition to having Dad continue his work with Axel, Gilmore wanted to team him with trumpet player Billy May because of Billy's humorous style. For Dad's first session, Heinie Beau had given the May touch to "Lean Baby." As Billy later recalled, "I had a moderate amount of success on records and found myself in the band business. When I got the call to work with Frank, I was with my band in Florida and couldn't do the gig. But I told Gilmore to feel free to let somebody else do the charts in the Billy May style." Trombonist/arranger Nelson Riddle—who had arranged Nat Cole's "Mona Lisa"—did the arrangements for Dad's "South of the Border" and "I Love You" á la Billy May but completed the set with arrangements for

> ## Dorothy Manners
> ### ON FS DURING THE LEAN YEARS:
>
> *Never did he lose that presence, that sense of being in charge of things. I was giving a little dinner in Chinatown— Jimmy Van Heusen, Frank and a few other friends. I went to pay the check and the man told me, "Mr. Sinatra's taken care of it." Later, we went to the Coconut Grove and he picked up that check. And he was broke.*

FRANK

ON GETTING THE ROLE OF MAGGIO:

I had the book and I was in Africa on a visit. I read it and reread it and it was a big book. And I loved it, it was a hell of a book. And then I spoke to Harry Cohn, who was then the head of Columbia Pictures and a friend. And I said, "I'd like to play that." He said, "Well, you've never done a dramatic role. You're a guy who sings and dances with Gene Kelly." And I said, "But that's the kind of thing I think I can do." "Well, let's make a test," he said. It was the barroom scene when Maggio went AWOL. That was an amazing afternoon because the director, Fred Zinnemann, said, "Well, what do we do here?" There was nothing in the script. He then said I should ad lib for two pages. I can't ad lib for a quarter of a page. And he said, "Well, do something. You know, what does a drunk do at the bar?" "Well, drunks do a lot of things at bars," I said. So I worked out some pieces of business with a couple of olives with the dice, and all that. And that was the test. And then I went to Africa. I heard that Eli Wallach, my dear friend, had also tested and I said, "Forget it!" I thought I was dead. He was such a good performer. In November, I did the Texaco Star Theater with Milton Berle, shopped for Ava's Christmas presents in New York and went to Montreal for a nightclub date. Harry Cohn called me there and said, "Come back, you've got the part."

Artist Paul Clemens

ON THE FRANK/AVA RELATIONSHIP:

The woman is suddenly in demand and the man is not. It's difficult to accommodate to that. And with Frank and Ava, there was always tension. The odds were against them. It was a stacked deck. Her career was thriving, and his, for the time being, was not. And they were both so passionate about everything, so much alike. It wasn't fair, really. It was as much unfortunate timing as anything else. But they had each other for a little while and they enriched each other's lives.

If we'd thought a bit of the end of it when we started painting the town, We'd have been aware that our love affair was too hot not to cool down.

"I've Got the World on a String" and "Don't Worry 'Bout Me" in his own style. It was the beginning of a musical partnership that would span decades and carry them through more than 90 recording sessions together. They would record 22 more songs—including "A Foggy Day," "They Can't Take That Away from Me" and "My Funny Valentine"—before the end of their first year together. Whenever Dad did a recording session, he sent me a set of rough dubs—test records made of lightweight acetate. I was proud that he was interested in my opinion. When he sent me the dubs from that first session at Capitol, I liked "I'm Walking Behind You" a lot. I called up to tell him so, but I also felt obliged to mention an Eddie Fisher version I had heard on the radio. Dad told me not to worry about it. As it happened, both versions sold, with Eddie's winning. But Pop was gaining ground. I could tell by the records and by the reactions of my friends at school.

APRIL 1953: Dad's rendition of "Three Coins in the Fountain"—his first stereo recording—was released by Capitol. The song became a huge hit and would go on to win the Academy Award.

Frank Jr.
ON SINATRA'S NEW SOUND:

Nelson began to pump a little more power into the sound. Instead of sounding like that silky-smooth crooner of the forties, now Pop was putting more energy into it, belting a little more. His voice lowered, too, got better, lost some of its sweetness. His whole attitude was becoming a little more hip now. The curly-haired, bow-tied image was gone. Now there was the long tie—and the hat....that Cavanaugh hat.

Nelson Riddle

ON WORKING WITH SINATRA:

He undoubtedly brought out my best work. Frank is stimulating to work with. You have to be right on your mettle all the time. The man somehow draws everything out of you. He has the same effect on the boys in the band; they know he means business, so they pull everything out. And he'd never give out compliments. He just isn't built to give out compliments. He expects your best.

APRIL 1953: The stars of *From Here to Eternity* flew to Hawaii to begin filming. Burt Lancaster remembered, "Deborah Kerr and me and Frank and Monty are sitting up in the front of the plane. And he and Monty are drunk. Monty, poor Monty, was this kind of a drinker—he'd chug-a-lug one martini and conk out. And Frank was, I believe, having a few problems, and so, when we arrived, these two bums were unconscious. They were gone! Deborah and I had to wake them up….This is the way they arrived, and Harry Cohn is down there with the press and everything. Well, we got through that, and now we start to do the picture. Every night, after work, we would meet in Frank's room. He had a refrigerator and he would open it and there would be these iced glasses. He would prepare the martinis with some snacks while we were getting ready to go to an eight o'clock dinner. We'd sit and chat about the day's work and he would try his nightly call to Ava, who was in Spain. In those days in Spain, if you lived *next door* to your friends, you couldn't get them on the telephone, let alone try to get them on the phone from Hawaii. He never got through. Not one night. When you finished your martini, he would take the glass from you, open up the icebox and get a fresh cold glass, and by eight o'clock he and Monty would be unconscious. I mean really unconscious. Every night. So Deborah and I would take Frank's clothes off and put him to bed. Then I would take Monty on my shoulders and we would carry him down to *his* room, take *his* clothes off and dump *him* in bed. And then she and I and the Zinnemanns would go out and have dinner."

MAY 1953: Ava broke away from filming *Knights of the Round Table* to join Frank for what she called a "second honeymoon" during his European singing tour, but transportation foul-ups and less-than-enthusiastic audiences prompted him to shorten the itinerary. He was booed in Italy when, according to Ava, the audience ignored his singing and "was on its feet going wild and yelling, 'Ava!

Left: Frank attempting to give fellow crooner—and former barber—Perry Como a trim.

Left: FS and actress Greer Garson at a fundraiser. Above: With actor pals Paul Douglas and Humphrey Bogart.

Director Fred Zinnemann

ON SINATRA AS MAGGIO:

In the beginning I wanted another actor for the part of Maggio—Eli Wallach, who had already made an excellent test. In the meantime Sinatra—who was at a low point in his life and his career, having played in two unsuccessful pictures and having divorced his wife Nancy—had begun a high-pressure campaign to get the part, sending telegrams signed "Maggio" to Harry Cohn, the president of Columbia Pictures, Buddy Adler the producer and me, the director, saying that he had been chosen by destiny to play the part. Cohn would have none of it. "He can't do it, he's just a hoofer," he said.

Sinatra was in Africa at this point visiting Ava Gardner, who was at work on Mogambo, John Ford's picture. Cohn, always a careful man with a penny, cabled Frank, saying that if he would return from Kenya at his own expense, he could do a test. Sinatra was back in a flash—four days, as all this was happening before the dawn of the jet age, and we shot a test that turned out OK. Cohn paid him a measly eight thousand dollars for playing the part.

The legend about a horse's head being cut off is pure invention, a poetic license on the part of Mario Puzo, who wrote The Godfather.

COLUMBIA PICTURES presents

FROM HERE TO ETERNITY

Copyright © 1953 by Columbia Pictures Corporation. All Rights Reserved. Country of Origin U.S.A.

Starring

BURT **LANCASTER** · MONTGOMERY **CLIFT**
DEBORAH **KERR** · FRANK **SINATRA** · DONNA **REED**

Screen Play by DANIEL TARADASH · Based upon the novel by JAMES JONES
Produced by BUDDY ADLER · Directed by FRED ZINNEMANN

Reprint

R 58 \ 125

Mario Puzo

ON "THE GODFATHER LEGEND":

In The Godfather, *Mario Puzo wrote that a popular singer many people believed was really my father got the big part that made his career in Hollywood only because a Mafia capo made the producer, an avid horse lover, "an offer he couldn't refuse": the head of his championship mount on his bed in a pool of blood.*

"The horse's head in the producer's bed was totally my imagination," *Puzo recalled. "I made it up based on Sicilian folklore. In the old days they would kill a man's favorite animal and hang it up as a warning."*

Ernest Borgnine
(Fatso Judson, the guy who kills Maggio):

I went to work the first day, and as luck would have it, my first scene was with Frank Sinatra and I'm dying inside, because here was the man who sang "Nancy" (I named my daughter Nancy because of that song). My idol, my everything. I loved him in everything he ever did. And I said, "How can I, a mere nothing, come on here?" But I knew I had to play this part as the meanest SOB that ever existed, otherwise the part won't play. So I was out there pounding the piano and everything else, and we started this scene. I'm looking around and I see Frank Sinatra dancing with this girl. And I see Montgomery Clift over with somebody else. And standing on the side were Deborah Kerr and Burt Lancaster talking to Fred Zinnemann. I was engulfed with stars. And I'm just shaking, you know. And Fred suddenly looked up and said, "OK, begin the scene!" So we started. I'm playing the piano and it came to the point where Frank says, "Come on, why don't you stop this banging on the piano, will ya? Give us a chance with our music." And I stood up to say my first line. I said, "Listen you little wop." He looked up at me, and as he looked up at me, he broke out into a smile and he said, "My God, he's 10 feet tall!" Do you know the whole thing just collapsed. His laughter broke the tension. It was so marvelous. I've never forgotten Frank for that. He was the most wonderful guy to work with that you ever saw in your life. He knew how I must have felt, you know. And because of it, he took the time to break that tension. That's something that I have done with everybody that I've ever worked with since. I break the ice for the other people. And I think it's nice, because it reverberates all down the line.

Ava! Ava!' The noise was so great he stopped singing. The orchestra stopped playing, Frank walked off. I got up, left the theater, and went back to the hotel. After a pause Frank came back on stage and finished the show." Their careers, which by necessity involved constant traveling, pushed them into a long-distance relationship. They relied on telephone lines to connect them a good deal of the time and, whenever possible, airplanes to bring them together for brief visits on location. Perhaps, at the end of it, the fact was that they simply couldn't stay together because they couldn't bear to be apart. Ultimately, it was healthier for them to pursue separate lives. All I do know is that Dad was so sad. He had a body full of sighs. And it took a long time for him to begin to live again. A long time. "What a period of time that was," he said. "It was all Mondays." I knew when I hugged him I was helping to heal the wound—but a hug from a daughter was only a Band-Aid, not a cure.

Burt Lancaster

ON SINATRA'S PERFORMANCE IN *FROM HERE TO ETERNITY*:

His fervor, his anger, his bitterness had something to do with the character of Maggio, but also with what he had gone through in the last number of years: a sense of defeat, and the whole world crashing in on him, his marriage to Ava going to pieces—all of those things caused this ferment in him, and they all came out in that performance. You knew this was a raging little man who was, at the same time, a good human being. Monty [Montgomery Clift] watched the filming of one of Frank's close-ups and said, "He's going to win the Academy Award." And that's what Monty felt was going to happen.

AUGUST 17, 1953: *From Here to Eternity* opened nationwide, on its way to grossing more than $80 million in its first year and becoming Columbia's biggest money-maker to date. So big was the box office that New York's Capitol Theater remained open 24 hours a day to accommodate the crowds. Topping the critics' choice of acclaimed performances: Sinatra as Maggio.

SEPTEMBER 1953: Dad returned from Europe with Ava at his side. He agreed to appear at Skinny D'Amato's 500 Club in Atlantic City, which in nightclub lore was partly owned by alleged Chicago mobster Sam Giancana. Skinny was a good friend of my father's and his club wasn't doing well, so when Skinny asked for help, Dad said yes. After his first performance, Ava wrote that Frank was introduced to Giancana, who praised his singing. Afterward, Ava asked Frank why he associated with hoodlums. "That hoodlum is responsible for giving me a job," he replied. On the last night of that engagement, it was reported in a fan magazine that he met three teenage girls from Brooklyn who came all the way just to glimpse him for a few minutes. It was past midnight, raining heavily, and none of the kids had umbrellas, raincoats or cab fare home, so, according to the article, Frank sent the girls safely back to Brooklyn in his own hired car.

OCTOBER 2, 1953: After attending the premiere of *Mogambo* together in New York, Dad and Ava flew to Hollywood, and she returned to Palm Springs alone. She told a friend: "When he was down and out, he was sweet. But now that he's successful again, he's become his old arrogant self. We were happy when he was on the skids."

OCTOBER 6, 1953: In the midst of all his personal angst, Frank made light of his tumultuous life in a weekly radio series called *Rocky Fortune*, in which he starred as a "footloose and fancy free young gentleman" who always seemed to get himself into—and out of—trouble. It remained on the air for the next 26 weeks.

OCTOBER 19, 1953: FS opened for a week in Las Vegas to SRO audiences at the Sands Hotel. He poured his heart into classics like "They Can't Take That Away from Me," "Day In, Day Out," "All of Me" and "Just One of Those Things." The Sands would become his Las Vegas home, but he was dividing the rest of his time between Los Angeles and New York.

OCTOBER 27, 1953: Acknowledging the inevitable, 11 months after their wedding, FS and Ava announced that "irreconcilable differences" had forced them to separate. As Ava wrote in her memoirs, "I'm pretty sure it was Howard Strickling, Metro's legendary publicity director, who issued what I thought was the most honest and sincere explanation for our impending divorce: 'Ava Gardner and Frank Sinatra stated today that having reluctantly exhausted every effort to reconcile their differences, they could find no mutual basis on which to continue their marriage. Both expressed deep regret and great respect for each other. Their separation is final and Miss Gardner will seek a divorce.'"

NOVEMBER 3, 1953: Within a month after debuting in his *Rocky Fortune* show, FS took on still another radio program, *Perfectly Frank*, a breezy, twice-weekly, 15-minute series in which he performed as both soloist and DJ for hits from other stars. This one had an eight-month run.

LATE NOVEMBER 1953: Unwilling to give up on his marriage, FS exhausted himself taping advance shows of his twice-weekly radio show in hopes of accompanying Ava to Europe for filming of *The Barefoot Contessa*, co-starring his dear friend

Red Buttons, Milton Berle and Frank Sinatra at a Capitol Records party honoring FS and the release of his movie and single, "From Here to Eternity."

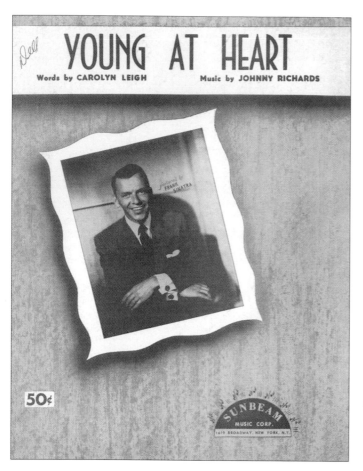

YOUNG AT HEART

Words by CAROLYN LEIGH   Music by JOHNNY RICHARDS

50¢

Humphrey Bogart, but he was taken to Mount Sinai Hospital in New York suffering from what the newspapers called "complete physical exhaustion, severe loss of weight and a tremendous amount of emotional strain."

DECEMBER 9, 1953: Dad's recording of "Young at Heart" climbed to the top of the singles hit parade. It was the first time he'd been back on the charts in several years. "Nelson told me he had a song that had been floating around Vine Street [Capitol Records] and other companies for weeks or months," Dad recalled. "'I think it's a good song,' Nelson said, 'but nobody wants to do it.' I didn't even ask him if I could hear it. I just said let's do it, and it turned out to be 'Young at Heart.' We did a single and it was a big hit."

DECEMBER 24, 1953: Ava wrote that when he recovered, he chartered a plane from London to visit her in Madrid in a final bid for reconciliation, but she was already preoccupied with a new flame, bullfighter Luis Dominguin, and was reluctant even to see her estranged husband.

JANUARY 1954: After a 14-month investigation, Dad's request to buy a two percent interest in the Sands Hotel for $54,000 was approved by the Nevada Gaming Commission. Among the other owners of the casino, according to FBI files, were front men for organized crime figures Frank Costello and Joe Adonis. Managing the establishment was Jack Entratter, my father's friend since the days when Entratter managed New York's famed Copacabana. Eleanor Roth, Entratter's longtime assistant, who was at the Sands from its opening day, December 5, 1952, until December 15, 1974 (three and a half years after Entratter's death), disputes the FBI: "Nobody connected with the Mob was ever on the license at the Sands. Carl Cohen, Eddie Levinson, Charlie Baron and Charlie Kandel were the other owners of the hotel. If Frank Costello owned the Sands, you'd think he would show up once in a while to check on his investment. He never came to the Sands. And Joe Adonis was dead long before the Sands opened." Dad's initial investment eventually grew to nine percent.

MARCH 25, 1954: At the long-awaited Academy Awards show, Dad's dream finally came true: With Frankie and me in the audience, he won the Oscar for Best Supporting Actor. It was the greatest moment of his professional life, and one of the most dramatic comeback stories in entertainment history. But almost as precious to him was the gift presented to him before the ceremony by Mom, Frankie, Tina and me—a gold medallion with a miniature Oscar in bas relief on one side, inscribed: DAD, ALL OUR LOVE FROM HERE TO ETERNITY, and on the other side a bust of St. Genesius, the patron saint of actors. When his name was announced, he kissed me on the cheek, kissed Frankie on the cheek and sprinted to the stage. Remembering the fight scene and the bully, Frankie turned to Dad after the Oscar ceremony and said, "You know, Dad, when I see that man, Fatso, I'm gonna kill him!" "No, son, you don't kill him," Dad said, "you kiss him. He helped me win the Academy Award."

FRANK

ON WINNING THE OSCAR®:

I've been up and down in my life more than a roller coaster on the Fourth of July. At 38 years old, I was a has-been. Sitting at a phone that wouldn't ring. Wondering what happened to all the friends who grew invisible when the music stopped. Finding out fast how tough it is to borrow money when you're all washed up. My only collateral was a dream. A dream to end my nightmare. And what a dream it was. It began when I read an absolutely fascinating book written by a giant, James Jones. More than a book, it was a portrait of people I knew, understood and could feel, and in it I saw myself as clearly as I see myself every morning when I shave. I was Maggio. No matter who said what, I would prove it, no matter how many tests I was asked to make, no matter what the money. I was going to become Maggio if it was the last thing I ever did.

FS with fellow Academy Award winner and co-star Donna Reed. Dad literally ran down the aisle to get his Oscar.

It was Mercedes McCambridge who woke me out of the dream. I'll thank her eternally for saying, "And the winner is Frank Sinatra for From Here to Eternity." Talk about being "born again." I couldn't even share it with another human being. I ducked the party, lost the crowds and took a walk. Just me and Oscar. I think I relived my entire life as I walked up and down the streets of Beverly Hills. Since that night, the roller coaster has evened out, and every day is the Fourth of July. I started out the decade as "the man least likely" and closed it out as a grateful human being, given a second shot at life.

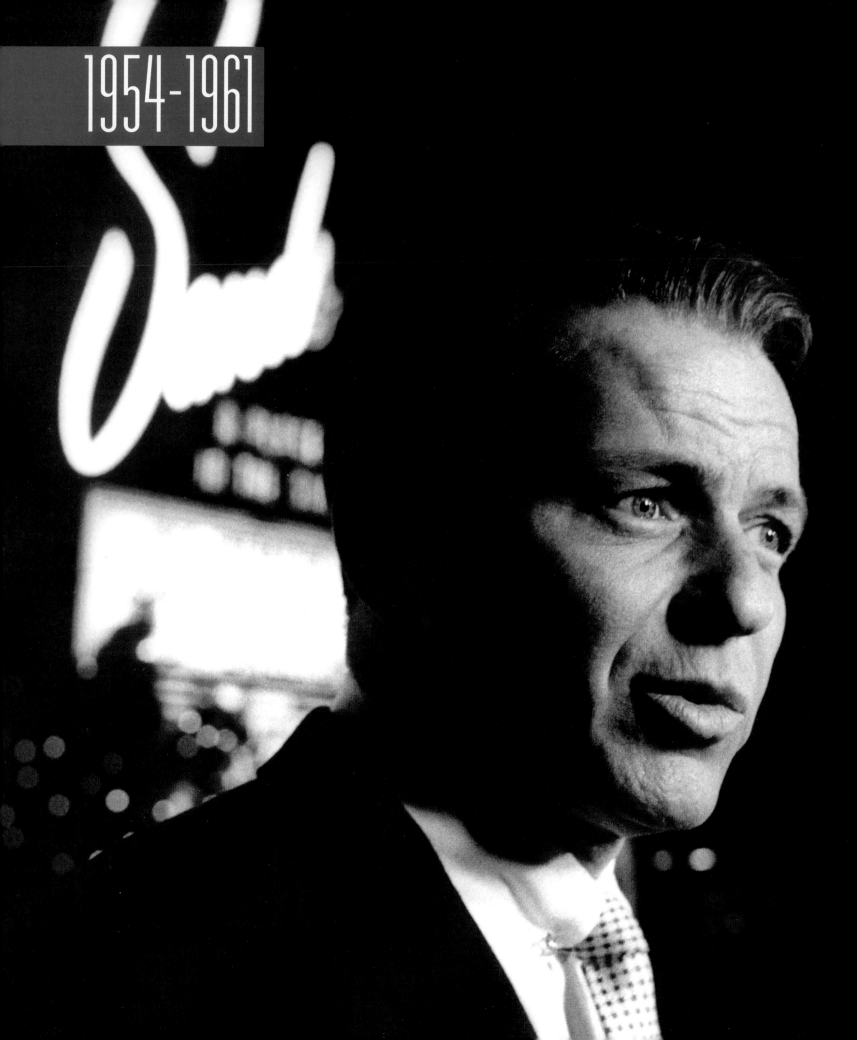

I've Got The World On A String

Though my father's face was beginning to show signs of the professional and personal struggles he had experienced, his spirit was alive and well. He put to use one of the touchstones of his life—"Don't despair"—something he strongly believes is a key to surviving even the most impossible situation. Strength is at the core of his character, strength of conviction and of principle. He seemed to reach deep down into that core to gain the strength to overcome his troubles and achieve a new success, a new life filled with quality work and outrageous fun. The Academy Award gave him the boost he needed and the respect of the Hollywood establishment and the public. But now what would he do with that hard-won attention?

As usual, it all began with the music. He seemed to be searching for perfection during his years at Capitol Records, and most people say he achieved it. During the onset of rock and roll, against the odds, he continued to push his way to the top of the charts and the top of the world. He succeeded because he had a unique talent for making incredibly brilliant recordings. The passion, the tumult, the pain of his roller-coaster relationship with Ava had changed Dad's way of working. Sammy Davis told me, "It was a quiet, morose time, and I think he solved it by keeping it inside him and filing it, putting it aside to use later in his art." And use it he did, in some of the most dramatic, heartfelt lyric interpretations of his career. People believed him, and they began to believe in him again.

His generous acts of charity, his friendships with important people, including the president of the United States, his battles with certain members of the media, his fights against intolerance were becoming legendary—all were part of his colorful, romantic mystique. The American public's love for the underdog made him even more powerful. They identified with him. They were rooting for him.

It was this influence—and the fact that his talent backed him up—that helped build the city of Las Vegas, and he took it as his own. He became King of the Strip—Las Vegas Boulevard—and the public wanted to know, and see with their own eyes, why he and his friends were having so damn much fun. So they went there in droves and joined in—spending a lot of money in the process.

It was a prolific time. An influential time. His music, his movies, his mountain of work, had made him powerful. Many people wanted to emulate him, be just like him, live the life he seemed to exemplify. The Capitol years were definitely, in many ways, the ultimate years. His storybook life had taken him, or perhaps he had taken it, from the streets of Hoboken to the palaces of the world, to the very pinnacle of power—to the top of his game.

"Take the chance, roll the dice, push your talent, love who you want to love, taste the wine, listen to the music, dance the dance. If you're knocked down, get up. Losing is nothing, for we all lose everything at the end. But we never win at all if we don't enter the fray."—*Pete Hamill*

EARLY 1954: Though he was living alone in a Wilshire Boulevard apartment—no longer a neighbor of Humphrey Bogart in West Los Angeles—FS became a member of Bogart's "Rat Pack." "In order to qualify," according to Lauren Bacall, "one had to be addicted to nonconformity, staying up late, drinking, laughing, and not caring what anyone thought or said about us. We were an odd assortment, but we liked each other so much, and every one of us had a wild sense of the ridiculous. The press had a field day, but we had the upper hand." Other members were David Niven and his wife Hjordis, restaurateur Mike Romanoff and his wife, Gloria, Swifty Lazar and Judy Garland and her husband, Sid Luft. "Frank was attracted to Bogie and to Spencer Tracy," remembered Bacall. "He admired them as men and as talents, and being with them gave him a feeling of solidity that his life lacked. He was a restless man, totally incapable of being alone."

Bogie
ON FRANK:

Frank's a hell of a guy. He tries to live his own life. If he could only stay away from the broads and devote some time to develop himself as an actor, he'd be one of the best in the business.

MARCH 30, 1954: Dad appeared on his last *Rocky Fortune* radio show.

APRIL 2, 7, 19, 1954: In three sessions, FS recorded songs for the *Swing Easy!* album, including "All of Me," "Taking a Chance on Love" and "Just One of Those Things," which, though recorded up-tempo, was, according to my Dad, "the saddest song ever written."

APRIL 10, 1954: Returning to the scene of his first triumph with the Hoboken Four, Dad made a brief appearance on the *Major Bowes Amateur Hour.*

JULY 2, 1954: Frank broadcast his last episode of his other radio show, *To Be Perfectly Frank.*

The Tower of Power: Celebrating the opening of the Capitol Records Tower, which my Dad called "Vine Street." Top row, left to right: Frank Sinatra, Danny Kaye, Gordon MacRae, Nat "King" Cole. Bottom row, left to right: Glenn Wallichs, Dean Martin, Stan Freberg.

Stan Cornyn
(later VP of Warner Bros. Records)

ON THE STATE OF CHANGING TECHNOLOGY:

The day of the long-playing, 10-inch, eight-song album had arrived. A new record-listening habit was created. People listened long rather than fast. The long-playing novelty became the Sinatra medium. He was building up, album by album, a body of poetic interpretations, preserved on records, such as no artist before him had done.

AUGUST 2, 1954: *Swing Easy!*, Dad's first 10-inch LP for Capitol, included classics like "Just One of Those Things" and "Taking a Chance on Love."

AUGUST 15, 1954: He guested on *The Gary Crosby Show*, a radio program starring Bing's son.

SEPTEMBER 1954: FS returned to weekly radio once again as host of his own show, broadcast on Wednesdays and Fridays, playing his records and singing his own songs.

SEPTEMBER 15, 1954: He did a comedy turn on radio's long-running series, *Amos and Andy*, which starred his friends Freeman Gosden and Charles Correll. No one, with the exception of Jack Benny, made him laugh as hard.

SEPTEMBER 24, 1954: Dad starred as a ruthless killer in *Suddenly*. Wrote *Newsweek*: "As an assassin, Sinatra superbly refutes the idea that the straight-role potentialities which earned an Academy Award for him in *From Here to Eternity* were one-shot stuff."

FALL 1954: Though he was on a roll as an actor, Dad didn't get one part he wanted most: Terry Malloy in *On the Waterfront*. He lost it to Marlon Brando.

NOVEMBER 5, 1954: At the request of his friend Joe DiMaggio, Frank drove him to a Hollywood address. According to *Confidential* magazine—the supermarket tabloid of its day, noted for its sensationalistic approach to journalism and its sometimes threatening tactics—DiMaggio, private investigators and several other men crashed into an apartment in which they believed Marilyn Monroe, then separated from DiMaggio, was having an illicit encounter. Marilyn wasn't there and the apartment belonged to Mrs. Florence K. Ross, a 39-year-old secretary who didn't even know Monroe. The detectives had pointed out the wrong door.

NOVEMBER 1954: Sammy Davis Jr. lost an eye in a serious car accident—and Dad was there for him. "I had no place to go except the hotel room I was living in," recalled Sammy, "so the first place I went was to Palm Springs, to Frank. You can have a tendency, at a time like that, for self-pity: 'Oh, what am I going to do?' He cut it off by making me laugh. The jokes started when I was in the hospital and they continued for years; an eye chart with the inscription, 'TO SMOKEY, PRACTICE, PRACTICE.' He called me Smokey because I smoke so much. A gift: half a pair of binoculars, with the other half sawed off for Jilly Rizzo, whose bad eye is on the opposite side. The card read: 'You guys should get together.' The only thing Sinatra

A 14-year-old on my first adult adventure, I accompanied my father on a concert tour of Australia. It was exciting. Just him and me for three whole weeks.

ever said of a serious nature was, 'Don't worry about nothing.' I had lost my equilibrium. He took me to the golf course and made me try to hit the ball. We would sit and he'd say, 'What did they teach you in the hospital? Did they give you this thing with pouring water?' And we'd go in the kitchen and he'd make me pour water in a glass. That kind of sensitivity is rare, rare. Another thing he does is anticipate for you. Meaning that by the time you get around to thinking about it, and go to say, 'Frank there's something I—' he says, 'I've taken care of that.' And he knows exactly what you're talking about because that's the kind of investment he puts into a friendship."

DECEMBER 1954: Back on top of the charts after a long slide from his heyday in the forties as a bobby-soxer heartthrob, FS swept *Billboard*'s disc jockey poll with best song ("Young at Heart") and best LP of the year (*Swing Easy!*), and he was named top male vocalist by *Billboard, Downbeat* and *Metronome*.

MID-JANUARY 1955: At 14, I accompanied Dad on a three-week concert tour of Australia. It was exciting. My mom made me a traveling suit in a comfortable navy-checked fabric for the 36-hour flight. My first road trip—halfway around the world. There was a whole troupe of us flying in a BOAC big-bellied Stratocruiser. Frank and company spent much of the flight in the belly of the big plane, because that's where the bar was. There were jam sessions and jokes, and I had the time of my life. The Australians gave Dad a warm, enthusiastic welcome. The audiences were big and very receptive, but the press assaulted him. It was as if they were laying for him! He was criticized, unbelievably, because "nobody swooned." He even was blamed for setting off a false fire alarm. This was my first exposure to the cruelty, inadvertent and intentional, of the press. I hated it. But nothing was going to spoil my vacation with my dad. I had him all to myself.

I was keeping a diary of the trip and writing letters home every day. One afternoon I ran out of hotel stationery in my bedroom, and I went into Dad's room looking for some. I opened the desk drawer. Inside was some intimate ladies' apparel, belonging, I found out later, to the girl singer on the tour. For the rest of the trip, I was destroyed. I was suddenly deeply saddened. I stopped writing in my little diary. I just didn't care. Dr. William Appleton, in his book *Fathers and Daughters,* calls this "The Theory of the Fall of Father." He writes, "When a man reveals his humanity to his daughter, when she is old enough to stand it, he actively prepares her for adulthood. By abandoning his role as her hero, he aids her in leaving him." It was time for me to begin growing up. I was badly shaken. And for a long time, I was angry at him. I never spoke with him about the episode. I should have said something right away. My mother finally asked me what was wrong and I told her. I'm sure she explained it to Dad. I couldn't. I was only 14.

JANUARY 15, 1955: In a dramatic musical role, Frank delivered a heartfelt performance as a down-and-out songwriter opposite Doris Day in the Warner Bros. musical romance *Young at Heart*, a remake of the John Garfield film *Four Daughters*. In addition to the title duet, he sang such wonderful songs as "She's Funny That Way," "Someone to Watch Over Me" and "One for My Baby." This was the first time Dad and Doris worked together since *Your Hit Parade* in 1949.

FEBRUARY 1955: Reliving his own personal heartbreak, Dad recorded one of his best albums, *In the Wee Small Hours,* including poignant interpretations of "I'll Be Around," "I Get Along Without You Very Well" and "When Your Lover Has Gone." This is my favorite album. From the liner notes: "Standing in front of the mike with his hands nearly always jammed into his pockets, his shoulders hunched a little forward, he sang. And as he sang, he created the loneliest early-morning mood in the world." Stan Cornyn later recalled, "For all his crashing self-assertion, through his art he was suggesting that man is still only a child, frightened and whimpering in the dark." He would record 36 other songs that year at the Capitol studios in Hollywood and New York. Among them: "Love and Marriage" and "(Love Is) The Tender Trap."

MARCH 7, 1955: Capitol released *Songs for Young Lovers,* an album that included such classics as "I Get a Kick Out of You," "A Foggy Day," "My Funny Valentine" and "They Can't Take That Away from Me."

MARCH 30, 1955: A year after winning the Oscar for his portrayal of Maggio in *From Here to Eternity,* Dad presented one to Eva Marie Saint for her performance in *On the Waterfront.*

MARCH 1955: After Bela Lugosi checked himself into a hospital to cope with his addiction to heroin, the horror-film star was astonished to receive a kind note and a basket of gourmet delicacies from Frank Sinatra. "It was a wonderful surprise," said Lugosi at the time. "I've never met Sinatra, but I hope to soon. He was the only star I heard from."

APRIL 27, 1955: He starred in a dramatic role in Max Liebman's *Kaleidoscope* television show.

JUNE 29, 1955: Dad's twice-weekly radio show, sponsored by Bobbi Home Permanent, went off the air. It was to be his last series on radio.

Actor Lee J. Cobb
ON FRANK
AS A FRIEND IN NEED:

After my heart attack in the summer of 1955, Frank moved into my life. I was in a low mental state then, divorced and pretty much alone in the world. I was sure my career had come to an end. But Frank— whom I knew mostly from having starred with me in The Miracle of the Bells in 1948—flooded me with books, flowers, delicacies. He kept telling me what fine acting I still had ahead of me. He built an insulating wall around me that shielded me from worry, tension and strain.

Disneyland's press preview day. Frankie and Pop in the Autopia.

DL 1000-20 DISNEYLAND

Robert Mitchum

ON SINATRA:

I had to fight with him for a scene in the movie. Frank is a tiger—afraid of nothing, ready for anything. He'll take on anybody, and about anything. He's the only man in town I'd be afraid to fight for real. I might knock him down, but he'd keep getting up until one of us was dead.

JULY 2, 1955: Co-starring with Olivia de Havilland, Robert Mitchum, Gloria Grahame, Broderick Crawford and Charles Bickford, FS delivered an impassioned performance as a dedicated surgeon in Stanley Kramer's *Not As a Stranger*. Though the picture wasn't well received by the critics, a reviewer credited Dad with saving the picture "through the sheer force of his personality."

JULY 11, 1955: With a group of friends that included Dean Martin, Sammy Davis Jr. and Humphrey Bogart, Dad attended a Judy Garland concert in Long Beach, and at the end they joined her on stage to take a bow.

AUGUST 15-20, 1955: FS prerecorded a number of songs for the movie *Carousel*, in which he was to appear with Shirley Jones for 20th Century Fox. But on the first day of shooting in Booth Bay, Maine, when Dad was informed that he would have to shoot the picture twice from beginning to end, once in 35 millimeter and once again in Cinemascope, he told the producers that he had no intention of giving them two movies for the price of one and quit on the spot. He was replaced by Gordon MacRae. The studio must have been furious after all of the preproduction involved.

AUGUST 29, 1955: Dad made the cover of *Time* magazine, which reported that although he listed his occupation in *Who's Who* as "baritone," he was "just about the hottest item in show business today." *Time* also said that he was on the verge of stepping into Bing Crosby's shoes as the "greatest all-around entertainer in show business." The magazine reported that my father's wardrobe was housed in a huge closet that stored his 100 suits, 20 hats and 50 pairs of shoes on a forest of individual shoe trees. He "carries nothing smaller than a $100 bill and peels them off like toilet paper." Despite a life of amazing contradictions, concluded *Time*, "There isn't any 'real' Sinatra. There's only what you see. You might as well try to analyze electricity. He is what he does. There's nothing inside—he puts out so terrifically that nothing can accumulate inside. Frank is the absolute genuine article, the diamond in the rough." Although *Time* was, in many ways, complimentary to my father, they stated many things about him as fact that were, in actuality, false.

SEPTEMBER 1955: *Confidential* magazine reported that during the wrong-door raid of 1954—which involved Joe DiMaggio—Sinatra had not stood by the car smoking a cigarette as he claimed but had entered the apartment along with the detectives who broke down the door. A few days after the magazine came out, thugs beat up 24-year-old Philip Irwin, one of the detectives involved in the raid. He told police he thought Sinatra was behind the attack because of rumors that Irwin had talked to *Confidential* reporters. He also claimed Sinatra had lied under oath when he said he hadn't gone into the apartment with the others. Dad said he was telling the truth and would never lie, especially under oath. My father's friend, music publisher Frank Military, who was present at the hearings, recently confirmed Dad's story: "Frank was totally innocent. He got suckered in by Joe." Most people refused to lend any credence to anything reported in that magazine.

LATE 1955: A California state senate committee launched an investigation into *Confidential*'s charges about the wrong-door raid, and Frank was called to testify. "I drove DiMaggio to the general area," he swore under oath. "I never knew the address. I parked at a curb and DiMaggio met Mr. [Barney] Ruditsky, a private investigator, and another man with a camera. I was not present. Someone later said they went into the wrong door." He also denied any involvement in the beating of detective Irwin. No indictments were issued, and that seemed to end the matter. But Dad hadn't heard the last of it.

SEPTEMBER 18, 1955: FS made an unscheduled guest appearance on *The Colgate Comedy Hour*, hosted that week by Dean Martin and Jerry Lewis.

SEPTEMBER 19, 1955: In a prestigious television appearance—aired in a new process NBC called "living color"—Dad played the Stage Manager in a television version of Thornton Wilder's *Our Town*, starring Paul Newman and Eva Marie Saint. One of the songs introduced in it, Sammy Cahn and Jimmy Van Heusen's "Love and Marriage," would win an Emmy and become one of Dad's biggest hits. This was Jimmy's first formal job for my father and he told me that "when the time came to run through the score for him, I went to your home. Conditions there made it slightly difficult to hear the seven songs for the first time. Tina and Frankie and you were all over his lap and your mother was in the kitchen getting some beautiful food ready and with the clatter of plates and kids underfoot it was not easy to impress him with my clever cantatas. Those were the lean years for him but there was nothing lean about his love for his family. And I watched it all, first with impatience because my cadenzas got clobbered, but later with the great wish that I were as lucky as he."

Rare photo of Frank Sinatra's wardrobe tests for the role he never played: Billy Bigelow in *Carousel*.

NOVEMBER 14, 1955: FS starred for MGM as the streetwise Nathan Detroit opposite Marlon Brando as Sky Masterson, Jean Simmons as Sister Sarah Brown and Vivian Blaine as Miss Adelaide in the film version of Frank Loesser's Broadway smash, *Guys and Dolls*. This is one of the finest scores ever written, with such great songs as "If I Were a Bell," "Sue Me" and "Sit Down, You're Rocking the Boat." Dad went into the project feeling that the picture would be a lot stronger if he, not Brando, had played Sky Masterson, the more vocal singing role; if singers, not movie stars, had played the other leads in the musical; and if more attention had been paid to

the great score. Sinatra and Brando: one an instinctual actor who revved himself up to do his very best on the first take, the other a Method actor, searching for motivation and perfection in take after take. The movie was a critical and box-office success.

NOVEMBER 17, 1955: Dad starred opposite Debbie Reynolds as a ladies' man in *The Tender Trap*. In my opinion they should have made more movies together because they made a good team. They were funny and romantic, and it's too bad nobody saw the potential. They never did another movie together. They are still friends.

NOVEMBER 19, 1955: Dad guested on the Milton Berle television show.

DECEMBER 4, 1955: While he was performing at the Sands in Las Vegas, Frank appeared as a guest on Dave Garroway's *Wide Wide World* show on NBC television.

JANUARY 9-10, 12, 16-17, 20, 1956: With Nelson Riddle, Dad recorded a new album, *Songs for Swingin' Lovers*, which included not only "You Make Me Feel So Young," "I Thought About You," "Anything Goes" and "We'll Be Together Again" but also a last-minute number arranged on the way to the studio: "I've Got You Under My Skin." Sinatra fans have voted it the best song he ever sang. It was released in March.

JANUARY 15, 1956: Giving possibly his best performance, Dad played Frankie Machine, a tormented heroin addict, opposite Kim Novak in Otto Preminger's *The Man with the Golden Arm* for United Artists. He earned a Best Actor nomination for what critic Arthur Knight called "a truly virtuoso performance," bringing to his character "a shade of sweetness, a sense of edgy indestructibility." It was demanding, a torturous piece of work, the only role he really wanted to play, almost needed to play, since Maggio. The Elmer Bernstein score is without question one of the finest ever written. This avant-garde, black-and-white gem has only one flaw: The entire film was shot on a soundstage and location shooting might have been better. The title, by the way, refers to Machine's card-dealing talent—not the fact that he

Frank Jr.

ON AN UNFORGETTABLE NIGHT IN THE STUDIO:

They'd been told how many songs to put on the album, and they were following instructions. They were supposed to finish the album on Friday night. Thursday, in the middle of the night, the A&R department called Sinatra and said, "We need three more songs for Swingin' Lovers. He says, "This is a helluva time to tell me." He called Nelson, who was living out in Malibu, and woke him up. Told Nelson they need three more arrangements. The next night, coming in from Malibu for the final date, Nelson's wife was driving and he was in the back seat with a flashlight, still writing out the parts. One of those arrangements was for "I've Got You Under My Skin." At the studio Nelson got up and started to conduct. Nelson Riddle was the kind of a guy, well, a volcano would go up next to him, he'd say, "How about that?" Absolutely unflappable. Now, Nelson conducted the set, and after they'd rehearsed "I've Got You Under My Skin," everybody just sat there. It was an old song, been recorded a thousand times, not a new song, right? But all the women had tears in their eyes and the whole orchestra, when they were done playing, stood up and applauded. For Nelson Riddle. This doesn't happen. But Nelson, he just stood there with cigarette ashes on him and said, "Yeah, how about that?"

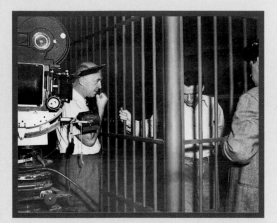

ON *THE MAN WITH THE GOLDEN ARM:*

I did some research on my part, and for about 40 seconds, through a peephole, I was allowed to see what happens to people when they try to kick heroin cold turkey—a youngster climbing a wall. It was the most frightening thing I've ever seen. I never want to see that again. Never. When we made the film, we wanted to show the real misery that drugs cause, so that people would not want to be involved. I've said this many times, but I thought I won an Oscar for the wrong picture. I thought in all fairness that I should have won it for The Man with the Golden Arm, *for which I was nominated. I felt if I ever deserved a prize, it should've been for that picture, because I did the finest work I ever did in my life on that film.*

is a drummer or that he shoots heroin. My favorite scene is the one in the jail cell when Machine, watching a screaming junkie, relives his own horror. My father's face is anguished here, not pretty. It's quite an amazing change.

JANUARY 24, 1956: Taking charge of his own movie career, Dad formed a production company—Kent Productions—to finance and produce films like his first release, *Johnny Concho*, in which he starred as a western gunslinger. A bunch of the boys—Sinatra, McGuire, Riddle, Sanicola—got together to make a cowboy movie. According to the *Los Angeles Examiner* he had signed heiress Gloria Vanderbilt, one of his occasional dates, to be his co-star, but she was eventually replaced by Phyllis Kirk.

FEBRUARY 29, 1956: Dad was devastated when Humphrey Bogart, a heavy smoker, was diagnosed with throat cancer.

APRIL 4, 5, 9, 1956: In the second group of marathon recording sessions with Nelson Riddle in this incredibly prolific year, Dad recorded 15 songs. Among them: "It Could Happen to You" and "Hey Jealous Lover." Total output for the year: 63 songs.

SPRING-SUMMER 1956: A dyed-in-the-wool liberal Democrat, Frank campaigned for a second time on behalf of presidential candidate Adlai Stevenson.

SUMMER 1956: FS appeared in a cameo role in the Dan Dailey-Cyd Charisse musical comedy, MGM's *Meet Me in Las Vegas*, filmed at the Sands Hotel.

JULY 30, 1956: Dad conducted his first album for Capitol, *Tone Poems in Color*, based on verses by poet Norman Sickel. Eight contemporary composers were commissioned to write a new composition based on the mood of a color. Victor Young wrote "White" and "Black," Gordon Jenkins "Green," Billy May "Purple," Jeff Alexander "Yellow" and "Brown," Alec Wilder "Gray" and "Blue," Nelson Riddle "Gold" and "Orange," Elmer Bernstein "Silver" and Andre Previn "Red." As the liner notes said, "In his direction of the symphony orchestra, Sinatra adds a brilliant new dimension to his stature."

> ### FRANK
> #### ON BING:
> *He was the father of my career, the idol of my youth—and the dear, dear friend of my maturity.*

> ### Bing Crosby
> #### ON FRANK:
> *A talent like that comes along once in a lifetime. Why in my lifetime?*

AUGUST 9, 1956: Back at MGM, Dad starred with Bing Crosby, by now a great friend, in the musical comedy *High Society*, John Patrick's adaptation of Philip Barry's *The Philadelphia Story* with a swell Cole Porter score that was recorded and released as an incredible soundtrack album. The Bing-Frank duet "Well, Did You Evah?" was the highlight of the movie. On the set, Frank was nicknamed "Dexedrine" because of his high energy level and Bing was nicknamed "Nembutal" because of his laid-back approach. It was also the beginning of a close friendship between FS and their co-star, the regal Grace Kelly, whom he affectionately called "Gracie."

AUGUST 12, 1956: After a reception for Eleanor Roosevelt in Chicago, Dad sang

Grace Kelly

ON SINATRA:

I'd always longed to do a musical and, of course, working with Bing and Frank was simply marvelous. They create a certain excitement and are two very strong personalities. So it was fascinating for me to be in the middle—watching the tennis match go back and forth from one to the other with tremendous wit and humor—each one trying to outdo the other...Frank and I did two numbers. He has an endearing sweetness and charm.

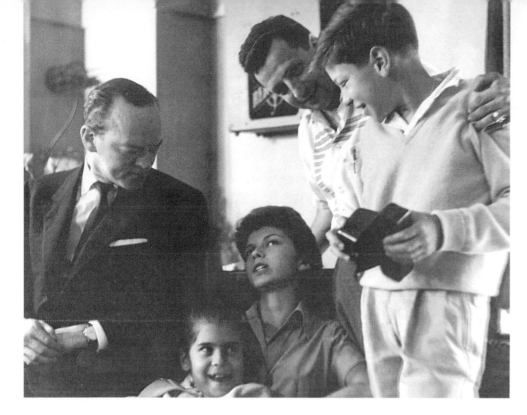

My brother, sister and I hung out in the hotel room in Atlantic City with Capitol executive and musician Dick Jones and Tony Consiglio. The photographer was Sammy Davis Jr.

the National Anthem at the Democratic Convention that nominated Adlai Stevenson. He was watching the convention with members of the Kennedy family when Stevenson locked up the nomination. The instant the '56 ticket was determined, he remembered Bobby Kennedy saying, "OK, that's it. Now we go to work for the next one." For the 1960 presidential election. Four years later. Not a minute to waste. Frank Sinatra was impressed.

AUGUST 15-21, 1956: In a sentimental reunion with the "Sentimental Gentleman of Song"—and a return to their old stomping grounds—FS appeared with Tommy and Jimmy Dorsey at the Paramount in New York. The movie playing on the screen during that engagement was *Johnny Concho*.

AUGUST 19, 1956: During his run at the Paramount, Dad appeared live between 8 and 9 p.m. on both *The Steve Allen Show* and *The Ed Sullivan Show*.

SUMMER 1956: Since his breakup with Ava, Dad was dividing his time between four homes: Los Angeles, New York and two desert homes. One desert home was a cozy two-bedroom condo on the 17th fairway of Tamarisk Country Club just beyond Palm Springs. But it was so close to the golf course that golfers would look into the living room window, and some clown actually drove a golf cart right into my father's pool. The other desert home was his suite at the Sands in Vegas, where he was the hottest act in town at a hotel that boasted such stellar entertainers as Dean Martin, Sammy Davis, Danny Thomas, Jerry Lewis and Red Skelton.

SEPTEMBER 14, 1956: FS was Edward R. Murrow's guest on his television interview show, *Person to Person*, filmed at Dad's new Coldwater Canyon home.

OCTOBER 5, 1956: He did a guest shot on NBC's *Dinah Shore Show*.

OCTOBER 17, 1956: Dad was one of many major stars in cameo roles—his was as a honky-tonk piano player—in the Mike Todd extravaganza, *Around the World in*

Someone's in rehearsal with Dinah.

80 Days. Marlene Dietrich also appeared in the scene with him. During the filming, he befriended one of the stars, young Shirley MacLaine, who became a great "buddy" soon afterward.

NOVEMBER 15, 1956: *This Is Sinatra*, a new album released by Capitol, was partly a compilation that featured "(Love Is) The Tender Trap," "The Gal That Got Away," "I've Got the World on a String," "Learnin' the Blues" and "Young at Heart."

NOVEMBER 1956: In a poll of jazz musicians—Frank Sinatra's toughest audience—*Metronome* named him Musicians' Musician of the Year.

DECEMBER 1956: In the annual *Motion Picture Herald* poll, Frank Sinatra was named among the Top 10 Money-Making Stars. That same month he returned to live performing in packed-house one-nighters at both the Sands and the Copa in New York.

JANUARY 14, 1957: Cancer claimed the life of Humphrey Bogart, and Dad was so grieved that he couldn't do his show at the Copa that night, saying, "I'm afraid I wouldn't be coherent." Friends Sammy Davis Jr. and Jerry Lewis filled in for him in sold-out performances with Marlene Dietrich and Joe DiMaggio in the audience.

Director George Sidney

ON FRANK'S BUSY SCHEDULE:

Frank is recording, he's making pictures, he's running the world. He's doing everything. I said, "Frank, tell me something. How do you do all these things?" He looked at me and said, "Very simple. One thing at a time." And that was it. Concentration. Amazing concentration. People think he's all over the place, but he's the most orderly person the world's ever known.

Jack Benny

ON SEEING FRANK AT THE SANDS:

I was in the audience, and he knew I was out there, and the place was jammed, and he said, "Ladies and gentlemen, I have a very dear friend in the audience," and he gives this very big buildup—and then he says, "My friend Jack Benny is in the audience." I took a bow and said, "Frank, can I say something?" He said, "Certainly, go ahead." I said, "This place is so packed I thought I was playing here." He fell on the floor laughing.

JANUARY 21, 1957: *Close to You*, released by Capitol, became a top 10 album for the year. Featuring the Hollywood String Quartet, it included "P.S. I Love You," "Everything Happens to Me," "Blame It on My Youth" and a song that was recorded as a practical joke on the Capitol execs and never meant to be released: "There's a Flaw in My Flue."

FEBRUARY 1957: Hearst Broadway columnist and CBS television personality Dorothy Kilgallen wrote a six-part series, "The Real Frank Sinatra Story," that purported to tell "heretofore unpublished episodes in Frankie's life." There was little new and even less substance in what came off as a typically mean-spirited hatchet job. Dad responded by taking personal digs at the columnist in his night-club act. He even sent Kilgallen a tombstone with her name carved on it. That was too much even for some Sinatra admirers, including columnist Louis Sobol, who wrote that his response to her attacks was "in bad taste" and "inexcusable." But Dad would publicly criticize Kilgallen for the rest of her life. And having been a victim of similar hatchet jobs myself, I can understand why he chose to finally fight back with the only forum he had, his microphone. I wish he had acted on these attacks much earlier.

MARCH 8, 1957: 1954's notorious wrong-door raid came back to haunt Frank once again when, according to the *Los Angeles Times*, a Los Angeles grand jury served him with a subpoena to testify at a hearing into private detectives and scandal magazines. Again, no indictments were brought against anyone in the entire affair and the whole sordid mess was finally put to rest.

MARCH 14, 1957: This year, Frank would record 56 new songs, including: "Autumn Leaves," "Witchcraft," "Have Yourself a Merry Little Christmas," "All the Way," "I Didn't Know What Time It Was," "Bewitched," "Come Fly with Me," "Time After Time," the classic "April in Paris" and a rerecording of "I'm a Fool to Want You," which critic George T. Simon called "the most emotional side of Frank I have ever heard." He sang it for Ava.

APRIL 7, 1957: He did another guest appearance on *The Bob Hope Show*.

SPRING 1957: Playing a nightclub singer and the definitive heel alongside Kim Novak and Rita Hayworth—perhaps two of Hollywood's most beautiful bookends—in

The role of Joey Evans was originated on Broadway by Frank's good friend Gene Kelly, and the fact that Dad played it on the screen enhanced their friendship, contrary to what such a situation might imply.

Rodgers and Hart's *Pal Joey*, Dad added "The Lady Is a Tramp" to his repertoire of classic hits. Director George Sidney recalled that "about billing, Frank was smart enough to say, put Rita first, and then me, and then Kim. Because here we had the big star, Rita, and then we had the new one coming up, Kim, and Frank in between the two. Every man in the world, whether he'd like to admit it or not, he says, 'Gee, I would like to be that fella...' What a sandwich!"

MAY 6, 1957: Another top 10 album, *A Swingin' Affair*, with great charts by Nelson Riddle, included "Night and Day," "I Wish I Were in Love Again," "The Lonesome Road" and "Nice Work If You Can Get It."

MAY 7, 1957: Dad was the subject of a three-part *Look* magazine cover story entitled "The Life Story of Frank Sinatra—Talent, Tantrums and Torment." Chronicling his meteoric rise to fame, author Bill Davidson acknowledged his subject's unquestioned gifts as a singer, actor and nightclub performer, but alluded repeatedly to his "emaciated" physique, thinning hair and frequent public displays of anger. "There is a generous Sinatra and a cruel Sinatra," wrote Davidson. "There is a Sinatra who fights for the underdog and a Sinatra who bullies his underlings. There is a cocky Sinatra, a scared Sinatra, a gay Sinatra, a brooding Sinatra. There is Sinatra the devoted family man and Sinatra the libertine." Dad promptly sued *Look* for libel, and though the suit was dropped a few months later—at the advice of his attorneys—he filed immediately for invasion of privacy, but that suit, too, was dropped. "I have always maintained that any writer or publication has a right to discuss or criticize my professional activities as a singer or actor," said Dad. "But I feel that an entertainer has a right to his privacy that is as inviolate as any other person's. Otherwise, it means that a 'public figure' is a second-class citizen in that he is denied rights which others enjoy." The fact is that public figures do not enjoy the same right to privacy as ordinary citizens. Davidson remembers the suit and the reason Dad decided not to pursue it. Prior to the *Look*

Sammy Davis Jr.

ON HIS FRIENDSHIP WITH FRANK:

I was the only black person that traveled in that sort of circle. Frank and I would talk about prejudiced people, and he'd say, "Aah, they're full of shit! Pay no attention to it." I can handle it all because of that learning experience, early in my life, with Frank. He forced me to learn. I was doing a gig at this nightclub in L.A., Ciro's. And Frank would bring all the heavyweights to see me. And then he started taking me around, introducing me to Gary Cooper, Judy Garland—all those people. I wanted to be like him so bad.

article, the U.S. Supreme Court had issued a ruling called "The Koussevitsky Decision," named after Boston Symphony conductor Serge Koussevitsky. The ruling stipulated that a public figure cannot sue for invasion of privacy. When I asked Davidson if he thought the ruling was fair, he said, "In retrospect, frankly, no. But I think it will eventually be reversed."

MAY 1957: This was the time of Frank Sinatra's concept albums: his invitations to *Come Fly with Me* and *Come Dance with Me* and to have *A Jolly Christmas*. His Capitol albums were averaging sales of 200,000 each, making him the most consistent seller of albums in the music industry. The reason, said conductor Nelson Riddle, was that he was getting better: "Where Sinatra used to sound like a muted violin, now he's like a fine cello." And Sinatra, known for his way with a melody, his beautifully enunciated and deeply felt reading of a lyric, is meticulous, too, about giving credit to the superlative composers, lyricists, arrangers, musicians, producers and directors with whom he has worked. He told writer John Bryson, "I believe in a team of people. Four heads are better than one. I want the best strength I can have behind me."

JUNE 8-9, 1957: On a short concert tour through the Northwest, Dad appeared in Vancouver, Portland and Seattle.

JUNE 14, 1957: At the end of a long and rocky road with Ava, his attorneys finally filed for divorce in Mexico City.

JUNE 16, 1957: Ending his tour, he did a major concert at the Cow Palace in San Francisco.

JUNE 17, 1957: Leaving for 16 weeks of location shooting in rural Spain, he played a guerrilla fighter, starring with Cary Grant and Sophia Loren in Stanley Kramer's costume epic *The Pride and the Passion*, again for United Artists. Said Kramer afterward: "He didn't appear to be happy, but he worked hard and insisted on doing a lot of things you'd normally expect a star would want a double to perform. He ran through explosions and fires. He often started scenes as though he didn't quite know what was going on. It seemed like a palpable case of lack of preparedness, but after a couple of minutes he was going like some high-precision machine."

Sophia Loren

ON FRANK:

The Pride and the Passion was my first contact with the American world. Frank Sinatra made me feel at ease with that world, with everybody. He could not have been kinder or more friendly, and I shall never stop being grateful to him for it.

Jack Entratter, Frank Sinatra and Kim Novak celebrate Lauren Bacall's birthday in Las Vegas.

JULY 5, 1957: The divorce decree from Ava was granted. She never remarried.

FALL 1957: According to Lauren Bacall, she and Dad were drawn together in the wake of Bogart's death and began dating. Their first date: an outing to a theater for a closed-circuit telecast of a prizefight between Sugar Ray Robinson and Gene Fullmer. "I had never thought much about celebrity after the insane exposure I'd had at the time of *To Have and Have Not* and my marriage to Bogie," she recalled. "I gave no thought to being noticed on such a quiet evening, even with Frank, but when we emerged from the theater, there were photographers waiting and the resulting pictures ended up in newspapers around the world." They soon became an item, and she played hostess at his small dinner parties. "It seemed to his friends and mine that we were crazy about each other," she later recounted, "that we were a great pair; that it wouldn't last; that Frank would never be able to remain constantly devoted, monogamous. But just then I was the center of his life. At least I felt I was. And I was happy."

SEPTEMBER 2, 1957: *Where Are You?*, a musical collaboration between FS and Gordon Jenkins, was a killer album: irresistibly sweet ballads of longing with deeply romantic orchestrations. Among them: "The Night We Called It a Day," "Laura," "Maybe You'll Be There" and "Baby Won't You Please Come Home?"

SEPTEMBER 9, 1957: It was reported in *Time* magazine that Frank Sinatra fired off a telegram to Florida Senator George Smathers of the Interstate and Foreign Commerce Committee, accusing Mitch Miller of confessing that he accepted payola in the form of "large sums of money" from songwriters whose songs Miller recorded at Columbia Records. Smathers introduced an amendment to the Federal Communications Act to prevent broadcasters from owning stock in publishing or record companies. It failed to become law.

SEPTEMBER 30, 1957: *A Jolly Christmas* from Frank Sinatra was quite simply the best Christmas album ever made—by anyone anywhere.

OCTOBER 13, 1957: With Louis Armstrong and Rosemary Clooney, Dad guested on his friend Bing Crosby's *Edsel Show*.

OCTOBER 14, 1957: Released two weeks after his last album, the soundtrack album from *Pal Joey*, with music by Richard Rodgers and Lorenz Hart, included "The Lady Is a Tramp," "I Could Write a Book," "There's a Small Hotel" and "I Didn't Know What Time It Was."

OCTOBER 18, 1957: Frank Sinatra debuted in *The Frank Sinatra Show*, a series of 21 one-hour musicals and 10 half-hour dramas on Friday nights on ABC television. Among his all-star roster of guests were such friends as Bob Hope, Peggy Lee, Kim Novak, Dean Martin, Bing Crosby, Dinah Shore, Robert Mitchum, Sammy Davis, Eddie Fisher, Ethel Merman, Joey Bishop, Ella Fitzgerald and Natalie Wood. The second show was to be the television debut of my nine-year-old sister, Tina, but she was too frightened to appear and I replaced her. Chesterfield Cigarettes and Bulova Watch Company signed up as sponsors. At the time, it was the most expensive half-hour in television history, and Dad set an ambitious schedule, shooting nine half-hour shows in just 15 working days. "One Friday I'll be a singer," he told *Newsweek*, "and another Friday I'll be an actor. If any bad mistakes are made, I want to be responsible for them." The financial aspects of the lucrative deal were widely publicized, and critics complained that the show appeared "unrehearsed." When reviewers wrote that the show looked "canned," Dad replied, "If they want audience reaction, I'll film the shows before an audience, the same as *I Love Lucy*. But I'm not going to gimmick up the show. I loathe phony soundtracks and canned applause. I'd rather quit than submit to them." Reviews for the series were disappointing, ratings were low and it was canceled after a single season. *The Frank Sinatra Show* was the last TV series he ever tried.

NOVEMBER 1, 1957: I sang with two of my girlfriends, Belinda Burrell and Jane Ross, on *The Frank Sinatra Show*. We called ourselves the Tri-Tones.

Scheduled for her TV debut, little Tina was OK during the dress rehearsal, but her last-minute attack of stage fright forced me to sub for her on the show—in my school clothes.

Strutting their stuff (right to left): Tri-Tones Belinda Burrell, Jane Ross and that other singing Sinatra.

The Frank Sinatra Show

The *Frank Sinatra Show*, an ambitious, big-budget series of one-hour musicals and half-hour dramas on ABC in 1957, showcased Dad's multiple talents, but the ratings and reviews didn't live up to audience expectations or his own.

Though it lasted only a season, the stellar list of guests who appeared on it made *The Frank Sinatra Show* worth watching.

The **FRANK SINATRA** *Show*

Left: Singing with Peggy Lee

Below: Like father, like son: Franks Sr. and Jr.

Clowning with Bing and Dean

Frank with two of the world's funniest men: Joe E. and Jerry Lewis (no relation).

NOVEMBER 10, 1957: The *New York Times Magazine* profiled FS, signaling his arrival as an Establishment icon. Estimating his income at about $4 million a year, Hollywood correspondent Thomas M. Pryor wrote that "Sinatra is perhaps the highest-paid performer in the history of show business."

DECEMBER 12, 1957: Starring with Mitzi Gaynor and Jeanne Crain, Dad took on another dramatic/musical role in Paramount's *The Joker Is Wild*, based on the true story of nightclub singer and close friend Joe E. Lewis, whose throat was cut after crossing the Mob, and who then made a comeback as a gravel-voiced standup comedian. This project was near and dear to all of us—we treasured Joe E. He was a fighter who won against great odds and Dad played the hell out of the role. Said Lewis after working with Frank during the production: "Frankie enjoyed playing my life more than I enjoyed living it." Lewis often co-starred with Sinatra in nightclubs.

JANUARY 6, 1958: *Come Fly with Me*, Dad's first stereo album, hit number one on the charts with songs like "Isle of Capri," "Moonlight in Vermont," "Autumn in New York," "Let's Get Away from it All" and "Blue Hawaii." This was the first time he actually worked with arranger Billy May. The last song they were recording one night was "The Road to Mandalay." They went through it, and when they did "And the dawn comes up like thunder—*Bong*—outta China... 'cross the bay," percussionist Lou Singer hit the gong cue with gusto. Billy May remembered, "That gong was big, like the one on the J. Arthur Rank movie logo. And when Lou hit it, it rang and rang. When Frank heard it the first time he said, 'Yeah! Let me hear it again.' BON-NGGG...He said, 'Yeah, Billy. Let's end it with the gong—and let the mother ring!'"

JANUARY 15-28, 1958: FS played two weeks at the Sands.

JANUARY 26, 1958: He was back on *The Dinah Shore Show*.

FEBRUARY 1, 1958: Dad did a guest spot on Dean Martin's *Club Oasis* television show sponsored by Oasis cigarettes, joining Dean in a duet of "Jailhouse Rock."

Nat "King" Cole helps Dad celebrate his 42nd birthday at Patsy D'Amore's Villa Capri restaurant in Hollywood.

Sammy Cahn

ON "ALL THE WAY":

Frank never turned down a song of mine. When Jimmy Van Heusen and I wrote "All the Way" for The Joker Is Wild, Jimmy and my agent Lillian Schary Small and I went up to Vegas to sing it for Sinatra. We were told he would hear it before breakfast, which meant four in the afternoon. Come 4:00 p.m. we were in the living room and he emerged from the bedroom looking like all the Dorian Grays. He looked at me much as he'd looked at Dorsey so many years before, grimaced and said, "You before breakfast—yechh." I looked back. "Hey, from where I'm standing, I'm not sure who's being punished more." Van Heusen gave me an intro and we went into "All the Way." When I'd sung the last immortal word and note, Frank turned and said, "Let's eat." We had a marvelous meal and left. Lillian Small had tears in her eyes. "How could he not like that song?" she said. I said, "Oh, he loved it." "How do you know?" "Because he loves them all." It won an Oscar.

Frank Jr.

ON THE NEW SOUNDS:

I can remember when Come Fly with Me *was released…waking up after this album had been shipped to the disc jockeys in L.A. and—during traffic hour, which is the biggest sales time on radio—I can remember the morning disc jockey at the top station in town playing the whole side of this album and saying, "We'll be back with the second side of this new Sinatra album after this commercial." Played the whole side of one album—and during traffic hour! Nobody did that.*

FEBRUARY 1958: Co-starring with Tony Curtis and Natalie Wood in *Kings Go Forth* for United Artists, FS was on location in France playing a World War II infantry lieutenant who comes home an amputee. Boris Karloff worked as Dad's unofficial acting coach while he was making this movie. He gave him advice that became invaluable: "You must learn to act with your *voice* as well as your face."

FEBRUARY 8, 1958: When he got word on location that his friend and mentor Manie Sacks was dying of leukemia, FS flew to Philadelphia to be at Manie's bedside. Manie's death the next day, so soon after Bogart's, was a blow that staggered my father for a long time to come. Manie Sacks' nephew Herman Rush remembered Dad's visit to the hospital: "The doctor had issued standing orders—no visitors—but one afternoon the rule was broken by a young man on the thin side who stopped by the hospital to see Manie. 'Just say Frank Sinatra's calling.' Unexpected, unannounced, Sinatra had suddenly closed down production of *Kings Go Forth*, a movie he was starring in, covered the cost of a two-day shutdown personally, and had flown to Philadelphia to see Manie."

MARCH 1958: Dad proposed marriage to Lauren Bacall. She accepted.

When Uncle Manie Sacks died, my father cried. He said, "When I holler for help, he ain't gonna be there anymore. There's a little bit of Manie in everything good that has ever happened to me."

MARCH 11-17, 1958: He played six nights to packed houses at the Hotel Fontainbleau in Miami Beach.

MARCH 19, 1958: FS starred in the first of Dean Martin's four Timex specials on NBC. Unlike Dean's previous live shows, which were kinescoped (filmed by focusing a 16-millimeter camera on a screen while the show was in production), these were on a new storage medium called videotape.

MARCH 19, 1958: The Federal Communications Commission approved the purchase of three radio stations by the Essex Corporation, a Sinatra company, for $2 million: KXL in Portland, Oregon, KJR in Seattle and KNEW in Spokane.

MARCH 29, 1958: Dad did a benefit for the Palm Springs Police Department.

MARCH 31, 1958: *This Is Sinatra: Volume II,* another top 10 album released by Capitol, was a compilation that included "Hey Jealous Lover," "How Little We Know," "If You Are but a Dream" and his theme song, "Put Your Dreams Away."

APRIL 9-22, 1958: Back at the Sands, he played two shows a night for two solid weeks to the usual SRO crowds.

MAY 29, 1958: Back in the studio with Nelson Riddle, my father recorded a couple

Bacall

ON THE RELATIONSHIP:

The last few months of Bogie's illness, a part of me needed a man to talk to, and Frank turned out to be that man. I not only began to depend on his voice on the other end of the phone, but looked forward to him. By the time Bogie died, my dependence on him became greater and greater. We continued for several months as close friends.

Then suddenly he didn't call for days. After a week the phone rang. That's when our relationship really changed. No promises were made, but we were together—a couple. I sold my house—I knew if I moved out of it he'd feel better. I knew Bogie's ghost would always come between us. Though his erratic behavior was very much part of him, I flatly refused to face what it might portend. Frank didn't know how to apologize, but he was fairly contrite, at least for him. He said he had felt somewhat trapped—was "chicken"—but now could face it. "Will you marry me?" He said those words and he meant them. I must have hesitated for at least 30 seconds. I was ecstatic—we both were.

Bacall

ON THE BREAKUP:

We went to have a drink with Swifty Lazar, and when Frank told him we were going to get married, I don't think he took it seriously until Frank started to plan the wedding. "We'll get married at the house and instead of our going away, we'll have our friends go away." A young girl came over for autographs. Frank handed me the paper napkin and pen. He said, "Put down your new name." So "Lauren Bacall" was followed by "Betty Sinatra." I often wondered what became of that napkin. Frank was leaving for a singing engagement in Miami—we'd work everything out on his return. Mum's the word until then. I was giddy with joy, felt like laughing every time I opened my mouth. I said nothing to anyone, but now I knew—my life would go on. The children would have a father, I would have a husband, we'd have a home again.

A few days later I went to the Huntington Hartford for an evening of Dickens. Swifty took me, and all Hollywood was there. At intermission Louella Parsons asked me if Frank and I were going to get married. I kept moving toward the ladies' room and said, "Why don't you ask him?" On my return I saw Swifty still talking to her. On the way home after the theater and supper we pulled up to a newsstand for the early edition of the morning paper. I saw enormous black letters jumping out at me from the Examiner: SINATRA TO MARRY BACALL. When I confronted Swifty, he just laughed. Frank didn't call for a few days, then finally one night he did, saying, "Why did you do it? I haven't been able to leave my room for days. The press are everywhere—we'll have to lie low and not see each other for a while."

There was nothing left to say to Frank. His attitude was remote, and clearly he thought I'd given it away—he couldn't deal with the press, they were driving him crazy, and under this circumstance the pressure was too great. He felt trapped. Though we met twice in the next six years, each time Frank looked right through me as if I wasn't there. We did not speak again until we met at one of Swifty's parties, where Frank told him, "You were responsible for what happened between her and me!" It was his way of admitting he knew it was Swifty who had spilled the beans. Actually, Frank did me a great favor—he saved me from the disaster our marriage would have been. He was probably smarter than I: He knew it wouldn't work. But the truth also is that he behaved like a complete shit. He was too cowardly to tell the truth: that it was too much for him and he couldn't handle it. But it turned out to be a tragedy with a happy ending. Now we're back on a friendly basis. I'll always have a special feeling for him, because the good times we had were awfully good.

of songs for the album *Frank Sinatra Sings for Only the Lonely*: "Guess I'll Hang My Tears Out to Dry," "Ebb Tide" and "Angel Eyes." He would record a total of 47 songs this year.

JUNE 7, 1958: Dad performed at a benefit in Monaco for his friend Princess Grace's favorite charity, and one of his: the United Nations Fund for Refugee Children.

JULY 2, 1958: Dad headlined "A Night with Sinatra" for the benefit of Cedars of Lebanon in Los Angeles. That same day, he attended the world premiere of *Kings Go Forth*. Playing a World War II Army radio operator, he falls in love with a French woman (Natalie Wood) who confesses that she's the daughter of a white mother and a black father. Tolerance is a theme that's close to his heart, and he talked about race relations that month in *Ebony* magazine: "Some of my friendships have given rise to some strange, quite cockeyed notions about me and the way I think. Because some of my good friends happen to be Negroes, it has been suggested that I have a preference for colored people, that I 'like' them. The fact is that I don't 'like' Negroes any more than I 'like' Jews or Moslems or Italians or any other group. I don't like according to the color of a man's skin or his place of worship. And I have never picked a friend because of his nationality. I simply like people, a lot of them, and my personal relationships are not determined by the boundaries of a country or what society thinks of certain kinds of human beings. I'd personally like to see more friendships forged across color and religious lines, for I feel this is the surest way to erase all the lines that divide people everywhere. The world is suffering from a shortage of love, between nations and individuals, and something drastic and dramatic is needed to meet this hunger."

Dad at my graduation from University High School in West Los Angeles. That's a Minox camera in his hand, not a lighter.

JULY 6, 1958: FS guested on *The Ed Sullivan Show* in New York.

AUGUST-SEPTEMBER 1958: FS was on location in Madison, Indiana, population 10,500, starring with Dean Martin and Shirley MacLaine in *Some Came Running* as a disillusioned war veteran and writer returning to a small Midwestern community after World War II. It was Dean's first major dramatic film role. My father so loves Shirley MacLaine's performance in this film that he screened it regularly for guests in his home.

OCTOBER 19, 1958: Dad was joined by Bing Crosby and Dean Martin on *The Frank Sinatra Timex Show* on ABC. The trio crooned "Together" and while Dean soloed with "Wrap Your Troubles in Dreams," he crossed his legs to reveal writing on the sole of his shoe. The camera zoomed in for a closeup: It said, "Eat at Dino's." This was a less than subtle commercial for Dean's Hollywood restaurant.

FS acted as master of ceremonies at the British premiere of the film *Me and the Colonel*. Attended by Queen Elizabeth, the event was a benefit for the British Cancer Fund.

From the bold, new novel by the author of "From Here To Eternity"

Dave was back and the whole town knew that trouble- and women- were close behind!

FRANK SINATRA

DEAN MARTIN

SHIRLEY MacLAINE

M·G·M presents A SOL C. SIEGEL PRODUCTION

...·"SOME CAME RUNNING"

with **MARTHA HYER** · **ARTHUR KENNEDY**

NANCY GATES · LEORA DANA

Screen Play by JOHN PATRICK and ARTHUR SHEEKMAN · Based On the Novel by JAMES JONES · In CinemaScope and METROCOLOR · Directed by VINCENTE MINNELLI

NOVEMBER 10, 1958: FS started shooting Frank Capra's *A Hole in the Head* with Eleanor Parker, Edward G. Robinson and Carolyn Jones in Miami. It's a family drama about a widower trying to raise his 11-year-old son while managing a run-down Miami Beach hotel. This is one of my favorite Sinatra movies. It makes me laugh and it makes me cry.

NOVEMBER 17, 1958: In a time of nothing but brilliance, how does one album outshine the others? I don't know. It seems to be a personal thing, like knowing exactly where you were and who you were with when you first heard a particular song. But many Sinatra fans feel *Only the Lonely* was his greatest album of ballads. This album is the one people remember today. Sammy Cahn and Jimmy Van Heusen, who composed the title song, wrote about Frank and loneliness: "The Frank Sinatra we know and have known (and hardly know) is an artist with as many forms and patterns as can be found in a child's kaleidoscope. A Sinatra singing a hymn of loneliness could very well be the real Sinatra." This album remained at number one for an amazing 120 weeks and prompted the *New York Post* to name Frank Sinatra "Love Voice of the Century." The cover won a Grammy.

DECEMBER 9-23, 1958: FS recorded the album *Come Dance with Me*, arranged by Billy May and Heinie Beau and produced by Dave Cavanaugh. All brass, reeds and rhythm. Great album. Great cover.

DECEMBER 14, 1958: He appeared at the Moulin Rouge in L.A. for the Friars' annual Christmas party for 750 orphans.

JANUARY 2, 1959: Dean Martin recorded a new album with FS conducting the Capitol Records orchestra. They used a new format: full dimensional stereo. The title: *Sleep Warm*.

JANUARY 28, 1959: Dad appeared at the Sands with Dean for the first time.

FEBRUARY 4, 1959: *Some Came Running* was released. Though panned by the critics, the film played to large and enthusiastic audiences, and Shirley MacLaine was nominated for her first Academy Award as the sweet, dumb floozy Ginny Moorhead.

MARCH-APRIL 1959: Frank toured the United States and Australia with a small jazz group led by Red Norvo.

APRIL 20, 1959: *Look to Your Heart*, still another top 10 album, was a collection of recordings from 1953 to 1955, including the singles "Anytime, Anywhere," "When I Stop Loving You" and "Same Old Saturday Night," along with the title song from *Not As a Stranger* and three numbers from the production of *Our Town*.

MAY 8, 1959: For the film *A Hole in the Head*, Dad recorded a Van Heusen-Cahn song, "High Hopes," that won the Oscar for Best Song of 1959. It was one of 23 songs he'd press that year for Capitol. Among them: "Stormy Weather," "None but the Lonely Heart," "I Love Paris" and "I'll Never Smile Again."

JULY 20, 1959: Wrote Ralph Gleason, the editor of *Jazz* magazine, in the liner notes for *No One Cares*, Dad's latest top 10 album for Capitol: "It is as certain a truth that Frank Sinatra is the greatest ballad singer of his generation as that Charlie Parker was a musical genius, Frank Lloyd Wright an architectural poet and Joe DiMaggio, hitting a ball, a thing of classic beauty." The songs included "A Cottage for Sale," "I Can't Get Started," "Here's That Rainy Day" and "When No One Cares."

JULY 1959: Co-starring with Steve McQueen, Gina Lollobrigida and Peter Lawford, FS played an embattled U.S. Army captain leading a guerrilla force during World War II in MGM's *Never So Few*. *Newsweek*'s Betty Voight caught up with Dad long enough to ask about his acting. "I wish I had some formal dramatic training, but I never have enough time. I have my own technique that I've evolved from discussing acting with some of my chums, like Spencer Tracy and Bogie, when he was still alive. Before starting to shoot a picture, I read the script half a hundred times. I pick it up and read maybe two or three pages one night and two days later I pick it up again and read halfway through it. By the time I start working I have a good idea of the dialogue and the story and the character I'm playing. Once we've begun shooting, I rarely open the script. I feel that you don't have to go by the script verbatim. If two good actors in a scene listen intently to what the other is saying, they'll answer each other intelligently. Actors who go only by the lines never seem to be listening to the other actor, so the scene comes out on the screen as if you can see the wheels going around in

Frank Jr.

ON *ONLY THE LONELY*:

For my money, this is the greatest blues album ever made. This album should be available in drugstores by prescription only—because this is death, this record. Photographer John Engstead, who shot our family portraits, used to have records playing in the background when he was photographing people. When we went to his studio one year, he had Only the Lonely sitting on the pile. I said, "Do you use that?" "No," he said, "I can't play that record anymore. I'd tell people to smile and nobody wanted to smile when this record was on."

Frank Capra

ON WORKING WITH FRANK:

He's a great singer and he knows it. The excitement of moving and reaching the hearts of live audiences with his lyrical virtuosity makes his blood run hot. Sinatra is also a great actor, and he knows that, too. But he cannot bewitch an audience of dispassionate cameramen, soundmen, script girls, makeup people, deadpan electricians who have seen it all before. If directors keep him busy, he maintains an easy truce, for having started something, Sinatra's next goal is to finish it—but fast. He bores easily; can't sit still or be alone; must be where the action is.

their heads." While he was filming a battle scene on location in the Philippines, the cornea of his left eye was scorched by muzzle blast from gunfire too close to his head. Temporarily blinded, he was led from the set by Lawford. A studio doctor said it was a close call and Dad was lucky not to have lost an eye.

JULY 25-AUGUST 1, 1959: With Red Norvo, FS appeared at his friend Skinny D'Amato's 500 Club in Atlantic City.

SEPTEMBER 1959: Dad was shooting 20th Century Fox's production of Cole Porter's *Can-Can*, again co-starring with Shirley MacLaine. This time he played an attorney who defends her character, a nightclub owner, when she's arrested with her dancers for performing the provocative can-can.

Dad, on stage with his accompanist Bill Miller, knocking out the audience at the 500 Club in Atlantic City.

SEPTEMBER 19, 1959: Dad hosted a luncheon honoring Soviet Premier Nikita Khrushchev and attended by more than 400 Hollywood stars where Khrushchev and 20th Century Fox president Spyros Skouras debated the relative merits of capitalism and communism. Visiting a movie set, the Khrushchevs enjoyed watching my father film a scene from *Can-Can*—but the Russian premier proceeded to denounce the can-can itself as a decadent example of Western culture. When they were denied permission to visit Disneyland for security reasons, my father offered to escort Mrs. Khrushchev there personally—an offer vetoed by the Secret Service. But later he sat with her and looked patiently at photos of her grandchildren.

SEPTEMBER 29, 1959: Dad guested with Peggy Lee and Louis Armstrong on television's *Bing Crosby Show*.

OCTOBER 19, 1959: Bing Crosby, Dean Martin and Mitzi Gaynor were guests on *The Frank Sinatra Timex Show*.

NOVEMBER 2, 1959: Once again, FS appeared as a guest on Dean's NBC television show.

Soviet Premier and Mrs. Nikita Khrushchev visit the set of *Can-Can* in 1959. Khrushchev called the can-can dance number "immoral." Reporting that advance ticket sales for the film were bigger than those for *Ben-Hur*, *Newsweek* added: "being condemned by Khrushchev may be an even bigger commercial asset than being banned in Boston."

In a scene from *Can-Can*, Frank Sinatra watches the "scandalous" dance on stage with co-stars Shirley MacLaine and Maurice Chevalier.

NOVEMBER 8, 1959: Frank and fellow Friars roasted Dean Martin in Los Angeles.

NOVEMBER 1959: According to her 1977 autobiography, *My Story*, 25-year-old Judith Campbell met FS at a Beverly Hills restaurant, Puccini, and he invited her to join him on a trip to Hawaii with Peter Lawford and Patricia Kennedy Lawford, Peter's wife of five years.

DECEMBER 13, 1959: On another of his Timex TV shows, Dad hosted an all-star cast that included Peter Lawford, Ella Fitzgerald, Nat "King" Cole and Dad's new girlfriend, Juliet Prowse, a dancer whom he had met on the set of *Can-Can*.

JANUARY 1960: The early sixties was their time and Las Vegas was their place. They made movies there and played nightclubs there and set a tone of arrogance and confidence, of energy and expectation that spoke to and for many of their generation. At the Sands, Dad and his pals—Joey Bishop, Sammy Davis Jr., Dean Martin and Peter Lawford—packed the room for two shows nightly. Guest stars of the highest magnitude dropped in unannounced: Bob Hope, Milton Berle, Dan Dailey, Harry James, Red Skelton, Shirley MacLaine and Danny Thomas, to name a few. Whenever a person of prominence was in the audience, Dad gave a colleague the honor of introducing him or her to the crowd. One time Dean would do it, another time Sammy, and so on. I remember the night Dean said to a room that was filled with extra excitement and a kind of tangible glow: "There's a senator here tonight, and this senator is running for president or something, and we play golf together, we go fishing together, and he's one of my best buddies." Then he turned to Dad and said, "What the hell is his name?" and Senator John Kennedy broke up laughing.

JANUARY 26-FEBRUARY 13, 1960: The members of the Summit

FRANK   SINATRA
DEAN   MARTIN
SAMMY   DAVIS JR.
PETER   LAWFORD
JOEY   BISHOP

Sammy Davis Jr.
ON THE SUMMIT:

We were like a team. The only thing missing was the marching band. We traveled as a group, man, and people couldn't get over it. And every night Frank would turn to me and say, "We're all men sitting here. Where are all the broads?" So one time I called up some friends and said, "I want 10 showgirls from the Stardust." Then I called for 10 from the Frontier. I had a big table set up in the lounge and when we walked in, here sat all these girls—oh, man! There must have been 25 of them. Frank was being Mr. Social, but by four-thirty, almost everybody was gone. I got a chick for myself, but every time I tried to make a move out of there, Frank would say, "Hey, where are you going, Smokey? Sit down! Listen, you remember this story..."and by six in the morning, my girl was gone and he was still telling me stories. I said to him, "I hope you're satisfied. There must have been 25 girls here." "Yeah," he said, smiling. So I said, "So why am I sitting here alone with you?"

"The Rat Pack" Becomes "The Summit"

After Bogart's death in 1957, Dad assumed leadership of the Holmby Hills Rat Pack, which had also included Bogart, Bacall, Judy Garland and Peter Lawford in addition to nonentertainers like restaurateur Mike Romanoff and literary agent Swifty Lazar. Over the next few years, as Frank's closest personal friends joined its ranks— Sammy Davis Jr., Dean Martin, Joey Bishop and Shirley MacLaine, along with associates like songwriter Jimmy Van Heusen—it evolved into such a tightly knit circle of high-profile performers that the press decided to rename it "the Clan." They resisted and resented having a club name. They called it "The Summit." When they worked together, it was a summit meeting indeed, a gathering—within the entertainment world—at the top.

Dean
ON FRANK:

Frank and I are brothers. We cut the top of our thumbs and became blood brothers. He wanted to cut the wrist. But I said, "What are you, crazy?"

Dean

ON SAMMY:

One night, Sammy came out on stage and did his dancing and then he jumped up on the piano and just sat there. He was through, but he wouldn't get off; he just sat there on the piano. Frank had to sing, so I just walked over and picked him up and went over to the mike and said, "I want to thank the NAACP for this wonderful trophy."

Sammy

ON SHIRLEY MACLAINE:

Crazy Shirley. She was one of the guys! None of us ever hit on her. She said once, "Here I am surrounded by the most attractive men in the world, and they make me feel like a boy!"

This haunting photograph of Marilyn Monroe sitting ringside at the Sands with Dean makes me think of the lyric from "Someone to Watch Over Me": "I'm a little lamb who's lost in the wood...I know I could always be good...to one who'll watch over me."

Lawford

ON THE GANG:

Everybody was on the same wavelength. We would do two shows a night, get to bed around five, get up again at seven or eight, and go to work on a movie. We'd come back, go to the steam room, get something to eat and start all over again—two shows a night. They were taking bets we'd all end up in a box.

filmed *Ocean's Eleven* on location in Vegas. It was the first of four films in which they starred together. FS played the ringleader of a gang of former Air Force buddies—including Dean, Sammy, Peter and Joey, along with Richard Conte and Henry Silva—who orchestrate a military-style holdup of five Las Vegas casinos. Of the Summit movies, my father said, "Of course they're not great movies. No one could claim that. We're not setting out to make *Hamlet* or *Gone with the Wind.* We gotta make pictures the people enjoy. Entertainment."

FEBRUARY 15, 1960: In another of his Timex television shows, Dad hosted a distinguished guest, Eleanor Roosevelt, in addition to Lena Horne and a repeat visit from his girlfriend Juliet Prowse.

FEBRUARY 1960: Joseph P. Kennedy, U.S. ambassador to England during World War II and father of Jack Kennedy, met with Dad to ask for his help in West Virginia, where JFK had to win the primary election in order to win the Democratic nomination for president. Since anti-Catholic sentiment ran high among voters there, the senior Kennedy suggested that my father ask Sam Giancana for help in swinging the election; if JFK won West Virginia, he would be considered an electable candidate despite his religion. My father approached Giancana, an old acquaintance, making it clear that this was a personal favor to him and not a quid pro quo with the Kennedys, and Giancana dispatched the 500 Club's Skinny D'Amato to get local sheriffs and powerful coal miners' unions to deliver 120,000 votes—and the election—to Kennedy. Dad and his closest friends— Sammy, Dean and Peter Lawford—proceeded to campaign for JFK throughout the country. In Jersey City, where Dolly Sinatra's name still opened doors, Frank enlisted the aid of Mayor John V. Kenny to swing the state party apparatus behind JFK's nomination.

FEBRUARY 7, 1960: According to her autobiography, Judith Campbell met John F. Kennedy at Dad's table in the lounge of the Sands Hotel in Vegas.

MARCH 1, 1960: Frank recorded three songs for the *Nice 'n' Easy* album with Nel-

Bill Miller

ON PLAYING AT THE SANDS WITH FRANK:

At the Sands, Frank was doing a number with just me, just the piano alone, and for some unknown reason, the sustaining pedal went out, and it clunked to the floor, and Frank heard that and kept right on singing. And then the piano began to creak, and he heard that; and he kind of looked back, but he kept on singing. And finally the right leg of the piano began to give, and all I could do was hold it up with my right knee till we finished the tune. It was a ballad, everything was quiet. We barely finished the tune, and I had to hop away from the piano because my leg was tired from holding it up, and I knew it was gonna fall, and I had to get out of the way, so I hopped away and the piano toppled over, and Frank—remember, he'd kept singing all the while—finally he acknowledges it. The piano topples and he turns around to me and says, "You having a little trouble back there?" Then he turns to the audience and says, "Look at this: 20 million dollar hotel, $1.98 piano."

son Riddle at the Capitol studios in Los Angeles: "You Go to My Head," "Fools Rush In" and "Try a Little Tenderness." Among the 30 other songs he'd record this year: "The Nearness of You," "Embraceable You," "How Deep Is the Ocean?," "When You're Smiling," "My Blue Heaven," "Always" and "Blue Moon."

APRIL 4, 1960: The soundtrack for *Can-Can*, released by Capitol, included such classics as "It's All Right with Me," "You Do Something to Me," "Let's Do It" and "I Love Paris."

SPRING 1960: As John Kennedy campaigned through hundreds of small towns across the country, his motorcade was preceded by a sound truck playing Frank Sinatra's revised recording of "High Hopes" with special JFK campaign lyrics.

MAY 12, 1960: In an ABC television special taped in Miami—with Lawford, Bishop, Davis and yours truly as his supporting cast—Dad met Elvis Presley for the first time by welcoming him back to civilian life from two years in the U.S. Army. On the show, Elvis sang "Witchcraft," complete with snapping fingers and classic crooning style, and Dad sang "Love Me Tender."

MAY 29, 1960: FS arrived in Tokyo for his first concerts in Japan.

MID-1960: FS wanted to produce and direct the film version of William Bradford Huie's book *The Execution of Private Slovik*, the story of the only U.S. soldier since the Civil War to be executed for desertion. It became a political cause célèbre when he hired a blacklisted screenwriter named Albert Maltz—who had written the screenplay for the Oscar-winning 1945 short, *The House I Live In*—to write it.

JULY 25, 1960: Another number-one album for Sinatra: *Nice 'n' Easy*, including "That Old Feeling," "You Go to My Head," "Fools Rush In" and "Dream," by Dad's favorite lyricist, Johnny Mercer.

JULY 1960: By earning $4 million a year, Frank Sinatra was, according to Richard Gehman in *Good Housekeeping*, the "greatest single male drawing card in the entertainment business." But Gehman went on to say that Dad was "not merely an entertainer and a personality, but an immensely powerful force—a law unto himself. He could spend the rest of his life making all the films offered to him in a single month." My father's influence in the recording industry was equally impressive: As the "acknowledged king" at Capitol Records, his new recordings were automatically played on radio from coast to coast. He had earned the right to pick his tunes and accompanists, dictate a midnight work schedule that required heavy overtime for musicians and engineers, even orchestrate the careers of other recording artists. "What all this means to you," concluded Gehman grandiosely, "is that Francis Albert Sinatra exercises a most powerful control over much of what you enjoy (or don't enjoy) in films, on television, on records, on the radio, in nightclubs—indeed, in every medium

Two phenomena, 1960: The Voice and The Pelvis. The two men shared the same passion for the underdog. Pete Hamill wrote these words about Frank, but they apply to Elvis as well: "The passive among us are redeemed by the active; the timid by those whose lives are propelled by the sense of adventure."

The "Execution" of Albert Maltz

Screenwriter Albert Maltz eagerly agreed when my father offered him the job of writing a screenplay for The Execution of Private Slovik, based on the classic book. Among the blacklisted "Hollywood Ten," Maltz had gone to prison for refusing to cooperate with the House Un-American Activities Committee and been denied industry employment for over a decade. "Frank's call was enormously exciting," recalled Maltz. "He said that if anyone tried to interfere with his hiring me, they were going to run into a buzz saw." But a New York Times report on March 21, 1960, on Maltz's involvement set off a firestorm of protest. Hearst columnists raked up all the old accusations against Frank Sinatra and demanded that he fire Maltz immediately. "What kind of thinking motivates Frank Sinatra in hiring an unrepentant enemy of this country who has never done anything to remove himself from the Communist camp?" sneered the New York Daily Mirror.

My father responded with a full-page ad in Variety defending his choice of Maltz, and while hundreds of clergymen excoriated him from pulpits around the country, he continued to stand firm. When General Motors, which was sponsoring three upcoming Sinatra television specials, threatened to cancel the shows, he told his business partners, "There will be other specials." Because of Sinatra's connection with the Kennedy campaign, however, JFK's political enemies soon linked him to Maltz. Cardinal Spellman of New York told Joseph Kennedy that "consorting with Communists" could kill his son's chance to win the presidency. When New Hampshire Governor Wesley Powell accused JFK of "softness towards communism," the ambassador called Frank to say, "It's either us or Maltz."

We were supportive as a family, but my brother, sister and I had problems at school, and my Dad didn't like the fact that his kids were being confronted and accused. After considerable inner torment, Frank issued a statement: "In view of the reaction of my family, my friends and the American public, I have instructed my attorneys to make a settlement with Albert Maltz. I had thought that the major consideration was whether or not the script would be in the best interests of the United States. My conversations with Maltz indicated that he has an affirmative, pro-American approach to the story. But the American public has indicated it feels the morality of hiring Maltz is the more crucial matter, and I will accept this majority opinion."

Ironically, had Maltz written the screenplay under an assumed name—as did Dalton Trumbo for Roman Holiday and The Brave One, both of which won Oscars—there would have been no uproar. This was one of the last vestiges of the chaos that followed Senator Joseph McCarthy's failed crusade. Dad paid Maltz in full for the screenplay but abandoned plans to direct or produce the film. It became a television milestone in the 1970s starring Martin Sheen, with a script by Richard Levinson and William Link.

More shenanigans at the Sands. This time Judy Garland joined in with the boys.

of entertainment except newspapers and magazines. His influence as a pacesetter is unparalleled in Hollywood." Gehman, like many other writers of the day, seemed overly impressed. He was either awestruck or misinformed because no one performer or producer had that kind of power. Case in point: the Maltz incident.

JULY 10, 1960: Dad and Judy Garland entertained at a $100-a-plate dinner for JFK in Chicago.

JULY 11, 1960: In one of his proudest moments, Dad sang "The Star-Spangled Banner" at the Democratic National Convention in Los Angeles, where JFK received his party's nomination for president.

SUMMER 1960: Dad campaigned hard for JFK at small fundraisers such as Janet Leigh's Key Women for Kennedy tea, and large ones such as the Democratic Governor's Ball in New Jersey, where he and other performers sang to an audience of many thousands.

JULY 22-31, 1960: Performing two shows a night, FS returned for nine nights at the 500 Club in Atlantic City.

AUGUST 23, 1960: Annoyed by repeated press references to his friends as "The Clan," FS issued a statement through press agent Warren Cowan. "As far as I know, the various guilds that are part of my professional life are the only organized groups to which I belong. 'The Clan' is a figment of someone's imagination. Naturally, people in Hollywood socialize with friends as they do in any community, but we do not gather together in childish fraternities as some people would like to think. There is no such entity as 'The Clan' and there never has been.

I am fortunate to have many friends and many circles of friends, but there are no membership cards."

AUGUST 27, 1960: Dad was among the headline attractions at the second annual Urban League Jazz Festival at Chicago's Comiskey Park.

SEPTEMBER 11, 1960: I became Mrs. Tommy Sands. Frank Sinatra gave me away with tears in his eyes. Just before he walked with me down the aisle, he presented me with a pair of star-shaped diamond earrings, "to match the stars in your eyes."

OCTOBER 12, 1960: Hawaii's Republican candidate for the House of Representatives, Frederick Titcomb, criticized show business people for making a farce out of serious politics. In Maui for the location shooting of *The Devil at Four O'Clock*—and to perform at a Kennedy for President show at the Waikiki Shell— Frank defended the right of entertainers to campaign for their political convictions: "The Hearst papers throughout the nation are campaigning for Nixon and throwing a lot of propaganda in. If this organization of newspapers can do it, then why shouldn't I just by singing? I've been campaigning for Democrats ever since I marched in a parade for Al Smith when I was a 12-year-old kid."

OCTOBER 19, 1960: Dad appeared with Eleanor Roosevelt on a radio show on behalf of JFK.

NOVEMBER 1960: After Kennedy's narrow victory over Nixon in the national elec-

When I married Tommy Sands, Dad didn't interfere or lecture on the hazards of getting married to a singer. We both, of course, realized the obvious parallels, but this was Hollywood, and I was definitely a Hollywood kid—my feet firmly rooted in celluloid, in glorious Technicolor.

Eleanor Roosevelt, the widow of one of my father's greatest heroes, graced the stage on his February 1960 television show.

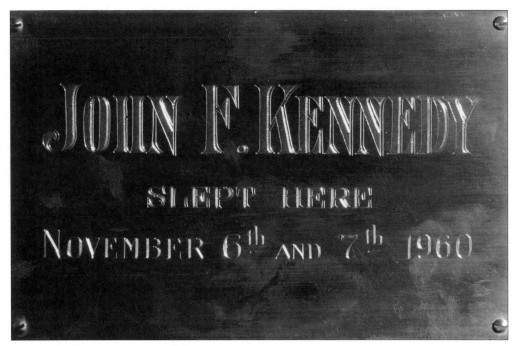

tion, he was a weekend houseguest at Dad's home in Palm Springs. After JFK left, my father placed a bronze plaque on the door of his guest room that read: "John F. Kennedy slept here November 6th and 7th, 1960."

NOVEMBER 13, 1960: Dad was the best man at the wedding of Sammy Davis Jr. and Swedish actress Mai Britt, which was held in Las Vegas. Sammy had always been part of our family. Sammy and I and Frankie and Tina and Dad went to Atlantic City together. A birthday in the Sinatra family, Sammy was there. A wedding, Sammy was there. A funeral, Sammy was there. He was a part of us. The color of his skin was never an issue. It was, though, with other people. And

This plaque, mounted on the door of a guest room at my father's house in Palm Springs, is evidence of the pride he felt when his friend Jack Kennedy visited him.

sometimes surprisingly so. Because Sammy was engaged to be married to Mai, Joe Kennedy put pressure on my father to persuade Sammy to postpone the wedding until after the election, which he did. Sammy loved JFK and would do anything for him, no matter how hurt he was.

DECEMBER 19, 1960: Although his contract with Capitol would not expire for two more years, Dad did his first session for his new, very own record label, Reprise Records. These sessions would eventually produce the album *Ring-a-Ding-Ding*. He formed Reprise in self-defense against the new technology that was becoming the vogue: overdubbing, multiple tracks, the sterility of studios dominated by machines, not energized by live audiences. It was important for him to have control of his dates, to fight off technicians who wanted to overproduce, to maintain the life and spontaneity of his work.

DECEMBER 1960: FS was asked to produce and star in JFK's inaugural gala. The

FRANK

ON RECORDING:

I adore making records. I'd rather do that than almost anything else. You can never do anything in life quite on your own—you don't live on your own little island. Making a record is as near as you can get to it—although, of course, the arranger and the orchestra play an enormous part. But once you're on that record singing, it's you and you alone. If it's bad and gets criticized, it's you who's to blame—no one else. If it's good, it's also you. I myself can't work well except under pressure. If there's too much time available, I don't like it—not enough stimulus. And I'll never record before eight o'clock in the evening. The voice is more relaxed then.

Sammy

ON THE WEDDING:

At my bachelor dinner, Frank cornered me and said, "Instead of paying you a straight salary for Sergeants 3, I'm going to give you $75,000 plus 7 percent of the action. It should be worth a quarter million to you. You'll have a wife and kids to think about." That's the kind of guy he is. Then, on the day of the wedding, people were leaning out of their windows all the way up the hill with telescopic lenses trained on my house. Reporters and newsreel men clustered in front of the door. Photographers perched in trees to get a free line of sight to the doorway. It's easy for others to say that it was only right for Frank to be there; "he's your friend." But it's not that simple. With all his independence, he still knows how quickly a career can go down the drain on the whim of the public. For him to state, "This is my friend, and you can stick it in your ear if you don't like it," means putting in jeopardy everything he's worked for, lost and regained, and must fight to hold on to. It was not a minor thing for Frank to be my best man.

Kennedys sent word to Dad that since Sammy had married Mai Britt, it would be better if he were not among the performers invited to appear at—or even attend—the gala. Dad's arguments that Sammy deserved an invitation fell on deaf ears. As Sammy recalled, "Peter Lawford called me on the phone. He said, 'Sam, I know you understand these things. They've got those rednecks down there and, well, The Man thinks it would just smack of—' 'The Man?' 'The president, yes.' I said, 'Hey, don't worry about it, man.' I never mentioned it, never brought it up with Frank." But Dad knew. He has confirmed the facts for me. He has told me it was one of the few times he ever felt at such a loss. In the past he'd always been able to help Sammy. He had been able to protest and bring about change. But now he could do nothing. Yes, he could have backed out of the inaugural, but Sammy would never have allowed that.

JANUARY 3, 1961: *Sinatra's Swingin' Session* was a fat album with up to 34 musicians recording everything from "When You're Smiling" and "It All Depends on You" to "September in the Rain" and "Blue Moon." It went into the top 10.

EARLY JANUARY 1961: FS and Peter Lawford arrived in Washington on the *Caroline*, JFK's private plane, to begin preparations for the inaugural gala. Pulling out all the stops in producing the event, Dad wasn't fazed by the news that Laurence Olivier and Ethel Merman couldn't make the date because they were appearing on Broadway in *Becket* and *Gypsy*, respectively. He bought all the seats and closed the shows for that night in both theaters.

JANUARY 19-20, 1961: Though deeply troubled by the Kennedys' treatment of his friend Sammy, the inaugural celebration was a milestone event for my father, not only as a lifelong Democrat but as a close personal friend of the man who was being sworn into the presidency of the United States. For the son of an immigrant Italian couple who had risen from the streets of Hoboken to become the biggest and most powerful star in show business, it was a moment to savor for a lifetime.

The Inauguration of John F. Kennedy

Frank Sinatra organized and produced the Inaugural Gala, amassing a remarkable group of performers. Said JFK, "We're all indebted to a great friend, Frank Sinatra. Long before he could sing he was pulling in votes in a New Jersey precinct...Tonight, we saw excellence."

Frank Sinatra rehearsing for the Inaugural Gala with a group of performers including Joey Bishop, Nat King Cole, Harry Belafonte and Jimmy Durante.

Above: Frank Sinatra, Senator Stuart Symington, Vice President Lyndon Johnson and President Kennedy.

Right: Big night. Big snowstorm. Frank Sinatra escorts First Lady Jacqueline Kennedy to the Inaugural.

Frank Sinatra and his friend, President John Fitzgerald Kennedy.

Put Your Dreams Away

When studying the life of Frank Sinatra one finds certain definite times of peace and success to be enjoyed with him, and others of chaos and turmoil, full of life-altering events that might have destroyed a man of lesser character. These three years started out well enough with the rallying cry of Ring-a-ding-ding, the "nothing's sacred/no holds barred" zany yet innocent irreverence of the Summit meetings in Las Vegas, the formation of Reprise Records and the continuing adoration of the people of the world.

But soon "The Chairman of the Board" faced seemingly insurmountable obstacles that would color his life forever. Prejudices of all types were still prevalent in the early sixties and my father himself was a victim "because my name ends a vowel." The stigma of "guilt by association" brought public humiliation and the loss of his dream, the Cal-Neva Lodge in Nevada. The cold-blooded murder of his friend and hero Jack Kennedy, worry about what that loss would mean to the future of his country—and the world—and the kidnapping of his only son brought 1963 to a brutally devastating conclusion.

Everybody knows his voice. It is truly one of a kind. Mimics can't capture the sound. It's the timbre, the structure of the throat. Frank works for every note, for every interval. He warms up, he rehearses, he studies.

With Sy Oliver (left) conducting, FS does his part for civil rights at a Carnegie Hall concert.

JANUARY 27, 1961: Dad was one of Dr. Martin Luther King Jr.'s earliest and most ardent supporters on behalf of nonviolent civil rights. Along with Dean and Sammy, he gave a benefit concert at Carnegie Hall for Dr. King's Southern Christian Leadership Conference.

FEBRUARY 1-14, 1961: Dad performed to packed houses for every show of a two-week run at the Sands in Las Vegas.

FEBRUARY 28-MARCH 13, 1961: He played two weeks at the Fontainebleau Hotel in Miami Beach.

SPRING 1961: Since he had his own record label now, I asked Dad to let me try my hand at a single. His chief executive, Mo Ostin, said he didn't want any rock and roll records. I replied that rock was here to stay, but I agreed to do a novelty record like Annette Funicello's. Mo said OK and put me with Annette's producer, Tutti Camaratta. My record was called "Cufflinks and a Tie Clip," and it was backed by a rhythm-and-blues song called "Not Just Your Friend." Tutti Camaratta picked

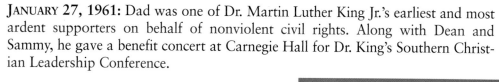

Ruta Lee

ON WORKING WITH THE SUMMITTEERS:

Sargeant's 3 was one of the happiest experiences of my life—but unfortunately all the men treated me like their kid sister! They all sipped pretty good, but I never saw them sloshed. Dino taught me to drink beer on the rocks and Frank taught me to take champagne the same way.

"Like I Do," another novelty number, for my second single—and we struck marinara. It didn't even get played in the States, but the record went to number one in Italy, Japan and other countries. Dad, my boss, was very pleased that his kid was making money for his new label, even if it wasn't very much. I assured him that one day I'd give Reprise its first number-one hit in the United States—if they'd lift their moratorium on rock. And I meant to keep my word.

APRIL 19-21, 1961: He performed benefit concerts in Mexico City.

MAY 1961: In six marathon sessions for Reprise, half arranged by Billy May and half by Sy Oliver, Dad recorded 24 songs. Billy May did the *Swing Along with Me* sessions: "Moonlight on the Ganges," "Granada," "Don't Cry Joe" and "The Curse of an Aching Heart," which was one of the songs the Hoboken Four sang in 1935. The album, produced by Neal Hefti, was retitled *Sinatra Swings* because of a Capitol Records injunction regarding their Sinatra album *Come Swing with Me*. The Sy Oliver sessions, which included "I'll Be Seeing You," "Imagination," "East of the Sun" and Tommy Dorsey's theme, "I'm Getting Sentimental over You," were part of the tribute album *I Remember Tommy*. "I really think this album has some of the best work I've ever done," recalled Frank. "I feel sentimental over Dorsey. I tried to sing the songs as he used to play them on his trombone."

A family portrait by the late Hollywood photographer John Engstead.

JUNE 24, 1961: He performed at a benefit for the County Sheriff's Rodeo at L.A.'s Memorial Coliseum.

JULY 9, 1961: Dad sang at another benefit for Cedars of Lebanon hospital in Los Angeles.

JULY 16, 1961: With Mervyn LeRoy—who helmed *The House I Live In*—as his director, my father starred opposite Spencer Tracy in Columbia's *The Devil at 4 O'Clock* as a convict redeemed by good deeds in the wake of a South Sea island volcanic eruption. Dad called Tracy "the Grey Fox." He said, "I learned a lot from him, everybody did." And Tracy said about Dad: "Nobody had his power. *The Devil at 4 O'Clock* was a Sinatra picture. Sinatra was the star. Although we worked very differently, he knew what he wanted. Some people said there would be fireworks, but there weren't."

Dad would have breakfast with early riser Spencer Tracy when his nighttime friends couldn't stay up anymore. Tracy would always lecture him about not sleeping.

Jimmy Van Heusen, FS and Jack Entratter in the carport of the Presidential Suite at the Sands Hotel.

AUGUST 7, 1961: Dad starred with Dean Martin at a concert in Frankfurt, Germany.

AUGUST 1961: He increased his share of the Sands Hotel in Las Vegas to 9 percent. This meant that his share was less than that of hotel president Jack Entratter and casino manager Carl Cohen but as much as or more than that of the resort's dozen other licensed shareholders.

AUGUST 15, 1961: Park Lake Enterprises, Inc. (doing business as Cal-Neva Lodge) was formed. The corporation had an authorized capital of 1,000 no par value shares, of which 540 were issued and owned as follows: Frank Sinatra, 270 shares; Henry W. Sanicola, 180 shares; and Sanford Waterman, 90 shares. The issuance price was $500 per share. The Board of Directors consisted of Frank Sinatra, president; Hank Sanicola, secretary; and Sanford Waterman, treasurer. It was expected that my father would eventually acquire all of the shares and become the sole owner. Dad liked Cal-Neva because it was unpretentious yet glamorous, homey yet exciting. He had the final say on every employee, choosing people who were honest and hardworking and who would turn the lodge into a wonderful getaway destination. Cal-Neva offered outdoor sports, nightlife, gambling and razzle-dazzle juxtaposed with nature's clear water, clean air, giant trees and purple mountains. Because heavy Sierra snowfalls on the narrow mountain roads kept the resort closed all winter, Dad and his partners decided that their best strategy for profitability was to help improve local roads and develop winter activities in order to turn the Cal-Neva into a year-round resort. He reveled in the fun of hotel, casino and stage ownership, throwing countless parties, even chartering planes to fly in friends such as Lucille Ball to share his enjoyment at ringside, and to bring in top names to the Celebrity Room: Dean Martin, Eddie Fisher, Lena Horne, Vic Damone, Red Skelton and Victor Borge were just a few of them.

AUGUST 1961: Dad was one of many guest stars—including Bing, Sammy, Dean, Joey, Peter Lawford, Kim Novak, Debbie Reynolds and Edward G. Robinson—all playing themselves in cameo roles opposite the great Mexican comedian Cantinflas in Columbia Pictures' *Pepe*.

AUTUMN 1961: Throughout the previous year, my father had been dating Juliet Prowse. She attended his recording sessions and spent time with Dad at his home in Coldwater Canyon. But both of them were wary of commitment and continued to date other people.

AUTUMN 1961: *Ring-a-Ding-Ding*, Frank Sinatra's

When profits from films produced by Dad's Park Lake Enterprises—including *4 for Texas, Robin and the 7 Hoods, Von Ryan's Express* and *Assault on a Queen*—were used to pay off losses incurred at his Cal-Neva Lodge in Lake Tahoe, his friend and partner Hank Sanicola was so infuriated that a major rift developed between the two friends. It never healed.

first Reprise album, was released. Produced by Felix Slatkin and arranged by Johnny Mandel, it turned to gold. With this album, Reprise introduced the quality product that would live up to its motto, "To play and play again." The album featured such great songs as "Be Careful It's My Heart," "In the Still of the Night," "A Fine Romance" and, of course, "Ring-a-Ding-Ding."

SEPTEMBER 23-24, 1961: Dad spent the weekend in Hyannisport with the Kennedy family. Joseph Kennedy was grateful for Frank's help in swinging the West Virginia primary that helped win his son the Democratic presidential nomination. Recently Frank recalled Joe Kennedy's concern about his overspending on clothes: "He would say, 'Francis, how many suits do you need?'" My father would ask, "Why do you call me Francis?" And Kennedy would say, "Because it's a good Catholic name."

OCTOBER 17, 1961: He surprised his friend Sammy with a brief walkon during his pal's run at the Sands Hotel in Las Vegas. Sammy would forget about the time and remain on stage too long, keeping the audiences away from the gambling tables. The casino bosses turned to Dad for help, and he tried various means to compel Sammy to shorten his show. One was an alarm clock placed on a stool on the stage. Another time he called Sammy on the backstage telephone during his show. Nothing seemed to work. One night Dad was in Las Vegas and got called down by the stage manager. Sammy was 40 minutes over. Frank got two six-foot-six-inch security guards who picked little Sammy up right there on the stage. My father took the microphone and said, "We're a little late. Good night, folks." And they all left the stage, three walking and one off the ground.

NOVEMBER 1-14, 1961: Dad did his own two weeks at the Sands. Eight of the shows were taped for a live album to be released by Reprise, but the album was scrapped.

NOVEMBER 20-22, 1961: During a 14-song recording session in Hollywood for the album *Sinatra & Strings*, Neal Hefti and Skip Martin produced a breathtaking Don Costa arrangement of "Stardust." Other songs recorded include "It Might as Well Be Spring," "Prisoner of Love," "Night and Day," "All or Nothing at All" and "Come Rain or Come Shine."

NOVEMBER 29-DECEMBER 2, 1961: Back in Australia, he performed for record crowds in a four-day series of concerts at Sydney Stadium. He was named *Playboy* magazine's Top Male Vocalist in their Jazz Poll, and had a few top 10 albums: *Sinatra's Swinging Session, All the Way, Ring-a-Ding-Ding, Come Swing with Me* and *Sinatra Swings.*

Dad and I share a yuletide hug.

Christmas 1961 at Mom's house at 700 Nimes Road in Bel Air: The tinsel took hours to apply. My Dad and his friends would come over late on Christmas Eve filled with Christmas cheer and they'd put the tinsel on the tree. It always looked like it had been thrown on, though, and my mother and I had to redo it.

JANUARY 7, 1962: He produced and starred in *Sergeants 3*, his second Summit movie. This one was a tongue-in-cheek remake of *Gunga Din* with American Indians. Dad, Dean and Peter played a trio of Army buddies caught up in the Indian wars of the late 1800s. Produced on location near Kanab, Utah, it also featured Sammy Davis Jr., Joey Bishop, Henry Silva, comics Buddy Lester and Sonny King

and Ruta Lee. Dad did his own stunts—even the one where he's being dragged under a wagon while Dean is inside it. Dad said, "I didn't mind the dragging, but what really bothered me was the way Dean kept stomping on my fingers as he was thrown back and forth."

JANUARY 9, 1962: Despite their mutual independence, Dad and Juliet Prowse were becoming closer as the months wore on. *Time* magazine reported that to celebrate their relationship, he took her to a quiet dinner at Romanoff's and slipped an elegantly beautiful diamond ring on the third finger of her left hand. When word of their engagement got out, he said to reporters: "Juliet has been my one romance. I'm 46 now—it's time I settled down."

JANUARY 1962: JFK announced plans to visit Palm Springs. With his official entourage, Kennedy planned to stay in our family's newly built guest quarters. My father was ecstatic. He had already been working with an architect to expand his house, and now, with the president coming, ordered a massive remodeling job, including the construction of a helipad and a pair of two-bedroom cottages by the pool. In fact, he redecorated every part of the house except his own bedroom.

Juliet Prowse with Dad in costume at the annual Boomtown party benefit for SHARE.

JANUARY 15, 1962: My father was one of the pallbearers at the funeral of a friend, the comedy genius Ernie Kovacs.

JANUARY 15-17, 1962: He turned out 12 songs for the *All Alone* album. Among them: "The Song Is Ended," "What'll I Do?," "When I Lost You" and the poignant "Are You Lonesome Tonight?" If you have this album and haven't thought about it for a long time, play it now. It's one of the best. Dad and I were in Palm Springs sitting at the bar one night listening to a "Sinatrathon" on the radio. The DJ introduced "What'll I Do," saying, "This is for the dark times, the short hours." My father listened to himself for a while, "What'll I do with just a photograph to tell my troubles to..." and he said quietly, "That was tough to do. I couldn't do that anymore. It takes great control." When you listen to "When I Lost You," remember that the day it was recorded, my Dad had just been a pallbearer for Ernie Kovacs.

JANUARY 21, 1962: As part of his executive responsibilities as president of Reprise, Dad hosted a sales meeting for his marketing representatives.

JANUARY 22, 1962: John Frankenheimer's mind-bending United Artists thriller *The Manchurian Candidate* began shooting, with Dad playing a former Korean War POW, tormented by recurring nightmares, who's swept into an assassination

Frank Sinatra and Laurence Harvey in a crucial scene from *The Manchurian Candidate*. The success of this film was due in part to John Frankenheimer's use of the innovative hand-held camera, which added greatly to the tension and suspense.

plot engineered by the Communists. This film is first-rate and Frankenheimer's best. Laurence Harvey is the Manchurian candidate. Angela Lansbury is devastating as his manipulative mother. At the time Dad said, "I'm more excited about this part than any other I've played. I'm saying things in this script that I've never had to speak on the screen before. Never had to speak at all for that matter. Long, wild speeches." And writer/producer George Axelrod recalled, "I thought it would be terrific to have that marvelous, beat-up Sinatra face giving forth long, incongruous speeches." During the filming of the karate scene with Henry Silva, Frank accidentally broke a dining room table with his hand and managed to break his finger, too. Nobody knew about the broken finger until after the scene was finished because he just kept on. Many years later, my father said about the film, "I think it's a damn good film. The screenplay was wonderful and it was based on the book by Richard Condon—one of the most interesting I ever read. The direction was superb. And Larry Harvey was a consummate, powerful actor. He had a great inner strength."

JANUARY 22, 1962: Dad guested on television's *Dick Powell Show*.

JANUARY 26, 1962: He did a comedy turn on ABC-TV's *The Soupy Sales Show* with the popular slapstick comic.

FEBRUARY 4, 1962: He made an appearance on ABC's *The Stan Freberg Show*.

FEBRUARY 5-6, 1962: The production company was in New York filming climactic scenes for *The Manchurian Candidate* at Madison Square Garden.

FEBRUARY 10, 1962: He appeared at a special benefit screening of *Sergeants 3* for handicapped children at the Capitol Theater in New York.

FEBRUARY 13, 1962: Ted Steele, a DJ and major fan, hosted a Sinatrathon on New York's WINS: 66 consecutive hours of Sinatra songs.

Because Frankie, Tina and I loved the Mack Sennett comedies so much, our father promised that one day he would do a slapstick pie-throwing show for us. Soupy Sales obliged.

"The Emperor," Michael Romanoff, with one of his loyal subjects in the pool at Dad's Palm Springs place.

FEBRUARY 14, 1962: Michael Romanoff was "the Emperor" and one of Hollywood's most colorful figures. Though born not in Russia but in Brooklyn, and not Romanoff but Gergenson, he adopted a royal Russian identity and bestowed gifts of land or water on his subjects, Frank, Sammy, Dean and Jimmy Van Heusen. If Dad did something especially well, Michael would say, "Well done, old boy," and make him a gift of the Ural Mountains or the Volga River. Michael and his wife were proprietors of Romanoff's restaurant in Beverly Hills. He was a unique, darling man with great style. Many years older than Frank, he became something of a father figure. It was reported that Romanoff threw the engagement party for Frank and Juliet on Valentine's Day at his restaurant.

Dean and Frank with Judy on her television show.

FEBRUARY 22, 1962: Weeks after they announced their engagement—and days after Romanoff's party in their honor—Dad and Juliet changed their minds because they couldn't agree on how much time she should devote to her career.

FEBRUARY 25, 1962: Dad appeared with Dean Martin on their friend Judy Garland's NBC television show.

FEBRUARY 27, 1962: According to Kenneth O'Donnell, an aide to JFK, the Secret Service had been asked to select a place for the president's visit to Palm Springs that had the necessary and best security. My father's place was open all around, but Bing Crosby's was backed up against a mountain and was ideal for their purposes. O'Donnell said that when the plan was announced, he heard that Peter Lawford was "hysterical" because the president had promised to stay with Sinatra. Lawford called O'Donnell and said, "Don't you realize Crosby is a Republican?" to which O'Donnell replied, "I don't care if he's a Red Chinaman—the Secret Service likes his place better than Sinatra's." Later, it was reported that the Attorney General had advised against staying at my dad's place "because of associations with known criminals." However according to O'Donnell, Robert Kennedy had called him urging that JFK stay at the Sinatra family residence, but even *that* didn't sway the Secret Service. The president came to Palm Springs and stayed at Crosby's house. He phoned Dad from Bing's.

MARCH 1962: Frank attended a tribute to Bob Hope by the Motion Picture Producers Association at the Beverly Hilton Hotel in Los Angeles.

MARCH 1962: He and Dean Martin made cameo appearances as visitors from another planet in the last of Hope and Crosby's celebrated "Road" pictures, *The Road to Hong Kong.*

APRIL 10-11, 1962: With Neal Hefti arranging, he recorded 12 new songs for Reprise. Among them: "I'm Beginning to See the Light," "I Get a Kick Out of You," "They Can't Take That Away from Me," "Love Is Just Around the Corner," "At Long Last Love," a new twist on that old standard, "Tangerine" and "Don'cha Go 'Way Mad" (with 10 "baby's" in succession and trombones playing the same pulsing note for 16 bars). Dad wanted to have a whole new sound and feel—more jazz. "I Get a Kick Out of You" was recorded at a much faster tempo than when he performs it on stage with the same chart. On this album, *Sinatra and Swingin' Brass,* Frank Sinatra once again reminds us of the importance of words: "The hardest thing is to pick the songs that mean something, and even when the words don't mean much, to sing them in such a way that they seem to."

APRIL 18-23, 1962: Dad and his band began a World Tour for Children. Before his departure, he told a press conference that he, as an "overprivileged adult, ought to help underprivileged children." He paid all of the expenses.

APRIL 24-28, 1962: *The Bob Hope Show*, taped in advance of his departure from L.A., was aired on the 25th while Dad was visiting children's hospitals and youth centers in Hong Kong. During his stay, he performed two con-

Various stops on Dad's World Tour for Children (right), and a rehearsal for his concert in London (top).

Frank and company rehearse for their London concert for children.

My father on his World Tour for Children.

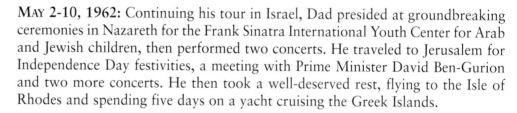

FS plants a tree in Israel in memory of his beloved friend and agent Bert Allenberg. Later, he was greeted by Prime Minister David Ben-Gurion (top, right).

certs at the new City Hall. On the second night, according to the trip diary, "The concert was a total success and the number of people wanting to attend couldn't be accommodated." So when it ended, he moved to another part of the hall and performed an additional concert. On the final day in Hong Kong, he did a matinee for children, an unqualified success. When it ended, he presented a check for $95,000 for charity.

MAY 2-10, 1962: Continuing his tour in Israel, Dad presided at groundbreaking ceremonies in Nazareth for the Frank Sinatra International Youth Center for Arab and Jewish children, then performed two concerts. He traveled to Jerusalem for Independence Day festivities, a meeting with Prime Minister David Ben-Gurion and two more concerts. He then took a well-deserved rest, flying to the Isle of Rhodes and spending five days on a yacht cruising the Greek Islands.

MAY 18-19, 1962: On to Greece for two concerts to capacity crowds in Athens at the Herod Atticus, an ancient Roman amphitheater. FS was presented with the Athens Medal of Honor and visited children's institutions that would benefit from the performances.

MAY 24-26, 1962: After a couple of days of rest, first in Milan, then in Nice, Dad and his entourage flew to Rome. This part of the trip was dubbed "Operation Roma," according to the trip diary: "Mr. S. had devised a master plan for entrance into Rome which would insure his privacy, allow him time to work and thwart the press. It succeeded admirably." He performed one concert in Rome, where he was presented with honors by both the mayor and the Chamber of Commerce, including the Italian Star of Solidarity. They then flew to Milan and performed two more concerts before stopping for another couple of days of rest in Geneva and Madrid.

MAY 30-JUNE 4, 1962: In London, his first night's concert at the acoustically perfect Royal Festival Hall, sponsored by Princess Margaret, was a triumph. The audience of several thousand was, as detailed in the diary, "on its feet and the clamor could still be heard long after Mr. S. had left the hall." But the most memorable moment occurred on a visit to the Children's Home for the Blind. A little blind girl asked my father, "What color is the wind?" She couldn't see the tears in his eyes as he answered, "No one knows because the wind moves too fast." Then came a concert at the Odeon Theatre and two more in one evening at the Hammersmith Gaumont Theatre. Between shows, he received the Gold Heart from the Variety Clubs as appreciation for his charitable work.

JUNE 5-7, 1962: In Paris, before he sang a note, he was presented with the Gold Medal of Paris by the Conseil Municipal. This distinguished award had previously been given to Dr. Albert Schweitzer and President John F. Kennedy. That evening he performed at the Lido. He again visited institutions that would benefit from the concerts and attended the Foundation Stone Ceremony dedicating the "Sinatra Wing" at the Summer Home of the St. Jean De Dieu for Crippled Boys at Bruyeres le Chatel. He gave his second concert at the Olympia Theatre to a wildly enthusiastic crowd of young Parisian admirers.

JUNE 9, 1962: While he was performing his last concert of the tour on stage in Monaco, excerpts of his concerts in Milan were shown in Rome on a special television broadcast.

JUNE 12-14, 1962: He recorded eleven songs in three sessions in Bayswater, England, for an album entitled *Great Songs from Great Britain*, which was never released in the United States. Included were "London by Night," "We'll Meet Again" and my favorite, "A Nightingale Sang in Berkeley Square."

JUNE 29-JULY 5, 1962: Dad was a big drawing card as the headliner at his Cal-Neva Lodge, which he had remodeled and expanded.

SUMMER 1962: Back in the States on an auto trip to Las Vegas from Palm Springs with Hank Sanicola, Hank worried aloud about Sam Giancana, who had been visiting Phyllis McGuire at Cal-Neva despite the fact that the Nevada Gaming Control Board had forbidden Giancana not only from having an association with a

At the Sporting d'Ete in Monte Carlo, my father welcomed Princess Grace and her husband, Prince Rainier, along with newlyweds Prince Juan Carlos of Spain and Princess Sophie of Greece. From the trip diary: "The evening was filled with red roses, white rococo palms, candlelight and a small amount of magic."

"...I've got my trouble and woe
But sure as I know the Jordan will roll
I'll get along
As long as a song is strung in my soul..."

hook and rode it to the floor. Dad's concern for Dean was short-lived, though. Before he could reach down to help his friend to his feet, he felt Dean's teeth gnawing at his ankle.

JUNE 6, 1963: *Come Blow Your Horn* was released nationally to positive reviews and good box office. Dad attended the world premiere at the Plaza Theatre in Palm Springs.

AUGUST 1963: Burt Lancaster, Tony Curtis, Kirk Douglas, Robert Mitchum and Dad made cameo appearances in John Huston's mystery-thriller *The List of Adrian Messenger.* Everyone in the cast and crew swore to preserve the secret identities of the cameo performers. Dad was a gypsy stableman. Even his own family had a hard time recognizing him.

Jilly Rizzo (in the striped shirt) and Frankie, with his arm around his grandmother Dolly, at one of her famous dinners in her Weehawken, New Jersey, home.

AUGUST 8, 1963: Booked into the Sands in Las Vegas, Dad was summoned to a meeting with the Nevada Gaming Control Board. Commissioner Ed Olsen told him the FBI had evidence that Sam Giancana had visited the Cal-Neva Lodge. Dad admitted that he'd run into Giancana when Sam was leaving Phyllis McGuire's cabin at the Cal-Neva, but that he had not invited Giancana to the lodge. Warned of the consequences, he agreed informally not to see Giancana in Nevada but insisted on his right to associate freely with anyone outside the state.

AUGUST 13, 1963: Dad attended Frankie's opening at the Flamingo Hotel in Las Vegas.

AUGUST 23-SEPTEMBER 8, 1963: With Dean and Sammy, he headlined a two-week engagement at the Sands.

LABOR DAY WEEKEND, 1963: Newspapers in Nevada and around the country reported that Frank Sinatra was under investigation by the state gaming commission. Commissioner Ed Olsen contacted Dad by phone, demanding that he appear at the government office. Countering, Dad insisted on an off-the-record meeting. When Olsen threatened him with a subpoena, Dad hung up. Later that evening, Gaming Control investigators arrived at the Cal-Neva, only to be ejected on orders from my father. The angry Olsen retaliated by bringing formal charges against Dad, accusing him of lying to the board, violating gaming laws by associating with Giancana and trying to intimidate government personnel.

In his newspaper column, *Las Vegas Sun* publisher Hank Greenspun responded with front-page editorials ridiculing the charges against my father: "Frank Sinatra is not a hoodlum, has never been accused of such and has not been identified by anyone as a member of any crime syndicate in the country. With the horrible record of criminal associations that many members of the gaming industry have—and which have not been severed—the only person chosen as a sacrifice to gaming rectitude is Frank Sinatra."

Los Angeles County Sheriff Peter Pitchess

ON INVESTIGATING SINATRA:

I have probably spent more time investigating Frank Sinatra than any other man or organization. First, because I was active in the intelligence section of the FBI when I was an agent; then as sheriff; then because Mr. Sinatra is my personal friend and I had to find out to protect my career. And let me tell you something: You might as well go home, because you're not going to confirm any of those things.

The Effect of the Cal-Neva Situation on Frank Sinatra

Frank Sinatra was the single most visible figure in Nevada in those days, so he took most of the flak. He took it because he was Sinatra and he survived it because, ultimately, he was innocent. But he paid an insurmountably high price for being Sinatra. He lost his license, he gave up his dream, Cal-Neva, and he suffered the pain of public criticism. But he never lost his self-respect because he knew he was innocent. In my mind, he never recovered from not being able to fight to save Cal-Neva—and his reputation. One of the keys to my father's personality is his ability— perhaps his need—to express his feelings, at the time, to the right person. In burying his desire to make this a fight to the finish (even though it would have hurt him financially), he buried a lot of anger. He wasn't used to harboring ill feelings forever, and it is this result of the Cal-Neva incident which he bore from then on. The press, of course, had a field day with the surrendering of the license, even though they did not know the reasons or details. Since they continually printed the wrong information, it became an additional piece of the Sinatra folklore. A new element had suddenly been forced into his core—one with which he had great difficulty. It took away what was left of naive beliefs; it encouraged him to carry a grudge. It made him defensive. Up until then, his problems with the press had been solved or resolved one at a time. From this point on, general statements were made—Frank Sinatra versus the American press—instead of small, separate disputes with individuals. The mythical war began. But he had made his choice. He never blamed anyone else. But for once he didn't get mad and he couldn't get even…He just hurt. The idea that as long as he was right he couldn't be touched no longer held. There was more vulnerability in his life now, and a push closer to the line between skepticism and cynicism.

Mickey Rudin (Frank's Attorney)

ON THE CAL-NEVA INCIDENT:

There was never a finding that he would lose his license and there was never a finding that he had invited Sam Giancana to Cal-Neva Lodge. Not withstanding those facts, for many years afterwards, whenever there was a mention of the name Frank Sinatra in conjunction with Las Vegas, or in conjunction with any other matter, there would be a tag line that Frank Sinatra lost his license in Las Vegas because he had invited Sam Giancana to the Cal-Neva Lodge. That blight on Sinatra newspaper publicity did not end until we actually went through a hearing in Nevada by applying for a license and had the true facts read upon the record. He was granted a license.

going to become associated with Warner Bros. and be listed as an executive, Warner did not want all of the newspaper publicity concerning Nevada and the Giancana incident. Warner said, "I know it's all bullshit about Giancana, but I'm tired of the image of Las Vegas. I like having Frank as a partner, but if he's going to become involved in Warner Bros. Pictures and own a third of Warner Bros. Records, I think he should not go on with the hearing."

Warner made it quite clear that if Dad did not surrender his license and thereby end the proceedings, the deal was to be called off. Warner's ultimatum left no room for discussion. And although he was "all warmed up to oppose the revocation of the license," ready to contest it and prove they were wrong, Mickey went to the lawyer in Nevada and said, "Reverse paths, turn in the license. I can't make both deals." Dad authorized Mickey to surrender the license. He never went to a hearing—just terminated the license. But a deeper reason he did not fight back, Dad told me, was not because of Warner Bros., but because the investigation was potentially embarrassing to his friend President Kennedy. He cared more about Kennedy than he did about proving he was right.

FALL 1963: Dad went to Rockford, Illinois, with Jerry Lewis to raise money for the family of a fireman who'd died in the line of duty.

OCTOBER 5-6, 1963: Dad shared top billing with Lena Horne in a concert at Carnegie Hall.

OCTOBER 31, 1963: Dad brought The Summit to Chicago to film *Robin and the 7 Hoods* with Sammy Davis Jr., Peter Falk, Victor Buono, Bing Crosby, and Edward G. Robinson in a cameo reprise of a Little Caesar-type character. This satirical twist on the Robin Hood story, a film as freewheeling as its stars, amplified the already growing notion that the Summit members were becoming folk heroes in some odd, wacky way.

With Dad and his pals in town, high-rolling good times spilled over to the Villa Venice. William Leonard, the *Tribune* nightlife critic, wrote that "The Rat Pack is in town—the Leader and all—for the first and possibly the only time, and nightlife is explosively exciting on the banks of the Des Plaines River at Milwaukee Avenue. The ancient Villa Venice has hit the jackpot with Sinatra, Martin and Sammy, who croon, carol, caper and clown to the biggest cabaret audience this town has seen in 30 years. Martin opens with 20 minutes of drinking songs, Sinatra fools everyone by coming on ahead of Davis with a quarter hour of old Frankie favorites that cause the ladies to whimper with audible delight. Davis does the impossible by making the next 10 minutes an electrical follow-up. Then the three unite for nearly an hour of corny comedy and swinging music. Outside, throngs show up about sundown looking for autographs or glimpses of the Leader or his clan."

From that moment on, virtually every Sinatra performance in Chicago became more than a mere concert; it became a kind of pop-culture event that crossed every boundary of generation, musical taste and politics. "I adore the place because it's a big city with the heart of a small town," said Dad. "There is no doubt in my mind that Dean, Sammy and the gang and I together had more laughs and got into more trouble there than any group of people anywhere."

Three of the 7 Hoods: Frank, Bing and Dean.

Jerry Lewis

ON MEETING FRANK SINATRA:

I was 15 years old and doing a "dumb act"—all I did was mime records—at a club called the Glass Hat, which was in the Belmont Plaza Hotel in New York City. I weighed about 106 pounds and with my bow tie and big shoulders I looked like Frank. And "All or Nothing at All" had just come out. It was one of the records that I mimed. Frank's mother, Natalie, came to my show three nights a week for 20 weeks. She was my biggest fan. She took me on my night off to see Frank with Harry James.

ON THE ROCKFORD BENEFIT:

He called me one evening and said, "What are you doing, Jew?" And I said, "Nothing in particular, Wop." He said, "Meet me tomorrow morning and bring your tools." We flew to Rockford, got to this coliseum seating 20,000. He's hired a 30-piece orchestra. We did the show, brought in about $100,000 and flew back to Los Angeles around four in the morning. This performance was for one fireman who had died, and his family. He said, "Thanks, you're a good friend." And I said, "You're a good man, Frank."

NOVEMBER 22, 1963: President Kennedy was murdered in Dallas. My father was finishing the film *Robin and the 7 Hoods* in a Burbank cemetery not far, eerily, from a gravestone bearing the name "Kennedy." Stunned when he was told the news, Dad got very quiet, then began to walk. And think. And walk. "Get me the White House," he ordered an aide. After a brief conversation with a presidential staffer, he returned to the waiting crew and said sadly, "Let's shoot this thing, 'cause I don't want to come back here anymore."

Dad went to Palm Springs after that and virtually disappeared—even I couldn't reach him. For three days while the Kennedys and the nation publicly mourned, my father grieved alone, locked away in his bedroom, the only part of the house that was still the same as when his friend, the president, had visited him.

NOVEMBER 26, 1963: A benefit for Dr. Martin Luther King Jr. starring Dad, Frank Jr. and the Count Basie band at the Santa Monica Civic Auditorium was canceled in the aftermath of the Kennedy assassination.

DECEMBER 1963: *4 for Texas* was released nationally to lukewarm reviews but red-hot business.

DECEMBER 3, 1963: In his final recording session of the year, Dad recorded two new singles in L.A., "Talk to Me Baby" and "Stay with Me."

DECEMBER 8-14, 1963: Sixteen days after the assassination of the president, another cataclysmic event occurred, this one striking the very heart of our family. My 19-year-old brother was kidnapped, and the next seven days plunged us all into the worst nightmare of our lives.

Said my father, after the president of the United States—his friend—was gone: "For a brief moment, he was the brightest star in our lives. I loved him." To this day, it still causes him pain to speak about it.

The Kidnapping of Frank Sinatra Jr.

President Kennedy died in Dallas on November 22, 1963. Sixteen days later, on December 8, 1963, my brother was appearing with Sam Donahue and The Tommy Dorsey Band at Harrah's Club in Lake Tahoe. Frankie and his friend, trumpet player John Foss, were having dinner before the show in Frankie's room at the lodge where Harrah's entertainers stayed. Shortly after nine o'clock there was a knock at the door. "Who is it?" asked Frankie.

"I have a delivery for Mr. Sinatra—a package."

He opened the door to find a .38 revolver pointed at him. Two men in ski parkas pushed their way into the room and told them to lie facedown on the floor with their hands behind their backs. The men taped John's and Frankie's hands, blindfolded them and took their wallets. Then the men untaped Frankie's hands and told him to stand up and put on a coat and shoes. As he was getting into his coat he heard one of the men say to John, "Don't make any noise for at least 10 minutes. If we don't make it to Sacramento, there will be trouble." Then my brother was dragged out into the darkness.

When John Foss was able to undo his taped wrists, he phoned the police. A dispatcher for the Nevada State Highway Patrol sent a message to the FBI: "According to the Douglas County Sheriff's Office, Frank Sinatra Jr. was kidnapped at Harrah's Club Lodge about half an hour ago. Two men were involved. They have him in a car. Roadblocks are being established."

The message was received at FBI headquarters in Washington, D.C., and forwarded to FBI Chief J. Edgar Hoover and Attorney General Robert F. Kennedy.

The car carrying Frankie quickly came upon a roadblock. The driver removed Frankie's blindfold and ordered him to pretend he was asleep. Frankie did not believe that John Foss had sufficient time to break free and notify the police. He thought the roadblock had been set up to make certain that cars were equipped with tire chains. Hearing the kidnappers threaten to shoot if any policeman gave them trouble, Frankie kept very still and did as he had been told. When the car passed through the roadblock, his blindfold was restored and he was forced to swallow two sleeping pills.

My mother was at home in Bel Air, having a relaxing Sunday night, when the phone call came from Frankie's manager, Tino Barzie, who had the room next door to 417. My sister heard Mom gasp. Tina: "After she hung up the phone, she began pacing up and down in disbelief." Mom somehow composed herself enough to make two phone calls. The first was to Dad in Palm Springs, the second to me in New Orleans.

There were other calls. One to Bobby Kennedy. He said, "Yeah, we're on to it. I have got two hundred and forty-eight men on it. There'll be more by tonight."

Next, Dad called Mickey Rudin and char-

tered a plane to Reno, where at midnight he met Charles W. Bates, special agent in charge of the San Francisco office of the FBI. By then the FBI agents at Mom's house had already put taps on her phones.

At the Mapes Hotel in Reno, Dad received some telephone advice from FBI Chief J. Edgar Hoover: "Just keep your mouth shut, Frank. Don't talk to anyone but law officers..." He also received a more personal call from Bobby Kennedy, one father to another.

I was in my room at the Roosevelt Hotel in New Orleans watching TV, while Tommy was singing in his show downstairs when Mom called. She told me to sit down because she had bad news. As I listened to her voice: "Brother...kidnapped...Dad...Reno...", she sounded far away and calm. She told me three FBI men were staying in her house and she had to get off the line in case the kidnappers tried to contact her. Kidnappers. FBI. These are words you never want to have crash into your life. I called the backstage extension and left word for my husband to call me as soon as he got offstage. My first thought was to pack and go home on the next plane, but then I grew frightened: What if it's a conspiracy? My life's been threatened before...people have threatened to kidnap me before...What should I do?

I really didn't know what to do. I also didn't know that FBI men already had arrived at the hotel to guard me. When Tommy came upstairs, we decided I shouldn't be moving around and should stay put and await instructions.

In New Jersey, Grandma and Grandpa heard the horrible news from their son.

The kidnap car was traveling toward Los Angeles while we waited nearly 17 hours—in California, Nevada, Louisiana and New Jer-

Snow had been falling all day. High winds had knocked down many of the tall Sierra trees. It was a dreadful, windy night. Under his coat my brother wore only a T-shirt, trousers and loafers—no socks. Freezing, he was shoved into the backseat of a car and made to lie down. They drove off into the storm.

Anguish and concern written on his face, Sinatra talks to reporters, telling them that a ransom has been paid.

sey—for the kidnappers to make contact.

Dad had been joined in Reno by Mickey Rudin, Jack Entratter and Dean Elson, special agent in charge of the FBI in Nevada. Dean Elson: "Sinatra would have gone anywhere, paid any amount, risked everything; all he wanted was his son back alive."

At 4:45 p.m. on December 9, he received his first phone call from the kidnappers. The FBI taped it:

"Is this Frank Sinatra?"

"Speaking. This is Frank Sinatra Senior."

"It doesn't sound like Sinatra."

"Well, it is. This is Frank Sinatra."

"Can you be available at 9 a.m. tomorrow morning?"

"Yes, I can."

"OK. Your son is in good shape, don't worry about him. See if you can do something about the roadblocks."

The next morning, the 10th, after another sleepless night, Dad received the second call.

"Hello."

"Sinatra?"

"Yeah."

A new voice: "Hello, Dad?"

"Frankie?"

"Yeah."

"How are you, son?"

"All right."

"Are you warm enough?" No response.

"You on the other end of the phone there—you on the other end of the phone there?"

"Yeah."

"You want to talk to me about making a deal? You want to resolve this thing?"

"Yeah, I do, but I can't do it now, Frank."

"Why not?"

"Gotta wait till around two o'clock."

"Well, do you have any idea what you want?"

"Oh, naturally we want money."

"Well, just tell me how much you want."

"Well, I can't tell you that now."

"I don't understand why you can't give me an idea so we can begin to get some stuff ready for you."

"Well, that's what I'm afraid of. I don't want you to have too much time to get ready."

"Well, I gotta have some time."

"I know. But you see, don't—don't rile me. You're making me nervous. I'll call you back about two o'clock."

"Well, can you call before that?"

"I don't think so. I gotta hang up now."

"Can I talk to Frankie again?"

Dial tone.

The next call ordered Dad to go to Ron's Service Station in Carson City. By the time he and Dean Elson arrived, the station attendant had already received four calls for Frank Sinatra—and figured one of the owner's friends was playing some kind of joke. The attendant was asked to leave the room while Dad answered the next call, which explained the ransom demand. When they left, Elson told the attendant not to mention to anyone what had happened.

In Beverly Hills, Al Hart, a close family friend and president of the City National Bank, had been alerted and was ready. The kidnappers demanded $240,000 in small used bills. All day, until dark, Al Hart and his people photographed each bill and made it ready for the drop. One of the FBI people said, "What are we going to put this money in, a paper bag?" The bills weighed 23 pounds. Al Hart said, "Go buy a valise." The man went to the department store, J.W. Robinsons, which remained open until 9 p.m., then returned and said he didn't have enough money to buy the $56 bag. Al Hart took some ransom money and gave it to him. They later put $239,985 into the new valise.

Daddy was instructed to go to Los Angeles to await the next call. Mom, Tina and Daddy, with other family members and several FBI agents, waited together in Mom's house. At 9:26 p.m. on the 10th, Dad was instructed to go to a gas station in Beverly Hills. There another phone call ordered him to have a courier bring the money to a phone booth in L.A. International Airport at 10 p.m. and use the name Patrick Henry.

Dad asked J. Edgar Hoover to send an FBI courier who would stay cool and not get Frankie in trouble. The agent went to the designated phone and waited.

"Patrick Henry? This is John Adams." The courier was directed to a gas station where he was to ask for a road map. "We'll be looking for you at the gas station. Hang around for five minutes and drive north on Sepulveda, stop at another gas station at Sepulveda and Olympic."

At the gas station, the FBI man was told that Frankie would be let go "four hours after you drop the money and get lost." The agent asked if he could "speak to Frank Jr." He was told no, because "he's not here, he's someplace else." And then the agent was told to go to still another gas station where the next call came. He was instructed to put the money between two school buses parked there, and then check into a hotel. He did so, after 10 p.m., December 10.

My brother was being held captive by a third man in a small house in the San Fernando Valley. He was cold and tired and frightened. By the night of the drop, he had had it. The original two kidnappers had gone off to collect the money while the third man guarded Frankie. After receiving a phone call at 10 p.m. the man said, "We got the money, but we got a problem. One of the guys got scared and ran. I think I better not let you go." Frankie said, "You let me go or I'll kill you. If you want to stop me, you'll have to kill me. One of us is going to die."

The next four hours seemed like 10 to the family. Mom, Dad and Tina in California, Tommy and me in New Orleans, Grandma and Grandpa in New Jersey were all hoping and praying that my brother, only 19 years old with his whole life before him, would be returned to us.

At 2 a.m., December 11, four hours after the ransom was paid, Daddy went to get his son. If he was afraid the kidnappers wouldn't keep their word he didn't show it to his family. He held Tina's face in his hands and said firmly, "I'm going to bring your brother home." And to Mom with greater conviction, "I'm going to bring him home." They clung together for a moment, sharing whatever it is parents share at a time like this, and then he left on the most important errand of his life and went looking for his boy. He got in his car as instructed—alone.

Frankie, meanwhile, had suggested to the man guarding him that perhaps the two other kidnappers were not coming back with the money. Perhaps they were leaving him to take the rap. That had persuaded the man to drive Frankie to the designated drop-off point in Los Angeles—but now, approaching the drop-off point, the man became apprehensive. Afraid someone had given him away, he told Frankie he was going to take him back. Frankie assured him that Frank Sinatra would not have told anyone.

At 2:35 a.m. Daddy returned to the house—alone. "Do you know what Dad's face looked like?" said Tina. "I've never seen a face like that." He thought the kidnappers had taken the money and not let Frankie go.

But the man driving Frankie did let him go—after the designated time—at the drop-off point on the San Diego Freeway at the Mulholland Drive exit. Terrified that the man might come back, Frankie pulled down his blindfold and ran for cover. He picked up a big rock and stuck it in his pocket; it was the only thing he could find in the desolate spot that resembled a weapon. He didn't see his father's car, so he decided he'd better walk toward Bel Air. Once off the freeway, he heard a car engine screaming up the hill and ducked behind a hedge out of range of the headlights. It was a bronze Ford sedan with men wearing overcoats and hats. By the time he realized they must have been FBI men, they were gone. He saw a morning paper in someone's driveway. It was dated December 11, 1963—one day before his father's birthday.

Another car came by, this time very slowly, and Frankie hid again. He was so scared. Then, realizing it was the private security service, the Bel Air Patrol, he shouted, "Hey!" The car stopped and Frankie identified himself and asked to be driven to his mother's home. The driver was security man George C. Jones. Shivering with cold from his two-mile walk, Frankie asked Jones to turn on the heat. He still had no socks and had lost weight. He was hungry, exhausted, terrified and freezing. But alive.

Because he had seen the press people crowding Mom's driveway for three days, Jones stopped the car near the Bel Air Patrol office and said he was concerned about getting Frankie through the reporters and photographers. "Suppose I get in the trunk," my brother said. "Then if we can't get through, we can go back to the office and do something else." Jones agreed.

George C. Jones: "Nobody knew I had the boy in the trunk. I drove on up to the home, passed the cars, the newspaper people, all the officers, into the parking area in the front of the house." He then backed the trunk of the car to within a few feet of the front door and told Frankie he was going to go get Mom or Dad. "I went to the door and knocked. Two men opened the door and I recognized Mrs. Sinatra inside. I looked at her and said, 'Mrs. Sinatra, I have your boy in the trunk of my car—and he is all right.' She gasped. She just stood there looking at me. Mr. Sinatra came to the door. I told him the same thing, that Frankie was OK, and in my trunk. He didn't smile. All he said was 'Let's get that trunk open.' Then Mr. and Mrs. Sinatra and five or six other people came out and I unlocked the trunk—and there was Frankie."

Sinatra Jr. Freed Unhurt; $240,000 Paid by Father

By GLADWIN HILL
Special to The New York Times

Accused: Sinatra Kidnap

John W. Irwin

Barry Worthington Keenan

Joseph Clyde Amsler

Frankie remembers seeing Dad's shoes first, then legs, chest and face. He climbed out and said, "Hi, Mom. Hi, Dad." They put their arms around him and began hugging and kissing him. They invited Patrolman Jones to come in. He later said, "I was sure tickled to see that boy come up to the car—and happier still when he went into his own house." Our prayers had been answered. Frankie was home. Happy Birthday, Dad.

Soon Bobby Kennedy called. He spoke to Dad and then to Frankie: "Are you all right son?"

"Yes, sir."

"Let me talk to one of my men." Elson took the phone and was told to "implement the ramrod." With Frankie home, the FBI began a full-scale search for the kidnappers.

My brother broke open the case. Frank Sinatra Jr.: "When the agents came to interview me the night I got away from those bastards, they told me to remember every little thing. I said, 'When they led me into the house I tripped on a piece of weather stripping at the door, on the ground.' I told them about hearing little airplanes overhead. I told them the make of the car: 'A Plymouth, a Plymouth station wagon.' My aunt used to have one and I remembered the sound of the back door; this one had the same sound. One of the guys led me around because I was blindfolded, and I could feel his hands. I told the Bureau, 'The man who has this hand works with harsh chemicals. He's a mechanic, a carpenter, or a painter 'cause it's like alligator scales inside his hand.' Turned out he was a painter. The FBI used all this stuff to break the case."

My brother was questioned for hours by

Dean Elson and the other FBI men who were at Mom's house. When he finally went to sleep, it was in Tina's room. His kid sister kept peeking at him as he slept, making sure he was really there—that she wasn't dreaming.

As soon as I knew Frankie was safe, I flew home. We had a tearful, laughing reunion. That night we got the news that the kidnappers were in custody, and we opened a magnum of champagne. My mother, who doesn't drink, drank most of it. She was so happy she didn't even have a headache the next day.

As J. Edgar wrote to me later: "I told your father how pleased I was that Frank Jr. has been safely returned. I recall pointing out to him that although he would now be besieged by inquiries from the news media, we still had numerous productive leads to pursue and would be able to do so only if the case received a minimum of publicity. Your father, of course, cooperated in every possible way. Within a short time, our investigation was completed and early in the morning of December 14th, I had the pleasure of telephoning your father again to inform him that the kidnappers were in custody."

The ordeal took its toll on my father. The lack of sleep. Little food. The dramatic temperature changes. Flying in the stormy skies. He had been distraught, even desperate— two things he had never been before. He handled each moment as it came. Even the worst one—when he'd gone to pick up his son and he wasn't there. I can't bear, even now, the image of him driving back to Mom's, alone in the car.

Afterward, his body reacted. He got sick. He went home to Palm Springs to recover. He spent the time healing. Reflecting. While mourners filed past the Eternal Flame at Arlington, while our country was still in shock, while Bobby and the other Kennedys were try-

ing to pick up the torn pieces of their lives, my father was trying to understand all these shattering events. It was all so emotionally draining—Jack, Frankie, Cal-Neva...overwhelming.

Although the kidnappers were later convicted—in near-record time by an angry federal jury—they defended themselves in court with the claim that they'd been hired to pull a publicity stunt to enhance Frank Jr.'s career. My father's only comment: "This family needs publicity like it needs peritonitis."

It took time for Frank Jr. to recover, too. It had never been easy being the son of Frank Sinatra, with all its privileges. And its illusions. We had all grown up in a cocoon, insulated from a world we never dreamed would touch us. Not like this. It changed us all, but no one more than Frankie himself. As he told a reporter in an interview for the Washington Post, "I want to look at things without distortion. It reminds me of a line in Becket when the king says, 'Why must you destroy all my illusions?' And the man answers, 'Because you should have none, my prince.'"

Christmas 1963: Dad received a note from a friend. In the midst of her own grief, Jacqueline Kennedy had taken time to send a note to my father.

Dec 3, 1963

Dear Frank
I do want to thank you for the enchanting pin you sent me for Christmas. You have always been so thoughtful.

The only happy thing that seems to have happened at the end of this year is the way your son was brought safely back to you

Please know I am so deeply happy about that—

With my appreciation—the very deepest—for all you did for Jack—and for believing in him from the beginning

Jackie—

FLY ME
TO THE MOON

The sale of Reprise to Warner Bros. gave Dad financial security, a corporate position, attractive quarters (they designed and built an attractive L-shaped office building for him on the studio lot) and, in the "Age of Aquarius" this Sagittarian's cycle was high. His wounds of 1963 were healing and his attitude—"You gotta love living, baby. Dying's a pain in the ass"—pretty much summed it up.

His influence on the music industry was growing: A picture that had been taken when Ray Charles and Frank Sinatra stopped briefly to chat in a recording studio appeared in a trade magazine with the caption "The recording industry as it stands today." When asked if he could explain his own brand of "Flower Power" he said, "I think I get an audience involved personally in a song, because I'm involved. It's not something I do deliberately. I can't help myself. If the song is a lament about the loss of love, I get an ache in my gut. I feel the loss myself and I cry out the loneliness, the hurt and the pain....Being an eighteen-carat manic-depressive and having lived a life of violent emotional contradictions, I have an overacute capacity for sadness as well as elation."

He continued to make films—fun ones: "It was all so nuts," Sammy Davis told me. "We were making one movie and Frank was told, 'This movie is too long.' So Frank grabbed the script and pulled out a fistful of pages and tore them up. 'There,' he said. 'It's shorter now!'"

He made serious ones, too—like *Von Ryan's Express*, *Tony Rome* and *The Detective*.

His ongoing love affair with his audiences thrived via television and personal appearances. He translated his ability to communicate to a new language of love with his much younger wife, Mia Farrow. Mia's mother, the beautiful actress Maureen O'Sullivan, told me, "The thing that impressed me most about your father was, I suppose, his 'correctness of life.' Everyone, everything had its place and was treated accordingly. He answered the telephone himself, read each letter he received and dictated an answer. He knew what the menu for dinner was and ordered it—often. Every person, every thing seemed to have its own niche in his plan."

For the first time he really discussed things openly. Serious things like religion and women and sex. My favorite quote from these potent, heady times: "I have a respect for life in any form. I believe in nature, in the birds, the sea, the sky, in everything I can see or that there is anything there is real evidence for. If these things are what you mean by God, then I believe in God. But I don't believe in a personal God to whom I look for comfort or a natural on the next roll of the dice. I'm not unmindful of man's seeming need for faith; I'm for anything that gets you through the night, be it prayers, tranquilizers or a bottle of Jack Daniels."

Then his father died. And, in 1971, my father decided to step out of the spotlight.

Paul Clemens: "A portrait is often a revelation to the painter as well as to the sitter. When I finished Frank's portrait, I found I had painted a man withdrawn into himself, thinking private thoughts. It is not a face of an extrovert; that face appears when the music and the fun start and he bares himself in song...never all of himself, but enough to captivate several generations and still remain an enigma to them and, perhaps, himself."

Sinatra Kidnap Defense: A Hoax

I Cooperated in Fear Of Bullet: Sinatra Jr.

Sinatra Jr. Insists Kidnap Was Real

WINTER 1964: At the trial of my brother's kidnappers, two of the attorneys for the defense created the idea that it all had been a hoax. This became the central theme of most reporting. Portions of the press even began to refer to it as "The Sinatra Trial."

The defense attorneys tried to keep recalling my father to the witness stand, because every time Sinatra took the stand the courtroom would be packed and the publicity would heat up again.

The trial of my brother's kidnappers lasted four weeks. Judge William G. East retired the jury saying, "I must comment: there is no direct evidence in this case by Frank Sinatra Jr. or persons in his behalf that prearrangements were made for his abduction."

The federal judge dismissed the hoax business in less than 40 minutes, and after several hours returned a verdict of guilty on all six counts. Two of the men received life sentences and the third, the man who let my brother go, was sentenced to 75 years.

Within months of the sentencing, my mother and father received a letter from the chaplain at the prison where two of the three men had been sent. He asked that my parents forgive the two men; that they regretted causing my parents suffering and anxiety during the kidnapping, "...as well as some embarrassment during the trial."

My father replied that he presumed a purpose of the letter was "that we take some action to express our forgiveness in order to alleviate the punishment" the court had imposed. He resented the implication that this had been a case of *Sinatra v. The Defendants* rather than *The People of the United States v. The Accused*. He said the use of the words "perhaps some embarrassment" caused him to wonder whether the defendants even afterward fully understood that by permitting their counsel to make opening statements about a hoax, and by doing the same thing outside with the press, they had caused the Sinatra family considerable anguish.

The conduct of the defendants during the trial had affected the way the press reported the case "and suspicion was created in the minds of many people as to the honesty and truthfulness of our son." Nothing had been done by the kidnappers since the trial to remove that suspicion. Not only were they insensitive to the harm done by the hoax claim, he went on, but such a charge meant that both the Department of Justice and the FBI were either parties to the hoax or "too stupid to realize" they were being taken in.

His words were as strong as his feelings. "In my opinion," he wrote, "my son has either gotten over the effects of the kidnapping or will easily get over [them] since he is a strong person; however, unless something affirmative is done by the defendants, the cloud of suspicion which hangs over his head will continue to affect adversely his life and career."

The cloud did exactly that. Frankie's reputation was ruined for a long time. Even people in the audience at his shows heckled him. It was awful. My brother suffered a terrible blow from the publicity. Once more some of the press had aimed their arrows at Frank Sinatra. This time they hit his son.

Trial Hurts Career, Young Sinatra Say

Frankie and me in rehearsal for a Smothers Brothers TV show. My father understands that it's not easy being a Sinatra kid, whatever the privileges. Frankie: "A lot of guys who could never get to Sinatra get to me because I'm more accessible."

The Director at work.

On location in Hawaii. The chair was a gift from me for his first directing job. His little visitor was Yul Brynner's daughter.

Right: On the set in Kauai with Clint Walker.

JANUARY-FEBRUARY 1964: Reprise had merged with Warner Bros. Records, and a new team was in charge: Mo Ostin, Mike Maitland, Joe Smith, Ed Thrasher and Stan Cornyn. Most of Frank Sinatra's recordings were done at Studio One at Western Recorders and Studios A and B at United Recorders, one block away on Sunset Boulevard in Hollywood. In a collaboration with Bing Crosby and Fred Waring and the Pennsylvanians, Dad recorded "America, I Hear You Singing." Sonny Burke gathered several arrangers for this flag-waver. I remember my excitement as I went to Dad's house to hear the album. I expected him to play it for me in sequence. But he had the tape cued up to "The Hills of Home," which was done a cappella by the Pennsylvanians. "Wait 'til you hear this, Chicken, you're gonna fall down." I did. By the way, Pop redid "The House I Live In." This one's even better than the first. I love my father's patriotism. I love the fact that he flies the flag daily at his house and that he is so open and honest about his feelings for and about our nation. This beautiful album is an example of his deep love for the U.S.A.

JANUARY 27-28, 1964: In two sessions in Los Angeles, Dad recorded 10 songs for the album *Frank Sinatra Sings 'Days of Wine and Roses,' 'Moon River' and Other Academy Award Winners*. Two of his own songs are here also, "All the Way" and "Three Coins in the Fountain."

FEBRUARY 15, 1964: Frank and Dean Martin appeared on Bing's CBS television special.

APRIL 8-10, 1964: In Los Angeles, Bing, Dean and Frank recorded the soundtrack album for *Robin and the 7 Hoods*.

APRIL 27, 1964: Dad began shooting *None but the Brave* for Warner Bros. on location in Hawaii. Making his directorial debut, he also starred with Clint Walker. The cast included my husband, Tommy Sands, and my cousin Dick Sinatra (son of bandleader Ray Sinatra). "*None but the Brave* is an anti-war story," Dad recalled, "that deals with a group of Americans and a group of Japanese stranded together on a

> # Bing
> **ON WORKING AT REPRISE:**
>
> *In 1964 I joined Reprise. Let's face it. Sinatra is a king. He's a very sharp operator, a keen record chief, and has an appreciation of what the public wants. I'm happy to be associated with him after all these years.*

Pacific island during the war. I have tried to show that when men do not have to fight, there is a community of interests."

MAY 10, 1964: During the location shooting for *None but the Brave*, Ruth Koch, wife of producer Howard Koch, went for a swim near the town of Lihue on the island of Kauai, and Dad watched from the beach because he had been warned about the treacherous undertow. A wave instantly swept Ruth about 75 yards out to sea. As Dad tried to swim to her, a second wave brought her back to shore and its undertow carried him 200 yards out. Although Frank is a strong swimmer, he couldn't fight his way back in. He struggled against the surf for 35 minutes. Jilly Rizzo raced to find a boat but there was none. A neighbor, Alfred Giles, plunged into the waves with his surfboard. County Supervisor Louis Gonsalves and Harold Jim swam out to Dad, and along with Giles on the surfboard, they struggled in the ocean until fire lieutenant George Keawe plunged into the surf, tossed a rope to the rescuers and managed to pull them to the beach. "In another five minutes he would have been gone," said Keawe. "His face was turning blue." When they pulled my father back to shore, he was put on a stretcher and carried to the house. "He is exhausted," an attending physician said, "but otherwise, his condition is satisfactory." When I got to the house, Dad was in his bed. He looked very pale. We went right to the basics. I said, "How are you doing?" He said, "I'm hungry." I said, "How about some peppers and eggs?" He said, "OK." We had pepper-and-egg sandwiches and watched TV together until he fell asleep. I wanted to ask him many questions, but I didn't. I wanted to tell him how much I loved him, but I didn't have to. After this ordeal, my father bought rescue equipment and a boat for the community.

JUNE 1964: During a marathon month of studio sessions in Los Angeles, Dad recorded 15 songs, including "Fly Me to the Moon," "Hello Dolly" and "I Can't Stop Loving You" with gifted arranger Quincy Jones for their *It Might as Well Be Swing* album, as well as sessions with Bing, Fred Waring and the Pennsylvanians for the album *The Twelve Songs of Christmas*. Together, they gave the world a beautiful Christmas present.

Quincy Jones
ON WORKING WITH SINATRA:

"I remember when I arranged the album for your Dad and Basie," recalled Quincy Jones (here with his wife, Ulla, in 1969). "We worked out at Warner Bros. Frank was in a bungalow, and next door was Dean's dressing room. Your dad put me in there to write arrangements. I stayed in one weekend, working. I fell asleep about seven o'clock on Monday morning. At about eight o'clock there was a knock on the door. And it was your dad in an Army uniform, saying, 'How do you like your eggs?' I'll never forget that. It was like waking up in a dream, Sinatra asking me, 'How do you like your eggs, Q?'"

For the speed at which it all worked, Q admired Dad's concentration and Basie's economy. He also felt the Basie band was a cohesive group that could not be touched by a studio band. Each time they wrote an arrangement they liked, "they just took it from there." They added a distinctive personality to the score. Quincy explained why he hired extra horn players for the album. "By having extra men on reserve, we don't have to disturb the singer's groove. There are times when a singer who is building a groove and building a picture on a song might have to stop until the blood comes back into the trumpet players' lips." About Basie and Sinatra, Jones noted that both have "the remarkable ability to eliminate the negative." And about my father, Q said, "So far as I can put the essence of Frank into words, I'd just say that he makes everything work. He makes everything fit."

JUNE 27, 1964: Warner Bros. released *Robin and the 7 Hoods*, the fourth and final movie by The Summit. Journalist John McClain wrote: "They are insanely generous and public-spirited...a crazy and wonderful part of America." *Robin* also gave birth to the tune that became Chicago's anthem: "My Kind of Town," arranged by Nelson Riddle, with music by Jimmy Van Heusen and lyrics by Sammy Cahn. Dad's hard-driving, hard-swinging rendition of this song in the film's final sequence, followed by his commercial recording and concert performances, made "My Kind of Town" an international hit.

JUNE 28, 1964: Dad guested on *The Ed Sullivan Show* on CBS television.

JULY 7, 1964: He flew to Tel Aviv, Israel, for the dedication of the Frank Sinatra International Youth Center for Arab and Jewish Children. He helped to raise money and was extremely proud to be there. That same day, once again, he also was voted Top Male Vocalist in the *Playboy* Jazz Poll.

JULY 13, 1964: He celebrated the 25th anniversary of his first recording.

JULY 31, 1964: Dad sang at a huge benefit for the NAACP at the Cow Palace in San Francisco.

SEPTEMBER 1964: He toured the French Riviera in a month devoted entirely to rest and recuperation.

OCTOBER 3, 1964: Returning to L.A., he logged a session with arranger Nelson Riddle, recording "Pass Me By," "Emily" and "Dear Heart," all for his *Academy Award Songs* album.

NOVEMBER 27-DECEMBER 10, 1964: Back at the Sands in Las Vegas for the first time in more than a year, Dad did two weeks to turnaway business with Count Basie and his band and Quincy Jones conducting.

DECEMBER 8, 1964: During his stand in Las Vegas, FS guested with Larry King for the first time in a phone interview on King's late-night radio talk show broadcast from Miami.

JANUARY 1965: *None but the Brave* was released nationally to positive reviews and a sizable box office. "Provocative and engrossing," wrote the *Los Angeles Times*.

It was 1965 and he was headed for 50. *Life* photographer John Dominis and writer Tommy Thompson caught it. Frank Sinatra said it, "You gotta love living baby. Dying's a pain in the ass."

FEBRUARY 1-14, 1965: Frank headlined with his old friend Joe E. Lewis in a two-week stand at the Eden Roc Hotel in Miami.

FEBRUARY 2, 1965: Flying into L.A. from Miami for the day, Dad spoke at a Beverly Hilton dinner honoring Associated Press correspondent Jim Bacon, one of the reporters on hand when he and Ava returned from Mexico in 1951 and their car and reporter William Eccles collided, creating a furor. With tongue planted firmly in cheek, he faced his adversaries and said, "I want to thank you for the privilege of appearing here. I think it is only fitting that I be invited to speak to a gathering of newspapermen, considering the marvelous relationship I have always had with the press. I believe in certain quarters of the Hearst empire I am known as the Eichmann of song. Now, many of you might have heard that I have in the past been harmful and brutal to members of the Fourth Estate. These are lies, vicious rumors started by a few disgruntled reporters I happened to run down with my car."

My father continued to expound on a subject that had long mystified and fascinated him: women. "Women, I've never met a man in my life who could give another man advice about women...I'm supposed to have a Ph.D. on the subject, but I've flunked more often than not. I'm very fond of women; I admire them. But, like all men, I don't understand them. Sex? There's not enough quantity and certainly not enough quality...If I'd had as many affairs as you fellas claim, I'd be speaking to you today from a jar in the Harvard Medical School."

Top left: Father and son sharing a personal moment backstage.

Above: Natalie Wood visits backstage.

FEBRUARY 17-MARCH 2, 1965: He and Lewis moved the act to the Sands for another two-week run.

FEBRUARY 28, 1965: Film clips of Dad's early appearances were included in a CBS special, *Cavalcade of Amateurs*.

MARCH 8, 1965: Dad began shooting Warner Bros.' *Marriage on the Rocks*, a comedy co-starring Deborah Kerr and Dean Martin. I was also in the film, playing—who else—Dad's daughter. At last I was actually able to be in a movie with my father and to observe firsthand the working Frank Sinatra. It was a good learning experience. I was very nervous. We had several scenes together and he was helpful, rehearsing with me and giving me suggestions. I must admit, I found the scenes we weren't in together much easier to do.

EASTER 1965: I thought Tommy Sands and I were happily married. But out of the blue, he said to me that he would never get over his fear of commitment and of family, so "I want you to get a divorce." Before I could even hear what he said, he was gone—and he never came back. Ironically, I was still on location with my father at

Sinatra, Durante, Burns and Lewis offer an impromptu toast to my 25th birthday at Chasen's restaurant.

the time with *Marriage on the Rocks*. My first day back on the picture I heard Dad's voice outside the makeup room. The sound of his voice triggered a spilling out of all the pent-up sadness and I broke down hard. The makeup man, Shotgun Britton, patched me up so Dad wouldn't know I had been crying.

APRIL 1965: When Dad's good friend, tough-guy actor George Raft, began his trial for federal income tax evasion, Dad signed a blank check and sent it to him with a note saying, "To use if you need it."

APRIL 23, 1965: *Life* magazine saluted Frank Sinatra with a 22-page cover story, the largest piece on an entertainer in the publication's history. Ever blunt, Dad told the interviewer, "I don't say that marriage is impossible, but if I would marry again it would have to be somebody out of show business, or who will get out of show business. I feel that I'm a fairly good provider. All I ask is that my wife looks after me, and I'll see that she is looked after."

APRIL-MAY 1965: During his first five sessions of the year, Dad recorded 17 songs. Among them: "September Song," "Last Night When We Were Young," "Hello Young Lovers," "When Somebody Loves You," "It Was a Very Good Year" and the title song of what became one of the best albums he ever made: *The September of My Years*. This album marks the first time I ever thought about what life would be like for me without my father, and as much as I loved it, it was painful to listen to. It would win four Grammy Awards: Album of the Year, Best Solo Vocal Performance, Best Arrangement for "It Was a Very Good Year" and Best Album Notes.

JUNE 16, 1965: Frank Sinatra received the Entertainer of the Year Award from the Conference of Personal Managers at the Beverly Hilton. This year he also was given the Commandeur de la Sante Publique by President Charles de Gaulle of France and he was again named Top Male Vocalist in the *Playboy* Jazz Poll.

JUNE 20, 1965: Frank, Dean, Sammy and Johnny Carson did a closed-circuit TV show for the Teamsters' favorite charity, St. Louis' Dismas House.

JUNE 23, 1965: Dad played an American Army colonel imprisoned in an Italian POW camp during World War II in 20th Century-Fox's exciting *Von Ryan's Express*, which premiered at Loew's State in New York. The colonel and his British counterpart, played by Trevor Howard, led a group of prisoners in a daring escape over the Swiss border that concluded with a heart-stopping sequence as the men commandeered a German train.

In the final scene, Fox president Richard Zanuck and his father, Darryl,

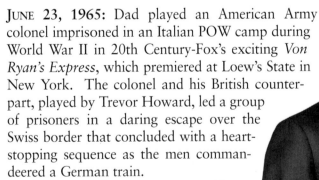

As busy as he was, my father was always there for us: my 25th birthday (left) and Tina's graduation from high school (right).

Dick Zanuck

ON SINATRA:

Despite his complexities, he is, more than anything, real. I've honestly never met anyone quite so real, and in this respect he is a totally unique personality, living in an all-too-real world inhabited for the most part by unreal people who are afraid to face the truth about their problems, about their lives and particularly about themselves as individuals. The great difference between Frank and the rest of us is that he is able to see himself, judge himself and others, judge life as it really is, and not as we would like it to be. And it is obvious that in doing so he becomes his own toughest critic. These are, perhaps, parts of his persistent problems with the lower orders of the press. He has a tendency to tell the truth and yet to be sensitive to the feelings of others, to keep it light and yet to be basically serious, and he must have naively expected this from others, including those with cameras, microphones and recorders. As his own critic, he doesn't need cheap shots. There have been countless words written about Frank in the past and surely a lot more will come—but whatever they say about him, the thing I know about him is that he's a real, complex, perplexing, loyal and generous man, and if he is in fact a son of a bitch, he's a true one and not a pretender.

Photographed at our Palm Springs house by Yul Brynner. Brynner was once introduced on an opening night by Sinatra as one of three Oscar winners in the audience (with Burt Lancaster and Rod Steiger). Yul signalled frantically to Frank, holding up four fingers, but Dad only looked puzzled. After the show he asked Yul what all the signalling was about. "There were not three Oscar winners in the room," said Brynner, "but four." "No," said Sinatra, saddened that he had failed to introduce someone. "Who else?" "You."

wanted an ending in which Colonel Ryan would get away safely to Switzerland along with the other prisoners, but since Ryan had been forced to kill a young woman in the course of his escape, Dad felt strongly that letting him live would be tantamount to letting him off the hook for that killing. They wanted Ryan to return in a sequel, but Dad won the argument, and he was right. As the train leaves the station at the end, Ryan is running desperately to catch up with it. Trevor Howard's character, Major Fincham, reaches out to grab his hand and pull him aboard. Shots ring out, and Ryan lies dying on the tracks as the train pulls away to freedom without him. It's the perfect ending to a fine movie, and it opened to boffo box office, fueling talk of another Oscar for Frank Sinatra.

JUNE 24, 1965: Dad traveled to Israel to begin filming United Artists' *Cast a Giant Shadow*, a saga about the founding of the Jewish state with Kirk Douglas as David "Mickey" Marcus, Israel's first general and a hero of the 1948 war. Playing a three-day cameo as a valiant bomber pilot, Dad took time out to renew his acquaintance with Israeli activist Teddy Kollek, who had become director-general of the prime minister's office and in charge of, among other things, promoting tourism.

SUMMER 1965: It was the age of Aquarius, the Beatles, Woodstock, Baez, Dylan, black power and flower power, the hip and the hippies, tuning out and turning on. It was an age of love—of love-ins and live-ins, of slogans about making love, not war. Frank Sinatra was 50 years old, I was 25, the new woman he

Dad took this picture of Mia Farrow on a boat trip.

loved was 20 and my father wanted to marry her. They met on the 20th Century-Fox lot. He was on the set of *Von Ryan's Express,* and she was on the soundstage next door, playing Allison McKenzie in ABC's prime-time soap opera, *Peyton Place.* "I liked him instantly," Mia, the daughter of director John Farrow and actress Maureen O'Sullivan, recalled later. "He rings true. He is what he is."

As I began to spend time with Mia and Pop—dinners, baseball games—I realized how good she was for him. She called him "Charlie Brown" and he called her "My Mia." Although Mia wasn't into material things or extravagances, Dad presented her with a light yellow Thunderbird—"to match your hair"—and she wrote poems for him. They were romantic, the swinger and the flower child. They were good together. Mia didn't like crowds, but she accompanied Dad on the road and sat in the audience where he could sing to her. Many times Tina and I would sit with her, and Dad would introduce "My daughter Tina, my daughter Nancy and my Mia." In our Sands hotel suite, Tina, Mia and I hung out in our pajamas until late in the day. We'd borrow each other's clothes and makeup and laugh a lot. It was like a dorm and we were three sisters.

JULY 4, 1965: As the closing act on the closing night of the SRO Newport Jazz Festival, Frank arrived by helicopter behind the stage, performed a knock-'em-dead set with the Basie band, then left the same way.

JULY 8-10, 1965: Playing to capacity crowds, he gave a three-night series of concerts with the Basie band at the Forest Hills Tennis Stadium on Long Island.

JULY 16, 1965: Moving on to Detroit, he played to a full house at Cobo Arena.

JULY 18, 1965: Concluding his short tour, he played two shows at the Arie Crown Expo Center in Chicago.

JULY 20, 1965: Dad invited Tina and me to join him at Grauman's Chinese Theater in Hollywood, where he ceremoniously placed his hands and feet in cement to screams of approval from the fans.

Sinatra, flanked by his two daughters, puts his name, hands and feet in concrete at Grauman's Chinese Theater in Hollywood. Tina and I put dimes in as well but they were later stolen.

Mia and Frank in New England.

AUGUST 1965: Dad played host to Mia on a cruise along the Eastern seaboard. Their traveling companions included Edie Goetz, Rosalind Russell and Claudette Colbert and their husbands as chaperones. In Mia's absence from *Peyton Place*, according to Hedda Hopper, "they have Allison McKenzie in a coma. She will linger in the state of suspended animation until Frankie decides her fate. If she returns to Hollywood unwed, she'll be revived. If she returns Mrs. Frank Sinatra, that may be the end of Allison McKenzie." They visited the Kennedy family at Hyannisport, and the late president's sisters Pat Lawford and Jean Smith joined them aboard the yacht for dinner. They were hounded unmercifully by the press. The resulting headlines were enough to force Mia and Frank to table their relationship for a while once the trip was over. The real tragedy occurred when crewman Robert Goldfarb drowned after his dinghy capsized in choppy seas after an outing on Martha's Vineyard.

AUGUST 1965: Bennett Cerf told me about "a boisterous and happy party" at Bill Styron's house on Martha's Vineyard, which ended with Frank and Bill trying persistently to get Fidel Castro via long distance to protest the fact that they couldn't seem to get decent Cuban cigars in New England anymore.

SEPTEMBER 6, 1965: *Newsweek* published a checklist of Dad's enterprises: Artanis ("Sinatra" spelled backward) Productions, which produced *None but the Brave*; Park Lake Enterprises, which produced *Four for Texas* and *Robin and the 7 Hoods*; Reprise Records; and Cal Jet Airways, a charter service.

SEPTEMBER 10, 1965: Dad appeared with Sammy in a predictable pie-throwing episode of *The Soupy Sales Show* taped earlier that summer in New York.

SEPTEMBER 16, 1965: Dad appeared as a guest star on the premiere of *The Dean Martin Show*, a new NBC variety program. Dean was in rare form that night, addressing my father by his new title, "Chairman of the Board." Dad, who had been called a lot of things in his life, was clearly tickled. The title stuck.

SEPTEMBER 20, 1965: In *Assault on a Queen*, Dad starred opposite Virna Lisi as a modern-day pirate who salvaged a sunken German U-boat in a bid to hijack the luxury liner *Queen Mary* and loot its cargo and its well-heeled passengers. The most memorable things about this film are the fact that Duke Ellington wrote the score and Rod Serling wrote the screenplay.

OCTOBER 4, 1965: Frank and Dean dropped in on Joey Bishop while he was guest-hosting the *Tonight Show*.

OCTOBER 11, 1965: In the first of two studio sessions this month, he recorded "Come Fly with Me," "I'll Never Smile Again" and "From Here to Eternity." Also this year, in addition to the Grammy-winning *September of My Years*, he produced two collectors' albums: *Sinatra '65*, a compilation including "I've Never Been in Love Before," "When Somebody Loves You" and "Luck Be a Lady"—from his best sessions throughout the sixties; and *My Kind of Broadway*, a bouquet of hit show tunes including "Golden Moment," "Hello Dolly," "They Can't Take That Away from Me," "Nice Work If You Can Get It" and "Without a Song."

OCTOBER 16, 1965: Frank hosted *The Hollywood Palace* and performed a spectacular 20-minute mini-concert with Count Basie.

NOVEMBER 16, 1965: Frank Sinatra was the subject of an hour-long CBS documentary, *Sinatra: An American Original*, hosted by Walter Cronkite.

NOVEMBER 20, 1965: In anticipation of my father's 50th birthday in December, he was honored with a special 100-page section of *Billboard*.

NOVEMBER 24, 1965: Dad did his one-man tour de force *A Man and His Music*, on NBC. The show won not only an Emmy Award for Outstanding Musical Program but also a Peabody Award for Distinguished Achievement in Video Programming.

NOVEMBER 29-30, 1965: He recorded 10 moon songs. Among them: "Moonlight Serenade," "Moonlight Becomes You," "The Moon Was Yellow" and "Oh, You Crazy Moon" for the 1966 album *Moonlight Sinatra*.

NOVEMBER 30, 1965: Reprise released its own version of *A Man and His Music*, a two-record retrospective with Frank narrating. It included a comprehensive discography of his more than 1,000 songs. The deluxe edition also featured a presentation book about his career in music. If you buy only one Sinatra album, this is it. Narrated and sung by FS, it is an anthology, a musical biography—31 songs and one comedy sketch. The arrangers are here: Riddle, Jenkins, May, Costa, Oliver, Mandel and Freeman. It won a Grammy for Album of the Year.

DECEMBER 1965: I recorded "These Boots Are Made for Walking." It reached number one in three weeks, becoming Reprise's second number-one record. Dean Martin's "Everybody Loves Somebody Sometime" was the first. My father was proud and happy.

Photographer Ron Joy took this picture of fellow photographer John Engstead taking our family portrait.

He'd call me up and say, "Hello, Star," or "Hiya, Record Seller." By the time "Boots" had topped the charts, he was introducing himself to audiences as "Nancy's father."

DECEMBER 11, 1965: The Armed Forces Radio Service broadcast a special tribute entitled *The Legend of Frank Sinatra.*

DECEMBER 12, 1965: On his birthday, *Look* magazine published a cover story called "Sinatra at 50." Dad agreed to sit down with *Look*'s John Bryson to talk about his life and times. In a rare moment of personal revelation, he admitted to sleeping badly and said that he often read the night away, consuming books on every subject from history to economics to fiction, countless magazines and an endless parade of film scripts. The chatty, admiring 10-page article described his Palm Springs home with its two bedrooms and a pair of two-bedroom guesthouses (*Look* wrongly reported that the guesthouses had five rooms), a saltwater swimming pool, a helicopter landing pad, tennis courts, an enormous, state-of-the-art kitchen with $100,000 worth of appliances and built-ins, books everywhere. Still visible was the red White House hotline telephone originally installed in anticipation of JFK's 1962 visit. My father was at the half-century mark, and his circle of friends included Yul Brynner, writer Harry Kurnitz, Michael Romanoff, financier Armand Deutsch, songwriter Jimmy Van Heusen, comedian Joe E. Lewis, producer William Goetz and their respective wives. *Look* estimated that Dad's one-man industry required the efforts of 35 full-time employees and grossed $3.5 million annually. If all the Sinatra records sold were stacked on top of each other, wrote Bryson, they would reach 187,500 feet.

My mother threw a 50th birthday party for Dad at the Beverly Wilshire Hotel. Everybody was there but Sammy. Dad thought he wasn't coming and that he was working on the road. But when we rolled out the giant birthday cake, Sammy popped out. Everybody sang Sammy Cahn parodies, including my sister and me. All of Hollywood show biz was there—and most of New York.

JANUARY 5-FEBRUARY 1, 1966: Frank Sinatra and Count Basie at the Sands in Las Vegas. Ten shows were recorded and edited by Reprise and later released as *Sinatra at the Sands,* arranged and conducted by Quincy Jones. The songs included "I've Got You Under My Skin," "September of My Years," "You Make Me Feel So Young," "Luck Be a Lady," "It Was a Very Good Year," "My Kind of Town," "One for My Baby," "Fly Me to the Moon," "Angel Eyes," "Where or When," "Come Fly with Me" and more. It won the Grammy for Stan Cornyn's liner notes.

FEBRUARY 1, 1966: Frank guested on *Sammy and His Friends,* an ABC television special.

FEBRUARY 24-MARCH 10, 1966: In high gear on the club circuit, he went straight into a two-week gig at the Fontainebleau in Miami Beach.

MARCH 19, 1966: *Cast a Giant Shadow* was released, starring Kirk Douglas and guest-starring Frank Sinatra, Yul Brynner and John Wayne.

APRIL 11, 1966: A classic Sinatra song was recorded, "Strangers in the Night," which was a smash single and the title cut of what was to become a number-one album for 73 weeks. The title song received four Grammys: Best Vocal Performance,

Dad in the Kennedy Room in our Palm Springs home.

Frank's 50th Birthday Party

Mom (left, with Dad) threw the party for Dad's 50th. Clockwise from below: I stand by as he prepares to cut the cake (Roz Russell is in the background); FS and Sammy(who earlier popped out of the cake); Tony Bennett; clowning with Milton Berle and Jilly Rizzo; Tina and me; and George Burns.

Record of the Year, Best Arrangement and Best Engineered Record. Once again he was named Top Male Vocalist in the *Playboy* Jazz Poll.

APRIL 13-MAY 3, 1966: Back to the Sands Hotel in Las Vegas.

MAY 1966: Dad made a guest appearance in the motion picture *The Oscar*, playing himself accepting an Oscar. I had a small part as my father's guest at the Academy Awards presentation.

MAY 11, 16, 1966: Nine songs in two sessions were recorded for the *Strangers in the Night* album, with arrangements by Nelson Riddle: "You're Driving Me Crazy," "My Baby Just Cares for Me," "Summer Wind," "Call Me," "On a Clear Day," "Downtown," "The Most Beautiful Girl in the World," a heartfelt new version of "All or Nothing at All" and more.

JUNE 5-6, 1966: *A Man and His Music, Part II* was taped at NBC in Burbank.

JULY 5, 1966: In London, he began filming *The Naked Runner*, a suspenseful drama in which he starred as a businessman who is forced to take part in an assassination attempt in order to save his young son.

JULY 14, 1966: The secret engagement of Mia Farrow to Frank Sinatra was announced.

JULY 19, 1966: Just before he married Mia, my father said to me, "I don't know, maybe we'll only have a couple of years together. She's so young. But we have to try."

Frank and Mia on their wedding day. The reception was held at the home of Bill and Edie Goetz. Above with Dean and Jeannie Martin and Richard Attenborough.

To Frank Sinatra
"a fine citizen,
a real friend"
Pat Brown
Oct. 66

Frank, Governor Pat Brown and Dean on the campaign trail.

Pat Brown

ON SINATRA THE CITIZEN:

I think the thing that impressed me most about Frank was a call I received from him stating he wanted to see me. I had no idea what he wanted, but he said let me fly up to talk to you. This was right after the Watts Riots. He told me he was willing to assist financially and in any other way he could the Governor of California in bringing about a better understanding between all people in this country. We spent two hours around the pool trying to determine what could be done. We finally decided we would assist a Negro minister in the Watts area. This we proceeded to do and although our efforts were not great, the enthusiasm he had stimulated me to a greater effort.

JULY 24, 1966: Before returning to London to resume shooting *The Naked Runner*, the groom took his bride to the South of France, where they visited friends Jack Warner, Loel Guiness and Fritz Lowe. Aboard Lowe's yacht Mia recalled being treated to flower-petal sandwiches.

JULY 27, 1966: *Assault on a Queen* premiered.

AUGUST 1966: My father hosted a fund-raiser for California Governor Edmund G. "Pat" Brown, who was seeking a third term and was being challenged by former Screen Actors Guild president Ronald Reagan. Dad campaigned hard for Brown, but Reagan won. Frank and Mia bought a house in Bel Air. They created a cozy, romantic home with dark wood and bright fabrics. The Old English home reflected Mia's love for the traditional. They also spent a lot of time at the Palm Springs home, where they added a tennis court, another two-bedroom bungalow, a projection/game room and a four-bedroom guesthouse, which he named "The Christmas Tree House" because of the big pine trees in front of it.

SEPTEMBER-OCTOBER 1966: He did two more fund-raisers for Governor Brown, one in San Francisco and one in Los Angeles.

NOVEMBER 1966: He returned to the Sands in Las Vegas, where he proudly introduced his new bride to his fans.

NOVEMBER 17-18, 1966: At two sessions in Hollywood, Dad recorded eight new songs produced by Jimmy Bowen and arranged by Ernie Freeman. They were destined for the album *That's Life*. "What Now My Love?," "I Will Wait for You" and "The Impossible Dream" help illustrate the subtitle: "An Assemblage of Songs Which Say Much and to Many..." The album and the title song were Top 10.

NOVEMBER 20, 1966: He performed at a charity benefit at the Hilton in Las Vegas for Danny Thomas' St. Jude's Children's Research Center.

NOVEMBER 27, 1966: Mr. and Mrs. Frank Sinatra were the guests on CBS' *What's My Line*, hosted by John Daly.

DECEMBER 1, 1966: FS guest-starred on NBC's *Dean Martin Show*.

DECEMBER 7, 1966: *A Man and His Music, Part II*, produced by Gary Smith and directed by Dwight Hemion, aired on CBS. This time he decided to share the spotlight—and I was the lucky guest.

JANUARY 12, 1967: FS hosted a big party at the Eden Roc Hotel in Miami Beach to celebrate the 65th birthday of his friend, boxing great Joe Louis.

JANUARY 20, 1967: Dorothy (Dot) Uhlemann's first day with Mr. S. Secretary extraordinaire, honcho, troubleshooter. When Dorothy is around everybody is literally no more than two phone calls away. FS: "Trying to explain Dorothy is like trying to explain every leaf in a tulip and what makes each color more beautiful than the other."

JANUARY 26, 1967: Subpoenaed by a Las Vegas federal grand jury looking into allegations that Mob-controlled casinos skimmed off millions in untaxed profits, my father testified behind closed doors. His remarks remained sealed and no indictments were handed down by the grand jury.

Antonio Carlos Jobim and Frank Sinatra flank "The girl from Ipanema?"

JANUARY 30-FEBRUARY 1, 1967: In three sessions arranged by Claus Ogerman and produced by Sonny Burke, the long dreamed-of album *Francis Albert Sinatra & Antonio Carlos Jobim* became a reality. Jobim—the brilliant Brazilian—said of Frank, "This man is Mount Everest for a songwriter." Stan Cornyn reported that at the sessions, Ogerman "tiptoed about ridding every song of clicks, bings, bips, all things sharp. Seemed like the whole idea was to out-hush each other." My dad said, "I haven't sung so softly since I had laryngitis." Cornyn added, "If he sang any softer, he'd have to be lying on his back." One trombone player, who had put his felt hat across his horn to muffle the sound, said after hitting a clam, "If I blow any softer, it'll have to come out the back of my neck." I would be remiss if I didn't mention Jobim's lovely vocals on four of the songs. Cornyn describes "Tone" (Dad's nickname for Antonio) as a "slight and tousled boy-man, speaking softly while about him rushes a world too fast. Antonio, troubled not by the clamor in the world, troubled more by the whisperings in his heart." Frank and Tone communicated quietly, with their eyes, their smiles, their hugs and looks of concern and triumph at what they had accomplished. Lyricist Gene Lees recalled the first time he heard the album: "One of the tracks, a Jobim song called 'Dindi,' sends chills up my arms and back. Sinatra's reading of it is one of the most exquisite ever to come out of American popular music. It is filled with longing. It aches. Somewhere within him Frank Sinatra aches. Fine. That's the way it's always been: The audience's pleasure derives from the artist's pain." At the end of the session, the A Team in the studio stepped aside, and Dad let me bring in my B Team to record a duet novelty song called "Somethin' Stupid." On the first take, Dad got silly, sounding his S's like Daffy Duck for fun, so we had to do a second take. Mo Ostin, the president of Reprise, bet him two dollars it would bomb. He lost his money: It went to number one, selling several million copies.

FEBRUARY 12, 1967: With only a piano as accompaniment, Dad appeared along with Ethel Merman, Gene Kelly, Garson Kanin and others at a benefit for the University of Southern California library: a glorious two-hour tribute to the genius of the late Cole Porter. He sang a lovely ballad version of "I've Got You Under My Skin."

On location in Florida for *Tony Rome*. Frank, Jill St. John and their stand-ins prepare for a scene.

FEBRUARY 16-MARCH 1, 1967: FS did another two-week stint at the Fontainebleau Hotel in Miami Beach. Before my month-long tour of Vietnam for the USO, I called my Dad and asked for his advice and blessing. I needed to have some guidelines, some information. I asked what he thought of my going on tour. He said, "Great idea. Just do what they tell you and don't do anything silly. Be aware." Be aware. The same words he had inscribed on the St. Christopher medal and key chain he gave me when I got my driver's license: "Be aware of everything around you." After my tour of Vietnam, having seen the horrors of war with my own eyes, I needed him again. I flew to Florida, got off the plane and went right to his show. When he spotted me, he introduced me to the audience and told them of my recent trip. They wouldn't stop applauding and he said, "Chicken, I think you'd better come up here." And I did, feeling out of place in my travel clothes in that elegant room. He said, "You'd better do something. How about 'My Buddy'?" Bill Miller, who knew the song, accompanied me.

FEBRUARY 24, 1967: FS was among the stars who took part in an internationally broadcast radio show honoring the 25th anniversary of the Voice of America.

APRIL 3, 1967: Dad returned to Miami to begin location work on *Tony Rome*, opposite Jill St. John and co-starring with Richard Conte, Gena Rowlands and Sue Lyon. Yours truly sang the title song. In this 20th Century-Fox release, FS played the title character, a private eye. Simultaneously, he performed again at the Fontainebleau for three weeks.

MAY 1967: Frank Sinatra was selected by the American-Italian Anti-Defamation League to head a national campaign to discourage identification of gangsters in ethnic terms. Their first effort: to persuade the ABC television network to stop using Italian-sounding names for thugs on their highly rated show *The Untouchables*. They were partially successful: Producers actually Americanized the names of several gangster characters.

MAY 1967: Ralph Salerno, a retired cop and a leading authority on organized crime, told the *New York Times* that Frank Sinatra "hardly matches the image the American-Italian Anti-Defamation League is seeking to project as representative of the 20 million Americans of Italian birth or ancestry." The *Times* then proceeded to rake up all of Dad's previously reported friendships and alleged connections with mobsters. It was obvious that Mr. Salerno had not done his homework, since my father had never been indicted for anything.

JUNE 11, 1967: FS performed at an all-star rally for Israel at the Hollywood Bowl.

JUNE 12, 1967: Another of Dad's heroes passed away, and he served as a pallbearer at Spencer Tracy's funeral in Los Angeles.

JUNE-JULY 1967: Jimmy Bowen did a mixed bag of songs such as "Born Free," "Don't Sleep in the Subway," "This Town" and "Some Enchanted Evening" with arrangers H.B. Barnum, Billy Strange, Claus Ogerman, Ernie Freeman and Gordon Jenkins. The album was called *Frank Sinatra*.

July 2-15, 1967: On the road again, traveling to Pittsburgh, Cleveland, Madison, Detroit, Chicago, Philadelphia and Baltimore.

July 7, 1967: *The Naked Runner* was released.

August 30-September 9, 1967: He did two weeks at the Sands, missing three nights because of fatigue.

Early September 1967: Howard Hughes purchased the Sands Hotel from the owners, listed as follows: Jack Entratter, Carl Cohen, Bryant R. Burton, Charles Baron, Charles Turner, Sanford Waterman, Hyman Abrams, Jerry Ross, George Reese, Michael Shapiro, Maxwell Rubin, Albert Parvin, Harry A. Goldman, Dean Martin, Michael Wichinsky, Harry Nobut, Morris Lewis and the estate of Aaron Weisberg.

September 1967: Eleanor Roth (President Jack Entratter's assistant at the Sands): "It was a Thursday morning when Carl Cohen came into Entratter's office and told him that General Edward Nigro, the general manager of the hotel, was going to cut off Frank Sinatra's credit in the casino because when Frank won, he took the chips, and when he lost, he didn't pay his markers. Why would they cut off his credit when he hadn't even been paid for the engagement? They could have taken the markers out of his salary without embarrassing him." Roth continued, "Jack Entratter didn't have the balls to tell Frank about the situation. On Friday evening, some of the Apollo astronauts came in to see the Sinatra show: Jack Swigert, Gene Cernan, Tom Stafford, Walt Cunningham, Wally Schirra and Ron Evans. After the show, Frank took them to the baccarat table, where he asked for credit. He was told that he no longer had credit in the casino, which humiliated him in front of his heroes. That's when the shit hit the fan. Frank pulled all of the wires out of the switchboard in the phone room and drove a golf cart through a plate-glass window. This got Carl Cohen's attention and prompted him to punch Frank in the mouth. It was all Entratter's fault for not telling Frank about the problem in the first place."

September 23, 1967: Back in Los Angeles, the Martin and Sinatra families got together for Dean's Christmas special.

Kirk Douglas
ON DAD'S FISTFIGHT AT THE SANDS:

In the wee hours of the morning, after more than a few drinks, Frank insisted on confronting the manager of the Sands, Carl Cohen, a very nice Jewish man. Carl Cohen punched Frank in the mouth and knocked him down. Most people avoided ever referring to this entire episode. But I couldn't resist. "Frank," I asked, "what happened? Did you and Carl Cohen really have a fight in Las Vegas?" Frank was in an embarrassing situation, and to me, that is the test of a man. Frank paused, looked at me with his steely blue eyes and said, "Yes." Then a twinkle came to his eyes and he added, "Kirk, I learned one thing. Never fight a Jew in the desert."

Rehearsing Martin's Christmas show: Dean, Dino, Frankie and Frank

Two American legends at work: Duke Ellington and Frank Sinatra.

OCTOBER 1-3, 1967: In Burbank, FS taped his third annual NBC special, *A Man and His Music + Ella + Jobim*. It aired five weeks later in mid-November.

OCTOBER 16, 1967: Filming began in New York for *The Detective*.

OCTOBER 19, 1967: He attended a huge benefit for the Italian-American league at Madison Square Garden.

NOVEMBER 11, 1967: *Tony Rome* premiered nationally.

NOVEMBER 22, 1967: Frank and Mia's separation was mentioned in the press.

DECEMBER 11, 1967: Along with Dean Martin and Sammy Davis Jr., my father guest-starred on my NBC television special, *Movin' with Nancy*.

DECEMBER 11-12, 1967: The Voice and The Duke—Sinatra and Ellington—collaborated on *Francis A. and Edward K.*, an album recorded in part on Dad's birthday in Hollywood and released the following year. It included elegant renditions of "Sunny," "I Like the Sunrise," "Follow Me" and "Poor Butterfly." By the way, the A is for Albert, the K is for Kennedy. Stan Cornyn's liner notes paint a vivid image of the session. "A birthday event, hosted by Francis and Edward, you go to with your shoes high polished. Duke confounds. Strolling through the door, six feet plus, dressed with wry urbanity. His blue socks rolled down to an inch above the ankle, and zoot! three inch cuffs on his slacks. Ellington moves across the studio floor to his permanent address: a pock-marked product of Steinway & Sons, once proud, now circle-scarred from years of forgotten coffee cups. For the next five minutes, Ellington lays out his cafeteria, including Cokes, cigarettes and Kleenex. Enter Sinatra. Wearing a vest, green and gold paisley tie at 3/4 mast. A break in recording *Indian Summer*. Sinatra ambles over to saxophone player Johnny Hodges, who asks if Frank ever recorded it before. He remembers doing it on the stand with Tommy Dorsey and how Dorsey refused to transpose the arrangement from Jack Leonard's key. And how 'my eyeballs'd fall out every time on the top note.' The birthday singer, at the peak of his powers. Moving gingerly through the lyrics. Caring about what's happening. This singer today is one year older. His singing, one year more profound. Francis A. and Edward K. Both already wise in the ways of birthdays. They hear back their music. Sinatra's eyes, when his song is happening, they also happen. And Duke, during playback, strutting. Playback finished, they turn to one another. 'Elegant record, Francis.' 'Always glad to hear that about that kind of carrying on,' Frank replied."

JANUARY 1968: FS was back in Miami for appearances at the Fontainebleau when he received an emergency call from Tony Bennett, who was preparing to step on stage for his opening night at the Waldorf-Astoria's Empire Room. Tony reported that a hysterical Judy Garland had just called him, crying that someone was threatening her life and she needed help—immediately! Dad reached out long distance with the singular Sinatra touch. While filming *The Detective* in New York City, he had befriended real-life detectives and members of the Police Department who had become his fans. Bennett's phone was still warm from his hand when Judy called him back. "I asked for help," she told him, "but this is ridiculous. There are a thousand police on the street outside my brownstone. And about 500 lawyers in my apartment!" Tony's next call was from Dad: "That all right, kid?" my father deadpanned. And the shows in Miami and New York went on.

FEBRUARY 1968: FS hosted an 82nd birthday party in Miami for his old friend Mike Romanoff.

Mia in the pool in Palm Springs.

FEBRUARY 26, 1968: Filming began in Miami for *Lady in Cement*, with Frank reprising his Tony Rome character. Director Gordon Douglas: "I had been continually rehearsing a scene with a young actress who had little experience and understandably was nervous. Frank, who was to be in the scene later, had the sensitivity to see it. He knew his being around would only make her more nervous, so he disappeared to the back of the set. I was concerned how the shooting of this scene would come across. Frank came over to me and said, 'Relax, she'll be fine.' And to top it all off, he did a little prophesying. 'She's also going to be a big star.' At that time I could not see it. But I'm sure that actress, who goes by the name of Raquel Welch, will forgive me."

MARCH 3-APRIL 6, 1968: Each day, after *Lady in Cement* wrapped, Frank did his nightclub act at the Fontainebleau.

MARCH 1968: Knowing my Dad was in trouble because of his separation from Mia, I went to Miami to spend a little time with him. He was sad. He was hurting. But he expressed his concern for Mia. "It will be harder for Mia to mend because of her age. When you get to be my age, you've built a wall around yourself. You don't hurt as much as you used to." We watched as President Lyndon Johnson gave a television talk. This was the startling "I shall not seek and I will not accept the nomination" speech. Afterward, we spoke, as we had before, about the war, politics, possibilities. My father believed strongly in Hubert Humphrey. He felt he should run. I, a supporter of Bobby Kennedy, said, "He must address the issue of Vietnam." "I agree," Dad said. "But he won't as long as he is Johnson's vice president. He will not embarrass LBJ by denouncing the war." I couldn't abide this—I had seen that atrocious war and I knew it had to stop. My father knew it, too. He also knew that Humphrey felt the same way.

Frank, Bill Goetz, Michael Romanoff, Freddie Brisson and Jilly Rizzo show off their golf duds in Palm Springs.

MAY 1-2, 1968: At a Big Brothers testimonial in Washington, D.C., for columnist Drew Pearson, Dad publicly announced his support of longtime friend Hubert Humphrey for president. He attended a benefit for Humphrey at the Shoreham Hotel.

MAY 19, 1968: FS hosted the Emmy Awards in Hollywood.

MAY 22, 1968: He headlined at a fund-raising rally and concert for Hubert Humphrey at the Oakland Coliseum.

JUNE 3, 1968: *The Detective* went into nationwide release, and critics praised the movie for its pungent, realistic dialogue.

Hubert Humphrey
ON DAD'S IDEALS:

My first recollection of your father was during the time of Roosevelt. He went to schools and talked to young people about all forms of prejudice and intolerance. Your dad was a hero to these kids. And he took this powerful message right to them—touching both their hearts and minds. I am convinced that this early dedication and activity helped create the political climate that made possible the passage of civil rights legislation in the 1960s. Thousands and thousands of boys and girls in the Forties who became parents and mature citizens in the Sixties had their eyes opened for the first time to the evils of prejudice by your dad. I recall the time when your father and I went to the White House very late one night. We went in the back entrance and up in the elevator to find the president in a characteristic posture for receiving visitors. He was in his bedroom, flat on his stomach, having a rubdown. He looked up and said, "Hiya, Frank. What have you and Hubert been conspiring to do tonight?" What we had been conspiring to do was a series of concerts in Watts, a war-torn ghetto in Los Angeles, the proceeds of which would be used for voter registration, to help implement the Voting Rights Act of 1965. What I recall most about your father is his great concern for the country, and particularly for black Americans who have been so long denied an equal opportunity...He is a solid, devoted American liberal in the tradition of Roosevelt and Truman, Kennedy and Johnson, and—if I can be immodest—myself.

Robert Francis Kennedy and Francis Albert Sinatra. FS: "The Top Cop. He helped me when my son was kidnapped. He made one of the first calls. He and John Edgar Hoover. 'We've got over 200 agents on it,' Kennedy said, 'and there will be more.'"

The cover photo of our family Christmas album.

JUNE 1968: Senator Robert Francis Kennedy was murdered in Los Angeles. The front-runner in the Democratic race for president, he was struck down at the Ambassador Hotel as he celebrated his victory in the California primary. When Bobby was killed, our nation was shredded. We had all taken too much. Nobody could be indifferent anymore. For a while after the assassination, my father, though campaigning for Humphrey, was quiet. I had supported Bobby for president but now sadly joined my father's team and went all out for Humphrey. "He's a decent man and he cares about people," my dad explained. "He cares about people that other people don't care about. I believe him and I believe in him—and that's what a man ought to feel about his president."

JULY 18-AUGUST 3, 1968: Dad went on a concert tour for Humphrey that went to Cleveland, Minneapolis, Baltimore, Detroit and Philadelphia.

AUGUST 12, 1968: In Hollywood, Dad shared the microphone with Tina, Frankie, the Jimmy Joyce Singers and me for the holiday album *The Sinatra Family Wish You a Merry Christmas*. Tina was scared, "in a coma," as she approached the mike for her solos. Dad joked, "You got one take, kid." We did "The Twelve Days of Christmas" as reworded by Sammy Cahn, "The Bells of Christmas," "The Christmas Waltz" and "It's Such a Lonely Time of Year," which was an anti-war song.

AUGUST 16, 1968: Dad was taping a TV special. I went to the studio to watch the "dress." It went very well and, as always, it was taped so that there could be editing options in case a few flaws slipped through during the taping of the final performance. I was in Dad's dressing room when he

Mia Farrow

When I think of the times we were alone together—my favorite times—it sounds too sentimental: crossword puzzles, spaghetti sauce, TV in bed, our puppies, walks, breakfasts, his incredible sweetness, the purity of his feelings...his smile. Looking back, I think that for us, our ages finally mattered. I was too ill at ease with his remoteness and unable to fathom his complexities. Although I knew how much he needed it, given my real immaturity I could not, I was not capable of being enough of a friend, however much I wanted to be. We had a great amount of love between us, but we lacked understanding in everyday life as well as of the major, deeper themes. Today he is still a part of me. I think of him often and wish him the very best because he deserves it and, of course, because I love him.

came off the set. His friend Jilly took him aside and told him that Mickey Rudin had called and that everything was over. He meant that Mia and Mickey had completed the final divorce proceedings in Nicaragua. Daddy asked Don Costa if the dress rehearsal had gone well for the orchestra. Then he looked around at the rest of us, took a long beat and said, "Let's go with the dress. I can't do it again now." It was as if someone had turned out the lights in his eyes. Their marriage was finished, but my friendship with Mia was not. I never had the feeling that I had to like her because she was my father's wife. I liked Mia for herself and for the way Dad had been when he was with her. After they split up, she sought solace in India with the Maharishi Mahesh Yogi, guru for the Beatles, and put her pain into a brilliant performance in *Rosemary's Baby*. Mia's best qualities were always right upfront. Today I love her for those same qualities: gentleness, intelligence, humor and a very quiet strength. She is my friend, and we still have long talks about the old days, about Pop and, of course, about our children. She still has no interest in material things. Her life is full of love and work.

AUGUST 1968: Once again, Frank Sinatra was broadsided, this time by a reporter named Nicholas Gage, who managed to link my father's name to every known gangster, infamous name and scurrilous incident having to do with the Mafia in America—from the early forties to the present day. One could almost understand such slander if it had appeared in a second-rate publication, but this was sanctioned by the *Wall Street Journal*, one of the most respected papers in America. Rumors were printed as fact and no quarter was given to the other side—except for a short

The Press vs. Frank Sinatra:

Most attacks in the newspaper are based on anonymous sources: "law enforcement officials," "police reports," "investigators." They have been written by "investigative" reporters whose idea of investigating is to accept material leaked from government agents—agents who are afraid to be named because they know their "reports" will not stand up in court as evidence of any crime. An example of this type of journalism was a story in the mostly respectable Wall Street Journal in August 1968, when my father was campaigning for Hubert Humphrey. The story, which was timed to appear shortly before the Democratic convention, embarrassed both Sinatra and Humphrey.

quote attributed to Frank's publicist at the time, Jim Mahoney, and buried deep within the two-page article: "These reports are rumors and vicious, unnecessary attacks. Mr. Sinatra has associated with Presidents, heads of state and hundreds of personalities much more interesting and copyworthy. It would be better if newspapers would do stories on these associations that we know are facts." As a result, Humphrey's advisers suggested that the candidate distance himself from my father, which hurt Frank deeply, precipitating not only a change in their friendship but in Dad's politics as well. Frank Sinatra is undoubtedly the most investigated public figure in American history with no legal result. Every charge against my father has died in the investigation stage because of lack of evidence. When evaluating the journalism about my father, I tried to keep in mind a maxim that guides the real investigative reporters whose work I have witnessed: "People who know, often don't say. People who say often don't know."

Frank with Patti and George Harrison, one of the men who was changing the look and texture of the record business.

SEPTEMBER 1968: In an impassioned campaign speech on the principles he shared with Hubert Humphrey, Dad said, "I don't know why we can't grow up. It took us long enough to get past the stage where we were calling Italians 'wops' and 'dagos,' but if we don't drop this 'nigger' thing, we just won't be around much longer."

NOVEMBER 11-14, 1968: Back in the studio, this time with Don Costa arranging, Dad recorded *Cycles*, an album of contemporary hits, including "Little Green Apples," "Gentle on My Mind" and "By the Time I Get to Phoenix." The title song was rerecorded in New York and I had the great pleasure of "producing" it at my dad's request "so that Don can be in the room with me." What an honor. From the liner notes by Hal Halverstadt: "Like the great American buffalo, the Sinatra brand of recording is diminishing. What's special to the spectator is the speed, utter professionalism, finesse and general excitement of a Sinatra session." This same year, FS also released the collection *Frank Sinatra's Greatest Hits:* "Strangers in the Night," "That's Life," "It Was a Very Good Year," "Somethin' Stupid," "Somewhere in Your Heart," "The World We Knew" and "Softly As I Leave You."

NOVEMBER 20, 1968: *Lady in Cement* was released by 20th Century-Fox.

NOVEMBER 25, 1968: His fourth annual television special, *Francis Albert Sinatra Does His Thing*, was aired on NBC, guest-starring Diahann Carroll. It was another ratings winner.

NOVEMBER 26-DECEMBER 19, 1968: Returning to Las Vegas for the first time since his fight with Carl Cohen at the Sands, Frank moved down the Strip to his new home,

"As I approach the prime of my life, I find I have the time of my life..."

Caesars Palace. The big Circus Maximus at Caesars offered him the opportunity to reach a bigger audience and to command a bigger salary. Caesars must have added rooms every time Sinatra appeared there. The place always seemed to be under construction. The marquee occasionally read "Guess Who." This finally evolved to a simple "He's Here." Nothing else needed to be said. The waiters, the bellmen, the guests, the whole place took on 10,000 volts of energy with each new Sinatra appearance. They called him "The Noblest Roman of Them All," and said so on the medallions they gave the guests. He packed every show, sometimes to the distress of the Las Vegas Fire Department, whose inspectors were constantly moving people out of the aisles and off stairways. And the bedlam spilled over to the other hotels. When Frank was in town, the whole town felt it.

DECEMBER 30, 1968: Dad ended the year by recording "My Way." In 1969, it hit the Top 10 in this country and in England, where it had the longest run of any song in British chart history—120 weeks! The song was co-written in French by François and Revaux. When Dad first played it for me at Caesars Palace in its original version, we thought it might be an important piece of material, though we didn't understand the words. Paul Anka wrote the English lyrics, and you know the rest. Dad was, at 54, young enough to sing the almost morbid words, "And now the end is near, and so I face the final curtain," without it depressing him or me. Now, almost 30 years later, I don't like to hear it anymore. I'd rather listen to "Mrs. Robinson" or "All My Tomorrows" from the 1969 *My Way* album. Ed Thrasher's photos and presentation are sensational. Also in 1968 Frank Sinatra was voted Top Male Vocalist in the *Playboy* Jazz Poll and inducted into the *Playboy* Hall of Fame.

JANUARY 20, 1969: FS appeared on *Rowan and Martin's Laugh-In*.

JANUARY 24, 1969: Two months after the election defeat of Hubert Humphrey, I was hosting a Kraft Music Hall special at NBC Studio 8H in New York when my Dad and Jilly walked in. I was surprised. I hadn't expected them. I raced over with my usual enthusiasm. "Daddy, I'm so happy to see you. What are you doing here?" I was hugging and kissing and smiling, and then I realized that he wasn't smiling. His eyes were red and tired. He said simply, "Please call your grandfather." He gave me the hospital phone number, which I called, but Marty, who was being examined by the doctor, said, "I'll call you back." When he did, I couldn't come to the phone because I was undressed, getting body makeup. I didn't know then how much I would regret not taking that call. By the time I was able to call him again, Grandpa was too ill to talk. Dad rushed him to Dr. Michael DeBakey in Houston, Texas, but Grandpa was beyond help. "Despite all our efforts to improve his condition over the next five days in order to perform an operation for his aneurysm of the aorta," Dr. DeBakey later informed me, "he unfortunately became progressively worse."

John Bryson:"He has fought his way through a lifetime of adulation, loathing, criticism, riches, scandal, decline, triumph...to a point where...the man is some kind of folk hero."

"Given a choice, I would choose to have a magic wand that I could use to draw a melody from that enchanted maze of brass and keys and wood and wind and steel. And I would stand there, big and brave, and quietly say, Gentlemen, play for me...Play for me..."
—Gordon Jenkins

Dad and Marty at the pool in Palm Springs.

The asthma that had plagued my grandfather all his life developed into emphysema. So, to compound his heart problem, his lungs were failing.

Dr. DeBakey told me that in all the years he'd spent watching people deal with their parents' grave illnesses, he had never seen anything like my father's devotion. He was moved by such concern, and especially by the unashamed displays of affection and tender love. For five agonizing days my father watched his father die. Each time he entered the room he said, "Hello, Dad," and kissed him. And he kissed him each time he had to leave the room. In between, he held Grandpa's hand. He caressed his face and he wiped his mouth. They had always been openly affectionate, men of few words, understanding each other easily. To lose your father out of your sight, to lose him on an operating table or in an accident, that must be wrenching enough. But to be at his side, holding his hand, hearing him gasp for air...to watch him die. I don't know. I just don't know and cannot imagine the magnitude of that grief or the torture for both men. I don't know what they went through individually, but they went through it together.

The man I call Dad had lost the man he called Dad. Hundreds of people showed up at the funeral, and the scene at Jersey City's Holy Name Cemetery was pure bedlam. Back at Grandma's house, Uncle Vincent, who had lived with Marty and Dolly for more than 50 years, brought out the food. About 60 of us went to the basement bar where Marty used to make his famous banana daiquiris, and where all the framed photographs on the walls reflected the rich, full life of the Sinatras. It was a sad night, but Daddy found comfort in his family and close friends. Like many Americans, my father had been silently strong through the assassinations of JFK and Bobby and Martin Luther King Jr. He had taken the loss of Mia and Hubert Humphrey's defeat. But when his father died, something snapped.

MARCH 19-20, 25, 1969: Dad's recording of *A Man Alone* was a symbiotic partnership between singer and songwriter. Arranged by Don Costa, with lyrics written by poet Rod McKuen, the album is a good example of what happens when the writer knows his singer. McKuen: "I would like to point out that your dad was given the latitude for some acting on this album—he is a fine actor." FS: "Real singing is acting. I sang well because I felt the lyrics here, here and here [pointing to head, heart and gut.] Whatever the man was trying to say in the song—I'd been there and back. I knew what it was all about." Dad had been in a state of flux when he and Rod started planning this project. He and Mia had parted, his father was ill, he was troubled and lonely.

MAY 9-25, 1969: Dad was back at Caesars for another extended run.

SUMMER 1969: My father met Vice President Spiro Agnew at a political convention in Palm Springs.

My favorite shot of my father and my grandfather.

AUGUST 16, 1969: At Houston's Astrodome, Frank performed in an all-star tribute to the triumphant Apollo 11 astronauts shortly after they returned from their lunar landing. Neil Armstrong, Buzz Aldrin and Michael Collins liked "Fly Me to the Moon" so much, it was played during their expedition via Mission Control. One of the great thrills of our lives was hearing Pop singing to us from outer space.

AUGUST 26, 1969: Dad recorded the album *Watertown*. Produced by Charlie Calello, written by Bob Gaudio for Frank, it was about Watertown, New York. Recalls Bob Gaudio: "It was designed to be a TV special, a story of a small town and a guy's trials and tribulations. It lost the impact and turned out to be an album that not too many people understood."

AUGUST 29, 1969: It was "The Night of the Thousand Sinatras" in Las Vegas. All three performing Sinatras were booked simultaneously: Dad at Caesars, Frank Jr. at the Frontier and me at the International (Hilton) for my first nightclub appearance. Dad flew in some friends from L.A., who saw my eight o'clock show. After a dinner break, I joined them for Dad's midnight show. And we all took in my brother's 2 a.m. show. Frankie then treated us to a chuckwagon breakfast.

OCTOBER 1, 1969: According to *Newsweek* magazine, FS refused to obey a subpoena from a New Jersey investigating committee in connection with a probe of organized crime in that state. Mickey Rudin: "There was considerable publicity about a subpoena from the New Jersey State Investigating Committee that he received while on a boat that stopped in New Jersey. This seemed to be the lark of an investigator who had a subpoena with him, filled it out on the spot, added Sinatra's name and served him with it."

Frank and the men he called "True American Heroes": The crew of Apollo 11: Edwin Aldrin, Neil Armstrong and Michael Collins.

The Night of the Thousand Sinatras.

On Frankie's TV special he sang "All or Nothing at All" with his dad.

OCTOBER 19, 1969: My brother starred in his own CBS television special, *Frank Sinatra Jr. and His Family and Friends*, with Jr. and Sr. performing together on stage at Caesars.

NOVEMBER 5, 1969: Dad starred—and performed solo—in another TV special simply entitled *Sinatra*. Also this year: Because he had established scholarships for young musicians, UCLA showed its gratitude by making him an Honorary Alumnus, and, once again, *Playboy* named him Top Male Vocalist in their Jazz Poll.

NOVEMBER 20, 1969: FS hosted a tribute to Jack Warner at the Burbank Studios.

JANUARY 14, 1970: Frank appeared as a guest on NBC's *Dinah Shore Show*.

EARLY FEBRUARY 1970: Dad attended a Democratic National Committee tribute to Harry Truman in Miami Beach.

Taping my brother's TV special: *Frank Sinatra, Jr. and His Family and Friends*.

Below: Tina thought her Dad was in Europe and would miss her 21st birthday party, but he surprised her.

Jack Warner, 1969: "I have been actively associated with Frank for approximately 15 years and I have always found him to be honorable, straightforward and with an abundance of integrity. Also, he is extremely charitable and never turns down any group, irrespective of race, creed or color, not only in the United States but in Mexico, Italy, Israel...as a matter of fact, worldwide. He is a gentleman and an important member of the human race." Warner, Jack Valenti and Sinatra (left).

Preparing a shot for my 1967 TV special *Movin' with Nancy*. I wanted a fast-moving, sharply edited, documentary-style show and decided to use film rather than tape. It was produced by Jack Haley, Jr. My guests: FS Sr., FS Jr., Dean and Sammy.

FEBRUARY 17, 1970: With a vote of 4-3, the Supreme Court rejected my father's appeal of a warrant to appear before the New Jersey State Committee investigating organized crime. He agreed to testify, but only at a secret midnight appearance that would minimize his exposure to the media. He testified to having met Meyer Lansky and Willie Moretti but not to knowing them. He confirmed that his many friends included Sam Giancana and Paul "Skinny" D'Amato but denied knowing that they, Joe Fischetti, Joe Adonis or Lucky Luciano were members of a criminal organization known as either La Cosa Nostra or the Mafia. After they embarrassed and humiliated my father and threatened to arrest him if he entered his home state, they asked him the same questions every other committee had asked him too many times before. The answers were a matter of public record, but they never took the time to research them. Instead, they chose to take full advantage of the publicity that the Sinatra name would bring to their hearings and dragged the man and his name through the mud once again. The ultimate irony was that once they ran out of questions, instead of dismissing my father, they asked him an irrelevant question about one of his movie roles: "Mr. Sinatra, was that really you running for the train at the end of *Von Ryan's Express*?" Mickey Rudin on the hearings: "When he finally appeared before that committee, they asked him nothing of any substance, had no evidence of affiliations with any criminals in New Jersey. And it was a complete bullshit questioning session. Nevertheless, there were resulting headlines about Sinatra and the Mafia." After 75 minutes in this vein, the committee chairman announced his satisfaction that Frank Sinatra had cooperated fully and ordered the contempt charge dropped.

FEBRUARY 24, 1970: Shooting began in Tucson on *Dirty Dingus Magee*, a period comedy western in which he played a thieving reprobate. FS in longjohns in Yerkys Hole, New Mexico, circa 1880. He needed this silliness after Grandpa died.

FEBRUARY 27, 1970: Frank performed at the Nixon White House as part of a tribute to Senator Everett Dirksen.

MARCH 8, 1970: FS joined in roasting his old friend Danny Thomas for the Friars Club.

EARLY 1970: He built a home for his mother in the Palm Springs compound.

APRIL 21, 1970: Frank did a week at Caesars in Vegas, but his right hand was bothering him. Doctors diagnosed it as Dupuytren's contracture, which he had surgically corrected later.

MAY 4-8, 1970: On the day Dad arrived in London for a series of concerts for charities with Count Basie at Royal Festival Hall, the BBC aired a documentary called *The Frank Sinatra Story*.

Dad prepares for a show under the watchful eye of Jerry Lewis' camera, June 1970.

MAY 30, 1970: At Danny Thomas' request, FS performed at "The Shower of Stars," a benefit for St. Jude's Children's Research Center, held at the Coliseum in Memphis.

JUNE 5, 1970: DJ Paul Compton, on Southern California's KGIL, aired a 48-hour Sinatra radio marathon.

JUNE 26, 1970: On WWDV in Philadelphia, DJ Sid Mark topped KGIL with 61 straight hours of Sinatra music, never repeating a single song.

JULY 8, 1970: Dad astonished his Democratic friends by coming out in support of Ronald Reagan in his bid for election to the governorship of California. Politically, my father's alliances had begun to change. This was a time of protest from the Left against the flag, remember. He was still a registered Democrat, and his liberal views still held in most areas (including the controversial question of terminating a pregnancy, which he believed should be up to the individual and her situation). Ronald Reagan, an old friend, welcomed his support in his 1970 campaign for re-election as California's governor. Frank Jr.: "Pop came out for him but advised him to move a little more to the middle of the road."

AUGUST 15, 1970: Dad did a benefit for Villa Scalabrini at the Chicago Civic Opera House, then flew to Los Angeles for another benefit on the 16th at the Hollywood Bowl for Nosotros, a Hispanic-American charitable organization.

AUGUST 29, 1970: In a repeat of their two-man 1963 benefit performance in Rockford, Illinois, Frank flew with Jerry Lewis to Richmond, Indiana, for a fund-raiser on behalf of the family of Dan Mitrione, an American who had been killed overseas.

SEPTEMBER 3, 1970: While at Caesars Palace for a two-week run, FS had an altercation with hotel executive vice president Sanford Waterman in Waterman's office, resulting in Waterman pulling a gun that he kept in his desk and aiming it at my father's face. My father, stunned that the old man would pull a gun on him—but keeping his cool—reached for the gun, saying, "I hope you like that gun, because you may have to eat it." Jilly Rizzo, who was also in the room, jumped over the desk at Waterman and took possession of the gun. My father threw up his hands and said, "That's it. I'm outta here." To this day, Dad wonders why Waterman was so frightened.

EARLY OCTOBER 1970: In Los Angeles, San Francisco and San Diego, he performed at three benefits for Ronald Reagan.

FS with the family of Dan Mitrione in Richmond, Indiana

OCTOBER 13, 1970: Seattle's KIRO topped all previous radio Sinatrathons with 71 consecutive hours of Sinatra music.

OCTOBER 26-NOVEMBER 2, 1970: He recorded many songs for the album *Sinatra and Company**. The asterisk is attached to some powerful names: Jobim, Costa, Deodato. Each side of this album was produced and arranged independently. "Wave," arranged by Deodato, is perhaps one of Dad's technical best. Some other titles: "One Note Samba," "Someone to Light Up My Life," "Close to You," "Bein' Green" and "Lady Day," which was produced by Frank Sinatra. Many of the Brazilian cuts were conducted by Columbia Pictures maestro Morris Stoloff.

NOVEMBER 16, 1970: Princess Grace of Monaco introduced Dad in the second of two one-man shows in London, which were taped for television by the BBC. That same day, on tape, FS was a guest on *The Bob Hope Show*. *Dirty Dingus Magee* also opened nationally, flopping with both critics and the public. Though it ranked as one of the worst pictures my father ever made, *Magee* at least provided Dad with a wealth of material for self-deprecating jokes.

NOVEMBER 18, 1970: Frank guested with Danny Thomas on *Make Room for Granddaddy*.

Frank, Dolly, Frankie, Hugh, his daughter Cody, me, Mom, Hugh's son Griff and Tina. Gowns by Hollywood designer Donfeld.

NOVEMBER 20, 1970: He performed a one-nighter at the Felt Forum in New York.

DECEMBER 12, 1970: Dad liked to give presents on his birthday, so I decided he should give me to Hugh Lambert. He did. Our wedding was held in St. Louis Catholic Church in Cathedral City, California. The church was normally filled on Sunday afternoons by the area's Mexican-American families. They were there as usual this Sunday but found the church closed and were milling about outside when my father drove up with Jilly and my brother. Frank Jr.: "These people were in their white dresses, carrying their little flowers, standing there, most of them speaking no English, and Pop wanted to know what was going on. The priest told him that

Governor and Mrs. Ronald Reagan, Vice President Spiro Agnew, Dolly and Frank cutting the ribbon on the medical building dedicated to my grandfather.

they had closed the church for the wedding party. The color came up in Pop's face and he said, 'You closed their church? To them?' He said, 'Open up the doors, let them all in. Don't keep them out of their church.'"

It was a beautiful day, but painful, too, because my grandpa wasn't there. I felt closer to Dad after he gave me away than ever before. He seemed more introspective, but at the same time more relaxed. He bought a piece of property in the mountains above Palm Springs and planned to build a house there so all of us could get away from the heat. He also bought back his Bowmont Drive home in Los Angeles. He sold his Grosvenor Square flat in London and his East 72nd Street apartment in New York. He re-established headquarters in Suite 2500 at the Waldorf Towers. He was beginning to plan for the future and I felt very much a part of it.

JANUARY 4, 1971: FS performed at a gala in Los Angeles to celebrate the election of Ronald Reagan as governor of California.

JANUARY 15, 1971: Dad realized a dream: the Martin Anthony Sinatra Medical Education Center in Palm Springs, for which he had raised the funds. At its dedication, he evoked the memory of Marty, his late father: "He's here," Dad said, pointing to his head. "And here," he added, pointing to his heart, "and this splendid structure is my dad's kind of dream, just as it is yours and mine. I remember a line in a childhood prayer that said, 'Send me blessed dreams and let them all come true.'" Governor Reagan of California spoke, too, and added to the thought of dreams. He said that two parents once invested their dreams in their son. "They saw the dreams come true, beyond anything they could have hoped. Then the son gave it back to them. Frank, you are living proof that life does begin when you begin to serve." The tears turned to laughter when Dr. Dan Kaplan made Frank an honorary staff member of the hospital. The gesture was probably unnecessary, said Dr. Kaplan, because "Frank's been operating for years."

JANUARY 29, 1971: Maintaining his practice of supporting the candidate of his

Accepting the Jean Hersholt Humanitarian Award, April 15, 1971. "I've been thinking about why you have to get famous to get an award for helping other people. If your name is John Doe, and you work night and day doing things for your helpless neighbors, what you get for your effort is tired. So, Mr. and Mrs. Doe, and all of you who give of yourselves to those who carry too big a burden to make it on their own, I want you to reach out and take your share of this because if I have earned it, so too have you."

choice, Dad attended a Democratic fund-raising dinner in honor of Senator John Tunney at the Beverly Hills Hotel.

MARCH 8, 1971: In New York, FS presented a Songwriters Guild Hall of Fame award to Richard Rodgers—and sang two Rodgers tunes.

MARCH 23, 1971: Dad was 55. A good time to pause and think. To think about the changes in the world at large and in his world—especially the loss of his father, his own priorities and his own mortality. For a long time he had been saying, "Will somebody please get me the hell off the road?" He was sick and tired of the traveling. So it didn't surprise me when he informed us that he would soon announce his retirement. The announcement to the public stated that although he'd enjoyed the exciting three decades of work, there had been "little room or opportunity for reflection, reading, self-examination and that need which every thinking man has for a fallow period, a long pause in which to seek a better understanding of changes occurring in the world."

APRIL 15, 1971: The Academy of Motion Picture Arts and Sciences, recognizing my father's lifetime of public philanthropy and private kindnesses, honored him on Oscar night with the distinguished Jean Hersholt Humanitarian Award.

JUNE 13, 1971: Surrounded by family and friends, he appeared at the Los Angeles Music Center in a benefit for the Motion Picture and Television Relief Fund that raised $800,000. Dad declared that this performance would be his farewell appearance. *Life* magazine made the event its cover story: "Sinatra Says Good-by and Amen, a farewell to 30 very good years." In deciding to step out of the spotlight, wrote Tommy Thompson in *Life*, he has "capped a career that included 58 films, 100 albums, nearly 2,000 individual songs." "I'm tired," he told Thompson. "It's been a helluva 35 years. I always sang a tough book. It's wrung me out." Said his friend Rosalind Russell, "He wanted to pause and think things over, to be without pressure for the first time in his active life."

Journalist Thomas Thompson
ON THE RETIREMENT CONCERT:

He was nervous. He had carefully orchestrated this finale. And being the most meticulous of men, he wanted it played with style and grace. He took the typewritten list of the 14 songs he would sing and he looked at it over and over again. He threw it down on the table and began doodling. His felt pen created a house, then he filled it with black strokes, covering the windows and doors, as if no one lived there anymore. He took a look back at the days he sang for cigarettes in Jersey: "So here I am tonight, 40 years later, going out the same way I came in—singing for nothing." He took exception to reports that he was retiring because of his health: "My health is spectacular. In fact, it's never been better. That's why those goddamn rumors burn me. It shows the irresponsibility of the American press." Is there anybody whose voice does for him what his has done for us, all of us over 30, all of us who recollect Sinatra drifting over from the phonograph in the corner of the living room, the fire low, the wine spent, Sinatra murmuring reassurances?. Sinatra, every man's advocate in seduction. Sinatra, every man's ally in romantic defeat.

Rosalind Russell: "We still have the blue eyes, those wonderful blue eyes, that smile; for one last time we have the man, the greatest entertainer of the 20th Century."

Before the Music Center show, *Life* reported, he was entertaining a parade of celebrity pals in his dressing room, including Cary Grant, Don Rickles and the 77-year-old Jack Benny, who strolled in playing his violin. "This man," he deadpanned, waving a hand at Dad, "endorsed Ronald Reagan for governor of California. Now I would have endorsed Reagan quietly, but Frank did it first. So I come out second with a little endorsement, and what do I get from Frank Sinatra the next day but a one-word telegram. It says, 'Copycat.'" Benny, master of timing, paused for effect. "Now I would like to retire," he said, starting to sputter, "only I can't!" Dad fell off the couch, holding his sides. The fun continued—all at my father's expense. Moments before showtime, as he was about to slip into his tuxedo jacket, Don Rickles called out, "Somebody help the old man on with his coat. Make way for the old-timer.

Sinatra Says Good-by and Amen

A farewell to 30 very good years

JUNE 25 · 1971 · 50¢

Help him go out in a blaze of glory. You're gonna be great out there. People love pity, Frank."

Roz Russell introduced him to the crowd that night: "He's worked long and hard for us with his head and his voice and especially his heart. But it's time to put back the Kleenex and stifle the sob, for we still have the man, we still have the blue eyes, those wonderful blue eyes, that smile; for one last time we have the man, the greatest entertainer of the 20th century." Dad said simply, "Might as well begin at the beginning." And then he sang "All or Nothing at All," "I've Got You Under My Skin," "I'll Never Smile Again," "The Lady Is a Tramp," "Ol' Man River" and his frequent closer, "My Way." And everybody offered up the deafening applause with which they would honor the end of his career. Then the world's greatest entertainer, the master tugger of heartstrings did one more—a rousing "That's Life." Again, the applause to usher out his era. But with the clear call for encores, perhaps for neverending encores, and in the tradition of respecting the audience, the song, the composer, the lyricist, the arranger, he did one last piece of work. Wrote Thomas Thompson: "He had built his career, he said softly, on saloon songs. He would end quietly on such a song. He slipped from his words into 'Angel Eyes,' surely a song for the short hours. He ordered the stage dressed in darkness, a pin spot picking out his profile in silhouette. He lit a cigarette in mid-sentence and its smoke enveloped him. He came to the last line. 'Excuse me while I...disappear.' And he was gone. It was the single most stunning moment I have ever witnessed on a stage."

"Excuse me while I disappear..."

Tributes to Frank Sinatra
Entered into the Congressional Record

SENATOR JOHN TUNNEY:

The man is a master of the performing arts. But there is more to Frank Sinatra than just a voice or a fleeting image on television or in the movies. The essence of Frank Sinatra is Sinatra the man, a man of deep feeling, a man who in a thousand silent acts has worked to better the lives of those around him. Whether it is helping children in America or in Europe or in Mexico or in Israel, whether it is building a hospital or a community service center, Frank Sinatra has always been there helping and doing so without fanfare.

SENATOR JACOB JAVITS:

I know of no person more able to express the joys and the happiness of the day-to-day life of Americans than Frank Sinatra.

SENATOR ALAN CRANSTON:

Frank Sinatra will always be remembered with warmth and affection as long as people like entertainment and entertainers. Unlike old soldiers, great entertainers never fade away. Their music goes on forever. The music of Frank Sinatra will go on forever. Some may say that Frank Sinatra is all voice. Those who know him well know that he is really all heart. They also know that he is all guts.

SENATOR HUBERT HUMPHREY:

Frank Sinatra gave and continues to give, and will continue to give for years to come, far more than the abilities with which he was blessed. His talent was a magical instrument with the power to help the unfortunate and the infirm as well as to mark the memorable milestones in the international world of entertainment.

Frank Sinatra and Bob Hope intersect once again.

JUNE 30, 1971: California Senator John Tunney entered a tribute to his friend Frank Sinatra into the Congressional Record. Several other senators also read eloquently beautiful testimonials to the work and the legacy of my father.

AUGUST 31-SEPTEMBER 1, 1971: Frank suffered the loss of two very dear friends, Random House founder and publisher Bennett Cerf and restaurateur Michael Romanoff.

SEPTEMBER 6, 1971: In Paris, Dad accepted the Award of the Century.

NOVEMBER 20, 1971: In New York, though retired, he sang 12 songs at a fund-raiser for the Italian-American Civil Rights League at Madison Square Garden.

NOVEMBER 25-27, 1971: Spiro Agnew and his family spent Thanksgiving weekend with Dad in Palm Springs.

FEBRUARY 8-MARCH 4, 1972: Stepping up his schedule of charity work, Dad joined Arnold Palmer in co-sponsoring a Day with the All-Americans benefit golf tournament in Palm Springs on behalf of the Tony Lima Scholarship Fund. He also hosted a benefit for the Palm Springs Police Department, then played a mixed doubles tennis match on behalf of a Palm Springs hospital.

APRIL 12, 1972: Dad competed on a pro-am team in the Dinah Shore Golf Tournament.

MAY 13, 1972: He was on the Friars dais at the Americana Hotel in New York to honor a couple of old friends, Jack Benny and George Burns.

Frank enjoying one of his favorite pastimes during his retirement.

MAY 18-19, 1972: Tina and Dad, invited by the Republican Party, went to Washington. Tina remembers making the rounds of the D.C. nightspots as well as political functions. "We were escorted by the Agnews to a reception at Pamela and Averell Harriman's home for Senator Jacob Javits of New York, who was so liberal I thought he was a Democrat. Dad and I went to dinner with Jim Mahoney and Eva Gabor at the Jockey Club, where Dad introduced me to Henry Kissinger and Barbara Howar. Afterward, we all went nightclubbing until Dad folded. At dawn, I took Eva to see the Lincoln Memorial." Tina wore her McGovern button to the Nixon White House.

JULY 1972: Though retired and still a registered Democrat, Sinatra followed more strongly than ever his practice of voting for the man, the candidate, not the party. Richard Nixon's announced policies made more sense to him than McGovern's, so it followed that Nixon was his man in 1972. He was drawn to Mr. Nixon because in the early sixties, President Kennedy had advocated recognition of China in his book *Strategy of Peace*. For years FS had felt that the United Nations was remiss in its stand on the issue. He supported the Republican president's decision to recognize the People's Republic of China.

JULY 18, 1972: At a gala at Baltimore's Lyric Theater for his friend Vice President Spiro Agnew, a U.S. marshal tried to serve FS with a subpoena to appear before the House Select Committee on Crime, which was investigating the influence of organized crime in professional sports. Democratic Senator John Tunney, a good friend of Dad's, intervened and prevented the summons from being served. My father then took the offensive. He let the congressional committee know that he'd gladly come "by invitation, not demand" and offered to answer questions about his $50,000 investment in the Berkshire Downs racetrack in Massachusetts, owned in part by New England Mafia boss Raymond Patriarca and New York capo Tommy Lucchese.

In his appearance before the committee in Washington, D.C., my father admitted having met Lucchese two or three times during his performances at the 500 Club in Atlantic City. Asked if he knew the man was a racketeer, he replied, "That's his problem, not mine. Let's dispense with that kind of question!" He let them know that he strongly objected to having to testify because of the impression of guilt it created in the public mind. "I won't have it!" he told them. "I'm not a second-class citizen. Let's get that straight."

AUGUST 22, 1972: Frank attended the GOP convention in Miami that nominated President Nixon as its candidate for re-election.

AUGUST 27, 1972: A reception for President Nixon at the western White House in San Clemente.

AUGUST 28, 1972: In a profile written for the *Saturday Review*, Dad himself made the briefest and best assessment of his own work: "I developed a certain way of singing, one that I hope won't die out after I'm gone." Expanding that thought, critic Gene Lees wrote that Sinatra was "first, last and always, a singer, a brilliant

Attorney Mickey Rudin

ON FRANK'S INVESTMENT IN BERKSHIRE DOWNS:

The fact of the matter is that it was a minor investment. Evidence developed that they were trying to use his name to promote the track. Even before there was any knowledge that the racetrack involved persons whom the newspapers would refer to as Mafiosi, and the fact that there was evidence of attempted bribery of the Massachusetts governor, a plan was made for the return of the investment. The money was returned. In anticipation that something might go wrong, we handed over the file to the FBI before any request was made for it. That is, we went to the law enforcement authorities and told them of our involvement before anybody could raise questions about that involvement. The results of that hearing are best described by a newspaper headline in the sports section of one of the Washington or Baltimore papers, which said that "The house committee on crime investigations appeared before Frank Sinatra." But many of the congressmen admitted that the charges and the publicity were unfair and that there was absolutely no evidence of wrongdoing.

Tina

He came out publicly one afternoon—I think it was a Friday. The report said, "Frank Sinatra endorses Richard Nixon"—and I hit the roof! I called him and said, "Goddamn it, I've been working for George McGovern for six months—I haven't swayed 20 voters and you just probably swayed two million." He said, "That's the way it goes, kid. Are you angry?" I said, "I'm very angry!" He said, "You work in your way, I'll work in mine. That's politics—it's a free country." I said, "I'm really upset." "Why don't you get in your car and come down here?" he said. I drove down to Palm Springs, loaded for bear, and he was ready to take me on. We had it out, but he let me know that he respected me and my efforts. He said, "Whatever it is you believe in, fight for it. Do the best you can and be as effective as you can. But I came out for my man, and if I swayed voters, I swayed voters, but I have to go public, too." Many times he said to me, "The older you get, the more conservative you get." He's still the street kid, but he's in a society that—well, some of his friends are so stuffy, but he likes it. It's a place, a standing in life that he, I think, wanted to attain.

singer, the most original and influential of his time." Quoting noted musicologist Henry Pleasants, the article went on to say that opera singers often collect my father's records. "Believe me, they know how good he is."

What really makes it all work, wrote Lees, "is Sinatra's way of singing phrases more for the meaning of the words than for the contours of melodic lines." This displacement of a note here and there to complete a lyric phrase "is a tiny detail, but it makes all the difference, and Sinatra is the man who perfected this kind of phrasing."

Lees concluded that "Sinatra created problems for the singers who came up after him, particularly the male singers. Indeed, he put them in an impossible position. If you don't phrase like him, it seems wrong. If you do phrase like him, you sound like him. Then there's his lovely enunciation: Once you've heard it, you know it's the right way to mouth the English language."

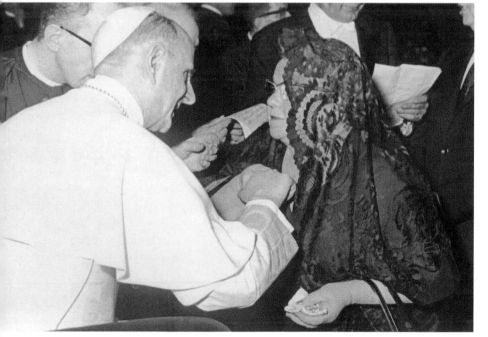

Pope Paul VI meets Dolly Sinatra.

SEPTEMBER 23, 1972: The Friars Club presented FS with its Humanitarian Award honoring his unstinting work and generous contributions to countless charitable causes, for which he invariably refused to accept any thanks or credit. When my grandmother returned from a visit to Italy years ago, she told us about her audience with the Pope, who said to her in Italian, "Your son is very close to God." She asked, "Why, Father, what do you mean?" And the Pope said, "Because he does God's work and he does not talk about it."

FALL 1972: The guest house had been renamed Agnew House, because it was where Ted and Judy Agnew stayed when they visited the desert. Tina recalled: "Agnew was at the Palm Springs house for a party, and I was running around getting voters to register for the '72 election. Every time I'd land a Democrat, I'd shout, 'Got one!' And Agnew would laugh. During Watergate

Frank Speaks Up on His Rights as a Citizen

In a letter published in the New York Times on July 24, 1972, my father wrote about his testimony before the Senate Select Committee on Crime:

"At one minute after 11, on the morning of July 18, I walked into a large hearing room in the Cannon Office Building in Washington to testify before a group called the Select Committee on Crime. The halls were packed with visitors; the rows behind me were sold out. And every member of the Congressional committee was present, an event which I'm told does not happen too often.

"The details of what happened that day have already appeared: the tedious questioning about a brief investment I made in a minor league race track ten long years ago; whether or not I knew or had met certain characters alleged to be in the crime business; whether I had ever been a officer of the Berkshire Downs race track, etc. With my lawyer providing some details that had been lost in the passage of time, I answered all questions to the best of my ability. Assuming that the committee even needed the information, it was apparent to most people there that the whole matter could have been resolved in the privacy of a lawyer's office, without all the attendant hoopla.

"But there are some larger questions raised by that appearance that have something to say to all of us. The most important is the rights of a private citizen in this country when faced with the huge machine of the central Government. In theory, Congressional investigating committees are fact-finding devices which are supposed to lead to legislation. In practice, as we learned during the ugly era of Joe McCarthy, they can become star chambers in which facts are confused with rumor, gossip and innuendo, and where reputations and character can be demolished in front of the largest possible audiences.

"In my case, a convicted murderer was allowed to throw my name around with abandon, while the TV cameras rolled on. His vicious little fantasy was sent into millions of American homes, including my own. Sure, I was given a chance to refute it, but as we have all come to know, the accusation often remains longer in the public mind than the defense. In any case, an American citizen, no matter how famous or how obscure, should not be placed in the position of defending himself before baseless charges, and no Congressional committee should become a forum for gutter hearsay that would not be admissible in a court of law.

"Over the years I have acquired a certain fame and celebrity, and that is one reason why so much gossip and speculation goes on about me. It happens to a lot of stars. But it is complicated in my case because my name ends in a vowel. There is a form of bigotry abroad in this land which allows otherwise decent people, including many liberals, to believe the most scurrilous tales if they are connected to an Italian-American name. They seem to need the lurid fantasy; they want to believe that if an entertainer is introduced to someone in a nightclub, they become intimate friends forever. But it is one thing to watch a fantasy for a couple of hours on a movie screen and then go home. It is quite another thing when the fantasies are projected on real, live human beings, because it doesn't say 'the end' when they are finished. Those human beings have to go on living with their friends, family and business associates in the real world.

"We might call this the politics of fantasy. Sitting at that table the other day, I wondered whether it was any accident that I had been called down to Washington during an election year, a year in which Congressmen have difficulty getting their names into the newspapers because of the tremendous concentration on the race for the Presidency. It certainly seemed that way.

"And I wondered if the people out there in America knew how dangerous the whole proceeding was. My privacy had been robbed from me, I had lost hours of my life, I was being forced to defend myself in a place that was not even a court of law. It wasn't just a question of them getting off my back; it was a question of them getting off everyone's back. If this sort of thing could happen to me, it could happen to anyone, including those who cannot defend themselves properly. I would hope that a lot of Americans would begin to ask their representatives, in the Government and in the media, to start separating fantasy from reality, and to bring this sort of nonsense to an end once and for all."

FS assisted his old friend Ronald Reagan in the California gubernatorial race. Comic Pat Henry is behind them.

I'd get on Daddy about Nixon. He'd say, 'Nobody's perfect.' He has loyalties. That lawyer, Charles Colson, who went to jail because of Watergate, and Vice President Agnew—he remained friendly with all of them. He loves underdogs; he is crazy about the guy who needs help."

He will defend anyone who has made a mistake. His attitude is this: "He's made mistakes. We've all made mistakes. The President of the United States is a human being and can make mistakes."

With Agnew, Dad flew to Cape Kennedy on Air Force Two to observe an Apollo moonshot launch.

OCTOBER 8, 1972: Agnew joined Dad, Bob Hope and Jack Benny for a round of golf in Palm Springs.

OCTOBER 20, 1972: FS sang at a Young Voters for Nixon rally in Chicago. He did "My Kind of Town (Chicago Is)," picking the right tune, as usual, for the right time and place.

NOVEMBER 1, 1972: In appreciation for his having raised $6.5 million in bond pledges for the state of Israel, Dad was presented with the prestigious Medal of Valor at the Century Plaza Hotel in Los Angeles. Also this year, the Screen Actors Guild gave Frank Sinatra their Highest Achievement Award.

NOVEMBER 7, 1972: The Nixon-Agnew ticket swept 49 states, demolishing George McGovern and Sargent Shriver, a brother-in-law of John and Robert Kennedy's.

DECEMBER 31, 1972: He attended a New Year's Eve party with Barbara Marx in Palm Springs at the home of Walter Annenberg, publisher of *TV Guide* and former ambassador to the Court of St. James.

JANUARY 1973: Staying at friend Peter Malatesta's home in Washington, Frank offered to cook dinner for the Agnews at their home. Barbara Marx was in Palm Springs and received a phone call from someone calling on behalf of Agnew's friend C.D. Ward, wondering what Frank was going to prepare for dinner. Barbara said, "Gee, I don't know, maybe his father's recipe Chicken Sinatra." The next day this information appeared in gossip columnist Maxine Cheshire's column in the *Washington Post*. Frank was annoyed because Cheshire had been targeting and badgering Agnew and he felt she had used his girlfriend to obtain information.

JANUARY 19, 1973: On the night before Nixon's inauguration, Dad and Barbara attended a cocktail party at Washington's Fairfax Hotel. Cheshire was in the crowded lobby. Barbara remembered: "She was harassing me in the hotel. I don't remember the questions and your father heard her. But she just kept baiting Frank as we were walking toward the door. She had a drink in her hand. He was polite at first, saying, 'Please leave us alone.' She kept hammering at him and he said, 'Will you back off and leave us alone.' But she kept baiting him the entire time. And Frank said, 'Please back off.' But she still kept picking at him and he turned and he said, 'You're nothing but a two-dollar broad. That's all you're worth. That's all you'll ever be worth.' And he stuffed two one-dollar bills in her glass. He should have socked her in the nose. I thought he was wonderful for the way he put her down. Henry Kissinger called the next day and said, 'Frank, you overpaid her.'"

FEBRUARY 7-11, 1973: The All-American Collegiate Golf Association, which raised money for scholarships, named him Man of the Year.

MARCH 28, 1973: My father was a pallbearer at the funeral of his dear friend Edward G. Robinson. Later that evening he received the Splendid American Award from the Thomas A. Dooley Foundation. He was also presented with the Man of the Year Award by the March of Dimes this year.

APRIL 17, 1973: Dad was invited by President Nixon to perform at a White House dinner for Giulio Andreotti, president of Italy. President Nixon wrote to me on January 30, 1984, that: "My most vivid memory is of that occasion when he sang at the White House after the dinner we gave for the president of Italy. When it was announced that he would sing, some of the critics wrote to me, objecting that because of his 'background,' he should not have been invited. I thought this was nonsense and responded in that vein...I felt that he was one of the nation's outstanding performing artists and that our guest from Italy could not feel more complimented than to have him perform on that occasion." Mr. Nixon said that he considered it one of his best decisions. And I wondered who some of the "critics" were. Apparently they had not read the *New York Times* on Dad's "politics of fantasy," or perhaps they were under a rock when members of Congress publicly apologized to him. Nixon warmly introduced my father as "The Washington Monument of Entertainment." With Nelson Riddle conducting, Dad sang "The House I Live In" and 10 other popular numbers over the next 40 minutes. "Once in a while," Nixon recalled, beaming with satisfaction, "there is a moment when there is magic in the room, when a singer is able to move us and capture us all. Frank Sinatra has done that tonight." Dad was moved to tears. At the end of the evening, Nixon took him aside and said, "You must get out of retirement." Dad replied, "Mr. President, after tonight, I'll have to think about it."

APRIL 1973: Slowly and inexorably, Frank Sinatra was moving back into his work. He'd had some time to relax and began to miss what had been for so long at the core of his life. Eventually he agreed to go along with the many requests made in the more than 30,000 letters he had received, many begging him to "at least make an album again."

APRIL 20-22, 1973: Dad's old friend Princess Grace and her husband, Prince Rainier, spent the Easter weekend as his houseguests in Palm Springs.

Both mother and son are meticulous, impeccable. My grandmother always wore White Shoulders cologne. I always keep a bottle of it to remind me of her. My father is a Yardley's Lavender kind of guy.

> # Nixon
> ### ON SINATRA AS A FRIEND:
>
> *Among the characteristics which impress me about Frank are his unfailing loyalty to his friends whether they are up or down, his refusal to be anybody but himself as distinguished from other celebrities who cannot resist putting on airs, and his unfailing candor and honesty in dealing with the media. I was even more impressed, however, when I heard of Frank's custom of reading the morning papers and circling names of individuals he didn't know who had suffered some physical mishap or bad luck. He instructed his secretary to send checks for $500 to each of them. His gifts were anonymous and were not deducted from his income tax as charitable contributions. That was the mark of a true gentleman.*

APRIL 25, 1973: He was best man at Dean Martin's wedding in Beverly Hills.

MAY 26, 1973: The Songwriters of America named Frank Sinatra Entertainer of the Century.

JUNE 4-5, 1973: In his first studio session since November 2, 1970, Frank recorded "Nobody Wins" and "Noah." The masters were destroyed.

JUNE 4-22, 1973: In four sessions, Sinatra, along with producer-arranger Don Costa and arranger Gordon Jenkins, recorded 11 songs, including "Send in the Clowns," "Winners" and "Let Me Try Again." The A Team was back at the incredible Stage 7 at Goldwyn studios, with Costa at the controls and Jenkins wielding the baton. Stan Cornyn: "As if anticipating the question and knowing there's no thunder roll of an answer to give if he's asked why he's doing this, he lays out the answer to everyone's most tiresome question and says, 'I just figured I'd do some work. No fun trying to hit a golf ball at eight at night.' A record exec. whispers how he wants to 'go on the road with this album and compare him to...to Lincoln.' Gordon Jenkins asks, 'Where did the baritone go?' And the baritone goes to his microphone. He sings with his hands on top of the music stand, holding firm on the music stand, trying hard. He sings and it's the voice that brings it all back and you realize that not one—isn't it curious?—not one other voice so clear and clean in all the years has come along, not one other. He is still, no contest, the best this world knows. He is, to his audience, as he sings, a real and enduring value, a firm handhold in a very slippery, very anonymous world." There had been a great deal of discussion in our family about the title for the album, and when I saw his list of songs, I suggested that he call the album *Let Me Try Again.* He looked at me with that deep stare of his as if to say, "Will you get out of here with that corny stuff?" Then he said, "I've already got the title." I asked, "What? What?" He told me. I hated it. I said, "You're kidding. That's awful." His choice prevailed. The album was called *Ol' Blue Eyes Is Back*, a phrase that has become a part of American folk culture.

JUNE 23, 1973: Dad was among the dignitaries who attended a dinner at the western White House for Soviet Premier Leonid Brezhnev.

MID-SUMMER 1973: In Watergate testimony before Congress, former White House attorney John Dean alleged that Nixon attempted to obtain tax favors for a list of prominent personal friends in the entertainment industry: Ronald Reagan, Jerry Lewis, Fred MacMurray, Frank Sinatra, Lucille Ball, Peter Lawford and Sammy Davis Jr. Said Mickey Rudin: "There has never been a tax evasion charge against your father. There have been numerous investigations, each of which ended as just

The cover to Frank Sinatra's comeback album, *Ol' Blue Eyes Is Back*. Charles Stackhouse, a returning POW, wrote my father about his ordeal in the "Hanoi Hilton" prison. He said that the only thing that got him through was an old scratchy Sinatra LP. President Nixon, in a letter sent to Frank in June 1973, wrote "It is a remarkable thing to learn that something we have done—though it may not seem particularly important or unusual at the moment—can so profoundly touch another whom we may not know and who is so far removed from us in time and place. You have done so not only in this instance, but also I would imagine on countless other occasions we will never hear about."

that, investigations." Business Manager Nathan Golden: "Nixon didn't do tax favors for anybody. There were a lot of people who gave more money than the law allowed by making donations in more than one state. When they called us on it, we hired an attorney, went to court and we paid a penalty."

SEPTEMBER 10, 1973: Dad was interviewed on ABC's *Wide World of Sports* at the Muhammad Ali-Ken Norton heavyweight title bout at the Forum in Inglewood, California.

SEPTEMBER 20, 1973: My husband, Hugh Lambert, did the choreography and staging for the television event *Ol' Blue Eyes Is Back*. Gene Kelly was Frank's special guest star. The audience invited to the taping was jeweled, black-tied and glamorous—a who's who of Hollywood, a guest list that could unnerve even the most seasoned performer. Gene and Frank were visibly excited and nervous. The show was a hit. But Dad said later, "When I haven't sung for a while, my reed gets rusty. If you don't sing all the time, when you go back it's a whole new voice. No bottom; you gotta pound on it for a while." He reached out to his old friend, Metropolitan Opera star Robert Merrill, for help: "We met at his hotel, the Waldorf Towers. He sang for me and I gave him exercises—scales to do to relax his throat. See, the trick of singing well is to have the throat open, relaxed."

OCTOBER 10, 1973: Agnew resigned his office as Vice President because of a criminal investigation.

OCTOBER 13, 1973: With Dinah Shore, FS co-hosted the Friars Club roast of Milton Berle on the occasion of Berle's 60th anniversary in show business.

NOVEMBER 1973: In an interview with Dwight Whitney of *TV Guide*, Sinatra said that even in retirement he couldn't escape the press. "I'm blunt and honest. I call them pimps and whores—the columnists without a conscience, the reporters who take long shots based on the idea that where there's smoke, there's fire."

NOVEMBER 18, 1973: *Ol' Blue Eyes Is Back* aired on NBC. Kay Gardella of the New York *Daily News* wrote: "We thought we were through writing love letters to Frank Sinatra. Here we go again!" Said Dad: "I didn't realize how much I'd miss the business—the records, the movies, the saloons. So here I am for all the young people who wanted to know what I used to work like."

DECEMBER 10, 1973: Dad recorded two songs in Hollywood: "Bad, Bad Leroy Brown" and "I'm Gonna Make It All the Way."

CHRISTMAS EVE 1973: Hugh and I spent a lot of time in Palm Springs. The glow I had from carrying my

Robert Merrill: "You have to let [the voice] flow. It's like getting out of a sickbed and trying to walk right away. You have to practice and vocalize. Frank understood and he did the exercises and his ten performances with no problems. Then he went on TV and talked about the trouble he'd had and said, 'I have a great teacher—Bob Merrill.' Well, I'm not a teacher professionally, and suddenly I started getting calls from all sorts of people who wanted to study with me."

Dad and Gene rehearsing "Can't Do That Anymore" for *Ol' Blue Eyes Is Back*.

Laughing and crying at the same time, my beautiful baby sister walks down the aisle on her father's arm to her waiting bridegroom.

Tina, Mom, Dolly and me (pregnant with A.J.); Wes, Dad and Hugh. Gowns by Holly Harp.

first baby added to the ever-present warmth of my family. We finished our late show at the Sahara in Las Vegas, then boarded Dad's plane at 2:30 a.m. We headed to Palm Springs, tired, hoping that Dad's gardener, Angel, would be at the airport to pick us up. Arriving, we saw a small crowd on the runway: Mom, Tina, Frankie, assorted friends and a mariachi band led by Guess Who singing "Jingle Bells." The house was ablaze with Christmas lights outside and in. It was beautiful. We sat by the big fireplace and had hot toddies and sandwiches until 6 a.m. After a big brunch on Christmas Day, Grandma's birthday, we prepared for a trip to the mountain house. As we left I said, "Where's Grandma?" "She doesn't want to come," said Dad. "And I don't know what to do with her when she gets like that." Hugh and I walked over to Grandma's. "I'm not going up that goddamn mountain," my grandmother said. "I don't care if it is my birthday and Christmas." We pleaded, not wanting to leave her alone, but she had made up her mind. Since the Christmas/birthday had been planned for the mountain house and the presents were already there under the tree, the rest of us had to go without the birthday girl. We were quite accustomed to these little wars between Dad and Dolly, but it still was hard leaving her. For me the most vivid memory of that Christmas is my parents' beaming faces as they sang "Jingle Bells."

JANUARY 25-31, 1974: Sanford Waterman, who had pulled a gun on Frank in 1970, had been indicted for racketeering, so Frank Sinatra was back at Caesars Palace.

JANUARY 26, 1974: Dad gave his second daughter away when Tina married record executive Wes Farrell in Cliff Perlman's penthouse apartment at Caesars Palace. As they walked down the aisle, Tina felt panic. "Oh, my God," she whispered. "What's wrong?" her father asked. Tina answered, "Oh, Daddy." Aware of her anxiety, he broke the tension by whispering back, "Don't worry, Pigeon, you can always get a divorce." It worked, and Tina laughed her way down the aisle on her father's arm.

FEBRUARY 1974: George Burns and several other guests celebrated Jack Benny's 80th birthday at Frank's house in Palm Springs.

MARCH 9, 1974: He did a benefit concert in Santa Clara, California, that raised more than $200,000 to build a college gymnasium. He reached into his own pocket to pay for the orchestra, the supporting acts and all travel expenses. Why? Because some 10 years earlier, he'd made an offhand remark to a university official that someday he would help the school raise money.

MARCH 13, 1974: Frank hosted a wonderful American Film Institute Salute to James Cagney in Hollywood, where Cagney was presented with the AFI Lifetime Achievement Award.

APRIL 8-27, 1974: Frank began a tour to benefit the Variety Clubs International, appearing for the first time since 1963 at New York's Carnegie Hall. In *Variety* one critic wrote: "He did everything right. They shook, yelled, stomped, clapped together, stood up at least five times." Mary Campbell of the Associated Press added, "He proved he's still Chairman of the Board." At $150 a head, the show brought in $250,000 for the show-business charity that protects homeless, abused and orphaned children. The tour took him next to Providence, Detroit, Philadelphia, Washington, D.C., and Chicago.

MAY 1974: MGM released *That's Entertainment*, producer-director Jack Haley Jr.'s masterpiece. Fred Astaire, Bing Crosby, Gene Kelly, Peter Lawford, Liza Minnelli, Donald O'Connor, Mickey Rooney, Debbie Reynolds, James Stewart and Elizabeth Taylor all co-hosted with Frank Sinatra. My father's MGM films are well represented.

Sinatra, George Raft and James Cagney

MAY 1974: In five sessions in Hollywood, Dad recorded *Some Nice Things I've Missed*, produced by Costa, Bowen and Burke. It featured "You Turned My World Around," "Sweet Caroline," "You Are the Sunshine of My Life," "The Summer Knows," "If" and more. "The Summer Knows" and "If" were a study in contrasts. The first was done in 18 takes. (So much for one-take Sinatra. That's for movies; for songs, he has done as many as 25 or 30 takes.) "If" was done in two. It would have been done in one, except that Dad noticed some "sand" in it. Not enough of the gravel quality "to sell to a dealer," he said, "but I think we need another one."

I was with Mom and Hugh in Palm Springs waiting out the last two weeks of a difficult pregnancy when Dad recorded this album. John Brady described the end of one session: "He said goodnight to some of the soft, pretty ladies, and to Father O'Connell [Grandma's priest] he said, 'Say a couple of small prayers for my Nancy, OK? I'm gonna be a granddad, you know.' "

MAY 22, 1974: My first daughter, Angela Jennifer, was born. Ol' Blue Eyes met Baby Blue Eyes at Cedars of Lebanon Hospital in Los Angeles. When he held her in his arms for the brief moment they would allow him, I knew we had given him the greatest possible gift. He had given me life, and now I had enriched his own.

My father's name is on records, films, buildings, hospital wings, orphanages, TV shows, books. And yet, until my first child was born, he had no real link to the future.

Frank Sinatra: "I said a silent prayer that the world would be as good to this little angel as it's been to me. I guess what makes me the happiest about all this, of course, is that our little beauty was born safely and well, and that her mother, my own Nancy with the laughing

SEPTEMBER 27, 1974: Frank gave a benefit concert for the proposed Cedars-Sinai Medical Center at the Universal Amphitheater in Los Angeles.

OCTOBER 1974: *McCall*'s profiled my father in an article by Thomas Thompson, who wrote that one key to Dad was that "he relishes power. He revels in it more than any public figure I can think of, with the possible exception of the late Lyndon Johnson." But Thompson also conceded that "Sinatra has never been anything less than fair and courteous. The only problem I ever encountered was in cutting through the layers of press agents, hangers-on and security men who surround him like those little remora fish that hang around sharks waiting for the left-overs." Thompson described Dad's evolution from ring-a-ding-ding liberal in Sy Devore's party attire to Saville Row-tailored political conservative and detailed his many private acts of grace. "One way to heal the wounds between him and the press would be for the media to ignore him. All together now, repeat after me: We will not review his records, not mention his television appearances. We vow to overlook his films, not announce his benefits. He will become the Man Without a Country, the Philip Nolan of American journalism, condemned to anonymity, cast away on a sea of indifference. But of course we won't. We can't. He fascinates. He endures. He commits excesses, but he has the talent and the charm to back them up. Frank Sinatra will not go silently into the night, and I, for one, am rather glad."

October 13, 1974: On his way to the ring at Madison Square Garden to tape "The Main Event."

OCTOBER 2-29, 1974: Frank launched a nine-city Eastern tour with bandleader Woody Herman and his Young Thundering Herd.

OCTOBER 13, 1974: At Madison Square Garden in New York City, "The Main Event" was staged in a boxing ring and hosted by sportscaster Howard Cosell. The show, the idea of promoter Jerry Weintraub, was broadcast live around the world. It was followed by an album of the same name, released on November 1st. Weintraub: "He wasn't too keen on doing TV. He didn't want to rehearse, he didn't want to bother with it. I went to Vegas to meet with him, and I went up to his suite and we had a cup of coffee. He said, 'What do you want, pal?' I said, 'I want you to do a TV special.' He said, 'Aw, I don't want to do a TV special.' 'Come on,' I said. 'We'll do it live from Madison Square Garden and we'll call it "The Main Event." And we'll make it like a boxing ring. We'll get Howard Cosell to do the announcing. [That's what did it.] You are the main event, you are the greatest singer in the world, you'll be the main event.' He said, 'I like it. Do it.'

"We put the thing together and we went into New York and we had 350 technicians

Producer George Schlatter

ON FRANK SINATRA:

Frank himself is an event. He's more than a singer, more than a person. There is that energy he exudes. He's one of our national treasures. Anywhere you go in the world, when you talk about America, they know Coca-Cola, they know the Statue of Liberty, they know Sinatra. And yet, with all of that, there is an innocence to him. He loves cherry bombs. He loves birthdays. He loves Christmas. He's patriotic. And he loves to laugh!

working on that show. I was producing it, and I was over at the Garden and Frank never came over. I had all these people and it was a live show and we were doing an album and we were going to broadcast around the world as well. So it was not a little thing that we were doing here. And I called him at the hotel and said I needed the lineup of songs, but he kept stalling me.

"Finally I got a call from his secretary, and she gave me a bunch of songs. And they're none of his songs. No 'Chicago,' no 'My Way.' Nothing. None of his stuff. I said, 'My God, I have got to talk to him.' So I run over to his hotel, walk into his suite, and he is sitting there in a bathrobe reading the newspaper. I said, 'Frank, what are you doing?' He said, 'I wanted to see ya, I figured it was the only way to get you over here.' Then he gives me his songs, his regular lineup. And he says to me, 'I'll see you over there. What time are we starting?' I said, 'Nine o'clock we're on the air live, around the world.' He said, 'Great, I'll be there. Don't worry about it.' "

Jerry worried. "Twenty till nine, his limousine pulls up. He gets out of the car, and he walks backstage, and he says to me, 'Pal, you don't look too good.' I said, 'We got a lot of work to do, you know. I'm in a panic.' And he said to me, 'Who's gonna put up a card when we have five minutes to go, so I can start "My Way"? Put him in a red shirt so I can see him.'

"We start the show, and we're walking down the aisle and we get to the curtain where his music is supposed to start, and he turned to me and he said, 'Jerry, you look white as a sheet.' I said, 'I'm scared to death.' And he looked up and he pinched my cheek, and he said to me, 'Don't worry about it, pal. You got me into this and I am gonna get you out of it.' "

With more than 20,000 people inside the arena and a second live audience stretching from Nova Scotia to Rio de Janeiro, Frank Sinatra put on a landmark performance. John Rockwell of the *New York Times* summed up the press reaction when he called the show "superb," the audience "rapturous" and the singer "master of his generation."

FALL 1974: Frank sang nine songs at a fundraiser for Republican Congressman Hugh Carey of New York, who later became governor of that state.

New York City Mayor Abe Beame, Governor Hugh Carey and FS on the dais at a fundraiser. In the back row are Producer Jerry Weintraub, John Denver and Frankie.

Buck Buchwach, the Honolulu newspaperman

ON FRANK'S GENEROSITY:

In Fall of 1974, Dad learned that his old friend Buck Buchwach, the Honolulu newspaperman, was having heart problems. "I hear you've been having trouble with your heart," Dad said. "Yep, but I've been feeling OK for the past few months and I've been working full-time at the newspaper," Bucky responded. "Never mind," my father said. "Here's what you're going to do. Clean up whatever you have to at the office, then hop on a plane to Houston and see Dr. DeBakey. I'll phone. He'll be expecting you." The day after that, Dr. DeBakey performed a double bypass on Buchwach. Said Buck: "Every single day I was recuperating in Portland, I received a phone call in the early afternoon from Frank, wherever he was, inquiring about my condition, kidding me, boosting my spirits, massaging my ego and transmitting as much encouragement as anyone ever got over a phone line. I was scared. I thought I was going to die. Those calls were life-restoring doses, far more effective than any prescription. I never had a friend who asked so little and gave so much of himself."

DECEMBER 20, 1974: Frank visited former president Nixon at his home in San Clemente.

DECEMBER 26, 1974: Jack Benny died and my father served as a pallbearer at his funeral.

DECEMBER 31, 1974: Frank ended the year with a performance at the Diplomat Hotel in Hollywood, Florida.

JANUARY 10-22, 1975: Back at Harrah's in Lake Tahoe.

FEBRUARY 1975: Frank was given the prestigious Cecil B. DeMille Award by the Hollywood Foreign Press at their annual Golden Globes ceremony, which he could not attend. My sister, Tina, accepted the award from Joan Crawford.

FEBRUARY 9, 1975: With Frank hosting the ceremony, Orson Welles received the Lifetime Achievement Award from the American Film Institute in Los Angeles.

FEBRUARY 14-17, 1975: Dad performed again at Harrah's in Lake Tahoe.

MARCH 5, 1975: Three new songs were recorded: "Anytime (I'll Be There)," "The Only Couple on the Floor" and "I Believe I'm Gonna Love You." Arrangements were by Don Costa, and the orchestra was conducted by Bill Miller.

MAY 13-JUNE 2, 1975: Frank began a European tour that included Paris, Vienna, Munich, Frankfurt, London, Brussels and Amsterdam. He played to rapturous SRO audiences.

JUNE 19-JULY 2, 1975: Frank went on to Caesars Palace in Las Vegas.

My "Uncle" Jack Benny, part of my dad's extended family, was beloved by all of us—a decent, kind and loving man.

JUNE 20, 1975: The U.S. House of Representatives Government Operations Committee, investigating improper Internal Revenue Service enforcement activity such as conducting illegal wiretaps and unwarranted surveillance, released a "master list" of people and organizations under scrutiny by the IRS. The list included Los Angeles Mayor Tom Bradley, Walter Annenberg, the American Legion, the American Civil Liberties Union and such high-profile entertainers as Doris Day, Dean Martin, Jill St. John, Frank Sinatra and John Wayne. Congress ordered the probe shut down.

AUGUST 1-7, 1975: A record 672,412 people requested seats for a week of back-to-back, sold-out performances by Frank Sinatra and John Denver at Harrah's in Lake Tahoe.

AUGUST 15-25, 1975: As part of a four-month tour, Dad did a series of one-nighters in Detroit, Washington, D.C., Toronto, New Jersey and Saratoga.

AUGUST 31, 1975: My father appeared on the Jerry Lewis Telethon for Muscular Dystrophy, helping to raise a record sum, and making a pledge in his new grand-daughter's name.

SEPTEMBER 8-20, 1975: FS, Count Basie and Ella Fitzgerald co-headlined for two hugely successful weeks at New York's Uris Theater, grossing more than $1 million. After one show, Dad escorted Jacqueline Onassis to the "21" Club.

Fitzgerald, Basie and Sinatra.

FRANK

ON ELLA FITZGERALD:

I love working with Ella. She's as good a musician and vocalist as anybody will ever hear for the next hundred years. She is so free and thinks so freely and is completely wrapped up in what she does—that's all she ever thinks about. In that way, she's like Benny Goodman, who thought only about the clarinet. Like Ella, he was what he does—a very bright and erudite man, sure, but his life was the clarinet. Once, many years ago, when we were at a Madison Square Garden Christmas benefit, I caught up with him off in a corner, quietly noodling on the licorice stick. Everybody else was sitting around having a sip of booze or something, and I walked over and said, "Every time I see you, Benny, you're practicing. Why do you do that so often?" He said, "Purely because if tonight I'm not great, I'm at least good." I never forgot that, because it's true. If you work hard at it all the time and you have a slow period, whether it's your own emotional problems or you're thinking, I don't feel like working as hard as I did last night, you work and it's still never below the standard, still better than the other guy. I've tried to live up to that, and I know Ella has, too.

SEPTEMBER 22-24, 1975: Ella, Basie and Frank played Philadelphia, Cleveland and Chicago, where Mayor Richard J. Daley presented Dad with the gold Medallion of Citizenship in a City Hall ceremony recognizing Dad's role in letting the world know that Chicago is "My Kind of Town."

OCTOBER 5, 1975: He performed at a benefit for St. Jude's Children's Research Center honoring Danny Thomas. This year the Frank Sinatra Child Care Unit was established at St. Jude's in Memphis, Tennessee, with funds raised by my father.

OCTOBER 17-23, 1975: Back to Harrah's at Lake Tahoe.

OCTOBER 24, 1975: Frank recorded "Christmas Mem'ries" and "A Baby Just Like You" for his granddaughter. Her picture appears on the sleeve.

OCTOBER 25, 1975: He attended a Friars dinner honoring Gene Kelly at the Century Plaza Hotel in Los Angeles.

OCTOBER 30-NOVEMBER 2, 1975: And on to Caesars Palace in Las Vegas.

NOVEMBER 5, 1975: At the Century Plaza Hotel in L.A., Dad was master of ceremonies as the Scopus Award was presented to the great piano virtuoso Artur Rubinstein by the American Friends of the Hebrew University of Israel.

NOVEMBER 13-20, 1975: The London Palladium received 350,000 requests for 15,000 available seats for concerts featuring Sarah Vaughan, Count Basie and Frank Sinatra.

NOVEMBER 23-30, 1975: Former vice president Agnew accompanied Dad and Barbara Marx to Tehran, where Frank was to perform. Then it was on to Israel for two charity shows on behalf of the Frank Sinatra Youth Center for Arab and Jewish Children.

Frank Opens Up

On September 22, 1975, in his first in-depth television interview, Frank Sinatra spoke with Bill Boggs on WNEW in New York:

ON RETURNING FROM RETIREMENT:

I was struggling, really fighting my way out of the doldrums. Because when I quit, I let everything go. And it all fell down. It's like somebody who lifts weights and then stops for a while—a matter of consistency, you have to do it every day. The greatest training that any youngster can have, if he really wants to become a pop singer, is to sing all the time, every day. So I was having a tough time vocally, trying to do what I wanted to do. But I was working very hard at it, and when I appeared at the Uris Theater it was purely like I was back in the very beginning of my career as a vocalist. I had to really concentrate hard.

ON PREPARING FOR A CONCERT:

It begins by keeping in physical condition. I vocalize about an hour and a half a day, every day. I break it up in stages. Just to keep the muscles warm. I keep thinking to myself, Am I warm enough? Am I really ready to pitch? Or, if I've got 10 minutes to curtain, should I run into the dressing room and get a hold of Bill Miller and sing four or five minutes of exercises—the middle area of the scale? I'll go up to an F and hit it once or twice and know that I'll probably never use it, but it's there if I need it. Which is what I didn't do during retirement. I wouldn't even hum for anybody. Not a [musical] sound did I make. And I really didn't miss singing. But I had a great time for almost two years, the most wonderful time of my life. I just wanted to stop working for a while.

ON HIS MUSICAL ROLE MODELS:

I go back to Mabel Mercer, Billie Holiday, Bob Eberly—and Jack Leonard, when he was with Tommy Dorsey. He did some marvelous pieces of phraseology that went on and on. It was fascinating to hear him do it. And Robert Merrill, who is probably the greatest baritone I've ever heard. Even now, every once in a while when I feel that I'm faulting myself, we meet and we do a clinic. And he straightens me out about something. I'd like to do it more, but he's busy, too. And I don't want to hang him up by trying to make him just a teacher.

ON TODAY'S POPULAR SINGERS:

One of the things that I think is sad about the new school of singing is that the kids have nowhere to go to learn. There are no orchestras that do one-nighters 300 dates a year. But when you work every single night, you're learning something every time. And if you want to go into the acting business, you begin to learn to use the lyric of a song as a script for a scene in a movie. I didn't know that at the time, but that's what I was doing.

ON SELECTING SONGS FOR A PERFORMANCE:

I choose the material that I think is best and also material that I think my audience wants to hear. Strangely enough, I often find myself thinking like a baseball pitcher when I'm performing. I will turn around and say to Bill Miller, "Skip the next two tunes and go to the third one," because there's something about the audience—I'm not getting vibes from anybody, so we go to something that might grab them a little bit more. So you throw a knuckler, and you throw a slider and you throw a fast ball. And that way it not only amuses them and entertains them, but it mystifies them a little. They don't quite understand why you're switching around like that.

ON HEARING HIS OWN RECORDS:

I can't stand that. If I'm out visiting someone, I say to them, "If you play my records, I'm going home." Because often I was a little impatient in making a record, and I said, "That's it, press it, print it." And there was one little note in it that isn't right. And every time I hear that record, it comes back to me. If I'm in my car listening to the radio, I cringe before the note comes and I think to myself, Why didn't we do it one more time? Just one more time.

ON BEING A PUBLIC FIGURE:

I think if you handle it carefully and tastefully, it can be done. That doesn't mean that if I wanted to go to Coney Island for an afternoon, I could go. I can't go—that would be absolute bedlam. But I can go shopping, I can walk up Fifth Avenue and go in and out of shops and people say, "Hello, how are you?" It's fine. Sign an autograph, fine. That's never any problem. That's a great delight, as a matter of fact, great flattery. And yet I know performers, who will be nameless, who just refuse to sign an autograph. And I really don't understand why. It's a simple thing to make somebody happy. And then I have the quiet moments. For instance, many times through the years, when I'm in New York, I like to take a walk at night when there's nobody around. I love to take a walk up Park Avenue or Fifth Avenue. And look in the windows at Saks. There are other strollers, you know, and I know they're saying, "Is that really him?" But of course there comes the other side, which is, by the way, extremely rare, where you get the rude guy who comes up when you've got your steak on a fork halfway to your mouth, and he says "Could you come over to my table for a minute?" And you say, "Would you please get away from here or I'm gonna have the guy throw you out of the restaurant." You either get that blunt or you say to him, "May I finish my dinner and I'd be delighted to come over." But that's terribly rare because most people have better sense than that, they really do.

ON HIS GRATITUDE TO HIS FANS:

I've been overly rewarded in my lifetime, and that's not buttering anybody up, it's a fact. I appreciate what's happened to me, and I wish everybody who is viewing us, or even if they aren't, if they just hear about it, I wish them thousands of times more than I've gotten in my life. And I wish everybody in the world a lot of sweet things, and pleasant dreams, and soft touching, hugging and kissing.

Amanda Kate obviously already falling in love with the first man in her life, her daddy.

When Grandpa Frank rocked Amanda to sleep, he would sing "It Had to Be You."

FEBRUARY 1976: The Friars Club selected Frank Sinatra as Top Box Office Name of the Century.

FEBRUARY 26-MARCH 14, 1976: He played Caesars Palace in Las Vegas and Harrah's in Lake Tahoe.

MARCH 17, 1976: Amanda Katherine, Dad's second granddaughter, made her entrance into the world.

MARCH 29, 1976: The Frank Sinatra-John Denver TV special aired on ABC.

APRIL 1976: *That's Entertainment Part Two* was released. The segment devoted to FS included excerpts from *Anchors Aweigh, Till the Clouds Roll By, High Society, The Tender Trap* and *It Happened in Brooklyn.*

EASTER 1976: Easter in Palm Springs—Mom, Dad, A.J., Amanda, Hughie and me—was lovely. I enjoyed seeing my babies in the arms of their grandparents and great-grandmother. Dolly, who liked to give cash, always insisted on putting money into the hand of the recipient. One night, she folded up some bills and put them in two-year-old A.J.'s hand. And then she did the same thing with her two-week-old great-granddaughter. Amanda Kate couldn't grasp the money, but Dolly managed to hold it against her tiny palm long enough to say, "Here, baby. Here's your first present from your great-grandma." Dolly believed in simple, basic things, like cash. She was so proud. We were a fabulous family. My parents looked so right together, and I saw a glimpse of that happy ending.

MAY 1976: At the same time that my father became engaged to Barbara Marx, his mother, Dolly, moved to Palm Springs to be closer to her family.

MAY 1-10, 1976: A short tour of the United States and Canada with Count Basie, which concluded at the Grand Ole Opry in Nashville.

MAY 13-15, 1976: Continuing his tour without Count Basie, he played the Saber Room in Hickory Hills, Illinois.

MAY 20-25, 1976: Again at Caesars Palace in Las Vegas.

MAY 23, 1976: The University of Nevada saluted Dad by granting him an honorary Doctorate of Humane Letters. Not bad for a grade-school dropout from the Hoboken school system! Dad called Grandma Dolly to say, "Ma, I graduated today."

MAY 27-30, 1976: Then on to the Latin Casino in Philadelphia.

JULY 11, 1976: Three months before their scheduled wedding date, Dad and Barbara exchanged vows before 130 carefully selected guests in Rancho Mirage at Sunnylands, the estate of Walter Annenberg. Both families attended the ceremony: Grandma Dolly, Tina and me; Barbara's son Bob Marx represented her family. Best man was Freeman Gosden (known for his role as Amos on the old *Amos and Andy* radio show). Also in attendance were Spiro Agnew, Ronald Reagan, the Gregory

Pecks, Kirk Douglas, heart surgeon Michael DeBakey and former Dodger manager Leo Durocher. As wedding presents, the bride and groom exchanged rings. Dad also gave Barbara a peacock blue Rolls-Royce, and she gave him a gray Jaguar XJS.

During the ceremony, Judge James H. Walsworth asked the bride, elegant in a Halston beige chiffon, if she would take Dad "for richer or poorer." Dad broke in, "Richer, richer."

SUMMER 1976: The newlyweds honeymooned with half a dozen friends in our mountain house.

AUGUST 1976: For the month of August, Grandma invited my family to La Jolla, California, where she always spent the summer. Dolly enjoyed going to the track in Del Mar. When she had a winner, she would press the winnings into the tiny hand of one of her great-granddaughters. Frank and Barbara visited us one day on their way back from Newport Beach, where Dad had done a photo session with his old friend John Wayne. They looked happy—Barbara blond and pink, Dad, tan and smiling, his blue eyes bright. I was happy for them. I looked at the sea and asked Grandma Dolly if we could spend the whole summer with her the following year. She sighed, just the way Daddy does, and said, "I won't be here next summer." "Why not?" I asked. "You hate the desert heat, you love the track. Why wouldn't you rather be here?" She said matter-of-factly, "I won't be anywhere." I sort of laughed it off: "Oh, c'mon, Gram." But Dolly was serious. She said, "I'm tired, baby. I miss Marty."

Mr. and Mrs. Wes Farrell, Mr. and Mrs. Frank Sinatra, Bob Marx and Mr. and Mrs. Hugh Lambert.

I took this picture of Dolly and her great granddaughters when we visited her in La Jolla.

*"Fly me to the moon and
let me play among the stars.
Let me see what spring is like
on Jupiter and Mars.
In other words, hold my hand…"*

AUGUST 24-29, 1976: Frank did one-nighters at the Canadian National Expo in Vancouver, then at the Saratoga Performing Arts Center, New Jersey's Garden State Arts Center and Riverfront Coliseum in Cincinnati.

SEPTEMBER 2-8, 1976: While at Caesars Palace, Frank performed another good deed. He made his usual appearance on Jerry Lewis' Labor Day Telethon for Muscular Dystrophy, singing "Stargazer" and Eric Carmen's "Never Gonna Fall in Love Again." Then, capping three months of elaborate secret planning, he said to Jerry, "Listen, I have a friend who loves what you do every year…Would you send my friend out, please? Where is he?" Out strolled Jerry's former partner, Dean Martin. The two had not seen or spoken to each other in more than 20 years. As they warmly embraced, Dad said, "I think it's about time, don't you?" To which Jerry replied, wiping away tears, "You son of a bitch." To Dean, Jerry said, "So, how ya been?" And Dean replied, "You know, it seems like we haven't seen each other for 20 years." Then Frank and Dean did a 10-song medley. Afterward, Jerry commented, "When Francis Albert is around, usually there's gonna be excitement."

SEPTEMBER 10-16, 1976: Back to Lake Tahoe with John Denver at Harrah's.

SEPTEMBER 24-OCTOBER 2, 1976: Frank played to packed houses at the Westchester Premier Theater in Tarrytown, New York, 25 miles north of NYC.

Displaying his gifts of heart and timing and showmanship, Frank reunites Jerry and Dean, allowing the world to share the moment.

OCTOBER 7-20, 1976: His tour took him to Hartford, Binghamton, Pittsburgh, Providence, New Haven, Montreal, Syracuse, Norfolk and Richmond.

OCTOBER 1976: Norman Rockwell painted Dad's portrait, which appeared in *Ladies' Home Journal* with a perceptive and revealing story written by actress Rosalind Russell entitled "Sinatra: An American Classic." The article noted that when my father went into his short-lived "retirement," he had completed 58 movies, 100 record albums, more than 2,000 individual recordings and more benefit concerts than he could count. Russell, a friend since 1940 when Dad sang "I'll Never Smile Again" to her and her husband, wrote that there are "several Frank Sinatras. Perhaps this is what makes him both fascinating and controversial. He is tempestuous, tender, searching, indefatigable, unexpected."

Portraits of FS by sculptor Robert Berks and Norman Rockwell. Of the Berks sculpture, Frank said, "When I give replicas of this away, it will be the nearest thing I can give of me...The way I feel—pain and joy at the same time."

NOVEMBER 12, 1976: "Evergreen" and "I Love My Wife" were recorded in Hollywood. The former was never released.

NOVEMBER 14, 1976: Frank received the Scopus Award from the American Friends of the Hebrew University of Israel because of his work for that country. Prime Minister Menachem Begin: "My personal appreciation to you for all you have done to encourage peace in the land so dear to us all...Men of good will everywhere applaud your generosity. None more enthusiastically than I." He was appearing at the Copacabana in 1948, when he was given a package and told to take the third taxi, which he did. The driver took him to a deserted pier where he left the bag as instructed. He never knew that what he was carrying was money for arms for Israel, until 30 or so years later, when he was visiting that country and a tearful Menachem Begin walked around his desk, hugged Frank and said, "Thank you."

In 1969, John Wayne wrote: "On locations I use a mobile home to travel to the set. The first requisite is not coffee or tea or an air conditioner or a heater, but a selection of Sinatra tapes for our recorder."

NOVEMBER 28, 1976: Another of Dad's dearest friends, Rosalind Russell, passed away in Los Angeles, and he delivered the eulogy at her funeral. The last time I saw Rosie, as Dad called her, was in Palm Springs. When I asked how she was feeling, she said to me, "Nancy, just don't ever get old. It's no fun."

DECEMBER 1976: We celebrated Christmas and Grandma's 82nd birthday in Palm Springs. None of us had a camera handy, and sadly no pictures were taken.

JANUARY 6, 1977: Dad opened once again at Caesars Palace. He flew to Las Vegas early in the day with a group of friends from Palm Springs. Grandma and her friend Anne Carbone were supposed to have gone with Dad, but—and this is so unlike her—Grandma didn't feel like it. She said she wanted to go later. She said she would come to the showroom directly from the airport.

When Dad left, a coming storm was already sweeping Los Angeles. Clouds and fog had darkened the pass and were coming in over the desert valley. That's when Grandma went on her odd errand. She asked Dad to give her the few pieces of jewelry she kept in his safe, because she now wanted to put them in her safe deposit box in the bank. As if moved by some strange premonition, she ran that errand and a couple of others. Then she went home to dress.

Dolly was meticulous—again, like her son. Her hair was groomed at all times. I never saw her with curlers or pin curls. Once in a while I saw a clip holding an already carefully designed wave, but that was all. She had small hairpieces that augmented the upswept curls on her crown. She wore one this day. Her maid, Maria, watched her put it on.

Grandma bathed and splashed on her favorite White Shoulders cologne. She dressed in her black brocade outfit and put on a pair of those funny little boots of hers. When my song "Boots" was climbing the charts, she used to say it was

Frank Sr. and Frank Jr. in late 1976.

because of her boots. She had the boots made to order because the high tops helped to control a chronic swelling in her ankles.

Grandma did all the things she always did when she was going out, but this time she took longer to do them. She packed her rosary, her white lace handkerchief with the N on it, an extra pair of glasses, some breath mints, her allowance check, her money purse, her tiny religious medals, some small bobby pins and her compact in her black ostrich double-strapped handbag. Concerned about the time, Maria asked her if she needed help. Maria had not seen Mrs. S. like this before. Grandma was never late.

By the time she had buttoned her black broadtail coat and wrapped her kerchief around her head, the sky was black. It was the worst storm in years. Dolly was one hour late for the chartered plane that was to take her to Vegas. She said goodbye to Maria, then told her to remember that "if anything happens to me, everything goes to my grandson." She got in the car with Anne.

Our gardener, Angel, a dear, gentle man who has been part of our family for 25 years, drove them to the steps of the jet. Grandma said to Angel, "Remember, everything goes to my grandson."

I know how difficult it was for her to climb those steps. According to her doctor, she was only weeks away from needing a walker.

The plane taxied down runway three-zero and waited for clearance. Visibility was not good, with a low cloud cover on the ground. When they were airborne, visibility was almost zero. It was to be instruments all the way. They could see little from the starting end of the runway.

The Palm Springs Airport lies in the Coachella Valley, at a point where two mountain ranges come together, forming a V, or a pass. Looking toward L.A., Mount San Jacinto is on the left and Mount San Gorgonio is on the right. To fly to L.A. from runway three-zero, planes proceed due west, or left, heading for the pass. To fly to Las Vegas, however, the plane would have to turn northeast, or right, almost immediately and climb above 12,000 feet.

At 5:50 p.m. my mom phoned me. Mickey Rudin had called her to report that Grandma's plane was overdue. It had left Palm Springs at 5 p.m. and had been due in Las Vegas at 5:20 p.m. There had been no communication with it since 5:02.

We all knew it was over. We all hoped for a miracle.

Frank Sinatra did his opening show that night. I know he did it for his mother.

The morning after the plane disappeared, my dad summoned Frankie, Tina and me. Hugh and I drove down. We kept the car radio and a second portable radio turned

Dolly and Frank at his wedding reception.

to the local news station, hoping to hear of that miracle. We went past the turnoff to the Rialto Airport at the foot of the San Bernardino Mountains. I couldn't take my eyes off those mountains. They were on our left and a little ahead of us for a while as we drove. They were majestic, covered with the whitest, heaviest snowfall I had ever seen up there. It was a little eerie, looking up at snow-covered mountains while we were riding in 80- or 90-degree heat.

I remember crying a lot on that drive and saying things like, "Maybe they were able to land," and "Maybe they're freezing up there." I remember needing my mother and missing my children. But mostly I remember a feeling I had never had before—as if I might explode, as if my body might blow apart. I think now that it was panic.

My brother was about 30 minutes ahead of us and had stopped at the rescue command center at the Rialto Airport. He spoke to a few of the volunteers and some reporters who were waiting for word. There was none. Mickey Rudin and Jilly Rizzo, who had flown into Rialto by helicopter, rode with Frankie to Palm Springs and slept all the way. They were exhausted; they had been up all night, trying to help.

When Hugh and I got to Palm Springs, we walked into a private Mass said by Father Geimer in Dad's living room. Dad was sitting in a chair, reading his missal. I sat down quickly and waited for some sort of calm to come, but none did. Everything seemed to be moving in slow motion. We were in a capsule, sort of floating.

After Mass, Dad and I held on to each other. I said, "Daddy, I don't know how to help you." And he said, "Just be here." I felt safe in his arms, my cheek resting on his soft beige pullover. He asked why I hadn't brought the children. I told him I had thought I should leave them home because at two-and-a-half years and 10 months old, they were very normal, very noisy. He just said, "Oh, OK."

Hugh and I looked at each other, understanding. The next day, Hugh went to Los Angeles and came back with the girls. I realized later, as I held them, that we needed their noises and smells and energy. Their mere presence gave us faith: They were still so fresh from God. I felt the same "safe" feeling with them in my arms.

There was no word about the plane. My brother spent most of his time in his room in the Christmas Tree House. My sister and I just sat or roamed around. People came by but didn't stay, an endless chain of sad, worried faces.

Angel and his son came. The boy, Ruben, had just come from the mountain, where he had been searching for "Mama." His clothes were still soaked from the snow and he was crying. He broke my heart.

In desperation, Tina and I spoke by phone with the famous psychic Peter Hurkos. He promised to concentrate on the problem and call back. Dad went up in a helicopter to help in the search. He found nothing. I was grateful for that.

The second night I sat with him in front of the fire. I asked what rescuers do when they find a plane down. I asked rather general questions, but he sensed my need and answered in specifics. He told me that if there were no survivors, they try to identify body parts and put them into separate bags. He told me carefully but thoroughly what the procedure is and how it is done. I wondered if he had asked someone the same thing that day. There was an odd comfort in hearing such matter-of-fact details.

By the third day we were all accepting the inevitable, I think, but as we admitted later, each had his or her own private bit of hope. Peter Hurkos phoned with a description of the location of the wreckage. I'll never forget the scene. Dad, Jilly, Tina, all of us leaning on the bar, studying the map with eyes open wide, ears hanging on Peter's every word, trying to pinpoint the spot on our map. He said the reason that the plane hadn't been spotted was that it had not gone straight but made

Mt. San Gorgonio, which we renamed Grandma's Mountain, also claimed the life of Dean Martin's son Dean Paul in 1987. Young Dino, an aspiring pilot, said when Grandma died, "That mountain shouldn't be there. It should be moved. It's a hazard to all pilots."

a quick, sharp left turn. Was this our miracle? I conjured up a picture of Grandma, Anne and two pilots huddled together, trying to keep warm. I mean, they made a crash landing, they're injured, but they are alive.

Nothing useful came of the Hurkos call, but it was something to do. We went to bed without any resolution. We were saddened about the pilots, too. They were not just pilots, but human beings, with frailties, abilities, families. I thanked God for my children, for the continuity of life.

At 11:30 p.m. the intercom buzzed in our room. Barbara's voice said, "They found it."

It's amazing what hope can do for the human face and what the absence of hope does to that same face. I'll never forget coming from my room and seeing my father's face.

The wreckage had been located just yards away from where Dad had been up in the chopper the day before. In the last couple of seconds, the pilots must have seen the mountain because they pulled back on the stick to try to avoid crashing. They broke off treetops before they hit. The plane had split in two. The nose was shattered. The fuselage was pretty much intact. The pilots' bodies disintegrated on impact. There was nothing left of them to put into body bags. "Grandma was found strapped to her seat," Mickey said. I forced myself to believe that.

I kept thinking that somebody should go and look at the remains, make sure. "Mickey's going," someone said. "Jilly's going," someone else said later. As it turned out, nobody went. Nobody could face up to it.

A subsequent investigation and lawsuit disclosed that a controller at the Palm Springs Airport had used confusing language, which could have caused the pilot to think that he should maintain the current altitude and heading. Because of other air traffic in the area, he was required to keep to a 9,000-foot altitude. When he finally received clearance to increase his altitude, it was too late. With these problems and poor visibility, the little plane had gone almost straight into the mountain at full takeoff speed. The liability was divided approximately equally between the controller and the pilot, who had the final responsibility to know the airport and the surrounding terrain.

After the investigation, I was given Grandma's black double-strapped handbag, bent and twisted out of shape. But it wasn't burned. I still have it. And the few things she had so carefully put into it as she was dressing that day were unharmed.

When somebody he loved died, Daddy always needed to be alone for a while. Nobody could comfort him. But this time it was different. He needed us with him. The image of his mother blown to bits or twisted and broken or whatever happens in a plane crash must have almost destroyed him. The suddenness of it—alive one instant, dead the next—that's not the way you expect people to die. He had hired the plane for her. I'm sure he must have carried a lot of guilt about that. And Anne, Dolly's good friend from New Jersey, Dr. Carbone's wife—Dad had known her practically all his life.

Daddy doesn't talk much about his boyhood anymore. He used to, when Grandma was alive. And a lot of laughter has gone from his life. Yet there still must be solace somehow in looking up at that mountain, so much more beautiful and lasting a memorial than any graveyard, and getting a peaceful feeling from living in the shadow of Grandma's mountain.

JANUARY 12, 1977: We joined Dad in a Palm Springs funeral service to bury his beloved mother beside her husband. That moment was almost certainly the most painful one of his life.

At his mother's funeral.

Dad's Relationship with Dolly

It was a crucial loss. They'd fought through his childhood and continued to do so to her dying day. But I believe that to counter her steel will, he'd developed his own. To prove her wrong when she belittled his choice of career, he'd transcended more fame than any American entertainer had ever achieved. Their friction first had shaped him, then, I think, remained to the end a litmus test of the grit in his bones. It helped keep him at the top of his game. There had been security in her strength and a sense of worth in being able to take care of her. Now there was a vast void of love and reliance and responsibility. And he was closer now, with both parents gone, to running out of his own seasons.

1977-1985

"...There were times,
    I'm sure you knew,
When I bit off more
    than I could chew.
But through it all,
    when there was doubt,
I ate it up,
    and spit it out.
The record shows
    I took the blows,
And did it my way..."

September Of My Years

After Dolly died, Dad's spirit, though severely wounded, continued to move him along. Inspired by the continuity of life he saw and felt through his granddaughters, he took on a schedule that might have crushed a much younger man. His work, prolific and of great quality, continued at a hectic pace: Films, recordings, concerts, television specials, campaigning, producing, aiding his favorite charities and family life left little room for hobbies or rest. He seemed more driven than ever. His name was on marquees, book jackets, records, the lips of senators, presidents and princes and buildings and hospital wings. Although it was not the kind of immortality he was seeking, it was indeed immortality.

On December 12, 1985, Frank Sinatra celebrated his 70th birthday. It had been a long and bumpy road. Along the way he had won some and lost some, cried some and laughed some. It had been a wild ride so far. At the age when most people retire, Frank Sinatra was kicking ass, from one end of the world to the other. The proudest moment came when he received the highest honor of his life, the highest honor his country can bestow to a civilian: The Medal of Freedom.

His style during his personal hours may have been changing. He was calming down. But the style onstage still had enormous impact. And the response had its impact on Sinatra.

Easter 1977 at the Palm Springs house.

JANUARY 12, 1977: My grandmother's funeral was a requiem High Mass at St. Louis's Catholic Church in Cathedral City. Danny Thomas, Dean Martin and Jilly Rizzo served as pallbearers. His friends and family offered the only comfort my father could find in those dark days.

JANUARY 1977: Dad began a new life. I had trouble coming to grips with the fact that his expressive love for my mother had not led to their remarriage. Finally, I resolved that his affection for her was genuine and would continue forever, yet it took time to understand its depths and limits. But what made things more difficult was that shortly after my grandmother's death, Barbara requested that Dad get his marriage to my mother annulled so they could marry in a Catholic ceremony. I found the concept of annulment shocking, and my brother, sister and I were concerned about how it would affect our mother.

JANUARY 24-30, 1977: Still in mourning for his mother, Dad canceled two weeks of scheduled appearances and recording sessions. During the last week of January, however, he performed at the Sunrise Musical Theater in Fort Lauderdale before flying to Barbados on the 31st to spend a few days with his old friend Claudette Colbert.

FEBRUARY 1977: Returning to New York, he was at Media Sound with Charles Calello, recording "Everybody Ought to Be in Love," among other songs.

FEBRUARY 28-MARCH 5, 1977: Dad went to London to give a series of concerts on behalf of the National Society for the Prevention of Cruelty to Children. Two princesses were in his audiences: Margaret and Anne, Queen Elizabeth II's sister and daughter, respectively. Frank Sinatra's popularity in London was so great that a group of British fans started a movement to change the name of the Royal Albert Hall, where he performed, to the Francis Albert Hall.

MARCH 7, 1977: He flew on to Amsterdam for a performance at the Concertgebouw before returning to Palm Springs for a rest.

MARCH 9, 14, 1977: With Nelson Riddle, he recorded five songs for a planned album that was never released: "Emily," "Linda," "Sweet Lorraine," "Barbara" and "Nancy."

MARCH 17-31, 1977: A week at Caesars was followed by a week at Harrah's.

APRIL 1, 1977: FS hosted and performed at a benefit for the Friends of the Eisenhower Medical Center at the Gene Autry Hotel in Palm Springs.

APRIL 6, 1977: He taped a portion of the television special *Frank Sinatra and Friends* at NBC studios in Burbank.

APRIL 7, 1977: He sang the National Anthem at Dodger Stadium, then went back to NBC to finish taping *Frank Sinatra and Friends,* which aired later in the year.

APRIL 12-MAY 23, 1977: After a week at home, Dad went on the road with a series of appearances in small venues: the Circle Star Theater in San Carlos, California, the Latin Casino in Cherry Hill, New Jersey, and a week with Dean Martin at the Westchester Premier Theater in Tarrytown, New York.

APRIL 15, 1977: In San Francisco, FS threw out the first ball at Candlestick Park during the Giants-Dodgers game.

APRIL 27, 1977: A benefit at Carnegie Hall for the Institute of Sports Medicine and Athletic Trauma.

APRIL 29-MAY 8, 1977: FS performed again at the Latin Casino.

MAY 17-29, 1977: He performed at the Westchester Premier Theater.

MAY 23, 1977: FS and Dean Martin were onstage at the Terrace Theater in New York City for the New York State Lottery drawing.

MAY 24, 1977: Along with Muhammad Ali, FS appeared as a guest of entertainment columnist Suzy Knickerbocker in a television special entitled *Suzy Visits*.

MAY 31-JUNE 10, 1977: Continuing his short tour with Dean, Dad returned to the Latin Casino, then went on to the Saber Room in Hickory Hills, Illinois.

JUNE 21, 1977: In New York, Frank began shooting his first made-for-television movie, the three-hour *Contract on Cherry Street*. He starred as a New York City police officer.

JULY 4, 1977: Dad was honored with the Freedom Medal at Independence Hall in Philadelphia.

JULY 13-14, 1977: For a 24-hour period, a blackout hit all of New York City. FS was on the 38th floor of the Waldorf Towers. He took the stairs all the way down to the street for location filming of *Contract on Cherry Street*, then walked back up eight flights to the NBC studios for rehearsals, and back down again. Upon his arrival on the set, the cast and crew gave him a standing ovation.

JULY 15-16, 1977: FS headlined a show with Milton Berle at Forest Hills Tennis Stadium.

AUGUST 16-17, 1977: Frank and Milton took their show to the Alpine Valley Music Theater, Wisconsin.

AUGUST 25-31, 1977: After a benefit performance at the Aladdin Hotel for the University of Nevada, Las Vegas, FS opened for a week's run at Caesars Palace.

SEPTEMBER 4, 1977: Dad sang four songs on the Jerry Lewis Muscular Dystrophy Telethon.

SEPTEMBER 30, 1977: He taped comedy spots for *Rowan and Martin's Laugh-In*.

Frank's 40th anniversary in show business was a very big birthday party at Caesars Palace in Las Vegas.

At the Caesars celebration, FS clowns with Dean, Milton Berle and Rich Little.

OCTOBER 1, 1977: FS and John Denver performed in Los Angeles at the Beverly Hilton for a benefit honoring Jane Levintraub as Mother of the Year.

OCTOBER 4, 1977: At Dodger Stadium, Dad threw out the first ball at a Dodgers-Phillies playoff game. Later that evening he presented the March of Dimes Award to George Burns during the Jack Benny Memorial Dinner at the Beverly Hilton Hotel.

OCTOBER 14-16, 1977: He attended three games of the World Series at Dodger Stadium. Arriving for dinner at Patsy's Restaurant in New York after a losing game, Frank was informed—cautiously—that the upstairs dining room was packed solid with Yankees, celebrating their victory over the Dodgers. FS said, "Good. Tell them the British are coming." He encountered Bucky Dent, who stood speechless. "Kid, you cost me a lot of money," Dad said, "but you played a great game." To Lou Piniella: "You're Barbara's favorite. She says you're cute." To Mickey Rivers: "Man, you have got to be the kookiest cat in the outfield." To Billy Martin: "You did a great job in managing these monkeys to victory." Joseph Scognamillo, the restaurant's proprietor, wrote: "Nancy, we all know your father's a winner. But he's also a good loser. He treated the whole Yankee team to dinner."

OCTOBER 21-NOVEMBER 16, 1977: Another week at Harrah's in Lake Tahoe, followed by a few days off. During a two-week run in Las Vegas, he commuted to L.A. to present the Hebrew University Scopus Award to John Wayne at the Century Plaza Hotel. Back in Las Vegas, he was "honored" in a Dean Martin roast taped at the MGM Grand. He returned to Burbank to host the *Tonight Show* for one night.

NOVEMBER 2, 1977: A memorial dinner for Dolly Sinatra to benefit Villa Scalabrini was held at Las Vegas's Stardust Hotel, and hosted by Robert Conrad.

NOVEMBER 19, 1977: *Contract on Cherry Street* aired on NBC. Critic Leonard Maltin wrote: "Sinatra's first TV movie has him well cast as an NYC police officer who takes on organized crime in his own fashion after his partner is gunned down. Aces to this fine thriller."

NOVEMBER 20-21, 1977: Filling in for Paul Anka, FS performed at Caesars Palace.

DECEMBER 2, 1977: In Washington, D.C., he gave a benefit performance on behalf of his old friend Hubert Humphrey.

DECEMBER 5-10, 1977: Back for another gig at Caesars, then home to Palm Springs to celebrate his 62nd birthday.

JANUARY 12-18, 1978: Another week at Caesars.

JANUARY 15, 1978: Frank appeared on Gene Kelly's TV special, taped at the Ambassador Auditorium in Pasadena, California.

JANUARY 23, 1978: Dad performed at a fundraiser for L.A. County Sheriff Peter Pitchess at the Century Plaza Hotel in Los Angeles.

FEBRUARY 1-8, 1978: Frank returned to Caesars for another week.

MARCH 2-8, 1978: Back for yet another week at Caesars.

MARCH 10, 1978: He attended a birthday party for Walter Annenberg in Palm Springs.

MARCH 13-14, 1978: Dad opened at the Sunrise Musical Theater in Fort Lauderdale. After two nights a sore throat forced him to postpone the rest of his one-week engagement. He also had to cancel his appearance at a benefit honoring Nelson Riddle that had been scheduled for March 18 at the Century Plaza Hotel in L.A.

MARCH 20-28, 1978: He vacationed in Barbados.

APRIL 2, 1978: He appeared in Manhattan at a benefit honoring New York Governor Hugh Carey, then flew to Israel.

Tina Sinatra

ON THE TRIP TO ISRAEL:

It was called the "Sinatra Caravan" and it was the first of the so-called Hollywood junkets to Israel. We left on the night of the Academy Awards, which is why Gregory Peck (who joined us later) and Johnny Carson did not go with us. Joanna Carson, Ed McMahon's wife Victoria, Totie Fields, who was in a wheelchair; about 100 people were on that airplane. We stayed at the Jerusalem Hilton. There was heavy security which made sightseeing impossible. Our itinerary was very rigid and would only change in the event of military activity. Because of bombings, a backfire would make us want to dive under a table.

Men didn't wear coats except for security guys, because guns could be hidden under coats. Dad didn't go out very often; it was too risky. He was too good a target.

They never told us where we were going. We broke into small groups and traveled in cars through desolate yet beautiful terrain. One day we went to an air base where we saw the nuts and bolts of war. Emotion was building. The Phantom jets flew directly over our heads at a low altitude. The aerobatics shook our guts.

It was a war of the elders, not of the young. It felt old. It felt unfair to the youth of Israel. The planes may have seemed sophisticated and state-of-the-art, but the pilots were young and frightened. They were babies whose one wish was to return to the place where they learned how to fly, the Arizona desert in the United States. The one place they did not want to be was where they were; they were discontented and scared and did not mince words about it either.

Dad asked me to fly back to Jerusalem with him in the Chinook helicopter. During the 20-minute trip, the young pilot turned to us and said, "We're flying over Bethlehem." I looked down at the place I'd heard about all my life and I thought about the baby born there that Christmas night so long ago, and I remembered the young jet pilots, babies themselves, freshly scrubbed and beautiful—and how unfair the whole idea of war was—and I started to cry. I snapped. I broke. Dad said, "Are you all right?" I looked at him with no words and said, "I don't know. I'm overwhelmed." He said, "This place'll do that to ya." Later, when I was able to speak and tell him how I felt, he said, "It's not easy seeing babies fight. Babies are always the ones who fight—and the ones to die."

APRIL 9, 1978: In Jerusalem, he dedicated the Frank Sinatra International Student Center at the Hebrew University on Mount Scopus. He also visited the Youth House he built in Nazareth, met with Prime Minister Menachem Begin and spent time with his dear friend Teddy Kollek, mayor of Jerusalem.

APRIL 13-16, 1978: He completed his postponed engagement at the Sunrise Musical Theater in Fort Lauderdale.

APRIL 25-30, 1978: He played a week at the Circle Star Theater in San Carlos, California.

MAY 3-16, 1978: One week each at Caesars Palace in Las Vegas and Harrah's in Lake Tahoe.

Israeli Prime Minister Menachem Begin welcomes American emissaries Frank Sinatra and Gregory Peck.

MAY 20, 1978: With Dean and Sammy, he headlined the SHARE Boomtown Party at the Santa Monica Civic Auditorium. SHARE stands for Share Happily and Reap Endlessly. The SHARE Girls—Janet Leigh, Ruth Berle, Gloria Cahn, Jeannie Martin, Miriam Nelson and so many more—put on a great show every year on behalf of emotionally challenged children. The highlight of each show was when the SHARE Girls did a Busby Berkeley/Rockettes finale. SHARE parties are still held today.

MAY 23-29, 1978: A performance at the Latin Casino in Cherry Hill, New Jersey.

JUNE 15-25, 1978: Another midwestern road tour took him on a series of one-nighters in Cleveland, Kalamazoo, Cincinnati, Washington, D.C., Huntington (West Virginia) and Terre Haute.

Pat Henry

ON WORKING WITH SINATRA:

I worked for a while as Frank Sinatra's opening act. You never know what's going to happen when you're with Frank. One day he came to New York, called me and said, "Pat, have you got a passport?" I said, "Why?" He said, "In case we ever go to England. We may do something over there." I said, "Yeah, I got one." He said, "Well, come with me to Marino's. I'm having dinner with Kirk Kerkorian and the guys. Bring your passport. Let me see it." Like an idiot, I go. I have $37 and a passport and I'm sitting there having dinner and Frank said, "We're gonna go see Kirk's new plane; he's got a DC-9 and we're gonna go out to LaGuardia and look at it." So I said, "Good." We go out and he said, "We're gonna give it a test run." I said, "Wonderful." We get on the plane, we're giving it a test run, and soon it's two hours later. I asked, "How long are we gonna test this plane?" Frank says, "Oh, I forgot to tell you—we're going to England." I said, "Are you crazy? I only got one suit to my name, what I'm wearing. That's all I've got." "So," he said, "we won't go to the same place twice."

JUNE 28, 1978: He attended the wedding of Princess Grace and Rainier's daughter Caroline in Monaco.

JUNE 30-JULY 7, 1978: FS vacationed with friends on the East Coast aboard the yacht *Blackhawk*.

JULY 24-26, 1978: A short gig at Harrah's in Reno.

JULY 31-AUGUST 10, 1978: Sarah Vaughan and Frank co-headlined at L.A.'s Universal Amphitheater.

AUGUST 27-SEPTEMBER 6, 1978: A series of one-nighters in the Northeast: the New York State Fair in Syracuse, the Saratoga Performing Arts Center in Saratoga Springs, the Pine Knob Theater in Clarkston, Michigan, and the Garden State Arts Center in Holmdel, New Jersey.

SEPTEMBER 11-16, 1978: After a brief break, he was back on the road, this time in London for an engagement at the Royal Festival Hall.

OCTOBER 13, 1978: FS, Pat Henry and the 5th Dimension performed at the World Mercy Fund benefit at the Waldorf.

OCTOBER 14-22, 1978: Back to New York for a week at Radio City Music Hall.

OCTOBER 26-31, 1978: A series of one-nighters at the Civic Center in Providence, Rhode Island, Ohio's University of Toledo, Atlantic City's Medical Center and, finally, Chicago Stadium.

NOVEMBER 9, 1978: He performed at a tribute to boxing great Joe Louis at Caesars Palace.

NOVEMBER 10-14, 1978: Dad was back at Caesars Palace for a six-day run, but exhaustion forced him to cancel the final night.

DECEMBER 29, 1978-JANUARY 7, 1979: Dad worked through the New Year's holiday at the Sunrise Musical Theater in Fort Lauderdale. Then he and Barbara flew to Barbados for a brief vacation.

FEBRUARY 13-18, 1979: Six nights at Chicago's Arie Crown Theater.

MARCH 5-11, 1979: His next engagement: Philadelphia's Valley Forge Musical Theater.

MARCH 15-21, 1979: He returned for a week at Caesars in Las Vegas.

My father raised money for the Atlantic City Medical Center and, in gratitude, they named a wing for him.

My dad is lovingly giving his old friend, boxer Joe Louis, a shot in the bread-basket. They were helping out on the Jerry Lewis telethon.

To Frank Sinatra, a great performer— from a fan, Jimmy Carter 5-79

On the occasion of Frank's 40th year in show business, President Carter wrote: "…The sound of your voice has long been a part of my life…When we recall the great events of our times or the important moments of our individual lives, it is always with the accompaniment of a song—sung your way."

APRIL 12-15, 20-21, 1979: He performed for six nights at Resorts International in Atlantic City.

MAY 3-6, 1979: Dad performed for four nights at the Circle Star Theater in San Carlos.

MAY 10-16, 1979: Back to Las Vegas for a week at Caesars Palace.

MAY 30, 1979: A benefit show for the University of Nevada in Las Vegas at the Aladdin Hotel.

MAY 31-JUNE 6, 1979: Another week at Caesars.

JUNE 9, 1979: Frank performed in Denver at a benefit for the Juvenile Diabetes Foundation.

JUNE 11-17, 1979: Back at the Universal Amphitheater in Los Angeles.

JUNE 13, 1979: The Italian Consul General presented FS with the Cavaliere Officiale, the highest award from the Italian government.

JUNE 22-JULY 3, 1979: One-nighters in upstate New York, Long Island, New Jersey and Michigan.

JULY 16-18, 1979: Three sessions in the studio. The only songs released from these dates, "I Had the Craziest Dream" and "It Had to Be You," were destined for the album *Trilogy*.

AUGUST 20-22, 1979: At Columbia studios in New York City for three recording sessions for the *Trilogy* collection, Record 2—*The Present*. The songs recorded: "You and Me," "Summer Me, Winter Me," "Love Me Tender," "Just the Way You Are" and a duet with opera singer Eileen Farrell, "For the Good Times." From the liner notes, beautifully written by David McClintick: "In a cavernous CBS studio on East 30th Street, Sinatra is going about the risky business of recording songs that other performers, with styles completely different from his, have made famous. Framed by sound partitions, he stands behind a microphone and music stand facing Don Costa, who is perched on a podium surrounded by 50 musicians. 'Ready, Frank?' asks Sonny Burke from behind a cloud of cigarette smoke in the control room. 'I've been ready since I was 12.'"

SEPTEMBER 3-9, 1979: More shows at Atlantic City's Resorts International.

SEPTEMBER 17-19, 1979: More recording sessions for the *Trilogy* collection, this time at Western Recorders in L.A. The songs: "The Song Is You," "But Not for Me," "Street of Dreams," "More Than You Know," "New York, New York" and "My Shining Hour." McClintick: "Outside the recording studio on Sunset

FS with the *Trilogy* arrangers: Billy May, Don Costa and Gordon Jenkins.

Boulevard the temperature hovers just under 90 degrees. Brush and forest fires are sprinkling soot on this seedy and vaguely menacing stretch of Hollywood from a sky that has turned from beige to rust to black as the sun has set. It is a Nathanael West sort of evening, and thus is a perfect foil for the magical contrast one finds inside the studio. For inside, it is unmistakably a Mabel Mercer sort of evening. Frank Sinatra, Billy May, a twelve-voice choir and a 55-piece orchestra are making a record of 'My Shining Hour,' an extraordinary song composed for the Fred Astaire film *The Sky's the Limit* in 1948. 'I can't believe we never got to this one—I've been wanting to do it for 35 years,' says Sinatra. On these sooty September evenings Sinatra is rerecording several renditions that he and May had completed two months earlier and that seemed perfectly acceptable then. But after listening repeatedly to cassettes of the July recordings, Sinatra decided he could do better. He changed a few keys, slowed a few tempos and generally gained further internal command of the songs."

SEPTEMBER 24-27, 1979: Frank and Barbara dined with President and Mrs. Anwar Sadat in Cairo, where Dad played "the biggest room I've ever played" at the foot of the great pyramids in Giza. After the event, held on behalf of the Faith and Hope Rehabilitation Center, a charity favored by Mrs. Sadat, President Sadat sent Dad a telegram calling his performance an "unforgettable experience. The money you raised [more than half a million dollars] is already working to help the orphans at Wafa Wa Amal Hospital in the desert...Wafa Wa Amal means Faith and Hope. You are both."

OCTOBER 6, 1979: FS received the Humanitarian Award at a Columbus Day dinner at the Waldorf-Astoria. Also this year he received the Pied Piper Award from ASCAP; the Trustees Award from NARAS; the International Man of the Year Award, presented by former President Gerald Ford; and the Grand Ufficiale Dell'Ordine Al Merito Della Repubblica Italiana, Italy.

The Chairman of the Board and one of the Seven Wonders of the World. It's right that they should have found each other.

Robert Merrill

ON SINATRA'S FAME:

You go through a stage door and out into a crowd with Frank and you can feel a certain tension. Frank has said to me, "God, I'd love to walk on the Via Veneto, just walk. Or Fifth Avenue. Or the Champs-Elysées." But he can't. After an event he needs people with him; he needs guards. My wife, Marion, and I left Carnegie Hall with him after a concert and there were hundreds of people waiting. And, as we left, this crowd—I don't know how to say it—it was like a rainstorm, like a dark cloud. It gathered and practically attacked us. There was a limousine waiting and Frank was behind us. He put his arms around Marion. He was concerned that she was going to get hurt. And he shoved us—actually, physically—into the car. We'd have been hurt. They mean well, but there's this tremendous adulation. People love him so, they forget he's a human being. And this is because he's a storyteller and a very compassionate man. He's sensitive—so automatically he's sensitive to words, to the story that they tell. What you are comes out in your music.

I remember being backstage at the Met before he performed a concert. He had a lot of press there and he handled everyone beautifully. Then one girl from a local station put a microphone in front of his face. She said, "Mr. Sinatra"—he was very nice to her, very pleasant—"What are you doing at the Metropolitan? What could you do at the Metropolitan?" Now, I held Francis's hand, you know. I sort of wanted to hold him back, but he was very pleasant. "Well," he said, "I do a little singing and I dance and I do comedy and I juggle." And she said, "Come on, now! Do you belong in the Metropolitan?" She was insulting him, hurting him, trying to get something controversial. She was trying to pick a fight. But he was very nice. Very controlled. But I wasn't. I got angry! I grabbed the mike, and her, and shoved her off.

Thirty-five years after he caused the Columbus Day Riots, Frank Sinatra marches, along with Governor Hugh Carey, in New York's parade.

OCTOBER 8, 1979: He served as Grand Marshal of the Columbus Day Parade in New York City.

OCTOBER 12, 1979: He co-starred with Flip Wilson, Natalie Cole and Robert Merrill in a benefit performance at the Waldorf-Astoria for the World Mercy Fund, which was founded by Bishop Murray in Africa in 1969. FS received the Primum Viveré (Life First) Award from World Mercy. The award is given to men or women in various fields who have excelled in their chosen profession and who have supported humanitarian causes, especially in the Third World. Engraved on the award are the words, "The Greatest Good You Can Do for Another Is Not Just to Share with Him Your Riches But to Reveal to Him His Own."

OCTOBER 13-27, 1979: Another short concert tour to New Haven, Providence, Portland (Maine), Montreal, Buffalo and Binghamton, then back to Resorts International in Atlantic City.

OCTOBER 28, 1979: Dad starred in "Sinatra at the Met," a white-tie benefit performance with Robert Merrill and Beverly Sills at New York's Metropolitan Opera House that raised $1.1 million for the Memorial Sloan-Kettering Cancer Center, an institution he had supported for years. It seemed as though almost all of Dad's concerts in these years were benefits for some charity or other, usually related to medicine or social service organizations.

NOVEMBER 2, 1979: FS and Dean Martin went on the campaign trail for Ronald Reagan at a benefit in Boston. Although he'd been a fundraiser for both Nixon and Ford, it was the first time he'd actually stumped this hard for a candidate and friend since John F. Kennedy in 1960. All told, his efforts would yield about $500,000 to the campaign's coffers.

NOVEMBER 8-14, 1979: Another week at Caesars Palace.

NOVEMBER 19-25, 1979: He was back at Resorts International in Atlantic City. During this engagement he had a reunion with some of the guys from the Rustic Cabin days.

Irwin "Ruby" Rubinstein and Leo Durocher—two of the older men my father relied on for advice, fun and friendship—at Ruby's Dunes restaurant on Palm Canyon Drive in the heart of Palm Springs.

NOVEMBER 1979: Dad's dear friend Irwin Rubinstein—Uncle Ruby of Ruby's Dunes restaurant in Palm Springs—died. My brother recalled: "It was Thanksgiving weekend. Pop called the cemetery and the guy in charge said, 'My gravediggers are off until next Tuesday.' And my father said to this man, 'You never buried somebody who was Jewish? You have no knowledge of the fact that tradition dictates that when a man dies, he's buried by sunset on the day after his death? You're not familiar with this tradition that goes back to the time of Abraham? You're going to break this tradition? I will pay the extra wages—overtime, double hours, triple, golden hours, platinum hours, whatever you want to call it.' Well, the guy that ran the cemetery didn't budge. My old man got off the phone and said, 'I'm going to go over there and punch that son of a bitch right in his nose, and if he's too old, I'll punch his son in the nose!' He said the last jokingly. But I said, 'Pop, let's cool off.' He said, 'The man was like a father to me.' Ruby was. He said, 'Here's a tradition that's gone on now for 4,300 years, and this guy wants to quote me holiday regulations all of a sudden.' And he couldn't believe it, you know—it bugged him so much. The principle of the thing. In the eulogy Pop delivered, he called Ruby 'a warm feast in a cold forest.'"

DECEMBER 12, 1979: Dad celebrated 40 years in show business on his 64th birthday with a huge celebration at Caesars Palace in Las Vegas. The event was a sellout that drew some of his oldest and dearest friends. It was taped for a two-hour TV special on NBC. Among the 1,000 people in attendance were Cary Grant, Lucille Ball, Glenn Ford, Orson Welles, Don Rickles, Milton Berle and Dean Martin, as well as Egyptian and Israeli diplomats who read telegrams of congratulations from Anwar Sadat and Menachem Begin.

Cary Grant

ON SINATRA:

Frank is a unique man. Utterly without hypocrisy. Bluntly yet loyally opinionated. Unaffected and, to me, uncomplex despite everything written. It's almost frightening to some, to be faced with honesty. Frank fascinates the curious: the writers who try to analyze an enigma that is not an enigma; perhaps hoping to discover those qualities responsible for the man's personal appeal. Well, I think I know the quality. It's truth. Simple truth. Without artifice. I remember reading somewhere that in a world of lies a truth seems like a lie. I've read more nonsense about Frank Sinatra than about possibly anyone else in our time.

Frank Sinatra, Cary and Barbara Grant.

A.J. comforting her sister Amanda at Christmastime.

DECEMBER 17-18, 1979: More recordings for the *Trilogy* collection, Record 3—*The Future: Reflections on the Future in Three Tenses.* This suite was composed, arranged and conducted by Gordon Jenkins with a 154-piece Philharmonic Symphony Orchestra and mixed chorus. McClintick again: "It is difficult to conceive of a more daunting assignment for a composer than being asked to write a suite of music about the future. There can be no question, however, that *Future* includes the most stirring and imaginative music and lyrics that Gordon Jenkins has ever written. It explores not only dreams like world peace and space travel but also some of Sinatra's most private musings about his own future and, implicitly, about his past." During the 1979 Christmas season in Palm Springs, my family heard the rough tapes of *Trilogy.* Four-year-old A.J. and not-quite-three-year-old Amanda snuggled with their "Pop-Pop." Frankie and Tina and I paced the floor of the Great Hall, our projection/game room. We laughed and cried and shared this unequaled gift of talent and music. It was an evening that lingers. Though each record stands on its own, the way to listen to *Trilogy* is all at once in one sitting.

JANUARY 1, 1980: FS was Grand Marshal of the Tournament of Roses Parade in Pasadena. Also this year, he was the first member of the Simon Wiesenthal Center Fellows Society; he received the Johnny Mercer Award from the Songwriters Hall of Fame; he narrated a documentary film for the World Mercy Fund in West Africa; and he became national campaign chairman for the National Multiple Sclerosis Society, a position he held for three years.

JANUARY 3-9, 1980: He kicked off the year at Caesars Palace in Las Vegas.

JANUARY 22-25, 1980: He performed at the Rio Palace in Rio de Janeiro, Brazil, for four shows. When he went to do the concert in Rio, he encountered a reaction like nothing he had ever seen—not at the Paramount, not with Dorsey, nor the television specials, nor in Vegas. This was its own special encounter.

JANUARY 26, 1980: The then-largest paying audience ever assembled for a solo performer—180,000 people—gathered at Maracaña Stadium in Rio de Janeiro to hear Frank Sinatra sing. (The feat was listed in *The Guinness Book of World Records.*)

FEBRUARY 2, 1980: The University of Santa Clara in Northern California established a $250,000 trust fund for a proposed Frank Sinatra Chair in Music and Theater Arts. It was "one of the nicest things that ever happened to me in my show business career," my father said at a benefit concert in Santa Clara. He said he had performed "in some places that didn't even give me a chair to sit on."

FEBRUARY 3, 1980: Dad shared the stage with Dean Martin at L.A.'s Shrine Auditorium in another fund-raiser for Ronald Reagan.

FEBRUARY 15, 1980: A benefit for the Desert Hospital at the Canyon Country Club and Hotel in Palm Springs.

MARCH 10, 1980: After a three-year absence from the screen, Dad started shooting *The First Deadly Sin*, based on the Lawrence Sanders best-seller.

Frank

ON THE CONCERT IN RIO:

I had never been to Rio. My records had been popular there for years, going back to when FDR was President, when they received our broadcasts. I had been all over the world, but for some reason, never to Brazil.

You know, there was an expression they used down there. When a young man was courting a woman, and things would get pretty far along, and the girl would put on the heat about doing something with marriage, the young man would stall her with, "When Frank Sinatra comes to Brazil..."

Well, when we did get there, a lot of weddings and babies date from about that time.

The day of the concert, it was raining. I kept looking out the window all day, wondering whether it would let up. But it kept on coming down. Not a light rain; a real downpour. And, do you know, the people started taking their seats at eight o'clock in the morning and they kept coming in, sitting there all day in the rain.

When we got to the stadium at night for the concert, it was still raining—and I have never seen a place as big as Maracaña. It was a soccer stadium, of course, and there were 175,000 people in it. It was immense. They had a huge center stage with six wings, all miked, and while I sang, I had to keep running from one wing to another to each

mike, until I was out of breath. But before that, there was a long walk to the stage and when I got there, and picked up the first mike, the rain stopped. At that instant.

Everybody gasped.

I looked up to the sky, toward heaven, and I said, "Thank You." They dissolved. Brazilians are a religious people, you know...

The concert went well and I was in the midst of singing a song I know as well as my hand when I lost the lyric. Just blew it. Nothing. I had been singing "Strangers in the Night" and when I stopped and couldn't remember how it went, the whole stadium started to sing it for me—in English.

I was touched...

Near the end of the program, I heard a pounding noise and turned around and there was this mountain of a guy, running at me. I thought, Okay, this is it. But he ran up to me and kissed me (on the cheek) and then ran off.

I learned later that in Brazil they have this guy who's called the Kissing Bandit or something like that and he kisses everybody, had kissed the Pope's shoe, and so on...

And then, when I finished the last song, did the encore, I put the mike down. And the rain started again.

The immense soccer stadium in Rio, Maracaña, was the setting for a special experience—a gift from the heavens, a lyric sung by the crowd and a kiss by a bandit.

The cover of *Trilogy*, designed by the legendary Saul Bass.

MARCH 26, 1980: Frank Sinatra released his *Trilogy* collection. Produced by Sonny Burke and engineered by Lee Herschberg, this was his first studio release since 1973. The album cover was designed by Saul Bass. From David McClintick's introduction entitled "Odyssey to Trilogy": "Twenty years into the rock era, Sinatra felt more intimidated than ever by the increasingly complex musical marketplace. He was gripped by doubts about what to record and about the nature of the contemporary audience for his records…It was a struggle that only superior artists endure." *Trilogy* went to Number One and garnered six Grammy nominations.

MARCH 28-30 AND APRIL 13-15, 1980: In Atlantic City, he performed nine shows over a six-day period at Resorts International.

APRIL 1980: Pete Hamill wrote a long article about my father for *New York* magazine. Hamill made one of the most astute observations I can remember about the tiresome lie of my father's "relationship" with the Mob: "He is the most investigated American performer since John Wilkes Booth, and although he has never been indicted or convicted of any Mob-connected crime, the connection is part of the legend." Several years earlier, late one winter night, after dropping off a date, Frank was in his limousine with Hamill, who described the ride: "'You have to go home?' Frank asked. I said no. And so for more than an hour, on this rainy night in New York, we drove around the empty streets. 'It's sure changed, this town,' he said…'Ah, well,' I said. 'Babe Ruth doesn't play for the Yankees anymore.' 'And the Paramount's an office building,' he said. 'Stop. I'm gonna cry.' I said."

Frank went on, "'You like people and they die on you. I go to too many goddamn funerals these days. And women,' he said, exhaling and chuckling again. 'I don't know what the hell to make of them, do you?' 'Every day I know less,' I said. 'Maybe that's what it's all about,' he said. 'Maybe all that happens is you get older and you know less.'"

APRIL 24, 1980: At the Century Plaza Hotel in Los Angeles, Variety Clubs International presented Frank Sinatra with the Humanitarian Award. He received it from Henry Kissinger.

MAY 23-26, 1980: After wrapping the location shoot for *The First Deadly Sin* in New York, he returned for four more nights at Resorts International in Atlantic City.

JUNE 13-26, 1980: Frank played two solid weeks at Carnegie Hall. Tickets for the entire engagement sold out in one day, breaking all previous sales records in the landmark theater's 90-year history.

JULY 3-8, 1980: Sergio Mendes and Brazil '88 joined Frank onstage at the Universal Amphitheater in Los Angeles.

JULY 11, 1980: Frank appeared at a Los Angeles fund-raiser for the St. Jude's Children's Research Center. The charity collected $2 million, and Frank received a St. Jude's plaque inscribed with the words: "To the legend and the man."

Secretary of State Henry Kissinger appreciated Frank's reaction to a misguided reporter.

The Sinatras at the Sporting Club in Monte Carlo for a Red Cross Gala.

JULY 16, 1980: Dad attended the Republican Convention in Detroit, where Ronald Reagan received the nomination.

JULY 24-30, 1980: Back at Caesars Palace in Las Vegas.

AUGUST 8, 1980: He did a Red Cross benefit in Monaco for his old friend Princess Grace.

AUGUST 24-31, 1980: During his engagement at Resorts International in Atlantic City, Dad took the time to join Jerry Lewis on his Labor Day Telethon for Muscular Dystrophy.

SEPTEMBER 8-20, 1980: Frank returned to London for memorable concerts at the Royal Festival and Royal Albert Halls. Critic Derek Jewell of the Sunday *Times* wrote: "Sinatra has become the keeper of the flame for everyone from 40 to 80. His songs distill the youth, the nostalgia of millions. He also happens to be the best at it: an artist of colossal stature. He shapes songs like no one else. That's genius."

SEPTEMBER 30, 1980: In a pre-election tribute to Ronald Reagan and George Bush, Dad and Dean sang to a gathering of more than 1,000 people at the Waldorf-Astoria in New York. Among the guests was artist Andy Warhol, who admitted he was only a Sinatra fan, not a Republican.

OCTOBER 3-8, 1980: Another string of shows at Caesars.

OCTOBER 22, 1980: He made a campaign appearance for Ronald Reagan in Syracuse, New York.

OCTOBER 23, 1980: *The First Deadly Sin* premiered at Loew's State Theater in Times Square. The screening was a benefit for the Mother Cabrini Medical Center. Directed by Brian G. Hutton with music by Gordon Jenkins, the film co-starred Faye Dunaway, David Dukes, Brenda Vaccaro, Martin Gabel and James Whitmore. My father was so excited about this one. He had been away from making feature films for 10 years and hadn't had a good role since *The Detective* in 1968.

From the stage in London, Frank greets close friend Claudette Colbert, who wrote: "Frank has had a very special corner of my heart for a long time."

NOVEMBER 11, 1980: He did a benefit at the Aladdin Hotel in Las Vegas for the University of Nevada.

NOVEMBER 14, 1980: Benefit in Las Vegas for the St. Jude's Ranch.

Take Me Out to the Ball Game

There still were flashes of the old days—like the baseball game in Atlantic City at three o'clock in the morning between players in sweatshirts reading "Ol' Blue Eyes" (Dad's team) and "Ol' Red Eyes" (Dean's team). "The game was called," said Dean, "on account of light."

65th Birthday Party Hoedown: Above, FS clowns with Johnny Carson. Right: He cuts the cake with the family by his side.

DECEMBER 8-10, 1980: FS filled in for an ailing Liza Minnelli at the Riviera Hotel in Las Vegas.

DECEMBER 12, 1980: Barbara surprised Frank with a 65th birthday party—a country-western barbecue for 250 friends—at her stables in Rancho Mirage.

DECEMBER 27, 1980-JANUARY 1, 1981: FS celebrated New Year's Eve with his audience at Resorts International in Atlantic City.

JANUARY 10, 1981: He performed at Radio City Music Hall for the benefit of the Memorial Sloan-Kettering Cancer Center. He continued doing these concerts for five years, raising enough money for a new wing, which was named for him.

JANUARY 19, 1981: Confirming his switch to the Republican Party, though still a registered Democrat, Frank Sinatra produced the Inaugural Gala for President-elect Ronald Reagan at the Capitol Center in Landover, Maryland. My father invited the Washington-area families of the Iran hostages to the rehearsal. The hostages were released on January 20. The Gala was a tremendous success. In a letter dated January 23, President Reagan wrote, "...I still feel the magic of the 'Gala.' And it truly was magic. For a time Nancy and I both thought maybe we were the only ones who felt the spell. We know now it was felt by everyone. We can never thank you enough for all that you did. This certainly wasn't just another benefit. It was produced, and masterfully so. Every minute was sheer magic and that was due to you." Later, Frank was appointed to The President's Committee on the Arts and Humanities.

JANUARY 21, 1981: Frank and Barbara were the guests of honor at a White House reception hosted by the Reagans.

JANUARY 29-FEBRUARY 4, 1981: Back at Caesars Palace in Las Vegas.

JANUARY 30, 1981: Tina married businessman Richard Cohen at my mother's Beverly Hills home. A.J. and Amanda were flower girls. Later in New York, they repeated their vows at Dad's apartment in a second wedding.

January 19, 1981: President Reagan's Inaugural Gala at the Capitol Center in Maryland.

FEBRUARY 5, 1981: Dad returned to Washington, D.C., for President Reagan's 70th birthday celebration at the White House.

FEBRUARY 12-18, 1981: Back onstage for another week at Caesars Palace.

FEBRUARY 19, 1981: Nearly 20 years after turning in his Nevada gaming license, Dad won it back, but not without some unpleasant scrutiny related, once again, to the Mob connection charges. Some members of the press made a big deal out of a charge—never substantiated—that Dad had been involved in skimming revenues from a Westchester, New York, theater in 1976. Lawyer Mickey Rudin: "The Westchester case is another unfortunate incident. When the theater first opened, I made no arrangements for your father to play there because it was an untested facility. After it was open for some time and proved to be a successful venue, a deal was made for Frank's appearance. He received the most money he had ever received for an appearance at a facility of that size. There were subsequent deals. When the facility got in trouble, Frank made some appearances there with Dean Martin, for which they were well paid. We permitted the sale of t-shirts and other souvenirs in the hope that the facility would make enough money to stay out of bankruptcy. At one of the performances somebody brought Carlo Gambino backstage with his granddaughter, who was named Sinatra, to take some pictures. A lot of pictures were taken of a lot of different people backstage. Unfortunately, they got into the hands of the press. One of the pictures was introduced as evidence in

FS and his gal Friday, Dorothy Uhlemann, at the Waldorf-Astoria in New York, January 1981.

the trial of certain people who were accused of bankruptcy fraud and tax fraud in connection with the Westchester Theater. That started the Mafia hue and cry all over again. Insofar as Frank's involvement in that case, neither he nor I was ever subpoenaed to testify before the grand jury with respect to this matter. However, the press made much of the picture and constantly brought Frank's name into the Westchester proceedings." Guilt by association again.

At the hearing, then L.A. County Sheriff Peter Pitchess testified that "If Mr. Sinatra is a member of the Mafia, I am the godfather." And Gregory Peck said, "Frank is one of the finest men and most trustworthy, truthful and reliable men I have known." The commission was unanimous in its approval for Dad to be licensed as a "key" employee at Caesars Palace, a necessary status for casino ownership.

MARCH 10, 1981: Atlanta, Georgia: Several of the city's children had been brutally murdered, and money was desperately needed to help the investigation. Learning that Sammy Davis Jr. had interrupted a Las Vegas engagement to appear at an Atlanta Task Force benefit at the Civic Center, my father called him and said, "When do you want me to be there?" They raised $200,000. Knowing that words were

Veronique and Gregory Peck visit my dad often. Greg, who is the same age as Frank, still likes to surf. The last time I saw him he was on his boogie board riding the waves.

Frank Sinatra Wins the Fight

In 1981 Sinatra applied for a gaming license in Nevada, and this time he had important facts read into the record. Here is how he brought that about: First, exercising his right under the Freedom of Information Act, he had the government disclose all their files on Frank Sinatra. He then turned these files over to the state of Nevada. In the past, the FBI had refused to turn over their files. (Part of their refusal may have been motivated by their knowledge that there was nothing incriminatory in them.)

The FBI files indicated that my father had been investigated endlessly for 30 years. (The early FBI files have him listed as a "Communist" because he appeared at a rally with Mrs. Eleanor Roosevelt and because he sang "The House I Live In.")

The files disclosed that there was no evidence of Mafia membership, Mafia affiliation or doing business with the Mafia. The FBI files also showed that the stories about Sinatra and members of the Mafia had come out originally as rumors printed in newspaper articles—rumors that were reported as rumors but were subsequently reported over and over until they were accepted as "facts."

At the conclusion of the hearing, Frank Sinatra was given a gaming license. He had generally tried to take the position of no comment, or, as he would put it, "Look, I'm not going to deny every piece of crap that comes along. I'm not going to dignify them with a response."

At various times, because of his loyalty to others or his refusal to dignify his attackers, he had sometimes lashed back, but most often he suppressed his feelings. I had learned, as he had long ago, that to most columnists it's not news that my father can be a nice guy or a decent kid. The many benefactions didn't start to come out until late in life. Without a newspaper or a TV station at his command, the only forum open to him, he thought, was his microphone. So he used it to vent some of his anger, sometimes humorously, sometimes viciously. He reached only a few thousand people, whereas the accusers reached millions through their media. But it was a healthy outlet for him. And for those who shared and understood his plight, each little jab he struck was significant and understandable. Though some remarks were not in good taste, I saw the set-to as a David vs. Goliath kind of thing, a mighty blow from a man some saw as mighty himself but who was, in dueling with the coarser members of the press, a little guy up against a giant.

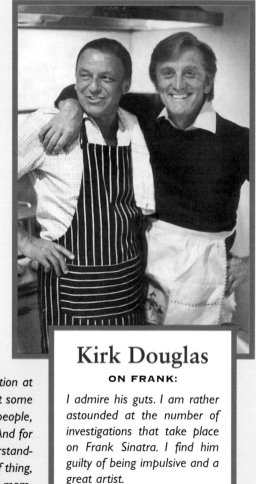

Kirk Douglas

ON FRANK:

I admire his guts. I am rather astounded at the number of investigations that take place on Frank Sinatra. I find him guilty of being impulsive and a great artist.

inadequate, Frank still tried to offer some solace. He said, "I will never waiver in my conviction that justice will prevail against dishonorable deeds. I love you and grieve for you and pray that all of you will live in the sunshine of an eternity of peaceful tomorrows."

MARCH 12-18, 26-30, 1981: Caesars Palace in Las Vegas. Frank canceled his last night's appearance when President Reagan was shot. Nancy Reagan: "When my husband was shot, your father was playing an engagement somewhere—I've forgotten where—perhaps in Vegas...Frank never called to say, 'Do you want me to come?' He just came. He shut down his show and just came. The next thing I knew, he was in Washington to be of support and help to me. It meant a great deal to me, and I'll always be grateful."

APRIL 8, 1981: In his first recording session since 1979, Dad recorded three songs in Hollywood: "Bang, Bang," "The Gal That Got Away"/"It Never Entered My Mind" and "Everything Happens to Me," which was never released. These were to appear on the album *She Shot Me Down*.

APRIL 9, 1981: He attended opening day of baseball season at Dodger Stadium.

The smiles tell the whole story. In giving, there is a big reward.

APRIL 14, 1981: FS was at California's Edwards Air Force Base for the landing of the space shuttle Columbia. I think if the Air Force would have allowed him to, Frank would have gone along for the shuttle ride.

APRIL 16, 1981: At the funeral of boxing great Joe Louis, Frank delivered the eulogy and served as a pallbearer.

APRIL 17-18, 1981: Princess Grace and Rainier spent the weekend with Dad in Palm Springs as they celebrated their 25th wedding anniversary.

APRIL 23, 1981: FS attended a dinner at the Century Plaza Hotel in L.A. for Vice President George Bush.

APRIL 25, 1981: At Metromedia Square in Hollywood, Dad was one of 200 Los Angeles people who were honored at "A Tribute to Men and Women of Achievement." According to Metromedia Chairman John Kluge, "Members of the press, as specialists within the media, were invited to nominate representative individuals from the many community achievers who have risen to the pinnacle of their endeavors."

The Rainiers visiting Palm Springs.

APRIL 29-MAY 3, 1981: Back to the Sunrise Musical Theater in Fort Lauderdale.

MAY 7, 1981: FS sang at a luncheon honoring Mrs. Reagan at the Congressional Club in Washington, D.C.

MAY 8-14, 1981: Continuing his tour, he performed at Pennsylvania's Valley Forge Theater.

"…You'd never know it,
   but buddy I'm a kind of poet,
   and I've got a lot of things to say,
And when I'm gloomy,
   you've got to listen to me
   until it's talked away…"

A.J., Pop Pop and Amanda watching television in Palm Springs.

MAY 20-25, 1981: After a quick return to L.A. to appear at an NBC affiliates' convention, he began another engagement at Resorts International in Atlantic City.

JUNE 2-7, 1981: On to Boston's Metropolitan Center.

JUNE 8, 1981: He presented the Sinatra/UCLA Music Awards, which are scholarships for outstanding music students. He had given these grants since 1968.

JUNE 10-17, 1981: He headlined a benefit for the University of Nevada at the Aladdin Hotel before opening at Caesars Palace.

JUNE 19-20, 1981: He attended a fund-raiser in San Francisco.

JULY 4-6, 1981: FS flew to Washington, D.C., to celebrate the July 4th weekend and to attend Nancy Reagan's birthday on July 5.

JULY 20-21, 1981: FS recorded five songs at the Columbia recording studios in New York City: "Thanks for the Memory," "I Loved Her," "A Long Night," "Say Hello" and "South to a Warmer Place." These were also destined for the *She Shot Me Down* collection. Produced by Don Costa and arranged by the Big Three—Costa, Jenkins and Riddle—this album very nearly recaptured the magic of the earlier theme albums.

JULY 24-AUGUST 2, 1981: Dad's performances at a Sun City resort in the independent tribal homeland of Bophuthatswana raised eyebrows. During apartheid, some people believed the Bophuthatswana republic was a puppet of the white supremacist government of South Africa. FS received the Order of the Leopard from President Lucas Mangope. He was the first white person to receive this honor. His sold-out audiences represented a mix of races, and when he was confronted with the inevitable questions, Dad said, "I play to all people of any color, creed, drunk or sober." He also said he didn't believe that "any human being—black, brown, white or yellow—should ever be called a second-class citizen."

AUGUST 5-13, 1981: Frank played five nights at the Luna Park Stadium in Buenos Aires and four nights at the Maksaud Plaza Hotel in São Paulo, Brazil.

AUGUST 19, 1981: In New York City, he recorded "Good Thing Going."

AUGUST 24-30, 1981: Back to Resorts International in Atlantic City.

AUGUST 28, 1981: While at Resorts, the Muscular Dystrophy Association taped three songs, which were played on the Labor Day Telethon.

SEPTEMBER 8-20, 1981: He played a two-week engagement with George Shearing at Carnegie Hall. George, who was blind, called Frank "Old Blue Eyes" and himself "Old No Eyes."

SEPTEMBER 15, 1981: He taped a Chrysler commercial and on the same day appeared on Arlene Francis's WOR radio show.

Frank and Barbara visit President Sadat. When Sadat was murdered, my father called him, "The single man of the desert who has stood tall in the sand begging for peace."

SEPTEMBER 22, 1981: Frank and Barbara attended the National Multiple Sclerosis Society Ball in Washington, D.C., with President and Mrs. Reagan.

SEPTEMBER 25-26, 1981: He performed at Hartford Civic Center in Connecticut.

OCTOBER 6, 1981: When Dad's friend, Egyptian president Anwar Sadat, was assassinated, my father wrote, "In the course of my lifetime, I have awakened too many mornings to a world that has lost another good man. But President Sadat's vicious murder hits me hardest now...for it is the loss of the single man of the desert who has stood tall in the sand begging for peace. I pray to God that He will prove that justice still works—even if I doubt it in these weeping hours. For no punishment will bring my brother back to life or heal the agony of Madame Sadat."

OCTOBER 12-18, 1981: Engagements at Kansas City's Municipal Auditorium, Wichita's Century Two Convention Hall, Houston's Jones Hall, New Orleans' Municipal Auditorium and a benefit performance at the Carousel Ball in Denver for the Diabetes Association.

OCTOBER 25, 1981: After attending Game 5 of the World Series with his family at Dodger Stadium, Dad performed at a fund-raising dinner for L.A. County Sheriff Sherman Block, who was running for re-election.

OCTOBER 28-29, 1981: He taped the TV special *Sinatra: The Man and the Music* at NBC studios in Burbank. In this hour-long show, Dad sang 14 selections from his greatest albums with Count Basie and his band playing backup. Among the highlights: "Pennies from Heaven," "I Get a Kick Out of You" and "New York, New York."

Dad had taken me to baseball games from the time I was the age of my daughters in these pictures. In those days, our team was the Hollywood Stars of the Pacific Coast League and my favorite player was Frank Kelleher. Now we are all Dodger fans.

Right: Hugh, Tina, A.J., Amanda, Dad and me going to the 1981 World Series.

Tommy Lasorda

ON SINATRA:

He is the most generous man I've ever met, the greatest singer that ever lived and I never saw anyone who did more for charity. He is a legend. To me, he is the one who made all us Italians very proud. We love him and think he is the greatest. I have been with Frank on many, many occasions and he has an electrifying personality. I've never seen an entertainer like him. He makes the audience feel like he is singing to each of them personally. I am proud and honored to say that I know Frank Sinatra. He is a brilliant, brilliant man.

OCTOBER 30, 1981: He played a benefit at the Beverly Hilton for St. John's Hospital. Hollywood legend Irene Dunne, one of the original founders of the hospital, wrote my father: "I don't think there is a performer living who gives as much of himself. I am sure the nuns at St. Johns are going to see that you get a special place in heaven."

OCTOBER 31, 1981: FS and Johnny Carson modeled in a fashion show at a dinner dance benefit for Jack Benny's Diabetes Foundation.

NOVEMBER 5-11, 1981: Back at Caesars Palace. He was forced to cancel the last three nights because of illness.

NOVEMBER 15, 1981: In Los Angeles, FS led the singing of "America the Beautiful" at a Scopus Award presentation to Nancy Reagan from the American Friends of Hebrew University of Israel.

NOVEMBER 22, 1981: NBC aired *Sinatra: The Man and the Music*, produced by Paul Keyes.

DECEMBER 5, 1981: In L.A., Frank recorded a Don Costa arrangement of Joe Raposo's "To Love a Child" for Nancy Reagan's Foster Grandparents Program.

Frank greeting Queen Noor and King Hussein of Jordan.

DECEMBER 31, 1981: Frank and Barbara celebrated New Year's Eve at the Palm Springs home of Walter and Lee Annenberg.

JANUARY 7-13, 1982: During an engagement at Caesars Palace, my father traveled to Los Angeles to attend the wedding of Dean Paul Martin to Dorothy Hamill on the 8th. On the 10th he traveled to Palm Springs for a benefit for Temple Isaiah at the Sheraton Plaza.

Frank and the great Nazi-hunter Simon Wiesenthal.

JANUARY 17, 1982: In Washington, he attended a benefit for Holocaust crusader Simon Wiesenthal. Two weeks later he hosted the world premiere of the film *Genocide* at the Kennedy Center.

JANUARY 24, 1982: George Shearing, Luciano Pavarotti and Frank performed at Radio City Music Hall in a benefit for the Memorial Sloan-Kettering Cancer Center.

JANUARY 31, 1982: Dad participated in a television special entitled *Let Poland Be Poland.* He said, "I'm not a politician, I'm a singer, but when I see people being forced from their homeland to seek freedom someplace else, it makes me realize all over again how grateful I am for the freedom I have—and how terrible I would feel if I had to leave the country I love. When the troubles began in Poland this winter, I remembered a song I recorded some time ago. It's based on a Polish folk song. I sang it in both English and Polish. If I were a politician I would probably make a speech right now. But since I'm not, here's the song. The title is 'Ever Homeward.'" President Reagan wrote: "An estimated 172 million people in 42 countries saw the production and some 100 million heard it on radio...It was a forum for the champions of human freedom throughout the world. Because of people like you who care, the message will continue to ring loud and clear."

FEBRUARY 3, 1982: In Detroit at Cobo Arena.

FEBRUARY 11-17, 1982: Comedian Pat Henry, a longtime friend of Dad's who frequently opened for him, died in his sleep during an engagement at Caesars Palace.

The Tenor and The Baritone. Pavarotti wrote: "Frank Sinatra is the biggest star in the universe of stars in the singing business of yesterday, of today, of always. And the Mozart of popular music."

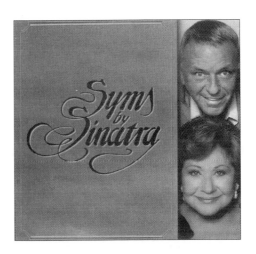

On the road with Dad—and the kids. There were times of chaos and times of joy.

FEBRUARY 20, 1982: FS and Bob Newhart performed at a Myasthenia Gravis tribute to Ed McMahon.

MARCH 4-17, 1982: He returned to Caesars Palace for a two-week run with Shields and Yarnell and me. He said to me, "Go on tour with me for a year and let's see what happens." We both agreed it would be fun for my kids to see what the road was about, and when they weren't in school they traveled on the road with us.

MARCH 25, 1982: Dad and Perry Como sang at a White House state dinner in honor of President Sandro Pertini of Italy.

MARCH 31, 1982: Frank and Bob Hope performed at a tribute to Princess Grace in her hometown, Philadelphia.

APRIL 1-4, 1982: An engagement at Resorts International in Atlantic City.

APRIL 5-8, 1982: In New York FS conducted Sylvia Syms's recording session for the album *Syms by Sinatra*. Produced by Frank Sinatra and Don Costa for the brilliant song stylist, this collaboration was the culmination of a dream that began in the early 1940s when Sylvia and Frank met on 52nd Street, where they had gone to hear Billie Holiday. "Lady Day" herself introduced them to each other, then took the aspiring Sylvia and Frank, who had just joined Tommy Dorsey's band, across the street to see Mabel Mercer. Sylvia Syms: "Mabel was not a great singer, but she had a way with words and phrasing that was unique. Lady Day, whose talent was just the opposite, had an animal instinct about Mabel and enjoyed bringing people to listen to her. As a conductor, your papa put phrasing into my mouth that had never occurred to me—and it became incredibly simple. He is the greatest delineator of words. I sit and watch him even now, as a performer watching another performer, not believing the lessons I'm learning." My father admired Holiday and Mercer, and both he and Sylvia were influenced by them. Dad produced and conducted this album for "Buddha," as he called Syms. Don Costa had a heart attack just before the recording sessions began. These were the last arrangements he wrote.

Backstage at Resorts International in Atlantic City, A.J., Amanda and I had the very good fortune to meet Frank Garrick and his wife. Frank, Dad's godfather, was the one who gave him one of his first jobs.

The great moments were when he'd bring me back for an extra bow, sharing the tumultuous applause that greeted his sudden appearance on stage. These would be wonderful gestures for any performer who wasn't his kid...but for me...

Gregory Peck, Cary Grant and FS aboard the Fabergé jet.

APRIL 28, 1982: A benefit for the Musicians Emergency Benevolent Fund, Local 369, at the Aladdin Hotel.

MAY 4-17, 1982: On another short tour, he played Philadelphia, Pittsburgh, Buffalo and Providence, Rhode Island.

MAY 16, 1982: In New York he hosted a Friars Club tribute to his old friend Cary Grant.

MAY 27-JUNE 19, 1982: Caesars Palace in Las Vegas, then a week in Palm Springs and 10 days at Resorts International in Atlantic City.

JUNE 3, 1982: FS performed at a University of Nevada, Las Vegas, benefit show at the Aladdin Hotel.

JUNE 26, 1982: He received a special award at a National Multiple Sclerosis Society meeting in Houston, still serving as its national campaign chairman.

JULY 16-21, 1982: Another week at Caesars Palace.

JULY 1982: Frank Sinatra was the first to perform in the newly enclosed Universal Amphitheater in Los Angeles. "A Legendary Evening with Frank Sinatra" lived up to its billing when a host of Hollywood legends turned out for Dad's benefit performance at the amphitheater. Cary Grant, Charlton Heston, Dorothy Lamour and Jimmy Stewart joined Ernest Borgnine and Angie Dickinson in raising more than $1 million for a variety of charities. Dressing backstage before the performance, my father asked Jilly Rizzo, "What's it look like?" "SRO," Jilly replied. "I mean Dodgers and Atlanta," Dad said, ever the baseball fan.

JULY 30-AUGUST 7, 1982: FS officially opened the Universal Amphitheater with two opening acts: comedian Charlie Callas and me.

AUGUST 10, 1982: In Chicago he headlined "Chicago Fest" at the Navy Pier.

August 20, 1982: In the Dominican Republic he gave a concert that was later shown on U.S. television as *The Concert for the Americas.*

August 21-29, 1982: He vacationed in Monaco with Princess Grace and Rainier.

September 1982: *Syms by Sinatra* was released. He once said of her, "If every modern-day female vocalist in America would take a one- or two-year hiatus from their jobs and study the vocalizing of Sylvia Syms, the world would be better for it."

September 11, 1982: A hospital benefit in Ottawa, Canada, with Rich Little.

September 12, 1982: At the Hilton in New York, Frank Sinatra was inducted into the Broadcasters Hall of Fame.

September 13, 1982: With Buddy Rich and Charlie Callas at a Carnegie Hall benefit for the World Mercy Fund.

September 13-23, 1982: At a Carnegie Hall concert, a young woman who was an admitted fan of rock music was quoted by the *New York Times* as saying, "Frank Sinatra is one thing I can agree with my parents about. They've been playing his records since I was born, and I don't ordinarily like that kind of music much, but he's a great singer."

September 15, 1982: Princess Grace of Monaco died in an automobile accident. Dad was unable to attend the funeral but he sent the following words of comfort to her family: "...I feel as though the sword of suffering pierced my heart...God is a jealous lover and wanted Grace now. Indeed our hearts are restless until they rest in Him."

September 25, 1982: During a rainstorm, at a benefit for the developmentally disabled at the Irvine Meadows Amphitheater in California, Dad sang for 45 minutes before the event had to be stopped because of the weather.

September 30-October 6, 1982: Caesars Palace in Las Vegas.

October 14-24, 1982: Resorts International in Atlantic City. He went to Washington, D.C., on the 19th for a luncheon for Nancy Reagan's Foster Grandparents Program, where he sang "To Love a Child." The proceeds from the event went to the charity.

In a valuable photograph, four Presidents inscribe best wishes to citizen Sinatra.

OCTOBER 31, 1982: He attended a presentation of the Hebrew University Scopus Award to his lawyer Milton "Mickey" Rudin.

NOVEMBER 4-13, 1982: FS did his final stand of the year at Caesars Palace.

DECEMBER 2, 1982: FS and the Les Brown Orchestra performed at a benefit for the American Cancer Fund, Tri-State branch, at the Beverly Hilton.

DECEMBER 8-10, 1982: He performed at the Golden Nugget in Atlantic City.

DECEMBER 26, 1982-JANUARY 1, 1983: On vacation in Acapulco.

DECEMBER 31, 1982: He celebrated New Year's Eve at Walter Annenberg's Palm Springs home.

JANUARY 3, 1983: FS conducted a recording session for his lead trumpeter Charlie Turner at Evergreen Studios in Los Angeles.

JANUARY 6-12, 1983: Dad returned to Caesars Palace.

JANUARY 14-16, 1983: Harrah's in Lake Tahoe.

JANUARY 19, 1983: Don Costa had passed away, and the sessions he was working on with Dad were canceled.

JANUARY 23, 1983: Performing with Victor Borge at a Radio City Music Hall benefit for the Memorial Sloan-Kettering Cancer Center.

JANUARY 24, 1983: A memorial service was held for Don Costa.

JANUARY 25, 1983: The remaining Don Costa session, with "Here's to the Band" and "All the Way Home" (which was not released) was arranged and conducted by Joe Parnello.

JANUARY 26-JANUARY 29, 1983: He made his second appearance at Steve Wynn's Golden Nugget in Atlantic City. He became a spokesperson for the casino/hotel and appeared in nationally televised commercials with Wynn. The resort's New Jersey revenues jumped 42 percent in

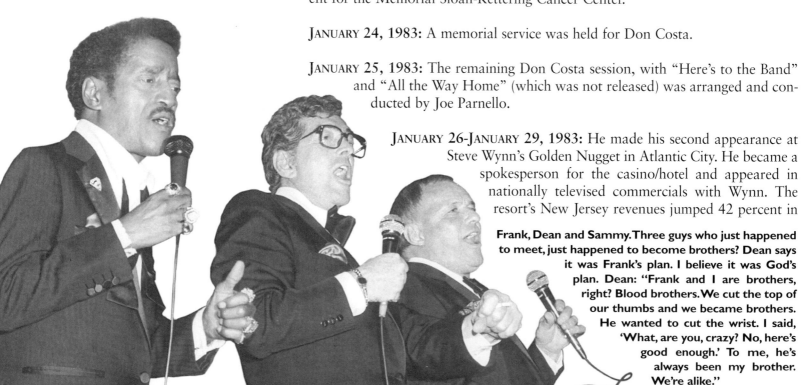

Frank, Dean and Sammy. Three guys who just happened to meet, just happened to become brothers? Dean says it was Frank's plan. I believe it was God's plan. Dean: "Frank and I are brothers, right? Blood brothers. We cut the top of our thumbs and we became brothers. He wanted to cut the wrist. I said, 'What, are you, crazy? No, here's good enough.' To me, he's always been my brother. We're alike."

Letter to Nikka: (Don Costa's daughter)

January 31, 1983

Dear Nikka,

I've purposely waited these few days to give you time to dry your tears and start to live in a world without your father…that dear, decent and talented man.

Not that the tears will ever stop when you remember how you love him, but at least the storm of your crying is over. And thanks to our wise and loving God, while there always will be some tears, hopefully the rest will come only in scattered showers. Maybe time doesn't completely heal all wounds but at least it softens them. We can thank God for that too.

Your father was one of the finest and dearest men I ever knew. I pray for him every day. Every hour of every day. He helped me more than you'll ever know. Without his talents, his friendship, and his genius, my life would have been a lot different. For the worse, I might add.

When my own mother died a few years ago I thought I'd never get over the sadness. I'm sure you think that way now after your father's death. So I want to tell you how I manage to keep on living. I live a little of every day for my mother. A quiet prayer now and then. A kind deed she would have been proud of. Happy memories of her whenever I close my eyes. All these help me. And they will help you, Nikka. I promise you that.

And don't forget how painful these days are for your mother. For your wonderful mother. She lost a good man too. You can help her. You can help her more than anyone in the world. And I know you will. And I know your father will smile on you for helping her. Sometimes think of it this way. We're all better people because we knew and loved Don. I'm a better man because of him. Let's remember that always. Both of us. And remember this also, Nikka dear, he's happy where he is now—in that beautiful land of eternity. Where he will live forever and ever in peace and where we will see him again when God calls us.

I love you Nikka.

Uncle Frank

a year. For Dad, who also got the use of Wynn's Boeing 727, helicopters, limousines and lavish high-roller suites, it hardly seemed like work. One newspaper reported that he was drawn to the arrangement because of what he called Wynn's "moxie." According to the article, he told Wynn, "Steve, this is what I always wanted to do, but nobody ever asked me. All they wanted me to do was sing and then sit in my room all day."

FEBRUARY 3-9, 1983: Again at Caesars Palace in Las Vegas.

FEBRUARY 12, 1983: At the "Love In II" benefit at the Canyon Country Club and Hotel for the Desert Hospital, FS performed with Dean Martin, Sammy Davis Jr., George Kirby and me.

FEBRUARY 13, 1983: Temple Isaiah honored FS at a groundbreaking ceremony in Palm Springs.

Her Majesty Queen Elizabeth, Nancy Reagan and Prince Philip greet Perry, Frank, Dionne and George on Stage 9 at Fox. The dinner menu included: Papaya with Bay Shrimp, Chicken Pot Pie, Fresh Spinach with Bacon and a Toasted Coconut Snowball.

FEBRUARY 27, 1983: In a command performance for Queen Elizabeth at 20th Century Fox in Los Angeles, Dad shared the bill with Perry Como, Dionne Warwick and George Burns.

FEBRUARY 28, 1983: Frank, with guitarist Tony Mottola, recorded "It's Sunday." That evening he attended a dinner party for Queen Elizabeth aboard the *Brittania*, which was docked in Long Beach.

MARCH 3-14, 1983: He returned for a week at Caesars Palace in Las Vegas, then moved on to Harrah's in Tahoe. John Denver filled in for him on the 13th because of Frank's sore throat.

APRIL 8, 1983: FS and Jackie Gayle performed at Arizona State University in Tempe.

APRIL 9, 1983: A collection of Dad's paintings was auctioned off for charity at the Sheraton Plaza in Palm Springs. The proceeds went to a local family counseling service.

APRIL 15, 1983: In Boston, FS, Dionne Warwick and Marvin Hamlisch performed at a benefit for ailing Red Sox outfielder Tony Conigliaro to help cover his huge medical expenses.

APRIL 18-21, 1983: He played a prestigious four-day engagement at the Kennedy Center in Washington, D.C.

APRIL 23, 1983: In New Jersey at the Meadowlands, FS performed with Buddy Rich.

APRIL 27-MAY 1, 1983: At the Golden Nugget in Atlantic City.

MAY 3-7, 1983: He finished an engagement at the Arie Crown Theater in Chicago despite a broken blood vessel in his throat.

MAY 20, 1983: With Red Buttons, he performed in a benefit at the Waldorf-Astoria in New York for the Hospital for Special Surgery.

MAY 22, 1983: While at Perry Como's charity golf tournament in Durham, North Carolina, FS and Perry performed in Duke University's Children's Classic Concert. Later, Dad was on the dais at the Waldorf in New York City for a Friars Club tribute to Elizabeth Taylor.

Gentle and brilliantly talented guitarist Tony Mottola and Frank first worked together when they were in their early 20s. Here, Tony is rehearsing "Autumn Leaves" at Caesars Palace in 1983.

JUNE 8-12, 1983: Again at the Golden Nugget in Atlantic City.

JUNE 15-19, 1983: At the Universal Amphitheater in Los Angeles with the Buddy Rich Orchestra.

JULY 1983: Dad flew to Tucson for one day to film a cameo role in Burt Reynolds's movie *Cannonball Run II*. He spent one night and worked for only four hours. He would have done more if they had asked him to. Sammy had asked him if he would do a bit part in the film because, after years of searching, nobody had come up with a story for another Summit movie. *Cannonball II* would unite them on film again, sadly, for the last time.

JULY 3, 1983: At Hillside Memorial Park in Los Angeles, Dad attended the funeral of Mary Livingstone, the late Jack Benny's beloved wife and a dear friend for many years.

JULY 7, 1983: Stricken with the second loss in only a few days, he went to a funeral for his mentor: bandleader Harry James.

JULY 17-AUGUST 14, 1983: He vacationed on the French Riviera.

AUGUST 5, 1983: FS performed with Sammy at a benefit in Monte Carlo for his late friend Princess Grace's favorite charity, the Red Cross.

SEPTEMBER 21-25, 1983: He returned to the Golden Nugget in Atlantic City with Dean Martin.

OCTOBER 1983: Capitol Records released a $350 boxed set of 16 of my father's LPs from 1953 to 1962. A review in *Atlantic Monthly* noted that "the albums explore: knowledge, reflection, friendship, travel, swinging and, finally, accomplishment and power, every avenue except religion. These albums are about continuing, and not only continuing but trying to get better in spite of the realities of aging. They are heroic feats of self-generation, of finding more with less and gaining in the struggle a reason for going on."

NOVEMBER 20, 1983: "The Variety Clubs All-Star Party" for FS was taped at NBC studios in Burbank and was produced by Paul Keyes. It was announced that all the funds Dad had raised for Variety Clubs International over the years had made it possible for them to build a wing at the Seattle Children's Orthopedic Hospital called the Sinatra Family Children's Unit for the Chronically Ill. Cary Grant, Milton Berle, Danny Thomas and many more headliners attended, honoring Frank Sinatra's music and humanitarian works. With words written by Paul Keyes, Richard Burton movingly acknowledged the man called "Mr. Anonymous": "I have never sung song with Frank Sinatra. Never acted with him, shared his stage nor been a member of an orchestra under his baton.

The Variety Clubs tribute was a great night in Frank's life. Here he is surrounded by: Top: Foster Brooks, Ricardo Montalban, Julio Iglesias, Richard Burton, Bob Newhart, Cary Grant, Jimmy Stewart. Middle: Tommy Lasorda, Monty Hall, Steve Lawrence. Bottom: Vic Damone, Carol Burnett, Florence Henderson and Michele Lee.

"We are, however, old friends of some thirty years and I have risen to my feet to applaud his blazing artistry, at numerous charity performances raising countless millions for the victims of the world.

"Frank is a giant. Among the givers of the world, he stands tallest. He has more than paid rent for the space he occupies on this planet, forged as he is from legendary loyalty and compassion carefully hidden...hidden because he has ordered it. Mr. Anonymous you have asked to be; Mr. Anonymous you shall be called. At risk of further offending you, I appear as the herald of grateful multitudes who have opened those unexpected envelopes...special-delivering answers to their prayers...those awakened by late-night phone calls which remedied their problems only on condition they share your covenant of secrecy...those who were surprised by signed checks with amounts not filled in...those performers down on their luck, who suddenly landed that role they never expected and still don't know whom to thank...and for untold beneficiaries of the caring and kindness of this splendid man who truly is his brother's keeper. And they are legion...those whose lives took a turn for the better...because of this man.

"A street corner poet burnt to the bone with the fury of his own ambition. Hoping someone would notice you. And they did notice you, Maggio. Thank you, Blue Eyes. God bless you, Mr. Anonymous."

And a medley entitled "Sinatra from A to Z" was performed by Steve Lawrence and Vic Damone, with an orchestra led by Nelson Riddle—from "All or Nothing at All" to "Zing Went the Strings of My Heart."

NOVEMBER 25-28, 1983: Worcester, Massachusetts, Hartford, Connecticut, and Nassau Coliseum in Long Island, New York.

NOVEMBER 30, 1983: During an engagement at the Golden Nugget in Atlantic City, Frank and Barbara and Dean and his manager, Mort Viner, sat down at an empty blackjack table, where the cards had been splayed face-up on the felt. Mort Viner remembers, "Frank was sitting to my right, Dean on my left. Frank asked the dealer not to take the time to place the decks back in the shoe and to please deal with one deck from her hand instead. The dealer said no, without explaining that there

Sinatra From A to Z

All or Nothing at All	**J**ust One of Those Things	**S**trangers in the Night
Bewitched, Bothered and Bewildered	A **K**iss Goodnight	**T**his Love of Mine
Come Fly with Me	The **L**ady is a Tramp	**U**nder a Blanket of Blue
Day In, Day Out	**M**y Kind of Town	**V**iolets for Your Furs
Embraceable You	**N**ew York, New York	**W**hen You're Smiling
A **F**oggy Day	**O**h, Look at Me Now	**EX**actly Like You
Get Happy	**P**ut Your Dreams Away	**Y**oung at Heart
Here's That Rainy Day	**Q**uiet Nights	**Z**ing Went The Strings of My Heart
I'll Never Smile Again	**R**ing-A-Ding-Ding	

...And that's "Sinatra from A to Z"

A Night to Remember at the Kennedy Center

A dinner hosted by Secretary of State George Shultz and a White House reception hosted by the Reagans were followed by the awards presentation at the Kennedy Center. Dad shared the honors that year—and the presidential box—with Katherine Dunham, Elia Kazan, Virgil Thomson and his old friend Jimmy Stewart.

During his segment of the program, Mikhail Baryshnikov danced to Twyla Tharp's new ballet, "The Sinatra Suite." Gene Kelly, a 1982 honoree, told the audience that when he first met Dad, his first impression was that "he was a skinny runt—but then he opened his mouth, and it was awesome." And Perry Como, accompanied by a children's chorus, sang "Young at Heart," but with lyrics penned especially for the occasion: "Though you once were the rage on the Paramount stage, though you're past middle age, Frank, you'll always be among the very young at heart."

Earlier, at the White House, President Reagan called Dad and Jimmy Stewart "special friends of Nancy's and mine," and remembered how Dad had sung for peanuts when he was coming up. "Let me repeat that," the President joked. "Frank Sinatra worked for $15 a week. But it paid off. He got a $10 a week raise." He also recalled some of Dad's film roles, including High Society, then remarked, "You know, Frank, if they'd only given me roles like that, I'd never have left Hollywood."

was a rule against it, which Frank and Dean didn't know. She spoke with the Pit Boss, who told her to go ahead and deal from your hand. They played maybe five or six hands in about six minutes and quit because they had lost $600. The hotel reported the incident to the gaming commission to cover themselves, because the Pit Boss made a mistake in telling the dealer to deal with the one deck—it was against New Jersey Gaming Commission rules, again unbeknownst to Frank or Dean. Nobody told them. It was a 'Non-event.' The Nugget, by reporting it, made it the big deal it became. Newspapers reported that there was a big argument with Frank losing his temper and threatening not to perform and that Frank and Dean lost four or five hundred thousand dollars, none of which is true. When Steve Wynn went to their dressing room to explain why the hotel reported the Pit Boss and the dealer, Dean and Frank felt terrible and apologized."

DECEMBER 3-4, 1983: Dad was thrilled to be named one of a handful of annual recipients of the Kennedy Center Honor for Lifetime Achievement. Other honorees were actor James Stewart, choreographer Katherine Dunham, director Elia Kazan and composer Virgil Thomson. He invited the entire family—Barbara, her son Bob, Tina and Frankie, Hugh and I and our children—to join him in Washington, D.C., to share in the occasion. We stayed at the Madison Hotel. The night before the presentation, Secretary of State George Shultz hosted a state dinner in the

Said Reagan: "His love of country, his generosity for those less fortunate, make him one of our most remarkable and distinguished Americans."

Capitol. We laughed a lot trying to figure out which fork to use; there must have been nine forks at each setting. Everything was exquisite. The next night began at the White House, where the actual awards were presented. Then on to the Kennedy Center for the taping of the television special. The ceremony honored his lifetime in the arts. "There is not the remotest possibility," said Gene Kelly, who introduced him, "that he will have a successor." It was a summation of his nearly 70 years. Mikhail Baryshnikov and Elaine Kudo danced "The Sinatra Suite," choreographed by Twyla Tharp to the music of "All the Way," "That's Life," "My Way" and "One for My Baby."

Choreographer Twyla Tharp

ON THE SONGS OF SINATRA:

[I wanted] access to all that sentiment and emotion...as well as all those things societally we attach to those songs. There's a certain morality and a certain kind of period, so that [they] serve as a set, almost a visual set for the piece. Those songs mean more than music. They stand for whole generations. And his career is extraordinary in spanning [them]...I listened to everything I could get hold of. One had to be the narrative of the piece. I see it as a statement about one long developing relationship, danced by different couples. It also had to make sense musically, so that it wouldn't be an affront to his ear or my ear or anyone's ear. The songs are: "Softly, As I Leave You"; "Strangers in the Night"; "One for My Baby"; then the first "My Way," which was early and aggressive; and "Something Stupid," the only one I think of as specifically humorous; and then, "All the Way"; "Forget Domani"; "That's Life"; and then the last "My Way," which is later and much more mellow...I've always heard the sentiment of that song differently, not as a selfish statement but in context, as the only way people can relate to one another...Unless an individual in a relationship can do it "their way" and "theirs" is also their partner's way, it doesn't work...

I've listened to those songs by now thousands of times and they still have resonance and meaning. I feel he's given so much to the culture and his songs mean so much to so many people, that it's a privilege...to say nothing of the fact that the genuine emotion he recorded into these songs keeps itself alive time after time.

You know, I sit in my dressing room and listen to those songs coming through the squawk box and they still move me. I felt I knew him intimately. When we met, I asked, "How'd you learn to sing so big?" And he had a simple and appropriate answer, "I like to sing." Which makes sense because singing is obviously something he understands in a fundamental way. It is something that is really in him to do. Those songs mean a lot to me, too, and I'm happy to share with people anything I may understand about them. Which is one of the reasons why the dance piece is so popular. Audiences love it. They have a great time and they're happy. What more could you ask for? They're happy and they're moved. And they recognize things in themselves. That means a community of spirit. And that's what I think theater should be.

DECEMBER 8, 1983: FS performed at the Meadowlands in New Jersey.

DECEMBER 12, 1983: With Sarah Vaughan, Count Basie and Ed McMahon, FS performed at a benefit for the City of Hope BRAVO (Blood Revolves Around Victorious Optimism) chapter at the Beverly Wilshire Hotel. Frank, Sarah and Basie also received the Spirit of Life Award. After the benefit, Dad celebrated his birthday at Matteo's restaurant in Westwood.

DECEMBER 14, 1983: In San Diego at the Sports Arena.

DECEMBER 15, 1983: On to a concert at the Long Beach Convention Center.

My father is never blasé about working with talented people. He was in awe of these two legends: Bill "Count" Basie and Sarah Vaughan.

DECEMBER 16, 1983: Dad appeared with Sammy, Dean and Diana Ross at a benefit for the University of Nevada, Las Vegas.

DECEMBER 18, 1983: FS and Alan King performed at a benefit for Temple Isaiah in Palm Springs.

JANUARY 11, 1984: FS and Buddy Rich appeared at the Hyatt Regency Houston, Texas, for the Wortham Theater Center Benefit for Arts and Humanities.

JANUARY 12, 1984: He performed at the Reunion Center in Dallas, Texas.

JANUARY 21, 1984: In Tampa, Florida, he did two shows at the Sun Dome Theater.

FEBRUARY 16, 1984: FS, Dean and Sammy performed at a benefit for St. John's Hospital at the Century Plaza Hotel in Los Angeles.

MARCH 10, 1984: He was in New York to attend the Friars Club Dinner at the Waldorf-Astoria Hotel honoring DJ William B. Williams.

MARCH 15, 1984: A performance at the Riverfront Coliseum in Cincinnati, Ohio.

MARCH 18, 1984: He appeared with Luciano Pavarotti, Diana Ross, Buddy Rich and Montserrat Caballe at Radio City Music Hall for another benefit performance for the Memorial Sloan-Kettering Cancer Center. "The reason I and other Italian opera singers admire Frank Sinatra," Pavarotti was quoted as saying, "is not just for his star quality and the beauty of his voice, but because his phrasing is very close to Italian bel canto."

MARCH 20, 1984: In New Haven he performed at the Veterans Memorial Coliseum.

MARCH 23-24, 1984: At the Premier Entertainment Center in Detroit.

APRIL 9, 1984: At the Academy Awards ceremony at the Music Center's Dorothy

FS, Diana Ross, Pavarotti and Montserrat Caballe performed at a benefit for Sloan-Kettering Cancer Center.

Chandler Pavilion, FS presented the Jean Hersholt Humanitarian Award to Columbia Pictures' Mike Frankovich.

APRIL 11, 1984: With Tom Dreesen and Buddy Rich, he performed at the Civic Center in Pittsburgh.

APRIL 13, 1984: FS and Quincy Jones joined to record the album *L.A. Is My Lady* in New York City at A&M studios. Songs: "Until the Real Thing Comes Along," "After You've Gone" and "L.A. Is My Lady."

APRIL 14, 1984: At the Spectrum Arena in Philadelphia with Tom Dreesen.

APRIL 16-17, 1984: FS and Quincy Jones continued recording sessions for *L.A. Is My Lady.* Songs: "A Hundred Years from Today," "The Best of Everything," "It's All Right with Me," "Teach Me Tonight," "If I Should Lose You" and "Mack the Knife."

APRIL 19, 1984: In Lincoln, Nebraska, he performed at the Devaney Sports Arena.

Frank and Charlie Callas guest on Jerry Lewis's talk show.

APRIL 20, 1984: He was a guest on Jerry Lewis's new talk show in Los Angeles.

APRIL 28, 1984: FS, Dean, Sammy and Lionel Richie performed at the SHARE Boomtown Benefit at Pauley Pavilion on the UCLA campus.

APRIL 30, 1984: FS attended Bill "Count" Basie's funeral.

MAY 1-5, 1984: At the Golden Nugget in Atlantic City.

MAY 8-12, 1984: Five shows at the Arie Crown Theater in Chicago with Tom Dreesen and Buddy Rich.

MAY 14, 1984: Performed at the Mecca Arena in Milwaukee, Wisconsin.

MAY 15, 1984: In Washington, D.C., he appeared at Constitution Hall for AT&T.

Frank Sinatra receiving a Doctor of Fine Arts degree from Loyola Marymount University. It was a sweltering day and I worried about my dad wearing that heavy robe for over two hours in the L.A. sun. But he never complained, not a word.

Michael Jackson visiting FS during the recording of L.A. Is My Lady. This is the first time the two legends had met and it was orchestrated by Quincy Jones, who had produced them both. Quincy: "God can't waste His time giving everybody something unique or original, so he just picked a few people. He picked a Louis Armstrong, He picked a Duke Ellington, He picked a Frank Sinatra, He picked a Michael Jackson. There are very few people who get that. You're talking about big stuff now. And on top of it, Frank took the gift and developed it to its ultimate. He knows when to do his homework too. And he picks the right songs. Taste is one of the key words. Taste and style...I mean, the way he phrases...It freaks me."

MAY 17, 1984: He recorded "Stormy Weather" and "How Do You Keep the Music Playing?" for *L.A. Is My Lady* with Quincy Jones at Ocean Wave studios.

MAY 26, 1984: He received an honorary Doctor of Fine Arts degree at Loyola Marymount University. While there, he spoke to the graduate students at the university.

JUNE 1, 1984: At the Fox Theater in Atlanta, FS performed for AT&T.

JUNE 1984: Frank did 13 nights at Carnegie Hall.

JUNE 17, 1984: He attended a White House dinner in honor of President Junius R. Jayewardene of Sri Lanka.

JUNE 23, 1984: A planned seven-day engagement began at the Golden Nugget in Las Vegas with Willie Nelson, but Frank became ill and canceled after one night.

JULY 9, 1984: In FS's Los Angeles office, he took photographs with children from the Boys' Republic Della Robbia Wreath Program, of which he was the 1984 national chairman.

JULY 15, 1984: With Buddy Rich at Davies Symphony Hall in San Francisco for AT&T.

JULY 17, 1984: In Costa Mesa, California, at the Pacific Amphitheater.

JULY 25, 1984: At the Garden State Arts Center in New Jersey.

JULY 26, 1984: FS appeared at a Republican Party fund-raiser in New Jersey with President Reagan.

JULY 31-AUGUST 21, 1984: In Monte Carlo on vacation.

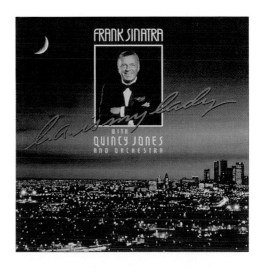

Two legends meet for a cause. Elton John and FS at a Red Cross gala in Monte Carlo.

AUGUST 10, 1984: Frank Sinatra and Elton John performed at a Red Cross gala in Monte Carlo for Prince Rainier.

AUGUST 1984: *L.A. Is My Lady* was released. The reviews were excellent. Quincy Jones's production and my father's signature singing proved to be a winning combination. Contemporary recordings are made track by track, and recording albums can take weeks of serial studio sessions. But *L.A. Is My Lady* was an old-fashioned effort, with my father and the musicians recording simultaneously. As the *New York Times* reported, the result was a disc that "swings the way an all-star jazz orchestra ought to. Mr. Sinatra sounds comfortable, bouncing his phrases off the jazzmen's syncopations like a singer who's been doing jazz sessions for years. The album is a lot of fun—the most enjoyable Frank Sinatra album in a long while."

AUGUST 22-23, 1984: Frank and Barbara attended the Republican Convention in Dallas.

SEPTEMBER 2, 1984: In the pouring rain, FS, Buddy Rich and Tom Dreesen performed at the Canadian National Exhibition in Toronto.

SEPTEMBER 13, 1984: FS was master of ceremonies at a Friars Club tribute to Dean Martin.

SEPTEMBER 16, 1984: In London, U.S. Ambassador and Mrs. Price held a dinner party honoring Frank and Barbara.

SEPTEMBER 17-22, 1984: Six shows at the Royal Albert Hall in London.

SEPTEMBER 25, 1984: He performed at the Moulin Rouge in Paris.

SEPTEMBER 26, 1984: U.S. Ambassador and Mrs. John Kenneth Galbraith honored Frank and Barbara at a dinner party.

OCTOBER 1-2, 1984: The mayor of Vienna invited FS to perform at the city's Stadthalle. President Reagan encouraged Frank to make an appearance as an expression of goodwill, so Dad agreed. The concert was sponsored by the U.S. embassy to benefit children's charities in Austria. Dad waived his salary and covered all expenses for Buddy Rich and his band. FS received the Medal of Honor for Science and Art First Class in Vienna, Austria. This award is Austria's highest civilian honor. That evening a State Dinner was held in his honor. In a letter to President Reagan, Ambassador Helene Van Damm wrote, "Frank took Vienna by storm! He performed before a sold-out concert hall to a roaring crowd of over 10,000, contributing not only his talent to this gala benefit for the children of Austria, but also bearing all travel costs for the musicians and then paying their salaries and per diem as well. How typical of Frank to always give above and beyond! Frank truly deserved receiving the highest award Austria has to offer. It was a highlight for U.S.-Austrian relations."

On the campaign trail with the President and First Lady.

OCTOBER 12-13, 1984: He did four shows at the Golden Nugget in Las Vegas.

OCTOBER 16-20 AND NOVEMBER 5, 1984: FS went to Chicago, Cincinnati, Cleveland, Hartford, Westchester, New York City, Washington, D.C., Sacramento and San Diego for Republican receptions and fund-raisers for President Reagan.

NOVEMBER 2-3, 1984: In Las Vegas at the Golden Nugget, he did four shows in two nights.

NOVEMBER 8, 1984: On Soundstage 15 at 20th Century Fox, FS performed in the Hollywood Park Horse Breeders Cup gala. John Forsythe and Cary Grant also participated in the program.

NOVEMBER 14-18, 1984: Five nights at the Universal Amphitheater in Los Angeles.

NOVEMBER 18, 1984: Before the closing show at the Universal Amphitheater, FS taped Variety Clubs International's "All-Star Party for Lucille Ball" at NBC studios.

NOVEMBER 26, 1984: The Boy Scouts of America honored FS with the Distinguished American Award at the Century Plaza Hotel in Los Angeles.

NOVEMBER 27, 1984: Dinner at the White House with President and Mrs. Reagan.

DECEMBER 27-30, 1984: At the Golden Nugget in Las Vegas.

JANUARY 12, 1985: In New York City, he performed on the Cerebral Palsy Telethon.

Frank and the kids in Palm Springs. It was our last Thanksgiving with Hugh.

The Grandfatherly one in action.

Wrote poet Amanda Lambert, (age 8):

"My Grandpa Francis Albert Sinatra

"My grandpa is a very well-known singer, for most of his albums like, 'L.A. is My Lady,' 'High Sosiety,' and 'New yorkNew york.' But I think he is the best grandpa in the whole wide world!!!

"My mother, Nancy Sinatra, is a well-known singer too, but one thing my grandpa liked best was…KIDS!!! Yep, always loved kids!

"By and by my grandpa became more and more famous!

But 'OL'BLUE EYES' will always be my grandpa!…And I love him to!!!!"

Frank tried to set up a tour of Russia but things didn't work out. At the Reagan Inaugural Gala, a bit of Russia embraces him—Mikhail Baryshnikov.

President Reagan, Nancy and Frank at the 1985 Inaugural Gala.

JANUARY 1985: Once again, before a political event—this time the presidential inaugural gala—the press attacked Frank Sinatra. The *Washington Post* dredged up in a rather desperate fashion the old boring, unfounded accusations of Mob connections. And with Dean Martin and Sammy Davis Jr. in town along with a group of Reagan's Hollywood friends, the *New Republic*, wanting its fair share of the headlines, called it "the Rat Pack inauguration."

JANUARY 18, 1985: He performed at Vice President George Bush's inaugural program. When asked by reporters about the incidents with the press, Bush said, "Leave him alone. Just leave him alone!" My father finally snapped at one interviewer but spoke to all the disreputable ones when he said, "You're dead. You're all dead for me." When I asked my dad what he meant, he told me, "They simply don't exist for me anymore."

JANUARY 19, 1985: Dad performed at the Presidential Inaugural Gala, "We the People," which he also produced. The Gala came off without a hitch.

JANUARY 20, 1985: He attended a White House reception.

FEBRUARY 7, 8, 10, 11, 1985: He appeared at the Sunrise Musical Theater in Ft. Lauderdale.

FEBRUARY 1985: In Miami Beach for the Miracle Ball benefit for St. Jude's Children's Research Center.

FEBRUARY 14-17 AND MARCH 15-16, 1985: In Las Vegas at the Golden Nugget.

MARCH 27, 1985: With Pete Barbuti at the Summit Arena in Houston, Texas.

MARCH 28, 1985: At Kemper Arena in Kansas City, Missouri, with Pete Barbuti.

APRIL 12-13, 1985: At the Golden Nugget in Las Vegas.

APRIL 17-19, 1985: FS performed in Tokyo at the Budokan.

APRIL 22, 1985: At the Imperial Hotel in Tokyo.

APRIL 25, 1985: In Hong Kong at the Hong Kong Coliseum.

MAY 23, 1985: Dad received an honorary engineering degree from the Stevens Institute of Technology in Hoboken. As a kid, he had hoped to attend this school because of his love for design. On this day, the campus carillon, traditional Westminster chimes, played "My Way." These Flemish bells are also programmed to play "It Was a Very Good Year" and "Send in the Clowns." All three songs are programmed to play on Dad's birthday through donations from his friends.

MAY 23, 1985: In a White House ceremony, President Reagan presented my father with the Medal of Freedom. He was in illustrious company. On the same day, the Medal was also presented to: Jacques-Yves Cousteau, Dr. Jerome Holland, Professor Sidney Hook, Ambassador Jeane J. Kirkpatrick, Dr. George M. Low, Frank Reynolds, S. Dillon Ripley, James M. Stewart, General Albert Coady Wedemeyer and General Charles E. Yeager.

MAY 24-27, 1985: Another engagement at the Golden Nugget in Las Vegas.

JUNE 1985: The *Los Angeles Times* was among 45 newspapers that refused to run Garry Trudeau's Doonesbury strip satirizing Frank as a friend of mobsters.

The proudest day of my father's life, the day he received the Medal of Freedom.

FRANK

ON GARRY TRUDEAU:

Garry Trudeau makes his living by his attempts at humor without regard to fairness or decency. I don't know if he has ever made any efforts on behalf of others or done anything to help the less fortunate in this country or elsewhere. I am happy to have the people of the United States judge us by our respective track records.

It is obvious that Trudeau's "comic strips" concerning me were irritating. However, I am used to the press taking "cheap shots" at me and, therefore, Trudeau's "comic strips" went from being irritating to annoying and upsetting because Trudeau, who makes great claim to being a liberal and someone against discrimination, is guilty of the worst type of ethnic slur possible.

Trudeau is guilty of ethnic prejudice, by making the point that I was thin skinned and criticizing him as a matter of self-interest. Moreover, when the publicity started, it was obvious that Trudeau and his syndicator were hoping that I would sue, but there was no reason for me to play into their hands by publicizing Trudeau which would have been the result of such a lawsuit.

AUGUST 8, 1985: He attended a Dodgers game with Jilly, Cary Grant and other friends.

AUGUST 18, 1985: In September of 1984 my husband, Hugh, had been diagnosed with throat cancer. My father was there for him through the entire ordeal. Hugh had eight weeks of radiation treatments to shrink the tumor. It was a nightmare. He suffered horrible burns on his neck and jaw. We spent that Thanksgiving in Palm Springs with Dad, and a lonely family Christmas: two frightened parents trying to make it a happy time for our young children. Surgery was scheduled for January 1985.

On the morning of the surgery, my father and Jilly were the first ones at the hospital. We were by Hughie's side as he was wheeled into the operating room at about 7:30 a.m. and Dad and Jilly stayed until the afternoon. It took the team of three surgeons a total of 18 hours to complete their task. My sister waited with me all night. Finally, the last doctor came out and pronounced the operation a success. I phoned my dad and told him the good news.

Over the next few months, we didn't see my parents much, mainly because Hugh really didn't wish to see anyone. He was unable to talk and could hardly turn his head, but he handled the whole situation with absolute grace and tremendous courage.

When Hughie seemed to be getting better, I took the kids and my mom to Laguna Niguel for a few days at the beach. One afternoon I got a call from the doctor. He said Hughie had collapsed and was in the hospital. I called my sister and my father and Hugh's older children, Griff and Cody, but I decided not to say anything to A.J. and Amanda. At ages 9 and 11, I thought it would be too much information for them to process. I dropped the girls and Mom off at her house and went to the hospital.

My dad and Tina were already there. As the hours went by, Hughie slipped away from us. X rays revealed a new tumor on his spinal cord at the base of the brain. Daddy stayed until very near the end. It was too sad for him. Hughie had been Dad's friend long before he became my husband. They had their own history and a great fondness for each other. Early on in the morning of August 18, Hughie passed away. I stayed with him for a while and then drove home alone to our little canyon house and went to our bed. I watched the daylight creep into our bedroom. I did not sleep. I had to face our children.

Dad and Tina took care of all the arrangements, from the choice of cemetery to the clothes for burial. I took Hughie's wedding ring and put mine on his little finger, and said goodbye. Dad ordered a good old-fashioned wake for his friend Hugh Lambert. He said we should celebrate Hughie's life and we did. The following June, on Father's Day, he took us to the cemetery. It was the first time we had been there since the funeral and Daddy knew the three of us could not go alone. He held his granddaughters' little hands and walked with them on the grounds of what he called a park. He answered their questions as directly as he answered mine when his mother died. He always told the truth. He taught me that communicating with children is just like communicating with adults. You should never talk down to them. I honestly believe Frank Sinatra is the "Great Communicator."

AUGUST 29-SEPTEMBER 1, 1985: In Las Vegas for six shows at the Golden Nugget.

SEPTEMBER 5-14, 1985: Dad played to sold-out audiences for his entire nine-show engagement at Carnegie Hall. Wrote one critic: "Through subtleties of gesture and of voice—a shift of tone, a way of rushing or delaying the beat—Mr. Sinatra brought to his songs a sense of hard-fought inner drama that made them character studies as well as musical gems."

SEPTEMBER 9, 1985: FS was interviewed at the Waldorf-Towers by Arlene Francis for her WOR radio show.

SEPTEMBER 13, 1985: After the show at Carnegie Hall, FS received the Italo-American Coalition Entertainer of the Year Award at the Waldorf-Astoria.

SEPTEMBER 15, 1985: FS was honored in New York City at the Players Club Pipe Night.

SEPTEMBER 26, 1985: In Los Angeles, FS sang one song at a benefit for the Entertainment Industry Council Against Drug Abuse at the Universal Premier Hotel. The evening was a tribute to Nancy Reagan's "Just Say No" antidrug campaign.

My husband Hugh and my father at a dinner following the Kennedy Inaugural Gala, which Hugh staged and choreographed and Frank produced and directed.

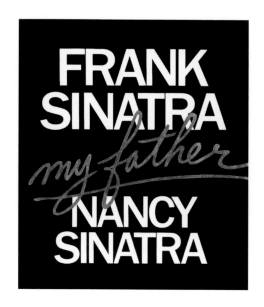

FALL 1985: After years of research, my book *Frank Sinatra: My Father* was published in hardcover.

OCTOBER 6, 1985: Nelson Riddle died as a result of liver failure. Two nights earlier he had conducted at the Hollywood Bowl for Ella Fitzgerald, and he was in the midst of recording his third album with Linda Ronstadt. While Frankie was at Nelson's funeral in Westwood, Frank was at Yul Brynner's funeral in New York and on the same day Orson Welles also died. Frankie: "When I talked to him on the phone about Orson, Dad was crying. He said, 'I don't know what I'm going to do without the fat guy.' They were like brothers and one of Orson's daughters was Frank's goddaughter."

OCTOBER 9-13, 1985: Seven shows at the Golden Nugget in Atlantic City.

OCTOBER 19, 1985: Frank Sinatra received another Life Achievement Award at the Washington Hilton. In his presentation, President Reagan said, "Francis Albert, I just want to tell you that I'm granting you full amnesty, complete forgiveness, for replacing all the Irish tenors in show business."

OCTOBER 22, 1985: As part of the promotion for my book, I interviewed Dad at my home for two segments of the TV show *Hour Magazine*.

OCTOBER 28, 1985: He attended the funeral of his good friend Morton Downey in Palm Beach, Florida.

OCTOBER 30, 1985: FS sang the parody "The Gentleman Is a Champ" for L.A. County Sheriff Sherman Block at a "Roast and Toast" at the Century Plaza Hotel.

NOVEMBER 3, 1985: In Los Angeles he attended the Princess Grace Foundation gala at the Beverly Wilshire Hotel.

NOVEMBER 11, 1985: He emceed a Friars dinner honoring Gene Kelly at the Beverly Hilton in Los Angeles.

NOVEMBER 15-16, 1985: At the Golden Nugget in Las Vegas.

NOVEMBER 21, 1985: Dad attended a Doubleday cocktail party at Nicky Blair's restaurant for my book.

NOVEMBER 30, 1985: He performed with Tom Dreesen in a show benefiting Barbara Sinatra's Children's Center in Palm Springs.

DECEMBER 1, 1985: In Los Angeles FS was master of ceremonies for Paul Keyes's Variety Clubs International "All-Star Party" television show for President Reagan.

DECEMBER 12, 1985: He taped an interview at his Rancho Mirage home for a Spencer Tracy tribute.

DECEMBER 15, 1985: FS was honored by Temple Isaiah in Palm Springs at a "Thank You, Frank" gala for all his help and support.

Sinatra at 70: A Journalist's Valentine

In the December 8, 1985, issue of the Chicago Tribune, one week before my father's 70th birthday, prize-winning columnist Bob Greene penned a heartfelt paean to his favorite singer.

The fact that Frank Sinatra is celebrating his 70th birthday this week is something that will cause many people to stop and think for a moment. Frank Sinatra—70 years old. It has less to do with Sinatra than with the rest of us. If Sinatra is 70, what has happened to us?

By the time I was old enough to appreciate Sinatra's music, he had long been established as an American legend. His image, to a generation much younger than he, was that of a sort of racy, brazen, distant uncle. It was as if at some point before we were aware of it, Sinatra had been voted the coolest guy in the world, and that the honor was sustaining—it never went away...

I started buying old Sinatra albums. I found a store that had some vintage 78 rpm Sinatra discs, and I bought them, too. Sinatra came to represent something to me: that the older guys really were a lot more savvy, a lot more experienced, a lot more comfortable with life. Most younger people see the older world only in terms of their parents and their parents' friends; the younger people aren't especially eager to join that world. Sinatra was the flip side of that: a hip, rich, slightly arrogant guy whose life was better than anybody else's—the ring-a-ding-ding image, all right, and a strong image it was.

I was on a college vacation in Miami Beach. Sinatra was in town making a movie with Raquel Welch; at night he was appearing in the La Ronde Room of the Fontainebleau Hotel on the beach. My college roommate and I tipped the headwaiter of the La Ronde Room to let us in, and we were given the very last table in the very last row of the showroom. A waiter brought us a bottle of Cutty Sark, a bottle of club soda and a bucket of ice. Frank Sinatra, in a black tuxedo, came onto the stage. We were in heaven.

It's hard to express what that meant: being in the same room where Frank Sinatra was singing in front of an orchestra. Breathing the same air. It felt much different than going to see one of the big rock bands of the era, because Sinatra had a history; he had been famous before we were born, and he didn't need us for his self-esteem. There weren't many other college people in the audience, but we didn't care. We were seeing Sinatra, and that was all that mattered.

In the years that followed, it seemed that the essence of Sinatra was diluted by all the controversial publicity; it was hard to concentrate on what he meant to the world as a singing man when you were reading all these things about the other side of his life. Somehow, though, that never mattered much.* Sinatra was still that sly older uncle whose life the rest of us would never match.

Which is why it's so hard to comprehend that now Sinatra is 70 years old. How are we supposed to think of him now? As a gentle, benevolent elder statesman of show business—sort of an American Maurice Chevalier? It's hard to imagine that, and I doubt that Sinatra would really want it that way. But Frank Sinatra is 70, and the world keeps turning, so we must not be so young anymore either. Oh well. Sneak me in the door and give me a table in the back row. Bring a bottle of Cutty Sark and turn down the lights. If Sinatra is 70, I want to be there to hear it.

*[From Nancy:] It is very interesting to me that even a fine writer of good reputation and credentials can fall into the irresistible trap of guilt by association and neglect to use the words "alleged" or "rumors" or even attempt to take issue with "all these things." In doing what he did, he put forward, once again—perhaps to a new generation—the idea that Frank might be a person of questionable ethics. It's ironic...so near, and yet so far away.

1986-1996

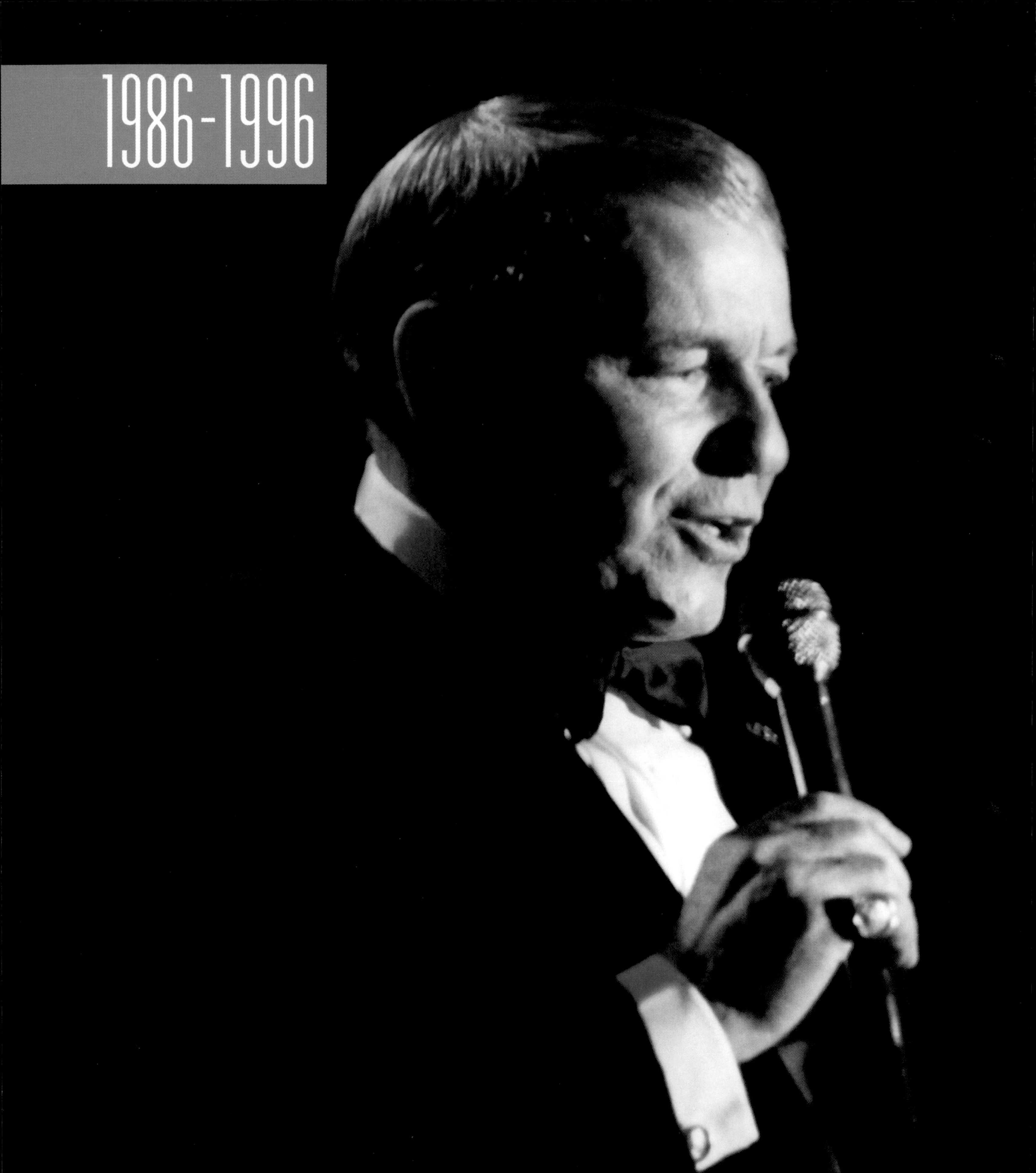

THE BEST
IS YET TO COME

This is the time for a retrospective look at the life and career of Frank Sinatra. In celebration of his 80th birthday, Columbia, Capitol and Reprise are releasing big packages chock-full of wonderful songs. This amazing mountain of work is a testament to his incredible talent and speaks volumes about him—in his own voice. This book will try to fill in the blank pages and chronicle his life and times.

The tributes are already pouring in. His fans are thanking him for all the joy and music he has brought into their lives, as usual. His detractors are criticizing him about any number of things, as usual. And his family and friends are thanking God for him, as usual. Virtually nothing has changed in the nearly six decades that he has been entertaining all of us. We still love him or loathe him. We still adore him or fear him. I think the one thing we all share, admirers and critics alike, is a basic, genuine respect for his talent. None of us can deny he is a musical genius, The Voice of this century.

Many in the nineties are trying to understand him and capture his essence. In the sixties, what Leo Rosten wrote about every man still comes closest, I believe, to capturing the unexplainable, complex yet simple man who is my father, Frank Sinatra—an American legend:

"In some way, however small and secret, each of us is a little mad...everyone is lonely at the bottom and cries to be understood. But we can never entirely understand someone else, and each of us remains part stranger even to those who love us...it is the weak who are cruel; gentleness is to be expected only from the strong...you can understand people better if you look at them—no matter how old or impressive they may be—as if they are children. For most of us never mature; we simply grow taller...The purpose of life is to matter—to count, to have it make some difference that we lived at all."

It would be impossible to calculate how many millions of dollars, pounds, francs and yen FS has raised for the sick, the hungry and the needy of this world. In just five concerts for one charity (The Memorial Sloan-Kettering Cancer Center) he raised more than $9 million. The Frank Sinatra Fund is used for people who cannot pay for the care they need.

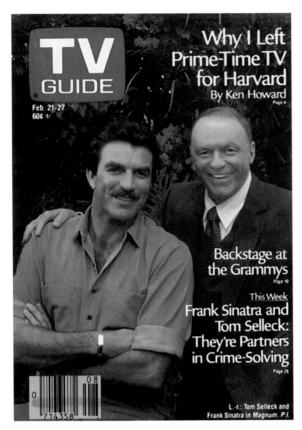

TV GUIDE Feb. 21-27 60¢

Why I Left Prime-Time TV for Harvard
By Ken Howard

Backstage at the Grammys

This Week
Frank Sinatra and Tom Selleck: They're Partners in Crime-Solving

L.-r.: Tom Selleck and Frank Sinatra in *Magnum, P.I.*

Dad had a great time in Hawaii working on this episode of *Magnum P.I.* In one of his best performances, he played a former cop whose granddaughter was brutally murdered.

FS, Sam, Gene Autry and Dean at a Century Plaza benefit for the Gene Autry Western Heritage Museum, February 21, 1987.

goal was to raise $30,000 and we raised $60,000. The next year we exceeded our goal. And it kept growing. I really got hooked when I started meeting the children. It was very sad. I realized they had to have a central meeting place and took it upon myself to find some land or a building. It really is very gratifying when you meet the children and see how they are when they first come in and how they change. It's really wonderful. Frank is our biggest fund-raiser."

NOVEMBER 9-16, 1986: Abdominal pains forced my father to curtail a performance at the Golden Nugget in Atlantic City. He flew home to Palm Springs and underwent emergency surgery for diverticulitis at Eisenhower Medical Center. Rumors were rampant but untrue. Everything was benign, the margins clean.

NOVEMBER 21-22, 1986: Back at work, he did four shows at the Golden Nugget in Las Vegas, and on the 21st he performed at the *Night of Stars* at Caesars Palace for the benefit of St. Jude's.

DECEMBER 12, 1986: Because he was still recovering from surgery, my father was unable to attend a black-tie dinner at Universal Studios in Los Angeles honoring Lew Wasserman on his 50th anniversary as chairman of MCA. Instead, Dad videotaped a special performance of "The Gentleman Is a Champ"—a parody of the old standard tailored to the evening's honoree—that was played at the ceremony. The recording was then pressed onto seven-inch souvenir records and handed out to the 800 guests along with their programs. These gold plastic discs have since become the most treasured Sinatra collectible on the market.

DECEMBER 15, 1986: Still recuperating but not wanting to miss the event, my father sang "New York, New York" at the grand opening of the second hundred years of Carnegie Hall. Two musical legends, conductors Leonard Bernstein and Zubin Mehta, also performed at the newly restored landmark. Dad commented that "I've worked here before, but this night has a special meaning for me."

JANUARY 4-9, 1987: He was in Hawaii to guest star in an episode of the CBS series *Magnum, P.I.*, which aired February 25.

MARCH 1, 1987: Frank Sinatra's third grandchild was born, named Michael Francis Sinatra. My brother and his longtime friend, Pat Fisher, both wanted a child and were worried about the passing of the years, so they made a commitment to conceive. Michael is just like Frankie was as a kid. Looks like him. Acts like him. Cute as a button. Smart as a whip.

MARCH 20, 1987: Dean Martin's son, Dean Paul, died when his Air Force Phantom jet crashed into the side of Mount San Gorgonio in the San Bernardino

National Forest. It was the same mountain on which Dolly Sinatra died in a private plane crash 10 years earlier. Dino's funeral was held at the Veterans Cemetery in West Los Angeles. My sister and I were cautioned by Dean's manager Mort Viner not to show any emotion at the funeral because Dino's family was devastated and trying desperately to stay calm and show courage in this public tribute. Tina and I sat two rows behind Dino's mother, Jeannie, her other children and Dino's son Alex. We squeezed each other's hand when one of us would start to cry, but managed to retain our composure until the flyover with the "Missing Man" formation (an incomplete V). We broke down. Jeannie, who didn't turn around but heard the soft sobs said later, with her arms around both of us, "I just knew it was the Sinatra girls." I believe this tragedy changed big Dean's life forever.

APRIL 1, 1987: Frank performed at the Dinah Shore/Nabisco Golf Tournament dinner at the Marriott Desert Springs Hotel.

APRIL 5, 1987: He attended the funeral of Buddy Rich in Los Angeles.

APRIL 6, 1987: He attended the Marvin Hagler/Sugar Ray Leonard title fight at Caesars Palace.

MAY 1987: FS canceled a summer concert tour of Scandinavia when the Swedish government announced plans to impose a tax on him for having performed in Bophuthatswana, South Africa, in 1981. Generally, foreign entertainers performing in Scandinavia were not taxed. Dad had eagerly been anticipating the concert tour, his first in Scandinavia in 35 years, but was deeply disappointed that unelected bureaucrats had the power to determine who should and should not perform in Sweden. As a lifetime defender of democratic rights, he felt it would be the height of hypocrisy to perform where people aren't made to feel welcome or treated with disrespect when they choose to exercise their legal rights.

MAY 14, 1987: In recognition of his humanism and his support for minorities over his long career, my father received a Life Achievement Award from the Los Angeles Chapter of the National Association for the Advancement of Colored People. The black-tie affair was marred, however, by the objections of an anti-apartheid organization that apparently believed Dad's South Africa appearances in 1981 undermined all the positive deeds he had done to address the plague of racism in the world.

In defending the selection of my father for the award, the president of the Los Angeles NAACP said, "I believe there has been a lot of misinformation. Frank Sinatra has made significant outcries against segregation, discrimination and bigotry," a sentiment most of my father's friends and fans believe describes him well. Sharing the dais with him were my sister, Tina, and his longtime friend Gregory Peck.

He condemned not only South Africa's racial policies but also those who objected to his receiving the Life Achievement Award, saying that "in the name of fighting apartheid [they] seek to divide not only blacks and whites but blacks themselves." Tellingly, Stevie Wonder and Sammy Davis Jr. both appeared at the event to acknowledge my father's achievements in interracial relations. "He was my

My nephew Michael at my house, Christmas 1994. In him we see the link to the future of the Sinatra name.

> **FRANK**
>
> **ON RACISM:**
>
> *Those of you who know me feel pretty secure about the way I think, the way I am. As far as anyone else is concerned, if my lifetime—more than half a century lived in the spotlight of public life—if those 50 years are not enough to show my covenant on the issue of civil rights, I am not going to waste my time defending the obvious or itemizing a laundry list of my deeds to benefit the brotherhood of man.*

Gregory Peck

I don't know anyone else who does things like Frank, and he does them all the time. First comes the impulse, then the follow-through. It is typical Sinatra behavior. Once he spent six hours in the kitchen, cooking up an Italian meal like Mama used to make for 24 dinner guests. Later on, when the guests had left, he demonstrated his remedy for sore, aching feet: Soak them in a pan of Scotch whiskey. You have to like a man like that. He is colorful. He is generous. He shows his feelings. I have known him since 1942. He is the friend I would call if I needed help in an emergency. I don't discuss Frank with the press. An interviewer asked me recently to explain our friendship. "Frank is so volatile," he said, "and you are so laid back. Frank is a Republican, and you are a Democrat." "And the interview is over," I said.

friend long before it became fashionable to be my friend," Sammy said. "You wouldn't see black dealers or black people living in hotels in Las Vegas if Sinatra hadn't spearheaded it all in 1946."

JUNE 2, 1987: Frank and Willie Nelson taped a public service announcement for NASA at the Las Palmas Theatre in Hollywood.

OCTOBER 18, 1987: Frank appeared at a benefit at the Las Vegas Convention Center for the 75th anniversary of the United Way.

NOVEMBER 29, 1987: He performed during a telethon for the Juvenile Diabetes Foundation at the Universal Sheraton.

DECEMBER 1, 1987: He attended a tribute to Buddy Rich at the Universal Amphitheater in Los Angeles.

DECEMBER 2, 1987: Frank performed at the Century Plaza Hotel at a dinner honoring industrialist Armand Hammer. Hammer thanked Frank in a letter dated December 3, 1987: "You made the evening sparkle and you assured that all of the guests left with the inspiration of Frank Sinatra's commitment to a great cause."

DECEMBER 6, 1987: He performed at the Kennedy Center Honors salute to Perry Como in Washington, D.C.

DECEMBER 1987: Dad, Sammy and Dean Martin held a news conference at Chasen's restaurant to announce their intention to tour together for the first time in 20 years.

MARCH 1988: Twenty-six years after it premiered in 1962, Dad's classic thriller *The Manchurian Candidate* was rereleased to a new moviegoing audience.

MARCH 13, 1988: Dad, Sammy and Dean kicked off their reunion tour at the Oakland Coliseum. It sold out within two hours. Joking about their advanced ages, according to the *Washington Post*, Dean and Sammy offered Dad a "golden age cocktail." "What the hell is a golden age cocktail?" he asked, playing straight man. Said Sammy, "Geritol and prune juice." "Gets you going," Dean added, "and keeps you going." When Sammy sang "Mr. Bojangles" and needed a hat for a prop, someone tossed one onto the stage. Sammy waved it at the exuberant crowd—it was a yarmulke. Dean sang "Amore," all the while gripping his everpresent drink in one hand. It reminded people of what he once considered "the breakfast of champions": bourbon and crackers. People wore T-shirts that read "Frank, Dean and Sammy: Together Again," and one woman said to the *Post,* "We feel like we kind of grew up with them." "This is like the Super Bowl," said one man. "An event," offered another. "It's like a once-in-a-lifetime deal."

APRIL 1988: Dad's first two 10-inch LPs—*Swing Easy* (1953) and *Songs for Young Lovers* (1954)—were rereleased by Capitol Records on compact disc.

MAY 11, 1988: Performed at the Irving Berlin Tribute at Carnegie Hall in New York City.

MAY 14, 1988: At the Waldorf Hotel in New York City, Frank performed with Liza at the Friars Tribute to Barbara Sinatra.

MAY 26, 1988: A portion of Dad's recording of "Just the Way You Look Tonight" was used as the voiceover in a commercial for Michelob beer. A lot of media watchers questioned the use of my father's voice because Michelob was positioned as a young person's drink and had previously featured such celebrities as Eric Clapton, Phil Collins, Roger Daltrey and Steve Winwood—all young rock-'n'-rollers. Michelob, however, felt that the campaign would get an added boost by featuring someone with timeless, upscale appeal. Said an Anheuser-Busch marketing manager, "We're trying to show the length and breadth of 'the night.'" And no one can sing about the night better than Frank Sinatra.

JUNE 5, 1988: In Beverly Hills at Jerry Weintraub's residence, Frank performed at a dinner honoring Vice President George Bush.

AUGUST 18, 1988: Attended the Republican Convention in New Orleans.

SEPTEMBER 13, 1988: Interviewed by *USA Today.*

Dean, Sam and Frank—The Summit once again. The tour proved to be too fatiguing for Dean, so he left before it ended.

Dad has known Liza since she was born. She calls him Uncle Frank. They tease each other about the song "New York, New York." Liza constantly reminds Dad, "It was written for me."

SEPTEMBER 15, 1988: Press question-and-answer session with Frank, Liza and Sammy.

NOVEMBER 3, 1988: "Legends in Our Time" convention, sponsored by Anheuser Busch, at the Shrine Auditorium in Los Angeles. Frank performed a few songs, accompanied by Sammy and Liza.

JANUARY 7, 1989: Frank, Lucille Ball and Jerry Weintraub chaired the JINSA/Roast/Tribute to Sonny Golden at the Century Plaza in Los Angeles.

JANUARY 1989: My father served as head of a group of artists, the Performers Rights Society of America, to lobby for musical royalty reform legislation. Broadcasters were opposed to the plan, which proposed that singers, lyricists and composers receive residual payments when their renditions of songs were played on the radio or when their records were played on jukeboxes and in discos. Dad's attorney, Robert Finkelstein, a co-founder of the group, spoke for its members when he said performance royalties should be a matter of equity. "Performers have to have some type of parity with other copyright owners," he told the Los Angeles Times. "There's such logic and such symmetry to this that I don't see it as morally or legally debatable."

JANUARY 19, 1989: Performed at President Bush's Inaugural Gala in Washington D.C., at the Convention Center.

JANUARY 25, 1989: FS received the Will Rogers Award at the 75th Anniversary of Beverly Hills at the Beverly Hills Hotel.

FEBRUARY 3-4, 1989: Frank Sinatra Celebrity Golf Invitational-Benefit for Desert Hospital, at the Canyon Country Club in Palm Springs.

APRIL 23, 1989: While in Paris, Frank was honored by the City of Paris, receiving the "Great Plate of the Bimillenary of Paris." The award was presented by Mayor Jacques Chirac.

JUNE 7, 1989: Revlon named my father and Barbara as its first "unforgettable couple." They joined such previous Revlon "unforgettables" as Oprah Winfrey, Brooke Shields, Audrey Hepburn and Liza Minnelli. Dad and Barbara joined the group in return for Revlon's support of the Barbara Sinatra Children's Center for abused kids in Palm Springs.

JULY 1989: Frank planned to introduce in the spring of 1990 a line of his own pasta sauces. "Over the years I've received some nice compliments about my cooking," Dad said at the company launch party, which was held at Morton's restaurant in Beverly Hills. "A few years ago, we made some pasta sauce for our friends during the holiday season, and it's become a tradition. I think it's terrific that the sauces and other items will be available to the public." The sauces were distributed by Armanino Foods of Distinction.

Dad and Frankie on the road. Frank says nobody knows the music better than his son.

OCTOBER 1989: When the Kremlin announced that it would not object if Hungary left the Warsaw Pact or if East Germany reunited with West Germany, Soviet Foreign Ministry spokesman Gennady Gerasimov appeared on a syndicated TV program and said, "Frank Sinatra has a very popular song, 'I Had It My Way.' So Hungary, Poland, every other country has its own way. They decide which road to take. It's their business. And we watch, watch closely, but we do not interfere." He called the new policy "the Frank Sinatra doctrine." Said Dad: "I'm honored to have my name associated with freedom of choice and people's dreams for a better life. I think it's marvelous." Vice President Dan Quayle said the Bush administration was encouraged by Mr. Gerasimov's comment, adding, "We hope that perestroika succeeds. But as they talk about the Frank Sinatra doctrine, also remember the Nancy Sinatra doctrine in song—'These Boots Are Made for Walking.'"

NOVEMBER 1989: Frank supported the local American Foundation of Musicians (AF of M) strike against the Las Vegas hotels, who were seeking to replace their house bands with taped music and synthesizers. In the *Los Angeles Times*, Frank was quoted as saying, "I am informed that a settlement of the strike is possible before the holidays. If such is the case I do not want to jeopardize these conversations and am deferring my decision to per-

I love this picture of my brother. In the eight years Frankie has been Dad's music director, he has also continued his own touring and singing—with an orchestra. Now he says, "I have the only band in town." With most Las Vegas hotels dropping their house bands, my brother is trying to keep alive a dying part of our culture. It's scary to think that young people might not want to take up the saxophone, the trumpet or the violin anymore.

form in Las Vegas." Dad's musical conductor, Frank Jr.: "Pop called me and said 'I want to go there to work. Get up there and take care of that strike.' I went up there and met with Mark Tully-Masagli, the president of Local 369 AF of M. We met at 1:00 a.m. at Ballys. He assured me that he was more than willing to cooperate. The following night after my show at the Four Queens, I went to Ballys and was given a sealed envelope from the musicians, which I took to my meeting with Bob Ostrovsky, head of Human Resources at Ballys. He read the terms and said, 'This is negotiable. This is workable.' I asked him if I had permission to tell my people that the outlook is hopeful. He said yes. All went well until Ostrovsky had to turn everything over to Ballys' attorneys in Atlantic City. They were the decision makers and couldn't have cared less about a strike 3,000 miles away. One of the attorneys said he wouldn't even take it to his superiors. He just said, 'No, we've made our minds up. We're not going to settle.' At which point I called him a little pencil-pushing, buck-passing, spineless bureaucrat. And the press attacked me for it. The strike was never resolved. It just ended. Tully-Masagli told me the five or six hotels said in essence, 'The boat has already sailed.' There are no more union contracts and no more house bands. The Desert Inn hired three staff musicians and the other hotels would hire on an a-la-carte (as needed) basis. Ballys fired Frank. They said he was 'undependable' because he had canceled three performances in support of the musician's union. Today, almost six years later, there are very few musicians living in Las Vegas."

NOVEMBER 13, 1989: A television special celebrating Sammy Davis Jr.'s 60th anniversary in show business was taped at the Shrine Auditorium in Los Angeles. Proceeds from the ticket sales were donated to the United Negro College Fund.

JANUARY 30, 1990: The new Knickerbocker Arena in Albany, New York, opened its doors to the public with a Frank Sinatra concert. Ten thousand tickets sold on the first day they were available.

A group shot from the 60th Anniversary tribute to Sammy. Clockwise from left: Ella Fitzgerald, Debbie Allen, Nell Carter, Bill Cosby, Gregory Peck, Jesse Jackson, Gregory Hines, Clint Eastwood, Tony Danza, Magic Johnson, Richard Pryor, Bob Hope. Middle row: Lola Falana, Diahann Carroll, Eddie Murphy, Shirley MacLaine, Dean Martin, Quincy Jones, Dionne Warwick, Whitney Houston. Front row: Mike Tyson, Frank Sinatra, Goldie Hawn, Sammy, Michael Jackson, Altovise Davis, Anita Baker, Stevie Wonder.

MAY 1990: In an appearance at Radio City Music Hall, fans rushed the stage to deposit flowers at my father's feet. "Sort of reminds me of the Paramount," Dad joked, recalling the old bobby-soxer days.

MAY 16, 1990: Dad lost a close friend when Sammy Davis Jr. died of throat cancer at the age of 64. Although he canceled the remaining four nights of his sold-out Radio City Music Hall concerts, while he was performing on stage he kept his emotions to himself as his friend lay dying in Los Angeles. He said, "I wish the world could have known Sam as I did. Sam never gave less than 100 percent when he was on stage, and he gave even more to those of us lucky enough to call him a friend. He was a class act, and I will miss him forever."

JUNE 1990: Frank performed at the London Arena and also held concerts in Glasgow, Scotland, and Stockholm, Sweden. My kids went with him. They said that Grandpa walked to London, pacing up and down the plane all night, covering people with blankets and giving them pillows and chatting with the flight attendants. He never sleeps on a plane. He's probably walked all over the world. The girls complained about not being able to sneak off without a security guard. They said they felt like the president's children with Secret Service agents hovering around them. I had to remind them that their grandfather believes in safety first.

AUGUST 1990: Frank's concert tour with pal Don Rickles began at Sacramento's Cal Expo Amphitheater. On stage both separately and together, their appearances invoked some of the fun of the old Summit get-togethers, like the time Dean and Sammy and Dad took Don's towel away from him at the Sands and shoved him out of the sauna, leaving him naked by the hotel pool.

AUGUST 1990: Dad signed an exclusive contract to appear at the Sands Hotel Casino and Country Club in Atlantic City for nine shows over two years.

OCTOBER 1990: Following his Sands deal on the East Coast, my father signed an exclusive two-year contract to appear at the Riviera in Las Vegas, including three New Year's Eve performances beginning in 1990.

OCTOBER 1990: The line of Frank Sinatra pasta sauces, which had only been available in California and Nevada, expanded their market to New York. His Sugo da Tavola Italian sauce was now available in three varieties: tomato basil with parmesan, marinara with mushrooms and Milano-style marinara.

DECEMBER 3, 1990: The Frank Sinatra Diamond Jubilee Tour kicked off a couple of days before his 75th birthday at the Meadowlands Arena in East Rutherford, New Jersey, with Steve Lawrence and Eydie Gorme as the opening act. Chivas Regal sponsored the world tour.

DECEMBER 12, 1990: What do you give a guy on his 75th birthday, a guy you love more than the moon, a guy who has achieved everything he ever dreamed of? I gave my dad...a tie. At a Los Angeles Kings hockey game, I saw a man wearing a

Amanda and her grandfather waiting to board the flight to London.

The Loss of My Uncle Sam

When I heard Sam had been taken to the hospital, I called Dad and then rushed over to see him. I found Sam wandering in the corridor in his hunter green velour robe. When he saw me, he padded over and gave me a bear hug. I said, "Sam, are you OK? What's wrong? You're scaring me." He said, "I'm all right, Nan, don't worry." That's all he would say. We visited a little while, and then I went to see another friend, Marilyn Lewis, owner of the Hamburger Hamlet restaurants, who was in the room next door. When I went back to Sammy's room, he was resting, so I left, not knowing anything except what was in my gut, and it was not a good feeling. He had lost too much weight and that was not a good sign.

The next time I saw him he was dying. Sammy's wife, Altovise, called and asked me to come over to the house. I called Jack Haley Jr. and asked him to go with me because I was afraid I wouldn't make it alone. I knew, because I had been with my husband as he lay dying, that it would be very difficult to see Sammy like this.

We went into the darkened room where Alto, Sammy's assistant Shirley Rhodes and his friend Murphy sat quietly. Sam was in a hospital bed, in a sitting position, covered only by a clean white sheet. He was sleeping. I pulled a chair up next to the bed and sat down. After a little while, he opened his eyes and recognized me. He reached out for my hand, and I got down on my knees on the floor next to him, taking his hand in both of mine. I rested my forehead on his arm—very gently because he was so frail and thin—and we stayed like that for a little while. As the minutes passed my heart went back through all of the wonderful times we had shared. I was able to recall very special images of him looking fit and full of energy, and those mem-ories sustain me to this day. After a time I felt him stir, so I pulled back a bit, still holding his hand. He weakly pulled it away, and seeing the tears in my eyes, slowly waved me away. I knew he didn't want me to see him like that, because he was a proud man, so I stood up to go. He reached for me once more. I took his hand and kissed it and whispered, "I love you, Sam." He was unable to speak, so he squeezed my hand as if to say, "I love you, too." Then he rested his hand at his side and closed his eyes, and I left.

The night before Sammy's burial service, my sister and I drove out to the cemetery for the private viewing. We sat with Altovise in the tiny chapel for a long time. She was suffering, and we felt so very helpless. Sammy was decked out in a natty outfit: suit and tie, a bright red shirt, the works. The room was filled with bright colors and lots of flowers. Murphy, who was pretty fragile himself, was so sad. When I approached to embrace him, he started to cry, a wailing kind of crying that only real, deep-down grief can bring out of the human body. I've heard it only a few times in my life, but it is unmistakable.

The funeral service was like a Hollywood production. It took place in a large, glassy chapel filled with flowers and celebrities and music and light. I was seated between Shirley MacLaine and my father. I was worried about my dad. He had lost so many friends, and now Smokey, who was like a brother to him, was gone, too. I was also concerned for him because the service was long and it was a hot day.

I do have one very vivid memory: As I was leaving the chapel to go to the limousine for the drive to the burial site, I heard heavy sobs. I turned to see a small, blond woman standing alone in the heat of the day. She had her face buried in her hands. Her body was heaving, racked with sobs. I went over to her, not knowing who she was, and I put my arms around her and she let go in my arms. She was so overcome with grief, I think she didn't know where she was or that a stranger had embraced her. When she quieted down, she pulled away from me and looked up into my eyes. I guess she wanted to see who this person was who held her. When I saw her face, I realized I had been consoling Sally Struthers, and when she recognized me, she fell back into my arms and cried some more.

To be completely honest, I don't remember much more about that day. It is one of those misty, blurry times of grief with tear-stained faces and hugging and lots of sobbing sounds, one of those days I purposely tried to strike from my life. Unfortunately, the memories that remain are all too real. Sammy, our treasured friend, really was gone.

cute tie decorated with M&Ms, Nestle's Crunch bars, Reese's Peanut Butter Cups, Hershey's Kisses and Life Savers. Showing absolutely no shame, I stopped him in the aisle and asked if he would give it to me. I just knew it was the perfect gift for Dad, who was a penny-candy kind of guy. Luckily, my audacious behavior was graciously rewarded: The guy promptly removed his neckwear, and Dad opened my gift with a delighted chuckle.

Father's Day, 1991: Mom, Dad (unwrapping his gifts) and Tina. We were also celebrating A.J.'s high school graduation.

DECEMBER 3, 1990: Some 1,200 people packed the International Ballroom of the Beverly Hilton to salute my father as recipient of the Ella, a lifetime achievement award bestowed upon him by the Society of Singers. The first lady of jazz herself, Ella Fitzgerald, serenaded Dad with "There Will Never Be Another You," and the two of them did a terrific duet of "The Lady Is a Tramp."

Others performed that night, too. As reported in the *Los Angeles Times*, Tony Bennett sang a moving rendition of "How Do You Keep the Music Playing?," Herb Jeffries sang "Flamingo" and Joe Williams, who is only a few years younger than Frank, had everyone snapping their fingers with "Alright, Okay, You Win." Ninety-something George Burns checked in with "Young at Heart." Peggy Lee and Jack Jones penned a ditty to Dad. Jo Stafford and the Hi-Lo's sang "I'll Never Smile Again," and Steve Lawrence and Eydie Gorme sounded great on two tunes Dad had co-written himself, "This Love of Mine" and "I'm a Fool to Want You."

It was an emotional evening and he was humbled by it. Luckily, the rest of America was able to share it a couple of weeks later in a CBS television special entitled *The Best Is Yet to Come*. The special was produced by my sister, Tina, and George Schlatter and included footage of Dad's performance at the Meadowlands on December 10.

JANUARY 12, 1991: At the American Cinema Awards, Frank presented the Humanitarian Award to Leo Jaffe.

JANUARY 13, 1991: Frank presented the Scopus Award to Quincy Jones at the Hebrew University Benefit.

MARCH 1991: *The Voice of Our Time*, a 90-minute special about Frank Sinatra's life and career, aired on public television.

MARCH 1991: "The Fascination of Frank Sinatra," a film retrospective at the School of the Art Institute of Chicago, featured 10 of Dad's movies. Although fairly limited in scope, the program, critics believed, delineated the depth and importance of his screen work. Wrote one critic, "Sinatra starred in several of the most psychologically probing films to come out of Hollywood....Like his singing, Sinatra's acting is subtle, understated and absolutely true."

APRIL 1991: In yet another tawdry tome, the swill was again dug up. This time the victim was former First Lady Nancy Reagan, who was accused of having an affair with Frank Sinatra in the White House. Offered as "proof" were claims that Mrs. Reagan always seated my father next to her at White House functions and had private lunches with him behind closed doors. My father's frequent visits to the White House had to do with the fact that he and the Reagans were warm and trusted long-

FS and Q with the Scopus Award.

My father loves dogs. He's had as many as eight at one time. Here he cuddles one of his King Charles Cavaliers.

time friends, and that for much of the Reagan administration Dad served on the President's Committee for the Arts and Humanities—facts the "author" chose to ignore.

JULY 4, 1991: In an essay for the op-ed section of the *Los Angeles Times* in commemoration of Independence Day, Dad wrote: "We are created equal! No one of us is better than any of us!...

"Why do innocent children still grow up to be despised? Why do haters' jokes still get big laughs when passed in whispers from scum to scum? You know the ones I mean—the 'Some of my best friends are Jewish...' crowd. As for the others, those cross-burning bigots to whom mental slavery is alive and well, I don't envy their trials in the next world, where their thoughts and words and actions will be judged by a jury of One....

"I'm a saloon singer, by self-definition. Even my mirror would never accuse me of inventing wisdom. But I do claim enough street smarts to know that hatred is a disease—a disease in the body of freedom, eating its way from the inside out, infecting all who come in contact with it, killing dreams and hopes of millions of innocents with words, as surely as if they were bullets....

"Take a minute. Consider what we are doing to each other as we rob friends and strangers of dignity as well as equality...For if we don't come to grips with this killer disease of hatred, of bigotry and racism and anti-Semitism, pretty soon we will destroy from within this blessed country....

"Don't just lip-sync the words to the song. Think them, live them. 'My country 'tis of thee, sweet land of liberty.' And when the music fades, think of the guts of Rosa Parks, who by a single act in a single moment changed America as much as anyone who ever lived....

"I'm no angel. I've had my moments. I've done a few things in my life of which I'm not too proud, but I have never unloved a human being because of race, creed or color. And if you think this is a case of he who doth protest too much, you're wrong. I couldn't live any other way...."

FRANK SINATRA'S DIAMOND JUBILEE WORLD TOUR

SEPTEMBER 26, 1991: In a meeting of classics, one archaeological, one musical, Dad sang among the ruins of Pompeii during his Diamond Jubilee tour of Europe. The concert almost didn't happen because conservationists were concerned about the ravages wreaked by fans climbing on the ashy residue from the eruption of Mount Vesuvius in A.D. 79. But organizers reached an agreement with concert promoters to take proper security precautions.

FALL 1991: Tina's book, *A Man and His Art*, was published. In it she exposed a hitherto unknown passion of my father's: painting. She wrote, "For Frank Sinatra, painting isn't an intellectual pursuit—it's visceral. It's more intangible, more essential than that. This book is the essence of him. Painting is a part of his talent that not many have seen before. This book is a way for him to share a very personal side of himself. It's a little like publishing a book of poetry. It's another window to his soul."

OCTOBER 1991: In anticipation of the upcoming holiday season, Dad's first recording in more than seven years was released. His version of "Silent Night" was one track on *The Christmas Album: A Gift of Hope*, proceeds from which would go to the San Diego-based Children's Hospital Foundation. My brother accompanied him on piano. The other performers on the album, which was produced by Michael Lloyd, included Reba McEntire, Barry Manilow, Willie Nelson, Kenny Loggins, Hank Williams Jr., Lou Rawls, Dionne Warwick and me.

DECEMBER 1991: Angie Dickinson, a friend of my father's for three decades, helped to promote his Chivas Regal telephone charity hotline on the radio. One DJ who interviewed her asked if she called Dad God. "No," replied Angie, who has a marvelous sense of humor. "I would never call him God. I would call him Mr. God."

JANUARY 21, 1992: Performed at a fund-raiser at the Waldorf-Astoria with Liza Minnelli and Shirley MacLaine for the New York mayoral candidacy of Andrew Stein.

APRIL 1992: Due to differences between Artanis and Armanino, the license was terminated. At the same time, we attempted to arrange for an orderly transition to TKI, who was already manufacturing the pasta sauce for Artanis in the East. TKI has since expanded the brand and optimistically we will have a very successful program.

MAY 6, 1992: Jilly Rizzo died in a fiery car accident in Palm Springs.

A MAN AND HIS ART
FRANK SINATRA
Introduction by TINA SINATRA

Tina: "Dad paints what he likes. He doesn't do it to please anybody."

The Death of Jilly Rizzo

It was the night of his 75th birthday and he was throwing himself a party. After cooking all evening with road manager Tony Oppedisano, Jilly left his house to visit his girlfriend Betty Jean. He was in her neighbor's Jaguar, which had been left with Betty Jean while the neighbor was on vacation. It was after midnight and the driver of the oncoming car had been drinking. He was traveling 85 mph when he hit Jilly in the white Jag, which had two rear gas tanks.

The impact produced sparks, igniting one gas tank and, as the car spun around, the other tank also exploded. Jilly was trapped inside, unable to open the door, which had been automatically locked. The fact that he had one eye made it impossible for him to see the door clearly, adding to his confusion in this car that was completely foreign to him.

All that was left of Jilly was his jewelry. The car was too hot to be touched for many hours after the crash. Tony identified the jewelry and what was left of the car, then he went back to Jilly's house to change. He phoned security at my father's house—it was very early—and told the guard what had happened and to make certain that Frank receive no phone calls.

After he showered, he called Jilly's children with the horrible news, and then Tony went to my father's house. He broke the news to Barbara and they decided not to wake Daddy up, but to wait until he came out of his room for breakfast. Although they were concerned that he might hear the news on television, they decided to risk it and let him sleep. Tony called me in Los Angeles, and I passed the news along to the rest of my family. Then I threw some clothes in my car—a Jaguar—and headed toward Palm Springs.

Before my dad woke up, Barbara called his doctor, Dr. Picchione; she was worried that the dreadful news would have a shattering effect on Frank and she felt the doctor might be necessary. She and Tony told Dad, who was devastated but strong. He asked about Jilly's daughter.

The driver who killed Jilly Rizzo did not have a license. It had been taken away because of three previous drunk driving convictions. Justice was sure and sweet. He's still in jail.

Tony: "As Jilly was getting into the car just after midnight I said, 'I want to be the first to wish you a happy birthday.'"

The Sinatra family, 1992.

JUNE 1992: Dad's European concert tour had mixed results. His London appearances in Albert Hall were warmly received, as usual, even by Prime Minister John Major, who met him during intermission at one of his performances.

SEPTEMBER 2, 1992: In Beverly Hills, Gregory Peck and Liza Minnelli presented FS with the Distinguished Life Achievement Award at the American Cinema Awards.

NOVEMBER 1992: CBS aired Tina's five-hour miniseries, *Sinatra*. Dad had given her his blessing, not to mention his cooperation, on the project, which dealt not only with his musical genius but with the controversies that had plagued him throughout his life. It spanned the years from 1920 to 1974, examining Dad's relationships with Sam Giancana, President Kennedy and his marriages. "Reading the script at various stages was painful for him," Tina said. "Now that it's done, he's going to have to face it."

The series itself underwent a painful conception and birth. Originally written as a 10-hour miniseries, it was revised and rethought and reorganized to meet with everyone's approval without sacrificing authenticity. Tina wanted to make a miniseries instead of writing a book because she felt Dad's life lent itself more naturally to a visual rendering than a literary one. The soundtrack included original recordings lip-synched by lead actor Philip Casnoff, who did a great job portraying Dad.

Although some critics said the story was a whitewash, Tina deleted material that would have given credence to that perception. In the 1950s, for example, Dad bought a house in Beverly Hills for Sammy Davis Jr., enabling him to be one of the first African-Americans to live there. But Tina opted to exclude that telling fact for fear that the film would come off as a list of his good deeds instead of a more psychologically compelling study.

JANUARY 9, 1993: The Career Achievement Award at the Palm Springs International Film Festival was bestowed on my father at the Riviera Hotel. Preceding the presentation of the award was an hourlong tribute with Robert Wagner serving as master of ceremonies. The tribute chronicled Dad's career through a number of his film clips, including scenes with Laurence Harvey

On the set of the miniseries *Sinatra*, Frank, Tina and Philip Casnoff, who played FS.

Tina Sinatra

ON THE MINISERIES:

He had been trying to get this produced since he worked with producer René Valenti on Contract on Cherry Street *and nothing ever happened. When we decided to go for it, I told him it wasn't going to be easy. He was involved in the writing of the script but wasn't prepared for the full impact of the scope of his life all in one sitting. When he looked at it I didn't hear from him for 36 hours. So I called him, asking, "Should I pack my bags and leave for Mexico?" He laughed and said, "No, No. I just had to digest it for a little while." I said, "You know, Mom reacted the same way." And Dad said, "I'll bet she did." I did this film not to exploit or to expose but to emotionalize this human being's life. A human being who happened to have been an American icon from the time he was 21. I wanted people to know what it was like to be in his skin.*

in *The Manchurian Candidate*, Shirley MacLaine in *Some Came Running* and Montgomery Clift in *From Here to Eternity*. At the ceremony, George Sidney, who directed Dad in two musicals, *Pal Joey* and *Anchors Aweigh*, paid him the ultimate compliment: "His first take is better than most people's tenth. He always went for the best and took risks."

JANUARY 21, 1993: In Los Angeles FS attended Mary Lazar's funeral.

JANUARY 22, 1993: Dad attended the funeral of Sammy Cahn, one of his best friends and favorite lyricists, who died of congestive heart failure at 79. "I've never known, never sung a Cahn song that didn't say something," my father wrote in the liner notes of one album.

APRIL 1993: *Frank Sinatra at the Movies*, a 19-song collection, was released by Capitol Records along with *Nat King Cole at the Movies*. Dad's collection included the title song for *From Here to Eternity*, the film that earned him an Oscar. Also part of the package were "Young at Heart" and "Someone to Watch Over Me" from *Young at Heart*, and the Oscar-winning "All the Way" from *The Joker Is Wild*.

JUNE 1993: His granddaughter A.J. accompanied him on tour to England, Germany and Sweden.

AUGUST 19-21, 1993: My father helped the town of Aurora, Illinois, usher in the high-rolling life. The Hollywood Casino, a two-boat center for gambling, dining and entertainment on the Fox River, had been open for a couple of months, but it wasn't until Dad appeared in concert for three days that its place in casino lore was truly established. According to one local booster, "Sinatra put us on the map." Said another customer: "Gambling and Frank seem to go together like scotch and soda."

SEPTEMBER 19, 1993: Dad and Barbara hosted a fund-raising dinner at Chasen's restaurant in Los Angeles to support the mayoral reelection bid of Teddy Kollek of Jerusalem. The affair, attended by such luminaries as Gregory Peck, Barbra Streisand and Marvin Davis, was another demonstration of my father's abiding dedication to Israel and to his friendship with Kollek.

OCTOBER 1993: His first new studio album in 10 years, *Duets*, featured tracks of my father singing 13 of his well-known songs with partners who represented the musical spectrum from swing to rock. Apart from its nontraditional mix of singing talent, the album was a technological accomplishment: None of the tracks was recorded with both singers present. Dad recorded his part in the Los Angeles studios of Capitol Records, and the other singers either recorded subsequently in the same studio or, in the case of some of the overseas musicians, phoned in their contributions courtesy of a digital system developed in part by George Lucas' Skywalker Sound.

The Voice in 1993

In the wake of his Duets smash, Frank Sinatra's continuing love of performing and his fans' continuing support inspired a wave of Sinatra analysis. It was no secret that Dad's vocal power at age 78 was not equal to that of his earlier years, but most critics were still blown away by what he continued to do. One fan said Sinatra's singing was "sort of like a beautiful antique. When you think about it, chances are you may buy something today that's better constructed, that may not have all the scratches, but the antique holds greater beauty and value." And a music journalist for the Pittsburgh Post Gazette posed the question: "Is Sinatra half the singer he was in 1942 or 1956? Actually, he's about three-fifths the singer he was—but that still makes him about twice the singer anyone else is."

Producer Phil Ramone and co-producer Hank Cattaneo worked with Patrick Williams on the arrangements, mostly by Nelson Riddle, of such songs as "The Lady Is a Tramp" (with Luther Vandross), "What Now My Love" (with Aretha Franklin), "I've Got You Under My Skin" (with Bono) , "I've Got a Crush on You" (with Barbra Streisand), "I've Got the World on a String" (with Liza Minnelli), "In the Wee Small Hours" (with Carly Simon), "New York, New York" (with Tony Bennett), "Come Rain or Come Shine" (with Gloria Estefan), "Witchcraft" (with Anita Baker) and "Summer Wind" (with Julio Iglesias).

NOVEMBER 1993: The Legacy division of Sony Music released *Frank Sinatra: The Columbia Years 1943-1952, The Complete Recordings*, a 12-CD boxed set of Frank's Columbia recordings from the 1940s and 1950s. Apart from its musical eclecticism, the 284-song album was notable for the fact that some of its material had been previously unavailable in any format. This is a fabulous collection. The purity of his voice on these early recordings is astounding, and the fact that most of these songs were done in one or two takes is a testament to the extraordinary technical skills of the orchestra and my father. Never a wrong note. Never a missed interval.

NOVEMBER 5, 1993: Taped the video for "I've Got You Under My Skin" with Bono in Palm Springs.

NOVEMBER 17-21, 1993: My father appeared at the Foxwoods Hotel and Casino in Ledyard, Connecticut, which is owned by the Mashantucket Pequot Indian tribe. Dad inaugurated the 1,480-seat showroom with five shows that also marked the opening of the casino's luxury hotel, shopping arcade, ethnic restaurant and entertainment complex. "It says about Foxwoods," commented a journalist who covered the gambling industry, "that it's a real player in the American gambling industry." Foxwoods was already the largest casino in the Western Hemisphere.

NOVEMBER 16, 1993: Within weeks of its release, *Duets* sold a million copies and rocketed to the number-one position on the *Billboard* chart. When *Duets* reached number one, Dad called me and said, "We're number one! We're number one!" He was so excited. He was like a little kid. By way of recognition, Capitol Records made Dad its first Tower of Achievement laureate.

JANUARY 6, 1994: Attended memorial service for Irving "Swifty" Lazar at the Westwood Village Memorial Park.

FEBRUARY 1994: *Duets* went multiplatinum.

MARCH 1, 1994: At the Grammy Awards show, Frank Sinatra accepted the Legend Award for lifetime achievement from *Duets* partner and new friend, U2's Bono, who had given him a wonderfully loony, warm, witty and beautifully written introduction, which he wrote on the plane. During Dad's speech, the TV broadcast suddenly went to commercial. Some people believed he was cut off because his comments, which included regret at not having been invited to perform on the show, were inappropriate. This wasn't true. Someone unwisely asked the producers to cut away if the speech ran too long. Unfortunately, their timing wasn't good because the rest of Frank's remarks were charming. He virtually

U2's Bono Introducing Sinatra At the Grammies

Frank never did like rock 'n' roll. And he's not crazy about guys wearing earrings either, but hey, he doesn't hold it against me and anyway, the feeling's not mutual.

Rock 'n' roll people love Frank Sinatra because Frank Sinatra has got what we want: swagger and attitude. He's big on attitude, serious attitude. Bad attitude. Frank's The Chairman of the Bad.

Rock 'n' roll plays at being tough, but this guy's...well, he's the Boss, the Boss of Bosses, the Man. Big Daddy. The Big Bang of Pop. I'm not gonna mess with him—are you?

Who is this guy that every city in America wants to claim as their own? This painter who lives in the desert, this first-rate, first-take actor, this singer who makes other men poets, boxing clever with every word, talking like America.

Speedy...straight up...in headlines...comin' through with the big shtick, the aside, the quiet compliment...the good cop/bad cop all in the same breath.

You know his story because it's your story.

Frank walks like America, cocksure...

It's 1945. The U.S. cavalry are trying to get their asses out of Europe, but they never really do. They are part of another kind of invasion. A.F.R. American Forces Radio, broadcasting a music that will curl the stiff upper lip of England and the rest of the world, paving the way for rock 'n' roll with jazz, Duke Ellington, the big band, Tommy Dorsey and, right out in front, Frank Sinatra.

His voice tight as a fist, opening only at the end of a bar, not on the beat, over it...playing with it, splitting it...like a jazz man, like Miles Davis...turning on the right phrase in the right song, which is where he lives, where he lets go, and where he reveals himself...his songs are his home and he lets you in...but you know, to sing like that, you gotta have lost a couple o' fights...to know tenderness and romance, you have to have had your heart broken.

People say Frank hasn't talked to the press. They want to know how he is, what's on his mind. But you know, Sinatra is out there more nights than most punk bands...selling his story through the songs, telling and articulate in the choice of those songs...private thoughts on a public address system...generous.

This is the conundrum of Frank Sinatra...left and right brain hardly talking, boxer and painter, actor and singer, lover and father, troubleshooter and troublemaker, bandman and loner, the champ who would rather show you his scars than his medals. He may be putty in Barbara's hand, but...I'm not gonna mess with him, are you?

Ladies and gentlemen, are you ready to welcome a man heavier than the Empire State, more connected than the Twin Towers, as recognizable as the Statue of Liberty...and living proof that God is a Catholic?

Will you welcome the King of New York City...FRANCIS... ALBERT...SINATRA!

ignored the TV cameras and spoke directly to the audience at Radio City about his love for them and for New York City.

MARCH 6, 1994: Dad collapsed on stage during a concert in Richmond, Virginia.

AUGUST 2, 1994: Before a concert at New Jersey's Garden State Arts Center, Dad was the first recipient of the Francis Albert Sinatra Tribute to the Performing Arts. The award recognized his long support of the Arts Center Foundation; he was honorary chairman of its Tribute Committee. The award was established to honor an individual, corporation or philanthropic foundation that had demonstrated dedication to improving the cultural life of New Jerseyans.

AUGUST 1994: RCA released a 5-CD collection, *The Song Is You*, which contained 120 of Dad's studio and radio recordings with Tommy Dorsey. According to Sony music project director Chuck Granata, "RCA's source material was in superior condition. Some of the 'Nature's Remedy' shows had not been heard since they were

> ### A.J. Lambert
> **ON MEETING BONO AFTER THE GRAMMYS:**
>
> *I told him about my concern regarding my desire to be a musician and my family name. He told me not to worry about it and to let connections be connections. Don't shun the help when I need it. But try to retain my own thoughts, my own voice and my independence at the same time.*

Road Manager Tony Oppedisano
ON FRANK'S COLLAPSE:

He wasn't even halfway through "My Way" when he turned to Frankie and asked for a chair. Frankie didn't quite hear him and ran into the wings to find out what he had said. We said, "He's looking for a chair." At that moment, he went to sit down on a stool that was there. He actually touched the corner of the stool, and very slowly, almost in slow motion, he fell. He didn't fall that far, maybe two feet. The audience gasped. There was a horrendous noise because he dropped the microphone. The orchestra continued to play for a few bars, then they stopped. No one moved. Everybody was frozen. Even Bill Miller was frozen. Tom Dreesen, Frankie and I ran to him and turned him over. I loosened his tie and shirt. And the first thing I remember him saying was, "What happened? Can the audience still see me?" That's what he was concerned about. As we took him off the stage, he asked me to step aside because he wanted to wave to the audience to let them know he was OK. The audience stood up and cheered. It was a night I'll never forget.

originally aired. They had a contest. Composers submitted songs. That's how Tommy Dorsey found 'I'll Never Smile Again.' Joey Bushkin, who played piano for Dorsey, entered the contest under an assumed name and won, with 'Oh! Look at Me Now.'" It's hard to believe some of these recordings are over 50 years old.

OCTOBER 21, 1994: I was in the audience when Dad performed at the Kiel Center in St. Louis. Dad gave a remarkable, flawless performance for a sell-out crowd of 18,000. We flew to Chicago right after the show. While we were having dinner in the Pump Room in the Ambassador East at about one o'clock in the morning, a few people were hanging out in the bar. By the time dinner was over, an hour or so later, the bar was jammed. Somebody had sent word that Frank was there. As he left to go up to his room, they all stood up and cheered him!

OCTOBER 22, 1994: The United Center, Chicago, Illinois. I had the distinct and slightly ominous feeling that this would be the last time Dad would perform in Chicago. I believed he had the same feeling; I could tell by the fact that he was putting all the energy he possessed into each number. The audience sensed it, too. The applause after each song was deafening, and the acoustics in the new arena—which were specially designed to magnify crowd noise during sporting events—made it almost frightening.

From my vantage point, stage left (from the performer's point of view), I could see the stage slightly above and to my right, and the entire horseshoe-shaped arena in front of me. I had the perfect SRO spot for crowd watching. There was the slightly more than middle-aged blonde with the pink rose in her ponytail who was too frozen with awe to even applaud and just stood there with her mouth open and tears running down her face. There was the man in the wheelchair giving everything he could possibly muster back to Frank. The Vegas-type guy with all the gold chains and the tan, whistling and waving. The college-age and teenage kids who were just learning about Frank and clamoring for him. The silver-haired senior citizens boogying and bopping to the beat. It was an eclectic mix of people, all there to witness history, to be able to tell their grandchildren, "Hey, I saw Sinatra. Yeah, I saw him the last time he came to Chicago—in '94." I figured Dad and Frankie would

August 1995: At La Dolce Vita restaurant in Beverly Hills, during one of our weekly family dinners, Dad gives grandfatherly advice to A.J. on the subjects of blue nail polish and tattoos.

decide to do "My Kind of Town" for the closer instead of "New York, New York," and the anticipation in the sell-out crowd was growing note by note. There was a feeling of such excitement in the air. It was a little bit like the eighth inning of a no-hitter. You're afraid to talk about it for fear of spoiling it. They did "New York, New York," which was welcomed by the audience with great delight. When he started the verse "Now this could only happen to a guy like me...And only happen in a town like this," well, it began, first as a low rumble... "So that is why I say to you most gratefully..." Then the rumble was amplified by little squeals of delight from the ladies and hands coming together and feet jumping up and down... "As I throw each one of you a kiss... This...is..." and by the time the word "my" came out of his mouth, 18,000 people of Chicago were on their feet cheering, stomping, whistling, clapping. The rumble grew into a roar and became a wave, a giant wave of screaming and bodies in motion, sweeping us all up in it. It felt like the building was going to lift off and implode on its occupants. The earthquake we experienced in Los Angeles in January 1994 with its ungodly, terrifying rumbling of a thousand oncoming trains had nothing on this feeling of love pouring out of this bunch of delirious Chicagoans. You would have thought the Bulls, the Bears and the Cubs had all won championships at the same time. I wasn't at the Paramount in New York when Dad thought the building was going to come down, but this must have been much more than that. Chicago pride was spilling out all over the place, and my father was the cause of all this commotion. I can't remember a more bittersweet moment. I celebrated with him, and I cried with him as he came down the steps of the stage to the thunderous goodbye of those grateful fans. He knew what he had done that night. He knew it, and he was humbled by the entire experience. The tears were still in his eyes and the audience was still voicing their emotional farewell as we drove toward the airport to fly home. It was a breathtaking moment, and I felt so blessed that I had been able to share it with him. I was never, ever more proud of my father than I was that night in the Windy City. "My kind of town, Chicago is..."

Frankie, me and Dad in the dressing room at the Sands Hotel in Atlantic City.

Road Manager
Tony Oppedisano

ON TWO MEMORABLE NIGHTS IN ST. LOUIS AND CHICAGO:

It's like he had those shows tucked in his back pocket since 1968. He wasn't under a lot of pressure. He was in a good mood.

NOVEMBER 1994: In a follow-up to 1993's *Duets* album, Capitol released *Duets II*. This time his featured singing partners included Stevie Wonder and Gladys Knight ("For Once in My Life"), Lena Horne ("Embraceable You"), Patti LaBelle ("Bewitched"), Jon Secada ("The Best Is Yet to Come"), Luis Miguel ("Come Fly with Me"), Jimmy Buffett ("Mack the Knife"), Frank Jr. ("My Kind of Town"), Willie Nelson ("A Foggy Day"), Neil Diamond ("The House I Live In"), Antonio Carlos Jobim ("Fly Me to the Moon"), Steve Lawrence and Eydie Gorme ("Where or When"), Linda Ronstadt ("Moonlight in Vermont"), Chrissie Hynde ("Luck Be a Lady") and Lorrie Morgan ("My Funny Valentine"/"How Do You Keep the Music Playing?").

The album debuted nationally at number 16 on the charts, and CBS aired a companion TV special that incorporated not only musicians from both *Duets* albums but also old footage of Dad singing with Perry Como, Bing Crosby, Ella Fitzgerald and Peggy Lee.

NOVEMBER 16, 1994: In Toronto, Canada, he did a cameo in Tina's CBS television movie, *Young at Heart*, starring Olympia Dukakis.

DECEMBER 10, 1994: He celebrated his 79th birthday at the Vintage Country Club in Indian Wells, California.

The three Sinatra grandchildren: A.J., Amanda and Michael.

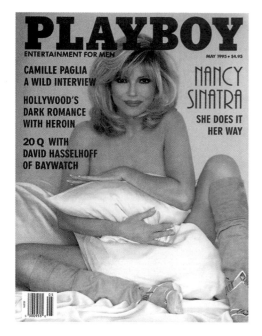

At the Palm Springs estate, each guest living area had a name. There was the "New York, New York" house. Dad's painting studio was called, "All the Way." "The Tender Trap" was the guest house built for President Kennedy. A screening room was appropriately named, "Send in the Clowns," and "My Way" was the office.

DECEMBER 19-20, 1994: Dad did two shows at Fukuoka Dome in Japan but Frankie recalls, "I had the sense he was very fatigued from the trip over. Plus the fact that one of our men, lead trombone Jim Huntsinger, and his wife Lynne, who was also in the orchestra, could not go to Japan because Jim was suffering from cancer. After the first concert, we received a fax that Jimmy had died. Jim and Lynne had met each other working for Dad and the news left him very down."

JANUARY 1995: Warner Records announced its plans to release, as its tribute to Sinatra on his forthcoming 80th birthday, a historic CD collection of Dad's finest work. The collection features more then 450 songs, including 70 numbers that have never been available on compact disc, 15 songs that have never been heard before, plus alternate takes and extended versions of some of his best-known classics.

FEBRUARY 1995: The Frank Sinatra Neckwear Collection was presented at the Magic Man Apparel Show in Las Vegas. Dad, always a snappy dresser with a particular fondness for ties, incorporated designs from his own artwork into the silk jacquard ties, on which his signature was stitched at the tip. "I have always been bewitched by shadows and contrasts," Dad said at the line's unveiling. "A bright bursting orange sun against a twilight blue sky, the rich shadow cast by a simple green leaf."

FEBRUARY 1995: Dad and Barbara decided to put the Palm Springs compound up for sale. Dad had owned the Palm Springs house since 1954, and it was an important part of my youth. Barbara: "Palm Springs has changed. We had a wonderful time there, and it's been a fabulous part of our lives. But it's time to move on. We're very happy now. We have two fabulous homes and lots of friends near us. I don't care what kind of possessions you have in life. It really doesn't mean anything unless you have good friends. And everybody is in the L.A. area now."

FEBRUARY 25, 1995: At the age of 79, before a VIP invitational audience in Palm Springs, Dad performed at a party on the last day of the Frank Sinatra Desert Classic golf tournament.

He stepped onto the stage, grabbed the mike and swung into Nelson Riddle's arrangement of "I've Got the World on a String." As written in *Esquire*, "Sinatra's voice is clear, tough, on the money. 'You Make Me Feel So Young' is sturdy, fabulously syncopated. 'Fly Me to the Moon' is automatic. Sinatra swings to his very center, in absolute control. 'Where or When' is performed by a 45-year-old man. It is everything that Sinatra wishes to convey. It is a ballad with tempo that gathers steam and explodes at its conclusion. He decides to sing an unplanned fifth song. 'Here's one that everybody knows,' Sinatra says, over the intro to 'My Kind of Town.' It's the equal of 'Where or When.' Then, for a final encore, Bill Miller slides into 'The Best Is Yet to Come.' His singing is high art. And then he's gone." Tony O': "It was a jubilant evening, reaching for notes and holding them. It was a phenomenal, phenomenal show. In the middle of songs he was making jokes. He was fantastic and made mincemeat out of the critics."

The performance was over. For a long time now, Dad has been talking about hanging it up for good—after all, he'll be 80 in December 1995—so if this is the final show he ever gives, he's ended in the style of a showman: on a classic high note. But his songs will be heard long after he stops singing them, and I can't help but remember his last line at another concert not long ago, a kind of blessing and a benediction to those who love the music that he's lived: "May you live to be 100 and the last voice you hear be mine."

JULY 24-26, 1995: A diverse group of artists joined together to celebrate Frank's 80th birthday in a program entitled: "Carnegie Hall Celebrates the Music of Frank Sinatra." Each evening had a different theme. Among the performers for the *Songs for Swingin' Lovers* show were Vic Damone, Burton Lane and Joe Williams. On the second night, *Come Fly with Me*, Betty Comden and Adolf Green, Maureen McGovern and Margaret Whiting saluted Frank. Rosemary Clooney and Linda Ronstadt headlined the third evening, *That's Life*. But this show culminated with my brother conducting a program entitled "As I Remember It." I was lucky enough to be there and he was wonderful.

JANUARY 1996: Reprise released an album entitled *Everything Happens to Me*. The 19 songs tell the story of a man, much like Frank Sinatra, who has loved and lost and loved again. The collection features "The Gal That Got Away"/"It Never Entered My Mind," "Once Upon a Time," "I Only Miss Her When I Think of Her," "Didn't We," "The Second Time Around" and others.

The last years were quiet ones for my father. His restlessness had abated a bit, and, though he missed the desert—which he called home—he was content with the sweetness of life in his two Los Angeles-area homes, one at the beach in Malibu and one in Beverly Hills. It was his first extended retirement in over 50 years, with the exception of the two-year break after his father died. His time was spent with family and close friends. He took the stage for the last time in December 1995 at a Shrine Auditorium celebration of his 80th birthday.

In May of 1996, A.J. graduated from USC, becoming the first Sinatra to finish college. Dad celebrated with her, the proudest grandpa in the world. He received his greatest personal tribute in 1997 when the United States Congress passed Congressman Jose Serrano's bill authorizing the Congressional Gold Medal. It is the highest civilian award, equivalent to the Congressional Medal of Honor. He held the bronze version of the medal in his hands six months before he died. In 1997, Frank conquered yet another medium—cyberspace. Our website, dedicated to everything Sinatra, will continue to provide information to his fans. Join us at **www.sinatrafamily.com.**

On January 26, 1998, I stood in for Daddy and accepted the American Music Award of Merit. When I left the house that night he said, "Give them all a big hug for me. *They* made *me* possible." I was staggered by the enthusiastic reception from the youthful audience. It was a testament to my father's extraordinary ability to touch everyone, no matter their age or musical tastes. The man who caused the first generation gap had reached yet another generation.

Amanda graduated with honors from Loyola Marymount University on Saturday, May 9. The last time I saw Daddy alive was May 10. A.J. and I walked to his house to tell him she had become engaged. When we broke the news, he just kept kissing A.J.'s hand and smiling and saying things like, "Oh, that's marvelous! That's wonderful news!" When A.J. told him how happy she was, Frank said, "I know! And you will be even happier! You will be so happy that flowers will grow out of your nose!"

MAY 14, 1998: My father died at 10:50 p.m. at Cedars-Sinai Medical Center of an acute heart attack. He was 82 years old. His last words were "I'm losing." It was a year to the day since President Clinton signed the bill that made Daddy's Congressional Gold Medal the law of the land. Leo Rosten wrote, "The purpose of life is to matter, to count, to have it make some difference that we lived at all." Frank Sinatra made a difference. For his final journey, we placed into his pockets a tiny bottle of Jack Daniels, a pack of Camels and his favorite candys. Most important, the people of the United States were with him, when a presidential envoy presented an American flag "on behalf of a grateful nation." I know my father would have cherished that more than anything.

"Our family and the country and the world mourn him now—as the loss of a part of what America is, and what the 20th century will be in history."

—A.J. and Amanda Sinatra Lambert

"Put your dreams away for another day, and I will take their place in your heart..."

FRANK ON THE ROAD 1986-1994

1986

1/23	Lloyd Noble Center, Oklahoma City
1/25	The University of New Orleans
2/15	The "Love-In III," Palm Springs
2/21-22	The Golden Nugget, Las Vegas
3/8-9	The Golden Nugget, Las Vegas
3/13	Stamford, CT
3/14	The Meadowlands, NJ
3/16	Radio City Music Hall
3/20-23	The Golden Nugget, Atlantic City
4/3	The Pacific Coliseum, Vancouver, BC
4/4	The Tacoma Dome
4/9-12	Circle Star Theater, San Carlos, CA
4/14	The Arena, St. Louis, MO
4/18-19	The Golden Nugget, Las Vegas
4/30-5/4	The Golden Nugget, Atlantic City
5/8	The Philadelphia Spectrum
5/22-26	The Golden Nugget, Las Vegas
6/21	The Worthington Hotel, Fort Worth, TX
6/22	The Pacific Amphitheater, Costa Mesa, CA
7/5-6	The Golden Nugget, Atlantic City
7/9-10	The Garden State Arts Center, Holmdel, NJ
7/26	Aloha Stadium, Honolulu
9/7	The Riverbend, Cincinnati, OH
9/10-14	The Chicago Theater
9/19-20	The Golden Nugget, Las Vegas
9/25	The Real Madrid Stadium, Madrid, Spain
9/27	The Palatrussardi, Milan, Italy
10/19	The McNichols Arena, Denver
10/23	Beverly Hilton, Beverly Hills
10/24-25	The Golden Nugget, Atlantic City
11/6-7	The Golden Nugget, Atlantic City
12/27-30	The Golden Nugget, Las Vegas

1987

2/21	Century Plaza Hotel, Los Angeles
3/28	Grand Canyon Resort Hotel, Palm Springs
4/3-6	The Golden Nugget, Las Vegas
4/18	Marriott Desert Springs Hotel
4/21-25	The Chicago Theater
4/26	Boston Symphony Hall
4/29-5/3	The Golden Nugget, Atlantic City
5/5	The Brendan Byrne Arena, NJ
5/8	The Capitol Centre, Landover, MD
5/9	The Sun Dome, Tampa, FL
5/22-24	The Golden Nugget, Las Vegas
6/13	Stadio di Calcio la Favorite, Palermo, Italy
6/16	Teatro Petruzelli Opera House, Bari, Italy
6/17	The Palazzo di Sport, Rome
6/20	The Arena di Verona, Rome
6/24	Palazzo di Sport, Genoa, Italy
6/26	Santa Margarita, Italy
8/19	The Pacific Amphitheater, Costa Mesa, CA
8/20-22	The Greek Theater, Los Angeles
8/26	The Riverbend Arena, Cincinnati, OH
8/28-29	The Garden State Arts Center, Holmdel, NJ
8/31	Pine Knob, Pontiac, MI
9/3-6	Ballys Grand Hotel, Atlantic City
9/10-19	Carnegie Hall, New York City
10/14	Nassau Coliseum, Garden City, NY
10/16	The Hartford Civic Center, CT
10/17	The Centrum, Worcester, MA
10/24	The Reunion Arena, Dallas
10/29-11/4	Ballys Hotel, Las Vegas
11/10	University of Notre Dame Arena, South Bend, IN
11/11, 1987	The University of Dayton Arena
11/12, 1987	The Chicago Theater
11/13, 1987	The Louisville Gardens, KY
12/4-5	The Brendan Byrne Arena, NJ
12/11-13	Ballys Golden Nugget, Atlantic City
12/26-1/2	Bally's Grand, Las Vegas

1988

1/9	Sanctuary Cove, Sydney, Australia
1/29-30	San Diego Sports Arena
2/11-17	Ballys Grand, Las Vegas
3/13	Oakland Coliseum
3/15	The Pacific Coliseum, Vancouver, BC
3/16	The Seattle Center Coliseum, Seattle, WA
3/18-20	The Chicago Theater
3/22	The Metro Center Arena, Bloomington, MN
3/25	The Joe Louis Arena, Detroit, MI
3/26	Pittsburgh Civic Arena
3/28	Cleveland Coliseum
3/29	The Riverfront Arena, Cincinnati, OH
3/31	The Capitol Center, Landover, MD
4/2	Providence Civic Center, RI
4/6-9	Radio City Music Hall
4/28-5/1	Ballys Grand, Reno
5/4-8	Ballys Grand, Atlantic City
6/26	Ballys, Atlantic City
7/6-10	Ballys Grand, Reno
8/19	The Charlotte Coliseum, NC
8/20	The Garden State Arts Center, Holmdel, NJ
8/23-29	Ballys Grand, Reno
9/1-4	Ballys Grand, Atlantic City
9/18-10/9	Phoenix, AZ
9/22	The Omni, Atlanta, GA
9/24	The Miami Arena
9/25	The Sun Dome, Tampa, FL
9/27-28	The Philadelphia Spectrum
9/30-10/1	The Brendan Byrne Arena, NJ
10/3-4	Nassau Coliseum, Uniondale, NY
10/15-16	The Centrum, Worcester, MA
10/26-30	Ballys Grand, Reno
11/4	The Summit, Houston, TX
11/11-13	The Circle Star Theater, San Carlos, CA
11/26	Los Angeles Forum
11/30-12/4	The Fox Theater, Detroit
12/8-11	Ballys Grand, Atlantic City
12/26-1/1	Ballys Grand, Las Vegas

1989

1/17	The Reunion Arena, Dallas
1/18	The Superdome, New Orleans
1/20-21	Miami Arena
1/26-28	Ballys, Las Vegas
2/4	Palm Springs
2/23	Castle Hall, Osaka, Japan
2/25	Tokyo Bay N.K. Hall
2/28-3/1	National Tennis Center, Melbourne, Australia
3/3-4	Sydney Entertainment Center, Australia
3/7-8	Blaisdell Arena, Honolulu
4/8	Ahoy Hall, Rotterdam, Holland
4/11	Stockholm, Sweden
4/13	Ekabas Hall, Oslo, Norway
4/15	Goteborg, Sweden
4/16	Ice Hockey Stadium, Helsinki, Finland
4/18-22	Royal Albert Hall, London,
4/25	The Paris Opera House
4/27	Holland Hall, Amsterdam
4/29	Olympic Hall, Munich, Germany
4/30	The Stadthalle, Vienna, Austria
5/3-4	"Lansdowne Road", Dublin, Ireland
5/18-21, 25-28	Ballys, Las Vegas
6/8	Aircraft carrier, "Intrepid," New York Harbor
6/14-18	Ballys Grand, Reno
6/22-25	Ballys, Las Vegas
7/1	Deer Creek Music Center, Indianapolis, IN
7/2	The Garden State Arts Center, Holmdel, NJ
7/13-15	Ballys Grand, Reno
8/31-9/3	Ballys Grand, Atlantic City
9/14-17	Ballys Grand, Reno
10/2	Skydome, Toronto, Canada

1990

1/17-21	Sunrise Musical Theater, Ft. Lauderdale, FL
1/23	Orlando Arena, FL
1/30	Knickerbocker Arena, Albany, NY

2/23-24	Palm Springs
3/8-11	Ballys Grand, Las Vegas
3/22	Kemper Arena, Kansas City, MO
3/24	Charlotte Coliseum, NC
4/6-7	Seattle, WA
4/19-22	The Open Fox Theater, Detroit, MI
4/27	The Starplex Theater, Dallas
4/28	Woodlands Pavilion, Houston
4/29	The Starplex Amphitheater, Dallas
5/3-6	Ballys, Las Vegas
5/12	Niagara Falls Civic Arena, NY
5/24-27	Ballys Grand, Reno
6/6	Capitol Music Center, Columbus, OH
6/8-10	The Fox Theater, St. Louis
6/14-17	Radio City Music Hall
6/30	Stockholm, Sweden
7/4-8	London Arena, England
7/10	Ibrox Stadium, Glasgow, Scotland
8/19	The Concord Pavilion, CA
8/23	Chastain Park, Atlanta, GA
8/25	The Garden State Arts Center, Holmdel, NJ
8/26	Jones Beach Theater, Long Island, NY
8/29	Great Woods in Mansfield, MA
8/31	The Riverbend, Cincinnati, OH
9/1	Poplar Creek, Hoffman Estates, IL
9/2	Marcus Amphitheater, Milwaukee, WI
9/6-7	The Greek Theater, Los Angeles
9/8	Pacific Amphitheater, Costa Mesa, CA
10/4-7	The Sands Hotel, Atlantic City
10/31	Metro Center, Rockford, IL
11/2	Assembly Hall, Champaign, IL
11/3	Hilton Coliseum, Ames, IA
12/31	The Riviera Hotel, Las Vegas

1991

1/23	Miami Arena
1/25	Orlando Arena
1/26	The Sun Dome, Tampa, FL
2/8	San Diego Sports Arena
2/10	The Long Beach Arena, CA
2/22-23	Palm Springs
3/2	The Sydney Entertainment Center, Australia
3/4	Brisbane Entertainment Center, Australia
3/6	Nat'l Tennis Center, Melbourne, Australia
3/10-11	Yokohama Arena, Tokyo, Japan
3/21-24	The Riviera Hotel, Las Vegas
4/5	Universal Amphitheater, Los Angeles
4/18	The Desert Sky Pavilion, Phoenix, AZ
4/20	The Centrum, Worcester, MA
4/21	Providence Civic Center, RI
4/26-28	The Circle Star Theater, San Carlos, CA
5/9	Olympic Saddledome, Calgary, Canada
5/15	The Nutter Center, Dayton, OH
5/16	The Civic Arena, Pittsburgh, PA
5/21	The Salt Palace, Salt Lake City
6/13-16	The Riviera Hotel, Las Vegas
6/20	The Hemisfair Arena, San Antonio, TX
6/22-23	Mexico City with Steve and Eydie
7/14	The World Music Center, Chicago IL
7/18-21	The Sands Hotel, Atlantic City
7/22	The Meriweather Post Pavilion, Columbia, MD
8/1	The Greek Theater, Los Angeles

8/8-11	The Riviera Hotel, Las Vegas
9/16	The Palau Santa Jordi, Barcelona, Spain
9/19	The Sports Palace, Anvers, Belgium
9/21	The Forum, Milan, Italy
9/23	Pallazzo dello Sport, Montecatina, Italy
9/24	Palazzio del Gilaccio, Rome
9/28	The Spectrum Arena, Oslo, Norway
10/1	The Ice Hockey Stadium, Malmo, Sweden
10/3	The Palais des Congre, Paris
10/5	The Festhalle, Frankfurt, Germany
10/7	The Hague, Netherlands
10/9-11	The Point, Dublin, Ireland
11/8	Joe Louis Arena, Detroit, MI
11/9	The Philadelphia Spectrum
11/12	Toronto Maple Leaf Gardens, Canada
11/13	Knickerbocker Arena, Albany, NY
11/15	Nassau Coliseum, Uniondale, NY
11/16	Madison Square Garden
11/21-24	The Sands Hotel, Atlantic City
12/5-8	The Riviera Hotel, Las Vegas
12/31	The Riviera Hotel, Las Vegas

1992

1/24	The Met Center, Bloomington, MN
2/12-16	The Desert Inn, Las Vegas
2/27-29	Palm Springs
3/12-15	The Sands Hotel, Atlantic City
3/18-22	Broward Center for the Performing Arts, FL
3/25	Palm Springs
4/8-12	The Desert Inn, Las Vegas
4/23	Roberts Stadium, Evansville, IN
4/25	Superdome, New Orleans
4/26	Jacksonville Coliseum. FL
5/14-16	The Circle Star Theater, San Carlos, CA
5/26-31	Royal Albert Hall, London
6/3	Monumental Mini Estadi, Barcelona, Spain
6/5	The Coliseum, La Caruña, Spain
6/7	Estadio des Autas, Porto, Portugal
6/9	The Marble Stadium, Athens, Greece.
6/24-28	The Desert Inn, Las Vegas
7/21	The Garden State Arts Center, Holmdel, NJ
7/23-26	The Sands Hotel, Atlantic City
8/7	Princess Grace "Red Cross Gala", Monte Carlo
9/17-18	The Greek Theater, Los Angeles
9/23-27	The Desert Inn, Las Vegas
10/1	The Warner Theater, Washington, DC
10/2	The Centrum, Worcester, MA
10/3	Providence Civic Center, RI
10/8-15	Radio City Music Hall
10/30 -11/1	Radio City Music Hall
11/5	The Bradley Center, Milwaukee, WI
11/7	Richfield Coliseum, Cleveland, OH
11/8	The Palace, Auburn Hills, MI
11/11-15	The Sands Hotel, Atlantic City
12/8-12	The Desert Inn, Las Vegas

1993

1/13-17	The Cerritos Arts Center, CA
1/29-31	The Desert Inn, Las Vegas
3/5-6	Palm Springs
3/23	Palm Springs
4/15-18	Kravis Center, West Palm Beach, FL

4/20	War Memorial, Rochester, NY
4/22-25	The Sands Hotel, Atlantic City
5/5-9	Desert Inn, Las Vegas
5/12-16	The Opera House, Chicago
5/29	The Scandinavium, Goteborg, Sweden
5/31	The Westfalenhalle, Dortmond, Germany
6/2	Derbypark, Hamburg, Germany
6/3	The Deutschlandhalle, Berlin, Germany
6/5	The Schloss Ehrenhof, Stuttgart, Germany
6/6	The Dom Square, Cologne, Germany
6/10-12	Westbury Music Fair, Westbury, NY
6/14-18	The Desert Inn, Las Vegas.
8/17	Chastain Park, Atlanta, GA
8/19-21	The Paramount Theater, Aurora, IL
8/23	The Garden State Arts Center, Holmdel, NJ
8/24	The Saratoga Performing Arts Center, NY
8/26-29	The Sands Hotel, Atlantic City
9/10	Western Washington State Fair, Pullyup, WA
9/12	The Long Beach Arena, CA
9/21-26	The Desert Inn, Las Vegas
10/6	Nassau Coliseum, Uniondale, NY
10/8	The Civic Center, Pittsburgh, PA
10/9	Copps Coliseum, Hamilton, Canada
10/26-31	The Desert Inn, Las Vegas
11/10-14	The Sands Hotel, Atlantic City
12/8	The San Diego Sports Arena
12/10	America West Arena, Phoenix, AZ
12/13-14	The Music Hall, Cincinnati, OH
12/27-1/1	MGM Grand, Las Vegas

1994

1/20-23	Broward Center for the Performing Arts, FL
1/25	Harborside Convention Hall, Ft. Myers, FL
1/27	Ocean Center, Daytona Beach, FL
1/29	The Omni, Atlanta, GA
2/4-5	Palm Springs
2/12-14	The Manila Convention Center, Philippines
3/5-6	The Mosque, Richmond, VA
3/24	The Mabee Arena, Tulsa, OK
3/26	The Mark, Moline, IL
3/27	Omaha, NE
4/14	The Azalea Festival, Wilmington, NC
4/16	Veteran War Memorial, Syracuse, NY
4/19-26	Radio City Music Hall
5/6, 10	The Hershey Park Arena, Hershey, PA
5/12-15	The Sands Hotel, Atlantic City
5/19-22	Foxwoods Casino, Ledyard, CT
5/27-29	MGM Grand, Las Vegas
6/28-7/11	The Folk Art Theater, Manila, Philippines
8/2	The Garden State Arts Center, Holmdel, NJ
8/4-6	The Sands Hotel, Atlantic City
8/29	The Meriweather Post Pavilion, Columbia, MD
8/31	Tanglewood, MA
9/1	Harborlights, Boston, MA
9/3	The Riverbend, Cincinnati, OH
9/23-24	The Greek Theater, Los Angeles
9/29-30	The Music Hall, Dallas
10/1	Hyatt Regency, Houston
10/4-5	Jones Hall, Houston
11/11-13	Foxwoods Casino, Ledyard, CT
11/18-20	The Sands Hotel, Atlantic City
12/19-20	Fukuoka Dome, Japan

Special Section: In Memoriam

Francis Albert Sinatra
Born Into Life December 12, 1915
Entered Into Eternal Life May 14, 1998

Prayer of St. Francis

Lord, make me an instrument of your peace.

Where there is hatred... let me sow love.

Where there is injury... pardon.

Where there is discord... unity.

Where there is doubt... faith.

Where there is error... truth.

Where there is despair... hope.

Where there is sadness... joy.

Where there is darkness... light.

O Divine Master, grant that I may not
*   so much seek*

To be consoled... as to console.

To be understood... as to understand.

To be loved... as to love
*   for*

It is in giving... that we receive.

It is in pardoning, that we are pardoned.

It is in dying... that we are born into eternal life.

THE WHITE HOUSE

WASHINGTON

May 20, 1998

Nancy Sinatra

Dear Nancy:

Hillary and I were saddened to learn of your father's death and wanted you to know we're thinking about you and your family.

Frank gave so much to so many through his music. He will remain an incredible legend, living on in the memories of those blessed to have known him and those who appreciated his talents.

We'll be holding you in our daily prayers.

Sincerely,

Bill

It's hard to put into words how much we loved Dad. He was so much a part of the Rickles. Not only was he a great friend but a man who was tremendously supportive of me in this competitive business. My Barbara and I remember so many good times we shared together. We felt special being in his company.

We know you will be warm inside, knowing we will all be listening to his music forever.

May God bless you and your family in these trying times and give you the comfort you deserve.

With love,
BARBARA AND DON RICKLES

My husband (now deceased), when a school boy, played hooky from school to go see Frank at the Paramount. Frank was his idol.

G.S.
NEW YORK

My heart goes out to you all. He will be missed not only by all of you but by his fans for over 60 years. I am proud to say I saw him in concert 5 times. He was great. Thank God we have his songs and the memories.

Peace and love.

His fan for over 60 years,
B.M.
INDIANA

It was with deep regret that I heard of your father's passing. I know how close the two of you were and that this is an irreparable loss to you. I admired all that he did throughout his life, especially for his family

and friends. He was one of a kind. My heartfelt sympathy goes out to you and your family. If there is a saving grace it is the comfort in knowing that he did it his way. I shall also miss him.

Sincerely,
PRISCILLA BEAULIEU PRESLEY

Actually, I wish I had written to the man himself. He showed us what it was supposed to look like. He laughed and worked with friends. He sang. They sang. And in our hearts, we sang. We felt the fun! His work was singing, and in that work, he rejoiced...so did we.

Love,
K.S.
NEW YORK

I was a fan before I met Frank over 45 years ago. And I am still. I treasure the time I shared with him professionally and socially. I grieve for your personal loss. And for

everyone's loss. There can only be one Frank Sinatra.

Thank God that with today's technology we will never have to be without his presence. He will be entertaining the world—from here to eternity.

Fondly,
JANET LEIGH

Please accept our deepest condolences for your great loss. Your father was indeed a very special human being. He was a giant among men. An exceptionally gifted performer and a devoted father.

Please know that you and your family are in our prayers, as is your beloved father. God bless his soul and may he rest in peace.

With all our love,
ANN-MARGRET AND ROGER

I am an English lady aged 70 who has been a life-long fan of your father—in fact, I have so many of his records collected over the years, my husband calls him, "the

lodger." The first money I ever earned at 14, I bought a Sinatra 78 of "The Moon Was Yellow and the Night Was Young." I have never heard it since, but I swooned over it—we only had a wind-up gramophone someone had given to my sisters and I. We played it over and over until my mother threatened to break it over my head! I always remember her saying, "He's just a five minute wonder—I don't know why you wasted your money—this time next year, he'll be forgotten!" She had to eat her words! I'm glad I lived in his lifetime and have all my memories to treasure. Please give him a red rose from me—he's been so much a part of my life.

Yours truly,
J.H.
ENGLAND

I want to express my deepest sympathy to you and to the other members of your family on the death of your father.

Although the world has lost one of its most memorable artists, and our Country one of its national treasures, words cannot properly express the many joys that Mr. Sinatra gave Americans for the past half-century. I was especially moved by the accounts of his anonymous generosity to the many charitable causes he favored.

Again, my thoughts are with you and your family during the coming days. With best wishes, I am

Sincerely yours,
TRENT LOTT, MAJORITY LEADER,
UNITED STATES SENATE

Christiane and I are terribly consternated about Frank's passing away and would like

to send you our love and sympathy. We will always remember him.

CHRISTIANE AND MIGUEL ALEMAN V.
MEXICO

Today I will make peppers and sausages, your favorite dish to cook in celebration of "your way" in heaven. "Viva tutti joya mia."
I.B.
CALIFORNIA

Pray
The Rosary
In Memory Of
Francis Albert Sinatra
December 12, 1915 - May 14, 1998

Your father gave me years of gentle, exhilarating, deep pleasure. I really "loved" him.
Sincerely,
P.S.
ENGLAND

No words can express our profound sorrow. We will miss him forever. He is the standard by which all human beings shall be measured. Thank you for "sharing" your father with all of us.
Much love,
W. AND M.L.
FLORIDA

We are so glad to have grown up with Frank Sinatra. I was a Hollywood teenager in the Forties and went to Wallach's Music City to listen to records and daydream. We've been to the Sands in Las Vegas, the Cal Neva in Tahoe many times, and last saw him in San Diego to celebrate our 50th anniversary! He's inspired our happy times and consoled us in our sad ones. We love him and share in your sadness. His music will live forever for all of us. God bless.
Gratefully,
CALIFORNIA

Wonderin' how you're doing, what with the demons and dragons...
Wishing you love and support.
Thanks for all these years...
BILL ROGERS MUSIC

I just heard of your dad's death and write to extend my condolences.

I'm sure millions of words will be spilled on this occasion, praising your father and reporting on the events and accomplishments of his life. Suffice it to say that he was one of a kind and his own way changed the century in which he lived. My guess is that—contrary to the pronouncements of Antony in Shakespeare's *Julius Caesar*—the good that your father did will outlive all other recollections.

You and your family are in our hearts and minds.

Sincerely,
STEPHEN JOEL TRACHTENBERG
PRESIDENT, THE GEORGE
WASHINGTON UNIVERSITY
WASHINGTON, D.C.

It's small comfort now, but someday the fact that millions of people—countless families—share the pain, the sense of loss, and the aching sense of unreality will help ease the sorrow.

There will always be an empty place in our hearts, but the warm memories and the priceless gifts of song, courage and honesty will help fill the void.

It's still Frank's world....

Love,
M. AND D.

May I say how sorry I was to hear of the death of your father.

The death of a parent is always sad, but to lose a father who had such worldwide renown must be very hard to bear. There may be small consolation in knowing that many millions of people all around the world are mourning with you. You will perhaps find solace in knowing that the pleasure your father gave is quite immeasurable. I have a number of Francis Albert's CDs and they are a constant joy to me. Merely to listen to one is to be transported into a world of musical per-

fection. I hope you do not mind that a complete stranger takes up a pen to write to you, but I felt you may be happier knowing that people everywhere are thinking of you.

Yours sincerely,
J.T.C.
ENGLAND

The millions of lovers of Frank have spoken but Helen and I wanted to add our small voice to those who will miss him forever. We loved him and we were part of his growing up. His voice will never be silenced nor will those who believed him to be the best there was. All our sympathy and much love,

DAVID BROWN
P.S. *We were in China when we heard the news and our television in Beijing instantly played one of Frank's concerts.*

The Lord gave him the gift of being able to touch our souls, and the ability to put wonderful dreams in our hearts. I thank the Lord for loaning Francis Albert Sinatra to all of us.

WITH LOVE AND PRAYERS,
MICHAEL AND PATTY LLOYD

May 14, 1998
"By day, I'll look to the sky
For the blue of your eyes;
By night, the twinkle..."
JAMES DARREN

I knew your dad since I was 9 (with my uncle Jule Styne), then worked with him (as arranger) on Anything Goes (NBC), then as director of the Danny Thomas special. I have fond memories of him always calling me "genius"—whenever I think of him I smile.

Yours,
BUDDY BREGMAN

I know you're probably out on the West Coast with your family tonight, but here in Manhattan, the lights of the Empire State Building are burning bright with a pale blue in honor of your father. I see them from my window as I sit here writing. I'm sorry for your loss...but the lights are still burning, just like his. I hope the idea that your dad had a fine long run gives you some comfort in your loss.

Warm regards,
C.

About 1944 Marty Melcher, a buddy at the time, was in my office in New York. He showed me a Zippo lighter someone had given him. Since neither Marty or I smoked, I asked if he would give it to me as another buddy, Axel Stordahl, smoked a pipe and this was the perfect lighter for pipes. He handed it over and when I offered it to Axel he said, "Thanks, but I already have one, but Frank smokes a pipe and has been trying to find one. Why don't you give it to him?" (The government requisitioned all these lighters for the servicemen and civilian stores could not get them.)

After a record date a few days later, I asked your dad if he would like to have my Zippo lighter. He was delighted and said,

"Where did you get it? I have been trying to find one, but no luck. Thanks buddy."

About two weeks later Ax and I saw Frank off at the Grand Central Station. While walking to the gate, he passed a gift shop and excused himself to buy something there. He came out with a package and before he entered the gate he handed it to me and said, "Here Mick, this is for you. See you guys!" And off he went to California.

After he left I opened it and it was a barometer, cased in a ship's wheel. I said to Ax, "What is this for?" Ax explained, "Frank is a funny guy. If you do something for him, he never forgets. This is his way of showing his gratitude."

Maybe he had a lot of Zippos over the years, but I still have that barometer. It is right behind my desk and it always brings back memories of that scene in the Grand Central Station.

Sincerely,
MICHAEL H. GOLDSEN, CEO
CRITERION MUSIC CORPORATION
HOLLYWOOD, CA

His life was as full as that of any four people, his magic so infectious that everyone who heard him has died a little bit. He was so kind to me and I am thinking of you...

Love,
TOM MANKIEWICZ

I was such a big fan of your Father's. I guess that I could be considered a "bobby soxer"—so many of his songs remind me of a carefree time in my life. I know that you have lost a Father, but the world has lost a giant. He had a heart of gold and I know that so many people of all ages will miss

him. He was proud of the legacy he left and I know that you will continue to be "keeper of his flame"—an empire that will live on for many years.

I know that you will find comfort in the many tributes that your Father will receive, but the biggest comfort of all should be that he made so many people happy with his many talents.

With warmest regards,
SENATOR DIANNE FEINSTEIN
WASHINGTON, D.C.

I am 75 years old, my daughter is 52 and my granddaughter is 27—we love your dad as though he were part of our family.

I was one of the adoring fans in my bobby sox and saddle shoes at the Paramount Theatre in the '40s. I shall never forget Frank Sinatra. Thank God we have the legacy of his music and films. My deepest sympathy to your mom, Tina and Frank, Jr.

Most sincerely,
F.L.
FLORIDA

I was devastated to hear about the loss of your beloved father. He is an idol to me. A legend that will live forever.

My deepest sympathy,
MARTIN SCORSESE

On behalf of the society in Dublin and the music lovers in Ireland, I would like to express our sympathy to yourself and the Sinatra family on the death of your father. He will be sadly missed by us all, but we have 59 years of recorded music to remem-

ber him by. There have been many tributes on Irish radio and TV, and I myself took part in a two-hour program on Dublin radio last night where we celebrated his life.

Please pass on our best wishes to the rest of the family.

Yours sincerely,
CHRIS HITCHCOCK
HON. SECRETARY
SINATRA MUSIC SOCIETY
DUBLIN BRANCH

Just when we want them most, words won't come. There is no way to express the loss—personal and professional—that we feel. And certainly no way to tell you how deep our sympathies are to you.

All the outpouring of love and loss doesn't begin to empty people's hearts of the emotion his passing has created. The emptiness will come... and last forever.

We send you our love.
ALAN AND MARILYN BERGMAN

This is one of those times everyone dreads but knows is inevitable. Your father used the clock of life in a style and fashion that few of us could ever attain. He was truly a phenomenon of this century and it was our pleasure to have been with him and share a few occasions we shall treasure always.

Our deepest love and understanding of your sorrow at this time. It seems that time has caught up with all of us.
ARTE AND GISELA JOHNSON

Frank Sinatra was not only one of the greatest performing artists of American history

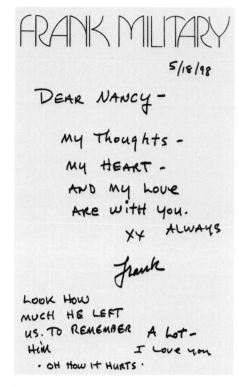

FRANK MILITARY

5/18/98

DEAR NANCY —

MY THOUGHTS -
MY HEART -
AND MY LOVE
ARE WITH YOU.
XX ALWAYS

Frank

LOOK HOW
MUCH HE LEFT
US. TO REMEMBER A LOT -
HIM   I LOVE YOU
· OH HOW IT HURTS ·

but also an outstanding exemplar of social responsibility in the arts and entertainment. My husband, Martin Luther King, Jr., and I appreciated his generous spirit in doing fund-raising benefits for the Civil Rights Movement, and he and Sammy Davis, Jr. also did a benefit for *The King Center* in 1969. His energetic humanitarian leadership served so many worthy causes and will provide a source of support and inspiration for many years to come. Frank Sinatra will be sorely missed, but we pray that his family and friends will find comfort in the knowledge that his vibrant legacy will live on in the hearts of all those he touched and in his many contributions to our nation.

Sincerely,
CORETTA SCOTT KING
THE KING CENTER

I am a daughter of a "bobby-soxer," which entailed growing up in the '50s and '60s listening to Frank Sinatra on the

"hi-fi." I learned to iron my dad's shirts to "Summer Wind," fold laundry to "High Hopes" and prepare dinner to "I Get No Kick From Champagne." As an adult I realize how lucky I am to have such fond "mother/daughter" memories. Just me, mom, and Frank Sinatra on the hi-fi.

All my best to you and your family.
Love,
J.F.
CALIFORNIA

It was a real honor to have worked for your dad. I thought the world of him. Now he knows something that no one on earth knows and that is "the secret of life…"

Aloha and God bless,
"PEPPER" MARTIN AND FAMILY
PAHOA, HAWAII
(SECURITY FOR FRANK SINATRA'S
HOME, RANCHO MIRAGE, '77-'89)

You were a special person here on Earth—and so your music shall follow you into Heaven, where you will sing with the angels…and we will feel your spirit forevermore.

L.T.
A FAITHFUL ADMIRER
CALIFORNIA

❖ ❖ ❖

I am so terribly sorry for your loss. I feel like I have lost someone dear to my heart. I just want to let you know that he will live on in our home forever, and not only am I teaching my three girls all of Mr. Sinatra's songs and movies, but one day I will be teaching my grandchildren about him, as my

grandmother and mother taught me.

We have all lost in his death. But we will all win by keeping his memory alive.

My deepest sympathy,
K.G. AND FAMILY
PENNSYLVANIA

People, events and things in life that bring the most joy bring the most sorrow when they are gone. Seeing your dad in concert and having my photo taken with him were some of the happiest days of my life. Losing him is one of the saddest. I look at the photos of him I have all over my house and I start to cry. I listen to his beautiful voice and I cry.

I want to offer you my condolences. There are no words to express the degree of my grief. Your dad kissed my cheek and shook my hand—and my mom's. He was so warm, so kind. I love him so much. A part of me died with him. Life will never be the same. He's happy in heaven, but losing him is sheer hell.

I know your memories of the love you shared will sustain you through this sorrow. God bless your dad and your family. You are in my prayers.

Love,
T.G.
PENNSYLVANIA

Your father sang a song, I think it's called "That's Life." That song has meant a lot to me over the past 10 years. My family has survived bankruptcy in 1988. Our home burning and never being rebuilt in 1990. And our youngest of five children nearly losing his hand in a moose hunting accident in 1996. That incident has put us in bankruptcy again from medical costs. But you know just like your father sang: "You pick yourself up and get back in the race, That's Life!" (It's my favorite Sinatra song!)

I've watched your interviews about Mr. Sinatra and it's refreshing and very special to hear the love in your voice for your father. And in seeing Frank Jr. talk about his father, it is obvious the trust and love in your family.

I realize I am among the millions who are your father's fans. For me I see your father's life contributions as the reflection of the Sinatra family values he was taught and then in turn lived and gave to his family and those he "touched."

I hope for you all that you will find com-fort in his memory and in each other. There are never the right words to express sorrow or grief; it's something private and personal that each person experiences and learns to live with. I pray God's blessings to be with you all.

Sincerely,
J.W.
ARKANSAS

Frank Sinatra, as an artist, belongs in the same class as Heifetz or Stokowski, to name two of the very few whose names are house-hold words and whose fame has been earned by unequaled accomplishments in their respective fields. But he is more. As a young star, he learned to use his influence with his mostly young and impressionable admirers to teach tolerance for all people at a time when to do so was not always easy, and with that he earned a place in America's heart that transcends art. Those of his generation, and some younger ones, know this; but it should not be forgotten by the youth of today who are beginning to rediscover his music yet may be unaware of the true stature of the man behind it. We at the Library of Congress cherish your father's legacy both as an artist and as a beloved cultural icon.

What a unique American. If American music has transformed the soundscape of the 20th century, he made it warm, accessible,

uman and wonderful. He arranged and
erformed as no other artist of this era.
Please give our deepest sympathies to all
he family.

Sincerely,

JAMES H. BILLINGTON
THE LIBRARIAN OF CONGRESS
WASHINGTON, D.C.

For about 35 years, Frank Sinatra was
resent in my life every day and he will be
forever.

He has brought me so much happiness that
I can't express at this moment.

On behalf of his numerous
French fans and particularly
those gathered in the Society of
France, I express to you and
your family our sincere condolences and deep sympathy.

MICHEL MACAIRE
SINATRA SOCIETY OF
FRANCE
(LES AMIS DE FRANK
SINATRA)

In 1939 I saw your Dad at the
Paramount. I knew then he would be someone special. We all loved him and he loved
us back.

Around 1956 I went to the Paramount
with my sister. That was the last time he
played there. We caught the last show. The
movie was Johnny Concho. He was a
coward in it and they called him "chicken."
After the movie, your father came out and
the place went wild. Finally we all quieted
down and the theater was completely dark
except for a light only on your father's face.
He started to sing, "I brought you violets for

your fur." Someone in the audience called
out, "Sing it chicken." Well, your father was
laughing with the audience, the music stopped,
and he started all over again. He was marvelous. He was on stage a little longer.

I will always have a place in my heart for
him. I tell my friends he was my first
boyfriend. I'm 74 years young because of
your father. God love him.

With love,

J.A.

Please accept the most sincere sympathy
from just one of Frank Sinatra's millions of
fans. Frank Sinatra was generous to so
many people and I was one of them. When
my husband Jim Gilliom, who was an L.A.
Dodger, passed away in 1978, he was most
gracious to my family. His life made an
impact on so many people. He was a wonderful, kind, and great personality.

May God bless you and your family.

Sincerely,

EDWINA GILLIOM
HIGGINBOTHAM

Your father's singing means much more to
me than I have told you. As a teenage student beginning college with a major in music,
I wanted something of an education I did
not see offered in the catalog of courses. The
musician I most respected then was a legendary jazz pianist, Lennie Tristano, who
had been a brilliant success in the 1940s
and then withdrew, mostly to teach. I went
to study with him. The first thing he did
was to teach one to listen, to memorize
recordings, and, whatever one's instrument,
to be able to sing what one learned.
All the great instrumentalists from
Louis Armstrong to Charlie Parker
were part of the course, but the first
musician to whom he introduced me
was Frank Sinatra, and I will
never forget the effect this discovery
had on me.

I still love to listen to
Sinatra's recordings, and I am
grateful for them. They are
art of the highest kind, and by
that I mean not only the art
of supreme technical mastery, but real
music that lifts the heart and makes one
glad to be alive.

It was once said about another musician,
"If it's in the music, it's in the man." That
is true, and by the measure of Sinatra's
music, the loss of the man to the world is
great indeed. We still have the music but you
who knew him so well will miss the man
very much. As one of his students, through
his records, and one of his great admirers, I
send to you and your family my heartfelt
condolences.

Sincerely,

JON NEWSOM
CHIEF, MUSIC DIVISION
THE LIBRARY OF CONGRESS
WASHINGTON, D.C.

I am not a fan, rather a friend. I am forty-three years old. My mother passed on her birthday March 31st, 1925 - March 31st, 1994. When Mr. Sinatra became ill in Virginia that year, my mother called me because she knew I would want to know about him. I was sixteen years old when I heard a song. A song which led me to purchase my first component set and subsequent albums one after another—all Sinatra. I lived in Atlanta after high school and a friend told me he was coming to town. I invited my mother from our home of Chester, SC, and my oldest sister to come to the Omni. I think I was the youngest person in the audience because when I yelled like a bobby-soxer he looked up into the stands as if he was for a brief moment taken back in time. In school I gave a presentation on his music and his voice by comparing past and present performances. Needless to say, the students were thrilled and the professor as well.

Last year, the company's awards convention was held in San Francisco. While there I bought Water Town on CD. I listened to this one again on my way back on the plane. It tells a story about someone leaving and is the one that comes to mind particularly now. On the twelfth of this month, I closed my store and, walking to my car in a neon lit parking lot, I hummed "That's All." I can feel things because the day before, while sitting in a meeting, I felt strange and somewhat ill. My

sister called me on that morning. I sat and cried on the side of my bed and have been crying and praying ever since. I'd like to say finally that my own personal consolation is that there is something special about people who come and go at this time of the season—it is a very good sign.

May God bless you all —
P.J.
NORTH CAROLINA

THE VICE PRESIDENT
WASHINGTON

May 18, 1998

Ms. Nancy Sinatra

Dear Nancy:

It is with tremendous sadness that I send my deepest condolences to you at the loss of your father. I understand that words are often of little consolation at this time, but I trust you will find solace in the strength of your wonderful family and comfort in the knowledge that your father was a truly exceptional American and an artist without peer.

Tipper joins me in sending our most sincere hopes for you and your family during this time, and I want you to know that you are all in our thoughts and prayers.

Sincerely,

Al Gore

God Bless.

❖ ❖ ❖

As a young man my father instilled many qualities in me that I would later see in a man that I would grow to love as a human being. The man was Frank Sinatra. In my

formative years I was exposed to his wonderful music and as I grew older, I was exposed to the man's contributions to this world. I, as many other fans can tell you, have my Sinatra stories, such as the first time I went to see him in concert at age 10 and then in 1991, at age 26. At the second concert with the legend, I was with a dear friend and to this day, we still discuss the love that was felt in the auditorium on that August night.

On the morning of May 15, 1998 I woke to see my son's television playing Frank's song "Young at Heart." I knew right then that we had lost Frank. The tears streamed down my cheeks as my heart broke in two. I had lost someone that was "family" and even though I never met him in person, I knew him as family all my life through the music and the many stories from my father, who had worked with Frank over the years.

If I was ever asked what single quality did I love in Frank the most, I would answer LOYALTY. The man is silent now, but the voice will live on forever. My prayers are with the entire Sinatra family.

In closing, I would like to say, "What is loved can never be lost and as long as we have a heart there will always be a place to keep Francis Albert Sinatra. *I LOVE YOU FRANK AND MISS YOU MORE THAN WORDS CAN DESCRIBE.*"
B.D.B.
VIRGINIA

FRANK SINATRA

The Officers, Governors and Members of the New York
Friars Club deeply mourn the loss of their beloved
Abbot Emeritus Frank Sinatra.

To the world he was the Chairman of the Board, but to
the Friars he was a friend who touched our lives, not
only in song, but also through his personal guidance.
He was fierce in his dedication and continued support of
humanitarian causes, which was always achieved with
modesty.

He helped us preserve the rich theatrical roots of the
Friars Club and his name belongs among the legendary
and immortal Friars like Jack Benny, George Burns,
Enrico Caruso, George M. Cohan, Cary Grant, George
Jessel, Joe E. Lewis, Dean Martin, Ed Sullivan and Mike
Todd and like them he shared a legacy of commitment
to the very best.

We are honored and proud to have been touched by the
legend that will always be Frank Sinatra.

Alan King, Abbot
Freddie Roman, Dean
Joe Cates, Prior
Frank Military, Scribe
David B. Cornstein, Treasurer
Jean Pierre Trebot, Executive Director

I have been meaning to leave you a note for the last few weeks or so. Your father has been on my mind and I knew something was the matter. I am heartbroken to hear the news this morning that your daddy left us. His presence in the music world and films are what legends are made of. What he did with lyrics could give wings to the heart of his listeners, certainly mine, and chase the fears of life away.

I join you in your sorrow and I am here for you if you need me.

Much love,

FRANCE NUYEN

When I decided to try to get legislation passed to award Mr. Sinatra the Congressional Gold Medal, I did it as a way of saying "thank you" for all of the joy that he had brought to my life and those of so many others.

When I was a child in Puerto Rico, my father came home from the U.S. Army and brought with him some 78 rpm records. This was my introduction to the English language and to the music of Mr. Sinatra. I fell in love with both. I work at improving my command of the English language every day, but I was smart enough not to try to imitate Sinatra's singing.

When my family moved to New York, as so many Puerto Ricans did at that time, I began to collect Sinatra records. Today my collection includes 309 long playing records, 78s, 45s, movies, books, photos and everything else that we Sinatra fanaticos collect. My e-mail address has the name Frank in it and Mr. Sinatra can be heard on my answering machine.

For this incurable romantic, Sinatra has supplied daily doses of the best singing in the world. The only way to round out this

"behavioral pattern" had to be for me to try to do something for him. The medal is a way for this fan and the nation to say "thank you" to this American institution.

My bill requires the U.S. mint to sell replicas of the medal to the public. As an additional tribute to Mr. Sinatra, we, his fans, can get together and raise a ton of money for the U.S. treasury.

My late father once told me, in Spanish, that the English language had taken a bad rap. People said that it was not a romantic language. He told me that it was, when it came out of the mouths of people who spoke it and sang it from the heart. My father was right and Mr. Sinatra showed us all how to do it in such a beautiful way.

CONGRESSMAN JOSÉ E. SERRANO

Congressman Serrano presents the Frank Sinatra National Medal to Nancy.

Dear Dad (Congressman Serrano),

I was deeply saddened to hear the news this morning of Frank Sinatra's passing. It touched me deeply not only because he was such a great entertainer, but because I know how much he means to you.

I know that he symbolized to you much more than music. His words and songs were your emotional outlet in which you, a hopeless romantic at heart, were able to dream, love, and sometimes hurt. He symbolized a passion that touched your inner soul to

awaken your desires to love and to be loved.

At a young age, he influenced you with his style and grace. His words introduced you to the beauty of the English language. You were deeply moved at his ability to put words together in beautiful harmony to convey a message of love and hope. His words seemed to flow so effortlessly, yet they were laced with a certain type of melancholy that only a true romantic could understand.

I know that his songs enriched your life in more ways than mere words can mention. Over the years his songs documented different times in your life, your loves, your losses, your hopes and your dreams, your triumphs and your tragedies—and through it all, Frank was there for you to keep you looking forward to another day and to another song. You could always count on him to sing to you and to say just the right things at just the right moment. At times, he was the only constant in your life.

He is such a huge part of my life because you are such a huge influence on mine. You raised me with the songs of Sinatra. So now when I think back to my younger years, I hear his tunes gently floating in the background of many of my memories. In his passing, let us raise our glasses in tribute, and not bow our heads in sorrow, for he has left the world a better place for people like you and me and every other person who dares to dream of love and romance.

Here's to Frank, the original swinger who has taught the world to dream.

JOSÉ MARCO SERRANO

I've always felt sending a condolence note to someone I don't really know that well to be somewhat perfunctory rather than heartfelt, but after several weeks of your father's passing I felt compelled to write. I couldn't help myself.

Your father stays in my head...too many moments that are special in my life are linked to him. As a teenager working in Atlantic City, I used to go to the 500 Club. Not having the money, we'd listen to him through the back door in the alley...the sound quality wasn't great but it was "Frank." One summer in the '60s I worked as a bellhop at the Cal Neva Lounge. Our uniforms—orange shirts and tan pants—were really cool for the time...the college parties with Sinatra on the record player...the dates with his music on the radio, but all my small personal experiences are nothing compared to what Frank Sinatra brought the world. It is so deeply embedded in the fabric of our time as to be linked for all time. To say he was special is an understatement. He may have begun just as the "voice"...he ended up as the voice of our time. You must feel very proud that he was your father.

Regretfully,
BARRY LEVINSON

Please accept our deepest condolences for the demise of our idol and icon...Frank Sinatra. And Frank, thank you for all the beautiful songs. Please pray and sing for us in heaven.

God bless you and your family.
HON. MIGUEL "MIKE" ROMERO
MANILA, PHILIPPINES

I grew up in the '60s and '70s with a father whose joie de vivre was inspired by your father. Frank Sinatra music in our home was not revered, nor unduly highlighted, but merely a part of the fabric of the Bocaccio family—and often the source of great debate between my uncles and grandfathers.

I want to tell you that on Friday morning, as I drove to a breakfast meeting and heard the news, I pulled over and immediately called my dad. We sat talking for 20 minutes, and relived seminal moments in our own father/son relationship—all somewhere punctuated by "Sinatra" music. We cried and your father once again brought us together in profound ways.

I just wanted to tell you that we were blessed by your father's presence on this planet—his was a life worth living.

Warmest personal regards,
GERARD BOCACCIO
THE BUBBLE FACTORY

My name is Anne "Skolnick" Stein. I am 80 years old, and today I am very, very sad.

I have known of Mr. Sinatra from the very start of his career and have loved him ever since.

You see, my brother, Sam Skolnick, was a top first trumpet player with Tommy Dorsey when Frank came aboard. Sam was in the back-up band at the Paramount when Frank sang there. I met Frank on one of the "one nite" stands in the '40s through my brother. I have loved his music, his humor, and his acting. I have very fond memories of him during my dancing days, and now I miss him and I cry.

Sincerely,
ANNE SKOLNICK STEIN
LOS ANGELES, CA

Frank Sinatra was playing at Bally's. Everybody told us not to see the show. Oddly, the dealers said that he would sing for 20 minutes and that was it. We went anyway. It was the greatest musical experience of my life. Sinatra was on fire. He did 1 hr. and 20 min. and it was amazing. We saw the years just fade away as he became young and vibrant right before our eyes. Each song was better and better. It was an amazing show. I'm so glad that I got to see Sinatra. I'm glad I didn't listen to the naysayers. Thanks for the great memory and the years of entertainment. To the family, my sympathy. I am sure that the memory of Sinatra is sweet as honey and in that way he will never perish.

J.A.
ILLINOIS

My 2-year-old daughter, Elizabeth, is a dedicated fan of "her friend, Frank." She loves his recordings and movies, and has pictures collected from websites and magazines in her room. She loves him so much that no one may sing along with his recordings. I am the luckiest mom in the world—I don't have to listen to Barney the Dinosaur! On her behalf and mine, please accept our condolences on Mr. Sinatra's passing.

J.N.
WASHINGTON

Deepest sympathy. My family and I shall miss him very much. He was with us each and every day for over 45 years. All celebrations and holidays, background music for family videos, etc. We are all so fortunate to have shared our lives with him. It was so much fun and thanks for it all. Love to you always.

G.M.
NEW JERSEY

This has been a terrible thing to lose you, Frank. Nobody will occupy your place. I give my deepest sympathy to the Sinatra family.

M.A.S.

GUATEMALA

Frank, I always loved your music although I am only 20 years old, so that I missed your big time. You will always be in my heart. You really did it YOUR WAY...goodbye.

G.R.

AUSTRIA

His eye is on the sparrow, but I know he watches me. God speed, Friend.

S.M.

NEW ZEALAND

I am 39 years old and have spent most of my life in radio as a broadcaster/dj. When I started as a 14-year-old disc jockey I saw all these albums from Old "Blue Eyes" and didn't realize that those albums would become my favorites one day. I hope the music that Frank left us will inspire the new artists. He set the "standard." Now it's up to our generation to reach up and grab the golden rings left there for us. I just want to wish God's peace to your family and hoping that someday, somewhere, we'll all enjoy and hear Frank again in person.

R.E.

WASHINGTON

Dear Frank,

All I can say is you have brought me joy by being an Italian American like myself, by making the most beautiful music I will ever hear, and by being such a great humanitarian. I know you are singing with the angels. May God keep you close to him like you have kept all of us close to you.

God bless you always,

M.A.S.

NEW JERSEY

Thanks, Mr. Sinatra, for the memories. Now that I'm older with children of my own and a lovely wife, I appreciate the words and music you've left behind. You'll always be missed, but I feel very fortunate that I was able to grow up in a time when you were still putting out the beautiful music that generations to come will grow to love.

D.F.

MISSOURI

I hope that the grandchildren will continue on with the projects that you have lined up for Frank's memory, and that the following generation of the Sinatra family will keep his memory and music alive for future generations to enjoy as we have over these many years. Love and may God bless all of you.

K.N.

NORTH CAROLINA

I loved Frank. His voice, his style, his quiet nature gave me inspiration. I never knew why I loved music from the '30s and '40s. As an African-American baby boomer, I was not supposed to be attracted to

his kind of voice or music, but now I know it is because of Frank Sinatra's presentation. I will miss him too.

O.H.

TEXAS

I am sincerely sorry, for all mankind has lost a big man. Now he'll be singing and dancing and joking in heaven with his friends as a new angel. May he rest in peace and may God give all the Sinatra relatives strength.

B.R.

MEXICO

Today is the day that your father Frank was laid to rest. He will live forever in our hearts and souls. I am 30 years old and played one of his CDs. My mother, who is in her 60s, wept. My father, who is 70, remained silent, and my daughter, who is 8, said, "I like this music, Mommy," while my son, 6, hummed to the lyrics. He is ageless and timeless, and my children are proof that his essence will span many generations to come. Thank you, Mr. Sinatra, for bringing happiness to four generations (my grandparents were fans as well). God speed to you.

K.S.

NEW JERSEY

Let the meteorites come. Frank Sinatra is gone.

CALIFORNIA

Encore

I've learned a few important things. Things are not always what they seem to be. Two reporters of great reputation, Tommy Thompson and Jimmy Cannon, told me separately that they too had been victims of Sinatra's distorted press. Thompson: "Some reporters insisted that wherever Sinatra went a wall of 'goons' and 'bodyguards' strong-armed a passageway." Thompson saw one newspaper photograph that identified two sturdy men as Sinatra's "bodyguards." "I knew they were actually two of his longtime musicians, one piano player, one guitarist. Frank said, 'Yeah, some bodyguards. They get drunk every night. They can't look after their own bodies much less mine.'" And Cannon told me that *Look* magazine ran a picture of Frank. "They described a guy in a navy blue suit and identified him as a 'bodyguard'. I was that guy."

I have also learned that good deeds are not always welcome. Burt Lancaster: "You sometimes feel like you want to run away from him because, if you say to Frank, 'I'm having a problem,' it becomes his problem. And sometimes maybe you'd like to try to work it out yourself."

Sinatra is considered a hero by many including Bill Fine, who wrote to Frank in 1985: "You pulled the Chrysler lever when your vote counted toward making that company go again—to say nothing of saving 35,000 jobs."

From Herbert Kalmbach, who appreciated Frank's offering a hand of friendship to Ted Agnew in his time of disgrace: "I feel certain that I am speaking for many in writing to tell you of my thanks for your kind loyalty, compassion and simple decency in standing by the Vice President."

And Jimmy Cannon again: "I know a guy whose life would have been ruined if Frank hadn't helped him. He was in a terrible financial jam. Frank could not go to the bank because he was in bad shape himself, but he went to a shylock and paid tremendous interest to get $10,000 to bail the guy out of his trouble."

From Richard Condon, who wrote *The Manchurian Candidate*: "Frank once told me that the only way to negotiate a dispute, figuratively, was to kick the opponent in the ankle and, as he hopped on one foot, belt him soundly across the chops."

The Sovereign Knights of Malta recognized my father for his "Aristocracy of Deeds" by knighting him in 1967.

Frank's motto, "Living well is the best revenge," helped create many sleepless nights. "He never sleeps much," actor Henry Silva told me. "I said to Frank one morning while we were working on a movie, 'How much sleep did you get last night?' He said, 'I went to bed at six and got up at seven-thirty.'"

My father thrives on work. Bing Crosby wrote to Dad on the occasion of his "retirement" in 1971. "The frantic schedule in which you have been engaged, professionally and socially, for the last twenty-five years must be a bonebreaker. I'd have been in traction long ago." And these words from Tennessee Williams describe Sinatra: "It is only in his work that an artist can find reality and satisfaction, for the actual world is less intense than the world of his invention and consequently his life, without recourse to violent disorder, does not seem very substantial. The right condition for him is that in which his work is not only convenient but unavoidable."

The music is still the important force. Charles Champlin wrote: "To listen to Sinatra today is to be reminded again that, among the things which are true about him, one is that he holds title to more of our musical memories than anyone else. Also, if he is made to seem like the last angry man from time to time, what he really is in a special sense is the last passionate man. The emotions he conveys may or may not be, in the nature of things, complex, but they are powerful and persistent and widely shared. There is always that remarkable sense of the inseparability of his own history and our own, the way in which, from the beginning, his cycles have, in different magnitudes, confirmed our own."

There are dichotomies. A public figure is rarely alone. He seldom has the opportunity to do any private work, to experiment without risk. After a time, everything is an event. "Frank is an extremely private man who has had to live his life as a totally public individual," writer-director Richard Brooks told me. Brooks sees Dad as a man with a compelling need to be free, caught in the claustrophobia of celebrity. "There are women who hand him flowers on stage and at the end of his shows. Most of them are not looking for romance with him. They are thanking him for some memory they have had in their lives. You can see it in their eyes. They would like him to know that he has made them feel something—probably something deep and very good. They're not there so they can say, 'I touched Frank Sinatra.' It's not that they touched Frank Sinatra. It's that somewhere, somehow, Frank Sinatra touched them."

In 1984, journalist Murray Kempton wrote, "When I hear Frank Sinatra, I have no basis for assuming that his particular lonely heart has learned its lesson, but, for the moment, every fiber of my being believes it has."

He was born fighting because he was born dying, and the prevailing fight has been with his own mortality. In the end, so much blurs into an unfinished portrait.

He is so outgoing, yet so withdrawn. His personality flows from a clash of extremes. A clash that stretches back to the little boy, assertive enough to run away to his cousin Buddy's house in order to escape his mother's anger, and troubled enough to bury himself beneath the covers and cry. That same little boy tried to track down the doctor who attended his birth because he blamed him for the scars on his face and neck. The man aggressively placing phone calls to Ava in Spain was the same man who collapsed from martinis to mask the pain. When Frank Sinatra flails out he is dealing as much with inner demons as with outer irritants. Now and then I wonder if, as some people believe, the camera can steal the soul, what can an audience of 175,000 do, or 20 million, or a hundred times that.

I am so blessed to have Frank Sinatra for my father. We read each other easily and communicate well. At six-thirty on the morning he was to have major surgery on his hand, he was already under sedation. I was on the road so there was no reason for him to think I was in town. He heard my footsteps in the hospital corridor and from his room called out, "Chicken?" He just knew it was me.

His words of advice have colored my life and I practice them. "Be aware. Be aware of everything around you," has helped keep me safe and centered in difficult situations. "Stay away from the dark thoughts, Chicken. Don't despair." This seems impossible to do sometimes, but with practice it can be put into one's life when needed, and be of great help in the darkest, loneliest of times.

I know him very well but I still have trouble identifying the driving force. The writer Garson Kanin told me, "What motivates him most is a driving need to communicate. You can hear that when you listen to his singing. I said to him once, 'Frank, what is your real, overall ambition in life? In the long view, what would you like to really feel you've accomplished?' And he thought for awhile and then he said, 'Well, I think my real ambition is to pass on to others what I know. You know, it took me a long, long time to learn what I now know, and I don't want that to die with me. I'd like to pass that on to younger people.'"

Poppa, it is my dearest hope that this book will help you do just that.

The Films Of Frank Sinatra

"**H**e sings prettily in an unphotogenic manner." That was George Simon's comment in *Metronome* reviewing Frank's first movie, *Las Vegas Nights*, in 1941. In the beginning, young people would have gone to see his films if he had been a lousy actor—but he wasn't. By the time *Newsweek* said, "Sinatra becomes a smoother performer every time out," in their review of his 1947 film *It Happened in Brooklyn,* Dad had established himself in Hollywood.

He had contracts with RKO (Radio Keith Orpheum—named for the Keith and Orpheum theatre chains) and MGM (Metro Goldwyn Mayer—named for Metro Pictures, Louis B. Mayer's company and Samuel Goldwyn Pictures). In 1945, one short film, *The House I Live In*, garnered him a special Academy Award. The talented people responsible for the production donated their time, and Dad insisted that the proceeds from the film go to charities. *Cue* magazine called it "a film that packs more power, punch and solid substance than most of the features ground each year out of Hollywood."

It is important to look closely at the films of Frank Sinatra because most of them were good, some excellent, and because, in a life so filled with marvelous music, the impression persists that he is a singer who has also done a little acting, a song-and-dance man who did a dramatic role now and then. Part of his appeal on the screen was the look: "His face," said the sculptor Jo Davidson in the early 1940s, "has a curious structure. Those cheekbones! Those bulges around the cheeks. That heavy lower lip...like a young Lincoln." And of course, those eyes and that keyboard grin! On a giant screen, it is important for an actor to use great economy of expression and movement, to be subtle. He was already a master of this and, believing brevity is not only "the soul of wit," but of drama as well, he was able to accomplish much without overacting or chewing the scenery. Perhaps the real key to his success in films was his ability to translate what he knew about expressing emotion in song to dialogue. He became as fine an actor and communicator on film as he was on acetate, wax, vinyl or tape.

My father doesn't think he deserved the Oscar for *From Here to Eternity*, and there are other roles he played that he wishes had been better received. But, as with everything else in life, you win some and you lose some. In the case of his movies Frank says it best: "I made some pretty good pictures...and I tried a few things that turned out to be mistakes..."

MAJOR BOWES AMATEUR THEATRE OF THE AIR
(1935)

RKO Pictures Release
  Producer and Director: John H. Auer
  Stats: Opened in October 1935 at Radio City Music Hall.

SYNOPSIS:

A series of short subjects filmed at Biograph Studios on Tremont Avenue, Bronx, New York. Sinatra appeared in two of them. In "The Nightclub," he played a nonsinging waiter, and in "The Big Minstrel Act," he wore a top hat and blackface with wide, white lips.

CAST:
The Three Flashes ....Jimmy Petrozelli
                                Patty Principe
                                Fred Tamburro
Waiter, Minstrel Man ....Frank Sinatra

LAS VEGAS NIGHTS
(1941)

Paramount Pictures
  Producer: William LeBaron
  Director: Ralph Murphy
  Screenplay: Ernest Pagano, Harry Clork
  Music Director: Victor Young
  Musical Arrangements: Axel Stordahl, Victor Young, Charles Bradshaw, Leo Shuken, Max Terr
  Musical numbers staged by: LeRoy Prinz
  Director of Photography: William C. Mellor
  Running time: 89 minutes
  Stats: Sinatra's first film.

SYNOPSIS:

A down-and-out vaudevillian named Stu Grant (Bert Wheeler) arrives in Las Vegas with three singing sisters. Although they're all broke, the women have a claim to their uncle's estate. They get lucky in a gambling casino, but when they turn over their winnings to Stu for safekeeping, he gambles most of it away. Fortunately, there's just enough money left for them to start a nightclub. More troubles ensue, however, when their club is wrecked and a crooked lawyer tries to cheat them out of their inheritance. Just before he succeeds, they manage to sell their uncle's property to a Los Angeles real estate developer. Sinatra performs as the male vocalist with Tommy Dorsey's orchestra.

CAST:
Norma Jennings ....Constance Moore
Stu Grant ....Bert Wheeler
Bill Stevens ....Phil Regan
Mildred Jennings ....Lillian Cornell
Patsy Lynch ....Virginia Dale
Hank Bevis.................................Hank Ladd

Tommy Dorsey and His Orchestra, Vocalist: Frank Sinatra

SONGS:
Sinatra sings "I'll Never Smile Again"

SHIP AHOY
(1942)

Metro-Goldwyn-Mayer
Producer: Jack Cummings
Director: Edward Buzzell
Screenplay: Harry Clork
Music Supervisor and Conductor:
  George Stoll
Musical Arrangements: Axel Stordahl,
  Cy Oliver, Leo Arnaud, George Bassman,
  Basil Adlam
Dance Director: Bobby Connolly
Running time: 95 minutes

SYNOPSIS:

In this musical comedy, Tallulah Winters (Eleanor Powell), the star of a dance troupe, has been hired—along with Tommy Dorsey's band—to perform in a floating nightclub in Puerto Rico. What Tallulah doesn't know is that she's been conned by foreign agents into carrying a magnetic mine that's been placed in her luggage. She thinks she's doing a service for her country and has no idea she's been duped. The suitcase containing the mine is accidentally exchanged for a bag belonging to an action-adventure writer named Merton K. Kibble (Red Skelton). When Tallulah finally discovers that she's been inadvertently enlisted as a spy, she tap-dances out a message in Morse code, which ultimately leads to the capture of the enemy agents. Sinatra appears as the male singer with Tommy Dorsey's orchestra.

CAST:

Tallulah Winters	Eleanor Powell
Merton K. Kibble	Red Skelton
Skip Owens	Bert Lahr
Fran Evans	Virginia O'Brien

Tommy Dorsey and His Orchestra, featuring Buddy Rich (drums), Ziggy Elman (trumpet), the Pied Pipers; Vocalists: Frank Sinatra, Connie Haines

SONGS:
Sinatra sings "The Last Call for Love" and "Poor You"

REVEILLE WITH BEVERLY
(1943)

Columbia Pictures
Producer: Sam White
Director: Charles Barton
Screenplay: Howard J. Green, Jack Henley,
  Albert Duffy
Music Director: Morris Stoloff
Art Director: Lionel Banks
Running time: 78 minutes
Stats: Although Sinatra sings only one
  song, this film helped establish him
  as a teenage heartthrob.

SYNOPSIS:

Beverly Ross (Ann Miller) is a former record-store salesgirl who finds herself sitting in for a disc jockey on an early morning radio program. Instead of playing classical music, she spins the popular songs of the day, knowing that they'll have more appeal for all the soldier boys stationed at nearby Army camps. Beverly's pop programming works so well that by the end of her first week on the air, her fan mail is overflowing at the local post office. When her radio show is heard by a rich inductee named Eddie Ross (Larry Parks), he's so enamored of her that he decides to switch identities with his former chauffeur, who's stationed at the same Army camp. Eddie then goes off in pursuit of Beverly, woos her and eventually wins her. Once again, Sinatra is seen only as a male vocalist.

CAST:

Beverly Ross	Ann Miller
Barry Lang	William Wright
Andy Adams	Dick Purcell
Vernon Lewis	Franklin Pangborn
Eddie Ross	Larry Parks

Bob Crosby and His Orchestra
Freddie Slack and His Orchestra, with Ella Mae Morse
Duke Ellington and His Orchestra
Count Basie and His Orchestra
Vocalists: Frank Sinatra, the Mills Brothers

SONGS:
Sinatra sings "Night and Day"

HIGHER AND HIGHER
(1943)

RKO Radio Pictures
  Producer and Director: Tim Whelan
  Screenplay: Jay Dratler, Ralph Spence
  Based on the play by: Joshua Logan,
    Gladys Hurlbut
  Music Director: Constantin Bakaleinikoff
  Musical Arrangements for Frank Sinatra:
    Axel Stordahl
  Vocal Arrangements: Ken Darby
  Running time: 90 minutes
  Stats: Sinatra's first important film and
    his first acting role.

SYNOPSIS:

When the wealthy Mr. Drake (Leon Errol) tells his servants that he's bankrupt and can't afford to pay them, his loyal staff comes to the rescue. The valet, Mike (Jack Haley), along with the others, hatches a plot to pass off Millie (Michele Morgan), the scullery maid, as their employer's debutante daughter. They hope she'll snare a rich husband and solve everyone's financial woes. The first likely suitor for the phony debutante is a well-heeled young man named Frank (Sinatra, playing himself) who happens to live next door. Another possible prospect is "nobleman" Fitzroy Wilson (Victor Borge), but he turns out to be as fake as the "debutante." The servants finally arrange for Millie's coming-out at the Debutantes' Ball, but Mrs. Keating (Elisabeth Risdon), a society matron, causes Millie's debut to backfire, thanks to her plans for her own debutante daughter, Catherine (Barbara Hale). Millie's deception is revealed when she and Mike realize they're in love with each other; Millie's been crazy about him for a long time. Catherine now sets her sights on Frank and wins him. Mr. Drake's money problems are solved when he discovers a secret storeroom of old liquor in his home—enough to open a tavern which his servants will run.

CAST:

Millie	Michele Morgan
Mike	Jack Haley
Frank	Frank Sinatra
Drake	Leon Errol
Fitzroy Wilson	Victor Borge
Sandy	Mary Wickes
Catherine Keating	Barbara Hale
Marty	Mel Torme
Byngham	Paul Hartman
Oscar	Dooley Wilson

SONGS:

Sinatra sings: "You Belong in a Love Song," "I Couldn't Sleep a Wink Last Night," "A Lovely Way to Spend an Evening," "The Music Stopped" and "I Saw You First"

STEP LIVELY
(1944)

RKO Pictures
  Producer: Robert Fellows
  Director: Tim Whelan
  Screenplay: Warren Duff, Peter Milne
  Based on the play "Room Service" by:
    Allen Boretz, John Murray
  Music Director: Constantin Bakaleinikoff
  Orchestral Arrangements: Gene Rose
  Musical Arrangements for Frank Sinatra:
    Axel Stordahl
  Vocal Arrangements: Ken Darby
  Running time: 88 minutes
  Stats: Sinatra's first screen kiss.

SYNOPSIS:

Sinatra plays Glen, a country bumpkin who dreams of becoming a playwright. He sends his play, along with a check for $1,500 toward its production, to a slick Broadway producer named Miller (George Murphy). Glen goes to New York to check on his play's progress and discovers Miller trapped in a Manhattan hotel because he can't pay his bill, and rehearsing another play with a cast of 22 hungry actors. A man named Jenkins (Eugene Pallette) arrives on the scene with a $50,000 check—from a mysterious backer—and a pretty protégée Miss Abbott (Anne Jeffreys), who falls for Glen. When Miller and his partners, Binion (Wally Brown) and Harry (Alan Carney), discover the check is bogus, they decide to open their new show within five days in order to beat the check before it bounces. While trying to avoid Glen, Miller suddenly discovers the young man has a voice that women find irresistible and offers him the lead in the show. Glen and the musical are a huge success. There's also a happy ending for him with Christine (Gloria DeHaven), the girl he's fallen in love with.

CAST:

Glen	Frank Sinatra
Miller	George Murphy
Wagner	Adolphe Menjou
Christine	Gloria DeHaven
Gribble	Walter Slezak
Jenkins	Eugene Pallette
Binion	Wally Brown
Harry	Alan Carney
Miss Abbott	Anne Jeffreys

SONGS:

Sinatra sings "Come Out, Come Out, Wherever You Are," "Where Does Love Begin?" "As Long as There's Music" and "Some Other Time"

ANCHORS AWEIGH
(1945)

Metro-Goldwyn-Mayer
  Producer: Joe Pasternak
  Director: George Sidney
  Screenplay: Isobel Lennart
  Music Supervisor and Conductor: George Stoll
  Frank Sinatra's Vocal Arrangements:
    Axel Stordahl
  Dance sequences created by: Gene Kelly
  Art Directors: Cedric Gibbons, Randall Duell
  Director of Tom & Jerry dance cartoon:
    Fred Quimby
  Running time: 143 minutes
  Stats: Sinatra's first Technicolor musical.
    His singing, dancing and acting won
    critical acclaim.

SYNOPSIS:
Two sailors, Clarence Doolittle (Frank Sinatra) and Joseph Brady (Gene Kelly), are spending their brief shore leave in Hollywood. There they meet up with a

precocious little boy named Donald Martin (Dean Stockwell), who lives with his aunt, Susan Abbott (Kathryn Grayson), a bit player in Hollywood movies. The outgoing Joseph tries to get the shy Clarence to fall in love with Susan, and vice versa. But his attempt at matchmaking goes awry when he realizes that he's fallen for Susan himself, and she tells him the feeling is mutual. Clarence, meanwhile, has come out of his shell and meets a pretty girl from Brooklyn whom he woos and wins. When their leave is over, both sailors go back to their ship, knowing they've now got new romances on shore.

CAST:
Clarence Doolittle ....Frank Sinatra
Joseph Brady ....Gene Kelly
Susan Abbott ....Kathryn Grayson
Donald Martin ....Dean Stockwell
Jose Iturbi ....Himself
Girl from Brooklyn..............Pamela Britton
Police Sergeant ....Rags Ragland
Cafe Manager ....Billy Gilbert

SONGS:
Sinatra sings "We Hate to Leave," "What Makes the Sunset?" "The Charm of You," "I Begged Her" and "I Fall in Love Too Easily"

THE HOUSE I LIVE IN
(1945)

RKO Radio Pictures
  Producer: Frank Ross
  Director: Mervyn LeRoy
  Screenplay: Albert Maltz
  Music Director: Axel Stordahl
  Running time: 10 minutes
  Stats: This short film was Sinatra's idea,
    and he arranged for the proceeds to
    go to charity. It won a special award
    from the Academy of Motion Picture
    Arts and Sciences.

SYNOPSIS:
The story's theme is racial and religious intolerance. Sinatra has just finished rehearsing a radio show. He steps out of the studio for a breath of fresh air. In the alleyway he discovers a group of boys chasing and beating up another kid because, as they tell Sinatra, "We don't like his religion." The crooner lectures

them on being tolerant of all races, creeds and religions, and then heads back to the studio. When one of the boys asks Sinatra what he does for a living, Sinatra demonstrates by singing the film's title song.

Frank Sinatra ....Himself

SONGS:
Sinatra sings "If You Are but a Dream" and "The House I Live In"

TILL THE CLOUDS ROLL BY
(1946)

Metro-Goldwyn-Mayer (Technicolor)
   Producer: Arthur Freed
   Director: Richard Whorf
   Screenplay: Myles Connolly, Jean Holloway
   Based on the life and music of Jerome Kern
   Music Supervisor and Conductor: Lennie
      Hayton
   Orchestrations: Conrad Salinger
   Musical numbers staged and directed by:
      Robert Alton
   Directors of Photography: Harry Stradling,
      George Folsey
   Art Directors: Cedric Gibbons, Daniel B.
      Cathcart
   Running time: 137 minutes
   Stats: "Ol' Man River" is sung twice in
      the film, once by Caleb Peterson and
      chorus, once by Sinatra.

SYNOPSIS:
This film biography on the life of the

legendary Jerome Kern (portrayed by Robert Walker) begins with the successful Broadway opening of his magnum opus, *Showboat*. On his way home after a party in his honor, Kern asks his chauffeur to stop at the old New York City brownstone where he lived when he was an aspiring songwriter. Woven into his story of musical success, a happy marriage and coming to Hollywood for the filming of *Showboat* are song-and-dance numbers performed by MGM's outstanding musical "guest stars," including Sinatra.

CAST:

Guest Star	June Allyson
Sally	Lucille Bremer
Marilyn Miller	Judy Garland
Magnolia	Kathryn Grayson
James I. Hessler	Van Heflin
Julie	Lena Horne
Bandleader	Van Johnson
Guest Star	Angela Lansbury
Gaylord Ravenal	Tony Martin
Ellie	Virginia O'Brien
Julie Sanderson	Dinah Shore

Guest Star	Frank Sinatra
Jerome Kern	Robert Walker

SONGS:
Sinatra sings "Ol' Man River"

IT HAPPENED IN BROOKLYN
(1947)

Metro-Goldwyn-Mayer
   Producer: Jack Cummings
   Director: Richard Whorf
   Screenplay: Isobel Lennart
   Music Supervisor and Director:
      Johnny Green
   Orchestrations: Ted Duncan
   Frank Sinatra's Vocal Arrangements:
      Axel Stordahl
   Musical numbers staged and directed by:
      Jack Donohue
   Piano solos arranged and played by:
      Andre Previn
   Running time: 104 minutes
   Stats: Critics applauded Sinatra's acting
      and comedic talent.

SYNOPSIS:
The war is over, and ex-GI Danny Miller (Sinatra) comes home to Brooklyn. Having no family of his own, Danny

moves in with an old friend, Nick Lombardi (Jimmy Durante), who works as a janitor at New Utrecht High School, where Anne Fielding (Kathryn Grayson) is a teacher. Danny and Anne are both aspiring singers, but both are discouraged about their chances of success. Jamie Shellgrove (Peter Lawford), the wealthy head of an aristocratic English family, comes to New York with a song

he's written, and he finally sees it successfully performed in a school recital. Jamie meets Anne and they fall in love, at which point Danny fondly remembers an ex-Army nurse who hails from Brooklyn. He looks her up and they, too, fall in love.

CAST:

Danny Webson Miller	Frank Sinatra
Anne Fielding	Kathryn Grayson
Jamie Shellgrove	Peter Lawford
Nick Lombardi	Jimmy Durante
Nurse	Gloria Grahame

SONGS:
Sinatra sings "The Brooklyn Bridge," "I Believe," "Time After Time," "The Song's Gotta Come from the Heart," "It's the Same Old Dream," "La Ci Darem la Mano," "Black Eyes"

THE MIRACLE OF THE BELLS
(1948)

RKO Radio Pictures
  Producer: Jesse L. Lasky, Walter MacEwen
  Director: Irving Pichel
  Screenplay: Ben Hecht, Quentin Reynolds
  Based on the novel by: Russell Janney
  Music: Leigh Harline
  Running time: 120 minutes
  Stats: Sinatra's first nonmusical acting part, but he sings one song a cappella.

SYNOPSIS:
Father Paul (Sinatra) is the priest in a little mining-town church in Pennsylvania. Bill Dunnigan (Fred MacMurray), a theatrical press agent, arrives in town to bury his former sweetheart, Olga (Alida Valli) beside her coal-miner father. Bill tells Father Paul that Olga was a struggling actress when he met her, and landed her the leading role in a major Hollywood movie. As soon as shooting was finished, Olga died of tuberculosis and the film's producer, Marcus Harris (Lee J. Cobb), decided to shelve the movie. Bill is determined to see the film released and asks Father Paul to have the church bells toll for four days in order to attract publicity, but Harris still says no. Then, at a morning Mass at the church, the congregation notices the statues of St. Michael and the Virgin Mary have turned to face Olga's coffin. No one knows, of course, that Father Paul is behind this "miracle." When news commentators tell the world about it, Harris finally changes his mind and releases Olga's first and last film.

CAST:
Father Paul ....Frank Sinatra
Bill Dunnigan ....Fred MacMurray
Olga Treskovna............................Alida Valli
Marcus Harris ....Lee J. Cobb

SONGS:
Sinatra sings "Ever Homeward"

THE KISSING BANDIT
(1948)

Metro-Goldwyn-Mayer
  Producer: Joe Pasternak
  Director: Laslo Benedek
  Screenplay: Isobel Lennart, John Briard Harding
  Music Supervisor and Conductor: George Stoll
  Musical Arrangements: Leo Arnaud
  Dance Director: Stanley Donen
  Costumes: Walter Plunkett
  Director of Photography: Robert Surtees
  Running time: 102 minutes
  Stats: Generally considered Sinatra's worst film.

SYNOPSIS:
The time is the 1830s in Spanish California. Ricardo (Sinatra) has just graduated from a Boston business school and arrives in California to take over his late father's innkeeping business. He quickly learns that his old man was really a bandit, and the gang he rode with expects Ricardo to become their new leader. His father also had a reputation as a Don Juan with all the ladies of the ranchos he robbed, thus making his a tough act to follow—until he meets Teresa (Kathryn Grayson), daughter of the don who rules the territory. Ricardo and his sidekick, Chico (J. Carroll Naish), pretend to be tax collectors from Spain in order to rob Don Jose, but they're caught and their disguise is revealed. Luckily, love conquers all: Ricardo is freed and forgiven and wins the beautiful Teresa.

CAST:
Ricardo ....Frank Sinatra
Teresa ....Kathryn Grayson
Chico....................................J. Carroll Naish
Isabella ....Mildred Natwick
Don Jose ....Mikhail Rasumny
General Torro ....Billy Gilbert
Dancers: Ricardo Montalban, Cyd Charisse, Ann Miller

SONGS:
Sinatra sings "What's Wrong with Me?"
"If I Steal a Kiss," "Senorita" and "Siesta"

TAKE ME OUT TO THE BALL GAME
(1949)

Metro-Goldwyn-Mayer
Producer: Arthur Freed
Director: Busby Berkeley
Screenplay: Harry Tugent, George Wells
Based on a story by: Gene Kelly, Stanley Donen
Music Supervisor and Conductor: Adolph Deutsch
Vocal Arrangements: Robert Tucker
Dance Directors: Gene Kelly, Stanley Donen
Art Directors: Cedric Gibbons, Daniel B. Cathcart
Running time: 93 minutes

SYNOPSIS:

In the early part of the century, vaudeville was flourishing, and so was baseball. And so were vaudeville's popular song-and-dance duo, Dennis Ryan (Sinatra) and Eddie O'Brien (Gene

Kelly), who are spending their summers as star players on the Wolves baseball team. A rivalry develops between Dennis and Eddie when both of them are smitten by the Wolves' new manager, K.C. Higgins (Esther Williams). Eddie's also involved with a double-crossing gambling kingpin, Joe Lorgan (Edward Arnold) who's out to destroy the baseball team. On top of this, Eddie takes a side job directing a nightclub chorus. When he breaks training, K.C. benches him. Lorgan tries to keep him from playing in the Wolves' big game but fails. Eddie goes on to help them win the pennant and the heart of K.C. Dennis, meanwhile, has fallen for a woman named Shirley (Betty Garrett), whose pursuit of him finally pays off.

CAST:

Dennis Ryan	Frank Sinatra
Eddie O'Brien	Gene Kelly
K.C. Higgins	Esther Williams
Shirley Delwyn	Betty Garrett
Joe Lorgan	Edward Arnold
Nat Goldberg	Jules Munshin

SONGS:

Sinatra sings "Take Me Out to the Ball Game," "Yes, Indeedy," "O'Brien to Ryan to Goldberg," "The Right Girl for Me," "It's Fate, Baby, It's Fate" and "Strictly U.S.A."

ON THE TOWN
(1949)

Metro-Goldwyn-Mayer
Producer: Arthur Freed
Director: Gene Kelly, Stanley Donen
Screenplay: Adolph Green, Betty Comden
Based on an idea by: Jerome Robbins
Music Supervisor and Conductor: Lennie Hayton
Arrangements: Conrad Salinger, Robert Franklyn, Wally Heglin
Music for "Miss Turnstiles" dance and "A Day in New York" ballet: Leonard Bernstein
Art Directors: Cedric Gibbons, Jack Martin Smith
Costumes: Helen Rose
Running time: 98 minutes
Stats: The first Hollywood musical filmed on location in New York City and considered one of MGM's finest. It received unanimous praise from critics and audiences.

SYNOPSIS:

Three sailors, Gabey (Gene Kelly), Chip (Sinatra) and Ozzie (Jules Munshin) are on shore leave for 24 hours in Manhattan. They're determined to see the whole city—"the Bronx is up and the Battery's down"—and to each find the perfect girl. Gabey's is Ivy Smith (Vera-Ellen), who has been named "Miss Turnstiles" and has her picture on New York's subway trains. Chip falls for a female taxi driver named Brunhilde Esterhazy (Betty Garrett) and Ozzie meets Claire Huddesen (Ann Miller), an anthropology student. The group's joyful whirlwind tour of New York's famous landmarks—the Empire State Building, the Statue of Liberty, Radio City Music Hall, Fifth Avenue, Coney Island—is the backdrop for their budding romances.

CAST:

Gabey	Gene Kelly
Chip	Frank Sinatra
Brunhilde Esterhazy	Betty Garrett
Claire Huddesen	Ann Miller
Ozzie	Jules Munshin
Ivy Smith	Vera-Ellen
Madame Dilyovska	Florence Bates

SONGS:

Sinatra sings "New York, New York," "Come Up to My Place," "You're Awful," "On the Town" and "Count on Me"

DOUBLE DYNAMITE
(1951)

RKO Radio Pictures
    Producer: Irving Cummings Jr.
    Director: Irving Cummings
    Screenplay: Melville Shavelson
    Original story: Leo Rosten
    Music: Leigh Harline
    Running time: 80 minutes

SYNOPSIS:

Bank tellers Johnny Dalton (Sinatra), and Mildred Goodhug (Jane Russell)—she's in the cage next to his—are in love but can't afford to marry on their combined salaries. Their waiter friend, Emile (Groucho Marx), suggests Johnny rob a bank for the much needed cash. Johnny would never do such a thing, but he does rescue a bookie who, in gratitude, bets on a horse in Johnny's name and wins $60,000. Johnny spends some of it on a new car and a mink coat for Mildred,

but then the bank discovers a shortage to the tune of $75,000. Although Johnny tells no one of his recent good fortune, Mildred is accused of embezzlement because the bank's shortage showed up on her adding machine. Charges against Mildred are dropped when the machine itself turns out to be the culprit, making errors all over the place. Finally, Johnny can reveal his good luck, and he and Mildred can marry.

CAST:

Mildred Goodhug ....Jane Russell
Emile J. Keck ....Groucho Marx
Johnny Dalton ....Frank Sinatra
Bookie ....Nestor Paiva

SONGS:

Sinatra sings "Kisses and Tears"

MEET DANNY WILSON
(1951)

Universal International Pictures
    Producer: Leonard Goldstein
    Director: Joseph Pevney
    Screenplay: Don McGuire
    Music Director: Joseph Gershenson
    Musical numbers staged by: Hal Belfer
    Director of Photography: Maury Gertsman
    Running time: 88 minutes
    Stats: Critics agreed that the Danny Wilson character and career were borrowed so freely from Sinatra's own life that he was literally playing himself.

SYNOPSIS:

Danny Wilson (Sinatra) is a brash and bad-tempered crooner who, along with his pianist, Mike Ryan (Alex Nicol), are barely earning a living performing at cheap beer joints. Then they meet singer Joy Carroll (Shelley Winters), who introduces them to racketeering nightclub owner Nick Driscoll (Raymond Burr), who wants 50 percent of all Danny's future earnings. Wilson goes on to great success as a singer while vying unsuccessfully with Mike for Joy's favor. Nick has gone into hiding from the law, but he continues to hound Danny for his promised percentage. When Nick threatens to shoot the singer, Mike intervenes, taking the bullet meant for Danny. To avenge his partner's death, Danny goes in search of the nightclub owner, finds him and, in deserted Wrigley Field at night, shoots and kills him.

CAST:

Danny Wilson ....Frank Sinatra
Joy Carroll ....Shelley Winters
Mike Ryan ....Alex Nicol
Nick Driscoll ....Raymond Burr

SONGS:

Sinatra sings "You're a Sweetheart," "Lonesome Man Blues," "She's Funny

That Way," "A Good Man Is Hard to Find," "That Old Black Magic," "When You're Smiling," "All of Me," "I've Got a Crush on You" and "How Deep Is the Ocean?"

FROM HERE TO ETERNITY
(1953)

Columbia Pictures
Producer: Buddy Adler
Director: Fred Zinnemann
Screenplay: Daniel Taradash
Based on the novel by: James Jones
Music Supervisor and Conductor:
Morris Stoloff
Director of Photography: Burnett Guffey
Running time: 118 minutes
Stats: Sinatra won an Oscar for Best
Supporting Actor, and the film won
seven more Academy Awards. It was a
milestone in Sinatra's acting career.

SYNOPSIS:

At an Army barracks in Honolulu—six months before Pearl Harbor is bombed—Private Robert E. Lee Prewitt (Montgomery Clift) is in trouble. Not only has Prewitt been demoted from head bugler, but his commanding officer also wants him to take part in a boxing match because Prewitt was once a top middleweight contender. Prewitt refuses—he once blinded a sparring partner and vowed never to fight again. As a result, he's given the "treatment" by his outfit, and only the feisty little Italian underdog, Private Angelo Maggio (Sinatra) befriends him. Meanwhile, Sergeant Milton Warden (Burt Lancaster) has begun a tempestuous affair with the captain's wife Karen (Deborah Kerr).

Prewitt, too, has fallen in love—with Lorene (Donna Reed), a prostitute who just wants to make enough money to get back to the States and marry a respectable man. Maggio's antics land him in the stockade, where he's brutally beaten by Sergeant "Fatso" Judson (Ernest Borgnine). Angelo escapes and dies in Prewitt's arms. The bugler goes after Fatso and kills him in a knife duel. Prewitt ultimately dies during the attack on Pearl Harbor when he tries to get back to camp. Warden gives up Karen for professional soldiering when she and Lorene return to the States. Onboard ship, Lorene introduces herself to Karen as Prewitt's grieving fiancée.

CAST:

Sgt. Milton Warden ....Burt Lancaster
Robert E. Lee Prewitt......Montgomery Clift
Karen Holmes ....Deborah Kerr
Lorene ....Donna Reed
Private Angelo Maggio...........Frank Sinatra
Sgt. "Fatso" Judson ....Ernest Borgnine
Captain Dana Holmes ....Philip Ober

SUDDENLY
(1954)

A Libra Production
Released by United Artists
Producer: Robert Bassler
Director: Lewis Allen
Screenplay: Richard Sale
Director of Photography: Charles G. Clark
Running time: 77 minutes
Stats: Sinatra won critical praise for his
first role as an unredeemable villain.

SYNOPSIS:

John Baron (Sinatra) has been paid $500,000 to assassinate the president of the United States during a fishing trip in the small town of Suddenly, California. Baron, along with his two henchmen, take over a house that has a sniper's view of the railroad station where the president will be arriving. They imprison the Benson family: Pop Benson (James Gleason), his daughter Ellen (Nancy Gates), and her young son, Pidge. During a security check at the Benson home, the Secret Service chief, Dan Carney, and the local sheriff, Tod Shaw (Sterling Hayden), are trapped by Baron and his men. Carney is killed and Shaw is wounded. A TV repairman arrives in response to an earlier call and he, too, is held captive. A horrified Ellen overhears Baron's plan to kill the president. When one of Baron's men goes to the railroad station to check the train schedule, he shoots a suspicious deputy and in turn is killed by the police. At the Benson house, when Baron's other partner is electrocuted while testing a rifle that has been hooked up to the TV set by the repairman, the enraged assassin kills the repairman. Then Baron turns on the others, but Ellen seizes a fallen gun and shoots him. The president's train is signaled by the police and rides on through its scheduled stop.

CAST:

John Baron ....Frank Sinatra

Tod Shaw ....Sterling Hayden
Pop Benson ....James Gleason
Ellen Benson ....Nancy Gates
Pidge Benson ....Kim Charney

YOUNG AT HEART
(1955)

An Arwin Production
Released by Warner Bros.
  Producer: Henry Blanke
  Director: Gordon Douglas
  Adaptation by: Liam O'Brien from the
    screenplay "Four Daughters" by Julius J.
    Epstein, Lenore Coffee
  Music Supervisor, Arranger and Conductor:
    Ray Heindorf
  Piano solos played by: Andre Previn
  Director of Photography: Ted McCord
  Running time: 117 minutes

SYNOPSIS:

Laurie Tuttle (Doris Day), her sisters and their father and aunt all live in quiet comfort in a small Connecticut town. Then Alex Burke (Gig Young), a handsome young composer, comes on the scene and he and Laurie fall in love. Alex invites Barney Sloan (Sinatra) to do the arrangements for a musical he's writing. Barney's a cynical saloon pianist and bitter about his rotten luck, but when he encounters the cheery sweetness of Laurie, he's smitten—even though Alex and Laurie are planning to marry. On her wedding day, Laurie finds out that one of her sisters is in love with Alex. The wedding is off, and Laurie runs off with Barney to New York City, where they get married. Their life together is difficult, and although Laurie has come to love Barney, he doesn't believe it's possible. He attempts suicide in a deliberate car crash but survives and finally acknowledges Laurie's love. The two start a new life together.

CAST:

Laurie Tuttle	Doris Day
Barney Sloan	Frank Sinatra
Alex Burke	Gig Young
Aunt Jessie	Ethel Barrymore
Fran Tuttle	Dorothy Malone

SONGS:

Sinatra sings "Young at Heart," "Someone to Watch over Me," "Just One of Those Things," "One for My Baby," "You, My Love"

NOT AS A STRANGER
(1955)

A Stanley Kramer Production
Released by United Artists
  Producer and Director: Stanley Kramer
  Screenplay: Edna and Edward Anhalt
  Based on the novel by: Morton Thompson
  Music composed and conducted by:
    George Antheil
  Film Editor: Fred Knudtson
  Running time: 135 minutes

SYNOPSIS:

When Lucas Marsh (Robert Mitchum) learns that he's going to be discharged from medical school because he can't pay his tuition, he marries a nurse named Kristina Hedvigson (Olivia de Havilland), who happens to have a great deal of money. After graduation, Lucas and his wife move to a small town, and he becomes an assistant to Dr. Runkelman (Charles Bickford) at a local hospital, where Alfred Boone (Sinatra) is also a doctor. Lucas, in his fierce dedication, makes a number of serious errors in medical judgment and ends up fighting with Kristina as a result. She asks him to leave. Dr. Boone is the one who tells Lucas that Kristina is three months pregnant. When Dr. Runkelman has a heart attack, Lucas operates and makes a fatal miscalculation; Runkelman dies. Lucas returns humbly to his wife, in desperate need of her love and support.

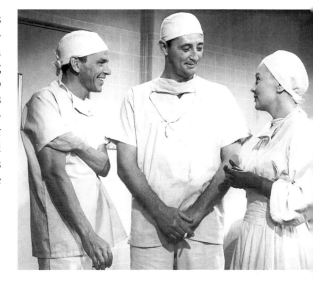

CAST:

Lucas Marsh	Robert Mitchum
Kristina Hedvigson	Olivia de Havilland
Alfred Boone	Frank Sinatra
Harriet Lang	Gloria Grahame
Dr. Aarons	Broderick Crawford
Dr. Runkelman	Charles Bickford

THE TENDER TRAP
(1955)

Metro-Goldwyn-Mayer
  Producer: Lawrence Weingarten
  Director: Charles Walters
  Screenplay: Julius J. Epstein
  Based on a play by: Max Shulman,
    Robert Paul Smith
  Music composed and conducted by:
    Jeff Alexander
  Director of Photography: Paul C. Vogel
  Running time: 111 minutes

SYNOPSIS:

Theatrical agent Charlie Reader (Sinatra) may have more girlfriends than he can keep track of, but he still envies the married life of his buddy Joe McCall (David Wayne). Charlie meets Julie Gillis (Debbie Reynolds), who not only is looking for a husband, she also has a timetable all worked out for catching one. Despite Joe's warnings, Charlie

begins dating Julie. When she's convinced that he's "trapped," she insists he marry her. Charlie declines the invitation, then discovers that all his former girlfriends are unavailable except for Sylvia (Celeste Holm). In a panic he proposes to both Sylvia and Julie, but when Julie learns what Charlie has done, she breaks up with him. He admits to Sylvia that he can't marry her—Julie is his true love. Joe then makes a play for Sylvia, but she's more interested in a bachelor she's just met on an elevator. Joe goes back to his wife, but at Sylvia's wedding Charlie catches her tossed bouquet and offers it to Julie. She accepts and Charlie's finally been tenderly trapped.

CAST:

Charlie Y. Reader	Frank Sinatra
Julie Gillis	Debbie Reynolds
Joe McCall	David Wayne
Sylvia Crewes	Celeste Holm
Poppy Matson	Lola Albright
Helen	Carolyn Jones

SONGS:

Sinatra sings "(Love Is) The Tender Trap"

GUYS AND DOLLS
(1955)

A Samuel Goldwyn Production
Released by MGM
  Producer: Samuel Goldwyn
  Director: Joseph L. Mankiewicz
  Screenplay: Joseph L. Mankiewicz
  From the musical play by: Jo Swerling,
    Abe Burrows
  Music and lyrics by: Frank Loesser
  Based on a story by: Damon Runyon
  Music Supervisor and Conductor:
    Jay Blackton
  Arrangements: Skip Martin, Nelson Riddle,
    Alexander Courage, Albert Sendrey
  Director of Photography: Harry Stradling
  Production Designer: Oliver Smith
  Choreography: Michael Kidd
  Running time: 150 minutes

SYNOPSIS:

Nathan Detroit (Sinatra), a lovable gambler who runs "the oldest established permanent floating crap game in New York," needs a thousand dollars to pay for a place the cops won't raid. He decides to win the money by betting fellow gambler Sky Masterson (Marlon Brando) that Sky can't get Salvation Army lass Sarah Brown (Jean Simmons) to go with him to Havana. Sky promises Sister Sarah that if she flies with him to the Cuban capitol, he'll fill her next prayer meeting with "genuine sinners." She relents, but once in Havana, she becomes tiddly after a drink and falls in love with the moonlight and Sky Masterson. He's so taken by her innocence that he doesn't seduce her. Back in New York City, Adelaide's trying unsuccessfully to get Nathan to marry her after a 14-year courtship. When Sky and Sarah return, he risks his bankroll against all the gamblers' promises to come to the prayer meeting. Everyone shows up, Sky wins his bet, he and Sister Sarah tie the knot and, at last, so do Nathan and Adelaide.

CAST:

Sky Masterson	Marlon Brando
Sarah Brown	Jean Simmons
Nathan Detroit	Frank Sinatra
Miss Adelaide	Vivian Blaine
Lt. Brannigan	Robert Keith
Nicely-Nicely Johnson	Stubby Kaye
Big Jule	B.S. Pully
Harry the Horse	Sheldon Leonard
Benny Southstreet	Johnny Silver

SONGS:

Sinatra sings "The Oldest Established (Permanent Floating Crap Game in New York)," "Guys and Dolls," "Adelaide" and "Sue Me"

THE MAN WITH THE GOLDEN ARM
(1955)

A Carlyle Production
Released by United Artists
   Producer and Director: Otto Preminger
   Screenplay: Walter Newman, Lewis Meltzer
   Based on the novel by: Nelson Algren
   Music composed and conducted by:
    Elmer Bernstein
   Director of Photography: Sam Leavitt
   Running time: 119 minutes
   Stats: Sinatra received an Academy Award
    nomination for Best Actor.

SYNOPSIS:

Frankie Machine (Sinatra), a former card dealer—so good at it that he's known as "the man with the golden arm"—has just come out of drug rehabilitation. He returns to his old haunts in Chicago, where a pusher, Louie, offers him a free "fix," but Frankie declines.

His wife, Zosh (Eleanor Parker), disabled from a drunk driving accident that Frankie caused, wants him to go back to dealing poker. He'd much rather work as a drummer but feels too guilty to oppose Zosh. He meets and falls in love with a "B-girl" named Molly (Kim Novak) but knows he can't leave Zosh. After getting a drum audition, he decides to quit dealing but takes on one last game—as well as Louie's offer of a fix. He's caught cheating, is beaten up, fails the audition, and is once again hooked on drugs. Louie discovers that Zosh can walk, and when he threatens to tell Frankie, she panics and pushes Louie down a stairwell to his death. Frankie spends three days with Molly going through the torture of drug withdrawal. He finally kicks the habit and tells Zosh that he's leaving but will send her money. She jumps from her wheelchair to go after him, but when she spots the police in the hallway, she leaps into the alley below. Frankie is with her as she dies, then walks away—followed by Molly.

CAST:

Frankie Machine	Frank Sinatra
Zosh	Eleanor Parker
Molly	Kim Novak
Sparrow	Arnold Stang
Louie	Darren McGavin
Schwiefka	Robert Strauss

MEET ME IN LAS VEGAS
(1956)

Metro-Goldwyn-Mayer
   Producer: Joe Pasternak
   Director: Roy Rowland
   Screenplay: Isobel Lennart
   Music Supervisor and Conductor:
    George Stoll
   Music for "Frankie and Johnny" ballet
    adapted by: Johnny Green
   Lena Horne's number arranged and
    conducted by: Lennie Hayton
   Orchestrations: Albert Sendry, Skip Martin
   Songs: Nicholas Brodszky, Sammy Cahn
   Dances created and staged by: Hermes Pan
    "Rehearsal Ballet" and "Sleeping Beauty
    Ballet" created and staged by: Eugene
    Loring
   Music coordinator: Irving Aaronson
   Director of Photography: Robert Bronner
   Running time: 112 minutes

SYNOPSIS:

When Nevada rancher Chuck Rodwell (Dan Dailey) keeps losing at the roulette table, he decides to do something to change his luck. Just before he places his next bet, he grabs the hand of Maria Corvier (Cyd Charisse), a ballet dancer who happens to be walking past him. He wins, and from that moment on doesn't want to let go of Maria. As they walk through the Sands Hotel, they see someone about to play a slot machine, but his back is to us. Chuck puts a coin in the machine, holding on to Maria's hand for good luck. The machine hits the jackpot, and as the overflowing money cascades to the floor, the astonished player turns around. It's Frank Sinatra.

CAST:

Chuck Rodwell	Dan Dailey
Maria Corvier	Cyd Charisse
MC at Silver Slipper	Jerry Colonna
Maria's manager	Paul Henried
Guest Stars at Sands Hotel	Lena Horne, Frankie Laine
Miss Hattie	Agnes Moorehead
Tom Culdane	Jim Backus

Unbilled guest appearances by: Frank Sinatra, Debbie Reynolds, Tony Martin, Peter Lorre, Vic Damone

JOHNNY CONCHO
(1956)

A Kent Production
Released by United Artists
  Producer: Frank Sinatra
  Director: Don McGuire
  Screenplay: David P. Harmon, Don McGuire
  Music composed and conducted by:
    Nelson Riddle

Director of Photography: William Mellor
Running time: 84 minutes
Stats: Sinatra's first film credit as producer.

SYNOPSIS:
The year is 1875 in Cripple Creek, Arizona. Johnny Concho (Sinatra), a bully, card cheat and coward, is the younger brother of the town's most notorious gunman. When Johnny's brother is killed in a duel, all of Cripple Creek is taken over by the gunman's killers, Tallman (William Conrad) and Walker (Christopher Dark). Instead of avenging his brother's death, Johnny runs away, but he can't escape his own cowardice. He meets a girl named Mary Dark (Phyllis Kirk) and a gun-toting preacher named Barney Clark (Keenan Wynn), who persuade Johnny to go back to Cripple Creek and avenge his brother's death. He exhorts the local citizenry to stop fearing the outlaws and to fight back against oppression. He himself is wounded in a showdown with his brother's killers, but the people of Cripple Creek come to his rescue and rid the town of the gunmen. Johnny is finally accepted as a man in his own right, no longer living in the shadow of his brother.

CAST:
Johnny Concho ....Frank Sinatra
Barney Clark..........................Keenan Wynn
Tallman ....William Conrad
Mary Dark ....Phyllis Kirk
Walker..............................Christopher Dark

HIGH SOCIETY
(1956)

Metro-Goldwyn-Mayer
  Producer: Sol C. Siegel
  Director: Charles Walters
  Screenplay: John Patrick
  Based on the play "The Philadelphia
    Story" by Philip Barry
  Music supervised and adapted by: Johnny
    Green, Saul Chaplin
  Orchestra conducted by: Johnny Green
  Orchestral Arrangements: Conrad Salinger,
    Nelson Riddle
  Director of Photography: Paul C. Vogel
  Costumes: Helen Rose
  Running time: 107 minutes

SYNOPSIS:
At the Newport, Rhode Island, mansion where the terribly rich and beautiful Tracy Lord (Grace Kelly) lives, a wedding is in its final stages of preparation. But Tracy's having a hard time deciding who she wants to marry. Her ex-husband, C.K. Dexter-Haven (Bing Crosby), is on the scene, along with George Kittredge (John Lund), the man she's planning to walk down the aisle with. Enter Mike Connor (Sinatra), a charming and brash reporter who's on assignment to cover the wedding for a slick magazine. When Tracy and Mike drink a little too much and she dives into a swimming pool, he jumps in and rescues her. She tries to go through with her wedding to the stuffy bore, George Kittredge, but finally realizes she doesn't want to be an ice maiden on a pedestal, but rather the woman that her ex-husband still loves. So she dumps Kittredge, and for the second time, she and Dexter-Haven get married.

CAST:
C.K. Dexter-Haven ....Bing Crosby
Tracy Lord................................Grace Kelly
Mike Connor..........................Frank Sinatra
Liz Imbrie ....Celeste Holm
George Kittredge ....John Lund
Uncle Willie ....Louis Calhern
Seth Lord ....Sidney Blackmer
Mrs. Seth Lord ....Margola Gilmore
Louis Armstrong..............................Himself

SONGS:
Sinatra sings "Who Wants to Be a Millionaire?", "You're Sensational," "Well, Did You Evah?" (duet with Bing Crosby) and "Mind If I Make Love to You?"

AROUND THE WORLD IN 80 DAYS
(1956)

A Michael Todd Production
Released by United Artists
  Producer: Michael Todd
  Director: Michael Anderson
  Screenplay: James Poe, John Farrow,
    S.J. Perelman
  Based on the novel by: Jules Verne
  Music: Victor Young
  Director of Photography: Lionel Lindon
  Special Effects: Lee Zavitz
  Running time: 178 minutes

SYNOPSIS:

In Victorian London, Phileas Fogg (David Niven) boasts to his fellow Reform Club members that he can circle the globe in 80 days. They bet him 20,000 pounds that he can't do it. Fogg takes the challenge and begins his journey accompanied only by his servant

Passepartout (Cantinflas). The adventure takes them around the world by every means of locomotion. Added to their amazing experiences is the pursuit of the two travelers by a British inspector who believes Fogg has robbed the Bank of England. In India, Phileas rescues Princess Aouda (Shirley MacLaine) from being burned alive, and she joins them on their madcap journey. In San Francisco they meet a Barbary Coast saloon singer (Marlene Dietrich) and her honky-tonk piano player (Sinatra). A triumphant Fogg returns to England only to be slapped into jail. By the time the inspector learns of his error, Fogg's 80 days are almost up. His only consolation is that he's about to marry the lovely Aouda. But then he discovers that he actually arrived back in London a day earlier because he had crossed the International Dateline. With ten minutes left, Fogg races to the club, arrives on the dot and claims his winnings.

CAST:

Phileas Fogg ....David Niven
Passepartout ....Cantinflas
Princess Aouda ....Shirley MacLaine
Inspector Fix ....Robert Newton

A host of stars make cameo guest appearances, including Marlene Dietrich, Frank Sinatra, Noel Coward, Ronald Colman, Charles Boyer, Sir John Gielgud, Joe E. Brown, Buster Keaton, George Raft, John Carradine, Trevor Howard, Jack Oakie.

THE PRIDE AND THE PASSION
(1957)

A Stanley Kramer Production
Released by United Artists
  Producer and Director: Stanley Kramer
  Screenplay: Edna and Edward Anhalt
  Based on the novel "The Gun" by:
    C.S. Forester
  Music: George Antheil
  Director of Photography: Franz Planer
  Running time: 132 minutes

SYNOPSIS:

After Napoleon's forces defeat Spain in the Peninsular Wars, a Spanish peasant named Miguel (Sinatra) decides to lead his people in an attack on the French-occupied fort at Avila. His weapon of destruction is a tremendous cannon that had been abandoned by the Spanish troops. Aiding him in dragging the cannon to the fort is a horde of peasants, as well as a British naval captain named Anthony Trumbull (Cary Grant), the only man who knows how to fire the enormous gun. Romance flowers when Miguel's girlfriend, Juana (Sophia Loren), is attracted to Trumbull, and he to her. The cannon is finally brought to the fortress and a bloody siege ensues, during which Miguel and Juana are killed. But the Spaniards are victorious, and Trumbull carries Miguel's body into the fort, then places his dead love, Juana, at the feet of the statue of Saint Teresa.

CAST:

Captain Anthony Trumbull ....Cary Grant
Miguel ....Frank Sinatra
Juana.......................................Sophia Loren
General Jouvet ....Theodore Bikel

THE JOKER IS WILD
(1957)

An A.M.B.L. Production
Released by Paramount
  Producer: Samuel J. Briskin
  Director: Charles Vidor
  Screenplay: Oscar Saul
  Based on the book by: Art Cohn
  Music composed and conducted by:
    Walter Scharf

Orchestrations: Leo Shuken, Jack Hayes
Orchestral arrangements of songs:
  Nelson Riddle
Director of Photography: Daniel L. Fapp
Costumes: Edith Head
Running time: 126 minutes
Stats: Sinatra bought the rights to the Art
  Cohn book when it was still in galley
  form. The movie's hit song, "All the Way"
  (written by Sammy Cahn and Jimmy
  Van Heusen), won an Academy Award.

SYNOPSIS:
This is based on the life of singer-turned-comedian Joe E. Lewis (Sinatra). A promising young performer, he becomes a pawn in fights between racketeers and nightclub owners. When he quits his job at a club to sing at a different one, mobsters beat him up and slash his throat, cutting his vocal cords. Sophie Tucker (playing herself) gets him a job on the burlesque circuit as a stand-up comedian. Although he's fallen in love with a wealthy society girl named Letty Page (Jeanne Crain) who wants to marry him, Joe never gets around to proposing. He does, however, marry a chorus girl named Martha Stewart (Mitzi Gaynor). She soon discovers that her husband is an alcoholic and that her greatest rival isn't another woman, it's Joe's drinking and gambling. Martha walks out on Joe, and so does his long-suffering best friend and piano accompanist, Austin Mack (Eddie Albert). Joe is finally forced to face himself and make the changes in his life that will start him on the comeback trail.

CAST:
Joe E. Lewis ....Frank Sinatra
Martha Stewart ....Mitzi Gaynor
Letty Page ....Jeanne Crain
Austin Mack ....Eddie Albert
Cassie Mack ....Beverly Garland
Swifty Morgan ....Jackie Coogan

SONGS:
Sinatra sings "I Cried for You," "If I Could Be with You," "Chicago" and "All the Way"

PAL JOEY
(1957)

An Essex-George Sidney Production
Released by Columbia Pictures
  Producer: Fred Kohlmar
  Director: George Sidney
  Screenplay: Dorothy Kingsley
  Based on the musical play by: John O'Hara
    (book) and Rodgers and Hart (music
    and lyrics)
  Music supervisor and conductor: Morris
    Stoloff
  Musical Arrangements: Nelson Riddle
  Orchestrations: Arthur Morton
  Director of Photography: Harold Lipstein
  Choreography: Hermes Pan
  Gowns: Jean Louis
  Running time: 111 minutes

SYNOPSIS:
An irresistible heel named Joey Evans (Sinatra) gets a job at the 626 Club in San Francisco and immediately sweeps

half the girls in the chorus line off their feet. Joey's charms, however, don't work on Linda English (Kim Novak), the newest dancer in the club's chorus. When Joey, the band and the girls perform at a charity event hosted by Vera Simpson (Rita Hayworth) at her Nob Hill mansion, Joe recognizes the wealthy widow as a famous former stripper. She's so enamored of Joey that she makes him an offer he can't refuse: She'll set him up in his own nightclub. Linda is to have a featured spot in the floor show at Chez Joey, but when Vera realizes that Joey and Linda are in love, she threatens to cancel the Club's opening unless he drops Linda. Joey calls her bluff and the nightclub doesn't open. Linda pleads with Vera to give Joey his chance, but Vera's not willing unless the chorus girl promises to break up with him. So determined is Vera to get her man, she even proposes marriage. But Joey declines the invitation, knowing that Linda is the only girl for him.

CAST:
Joey Evans ....Frank Sinatra
Vera Simpson ....Rita Hayworth
Linda English.............................Kim Novak
Gladys ....Barbara Nichols
Ned Galvin ....Bobby Sherwood

SONGS:
Sinatra sings "I Didn't Know What Time It Was," "There's a Small Hotel," "I Could Write a Book," "The Lady Is a Tramp," "Bewitched, Bothered and Bewildered," "What Do I Care for a Dame?"

KINGS GO FORTH
(1958)

A Frank Ross-Eton Production
Released by United Artists
  Producer: Frank Ross
  Director: Delmer Daves
  Screenplay: Merle Miller
  Based on the novel by: Joe David Brown
  Music composed and conducted by:
    Elmer Bernstein
  Orchestrations: Leo Shuken, Jack Hayes
  Director of Photography: Daniel L. Fapp
  Running time: 109 minutes

SYNOPSIS:

In this World War II opus set in 1944, Lieutenant Sam Loggins (Sinatra) and his radio operator, Britt Harris (Tony Curtis) are fighting the Germans in southern France. During weekend leave on the Riviera, Sam meets and falls in love with Monique Blair (Natalie Wood). When he asks her to marry him, she refuses, confessing that she's the daughter of a white mother and a black father. Loggins is shocked and resigned to losing her, especially when he finds out that she's in love with his buddy, Britt. Sam tells Britt of Monique's parentage and he seems unconcerned, but then just before the two embark on a dangerous Army mission, Britt admits to Monique that he never intended to marry her. She's devastated, and Sam vows to kill the man who has caused Monique so much heartbreak. The Germans, however, do the job for him during their mission: Britt is killed, and Sam himself loses an arm. When the war is over, he comes back to Nice and discovers that Monique, the girl he still secretly loves, has turned her villa into a school for war orphans.

CAST:

Lt. Sam Loggins........................Frank Sinatra
Sgt. Britt Harris..........................Tony Curtis
Monique Blair........................Natalie Wood

Mrs. Blair ....Leora Dana
Jazz Musicians........Red Norvo, Mel Lewis,
                   Pete Candoli,
                   Red Wooten,
                Richie Kamuca,
                Jimmy Weible

SOME CAME RUNNING
(1958)

Metro-Goldwyn-Mayer
  Producer: Sol C. Siegel
  Director: Vincente Minnelli
  Screenplay: John Patrick, Arthur Sheekman
  Based on the novel by: James Jones
  Music composed and conducted by:
    Elmer Bernstein
  Orchestrations: Leo Shuken, Jack Hayes
  Director of Photography: William H. Daniels
  Running time: 127 minutes

SYNOPSIS:

After his Army discharge, Dave Hirsh (Sinatra) returns to his hometown in Indiana with an unpublished manuscript and a lovable floozy named Ginny (Shirley MacLaine). Older brother Frank (Arthur Kennedy) resents his return, and Dave hates Frank for having put him in an orphanage when he was a child. Dave meets Gwen French (Martha Hyer), a

college teacher who wants to help him with his writing, and Bama Dillert (Dean Martin), a professional gambler who takes Dave on as his poker-playing, whiskey-drinking partner. Dave falls in love with Gwen, and although she gets his manuscript published, she has no romantic interest in him. Disappointed, hurt and feeling reckless, Dave goes on a spree with Ginny and Bama. They find Frank's teenage daughter, who has run away from home with her boyfriend, and Dave brings her back, tells off his brother and then proposes to Ginny. She's thrilled, but the marriage is short lived. A former boyfriend of hers comes to town and goes gunning for Dave at a local carnival. In an attempt to shield her husband, Ginny is fatally shot.

CAST:

Dave Hirsh ....Frank Sinatra
Bama Dillert ....Dean Martin
Ginny Moorhead..............Shirley MacLaine
Gwen French...........................Martha Hyer
Frank Hirsh.........................Arthur Kennedy
Dawn Hirsh ....Betty Lou Keim

A HOLE IN THE HEAD
(1959)

A Sincap Production
Released by United Artists
  Producer and Director: Frank Capra
  Screenplay: Arnold Schulman (based on
    his play)
  Music: Nelson Riddle
  Director of Photography: William H. Daniels
  Costumes: Edith Head
  Running time: 120 minutes
  Stats: The film's popular song, "High
    Hopes," won an Oscar.

SYNOPSIS:

Tony Manetta (Sinatra) owns a run-down Miami Beach hotel, but dreams of it becoming the Hilton. He's a widower with an 11-year-old son, Ally (Eddie Hodges), whom he treats like an adult. When Tony's about to lose his hotel, he turns for financial help to his rich but frugal older brother, Mario (Edward G.

Robinson). Mario offers the money on one condition: Tony has to let Ally live in New York with Mario and his wife; they don't approve of the way he's raising the boy. Tony refuses and then meets a wealthy widow named Mrs. Rogers (Eleanor Parker). When he falls in love with her, he realizes he can't marry her for her money. An old buddy of Tony's looks like a prospective angel for a while, but then Tony winds up in more trouble than ever before. He now wants to make his son hate him so that the boy will want to go to New York. But Mario comes through at the last minute, decides to retire in Miami, Tony gets his money, the whole family is reunited and everyone goes to the beach.

CAST:

Tony Manetta	Frank Sinatra
Mario Manetta	Edward G. Robinson
Mrs. Rogers	Eleanor Parker
Shirl	Carolyn Jones
Sophie Manetta	Thelma Ritter
Jerry Marks	Keenan Wynn
Ally Manetta	Eddie Hodges

SONGS:
Sinatra sings "All My Tomorrows" and "High Hopes"

NEVER SO FEW
(1959)

A Canterbury Production
Released by Metro-Goldwyn-Mayer
  Producer: Edmund Grainger
  Director: John Sturges
  Screenplay: Millard Kaufman
  Based on the novel by: Tom T. Chamales
  Music: Hugo Friedhofer
  Director of Photography:
    William H. Daniels
  Running time: 124 minutes

SYNOPSIS:

Captain Tom Reynolds (Sinatra) is serving with a group of soldiers and guerrillas who are fighting the Japanese in Burma during World War II. Reynolds and Captain Danny DeMortimer (Richard Johnson) are sent to Calcutta to obtain a doctor and medical supplies for their men. Reynolds acquires a jeep driver named Bill Ringa (Steve McQueen) and Captain Grey Travis (Peter Lawford). At the home of wealthy war profiteer Nikko Regas (Paul Henried), Reynolds meets Regas' mistress, Carla Vesari (Gina Lollobrigida), and is smitten. Once back at camp, while celebrating Christmas, they are attacked by the Japanese and Reynolds is wounded. Carla visits him in the hospital and starts warming up to him. Recovered and back on the battlefield, Reynolds and his men destroy a Japanese airfield but discover the convoy meant to support them was massacred by the Chinese. Reynolds leads his group into China, where, in a small village, he finds that Chiang Kai-shek's government is involved in selling U.S.-donated arms to the Japanese, who used them against the American troops. Reynolds is ordered not to attack the village, but when DeMortimer is killed, he's so enraged that he orders all prisoners shot and tells his superiors to "go to hell." Facing a court-martial, he rejects Carla's offer to have Regas intercede on his behalf. The American general finally has the charges dropped. Reynolds and

Carla have a brief reunion before he goes back to his men in the hills.

CAST:

Capt. Tom C. Reynolds	Frank Sinatra
Carla Vesari	Gina Lollobrigida
Capt. Grey Travis	Peter Lawford
Bill Ringa	Steve McQueen
Capt. Danny DeMortimer	Richard Johnson
Nikko Regas	Paul Henreid
General Sloan	Brian Donlevy
Sgt. John Danforth	Charles Bronson

CAN-CAN
(1960)

A Suffolk-Cummings Production
Released by 20th Century-Fox
   Producer: Jack Cummings
   Director: Walter Lang
   Screenplay: Charles Lederer, Dorothy Kingsley
   Based on the musical play by: Abe Burrows
   Songs by: Cole Porter
   Music Arranger and Conductor: Nelson Riddle
   Director of Photography: William H. Daniels
   Dances staged by: Hermes Pan
   Costumes: Irene Sharaff
   Running time: 130 minutes

SYNOPSIS:

Although an ancient French law has forbidden the dancing of the can-can, lawyer François Durnais (Sinatra), with help from sympathetic judge Paul Barriere (Maurice Chevalier), prevents the police from raiding the cafe owned by Simone Pistache (Shirley MacLaine). But a raid is planned anyway by Philippe Forrestier (Louis Jourdan), even though he has met and become infatuated with Simone. François helps free her after she's arrested, and Philippe asks Simone to marry him. Unfortunately, she's already in love with François, but, despite her persuasive charm, she cannot get him to marry her. At a party given by Philippe, Simone makes a spectacle of herself, thanks to a little scheme hatched by François and Barriere. But Philippe still wants to marry the cafe owner, thus forcing François to propose to Simone. Then, after her dancers give a specially staged performance before the Parisian court, the can-can is finally made legal.

CAST:

Francois Durnais ....Frank Sinatra
Simone Pistache ....Shirley MacLaine
Paul Barriere ....Maurice Chevalier
Philippe Forrestier ....Louis Jourdan
Claudine ....Juliet Prowse

SONGS:
Sinatra sings "I Love Paris," "C'est Magnifique," "Let's Do It" and "It's All Right with Me"

OCEAN'S ELEVEN
(1960)

A Dorchester Production
Released by Warner Brothers
   Producer and Director: Lewis Milestone
   Screenplay: Harry Brown, Charles Lederer
   Story: George Clayton Johnson, Jack Golden Russell
   Music composed and conducted by: Nelson Riddle
   Songs: Jimmy Van Heusen, Sammy Cahn
   Director of Photography: William H. Daniels
   Running time: 127 minutes

SYNOPSIS:

A daring plan to rob five Vegas casinos simultaneously on New Year's Eve is concocted by Danny Ocean (Sinatra) and ten of his former Army Air Force buddies. The ingenious robbery requires military precision and perfect timing. They plan to create a power blackout in Vegas and short-circuit the emergency

lighting in the casinos, thus causing the doors to the money vaults to open when the switches are thrown. Their booty will be dumped in garbage cans outside the casinos and picked up by Josh Howard (Sammy Davis Jr.) in a truck. As he waits for New Year's Eve, Danny misses his estranged wife, Beatrice (Angie Dickinson), and wires her that he's ill; she rushes to him. So does one of his old girl-friends, who accuses him of running out on her. When Beatrice insists that Danny come back to New York with her, he says he can't, and she leaves him again. New Year's Eve arrives and the holdup goes off without a hitch until one of the gang has a heart attack and dies. Unable to get their loot out of Vegas, they hide it in the dead man's coffin, not knowing that his widow has planned to have her husband cremated. Danny and his pals watch helplessly as their ill-gotten gains go up in flames.

CAST:

Danny Ocean ....Frank Sinatra
Sam Harmon ....Dean Martin
Josh Howard......................Sammy Davis Jr.
Jimmy Foster ....Peter Lawford
Beatrice Ocean..................Angie Dickinson
Anthony Bergdorf.................Richard Conte
Duke Santos ....Cesar Romero
"Mushy" O'Conners.................Joey Bishop
Spyros Acebos ....Akim Tamiroff

Cameo guest appearances by: Red Skelton, George Raft, Shirley MacLaine

PEPE
(1960)

A G.S.-Posa Films International Production
Released by Columbia Pictures
   Producer and Director: George Sidney
   Screenplay: Dorothy Kingsley, Claude Binyon
   Based on the play "Broadway Magic" by:
      Ladislas Bush-Fekete
   Music supervision and background score:
      Johnny Green
   Director of Photography: Joe MacDonald
   Running time: 195 minutes

SYNOPSIS:

Pepe (Cantinflas) has raised a beautiful white stallion named Don Juan from a colt. When the horse is to be auctioned, Pepe saves his meager earnings to buy the animal but is outbid by Hollywood director Ted Holt (Dan Dailey), who's hoping Don Juan will revive his sagging career. The innocent little Pepe follows his horse to Hollywood and meets up with a slew of filmdom's famous performers. When Holt sees how happy Don Juan is to see Pepe, he gives him the job of taking care of the horse. Unable to make a movie deal for himself, Holt goes to Las Vegas with Pepe in tow. With some gambling advice from Hollywood stars, Pepe wins enough money to produce Holt's picture himself. The film is finally completed and the star, Suzie Murphy (Shirley Jones), is a big hit. But Pepe, who has lost Don Juan, this time to a producer, regains him again, as well as all the newborns that Don Juan has sired.

CAST:

Pepe ....Cantinflas
Ted Holt.....................................Dan Dailey
Suzie Murphy ....Shirley Jones

Guest stars (as themselves) include: Frank Sinatra, Joey Bishop, Maurice Chevalier, Bing Crosby, Tony Curtis, JimmyDurante, Sammy Davis Jr., Peter Lawford, Kim

Novak, Janet Leigh, Debbie Reynolds, Jack Lemmon, Dean Martin, Edward G. Robinson, Greer Garson

---

THE DEVIL AT 4 O'CLOCK
(1961)

A Columbia Picture
   Producer: Fred Kohlmar
   Director: Mervyn LeRoy
   Screenplay: Liam O'Brien

Based on the novel by: Max Catto
Music: George Duning
Director of Photography: Joseph Biroc
Running time: 126 minutes

SYNOPSIS:

On a plane bound for Tahiti, three chained convicts, Harry (Sinatra), Marcel and Charlie, stop on a small French island that has an active volcano. The local priest, Father Doonan (Spencer Tracy), enlists the convicts to repair a chapel at a children's leper hospital, where Harry falls in love with Camille (Barbara Luna), a blind nurse. The next day the volcano erupts, and Doonan again asks the prisoners to help him rescue the children at the hospital. There's a schooner waiting for the outgoing tide that will get them all off the island at four o'clock the next afternoon. But rain, wind and earthquakes hamper the group's progress. When they take refuge in a hillside cave, Father Doonan marries Camille and Harry. The next day, Marcel and Charlie die, one drowning in a bog, the other killed by a collapsing bridge. Doonan is stranded on the island as Harry brings the children and his new bride safely to the schooner. He goes back to help Doonan, but the volcano erupts again and the entire island explodes, then sinks into the sea.

CAST:

Harry......................................Frank Sinatra
Father Doonan.......................Spencer Tracy
Jacques..........................Jean Pierre Aumont
Charlie ....Bernie Hamilton
Marcel ....Gregoire Aslan
Camille ....Barbara Luna
Father Perreau ....Kerwin Mathews

SERGEANTS 3
(1962)

An Essex-Claude Production
Released by United Artists
  Producer: Frank Sinatra
  Director: John Sturges
  Executive Producer: Howard W. Koch
  Screenplay: W.R. Burnett
  Music: Billy May
  Director of Photography: Winton C. Hoch
  Running time: 112 minutes
  Stats: Sinatra did his own stunts in this film.

SYNOPSIS:

Set in the Indian territory of Utah, circa 1873, this western is a remake of *Gunga Din*. American Cavalry Sergeants Mike Merry (Sinatra), Chip Deal (Dean Martin) and Larry Barrett (Peter Lawford) are inseparable buddies. During a barroom brawl, the three meet up with Jonah Williams (Sammy Davis Jr.), a recently freed slave who wants very much to hang out with the sergeants and follows them on their assignment to track down a tribe of Sioux Indians. Barrett, who is planning to marry Amelia Parent (Ruta Lee) as soon as this last expedition is completed, is tricked by his pals into signing on again for another stint in the cavalry. When Deal is captured and tortured by the Sioux, he's rescued by Merry, Barrett and Jonah. They also foil the planned Indian massacre when Jonah's bugle blowing alerts the U.S. Cavalry to the hordes of Sioux massed to attack. All three sergeants are decorated for bravery, and as Barrett rides off to meet his bride—not knowing he's still in the Army—Mike Merry turns in Barrett's re-enlistment papers and tells his officers that Sergeant Barrett is a deserter.

CAST:

Sgt. Mike Merry	Frank Sinatra
Sgt. Chip Deal	Dean Martin
Sgt. Larry Barrett	Peter Lawford
Jonah Williams	Sammy Davis, Jr.
Sgt. Major Roger Boswell	Joey Bishop
Mountain Hawk	Henry Silva
Amelia Parent	Ruta Lee
Willie Sharpknife	Buddy Lester

THE ROAD TO HONG KONG
(1962)

A Melnor Films Production
Released by United Artists
  Producer: Melvin Frank
  Director: Norman Panama
  Screenplay: Norman Panama, Melvin Frank
  Music composed and conducted by:
    Robert Farnon
  Director of Photography: Jack Hildyard
  Running time: 91 minutes

SYNOPSIS:

Harry Turner (Bing Crosby) and partner Chester Babcock (Bob Hope) are con artists in India, trying to sell an "Interplanetary Fly-It-Yourself Space Kit." When the police intervene, Chester is injured trying to prove the space kit works and ends up in a hospital suffering from amnesia. The two travel to a Tibetan "Lamasery" where the Grand Lama cures Chester and gives him a drug that makes him remember everything he sees. But before they can use Chester's supernatural ability in their vaudeville memory act, the duo get into various espionage escapades, which finally land them—via rocket—on a distant planet called Plutonius. With them is the beautiful Secret Service agent Diane (Joan Collins), whose boyfriend is a "spaceman" played by Sinatra in a cameo appearance.

CAST:

Harry Turner	Bing Crosby
Chester Babcock	Bob Hope
Diane	Joan Collins
Dorothy Lamour	Herself
The Leader	Robert Morley
Grand Lama	Felix Aylmer

Unbilled guest stars: Jerry Colonna, Dean Martin, David Niven, Peter Sellers, Frank Sinatra

THE MANCHURIAN CANDIDATE (1962)

An M.C. Production
Released by United Artists
   Producers: George Axelrod, John Frankenheimer
   Director: John Frankenheimer
   Executive Producer: Howard W. Koch
   Screenplay: George Axelrod
   Based on the novel by: Richard Condon
   Music composed and conducted by: David Amram
   Director of Photography: Lionel Lindon
   Art Director: Richard Sylbert
   Special Effects: Paul Pollard
   Running time: 126 minutes

SYNOPSIS:

During the Korean War, the Chinese Communists capture and brainwash two American soldiers, Bennett Marco (Sinatra) and Raymond Shaw (Laurence Harvey), into believing that Shaw led a successful patrol against the Reds and is a hero. Through further mindbending, Shaw is made to obey Communist orders without remembering his actions; obedience is triggered by the sight of the Queen of Diamonds. When back in the States, Marco's recurring nightmares and vague recollections lead him to visit Shaw. When Marco recognizes Shaw's houseboy as the Korean who betrayed them to the Communists, a karate fight follows; the houseboy ends up in the hospital and Marco is briefly put in jail. Shaw tells Marco of another patrol member who he's learned also has strange nightmares. Then he reveals his hatred for his mother (Angela Lansbury) and stepfather, Senator John Iselin, because of their right-wing politics. Marco believes Shaw has been programmed to explode at some imminent and important moment. With the Army's permission, he begins investigating and uses a psychiatrist's help to unlock the Queen of Diamonds "key." Marco then attempts to learn who's controlling Shaw. Unbeknownst to everyone, it's Shaw's own mother. She's planning to have her son kill the presidential nominee so that her husband, the vice presidential nominee, will take over. The assassination is set to occur at a Madison Square Garden rally. Despite Marco's attempts to convince Shaw that he's mind-controlled, Shaw obeys his mother's orders, first killing a senator and then the senator's daughter—Shaw's own wife. But at the last moment, instead of killing the presidential nominee, Shaw turns his high-powered rifle on his mother, stepfather and then himself.

CAST:

Bennett Marco ....Frank Sinatra
Raymond Shaw ....Laurence Harvey
Rosie ....Janet Leigh
Raymond's mother ....Angela Lansbury
Senator Iselin ....John Gregory

COME BLOW YOUR HORN (1963)

An Essex-Tandem Production
Released by Paramount Pictures
   Producers: Norman Lear, Bud Yorkin
   Director: Bud Yorkin
   Executive Producer: Howard W. Koch
   Screenplay: Norman Lear
   Based on the play by: Neil Simon
   Music composed and conducted by: Nelson Riddle
   Director of Photography: William H. Daniels
   Gowns: Edith Head
   Running time: 112 minutes

SYNOPSIS:

Young Buddy Baker (Tony Bill) is bored living at home with his old-fashioned parents—particularly his domineering father (Lee J. Cobb)—so he packs his bags and moves in with his older brother Alan (Sinatra), who lives in a luxurious Manhattan apartment. Alan is a hard-drinking, womanizing bachelor who never lets his work at his father's artificial fruit factory impede his playboy lifestyle. The senior Bakers are shocked at their sons, but Alan is so impressed with his kid brother's independence that he buys him a new wardrobe and introduces him to New York's night life. Buddy's such a good student that he's soon appropriating his brother's private stock of booze and women. Alan loses one girlfriend to Buddy, then is beaten up by the husband of another and is even dumped by his favorite date, Connie (Barbara Rush). When Alan tries to get Buddy to settle down, he's told to mind his own business. Their confrontation jolts Alan into proposing to Connie and marrying her, then patching up a marital spat between his parents and finally bequeathing his bachelor pad to the delighted Buddy.

CAST:

Alan Baker.............................Frank Sinatra
Papa Baker ....Lee J. Cobb
Mama Baker ....Molly Picon
Buddy Baker ....Tony Bill
Connie....................................Barbara Rush
Peggy...Jill St. John
Mr. Eckman............................Dan Blocker
Wino......................................Dean Martin

SONGS:

Sinatra sings "Come Blow Your Horn"

THE LIST OF ADRIAN MESSENGER
(1963)

A Joel Production
Released by Universal
  Producer: Edward Lewis
  Director: John Huston
  Screenplay: Anthony Veiller
  Based on the novel by: Philip MacDonald
  Music: Jerry Goldsmith
  Director of Photography: Joe MacDonald
  Makeup: Bud Westmore
  Running time: 98 minutes
  Stats: This film featured four guest stars in complete disguise, including Sinatra.

SYNOPSIS:

Adrian Messenger (John Merivale) gives a retired British intelligence officer, Anthony Gethryn (George C. Scott), a list of 11 names and asks him to check the whereabouts of these people. When Messenger is killed in a midair plane explosion, Gethryn discovers that everyone on the list has also met with an accidental death. Enlisting the help of Scotland Yard, Gethryn finds out that all the victims were former POWs whose escape plan was revealed to the Nazis by an informer, someone who now has plans for prominence and is therefore systematically killing those who knew of his notorious past. The clever killer wears a different disguise for each murder. Gethryn discovers that the murderer is one of the heirs to a great English estate, and only a small boy stands in his way—so the murderer plans to kill the boy during a fox hunt. But Gethryn closes in and the villain, George Brougham (Kirk Douglas), is killed by one of his own traps when he attempts to escape.

CAST:

Anthony Gethryn	George C. Scott
Lady Jocelyn Bruttenholm	Dana Wynter
Marquis of Gleneyre	Clive Brook
Sir Wilfred Lucas	Herbert Marshall
Mrs. Karoudjian	Gladys Cooper
George Brougham	Kirk Douglas

Guest stars in disguise:

Woman	Burt Lancaster
Italian	Tony Curtis
Jim Slattery	Robert Mitchum
Gypsy stableman	Frank Sinatra

---

4 FOR TEXAS
(1964)

A Sam Company Production
Released by Warner Bros.
  Producer and Director: Robert Aldrich
  Executive Producer: Howard W. Koch
  Screenplay: Teddi Sherman, Robert Aldrich
  Music composed and conducted by: Nelson Riddle
  Orchestrations: Gil Grau
  Director of Photography: Ernest Laszlo
  Running time: 124 minutes

SYNOPSIS:

Zack Thomas (Sinatra) and Joe Jarrett (Dean Martin) are heading to Galveston in 1870 when their stagecoach is attacked by bandits. After fending off their attackers, Zack shows Joe a bag containing $100,000, which Joe promptly relieves him of at gunpoint. Joe deposits his loot in a Galveston bank run by Harvey Burden (Victor Buono), a crook who wants Zack to become the town's gambling king. When Zack arrives, the stagecoach bandit tries to kill him, but Joe comes to the rescue. Zack finds out why Joe saved his life: He's planning to compete with Zack by opening a riverboat gambling saloon. Enraged, Zack pulls a gang together and plans to raid the boat on opening night. But Burden has plans, too: He's going to let Zack and Joe destroy each other, then move in with his stagecoach bandits and control everything. Although Zack and Joe are ready to fight on opening night, they discover what Burden is up to and go after him instead. The bad guys are defeated, Burden is arrested and Zack and Joe marry their girlfriends in a double wedding.

CAST:

Zack Thomas	Frank Sinatra
Joe Jarrett	Dean Martin
Elya Carlson	Anita Ekberg
Maxine Richter	Ursula Andress
Matson	Charles Bronson
Harvey Burden	Victor Buono
Croupier	Arthur Godfrey

Special guest stars: The Three Stooges, Teddy Buckner and His All-Stars

ROBIN AND THE 7 HOODS
(1964)

A P-C Productions Picture
Released by Warner Bros.
  Producer: Frank Sinatra
  Director: Gordon Douglas
  Executive Producer: Howard W. Koch
  Screenplay: David R. Schwartz
  Music composed and conducted by:
    Nelson Riddle
  Orchestrations: Gil Grau
  Director of Photography: William H. Daniels
  Choreography: Jack Baker
  Running time: 123 minutes

SYNOPSIS:

Robbo (Sinatra), a Chicago gangster in the late 1920s, warns rival gangster Guy Gisborne (Peter Falk) to stay off his turf. Gisborne doesn't, and the two end up wrecking each other's nightclubs. Robbo builds a new club that can be instantly transformed into a revival hall. When Gisborne persuades the police to raid the place, they find only a group of gospel singers. Marian (Barbara Rush), the daughter of a dead gangster, offers Robbo $50,000 to kill her father's murderers. Robbo tells his aide, Will (Sammy Davis Jr.), to dump the money. Will gives it to an orphanage which, thanks to the media, turns Robbo into a hero. The modern-day Robin Hood hires the orphanage official, Allen A. Dale (Bing Crosby), to run a charity for him. Robbo falls in love with Marian, only to discover she's a crook who runs a counterfeiting ring, using his charity as a front. When he orders Marian out of town, she hires Gisborne to kill him, but the plan fails. She then starts a women's reform movement, and they destroy Robbo's organization. He's reduced to street begging with his side-kicks, Will and John (Dean Martin), until a limo pulls up. Marian and Dale emerge and give the impoverished trio a wad of money. Then she and Dale go into her reform club together.

CAST:

Robbo....................................Frank Sinatra
Little John ....Dean Martin
Will ....Sammy Davis Jr.
Guy Gisborne.............................Peter Falk
Marian ....Barbara Rush
Sheriff Potts ....Victor Buono
Tomatoes ....Jack LaRue
Big Jim.......................Edward G. Robinson
Allen A. Dale ....Bing Crosby

SONGS:
Sinatra sings "My Kind of Town," "Style," "Mr. Booze" and "Don't Be a Do-Badder"

NONE BUT THE BRAVE
(1965)

An Artanis Production
Released by Warner Bros.
  Producer and Director: Frank Sinatra
  Executive Producer: Howard W. Koch
  Associate Producer: William H. Daniels
  Screenplay: John Twist, Katsuya Susaki
  Original story: Kikumaru Okuda
  Music: John Williams
  Director of Photography: Harold Lipstein
  Running time: 105 minutes
  Stats: Sinatra makes his directorial debut.

SYNOPSIS:

On a small deserted island in the South Pacific, a group of Japanese soldiers, led by Lieutenant Kuroki, maintain discipline and order while slowly building a boat to carry them back into occupied territory. When an American plane crash-lands on the island, there's an immediate skirmish between the two sides, but then a truce is agreed upon by the Japanese commander and the American pilot. Chief Pharmacist Mate Maloney (Sinatra) is called on to amputate the leg of one of the Japanese soldiers. Despite lack of radio communication, the Japanese insist that if either side is able to return to the war zone, the truce will no longer be in effect. The Americans repair their radio, make contact with the Army and a destroyer comes to rescue them. Despite the new friendships that had evolved on the island, the Japanese and Americans are now at war again. The ensuing battle kills all the Japanese and leaves only five Americans alive.

CAST:

Chief Pharmacist Mate Maloney ...Frank Sinatra
Capt. Dennis Bourke ....Clint Walker
2nd Lt. Blair............................Tommy Sands
Sgt. Bleeker ....Brad Dexter
Air Crewman Keller. ....Tony Bill
Lt. Kuroki ....Tatsuya Mihashi
Sgt. Tamura ....Takeshi Kato

VON RYAN'S EXPRESS
(1965)

A P-R Productions Picture
Released by 20th Century-Fox
  Producer: Saul David
  Director: Mark Robson
  Screenplay: Wendell Mayes, Joseph Landon
  Based on the novel by: David Westheimer

Music: Jerry Goldsmith
Director of Photography: William H. Daniels
Running time: 117 minutes

SYNOPSIS:
The scene is a POW camp in southern Italy in 1943, when the Allies are landing, the Italians are trying to get out of the war and the Nazis are attacking the Allied forces. When Italian rule collapses, the Fascist who ran the camp is ousted. A conflict arises between the British prisoners, led by Major Fincham (Trevor Howard), and the lone American, Colonel Joseph Ryan (Sinatra): The Brits think he's overly hostile to the Italians, even going so far as to put "Von" in front of his name. Tensions between the British and Ryan ease when the group engineers an escape plan. Impersonating Nazi troops, they seize a German train and try to make a run for the Swiss border. It's just within sight when the train is halted by German soldiers. In the battle that follows, most of the Germans are killed and a majority of POWs make it across the Swiss border—all except Ryan, who, while making a desperate run for the train, is shot by the Nazis and lies dying on the tracks as Von Ryan's express rides on to freedom.

CAST:

Colonel Joseph L. Ryan	Frank Sinatra
Major Eric Fincham	Trevor Howard
Gabriella	Raffaella Carra
Sergeant Bostick	Brad Dexter
Captain Oriani	Sergio Fantoni
Chaplain Costanzo	Edward Mulhare

MARRIAGE ON THE ROCKS
(1965)

An A-C Productions Picture
Released by Warner Bros.
  Producer: William H. Daniels
  Director: Jack Donohue
  Screenplay: Cy Howard
  Music composed and conducted by:
  Nelson Riddle
  Director of Photography: William H. Daniels
  Running time: 109 minutes
  Stats: Nancy Sinatra's first appearance in a film with her father.

SYNOPSIS:
While Dan Edwards (Sinatra) is waiting in a restaurant for his wife, Valerie (Deborah Kerr), to show up so they can celebrate their 19th wedding anniversary, she's with a lawyer telling him she wants to divorce her boring husband. He suggests the Edwardses go on a second honeymoon instead. The same suggestion is made by Dan's best friend, Ernie (Dean Martin). So Valerie and Dan fly off to Mexico, where an ambulance-chasing lawyer accidentally divorces them. They arrange to remarry, but first Dan has to go back to the States for an emergency business meeting. He sends Ernie to Mexico to explain the delay to Valerie, and these two are inadvertently married by the overzealous attorney. Valerie tries to make Dan jealous of her "marriage" to Ernie. But Dan's enjoying being a bachelor again, so they remain apart until Valerie discovers she's pregnant, and her ex-husband's definitely the father—thanks to their Mexican second honeymoon. The happy couple is reunited and plan to marry again—as soon as the divorce from Ernie is final.

CAST:

Dan Edwards	Frank Sinatra
Valerie Edwards	Deborah Kerr
Ernie Brewer	Dean Martin
Miguel Santos	Cesar Romero

Jeannie MacPherson	Hermione Baddeley
Jim Blake	Tony Bill
Tracy Edwards	Nancy Sinatra
Guest Star	Trini Lopez

CAST A GIANT SHADOW
(1966)

A Mirisch-Glenroc-Batjac Production
Released by United Artists
  Producer and Director: Melville Shavelson
  Co-producer: Michael Wayne
  Screenplay: Melville Shavelson
  Based on the book by: Ted Berkman
  Music composed and conducted by:
    Elmer Bernstein
  Music for "Next Year in Jerusalem":
    Dov Seltzer
  Running time: 139 minutes

SYNOPSIS:

In 1949 the British are planning to leave Palestine, which is about to become the new state of Israel. But Arabs are openly defying the Jewish homeland and threatening a war. Colonel David "Mickey" Marcus (Kirk Douglas), a West Point graduate and former military adviser to FDR, is asked by the British to turn the disorganized Israeli army into a fighting machine against the Arabs. Over the objections of his wife and a Pentagon official, Marcus goes to Israel. He meets with the premier, Jacob Zion (Luther Adler), and Israeli underground leader Asher Gonen (Yul Brynner). Marcus stays at the home of a beautiful female soldier, Magda Simon, and the two fall in love. Although the U.N. calls for a cease-fire between Arabs and Jews, Marcus is ordered to take the Israeli army into Jerusalem before the truce begins. They are so short on ammunition that when a bomber pilot named Vince (Sinatra) runs out of explosives, he starts spraying seltzer at the enemy planes, but he is finally shot down and killed. Marcus leads the Israelis to victory, and realizing he still loves his wife, says good-bye to Magda. Stopped by a sentry guard at a monastery, Marcus is challenged by the guard in Hebrew. Unable to speak the language, Marcus doesn't respond. As he continues walking, the sentry shoots and kills him—just hours before the truce goes into effect.

CAST:

Col. David "Mickey" Marcus...Kirk Douglas
Magda Simon...........................Senta Berger
Emma Marcus ....Angie Dickinson
Major Safir ....James Donald
Jacob Zion............................Luther Adler
Pentagon Chief of Staff............Gary Merrill

Guest Stars:

Vince..Frank Sinatra
Asher Gonen ....Yul Brynner
General Mike Randolph...........John Wayne

THE OSCAR
(1966)

A Greene-Rouse Production
Released by Embassy Pictures
  Producer: Clarence Greene
  Director: Russell Rouse
  Executive Producer: Joseph E. Levine
  Screenplay: Harlan Ellison, Russell Rouse,
  Clarence Greene
  Based on the novel by: Richard Sale
  Music: Percy Faith
  Director of Photography: Joseph
  Ruttenberg
  Gowns: Edith Head
  Running time: 119 minutes

SYNOPSIS:

Hollywood's big night—the Academy Awards ceremony—is in full swing. One of the Best Actor nominees is a ruthless egomaniac named Frankie Fane (Stephen Boyd) who will do anything to win the Oscar. A flashback reveals Frankie's past, starting when he and his best friend Hymie Kelly (Tony Bennett) worked in strip joints. Sophie Cantaro (Eleanor Parker) falls for Frankie and gets him a film job. His acting career's ascent is counterpointed by his abusive and heartless behavior toward the women in his life, including the one he marries. Then his career starts slipping and Frankie fights with everyone, including his best friend and agent, Kappy Kapstetter (Milton Berle). On the brink of despair, Frankie is nominated for an Oscar. The possibility that he'll be back on top again leads him to pull every stunt to get the coveted award. At the ceremony, when the actress announces "...and the winner is...," Frankie automatically rises from his seat, almost in a trance. The audience, thinking he's giving a standing ovation to the real winner, rise with him to applaud the actor who has actually won: Frank Sinatra. As a devastated Fane sits down, Sinatra claims the Oscar.

CAST:

Frank Fane ....Stephen Boyd
Kay Bergdahl.........................Elke Sommer
Kappy Kapstetter ....Milton Berle
Sophie Cantaro....................Eleanor Parker
Kenneth Regan ....Joseph Cotten
Hymie Kelly ....Tony Bennett
Laurel Scott...............................Jill St. John
Trina Yale.................................Edie Adams
Barney Yale........................Ernest Borgnine
Steve Marks..........................Peter Lawford

Guest Stars as themselves: Frank Sinatra, Merle Oberon, Hedda Hopper, Nancy Sinatra, Edith Head

ASSAULT ON A QUEEN
(1966)

A Sinatra Enterprises-Seven Arts Production
Released by Paramount Pictures
  Producer: William Goetz
  Director: Jack Donohue
  Screenplay: Rod Serling
  Based on the novel by: Jack Finney
  Music: Duke Ellington
  Orchestral Arrangements: Van Cleave,
    Frank Comstock
  Director of Photography: William H. Daniels
  Running time: 106 minutes

SYNOPSIS:

Mark Brittain (Sinatra), an ex-submarine officer, is hired by wealthy Italian Rosa Lucchesi (Virna Lisi) and her partners to dive for buried treasure off the coast of Florida. Instead of treasure they find a small sunken German submarine and salvage it in order to pull off a fantastic scheme: the hijacking of the *Queen Mary*. While they're getting the sub ready for action, Mark and one of Rosa's partners, Vic Rossiter (Tony Franciosa), become rivals for her attention. The sub goes to sea and intercepts the *Queen*. Mark, Rossiter and Lauffnauer (one of Rosa's men) pose as British officers and come on board the ship, threatening to torpedo it unless the purser's safe is opened. Loot in hand, they begin leaving the ship, but Rossiter grabs a passenger's diamond ring and is shot and killed. As Mark and Lauffnauer reach the sub, they spot an oncoming Coast Guard cutter, and Lauffnauer tells his submates that he's going to torpedo the Coast Guard boat. They stop him and Mark surfaces the sub, escaping with Rosa and another crew member in a rubber raft. The sub is destroyed by the cutter and the trio are left at sea, drifting toward South America.

CAST:

Mark Brittain	Frank Sinatra
Rosa Lucchesi	Virna Lisi
Vic Rossiter	Tony Franciosa
Tony Moreno	Richard Conte
Eric Lauffnauer	Alf Kjellin
Linc Langley	Errol John

THE NAKED RUNNER
(1967)

A Sinatra Enterprises Production
Released by Warner Bros.
  Producer: Brad Dexter
  Director: Sidney J. Furie
  Screenplay: Stanley Mann
  Based on the novel by: Francis Clifford
  Music: Harry Sukman
  Director of Photography: Otto Heller
  Running time: 103 minutes

SYNOPSIS:

American businessman and widower Sam Laker (Sinatra) lives in London with his 14-year-old son, Patrick. While planning to take the boy with him on a business trip to Leipzig, Sam is contacted by an old war buddy, Martin Slattery, now with British Intelligence. Slattery wants Sam—a former marksman—to kill a British spy who has defected to the Communists. When Sam refuses, Slattery asks him to at least deliver a message to an underground worker named Karen Gisevius, who turns out to be a woman who once helped Sam during the war. He relents, delivers the message and returns to his hotel only to find out that his son has been kidnapped and is being held hostage by the East Germans. They want Sam to assassinate a man in Copenhagen. To get Patrick back safely, Sam agrees, but the intended victim never shows up. The German officer tells Sam that his son is dead because the assignment wasn't carried out, leading Sam to seek revenge. He plans to kill the officer, using his telescopic rifle to shoot the German in his car as he's riding along a highway. When the car passes, Sam shoots and kills the occupant. As he makes his getaway, Slattery and the German officer appear and tell Sam that his son is safe. They also reveal that Sam was part of an elaborate plan to get him to kill the British spy-defector—which he did by shooting the man in the passing car.

CAST:

Sam Laker	Frank Sinatra
Slattery	Peter Vaughan
Colonel Hartmann	Derren Nesbitt
Karen	Nadia Gray
Ruth	Toby Robins

TONY ROME
(1967)

An Arcola-Millfield Production
Released by 20th Century-Fox
   Producer: Aaron Rosenberg
   Director: Gordon Douglas
   Screenplay: Richard L. Breen
   Based on the novel "Miami Mayhem" by:
   Marvin H. Albert
   Music: Billy May
   Director of Photography: Joseph Biroc
   Title song: "Something Here Inside of Me"
     by: Lee Hazelwood, Nancy Sinatra
   Running time: 110 minutes

SYNOPSIS:

A wisecracking, tough but romantic Miami private eye named Tony Rome (Sinatra) is asked by his ex-partner, Ralph Turpin, to remove Diana (Sue Lyon), a drunken socialite, from Turpin's motel and return her to her wealthy father, Rudolph Kosterman (Simon Oakland), and stepmother, Rita (Gena Rowlands).

Kosterman then hires Rome to find out what's wrong with his daughter. First Tony discovers that Diana's diamond pin is lost and a lot of people are looking for it. The pin is fake, as are all the Kosterman jewels. Then Turpin is murdered and Rome thinks the death is connected to Diana. His investigation is aided by predatory divorcee Ann Archer (Jill St. John), and they learn that Diana is giving money to her alcoholic mother, Lorna. After Rita unsuccessfully attempts to kill Rome, he discovers that her ex-husband, Nimmo, is blackmailing her because her divorce from him isn't legal. He also took her jewels, replacing them with fakes, but when he tries to retrieve Diana's lost pin, he's mortally wounded. Tony goes to the home of Diana's mother and her husband, Adam Boyd, and finds Boyd burying Nimmo. He confesses he wanted Kosterman killed so he could inherit the family fortune through Diana. After Boyd is arrested, the Kostermans promise to take care of Lorna. Tony wants to take a

well-deserved vacation with his divorcee girlfriend, but she decides to return to her ex-husband. Rome sails off alone on his boat, christened the *Straight Pass*.

CAST:

Tony Rome	Frank Sinatra
Ann Archer	Jill St. John
Lt. Santini	Richard Conte
Rita Kosterman	Gena Rowlands
Rudolph Kosterman	Simon Oakland
Adam Boyd	Jeffrey Lynn
Diana	Sue Lyon

THE DETECTIVE
(1968)

An Arcola-Millfield Production
Released by 20th Century-Fox
   Producer: Aaron Rosenberg
   Director: Gordon Douglas
   Screenplay: Abby Mann
   Based on the novel by: Roderick Thorp
   Music: Jerry Goldsmith
   Director of Photography: Joseph Biroc
   Running time: 114 minutes

SYNOPSIS:

Hard-bitten homicide detective Joe Leland (Sinatra) investigates the mutilation murder of a homosexual. After making the round of gay hangouts, Leland arrests a suspect, Felix Tesla (Tony Musante), and by gaining the man's confidence, extracts a confession. Tesla dies in the electric chair, and Leland is promoted, but remains disturbed about Tesla's guilt because he knows the gay man was psychotic. Leland's other problems are personal: His wife Karen (Lee Remick) is a nymphomaniac and their marriage dissolves, but Leland's still in love with her. Enter Norma MacIver (Jacqueline Bisset), who asks Leland to investigate her husband's death, which the police listed as a suicide. Leland discovers Colin MacIver was involved with city officials who bought ghetto property for private profit. A fellow detective tries unsuccessfully to stop Leland from further investigation. Then two hit men attempt to kill Leland, but he kills them

first. When a psychiatrist friend of Norma's also tries to stop Leland, he confronts the doctor and forces him to play tapes of sessions with MacIver. Tormented by his bisexuality, Norma's husband committed the murder for which Tesla was electrocuted. Shattered that he sent an innocent man to the chair, and appalled at the corruption in his police department, Leland leaves the force after 20 years as a detective. He decides to try and rebuild his life, pushing for police reforms—and a personal relationship with Norma.

CAST:

Det. Joe Leland	Frank Sinatra
Karen Leland	Lee Remick
Lt. Curran	Ralph Meeker
Lt. Dave Shoenstein	Jack Klugman
Chief Tom Farrell	Horace McMahon
Colin MacIver	William Windom
Felix Tesla	Tony Musante
Det. Mickey Nestor	Robert Duvall
Norma MacIver	Jacqueline Bisset

LADY IN CEMENT
(1968)

An Arcola-Millfield Production
Released by 20th Century-Fox
  Producer: Aaron Rosenberg
  Director: Gordon Douglas
  Screenplay: Marvin H. Albert, Jack Guss
  Based on the novel by: Marvin H. Albert
  Music composed and conducted by:
    Hugo Montenegro
  Orchestrations: Billy May
  Director of Photography: Joseph Biroc
  Running time: 93 minutes

SYNOPSIS:

Private eye Tony Rome (Sinatra) is back. This time he's looking for buried treasure off the Florida coast near Miami. What he finds is a dead woman, naked, her feet encased in cement. While trying to discover the identity of the "lady in cement," Tony meets up with an ex-con named Earl Gronsky (Dan Blocker) who was a former boyfriend of the dead woman. It's not too long before Rome becomes involved with beautiful, alcoholic heiress Kit Forrest (Raquel Welch) and former racketeer Al Mungar (Martin Gabel). Mungar has convinced Kit that she's the dead woman's murderer. With some help—and some hindrance—from his detective buddy, Lt. Santini (Richard Conte), Tony finally solves the murder mystery and takes off to the Bahamas with the lovely Kit.

CAST:

Tony Rome	Frank Sinatra
Kit Forrest	Raquel Welch
Earl Gronsky	Dan Blocker
Lieutenant Santini	Richard Conte
Al Mungar	Martin Gabel
Maria Baretto	Lainie Kazan

DIRTY DINGUS MAGEE
(1970)

Released by Metro-Goldwyn-Mayer
  Producer and Director: Burt Kennedy
  Screenplay: Tom and Frank Waldman,
    Joseph Heller
  Based on the novel "The Ballad of Dingus
  Magee" by: David Markson
  Music: Jeff Alexander
  Director of Photography: Harry Stradling Jr.
  Running time: 91 minutes

SYNOPSIS:

It's the 1880s in New Mexico and that thieving rascal, Dingus Magee (Sinatra), has just robbed Hoke Birdsill (George Kennedy). Hoke reports the robbery to the local mayor, Belle Knops (Anne Jackson)—who's also the madame of the town's sole industry, a whorehouse frequented by cavalrymen from the nearby fort. Belle appoints Hoke sheriff so he can go after Dingus. He finds Magee romping in the bushes with an Indian girl and throws him in jail. Belle's upset because the cavalry's heading off to battle, and that will probably ruin her business. When the Indian girl helps Dingus escape, Belle blames the local tribe and tells the cavalry to crush the "uprising." Now Hoke's after Dingus for robbing a stagecoach, the Indians are after him for refusing to trade his rifle for the girl and she's after him for another roll in the hay. Dingus is chasing Belle for her money and finally manages—after numerous chases, captures and escapes—to get out of town with Belle's cash and the pretty Indian girl.

CAST:

Dingus Magee	Frank Sinatra
Hoke Birdsill	George Kennedy
Belle Knops	Anne Jackson
Prudence Frost	Lois Nettleton
John Wesley Hardin	Jack Elam
Anna Hotwater	Michele Carey

THAT'S ENTERTAINMENT
(1974)

Released by Metro-Goldwyn-Mayer
  Producer, Director and Writer: Jack Haley, Jr.
  Executive Producer: Daniel Melnick
  Photography: Gene Polito, Ernest Laszlo,
  Russell Metty, Ennio Guarnieri, Allan Green
  Music adapted by: Henry Mancini
  Music Supervisor: Jesse Kaye
  Editors: Bud Friedgen, David W. Blewitt
  Running time: 137 minutes

SYNOPSIS:

With one hundred excerpts from MGM's classic musicals from 1929's *The Hollywood Revue* to 1958's *Gigi*, this is a nostalgic homage to the extraordinary talents—directors, choreographers, actors, dancers, singers, costume and set designers, composers, musicians and wonderful storytellers—who made MGM the legendary, star-studded studio that it was. These treasured moments

from *Anchors Aweigh*, *Wizard of Oz*, *Singin' in the Rain*, *An American in Paris*, the black-and-white *Broadway Melody* films, *Showboat*, *Good News*, *On the Town*, *Seven Brides for Seven*

Brothers, *Funny Face*, and so many more, are narrated and hosted by some of MGM's finest—including Sinatra—who take us on a sentimental journey as they walk around the dusty backlot and sound stages that were once home to the creators of an era of unparalleled musical entertainment—almost all of it in glorious Technicolor.

CAST:

  Host/Narrators:
  Fred Astaire, Bing Crosby,
  Gene Kelly, Peter Lawford,
  Liza Minnelli, Donald O'Connor,
  Debbie Reynolds, Mickey Rooney,
  Frank Sinatra, James Stewart,
  Elizabeth Taylor

CONTRACT ON CHERRY STREET
(1977)

An Artanis Production for Columbia Pictures Television
  Producer: Hugh Benson
  Director: William A. Graham
  Executive Producer: Renee Valente
  Screenplay: Edward Anhalt
  Based on the book by: Philip Rosenberg
  Music: Jerry Goldsmith
  Running time: 155 minutes
  Stats: Sinatra's first TV movie.

SYNOPSIS:

Frank Hovannes (Sinatra), an uncompromising, hard-driven New York deputy police inspector, is in charge of an elite branch of law enforcement known as the Office of Crime Control, an anti-Mafia crime unit. He's under growing pressure from his department brass to wipe out a local numbers racket. When his best friend and team partner Ernie Weinberg (Martin Balsam) is killed in a shootout, Hovannes goes over the edge. Unauthorized, he decides to go after some key Mafia gangsters, and pretty soon he and the men in his squad have become vigilantes. Hovannes realizes that his plan to nab the city's most notorious criminals has gotten out of control when a mobster who's not on his hit list is slain. He fears that he has set off a chain of events that will lead to disaster for everyone.

CAST:
Deputy Inspector Frank Hovannes..........Frank Sinatra
Tommy Sinardos ....Jay Black
Emily Hovannes ....Verna Bloom
Capt. Ernie Weinberg...........Martin Balsam
Vincenzo Seruto ....Joe DeSantis
Baruch Waldman ....Martin Gabel

THE FIRST DEADLY SIN
(1980)

An Artanis/Cinema Seven Production
Released by Filmways
  Producers: George Pappas, Mark Shanker
  Director: Brian G. Hutton
  Executive Producers: Frank Sinatra,
    Elliot Kastner
  Screenplay: Mann Rubin
  Based on the novel by: Lawrence Sanders
  Music: Gordon Jenkins
  Director of Photography: Jack Priestley
  Running time: 112 minutes
  Stats: Sinatra's first feature film after a
    10-year hiatus.

SYNOPSIS:

Just when Edward Delaney (Sinatra), a hard-boiled police detective, is getting ready to retire, he finds himself facing one of his most difficult cases, as well as a personal crisis. He's trying to solve a particularly grisly murder while caring for his dying wife, who grows weaker every day after a possibly bungled kidney operation. At the same time, he's trying to break in a new precinct commander who tends to do everything by the book. With the help of a police mortician and a weapons expert who works at the Metropolitan Museum, Delaney discovers that the murder was committed with a mountain climber's icepick. Delaney's now convinced he's on the trail of a psychopath and narrows down his list of suspects to one "Daniel Blank," the name Delaney assigns to the man. Obsessively, Delaney harasses Blank, who promises retaliation by claiming he has powerful friends. Finally, Blank goads Delaney into shooting him, and thereby destroys the detective's career.

CAST:

Lt. Edward Delaney ....Frank Sinatra
Barbara Delaney..................Faye Dunaway
Daniel Blank...........................David Dukes
Dr. Bernardi.............................George Coe
Monica Gilbert....................Brenda Vaccaro
Christopher Langley ....Martin Gabel
Capt. Broughton ....Anthony Zerbe

CANNONBALL RUN II
(1983)

A Golden Harvest Film
Released by Warner Bros.
  Producer: Albert S. Ruddy
  Director: Hal Needham
  Executive Producers: Raymond Chow,
    Andre Morgan
  Screenplay: Hal Needham, Albert S.
    Ruddy, Harvey Miller
  Based on characters created by:
    Brock Yates
  Music: Al Capps
  Director of Photography: Nick McLean
  Stunt Coordinator: Alan R. Gibbs
  Running time: 108 minutes

SYNOPSIS:

The semi-illegal Trans American Cannonball Run is being sponsored by the son of a Middle Eastern king, with a $1 million prize. Stunt-car racers J.J. McClure (Burt Reynolds) and his buddy "Chaos" (Dom DeLuise) enter the race not knowing that the sheik has it rigged so that his tribe will win. During the run from California to Connecticut, J.J. and Chaos meet up with a vast array of eccentric characters, including con men pretending to be priests, a metal-toothed giant, an inept Mafioso running his operation from a desert ghost town, a couple of fast-driving bimbos and a Las Vegas kingpin known as the Chairman (Sinatra), who helps the racers rescue the sheik after he's been seized by gangsters. The grateful sheik hands the one million over to the Chairman.

CAST:

J.J. McClure ....Burt Reynolds
Victor ("Chaos")....................Dom DeLuise
Blake......................................Dean Martin
Fenderbaum ....Sammy Davis Jr.
Sheik...Jamie Farr
Betty ....Marilu Henner
Hymie ....Telly Savalas
Veronica ....Shirley MacLaine
1st Fisherman.........................Foster Brooks
2nd Fisherman............................Sid Caesar
1st Chip.................................Tim Conway
2nd Chip ....Don Knotts
King ....Ricardo Montalban
Homer ....Jim Nabors
The Chairman ....Frank Sinatra

FRANK SINATRA
AN "A TO Z" DISCOGRAPHY

A BABY JUST LIKE YOU
(John Denver-Joe Henry)
Reprise Records
Arranged by Don Costa
Conducted by Bill Miller
Recorded: October 24, 1975

A COTTAGE FOR SALE
(Willard Robinson-Larry Conley)
Capitol Records
Arranged by Gordon Jenkins
Recorded: March 26, 1959

A DAY IN THE LIFE OF A FOOL
(Carl Sigman-Luis Bonfa)
Reprise Records
Arranged by Don Costa
Recorded: February 20, 1969

A FELLA WITH AN UMBRELLA
(Irving Berlin)
Columbia Records
Arranged by Axel Stordahl
Recorded: March 16, 1948

A FELLOW NEEDS A GIRL
(Richard Rodgers-Oscar Hammerstein II)
Columbia Records
Arranged by Axel Stordahl
Recorded: August 17, 1947

A FINE ROMANCE
(Jerome Kern-Dorothy Fields)
Reprise Records
Arranged by Johnny Mandel
Recorded: December 20, 1960

A FOGGY DAY
(George Gershwin-Ira Gershwin)
Capitol Records
Arranged by Nelson Riddle
Recorded: November 5, 1953

A FOGGY DAY
(George Gershwin-Ira Gershwin)
Reprise Records
Arranged by Johnny Mandel
Recorded: December 19, 1960

A FOGGY DAY
(George Gershwin-Ira Gershwin)
Reprise Records
With sextet accompaniment (Live recording)
Arranged by Neal Hefti and Billy May
Recorded: June 5, 1962 (Paris)

A FOGGY DAY
(George Gershwin-Ira Gershwin)
With Willie Nelson
Capitol Records
Arranged by Johnny Mandel
Orchestra conducted by Patrick Williams
Recorded: October 11, 1993

A FRIEND OF YOURS
(Johnny Burke-Jimmy Van Heusen)
With the Ken Lane Singers
Columbia Records
Arranged by Axel Stordahl
Recorded: March 6, 1945

A GARDEN IN THE RAIN
(Carroll Gibbons-James Dyrenforth)
Reprise Records
Arranged by Robert Farnon
Recorded: June 12, 1962

A GHOST OF A CHANCE
(Victor Young-Bing Crosby-Ted Washington)
Columbia Records
Arranged by Axel Stordahl
Recorded: December 7, 1945

A GHOST OF A CHANCE
(Victor Young-Bing Crosby-Ned Washington)
Capitol Records
Arranged by Gordon Jenkins
Recorded: March 24, 1959

A GOOD MAN IS HARD TO FIND
(Eddie Green)
With Shelley Winters
Film recording for: 'Meet Danny Wilson'
Universal-International
Columbia Records (Commercial issue)
Arranged by Joseph Gershenson
Recorded: June 21, 1951

A HUNDRED YEARS FROM TODAY
(Victor Young-Ned Washington)
Qwest Records
Arranged by Sam Nestico
Orchestra conducted by Quincy Jones
Recorded: April 16, 1984

A LITTLE IN LOVE
(C. O'Neill-J. Pelosa)
Victor Records
With Tommy Dorsey and his Orchestra
Recorded: August 3, 1940 (Radio aircheck)

A LITTLE LEARNIN' *(Is A Dangerous Thing)*
(Sy Oliver-Dick Jacobs)
With Pearl Bailey
Columbia Records
Arranged by Sy Oliver
Recorded: December 8, 1947

A LONG NIGHT
(Alec Wilder-Loonis McGlohin)
Reprise Records
Arranged and conducted by Gordon Jenkins
Recorded: July 20, 1981

A LOVELY WAY TO SPEND AN EVENING
(Harold Adamson-Jimmy McHugh)
Film recording for: 'Higher And Higher'
RKO Pictures
Arranged by Axel Stordahl
Orchestra conducted by Constantin Bakaleinikoff
Recorded: August 24, 1943

A LOVELY WAY TO SPEND AN EVENING
(Harold Adamson-Jimmy McHugh)
Columbia Records
With The Bobby Tucker Singers
Arranged and conducted by Axel Stordahl
Recorded: November 10, 1943

A LOVELY WAY TO SPEND AN EVENING
(Harold Adamson-Jimmy McHugh)
V-Disc recording
Columbia Records
Arranged by Alec Wilder
Recorded: November 21, 1943

A MAN ALONE
(Rod McKuen)
Reprise Records
Arranged by Don Costa
Recorded: March 20, 1969

A MAN ALONE (Reprise)
(Rod McKuen)
Reprise Records
Arranged by Don Costa
Recorded: March 20, 1969

A MILLION DREAMS AGO
(Lew Quadling-Eddy Howard-Dick Jurgens)
Capitol Records
Arranged by Axel Stordahl
Recorded: September 12, 1961

A NIGHTINGALE SANG IN BERKELEY SQUARE
(Eric Maschwitz-Manny Sherwin)
Reprise Records
Arranged by Robert Farnon
Recorded: June 13, 1962

A SINNER KISSED AN ANGEL
(Mack David-Ray Joseph)
Victor Records
With Tommy Dorsey and his Orchestra
Recorded: September 18, 1941

ACCIDENTS WILL HAPPEN
(Johnny Burke-Jimmy Van Heusen)
Columbia Records
Arranged by Axel Stordahl
Recorded: September 18, 1950

ADELAIDE
(Frank Loesser)
Film recording for: 'Guys and Dolls'
Samuel Goldwyn Productions
Arranged by Nelson Riddle
Orchestra conducted by Jay Blackton
Recorded: March 11, 1955

ADESTE FIDELES
(Traditional)
Columbia Records
Arranged by Axel Stordahl
Recorded: August 8, 1946

ADESTE FIDELES
(Traditional)
Capitol Records
With The Ralph Brewster Singers
Arranged by Gordon Jenkins
Recorded: July 10, 1957

(Theme From) **ADVISE AND CONSENT**
(Fielding-Washington)
Film recording for: 'Advise and Consent'
Columbia Pictures
Arranged by Jerry Fielding
Recorded: September 18, 1961

AFTER YOU'VE GONE
(Henry Creamer-Turner Layton)
Qwest
Arranged by Frank Foster
Orchestra conducted by Quincy Jones
Recorded: April 13, 1984

AIN'T SHE SWEET?
(Milton Ager-Jack Yellen)
Reprise Records
Arranged by Neal Hefti
Recorded: April 10, 1962

AIN'TCHA EVER COMIN' BACK?
(Paul Weston-Axel Stordahl-Irving Taylor)
Columbia Records
With The Pied Pipers
Arranged by Axel Stordahl
Recorded: March 11, 1947

ALL ALONE
(Irving Berlin)
Reprise Records
Arranged by Gordon Jenkins
Recorded: January 15, 1962

ALL I NEED IS THE GIRL
(Stephen Sondheim-Jule Styne)
Reprise Records
With Duke Ellington and his Orchestra
Arranged by Billy May
Recorded: December 11, 1967

ALL MY TOMORROWS
(Sammy Cahn-Jimmy Van Heusen)
Capitol Records
Arrangments by Nelson Riddle
Recorded: December 29, 1958

ALL MY TOMORROWS
(Sammy Cahn-Jimmy Van Heusen)
Reprise Records
Arranged by Don Costa
Recorded: February 18, 1969

ALL OF ME
(Seymour Simons-Gerald Marks)
V-Disc recording
Columbia Records
Arranged by Axel Stordahl
Recorded: July 8, 1944

ALL OF ME
(Seymour Simon-Gerald Marks)
Columbia Records
Arranged by George Siravo
Conducted by Axel Stordahl
Recorded: November 7, 1946

ALL OF ME
(Seymour Simon-Gerald Marks)
Columbia Records
Arranged by George Siravo
Conducted by Axel Stordahl
Recorded: October 19, 1947

ALL OF ME
(Seymour Simon-Gerald Marks)
Film recording for: 'Meet Danny Wilson'
Universal-International
Arranged by Joseph Gershenson
Recorded: June 13, 1951

ALL OF ME
(Seymour Simon-Gerald Marks)
Capitol Records
Arranged by Nelson Riddle
Recorded: April 19, 1954

ALL OF YOU
(Cole Porter)
Reprise Records
Arranged by Billy May
Recorded: September 17, 1979

ALL OR NOTHING AT ALL
(Arthur Altman-Jack Lawrence)
Columbia Records
Arranged by Andy Gibson
Recorded: August 31, 1939

ALL OR NOTHING AT ALL
(Arthur Altman-Jack Lawrence)
Reprise Records
Arranged by Don Costa
Recorded: November 22, 1961

ALL OR NOTHING AT ALL
(Arthur Altman-Jack Lawrence)
Reprise Records
Arranged by Nelson Riddle
Recorded: May 16, 1966

ALL OR NOTHING AT ALL
(Arthur Altman-Jack Lawrence)
Reprise Records
Arranged by Joe Beck
Recorded: February 16, 1977

ALL THE THINGS YOU ARE
(Jerome Kern-Oscar Hammerstein II)
V-Disc recording
Columbia Records
Arranged by Axel Stordahl
Recorded: July 8, 1944

ALL THE THINGS YOU ARE
(Jerome Kern-Oscar Hammerstein II)
Columbia Records
With the Ken Lane Singers
Arranged by Axel Stordahl
Recorded: January 29, 1945

ALL THE WAY
(Sammy Cahn-Jimmy Van Heusen)
Film recording for: 'The Joker Is Wild'
Paramount Pictures
Arranged by Nelson Riddle
Orchestra conducted by Walter Scharf
Recorded: October 3, 1956

ALL THE WAY
(Sammy Cahn-Jimmy Van Heusen)
Capitol Records
Arranged by Nelson Riddle
Recorded: August 13, 1957

ALL THE WAY
(Sammy Cahn-Jimmy Van Heusen)
Reprise Records
Arranged by Nelson Riddle
Recorded: April 29, 1963

ALL THE WAY HOME
(Teddy Randazzo)
Reprise Records
Arranged by Joe Parnello
Recorded: January 25, 1983

ALL THIS AND HEAVEN TOO
(Eddie DeLange-Jimmy Van Heusen)
Victor Records
With Tommy Dorsey and his Orchestra
Recorded: May 23, 1940

ALL THROUGH THE DAY
(Jerome Kern-Oscar Hammerstein II)
Columbia Records
Arranged by Axel Stordahl
Recorded: February 3, 1946

ALMOST LIKE BEING IN LOVE
(Alan J. Lerner-Frederick Lowe)
Columbia Records
Arranged by Axel Stordahl
Recorded: March 31, 1947

ALMOST LIKE BEING IN LOVE
(Alan J. Lerner-Frederick Lowe)
Capitol Records
Arranged by Heinie Beau
Orchestra conducted by Billy May
Recorded: March 22, 1961

ALWAYS
(Irving Berlin)
Columbia Records
Arranged by Axel Stordahl
Recorded: December 15, 1946

ALWAYS
(Irving Berlin)
Columbia Records
Arranged by Axel Stordahl
Recorded: January 9, 1947

ALWAYS
(Irving Berlin)
Capitol Records
Arranged by Nelson Riddle
Recorded: August 23, 1960

AMERICA THE BEAUTIFUL
(Katherine Bass-Samuel Ward)
Columbia Records
With the Ken Lane Singers
Arranged by Axel Stordahl
Recorded: August 27, 1945

AMERICA THE BEAUTIFUL
(Katherine Bass-Samuel Ward)
Reprise Records
With vocal chorus
Arranged by Nelson Riddle
Recorded: February 20, 1963

AMERICAN BEAUTY ROSE
(Redd Evans-Hal David-Arthur Altman)
Columbia Records
Arranged by Norman Leyden
Orchestra conducted by Mitch Miller
Recorded: March 10, 1950

AMERICAN BEAUTY ROSE
(Redd Evans-Hal David-Arthur Altman)
Capitol Records
Arranged by Heinie Beau
Orchestra conducted by Billy May
Recorded: March 21, 1961

AMONG MY SOUVENIRS
(Edgar Leslie-Horatio Nicholls)
Columbia Records
Arranged by Axel Stordahl
Recorded: July 30, 1946

AND THEN YOU KISSED ME
(Sammy Cahn-Jule Styne)
V-Disc recording
Columbia Records
Arranged and conducted by Axel Stordahl
Recorded: May 24, 1944

AN OLD FASHIONED CHRISTMAS
(Sammy Cahn-Jimmy Van Heusen)
Reprise Records
With Fred Waring and his Pennsylvanians
Arranged by Nelson Riddle
Orchestra conducted by Fred Waring
Recorded: June 16, 1964

ANGEL EYES
(Matt Dennis-Earl Brent)
Capitol Records
Arranged by Nelson Riddle
Orchestra conducted by Felix Slatkin
Recorded: May 29, 1958

ANGEL EYES
(Matt Dennis-Earl Brent)
Reprise Records
With Count Basie and his Orchestra (Live recording)
Arranged by Quincy Jones and Billy Byers
Recorded: January 26-February 1, 1966 (Las Vegas)

ANGEL EYES
(Matt Dennis-Earl Brent)
Reprise Records
With Woody Herman and the Young Thundering Herd (Live recording)
Arranged by Nelson Riddle
Orchestra conducted by Bill Miller
Recorded: October 4, 1974 (Buffalo)

ANYTHING
(Harry Rosenthal-Douglas Furber-Irving Caesar)
Victor Records
With Tommy Dorsey and his Orchestra
Arranged by Deane Kincaide
Recorded: September 9, 1940

ANYTHING GOES
(Cole Porter)
Capitol Records
Arranged by Nelson Riddle
Recorded: January 16, 1956

ANYTIME (I'LL BE THERE)
(Paul Anka)
Reprise Records
With vocal chorus
Arranged by Don Costa
Orchestra conducted by Bill Miller
Orchestral track recorded: February 4, 1975
Vocal track recorded: March 5, 1975

ANYTIME, ANYWHERE
(Carpenter-Adelson)
Capitol Records
Arranged by Nelson Riddle
Recorded: May 2, 1953

ANYTIME AT ALL
(Baker Knight)
With vocal chorus
Reprise Records
Arranged by Ernie Freeman
Recorded: November 10, 1964

APRIL IN PARIS
(Vernon Duke-Yip Harburg)
Columbia Records
Arranged by Axel Stordahl
Recorded: October 9, 1950

APRIL IN PARIS
(Vernon Duke-Yip Harburg)
Capitol Records
Arranged by Billy May
Recorded: October 3, 1957

APRIL IN PARIS
(Vernon Duke-Yip Harburg)
Reprise Records
With sextet accompaniment (Live recording)
Arranged by Neal Hefti and Billy May
Recorded: June 5, 1962 (Paris)

APRIL PLAYED THE FIDDLE
(Johnny Burke-James Monaco)
Victor Records
With Tommy Dorsey and his Orchestra
Arranged by Deane Kincaide
Recorded: April 10, 1940

ARE YOU LONESOME TONIGHT?
(Roy Turk-Lou Handman)
Reprise Records
Arranged by Gordon Jenkins
Recorded: January 17, 1962

AREN'T YOU GLAD YOU'RE YOU?
(Johnny Burke-Jimmy Van Heusen)
V-Disc recording
Columbia Records
Arranged and conducted by Axel Stordahl
Recorded: October 3, 1945

AROUND THE WORLD
(Victor Young-Harold Adamson)
Capitol Records
Arranged by Billy May
Recorded: October 8, 1957

AS LONG AS THERE'S MUSIC
(Sammy Cahn-Jule Styne)
Film recording for: 'Step Lively'
RKO Pictures
Arranged by Axel Stordahl
Orchestra conducted by Constantin Bakaleinikoff
Recorded: January 31, 1944

AS LONG AS THERE'S MUSIC
(Sammy Cahn-Jule Styne)
Film recording for: 'Step Lively'
RKO Pictures
With Gloria DeHaven and Chorus
Arranged by Axel Stordahl
Orchestra conducted by Constantin Bakaleinikoff
Recorded: February 25, 1944

AS TIME GOES BY
(Herman Hupfield)
Capitol Records
Arranged by Axel Stordahl
Recorded: September 12, 1961

AS YOU DESIRE ME
(Allie Wrubel)
Reprise Records
Arranged by Don Costa
Recorded: November 20, 1961

AT LONG LAST LOVE
(Cole Porter)
Capitol Records
Arranged by Nelson Riddle
Recorded: November 20, 1956

AT LONG LAST LOVE
(Cole Porter)
Reprise Records
Arranged by Neal Hefti
Recorded: April 11, 1962

AT LONG LAST LOVE
(Cole Porter)
Reprise Records
With sextet accompaniment (Live recording)
Arranged by Neal Hefti and Billy May
Recorded June 5, 1962 (Paris)

AT SUNDOWN
(Walter Donaldson)
Film recording for: 'The Joker Is Wild'
Paramount Pictures
Arranged by Nelson Riddle
Orchestra conducted by Walter Scharf
Recorded: October 3, 1956

AUTUMN IN NEW YORK
(Vernon Duke)
Columbia Records
Arranged by Axel Stordahl
Recorded: December 4, 1947

AUTUMN IN NEW YORK
(Vernon Duke)
Capitol Records
Arranged by Billy May
Recorded: October 3, 1957

AUTUMN IN NEW YORK
(Vernon Duke)
Reprise Records
With Woody Herman and the Young Thundering Herd (Live recording)
Arranged by Billy May
Orchestra conducted by Bill Miller
Recorded October 12, 1974 (New York City)

AUTUMN LEAVES
(Joseph Kosma-Jacques Prevert-Johnny Mercer)
Capitol Records
Arranged by Gordon Jenkins
Recorded: April 10, 1957

AVAILABLE
(Sammy Cahn-E. Wynn-H. Marks)
Reprise Records
With vocal chorus
Arranged by Ernie Freeman
Recorded: July 17, 1964

AVE MARIA
(Franz Schubert)
Columbia Records
With the U. S. Military WAVES Chorus
Arranged by Axel Stordahl
Recorded: March 28, 1945 (Radio aircheck)

AZURE-TE *(Paris Blues)*
(D. Wolf-B.Davis)
Columbia Records
Arranged by Heinie Beau
Orchestra conducted by Axel Stordahl
Recorded: June 3, 1952

BABY WON'T YOU PLEASE COME HOME?
(Charles Warfield-Clarence Williams)
Capitol Records
Arranged by Gordon Jenkins
Recorded: April 29, 1957

BAD, BAD LEROY BROWN
(Jim Croce)
Reprise Records
Arranged by Don Costa
Recorded: December 10, 1973

BAD, BAD LEROY BROWN
(Jim Croce)
Reprise Records
With Woody Herman and the Young Thundering Herd (Live recording)
Arranged by Don Costa
Orchestra conducted by Bill Miller
Recorded: October 13, 1974

BALI HA'I
(Richard Rodgers-Oscar Hammerstein II)
With vocal chorus
Columbia Records
Arranged by Axel Stordahl
Recorded: February 28, 1949

BANG, BANG
(Sonny Bono)
Reprise Records
Arranged by Gordon Jenkins
Recorded: June 4, 1973

BANG, BANG
(Sonny Bono)
Reprise Records
Arranged by Gordon Jenkins
Recorded: April 8, 1981

BARBARA
(Mack David-Jimmy Van Heusen)
Reprise Records
Arranged by Nelson Riddle
Recorded: March 14, 1977

BAUBLES, BANGLES AND BEADS
(Robert Wright-George Forrest)
Capitol Records
Arranged by Billy May
Recorded: December 22, 1958

BAUBLES, BANGLES AND BEADS
(Robert Wright-George Forrest)
Reprise Records
With Antonio Carlos Jobim
Arranged by Claus Ogerman
Recorded: January 30, 1967

BE CAREFUL IT'S MY HEART
(Irving Berlin)
Victor Records
With Tommy Dorsey and his Orchestra
Arranged by Axel Stordahl
Recorded: June 9, 1942

BE CAREFUL IT'S MY HEART
(Irving Berlin)
Reprise Records
Arranged by Skip Martin
Orchestra conducted by Johnny Mandel
Recorded: December 20, 1960

BEFORE THE MUSIC ENDS
(Gordon Jenkins)
Reprise Records
With the Los Angeles Philharmonic Symphony Orchestra
Arranged by Gordon Jenkins
Recorded: December 18, 1979

BEGIN THE BEGUINE
(Cole Porter)
Columbia Records
Arranged by Axel Stordahl
Recorded: February 24, 1946

BEIN' GREEN
(Joe Raposo)
Reprise Records
Arranged by Don Costa
Recorded: October 26, 1970

BEWITCHED
(Richard Rodgers-Lorenz Hart)
Film recording for: 'Pal Joey'
Columbia Pictures
Arranged by Nelson Riddle
Orchestra conducted by Morris Stoloff
Recorded: July 25, 1957

BEWITCHED
(Richard Rodgers-Lorenz Hart)
Capitol Records
Arranged by Nelson Riddle
Recorded: August 13, 1957

BEWITCHED
(Richard Rodgers-Lorenz Hart)
Reprise Records
Arranged by Nelson Riddle
Recorded: February 20, 1963

BEWITCHED
(Richard Rodgers-Lorenz Hart)
Capitol Records
With Patti LaBelle
Arranged and conducted by Patrick Williams
Recorded: May 17, 1994

BIM BAM BABY
(Sammy Mysels)
Columbia Records
Arranged by Axel Stordahl
Recorded: June 3, 1952

BLAME IT ON MY YOUTH
(Oscar Levant-Edward Heyman)
Capitol Records
With The Hollywood String Quartet
Arranged by Nelson Riddle
Recorded: April 4, 1956

BLUE HAWAII
(Leo Robin-Ralph Rainger)
Capitol Records
Arranged by Billy May
Recorded: October 8, 1957

BLUE LACE
(Riz Ortolani-Bill Jacob-Patti Jacob)
Reprise Records
Arranged by Nelson Riddle
Recorded: November 11, 1968

BLUE MOON
(Richard Rodgers-Lorenz Hart)
Capitol Records
Featuring Plas Johnson, tenor saxophone
Arranged by Nelson Riddle
Recorded: September 1, 1960

BLUE SKIES
(Irving Berlin)
Victor Records
With Tommy Dorsey and his Orchestra and band chorus
Arranged by Sy Oliver
Recorded: July 15, 1941

BLUE SKIES
(Irving Berlin)
With Tommy Dorsey and his Orchestra and Band Chorus
Film recording for: 'Ship Ahoy'
Metro-Goldwyn-Mayer
Arranged by Sy Oliver
Orchestra conducted by George Stoll
Recorded: December 18, 1941

BLUE SKIES
(Irving Berlin)
Columbia Records
Arranged by Axel Stordahl
Recorded: July 30, 1946

BLUES IN THE NIGHT
(Harold Arlen-Johnny Mercer)
Capitol Records
Arranged by Nelson Riddle
Recorded: June 24, 1958

BODY AND SOUL
(Edward Heyman-Robert Sour-Frank Eyton-Johnny Green)
Columbia Records
Featuring Bobby Hackett, cornet
Arranged by Axel Stordahl
Recorded: November 9, 1947

BONITA
(Antonio Carlos Jobim-Ray Gilbert)
Reprise Records
Arranged by Eumir Deodato
Orchestra conducted by Morris Stoloff
Recorded: February 12, 1969

BOP GOES MY HEART
(Walter Bishop-Jule Styne)
Columbia Records
With The Phil Moore Four
Arranged by Phil Moore
Recorded: December 15, 1948

BORN FREE
(Don Black-John Barry)
Reprise Records
Arranged by Gordon Jenkins
Recorded: July 24, 1967

BOTH SIDES NOW
(Joni Mitchell)
Reprise Records
Arranged by Don Costa
Orchestra conducted by Bill Miller
Recorded: November 14, 1968

BRAZIL
(Ary Barroso-Bob Russell)
Capitol Records
Arranged by Billy May
Recorded: October 8, 1957

BUT BEAUTIFUL
(Johnny Burke-Jimmy Van Heusen)
Columbia Records
Arranged by Axel Stordahl
Recorded: August 17, 1947

BUT NONE LIKE YOU
(Ray Noble)
Columbia Records
Arranged by Axel Stordahl
Recorded: December 26, 1947

BUT NOT FOR ME
(George Gershwin-Ira Gershwin)
Reprise Records
Arranged by Billy May
Recorded: September 18, 1979

BY THE TIME I GET TO PHOENIX
(Jimmy Webb)
Reprise Records
Arranged by Don Costa
Orchestra conducted by Bill Miller
Recorded: November 12, 1968

BYE BYE BABY
(Leo Robin-Jule Styne)
Columbia Records
With The Pastels
Arranged by George Siravo
Orchestra conducted by Hugo Winterhalter
Recorded: July 10, 1949

CALIFORNIA
(Sammy Cahn-Jimmy Van Heusen)
Reprise Records
With vocal chorus
Arranged by Nelson Riddle
Recorded: February 20, 1963

CALL ME
(Tony Hatch)
Reprise Records
Arranged by Nelson Riddle
Recorded: May 16, 1966

CALL ME IRRESPONSIBLE
(Sammy Cahn-Jimmy Van Heusen)
Reprise Records
Arranged by Nelson Riddle
Recorded: January 21, 1963

CAN I STEAL A LITTLE LOVE?
(Phil Tuminello)
Capitol Records
Arranged by Nelson Riddle
Recorded: December 3, 1956

CAN'T WE BE FRIENDS?
(Kay Swift-Paul James)
Capitol Records
Arranged by Nelson Riddle
Orchestra conducted by Bill Miller
Recorded: February 8, 1955

CAN'T YOU JUST SEE YOURSELF?
(Sammy Cahn-Jule Styne)
Columbia Records
Arranged by Dick Jones
Orchestra conducted by Axel Stordahl
Recorded: October 19, 1947

CASTLE ROCK
(Ervin Drake-Jimmy Shirl-Al Sears)
Columbia Records
With Harry James and his Orchestra
Arranged by Ray Conniff
Recorded: July 19, 1951

CATANA
(Alfred Newman-Eddie DeLange)
Columbia Records
Arranged by Axel Stordahl
Recorded: December 26, 1947

C'EST MAGNIFIQUE
(Cole Porter)
Capitol Records
Arranged by Nelson Riddle
Recorded: August 27, 1959

CHANGE PARTNERS
(Irving Berlin)
Reprise Records
With Antonio Carlos Jobim
Arranged by Claus Ogerman
Recorded: January 30, 1967

CHARMAINE
(Erno Rapee-Lew Pollack)
Reprise Records
Arranged by Gordon Jenkins
Recorded: January 15, 1962

CHATTANOOGIE SHOE SHINE BOY
(Harry Stone-Jack Stapp)
Columbia Records
With the Jeff Alexander Choir
Arranged by Axel Stordahl
Recorded: January 12, 1950

CHEEK TO CHEEK
(Irving Berlin)
Capitol Records
Arranged by Billy May
Recorded: December 22, 1958

CHERRY PIES OUGHT TO BE YOU
(Cole Porter)
Columbia Records
With Rosemary Clooney
Arranged by Axel Stordahl
Recorded: December 11, 1950

CHICAGO
(Sammy Cahn-Jimmy Van Heusen)
Capitol Records
Arranged by Nelson Riddle
Recorded: August 13, 1957

CHICAGO
(Sammy Cahn-Jimmy Van Heusen)
Reprise Records
With sextet accompaniment (Live recording)
Arranged by Neal Hefti and Billy May
Recorded: June 5, 1962 (Paris)

CHRISTMAS DREAMING
(Irving Gordon-Lester Lee)
Columbia Records
Arranged by Axel Stordahl
Recorded: June 26, 1947

CHRISTMAS DREAMING
(Irving Gordon-Lester Lee)
Columbia Records
Arranged by Axel Stordahl
Recorded: July 3, 1947

CHRISTMAS MEM'RIES
(Alan & Marilyn Bergman-Don Costa)
Reprise Records
With vocal chorus
Arranged by Don Costa
Conducted by Bill Miller
Recorded: October 24, 1975

CIRIBIRIBIN
(Rudolf Thaler-Alberto Pestalozza-Jack Lawrence-Harry James)
Columbia Records
With Harry James and his Orchestra
Arranged by Andy Gibson
Recorded: November 8, 1939

CLOSE TO YOU
(Al Hoffman-Jerry Livingston-Carl Lampl)
Columbia Records
With The Bobby Tucker Singers
Choral arrangement by Alec Wilder
Recorded: June 7, 1943

CLOSE TO YOU
(Al Hoffman-Jerry Livingston-Carl Lampl)
V-Disc recording
Columbia Records
With The Bobby Tucker Singers
Orchestral arrangement by Axel Stordahl
Recorded: December 26, 1943

CLOSE TO YOU
(Al Hoffman-Jerry Livingston-Carl Lampl)
With the Hollywood String Quartet
Capitol Records
Arranged by Nelson Riddle
Recorded: November 1, 1956

CLOSE TO YOU
(Burt Bacharach-Hal David)
Reprise Records
Arranged by Don Costa
Recorded: October 29, 1970

COME BACK TO ME
(Alan J. Lerner-Burton Lane)
Reprise Records
With Duke Ellington and his Orchestra
Arranged by Billy May
Recorded: December 11, 1967

COME BACK TO SORRENTO
(Ernesto DeCurtis-Claude Aveling)
Columbia Records
Arranged by Axel Stordahl
Recorded: October 9, 1950

COME BLOW YOUR HORN
(Sammy Cahn-Jimmy Van Heusen)
Film recording for: 'Come Blow Your Horn'
Paramount Pictures
Arranged by Nelson Riddle
Recorded: October 25, 1962

COME BLOW YOUR HORN
(Sammy Cahn-Jimmy Van Heusen)
Reprise Records
Arranged by Nelson Riddle
Recorded: January 21, 1963

COME DANCE WITH ME
(Sammy Cahn-Jimmy Van Heusen)
Capitol Records
Arranged by Billy May
Recorded: December 23, 1958

COME FLY WITH ME
(Sammy Cahn-Jimmy Van Heusen)
Capitol Records
Arranged by Billy May
Recorded: October 8, 1957

COME FLY WITH ME
(Sammy Cahn-Jimmy Van Heusen)
Reprise Records
With sextet accompaniment (Live recording)
Arranged by Neal Hefti and Billy May
Recorded: June 5, 1962 (Paris)

COME FLY WITH ME
(Sammy Cahn-Jimmy Van Heusen)
Reprise Records
Arranged by Billy May
Orchestra conducted by Sonny Burke
Recorded: October 11, 1965

COME FLY WITH ME
(Sammy Cahn-Jimmy Van Heusen)
Reprise Records
With Count Basie and his Orchestra (Live recording)
Arranged by Quincy Jones and Billy Byers
Recorded: January 26-February 1, 1966 (Las Vegas)

COME FLY WITH ME
(Sammy Cahn-Jimmy Van Heusen)
Capitol Records
With Luis Miguel
Arranged by Billy May
Orchestra conducted by Patrick Williams
Recorded: July 1, 1993

COME OUT, COME OUT, WHEREVER YOU ARE
(Sammy Cahn-Jule Styne)
Film recording for: 'Step Lively'
RKO Pictures
Arranged by Axel Stordahl
Orchestra conducted by Constantin Bakaleinikoff
Recorded: January 31, 1944

COME OUT, COME OUT WHEREVER YOU ARE
(Sammy Cahn-Jule Styne)
V-Disc recording
Columbia Records
Arranged by Axel Stordahl
Recorded: May 17, 1944

COME RAIN OR COME SHINE
(Harold Arlen-Johnny Mercer)
V-Disc recording
Columbia Records
Arranged by Axel Stordahl
Recorded: June 5, 1946

COME RAIN OR COME SHINE
(Harold Arlen-Johnny Mercer)
Reprise Records
Arranged by Don Costa
Recorded: November 22, 1961

COME RAIN OR COME SHINE
(Harold Arlen-Johnny Mercer)
Capitol Records
With Gloria Estefan
Arranged by Don Costa
Orchestra conducted by Patrick Williams
Recorded: July 1, 1993

COME UP TO MY PLACE
(Leonard Bernstein-Betty Comden-Adolph Green)
Film recording for: 'On the Town'
Metro-Goldwyn-Mayer
With Betty Garrett
Arranged by Saul Chaplin
Orchestra conducted by Lennie Hayton
Recorded: March 3, 1949

COME WALTZ WITH ME
(Sammy Cahn-Jimmy Van Heusen)
Reprise Records
Arranged by Gordon Jenkins
Recorded: January 17, 1962

COMME CI COMME CA
(Alex Kramer-Joan Whitney-Pierre Duden-Bruno Coquatrix)
Columbia Records
Arranged by Axel Stordahl
Recorded: December 12, 1948

COULD 'JA?
(Carl Fischer-Bill Carey)
Columbia Records
With The Pied Pipers
Arranged by Axel Stordahl
Recorded: May 28, 1946

COUNT ON ME
(Roger Edens-Betty Comden-Adolph Green)
Film recording for: 'On The Town'
Metro-Goldwyn-Mayer
With Jules Munshin, Ann Miller, Betty Garrett, Alice Pearce and Chorus
Arranged by Saul Chaplin
Orchestra conducted by Lennie Hayton
Recorded: March 24, 1949

CRADLE SONG *(Brahms' Lullaby)*
(Johannes Brahms)
Film recording for: 'Anchor's Aweigh'
Metro-Goldwyn-Mayer
Arranged by Axel Stordahl
Orchestra conducted by George Stoll
Recorded: June 6, 1944

CRADLE SONG *(Brahms' Lullaby)*
(Johannes Brahms)
V-Disc recording
Columbia Records
Arranged and conducted by Axel Stordahl
Recorded: July 8, 1944

CRADLE SONG *(Brahms' Lullaby)*
(Johannes Brahms)
V-Disc recording
Columbia Records
Arranged by Raymond Paige
Recorded: October 23, 1944

CRADLE SONG *(Brahms' Lullaby)*
(Johannes Brahms)
Columbia Records
Arranged by Axel Stordahl
Recorded: December 3, 1944

CRAZY LOVE
(Sammy Cahn-Phil Tuminello)
Capitol Records
Arranged by Nelson Riddle
Recorded: March 14, 1957

CYCLES
(Gayle Caldwell)
Reprise Records
With vocal chorus
Arranged by Don Costa
Recorded: July 24,1968

DANCING IN THE DARK
(Arthur Schwartz-Howard Dietz)
Capitol Records
Arranged by Billy May
Recorded: December 22, 1958

DANCING ON THE CEILING
(Richard Rodgers-Lorenz Hart)
Capitol Records
Arranged by Nelson Riddle
Conducted by Bill Miller
Recorded: February 8, 1955

DAY BY DAY
(Sammy Cahn-Axel Stordahl-Paul Weston)
Columbia Records
Arranged by Axel Stordahl
Recorded: August 22, 1945

DAY BY DAY
(Sammy Cahn-Axel Stordahl-Paul Weston)
Capitol Records
Arranged by Billy May
Recorded: March 20, 1961

DAY IN, DAY OUT
(Rube Bloom-Johnny Mercer)
Capitol Records
Arranged by Axel Stordahl
Recorded: April 2, 1953

DAY IN, DAY OUT
(Rube Bloom-Johnny Mercer)
Capitol Records
Arranged by Nelson Riddle
Recorded: March 1, 1954

DAY IN, DAY OUT
(Rube Bloom-Johnny Mercer)
Capitol Records
Arranged by Billy May
Recorded: December 22, 1958

DAY IN, DAY OUT
(Rube Bloom-Johnny Mercer)
Reprise Records
With sextet accompaniment (Live recording)
Arranged by Neal Hefti and Billy May
Recorded: June 5, 1962 (Paris)

DAYBREAK
(Harold Adamson-Ferde Grofe)
Victor Records
With Tommy Dorsey and his Orchestra
Arranged by Axel Stordahl
Recorded: July 1, 1942

DAYBREAK
(Harold Adamson-Ferde Grofe)
Reprise Records
Arranged by Sy Oliver
Recorded: May 2, 1961

DAYS OF WINE AND ROSES
(Henry Mancini-Johnny Mercer)
Reprise Records
Arranged by Nelson Riddle
Recorded: January 28, 1964

DEAR HEART
(Henry Mancini-Jay Livingstone-Ray Evans)
Reprise Records
With vocal chorus
Arranged by Nelson Riddle
Recorded: October 3, 1964

DEAR LITTLE BOY OF MINE
(Ernest R. Ball-J. Kiern Brennan)
Columbia Records
With The Mitch Miller Singers
Arranged by Mitch Miller
Recorded: June 28, 1950

DEEP IN A DREAM
(Jimmy Van Heusen-Eddie DeLange)
Capitol Records
Arranged by Nelson Riddle
Recorded: March 4, 1955

DEEP NIGHT
(Rudy Vallee-Charles E. Henderson)
Columbia Records
With Harry James and his Orchestra
Arranged by Ray Conniff
Recorded: July 19, 1951

DESAFINADO *(Off-Key)*
(Jon Hendricks-Antonio Carlos Jobim-N. Mendonca)
Reprise Records
Arranged by Eumir Deodato
Recorded: February 12, 1969

DEVIL MAY CARE
(Johnny Burke-Harry Warren)
Victor Records
With Tommy Dorsey and his Orchestra
Recorded: March 29, 1940

DIDN'T WE?
(Jim Webb)
Reprise Records
Arranged by Don Costa
Recorded: February 18, 1969

DIG DOWN DEEP
(Hirsh-Marks-Sano Marco)
Victor Records
With Tommy Dorsey and his Orchestra
Featuring The Pied Pipers
Arranged by Axel Stordahl
Recorded: June 17, 1942

DICK HAYMES, DICK TODD AND COMO
(Parody of "Sunday, Monday or Always")
(J. Burke-J. Van Heusen-S. Cahn)
V-Disc recording
Columbia Records
Arranged by Axel Stordahl
Orchestra conducted by Raymond Paige
Recorded: October 23, 1944

DINDI
(Antonio Carlos Jobim-Ray Gilbert)
Reprise Records
With Antonio Carlos Jobim
Arranged by Claus Ogerman
Recorded: January 30, 1967

DO I WORRY?
(Bobby Worth-Stanley Cowan)
Victor Records
With Tommy Dorsey and his Orchestra
Featuring The Pied Pipers
Arranged by Axel Stordahl
Recorded: February 7, 1941

DO YOU KNOW WHY?
(Johnny Burke-Jimmy Van Heusen)

Victor Records
With Tommy Dorsey and his Orchestra
Arranged by Deane Kincaide
Recorded: October 16, 1940

DOLORES
(Frank Loesser-Louis Alter)
Victor Records
With Tommy Dorsey and his Orchestra
Featuring The Pied Pipers
Arranged by Sy Oliver
Recorded: January 20, 1941

DON'CHA GO 'WAY MAD
(Jimmy Mundy-Al Stillman-Illinois Jacquet)
Reprise Records
Arranged by Neal Hefti
Recorded: April 11, 1962

DON'T BE A DO-BADDER *(Finale)*
(Sammy Cahn-Jimmy Van Heusen)
Film recording for: 'Robin and the 7 Hoods'
Warner Bros.
With Dean Martin and Sammy Davis Jr.
Arranged by Nelson Riddle
Recorded: October 18, 1963

DON'T BE A DO-BADDER
(Sammy Cahn-Jimmy Van Heusen)
Reprise Records
With Bing Crosby, Dean Martin, Sammy Davis Jr. and Chorus
Arranged by Nelson Riddle
Recorded: April 10, 1964

DON'T BE THAT WAY
(Benny Goodman-Edgar Sampson-Mitchell Parish)
Reprise Records
Arranged by Billy May
Recorded: May 19, 1961

DON'T CHANGE YOUR MIND ABOUT ME
(Adelson-Carpenter)
Capitol Records
With June Hutton and the Pied Pipers
Arranged by Nelson Riddle
Recorded: September 23, 1954

DON'T CRY JOE
(Joe Marsala)
Columbia Records
With The Pastels
Arranged by Sy Oliver
Orchestra conducted by Hugo Winterhalter
Recorded: July 10, 1949

DON'T CRY JOE
(Joe Marsala)
Reprise Records
Arranged by Billy May
Recorded: May 23, 1961

DON'T EVER BE AFRAID TO GO HOME
(Bob Hilliard-Carl Sigman)
Columbia Records
Probably arranged by George Siravo
Orchestra conducted by Axel Stordahl
Recorded: February 6, 1952

DON'T EVER GO AWAY
(Ray Gilbert-Duran-Antonio Carlos Jobim)
Reprise Records
With Antonio Carlos Jobim
Arranged by Eumir Deodato
Orchestra conducted by Morris Stoloff
Recorded: February 11, 1969

DON'T FORGET TONIGHT TOMOR-ROW
(Jay Milton-Ukie Sherin)
Columbia Records
With The Charioteers
Arranged by Axel Stordahl
Recorded: May 16, 1945

DON'T FORGET TONIGHT TOMOR-ROW
(Jay Milton-Ukie Sherin)
V-Disc recording
Columbia Records
With The Pied Pipers
Arranged by Axel Stordahl
Recorded: October 31, 1945

DON'T LIKE GOODBYES
(Harold Arlen-Truman Capote)
Capitol Records
With The Hollywood String Quartet
Arranged by Nelson Riddle
Recorded: March 8, 1956

DON'T MAKE A BEGGAR OF ME
(Al Sherman-Harry Goodman)
Capitol Records
Arranged by Axel Stordahl
Recorded: April 2, 1953

DON'T SLEEP IN THE SUBWAY
(Jackie Trent-Tony Hatch)
Reprise Records
With vocal chorus
Arranged by Ernie Freeman
Recorded: July 24, 1967

DON'T TAKE YOUR LOVE FROM ME
(Henry Nemo)
Capitol Records
Arranged by Heinie Beau
Orchestra conducted by Billy May
Recorded: March 20, 1961

DON'T TAKE YOUR LOVE FROM ME
(Henry Nemo)
Reprise Records
Arranged by Don Costa
Recorded: November 21, 1961

DON'T WAIT TOO LONG
(Sunny Skylar)
Reprise Records
Arranged by Gordon Jenkins
Recorded: April 13, 1965

DON'T WORRY 'BOUT ME
(Ted Koehler-Rube Bloom)
Capitol Records
Arranged by Nelson Riddle
Recorded: April 30, 1953

DON'T WORRY 'BOUT ME
(Ted Koehler-Rube Bloom)
Reprise Records
With Count Basie and his Orchestra
(Live recording)
Arranged by Quincy Jones and Billy Byers
Recorded: January 26-February 1, 1966
(Las Vegas)

DOWNTOWN
(Tony Hatch)
Reprise Records
Arranged by Nelson Riddle
Recorded: May 16, 1966

DREAM
(Johnny Mercer)
Columbia Records
With The Ken Lane Singers
Arranged by Axel Stordahl
Recorded: March 6, 1945

DREAM
(Johnny Mercer)
Capitol Records
Arranged by Nelson Riddle
Recorded: March 3, 1960

DREAM AWAY
(P. Williams-J. Williams)
Reprise Records
Arranged by Don Costa
Orchestra conducted by Gordon Jenkins
Recorded: August 20, 1973

DRINKING AGAIN
(Johnny Mercer-Doris Tauber)
Reprise Records
Arranged by Claus Ogerman
Recorded: February 1, 1967

DRINKING WATER *(Aqua De Beber)*
(Antonio Carlos Jobim-Gene Lees-Vinicius DeMoraes)
With Antonio Carlos Jobim
Reprise Records
Arranged by Eumir Deodato
Orchestra conducted by Morris Stoloff
Recorded: February 12, 1969

DRY YOUR EYES
(Neil Diamond-J.R. Robertson)
Reprise Records
With vocal chorus
Arranged by Don Costa
Orchestra conducted by Bill Miller
Recorded: September 27, 1976

EARLY AMERICAN
(Johnny Burke-Jimmy Van Heusen)
Reprise Records
With Fred Waring and his Pennsylvanians
Arranged by Nelson Riddle
Orchestra conducted by Fred Waring
Recorded: January 2, 1964

EAST OF THE SUN *(And West of the Moon)*
(Brooks Bowman)
With the Dorsey Sentimentalists and Band Chorus
Victor Records
Arranged by Sy Oliver
Recorded: April 23, 1940

EAST OF THE SUN *(And West of the Moon)*
(Brooks Bowman)
Reprise Records
Arranged by Sy Oliver
Recorded: May 3, 1961

EBB TIDE
(Robert Maxwell-Carl Sigman)
Capitol Records
Arranged by Nelson Riddle
Orchestra conducted by Felix Slatkin
Recorded: May 29, 1958

ELIZABETH
(Bob Gaudio-Jake Holmes)
Reprise Records
Arranged by Charles Calello
Recorded: October 31, 1969

EMBRACEABLE YOU
(George Gershwin-Ira Gershwin)
Columbia Records
Arranged by Axel Stordahl
Recorded: December 19, 1944

EMBRACEABLE YOU
(George Gershwin-Ira Gershwin)
Special film recording for: 'Lucky Strike' Promo Film
American Tobacco Company
With the Lucky Strike Quartet and The Hit Parade Orchestra
Recorded: July 27, 1947

EMBRACEABLE YOU
(George Gershwin-Ira Gershwin)
Capitol Records
Arranged by Nelson Riddle
Recorded: March 3, 1960

EMBRACEABLE YOU
(George Gershwin-Ira Gershwin)
Capitol Records
With Lena Horne
Arranged by Nelson Riddle
Orchestra conducted by Patrick Williams
Recorded: October 15, 1993

EMILY
(Johnny Mandel-Johnny Mercer)
Reprise Records
With vocal chorus
Arranged by Nelson Riddle
Recorded: October 3, 1964

EMILY
(Johnny Mandel-Johnny Mercer)
Reprise Records
Arranged by Nelson Riddle
Recorded: March 9, 1977

EMPTY IS
(Rod Mc Kuen)
Reprise Records
Arranged by Don Costa
Recorded: March 19, 1969

EMPTY IS *(Spoken Introduction)*
(Rod McKuen)
Reprise Records
Arranged by Don Costa
Recorded: March 21, 1969

EMPTY TABLES
(Johnny Mercer-Jimmy Van Heusen)
Reprise Records
Arranged by Gordon Jenkins
Recorded: June 22, 1973

EMPTY TABLES
(Johnny Mercer-Jimmy Van Heusen)
Reprise Records
Featuring Bill Miller, Piano
Solo piano arrangement by Bill Miller
Recorded: February 5, 1976

EVER HOMEWARD *(a cappella)*
(Sammy Cahn-Jule Styne)
Film recording for: 'The Miracle of the Bells'
RKO Pictures
Recorded: August 19-20, 1947

EVER HOMEWARD
(Sammy Cahn-Jule Styne)
Columbia Records
Arranged by Axel Stordahl
Recorded: December 8, 1947

EVERY DAY OF MY LIFE
(Morty Beck-Billy Hays-Harry James)
Columbia Records
With Harry James and his Orchestra
Arranged by Andy Gibson
Recorded: November 8, 1939

EVERY MAN SHOULD MARRY
(Benny Davis-Abner Silver)
Columbia Records
Arranged by Hugo Winterhalter
Recorded: July 14, 1949

EVERY MAN SHOULD MARRY
(Benny Davis-Abner Silver)
Columbia Records
Arranged by Morris Stoloff
Recorded: July 21, 1949

EV'RYBODY HAS THE RIGHT TO BE WRONG
(At Least Once)
(Sammy Cahn-Jimmy Van Heusen)
Reprise Records
Arranged by Torrie Zito
Recorded: August 23, 1965

EVERYBODY LOVES SOMEBODY
(Irving Taylor-Ken Lane)
Columbia Records
Arranged by Axel Stordahl
Recorded: December 4, 1947

EVERYBODY LOVES SOMEBODY
(Irving Taylor-Ken Lane)
Capitol Records
Arranged by Nelson Riddle
Recorded: November 25, 1957

EVERYBODY OUGHT TO BE IN LOVE
(Paul Anka)
Reprise Records
With vocal chorus
Arranged by Charles Calello
Recorded: February 16, 1977

EVERYBODY'S TWISTIN'
(Ted Koehler-Rube Bloom)
Reprise Records
Arranged by Neal Hefti
Recorded: February 27, 1962

EVERYTHING HAPPENS TO ME
(Tom Adair-Matt Dennis)
Victor Records

With Tommy Dorsey and his Orchestra
Arranged by Axel Stordahl
Recorded: February 7, 1941
EVERYTHING HAPPENS TO ME
(Tom Adair-Matt Dennis)
With the Hollywood String Quartet
Capitol Records
Arranged by Nelson Riddle
Recorded: April 4, 1956
EVERYTHING HAPPENS TO ME
(Tom Adair-Matt Dennis)
Reprise Records
Arranged by Gordon Jenkins
Recorded: September 24, 1974
EVERYTHING HAPPENS TO ME
(Tom Adair-Matt Dennis)
Reprise Records
Arranged by Gordon Jenkins
Recorded: April 8, 1981
FAIRY TALE
(Jay Livingstone-Dok Stanford)
Capitol Records
Arranged by Nelson Riddle
Recorded: July 29, 1955
FAITHFUL
(Jimmy Kennedy-Harry Stone)
Columbia Records
With The Skylarks
Arranged by Axel Stordahl
Recorded: January 16, 1951
FALLING IN LOVE WITH LOVE
(Richard Rodgers-Lorenz Hart)
V-Disc recording
Columbia Records
Arranged and conducted by Axel Stordahl
Recorded: July 8, 1944
FALLING IN LOVE WITH LOVE
(Richard Rodgers-Lorenz Hart)
Columbia Records
Arranged by Axel Stordahl
Recorded: August 8, 1946
FALLING IN LOVE WITH LOVE
(Richard Rodgers-Lorenz Hart)
Reprise Records
Arranged by Billy May
Recorded: May 19, 1961
FAREWELL, AMANDA
(Cole Porter)
Special film recording for: 'Adam's Rib'
Metro-Goldwyn-Mayer
Arranged by Axel Stordahl
Orchestra conducted by Johnny Green
Recorded: August 8, 1949
FAREWELL, FAREWELL TO LOVE
(D. Wolf-George Siravo)
Columbia Records
With Harry James and his Orchestra
Arranged by George Siravo
Recorded: July 19, 1951
FEELIN' KINDA SUNDAY
(Kathy Wakefield-Annette Tucker-Nino Tempo)
Reprise Records
With Nancy Sinatra and vocal chorus
Arranged by Don Costa
Recorded: November 2, 1970
FEET OF CLAY
(Bob Hilliard-Carl Sigman)
Columbia Records
Arranged by Axel Stordahl
Recorded: February 6, 1952
FIVE HUNDRED GUYS
(Canteen-Kosleff)
Capitol Records
With vocal chorus
Arranged by Nelson Riddle
Recorded: April 9, 1956
FIVE MINUTES MORE
(Sammy Cahn-Jule Styne)
Columbia Records
Arranged by George Siravo
Orchestra conducted by Axel Stordahl
Recorded: May 28, 1946
FIVE MINUTES MORE
(Sammy Cahn-Jule Styne)
Capitol Records
Arranged by Billy May
Recorded: March 22, 1961
FLOWERS MEAN FORGIVENESS
(White-Frisch-Wolfson)
Capitol Records
With vocal chorus
Arranged by Nelson Riddle
Recorded: January 12, 1956
FLY ME TO THE MOON
(Bart Howard)
Reprise Records
With Count Basie and Hhs Orchestra
Arranged by Quincy Jones
Recorded: June 9, 1964
FLY ME TO THE MOON
(Bart Howard)
Reprise Records
With Count Basie and his Orchestra (Live recording)
Arranged by Quincy Jones
Recorded: January 26-February 1, 1966 (Las Vegas)
FLY ME TO THE MOON
(Bart Howard)
Capitol Records
With Antonio Carlos Jobim
Arranged by Quincy Jones and Patrick Williams
Orchestra conducted by Patrick Williams
Recorded: October 12, 1993
FOLLOW ME
(Alan J. Lerner-Frederick Lowe)
Reprise Records
With Duke Ellington and his Orchestra
Arranged by Billy May
Recorded: December 12, 1967
FOOLS RUSH IN
(Johnny Mercer-Rube Bloom)
Victor Records
With Tommy Dorsey and his Orchestra
Arranged by Axel Stordahl
Recorded: March 29, 1940
FOOLS RUSH IN
(Johnny Mercer-Rube Bloom)
Columbia Records
Arranged by Axel Stordahl
Recorded: October 31, 1947
FOOLS RUSH IN
(Johnny Mercer-Rube Bloom)
Capitol Records
Arranged by Nelson Riddle
Recorded: March 1, 1960
FOR A WHILE
(Bob Gaudio-Jake Holmes)
Reprise Records
Arranged by Charles Calello
Recorded: October 31, 1969
FOR EVERY MAN THERE'S A WOMAN
(Leo Robin-Harold Arlen)
Columbia Records
Arranged by Axel Stordahl
Recorded: December 28, 1947
FOR ONCE IN MY LIFE
(Ronald Miller-Orlando Murden)
Reprise Records
Arranged by Don Costa
Recorded: February 24, 1969
FOR ONCE IN MY LIFE
(Ronald Miller-Orlando Murden)
Capitol Records
With Gladys Knight and Stevie Wonder
Arranged by Don Costa
Orchestra conducted by Patrick Williams
Recorded: October 12, 1993
FOR THE GOOD TIMES
(Kris Kristofferson)
Reprise Records
With Eileen Farrell
Arranged by Don Costa
Recorded: August 21, 1979
FORGET DOMANI
(Riz Ortolani-Norman Newell)
Reprise Records
Arranged by Ernie Freeman
Recorded: May 6, 1965
FORGET TO REMEMBER
(Teddy Rondazzo-Vincent Pike)
Reprise Records
Arranged by Don Costa
Recorded: August 18, 1969
FREE FOR ALL
(Matt Dennis-Tom Adair)
Victor Records
With Tommy Dorsey and his Orchestra featuring The Pied Pipers
Arranged by Sy Oliver
Recorded: June 27, 1941
FRENCH FOREIGN LEGION
(Aaron Schroeder-Guy Wood)
Capitol Records
Arranged by Nelson Riddle
Recorded: December 29, 1958
FROM HERE TO ETERNITY
(Freddie Karger-Robert Wells)
Capitol Records
Arranged by Nelson Riddle
Recorded: May 2, 1953
FROM PROMISE TO PROMISE
(Rod McKuen)
Reprise Records
Arranged by Don Costa
Recorded: March 21, 1969
FROM THE BOTTOM OF MY HEART
(Billy Hays-Andy Gibson)
Columbia Records
With Harry James and his Orchestra
Arranged by Andy Gibson
Recorded: July 13, 1939
FROM THE BOTTOM TO THE TOP
(Gene Wilson)
Capitol Records
With The Nuggets
Arranged by Dave Cavanaugh
Recorded: March 7, 1955
FROM THIS DAY FORWARD
(Eddie Greene-Leigh Harline)
Columbia Records
Arranged by Axel Stordahl
Recorded: February 24, 1946
FROM THIS MOMENT ON
(Cole Porter)
Capitol Records
Arranged by Nelson Riddle
Recorded: November 28, 1956
FUGUE FOR TINHORNS
(Frank Loesser)
Reprise Records
With Bing Crosby and Dean Martin
Arranged by Bill Loose
Orchestra conducted by Morris Stoloff
Recorded: July 29, 1963
FULL MOON AND EMPTY ARMS
(B. Kaye-T. Mossman)
Columbia Records
Arranged by Axel Stordahl
Recorded: November 19, 1945
FULL MOON AND EMPTY ARMS
(B. Kaye-T. Mossman)
Columbia Records
Arranged by Axel Stordahl
Recorded: November 30, 1945
GENTLE ON MY MIND
(John Hartford)
Reprise Records
Arranged by Don Costa
Orchestra conducted by Bill Miller
Recorded: November 12, 1968
GET HAPPY
(Harold Arlen-Ted Koehler)
Capitol Records
Arranged by Nelson Riddle
Recorded: April 19, 1954
GET ME TO THE CHURCH ON TIME
(Frederick Lowe-Alan J. Lerner)
Reprise Records
With Count Basie and his Orchestra (Live recording)
Arranged by Quincy Jones and Billy Byers
Recorded: January 26-February 1, 1966 (Las Vegas)
GIVE HER LOVE
(Jim Harbert)
Reprise Records
With vocal chorus
Arranged by Ernie Freeman
Recorded: November 17, 1966
GLAD TO BE UNHAPPY
(Richard Rodgers-Lorenz Hart)
Capitol Records
Arranged by Nelson Riddle
Conducted by Bill Miller
Recorded: February 8, 1955
GO TELL IT ON THE MOUNTAIN
(Traditional)
Reprise Records
With Bing Crosby and Fred Waring and his Pennsylvanians
Arranged by Jack Halloran
Orchestra Conducted by Fred Waring
Recorded: June 19, 1964
GOD'S COUNTRY
(Beasley Smith-Haven Gillespie)
Columbia Records
With the Jeff Alexander Choir
Arranged by Axel Stordahl
Recorded: January 12, 1950
GOIN' OUT OF MY HEAD
(Teddy Randazzo-Bobby Weinstein)
Reprise Records
Arranged by Don Costa
Recorded: August 18, 1969
GOLDEN MOMENT
(Kenneth Jacobson-Rhoda Roberts)
Reprise Records
Arranged by Nelson Riddle
Recorded: August 23, 1965
GONE WITH THE WIND
(Allie Wrubel-Herb Magidson)
Capitol Records
Arranged by Nelson Riddle
Recorded: June 24, 1958
GOOD THING GOING
(Stephen Sondheim)
Reprise Records
Arranged Don Costa
Recorded: August 19, 1981
GOODBYE
(Gordon Jenkins)
Capitol Records
Arranged by Nelson Riddle
Recorded: June 26, 1958
GOODBYE LOVER, GOODBYE
(Unknown)
Victor Records
With Tommy Dorsey and his Orchestra
Recorded: March 20, 1941 (Radio aircheck)
GOODBYE *(She Quietly Says)*
(Bob Gaudio-Jake Holmes)
Reprise Records
Arranged by Joseph Scott
Recorded: August 27, 1969
GOODNIGHT IRENE
(John Lomax-Huddy Ledbetter)
Columbia Records
With The Mitch Miller Singers
Arranged by Mitch Miller
Recorded: June 28, 1950
GOODY, GOODY
(Johnny Mercer-Matty Malneck)
Reprise Records
Arranged by Neal Hefti
Recorded: April 11, 1962
GOODY, GOODY
(Johnny Mercer-Matty Malneck)
Reprise Records
With sextet accompaniment (Live recording)
Arranged by Neal Hefti and Billy May
Recorded: June 5, 1962 (Paris)
GRANADA
(Augustin Lara-Dorothy Dodd)
Reprise Records
Arranged by Billy May
Recorded: May 23, 1961
GUESS I'LL HANG MY TEARS OUT TO DRY
(Sammy Cahn-Jule Styne)
Columbia Records
Arranged by Axel Stordahl
Recorded: July 30, 1946
GUESS I'LL HANG MY TEARS OUT TO DRY
(Sammy Cahn-Jule Styne)
Capitol Records
Featuring Al Viola, guitar
Arranged by Nelson Riddle
Orchestra conducted by Felix Slatkin
Recorded: May 29, 1958
GUESS I'LL HANG MY TEARS OUT TO DRY
(Sammy Cahn-Jule Styne)
Capitol Records
With Carly Simon
Arranged by Nelson Riddle
Orchestra conducted by Patrick Williams
Recorded: July 9, 1993
GUYS AND DOLLS
(Frank Loesser)
Film recording for: 'Guys and Dolls'
Samuel Goldwyn Productions
With Stubby Kaye and Johnny Silver
Arranged by Nelson Riddle
Orchestra conducted by Jay Blackton
Recorded: March 1, 1955
GUYS AND DOLLS
(Frank Loesser)
Reprise Records
With Dean Martin
Arranged by Bill Loose
Orchestra conducted by Morris Stoloff
Recorded: July 18, 1963
GUYS AND DOLLS *(Reprise)*
(Frank Loesser)
Reprise Records
With Dean MArtin
Arranged by Bill Loose
Orchestra conducted by Morris Stoloff
Recorded: July 25, 1963
HALF AS LOVELY (Twice As True)
(Lew Spence-Sammy Gallop)
Capitol Records
Arranged by Nelson Riddle
Recorded: May 13, 1954
HALFWAY DOWN THE STREET
(K. Gannon-G. Wood)
Victor Records
With Tommy Dorsey and his Orchestra
Recorded: July 20, 1940 (Radio aircheck)
HALLELUJAH, I LOVE HER SO
(Ray Charles)
Reprise Records
Arranged by Don Costa
Recorded: February 24, 1969
HARK! THE HERALD ANGELS SING
(Felix Mendelssohn)
Capitol Records
With the Ralph Brewster Singers
Arranged by Gordon Jenkins
Recorded: July 10, 1957
HAVE YOU MET MISS JONES?
(Richard Rodgers-Lorenz Hart)
Reprise Records
Arranged by Billy May
Recorded: May 18, 1961
HAVE YOURSELF A MERRY LITTLE CHRISTMAS
(Hugh Martin-Ralph Blane)
Columbia Records
Arranged by Axel Stordahl
Recorded: June 26, 1947
HAVE YOURSELF A MERRY LITTLE CHRISTMAS
(Hugh Martin-Ralph Blane)
Columbia Records
Arranged by Axel Stordahl
Recorded: July 3, 1947
HAVE YOURSELF A MERRY LITTLE CHRISTMAS
(Hugh Martin-Ralph Blane)
Capitol Records
With The Ralph Brewster Singers
Arranged by Gordon Jenkins
Recorded: July 16, 1957
HAVE YOURSELF A MERRY LITTLE CHRISTMAS
(Hugh Martin-Ralph Blane)
Special film recording for: 'The Victors'
Columbia Pictures
With vocal chorus
Arranged by Gil Grau
Orchestra conducted by Gus Levene
Recorded: July 16, 1963
HAVE YOURSELF A MERRY LITTLE CHRISTMAS
(Hugh Martin-Ralph Blane)
Reprise Records
Arranged by Gil Grau
Orchestra conducted by Gus Levene
Recorded: October 13, 1963
HEAD ON MY PILLOW
(Bissel Palmer-Fred Norman)
Victor Records
With The Dorsey Sentimentalists
Arranged by Axel Stordahl
Recorded: April 23, 1940
HEAR MY SONG VIOLETTA
(O. Klose-R. Luckesch-B. Bernier-B. Emmerich)
Victor Records
With Tommy Dorsey and his Orchestra
Arranged by Sy Oliver
Recorded: March 29, 1940
HELLO DOLLY
(Jerry Herman)
Reprise Records
With Count Basie and his Orchestra
Arranged by Quincy Jones
Recorded: June 10, 1964
HELLO YOUNG LOVERS
(Richard Rodgers-Oscar Hammerstein II)
Columbia Records
Arranged by Axel Stordahl
Recorded: March 2, 1951
HELLO YOUNG LOVERS
(Richard Rodgers-Oscar Hammerstein)
Reprise Records
Arranged by Gordon Jenkins
Recorded: April 13, 1965
HELP YOURSELF TO MY HEART
(Sammy Kaye-Sammy Timberg)
Columbia Records
Arranged by Axel Stordahl
Recorded: December 28, 1947
HERE COMES THE NIGHT
(Frank Loesser-H. Edelstein-C. Hohengarten)
Columbia Records
With Harry James and his Orchestra
Arranged by Andy Gibson
Recorded: August 31, 1939
HERE GOES
(Unknown)
Capitol Records
Arranged by Billy May
Recorded: March 3, 1958
HERE'S THAT RAINY DAY
(Johnny Burke-Jimmy Van Heusen)
Capitol Records
Arranged by Gordon Jenkins
Recorded: March 25, 1959
HERE'S TO THE BAND
(Artie Schroek-Alfred Nittoli)
Reprise Records
Arranged by Joe Parnello
Recorded: January 25, 1983
HERE'S TO THE LOSERS
(Bob Wells-Segal)
Reprise Records
Arranged by Marty Paich
Recorded: July 31, 1963
HEY JEALOUS LOVER
(Sammy Cahn-Bee Walker-Kay Twomey)
Capitol Records
With vocal chorus
Arranged by Nelson Riddle
Recorded: April 9, 1956
HEY LOOK, NO CRYING
(Jule Styne-Susan Birkenhead)
Reprise Records
Arranged by Gordon Jenkins
Recorded: September 10, 1981
HIDDEN PERSUASION
(Churchill)
Capitol Records
Arranged by Nelson Riddle

Recorded: August 31, 1960
HIGH HOPES *(And Finale)*
(Sammy Cahn-Jimmy Van Heusen)
Film recording for: 'A Hole in the Head'
United Artists
With Eddie Hodges
Arranged and conducted by Nelson Riddle
Recorded: February 12-13, 1959
HIGH HOPES
(Sammy Cahn-Jimmy Van Heusen)
Capitol Records
With Eddie Hodges and children's chorus
Arranged by Nelson Riddle
Recorded: May 8, 1959
HOME ON THE RANGE
(Traditional)
Columbia Records
Arranged by Axel Stordahl
Recorded: March 10, 1946
HOMESICK, THAT'S ALL
(Gordon Jenkins)
Columbia Records
Arranged by Axel Stordahl
Recorded: March 6, 1945
HOMESICK, THAT'S ALL
(Gordon Jenkins)
V-Disc recording
Columbia Records
Arranged by Axel Stordahl
Recorded: September 26, 1945
HOW ABOUT YOU?
(Ralph Freed-Burton Lane)
Victor Records
With Tommy Dorsey and his Orchestra
Arranged by Paul Weston
Recorded: December 22, 1941
HOW ABOUT YOU?
(Ralph Freed-Burton Lane)
Capitol Records
Arranged by Nelson Riddle
Recorded: January 10, 1956
HOW AM I TO KNOW?
(D. Parker-J. King)
Victor Records
With Tommy Dorsey and his Orchestra and band chorus
Recorded: November 28, 1940 (Radio aircheck)
HOW ARE YA FIXED FOR LOVE?
(Sammy Cahn-Jimmy Van Heusen)
Capitol Records
With Keely Smith
Arranged by Billy May
Recorded: March 3, 1958
HOW COULD YOU DO A THING LIKE THAT TO ME?
(Alan Roberts-Tyree Glen)
Capitol Records
Arranged by Nelson Riddle
Recorded: March 7, 1955
HOW CUTE CAN YOU BE?
(Carl Fischer-Bill Carey)
Columbia Records
Arranged by Axel Stordahl
Recorded: February 3, 1946
HOW DEEP IS THE OCEAN?
(Irving Berlin)
Columbia Records
Arranged by Axel Stordahl
Recorded: March 10, 1946
HOW DEEP IS THE OCEAN?
(Irving Berlin)
Film recording for: 'Meet Danny Wilson'
Universal International
Arranged by Joseph Gershenson
Recorded: June 13, 1951
HOW DEEP IS THE OCEAN?
(Irving Berlin)
Capitol Records
Arranged by Nelson Riddle
Recorded: March 3, 1960
HOW DO YOU DO WITHOUT ME?
(Joe Bushkin-John DeVries)
Victor Records
With Tommy Dorsey and his Orchestra
Arranged by Paul Weston
Recorded: September 18, 1941
HOW DO YOU KEEP THE MUSIC PLAYING?
(Alan & Marilyn Bergman-Michel Legrand)
Qwest Records
Arranged by Bob Florence
Orchestra conducted by Joe Parnello
Recorded: May 17, 1984
HOW INSENSITIVE
(Antonio Carlos Jobim-Ray Gilbert-Vinicius DeMoraes)
Reprise Records
With Antonio Carlos Jobim
Arranged by Claus Ogerman
Recorded: February 1, 1967
HOW LITTLE WE KNOW
(Phillip Springer-Carolyn Leigh)
Capitol Records
Arranged by Nelson Riddle
Recorded: April 5, 1956
HOW LITTLE WE KNOW
(Phillip Springer-Carolyn Leigh)
Reprise Records
Arranged by Nelson Riddle
Recorded: April 30, 1963
HOW OLD AM I?
(Gordon Jenkins)
Reprise Records
Arranged by Gordon Jenkins
Recorded: April 22, 1965
HUSH-A-BYE-ISLAND
(Harold Adamson-Jimmy McHugh)
Columbia Records
Arranged by Axel Stordahl
Recorded: April 22, 1946
I AM LOVED
(Cole Porter)
Columbia Records
Arranged by Axel Stordahl
Recorded: November 16, 1950
I BEGGED HER
(Sammy Cahn-Jule Styne)
Film recording for: 'Anchors Aweigh'
Metro-Goldwyn-Mayer
With Gene Kelly
Arranged by Axel Stordahl
Orchestra conducted by George Stoll
Recorded: June 13, 1944
I BEGGED HER
(Sammy Cahn-Jule Styne)
Columbia Records
Arranged by Axel Stordahl
Recorded: December 1, 1944
I BELIEVE
(Sammy Cahn-Jule Styne)
Film recording for: 'It Happened In Brooklyn'
Metro-Goldwyn-Mayer
With Jimmy Durante and Bobby Long
Orchestra conducted by Johnny Green
Recorded: October 21, 1946
I BELIEVE
(Sammy Cahn-Jule Styne)
Columbia Records
Arranged by Axel Stordahl
Recorded: October 31, 1946
I BELIEVE
(Sammy Cahn-Jule Styne)
Capitol Records
Arranged by Nelson Riddle
Recorded: November 25, 1957
I BELIEVE I'M GONNA LOVE YOU
(Gloria Sklerov-Harry Lloyd)
Reprise Records
With vocal chorus
Arranged by Al Capps
Orchestra conducted by Bill Miller
Recorded: March 5, 1975
I BELIEVE IN YOU
(Frank Loesser)
Reprise Records
With Count Basie and his Orchestra
Arranged by Quincy Jones
Recorded: June 9, 1964
I CAN READ BETWEEN THE LINES
(Ramon Getzov-Sid Frank)
Capitol Records
Arranged by Nelson Riddle
Recorded: May 2, 1953
I CAN'T BELIEVE I'M LOSING YOU
(Don Costa-Zeller)
Reprise Records
Arranged by Don Costa
Recorded: April 8, 1964
I CAN'T BELIEVE THAT YOU'RE IN LOVE WITH ME
(Clarence Gaskill-Jimmy McHugh)
Capitol Records
Arranged by Nelson Riddle
Recorded: August 23, 1960
I CAN'T GET STARTED
(Vernon Duke-Ira Gershwin)
Capitol Records
Arranged by Gordon Jenkins
Recorded: March 26, 1959
I CAN'T STOP LOVING YOU
(Don Gibson)
Reprise Records
With Count Basie and his Orchestra
Arranged by Quincy Jones
Recorded: June 12, 1964
I CONCENTRATE ON YOU
(Cole Porter)
Columbia Records
Arranged by Axel Stordahl
Recorded: January 9, 1947
I CONCENTRATE ON YOU
(Cole Porter)
Capitol Records
Arranged by Nelson Riddle
Recorded: August 22, 1960
I CONCENTRATE ON YOU
(Cole Porter)
Reprise Records
With Antonio Carlos Jobim
Arranged by Claus Ogerman
Recorded: January 30, 1967
I COULD HAVE DANCED ALL NIGHT
(Alan J. Lerner-Frederick Lowe)
Capitol Records
Arranged by Billy May
Recorded: December 23, 1958
I COULD HAVE DANCED ALL NIGHT
(Alan J. Lerner-Frederick Lowe)
Reprise Records
With sextet accompaniment (Live recording)
Arranged by Neal Hefti and Billy May
Recorded: June 5, 1962 (Paris)
I COULD HAVE TOLD YOU
(Arthur Williams-Carl Sigman)
Capitol Records
Arranged by Nelson Riddle
Recorded: December 9, 1953
I COULD MAKE YOU CARE
(Sammy Cahn-Saul Chaplin)
Victor Records
With Tommy Dorsey and his Orchestra
Recorded: July 17, 1940
I COULD WRITE A BOOK
(Richard Rodgers-Lorenz Hart)
Columbia Records
With the Jeff Alexander Choir
Arranged by Axel Stordahl
Recorded: January 7, 1952
I COULD WRITE A BOOK
(Richard Rodgers-Lorenz Hart)
Film recording for: 'Pal Joey'
Columbia Pictures
With Trudy Erwin
Arranged by Nelson Riddle
Orchestra conducted by Morris Stoloff
Recorded: June 14, 1957
I COULD WRITE A BOOK
(Richard Rodgers-Lorenz Hart)
Capitol Records
Arranged by Nelson Riddle
Recorded: August 13, 1957
I COULDN'T CARE LESS
(Sammy Cahn-Jimmy Van Heusen)
Capitol Records
Arranged by Nelson Riddle
Recorded: October 15, 1958
I COULDN'T SLEEP A WINK LAST NIGHT
(Harold Adamson-Jimmy McHugh)
Film recording for: 'Higher and Higher'
RKO Pictures
Featuring Stanley Wrightsman, Piano
Arranged by Axel Stordahl
Orchestra conducted by Constantin Bakaleinikoff
Recorded: September 8, 1943
I COULDN'T SLEEP A WINK LAST NIGHT
(Harold Adamson-Jimmy McHugh)
Columbia Records
With The Bobby Tucker Singers
Choral arrangement by Alec Wilder
Recorded: November 3, 1943
I COULDN'T SLEEP A WINK LAST NIGHT
(Harold Adamson-Jimmy McHugh)
V-Disc recording
Columbia Records
Arranged by Alec Wilder
Orchestra conducted by Axel Stordahl
Probably recorded: November 14, 1943
I COULDN'T SLEEP A WINK LAST NIGHT
(Harold Adamson-Jimmy McHugh)
Capitol Records
With the Hollywood String Quartet
Arranged by Nelson Riddle
Recorded: November 1, 1956
I COVER THE WATERFRONT
(Johnny Green-Edward Heyman)
Capitol Records
Arranged by Gordon Jenkins
Recorded: April 29, 1957
I CRIED FOR YOU
(Gus Arnheim-Abe Lyman-Arthur Freed
Special film recording for: 'The Joker Is Wild'
Paramount Pictures
Arranged by Nelson Riddle
Orchestra conducted by Walter Scharf
Recorded: October 3, 1956
I DIDN'T KNOW WHAT TIME IT WAS
(Richard Rodgers-Lorenz Hart)
Film recording for: 'Pal Joey'
Columbia Pictures
Arranged by Nelson Riddle
Orchestra conducted by Morris Stoloff
Recorded: May 23, 1957
I DIDN'T KNOW WHAT TIME IT WAS
(Richard Rodgers-Lorenz Hart)
Capitol Records
Arranged by Nelson Riddle
Orchestra conducted by Morris Stoloff
Recorded: September 25, 1957
I DON'T KNOW WHY
(Roy Turk-Fred Ahlert)
Columbia Records
Arranged by Axel Stordahl
Recorded: July 30, 1945
I DREAM OF YOU
(Marjorie Goetschius-Edna Osser)
Columbia Records
Arranged by Axel Stordahl
Recorded: December 1, 1944
I FALL IN LOVE TOO EASILY
(Sammy Cahn-Jule Styne)
Film recording for: 'Anchors Aweigh'
Metro-Goldwyn-Mayer
Arranged by Axel Stordahl
Orchestra conducted by George Stoll
Recorded: September 5, 1944
I FALL IN LOVE TOO EASILY
(Sammy Cahn-Jule Styne)
Columbia Records
Featuring Dave Mann, piano
Arranged by Axel Stordahl
Recorded: December 1, 1944
I FALL IN LOVE WITH YOU EV'RY DAY
(Sammy Stept)
Columbia Records
Arranged by Axel Stordahl
Recorded: March 10, 1946
I FALL IN LOVE WITH YOU EV'RY DAY
(Sammy Stept)
V-Disc recording
Columbia Records
Arranged by Axel Stordahl
Recorded: April 10, 1946
I GET A KICK OUT OF YOU
(Cole Porter)
Capitol Records
Arranged by Nelson Riddle
Recorded: November 6, 1953
I GET A KICK OUT OF YOU
(Cole Porter)
Reprise Records
Arranged by Neal Hefti
Recorded: April 10, 1962
I GET A KICK OUT OF YOU
(Cole Porter)
Reprise Records
With sextet accompaniment (Live recording)
Arranged by Neal Hefti and Billy May
Recorded: June 5, 1962 (Paris)
I GET A KICK OUT OF YOU
(Cole Porter)
Reprise Records
With Woody Herman and the Young Thundering Herd (Live recording)
Arranged by Nelson Riddle
Orchestra conducted by Bill Miller
Recorded: October 13, 1974 (New York City)
I GET ALONG WITHOUT YOU VERY WELL
(Hoagy Carmichael)
Capitol Records
Arranged by Nelson Riddle
Recorded: February 17, 1955
I GOT A GAL I LOVE
(Sammy Cahn-Jule Styne)
Columbia Records
Arranged by Axel Stordahl
Recorded: October 31, 1946
I GOT IT BAD AND THAT AIN'T GOOD
(Duke Ellington-Paul Francis Webster)
Capitol Records
Featuring Juan Tizol, trombone
Arranged by Nelson Riddle
Recorded: November 28, 1956
I GOT PLENTY O' NUTTIN'
(George Gershwin-Ira Gershwin)
Capitol Records
Arranged by Nelson Riddle
Recorded: November 15, 1956
I GOTTA RIGHT TO SING THE BLUES
(Harold Arlen-Ted Koehler)
Capitol Records
Arranged by Skip Martin
Recorded: March 6, 1962
I GUESS I'LL HAVE TO CHANGE MY PLAN
(Arthur Schwartz-Howard Dietz)
Capitol Records
Arranged by Nelson Riddle
Recorded: November 20, 1956
I GUESS I'LL HAVE TO DREAM THE REST
(Harold Green-Mickey Stoner-Martin Block)
Victor Records
With Tommy Dorsey and his Orchestra
Featuring The Pied Pipers
Arranged by Axel Stordahl
Recorded: June 27, 1941
I GUESS I'LL HAVE TO DREAM THE REST
(Harold Green-Mickey Stoner-Martin Block)
Columbia Records
With The Whippoorwills
Arranged by Axel Stordahl
Recorded: October 9, 1950
I HAD THE CRAZIEST DREAM
(Mack Gordon-Harry Warren)
Reprise Records
With vocal chorus
Arranged by Billy May
Recorded: July 17, 1979
I HADN'T ANYONE TILL YOU
(Ray Noble)
Reprise Records
Arranged by Don Costa
Recorded: November 20, 1961
I HAVE BUT ONE HEART
(Marty Symes-Johnny Farrow)
Columbia Records
Arranged by Axel Stordahl
Recorded: November 30, 1945
I HAVE DREAMED
(Richard Rodgers-Oscar Hammerstein II)
Reprise Records
Arranged by Nelson Riddle
Recorded: February 19, 1963
I HAVEN'T TIME TO BE A MILLIONAIRE
(Johnny Burke-James Monaco)
Victor Records
With Tommy Dorsey and his Orchestra
Arranged by Deane Kincaide
Recorded: April 10, 1940
I HEAR A RHAPSODY
(George Fragos-Jack Baker-Dick Gasparre)
Victor Records
With Tommy Dorsey and his Orchestra
Recording date unknown (Radio aircheck 1940-1942)
I HEAR A RHAPSODY
(George Fragos-Jack Baker-Dick Gasparre)
Columbia Records
With the Jeff Alexander Choir
Arranged by Axel Stordahl
Recorded: January 7, 1952
I HEARD THE BELLS ON CHRISTMAS DAY
(Henry Longfellow-Johnny Marks)
Reprise Records
With Fred Waring and His Pennsylvanians
Arranged by Nelson Riddle
Orchestra conducted by Fred Waring
Recorded: June 16, 1964
I LEFT MY HEART IN SAN FRANCISCO
(George Corey-Douglas Cross)
Reprise Records
Arranged by Nelson Riddle
Orchestra conducted by Neal Hefti
Recorded: August 27, 1962
I LIKE THE SUNRISE
(Duke Ellington)
Reprise Records
With Duke Ellington and his Orchestra
Arranged by Billy May
Recorded: December 12, 1967
I LIKE TO LEAD WHEN I DANCE
(Sammy Cahn-Jimmy Van Heusen)
Reprise Records
Arranged by Nelson Riddle
Recorded: April 8, 1964
I LOVE MY WIFE
(Cy Coleman-Michael Stewart)
Reprise Records
Arranged by Nelson Riddle
Recorded: November 12, 1976
I LOVE PARIS
(Cole Porter)
Capitol Records
With Maurice Chevalier
Arranged by Nelson Riddle
Recorded: October 13, 1959
I LOVE PARIS
(Cole Porter)
Capitol Records
Arranged by Nelson Riddle
Recorded: April 13, 1960
I LOVE PARIS
(Cole Porter)
Reprise Records
With sextet accompaniment (Live recording)
Arranged by Neal Hefti and Billy May
Recorded: June 5, 1962 (Paris)
I LOVE YOU
(Webb)
Columbia Records
Arranged by Axel Stordahl
Recorded: July 30, 1946
I LOVE YOU
(Harry Archer-Harlan Thompson)
Capitol Records
Arranged by Nelson Riddle
Recorded: April 30, 1953

I LOVE YOU
(Cole Porter)
Reprise Records
Arranged by Neal Hefti
Recorded: April 10, 1962

I LOVED HER
(Gordon Jenkins)
Reprise Records
Arranged by Gordon Jenkins
Recorded: July 20, 1981

I NEVER KNEW
(Gus Kahn-Ted Florito)
Reprise Records
Arranged by Billy May
Recorded: May 19, 1961

I ONLY HAVE EYES FOR YOU
(Al Dubin-Harry Warren)
V-Disc recording
Columbia Records
With The Bobby Tucker Singers
Arranged and conducted by Axel Stordahl
Recorded: October 17, 1943

I ONLY HAVE EYES FOR YOU
(Al Dubin-Harry Warren)
Columbia Records
With The Ken Lane Singers
Arranged by Axel Stordahl
Recorded: August 27, 1945

I ONLY HAVE EYES FOR YOU
(Al Dubin-Harry Warren)
Reprise Records
With Count Basie and his Orchestra
Arranged by Neal Hefti
Recorded: October 3, 1962

I SAW YOU FIRST
(Harold Adamson-Jimmy McHugh)
Film recording for: 'Higher And Higher'
RKO Pictures
With Marcy McGuire
Arranged by Gene Rose
Orchestra conducted by Constantin Bakaleinikoff
Recorded: August 24, 1943

I SEE IT NOW
(Alec Wilder-Bill Engvick)
Reprise Records
Arranged by Gordon Jenkins
Recorded: April 14, 1965

I SEE YOUR FACE BEFORE ME
(Arthur Schwartz-Howard Dietz)
Capitol Records
Arranged by Nelson Riddle
Recorded: February 16, 1955

I SHOULD CARE
(Sammy Cahn-Paul Weston-Alex Stordahl)
Columbia Records
Arranged by Axel Stordahl
Recorded: March 6, 1945

I SING THE SONGS
(Bruce Johnstone)
Reprise Records
Arranged by Don Costa
Orchestra conducted by Bill Miller
Recorded: February 5, 1976

I THINK OF YOU
(Jack Elliot-John Marcotte)
Victor Records
With Tommy Dorsey and his Orchestra
Arranged by Paul Weston
Recorded: September 18, 1941

I THINK OF YOU
(Jack Elliot-John Marcotte)
Capitol Records
Arranged by Gordon Jenkins
Recorded: May 1, 1957

I THOUGHT ABOUT YOU
(Johnny Mercer-Jimmy Van Heusen)
Capitol Records
Arranged by Nelson Riddle
Recorded: January 9, 1956

I TRIED
(Carl Nutter-Paul Hand-Clark Dennis)
Victor Records
With Tommy Dorsey and his Orchestra
Arranged by Axel Stordahl
Recorded: January 20, 1941

I WANNA BE AROUND
(Johnny Mercy-Sadie Vimmerstett)
Reprise Records
With Count Basie and his Orchestra
Arranged by Quincy Jones
Recorded: June 9, 1964

I WANT TO THANK YOUR FOLKS
(Benny Benjamin-George Weiss)
Columbia Records
Arranged by Axel Stordahl
Recorded: December 15, 1946

I WENT DOWN TO VIRGINIA
(Redd Evans-Dave Mann)
Columbia Records
Arranged by Axel Stordahl
Recorded: November 25, 1947

I WHISTLE A HAPPY TUNE
(Richard Rodgers-Oscar Hammerstein II)
Columbia Records
Arranged by Axel Stordahl
Recorded: March 27, 1951

I WILL DRINK THE WINE
(Paul Ryan)
Reprise Records
With vocal chorus
Arranged by Don Costa
Recorded: October 26, 1970

I WILL WAIT FOR YOU
(Michel Legrand-Norman Gimbel)
Reprise Records
Arranged by Ernie Freeman
With vocal chorus
Recorded: November 18, 1966

I WISH I WERE IN LOVE AGAIN
(Richard Rodgers-Lorenz Hart)
Capitol Records
Arranged by Nelson Riddle
Recorded: November 20, 1956

I WISH YOU LOVE
(Lee Wilson-Charles Trenet)
Reprise Records
With Count Basie and his Orchestra
Arranged by Quincy Jones
Recorded: June 10, 1964

I WISHED ON THE MOON
(Dorothy Parker-Ralph Rainger)
Reprise Records
Arranged by Nelson Riddle
Recorded: November 30, 1965

I WON'T DANCE
(Jerome Kern-Dorothy Fields-Jimmy McHugh)
Capitol Records
Arranged by Nelson Riddle
Recorded: November 15, 1956

I WON'T DANCE
(Jerome Kern-Dorothy Fields-Jimmy McHugh)
Reprise Records
With Count Basie and his Orchestra
Arranged by Neal Hefti
Recorded: October 2, 1962

I WOULD BE IN LOVE (ANYWAY)
(Bob Gaudio-Jake Holmes)
Reprise Records
Arranged by Joseph Scott
Recorded: August 25, 1969

I WOULDN'T TRADE CHRISTMAS
(Sammy Cahn-Jimmy Van Heusen)
Reprise Records
With Nancy, Frank Jr. and Tina Sinatra
Arranged by Nelson Riddle
Recorded: August 12, 1968

I'D KNOW YOU ANYWHERE
(Johnny Mercer-Jimmy McHugh)
Victor Records
With Tommy Dorsey and his Orchestra
Arranged by Deane Kincaide
Recorded: September 17, 1940

IF
(David Gates)
Reprise Records
Arranged by Gordon Jenkins
Recorded: May 7, 1974

IF I COULD BE WITH YOU
(Jimmy Johnson-Henry Creamer)
Special film recording for: 'The Joker Is Wild'
Paramount Pictures
Arranged by Nelson Riddle
Orchestra conducted by Walter Scharf
Recorded: October 3, 1956

IF I EVER LOVE AGAIN
(Russ Carlyle-D. Reynolds)
Columbia Records
With The Double Daters
Arranged by Hugo Winterhalter
Recorded: July 14, 1949

IF I FORGET YOU
(Irving Caesar)
Columbia Records
Arranged by Axel Stordahl
Recorded: December 30, 1947

IF I HAD THREE WISHES
(Lew Spence-Claude Baum)
Capitol Records
Arranged by Nelson Riddle
Recorded: March 7, 1955

IF I HAD YOU
(Ted Shapiro-Jimmy Campbell-Reg Connelly)
Columbia Records
Arranged by Axel Stordahl
Recorded: August 11, 1947

IF I HAD YOU
(Ted Shapiro-Jimmy Campbell-Reg Connelly)
Capitol Records
Arranged by Nelson Riddle
Recorded: November 26, 1956

IF I HAD YOU
(Ted Shapiro-Jimmy Campbell-Reg Connelly)
Reprise Records
Arranged by Robert Farnon
Recorded: June 12, 1962

IF I LOVED YOU
(Richard Rodgers-Oscar Hammerstein II)
Columbia Records
Arranged by Axel Stordahl
Recorded: May 1, 1945

IF I ONLY HAD A MATCH
(Lee Morris-Arthur Johnston-G. Mayer)
Columbia Records
Arranged by Axel Stordahl
Recorded: November 25, 1947

IF I SHOULD LOSE YOU
(Leo Robin-Ralph Rainger)
Qwest Records
Arranged by Sam Nestico
Orchestra conducted by Quincy Jones
Recorded: April 17, 1984

IF I STEAL A KISS
(Edward Heyman-Nacio Herb Brown)
Film recording for: 'The Kissing Bandit'
Metro-Goldwyn-Mayer
Arranged by Leo Arnaud
Orchestra conducted by George Stoll
Recorded: May 8, 1947

IF I STEAL A KISS
(Edward Heyman-Nacio Herb Brown)
Columbia Records
Arranged by Axel Stordahl
Recorded: December 4, 1947

IF IT'S THE LAST THING I DO
(Sammy Cahn-Saul Chaplin)
Capitol Records
With The Hollywood String Quartet
Arranged by Nelson Riddle
Recorded: March 8, 1956

IF ONLY SHE'D LOOK MY WAY
(I. Novello-F. Melville)
Columbia Records
Arranged by Axel Stordahl
Recorded: September 21, 1950

IF YOU ARE BUT A DREAM
(Moe Jaffe-Jack Fulton-Nathan Bonx)
V-Disc recording
Columbia Records
Arranged by Axel Stordahl
Orchestra conducted by Raymond Paige
Recorded: October 23, 1944

IF YOU ARE BUT A DREAM
(Moe Jaffe-Jack Fulton-Nathan Bonx)
Columbia Records
Arranged by Axel Stordahl
Recorded: November 14, 1944

IF YOU ARE BUT A DREAM
(Moe Jaffe-Jack Fulton-Nathan Bonx)
Special film recording for: 'The House I Live In'
RKO Pictures
Arranged by Axel Stordahl
Recorded: May 8, 1945

IF YOU ARE BUT A DREAM
(Moe Jaffe-Jack Fulton-Nathan Bonx)
Capitol Records
Arranged by Nelson Riddle
Recorded: December 11, 1957

IF YOU GO AWAY
(Rod McKuen-Jacques Brel)
Reprise Records
Arranged by Don Costa
Recorded: February 20, 1969

IF YOU KNEW SUSIE
(Sammy Cahn-Jule Styne)
Special film recording for: 'Anchors Aweigh'
Metro-Goldwyn-Mayer
With Gene Kelly
Arranged by Axel Stordahl
Orchestra conducted by George Stoll
Recorded: June 13, 1944

IF YOU NEVER COME TO ME
(Antonio Carlos Jobim-Ray Gilbert)
Reprise Records
With Antonio Carlos Jobim
Arranged by Claus Ogerman
Recorded: January 31, 1967

IF YOU PLEASE
(Johnny Burke-Jimmy Van Heusen)
Columbia Records
With The Bobby Tucker Singers
Choral arrangement by Alec Wilder
Recorded: June 22, 1943

IF YOU STUB YOUR TOE ON THE MOON
(Johnny Burke-Jimmy Van Heusen)
Columbia Records
With The Phil Moore Four
Arranged by Phil Moore
Recorded: January 4, 1949

I'LL BE AROUND
(Alec Wilder)
V-Disc recording
Columbia Records
Arranged by Alec Wilder
Orchestra conducted by Axel Stordahl
Recorded: November 14, 1943

I'LL BE AROUND
(Alec Wilder)
Capitol Records
Arranged by Nelson Riddle
Orchestra conducted by Bill Miller
Recorded: February 8, 1955

I'LL BE HOME FOR CHRISTMAS
(Walter Kent-Kim Gannon-Buck Ram)
Capitol Records
With The Ralph Brewster Singers
Arranged by Gordon Jenkins
Recorded: July 17, 1957

I'LL BE SEEING YOU
(Irving Kahal-Sammy Fain)
Victor Records
With Tommy Dorsey and his Orchestra
Arranged by Paul Weston
Recorded: February 26, 1940

I'LL BE SEEING YOU
(Irving Kahal-Sammy Fain)
Reprise Records
Arranged by Sy Oliver
Recorded: May 1, 1961

I'LL BE SEEING YOU
(Irving Kahal-Sammy Fain)
Capitol Records
Arranged by Axel Stordahl
Recorded: September 11, 1961

I'LL FOLLOW MY SECRET HEART
(Noel Coward)
V-Disc recording
Columbia Records
Arranged by Axel Stordahl
Recorded: July 8, 1944

I'LL FOLLOW MY SECRET HEART
(Noel Coward)
Reprise Records
Arranged by Robert Farnon
Recorded: June 12, 1962

I'LL MAKE UP FOR EVERYTHING
(Ross Parker)
Columbia Records
Arranged by Axel Stordahl
Recorded: October 22, 1947

I'LL NEVER BE THE SAME
(Matty Malneck-Frank Signorelli-Gus Kahn)
Capitol Records
Arranged by Nelson Riddle
Recorded: March 4, 1955

I'LL NEVER LET A DAY PASS BY
(Victor Schertzinger-Frank Loesser)
Victor Records
With Tommy Dorsey and his Orchestra
Recorded: May 28, 1941

I'LL NEVER SMILE AGAIN
(Ruth Lowe)
Victor Records
With Tommy Dorsey and his Orchestra
Featuring The Pied Pipers
Arranged by Fred Stulce
Recorded: April 23, 1940

I'LL NEVER SMILE AGAIN
(Ruth Lowe)
Victor Records
With Tommy Dorsey and his Orchestra
Featuring The Pied Pipers
Arranged by Fred Stulce
Recorded: May 23, 1940

I'LL NEVER SMILE AGAIN
(Ruth Lowe)
Victor Records
With Tommy Dorsey and his Orchestra
Recorded: June 12, 1940 (Radio aircheck)

I'LL NEVER SMILE AGAIN
(Ruth Lowe)
Film recording for: 'Las Vegas Nights'
Paramount Pictures
With Tommy Dorsey and his Orchestra
Featuring The Pied Pipers
Arranged by Fred Stulce
Orchestra conducted by Victor Young
Recorded: November 24, 1940

I'LL NEVER SMILE AGAIN
(Ruth Lowe)
V-Disc recording
Columbia Records
Featuring Tommy Dorsey, trombone and The Pied Pipers
Arranged by Axel Stordahl
Recorded: October 24, 1945

I'LL NEVER SMILE AGAIN
(Ruth Lowe)
Capitol Records
Arranged by Gordon Jenkins
Orchestra conducted by Nelson Riddle
Recorded: May 14, 1959

I'LL NEVER SMILE AGAIN
(Ruth Lowe)
Reprise Records
With vocal chorus
Arranged by Fred Stulce
Orchestra conducted by Sonny Burke
Recorded: October 11, 1965

I'LL ONLY MISS HER WHEN I THINK OF HER
(Sammy Cahn-Jimmy Van Heusen)
Reprise Records
Featuring Laurindo Almeida, guitar
Arranged by Torrie Zito
Recorded: August 23, 1965

I'LL REMEMBER APRIL
(Don Reye-Gene DePaul-Patricia Johnston)
Capitol Records
Arranged by Heinie Beau
Recorded: September 12, 1961

I'LL SEE YOU AGAIN
(Noel Coward)
Capitol Records
Arranged by Axel Stordahl
Recorded: September 11, 1961

I'LL TAKE TALLULAH
(Burton Lane-Yip Harburg)
Victor Records
With Tommy Dorsey and his Orchestra
Featuring The Pied Pipers
Arranged by Sy Oliver
Recorded: February 19, 1942

ILL WIND
(Harold Arlen-Ted Koehler)
Capitol Records
Arranged by Nelson Riddle
Recorded: February 16, 1955

I'M A FOOL TO WANT YOU
(Jack Wolf-Joel Heron-Frank Sinatra)
Columbia Records
With The Ray Charles Singers
Arranged by Axel Stordahl
Recorded: March 27, 1951

I'M A FOOL TO WANT YOU
(Jack Wolf-Joel Heron-Frank Sinatra)
Capitol Records
Arranged by Gordon Jenkins
Recorded: May 1, 1957

I'M BEGINNING TO SEE THE LIGHT
(Harry James-Duke Ellington-J. Hodges-D. George)
Reprise Records
Arranged by Neal Hefti
Recorded: April 10, 1962

I'M GETTING SENTIMENTAL OVER YOU
(George Bassman-Ned Washington)
Reprise Records
Arranged by Sy Oliver
Recorded: May 1, 1961

I'M GLAD THERE IS YOU
(Paul Madeira-Jimmy Dorsey)
Columbia Records
Arranged by Axel Stordahl
Recorded: November 9, 1947

I'M GONNA LIVE TILL I DIE
(Al Hoffman-Walter Kent-Mann Curtis)
Capitol Records
With Ray Anthony and his Orchestra
Arranged by Dick Reynolds
Recorded: December 13, 1954

I'M GONNA MAKE IT ALL THE WAY
(Floyd Huddleston)
Reprise Records
Arranged by Don Costa
Recorded: December 10, 1973

I'M GONNA SIT RIGHT DOWN AND WRITE MYSELF A LETTER
(Fred Ahlert-Joe Young)
Capitol Records
Arranged by Nelson Riddle
Recorded: April 7, 1954

I'M GONNA SIT RIGHT DOWN AND WRITE MYSELF A LETTER
(Fred Ahlert-Joe Young)
Reprise Records
With Count Basie and his Orchestra
Arranged by Neal Hefti
Recorded: October 3, 1962

I'M NOT AFRAID
(Rod McKuen-Jacques Brel)
Reprise Records
Arranged by Lennie Hayton
Recorded: October 28, 1970

I'M SORRY I MADE YOU CRY
(N.J. Clesi-Theodore Morse)
Columbia Records
Arranged by Axel Stordahl
Recorded: October 24, 1946

I'M WALKING BEHIND YOU
(Bill Reid)
Capitol Records
Arranged by Axel Stordahl
Recorded: April 2, 1953

IMAGINATION
(Johnny Burke-Jimmy Van Heusen)
Victor Records
With Tommy Dorsey and his Orchestra
Arranged by Axel Stordahl
Recorded: April 10, 1940

IMAGINATION
(Johnny Burke-Jimmy Van Heusen)
Reprise Records
Arranged by Sy Oliver
Recorded: May 1, 1961

IMAGINATION
(Johnny Burke-Jimmy Van Heusen)
Reprise Records

With sextet accompaniment (Live recording)
Arranged by Neal Hefti and Billy May
Recorded: June 5, 1962 (Paris)

IN THE BLUE OF EVENING
(Tom Adair-Alphonso d'Artega)
Victor Records
With Tommy Dorsey and his Orchestra
Arranged by Axel Stordahl
Recorded: June 17, 1942

IN THE BLUE OF EVENING
(Tom Adair-Alphonso d'Artega)
Victor Records
With Tommy Dorsey and his Orchestra
Recorded: August 6, 1942 (Radio aircheck)

IN THE BLUE OF EVENING
(Tom Adair-Alphonso d'Artega)
Reprise Records
Arranged by Sy Oliver
Recorded: March 21, 1961

IN THE COOL, COOL, COOL OF THE EVENING
(Hoagy Charmichael-Johnny Mercer)
Reprise Records
Arranged by Nelson Riddle
Recorded: January 27, 1964

IN THE STILL OF THE NIGHT
(Cole Porter)
Reprise Records
Arranged by Johnny Mandel
Recorded: December 19, 1960

IN THE STILL OF THE NIGHT
(Cole Porter)
Reprise Records
With sextet accompaniment (Live recording)
Arranged by Neal Hefti and Billy May
Recorded: June 5, 1962 (Paris)

IN THE WEE SMALL HOURS OF THE MORNING
(Dave Mann-Bob Hilliard)
Capitol Records
Arranged by Nelson Riddle
Recorded: February 17, 1955

IN THE WEE SMALL HOURS OF THE MORNING
(Dave Mann-Bob Hilliard)
Reprise Records
Arranged by Nelson Riddle
Recorded: April 29, 1963

INDIAN SUMMER
(Victor Herbert-Al Dubin)
Reprise Records
With Duke Ellington and his Orchestra
Featuring Johnny Hodges, alto sax
Arranged by Billy May
Recorded: December 11, 1967

INDISCREET
(Sammy Cahn-Jimmy Van Heusen)
Reprise Records
Arranged by Gordon Jenkins
Recorded: January 16, 1962

ISLE OF CAPRI
(Will Grosz-Jimmy Kennedy)
Capitol Records
Arranged by Billy May
Recorded: October 1, 1957

ISN'T SHE LOVELY
(Stevie Wonder)
Reprise Records
Arranged by Don Costa
Recorded: August 22, 1979

IT ALL CAME TRUE
(Sunny Skylar)
Columbia Records
Arranged by Axel Stordahl
Recorded: July 3, 1947

IT ALL CAME TRUE
(Sunny Skylar)
Columbia Records
With Alvy West and the Little Band
Arranged by Alvy West
Recorded: September 23, 1947

IT ALL DEPENDS ON YOU
(Buddy DeSylva-Lew Henderson-Ray Brown)
Columbia Records
Arranged by George Siravo
Orchestra conducted by Hugo Winterhalter
Recorded: July 10, 1949

IT ALL DEPENDS ON YOU
(Buddy DeSylva-Lew Henderson-Ray Brown)
Capitol Records
Arranged by Billy May
Recorded: September 30, 1958

IT ALL DEPENDS ON YOU
(Buddy DeSylva-Lew Henderson-Ray Brown)
Capitol Records
Arranged by Nelson Riddle
Recorded: August 23, 1960

IT CAME TO ME
(Louis DePyro)
Victor Records
With Tommy Dorsey and his Orchestra
Recorded: August 3, 1940 (Radio aircheck)

IT CAME UPON A MIDNIGHT CLEAR
(Willis)
Capitol Records
With The Ken Lane Singers
Arranged by Axel Stordahl
Recorded: December 28, 1947

IT CAME UPON A MIDNIGHT CLEAR
(Willis)
Capitol Records
With The Ralph Brewster Singers
Arranged by Gordon Jenkins
Recorded: July 10, 1957

IT COULD HAPPEN TO YOU
(Johnny Burke-Jimmy Van Heusen)
Capitol Records
With The Hollywood String Quartet
Arranged by Nelson Riddle
Recorded: April 5, 1956

IT GETS LONELY EARLY
(Sammy Cahn-Jimmy Van Heusen)
Reprise Records
Arranged by Gordon Jenkins
Recorded: April 22, 1965

IT HAD TO BE YOU
(Gus Kahn-Isham Jones)
Reprise Records
Arranged by Billy May
Recorded: July 18, 1979

IT HAPPENED IN MONTEREY
(Mabel Wayne-Billy Rose)
Capitol Records
Arranged by Nelson Riddle
Recorded: January 12, 1956

IT HAPPENS EVERY SPRING
(Mack Gordon-Josef Myrow)
Columbia Records
Arranged by Axel Stordahl
Recorded: April 10, 1949

IT MIGHT AS WELL BE SPRING
(Richard Rodgers-Oscar Hammerstein II)
Reprise Records
Arranged Don Costa
Recorded: November 21, 1961

IT MIGHT AS WELL BE SPRING
(Richard Rodgers-Oscar Hammerstein II)
Reprise Records
Arranged by Nelson Riddle
Recorded: January 28, 1964

IT NEVER ENTERED MY MIND
(Richard Rodgers-Lorenz Hart)
Columbia Records
Arranged by Axel Stordahl
Recorded: November 5, 1947

IT NEVER ENTERED MY MIND
(Richard Rodgers-Lorenz Hart)
Capitol Records
Arranged by Nelson Riddle
Recorded: March 4, 1955

IT NEVER ENTERED MY MIND/ THE GAL THAT GOT AWAY *(Medley)*
(Richard Rodgers-Lorenz Hart)
Reprise Records
Arranged by Nelson Riddle
Conducted by Vincent Falcone, Jr.
Recorded: April 8, 1981

IT ONLY HAPPENS WHEN I DANCE WITH YOU
(Irving Berlin)
Columbia Records
Arranged by Axel Stordahl
Recorded: March 16, 1948

IT STARTED ALL OVER AGAIN
(Carl Fischer-Bill Carey)
Victor Records
With Tommy Dorsey and his Orchestra
Featuring The Pied Pipers
Arranged by Axel Stordahl
Recorded: July 1, 1942

IT STARTED ALL OVER AGAIN
(Carl Fischer-Bill Carey)
Reprise Records
Arranged by Sy Oliver
Recorded: May 3, 1961

IT WAS A VERY GOOD YEAR
(Ervin Drake)
Reprise Records
Arranged by Gordon Jenkins
Recorded: April 22, 1965

IT WAS A VERY GOOD YEAR
(Ervin Drake)
Reprise Records
With Count Basie and his Orchestra (Live recording)
Arranged by Quincy Jones and Billy Byers
Recorded: January 26-February 1, 1966 (Las Vegas)

IT WORRIES ME
(Fritz Schultz-Reichel-Carl Sigman)
Capitol Records
Arranged by Nelson Riddle
Recorded: May 13, 1954

IT'S A BLUE WORLD
(Bob Wright-Chet Forrest)
Capitol Records
Arranged by Heinie Beau
Orchestra conducted by Axel Stordahl
Recorded: September 12, 1961

IT'S A LONESOME OLD TOWN
(Charles Kisco-Larry Tobias)
Capitol Records
Arranged by Nelson Riddle
Recorded: June 26, 1958

IT'S A LONG WAY FROM YOUR HOUSE TO MY HOUSE
(Sid Tepper-Nick Brodsky)
Columbia Records
Arranged by Axel Stordahl
Recorded: May 10, 1951

IT'S A LOVELY DAY TOMORROW
(Irving Berlin)
Victor Records
With Tommy Dorsey and his Orchestra
Arranged by Axel Stordahl
Recorded: April 23, 1940

IT'S A WONDERFUL WORLD
(Jan Savitt-Harold Adamson-Johnny Watson)
Reprise Records
Arranged by Billy May
Recorded: May 19, 1961

IT'S ALL RIGHT WITH ME
(Cole Porter)
Capitol Records
Arranged by Nelson Riddle
Recorded: August 27, 1959

IT'S ALL RIGHT WITH ME
(Cole Porter)
Qwest Records
Arranged by Sam Nestico
Orchestra conducted by Quincy Jones
Recorded: April 16, 1984

IT'S ALL UP TO YOU
(Sammy Cahn-Jimmy Van Heusen)
Columbia Records
With Dinah Shore and vocal chorus
Arranged by Axel Stordahl
Recorded: November 7, 1946

IT'S ALWAYS YOU
(Johnny Burke-Jimmy Van Heusen)
Victor Records
With Tommy Dorsey and his Orchestra
Recorded: January 15, 1941

IT'S ALWAYS YOU
(Johnny Burke-Jimmy Van Heusen)
Reprise Records
Arranged by Sy Oliver
Recorded: May 3, 1961

IT'S EASY TO REMEMBER
(Richard Rodgers-Lorenz Hart)
Capitol Records
With The Hollywood String Quartet
Arranged by Nelson Riddle
Recorded: November 1, 1956

IT'S FATE, BABY, IT'S FATE
(Roger Edens-Betty Comden-Adolph Green)
Film recording for: 'Take Me Out To The Ball Game'
Metro-Goldwyn-Mayer
With Betty Garrett
Arranged by Robert Tucker
Orchestra conducted by Adolph Deutsch
Recorded: August 12, 1948

IT'S FUNNY TO EVERYONE BUT ME
(Jack Lawrence)
Columbia Records
With Harry James and his Orchestra
Arranged by Andy Gibson
Recorded: August 17, 1939

IT'S NICE TO GO TRAV'LING
(Sammy Cahn-Jimmy Van Heusen)
Capitol Records
Arranged by Billy May
Recorded: October 8, 1957

IT'S ONLY A PAPER MOON
(Billy Rose-Yip Harburg-Harold Arlen)
Columbia Records
Arranged by George Siravo
Recorded: April 24, 1950

IT'S ONLY A PAPER MOON
(Billy Rose-Yip Harburg-Harold Arlen)
Capitol Records
Arranged by Nelson Riddle
Recorded: August 31, 1960

IT'S ONLY MONEY
(Sammy Cahn-Jule Styne)
Film recording for: 'Double Dynamite'
RKO Pictures
With Groucho Marx
Arranged by Leigh Harline
Orchestra conducted by Constantin Bakaleinikoff
Recorded: January 28, 1949

IT'S ONLY MONEY *(FINALE)*
(Sammy Cahn-Jule Styne)
From: 'Double Dynamite'
RKO Pictures
With Groucho Marx and Jane Russell
Arranged by Leigh Harline
Orchestra conducted by Constantin Bakaleinikoff
Recorded: January 31, 1949

IT'S OVER, IT'S OVER, IT'S OVER
(Matt Stanford-Dok Stanford)
Capitol Records
With vocal chorus
Arranged by Nelson Riddle
Recorded: April 13, 1960

IT'S SUNDAY
(Jule Styne-Susan Birkenhead)
Reprise Records
Featuring Tony Mottola, guitar
Solo guitar arrangement by Tony Mottola
Recorded: February 28, l983

IT'S THE SAME OLD DREAM
(Sammy Cahn-Jule Styne)
Film recording for: 'It Happened In Brooklyn'
Metro-Goldwyn-Mayer
With The Starlighters
Arranged by Axel Stordahl
Orchestra conducted by Johnny Green
Recorded: September 27, 1946

IT'S THE SAME OLD DREAM
(Sammy Cahn-Jule Styne)
Columbia Records
With Four Hits and A Miss
Arranged by Axel Stordahl
Recorded: October 24, 1946

IT'S THE SAME OLD DREAM
(Sammy Cahn-Jule Styne)
Capitol Records
Arranged by Nelson Riddle
Recorded: November 25, 1957

I'VE BEEN THERE
(Gordon Jenkins)
Reprise Records
With The Los Angeles Philharmonic Symphony Orchestra
Arranged by Gordon Jenkins
Recorded: December 17, 1979

I'VE BEEN TO TOWN
(Rod McKuen)
Reprise Records
Arranged by Don Costa
Recorded: March 19, 1969

I'VE GOT A CRUSH ON YOU
(George Gershwin-Ira Gershwin)
Columbia Records
Featuring Bobby Hackett, cornet
Arranged by Axel Stordahl
Recorded: November 5, 1947

I'VE GOT A CRUSH ON YOU
(George Gershwin-Ira Gershwin)
Film recording for: 'Meet Danny Wilson'
Universal International
With The Ebonaires Quartet
Arranged by Joseph Gershenson
Recorded: July 11, 1951

I'VE GOT A CRUSH ON YOU
(George Gershwin-Ira Gershwin)
Capitol Records
Arranged by Nelson Riddle
Recorded: March 3, 1960

I'VE GOT A CRUSH ON YOU
(George Gershwin-Ira Gershwin)
Reprise Records
With Count Basie and his Orchestra (Live recording)
Arranged by Quincy Jones & Billy Byers
Recorded: January 26-February 1, 1966 (Las Vegas)

I'VE GOT A CRUSH ON YOU
(George Gershwin-Ira Gershwin)
Capitol Records
With Barbra Streisand
Arranged by Patrick Williams
Recorded: July 6, 1993

I'VE GOT A HOME IN THAT ROCK
(Traditional)
Columbia Records
With The Charioteers
Arranged by Axel Stordahl
Recorded: May 16, 1945

I'VE GOT MY LOVE TO KEEP ME WARM
(Irving Berlin)
Reprise Records
Arranged by Dick Reynolds
Orcehstra conducted by Johnny Mandel
Recorded: December 21, 1960

I'VE GOT THE WORLD ON A STRING
(Harold Arlen-Ted Koehler)
Capitol Records
Arranged by Nelson Riddle
Recorded: April 30, 1953

I'VE GOT THE WORLD ON A STRING
(Harold Arlen-Ted Koehler)
Capitol Records
With Liza Minnelli
Arranged by Nelson Riddle
Orchestra conducted by Patrick Williams
Recorded: July 1, 1993

I'VE GOT YOU UNDER MY SKIN
(Cole Porter)
Capitol Records
Featuring Milt Bernhart, trombone
Arranged by Nelson Riddle
Recorded: January 12, 1956

I'VE GOT YOU UNDER MY SKIN
(Cole Porter)
Reprise Records
With sextet accompaniment (Live recording)
Arranged by Neal Hefti and Billy May
Recorded: June 5, 1962 (Paris)

I'VE GOT YOU UNDER MY SKIN
(Cole Porter)
Reprise Records
Featuring Dick Nash, trombone
Arranged by Nelson Riddle
Recorded: April 30, 1963

I'VE GOT YOU UNDER MY SKIN
(Cole Porter)
Reprise Records
With Count Basie and his Orchestra (Live recording)
Arranged by Quincy Jones & Billy Byers
Recorded: January 26-February 1, 1966 (Las Vegas)

I'VE GOT YOU UNDER MY SKIN
(Cole Porter)
Reprise Records
With Woody Herman and the Young Thundering Herd (Live recording)
Arranged by Nelson Riddle
Orchestra conducted by Bill Miller
Recorded: October 13, 1974 (New York City)

I'VE GOT YOU UNDER MY SKIN
(Cole Porter)
Capitol Records
With Bono
Arranged by Nelson Riddle
Orchestra conducted by Patrick Williams
Recorded: July 1, 1993

I'VE HAD MY MOMENTS
(Walter Donaldson-Gus Kahn)
Capitol Records
With The Hollywood String Quartet
Arranged by Nelson Riddle
Recorded: April 4, 1956

I'VE HEARD THAT SONG BEFORE
(Sammy Cahn-Jule Styne)
Capitol Records
Arranged by Billy May
Recorded: March 21, 1961

I'VE NEVER BEEN IN LOVE BEFORE
(Frank Loesser)
Reprise Records
Arranged by Nelson Riddle
Orchestra conducted by Morris Stoloff
Recorded: July 18, 1963

JEEPERS CREEPERS
(Harry Warren-Johnny Mercer)
Capitol Records
Arranged by Nelson Riddle
Recorded: April 19, 1954

JESUS IS A ROCK *(In A Weary Land)*
(Traditional)
Columbia Records
With The Charioteers
Arranged by Axel Stordahl
Recorded: May 16, 1945

JINGLE BELLS
(James Pierpoint)
Columbia Records
With The Ken Lane Singers
Arranged by Axel Stordahl
Recorded: August 8, 1946

JINGLE BELLS
(James Pierpoint)
Capitol Records
With The Ralph Brewster Singers
Arranged by Gordon Jenkins
Recorded: July 16, 1957

JUST A KISS APART
(Victor Herbert-Buddy DeSylva)
Columbia Records
Arranged by Morris Stoloff
Recorded: July 21, 1949

JUST AN OLD STONE HOUSE
(Alec Wilder)
Columbia Records
Arranged by Mitch Miller
Recorded: November 15, 1945

JUST AS THOUGH YOU WERE HERE
(John Benson Brooks-Eddie DeLange)
Victor Records
With Tommy Dorsey and his Orchestra
Featuring The Pied Pipers
Arranged by Axel Stordahl
Recorded: May 18, 1942

JUST AS THOUGH YOU WERE HERE
(John Benson Brooks-Eddie DeLange)
Victor Records
With Tommy Dorsey and his Orchestra
Featuring The Pied Pipers
Recorded: August 6, 1942 (Radio aircheck)

JUST AS THOUGH YOU WERE HERE
(John Benson Brooks-Eddie DeLange)
Reprise Records
Arranged by Gordon Jenkins
Recorded: September 24, 1974

JUST CLOSE YOUR EYES
(L. Rodgers-J. Elliott-S. Mineo)
V-Disc recording
Columbia Records
Arranged by Axel Stordahl
Recorded: October 18, 1944
JUST FOR NOW
(Dick Redmond)
Columbia Records
Arranged by Axel Stordahl
Recorded: October 26, 1947
JUST FRIENDS
(John Klenner-Sam Lewis)
Capitol Records
Arranged by Gordon Jenkins
Recorded: March 26, 1959
JUST IN TIME
(Jule Styne-Betty Comden-Adolph Green)
Capitol Records
Arranged by Billy May
Recorded: December 9, 1958
JUST ONE OF THOSE THINGS
(Cole Porter)
Capitol Records
Arranged by Nelson Riddle
Recorded: April 7, 1954
JUST ONE OF THOSE THINGS
(Cole Porter)
Film recording for: 'Young At Heart'
Warner Bros.
Featuring Andre Previn, piano
Recorded: July 13-14, 1954
JUST ONE WAY TO SAY I LOVE YOU
(Irving Berlin)
Columbia Records
Arranged by Axel Stordahl
Recorded: May 6, 1949
JUST THE WAY YOU ARE
(Billy Joel)
Reprise Records
Arranged by Don Costa
Recorded: August 22, 1979
KISS ME AGAIN
(Henry Blossom-Victor Herbert)
V-Disc recording
Columbia Records
Arranged by Axel Stordahl
Recorded: October 17, 1943
KISS ME AGAIN
(Henry Blossom-Victor Herbert)
Columbia Records
Arranged by Axel Stordahl
Recorded: December 19, 1944
KISSES AND TEARS
(Sammy Cahn-Jule Styne)
Film recording for: 'Double Dynamite'
RKO Pictures
With Jane Russell
Arranged by Leigh Harline
Orchestra conducted by Constantin Bakaleinikoff
Recorded: December 2, 1948
KISSES AND TEARS
(Sammy Cahn-Jule Styne)
Columbia Records
With The Phil Moore Four
Arranged by Phil Moore
Recorded: January 4, 1949
KISSES AND TEARS
(Sammy Cahn-Jule Styne)
Columbia Records
With Jane Russell and The Modernaires
Arranged by Axel Stordahl
Recorded: February 23, 1950
L.A. IS MY LADY
(Alan & Marilyn Bergman-Quincy Jones-Peggy Lipton Jones)
Qwest Records
Arranged by Quincy Jones, Dave Matthews, Jerry Hey, Torrie Zito
Orchestra conducted by Quincy Jones
Recorded: April 13, 1984
LA CI DAREM LA MANO
(Wolfgang A. Mozart-Lorenzo da Ponte)
Film recording for: 'It Happened In Brooklyn'
Metro-Goldwyn-Mayer
With Kathryn Grayson
Arranged by Axel Stordahl
Orchestra conducted by Johnny Green
Recorded: July 18, 1946
LADY DAY
(Bob Gaudio-Jake Holmes)
Reprise Records
Arranged by Charles Calello
Recorded: August 25, 1969
LADY DAY
(Bob Gaudio-Jake Holmes)
Reprise Records
Arranged by Don Costa
Recorded: November 7, 1969
LAST NIGHT WHEN WE WERE YOUNG
(Harold Arlen-Yip Harburg)
Capitol Records
Arranged by Nelson Riddle
Recorded: March 1, 1954
LAST NIGHT WHEN WE WERE YOUNG
(Harold Arlen-Yip Harburg)
Reprise Records
Arranged by Gordon Jenkins
Recorded: April 13, 1965
LAURA
(Johnny Mercer-David Raskin)
Columbia Records
Arranged by Axel Stordahl
Recorded: October 22, 1947
LAURA
(Johnny Mercer-David Raskin)
Capitol Records
Arranged by Gordon Jenkins
Recorded: April 29, 1957
LEAN BABY
(Billy May-Roy Alfred)
Capitol Records
Arranged by Heinie Beau
Recorded: April 2, 1953
LEARNIN' THE BLUES
(Delores Vicki Silvers)
Capitol Records
Arranged by Nelson Riddle
Recorded: March 23, 1955
LEARNIN' THE BLUES
(Delores Vicki Silvers)
Reprise Records
With Count Basie and his Orchestra
Arranged by Neal Hefti
Recorded: October 2, 1962
LEAVING ON A JET PLANE
(John Denver)
Reprise Records
Arranged by Don Costa
Recorded: October 29, 1970
LET IT SNOW, LET IT SNOW, LET IT SNOW
(Sammy Cahn-Jule Styne)
Columbia Records
With The B. Swanson Quartet
Arranged by Axel Stordahl
Recorded: November 5, 1950
LET ME LOVE YOU TONIGHT
(Mitchell Parish-Rene Touzet)
V-Disc recording
Columbia Records
Arranged by Axel Stordahl
Recorded: October 18, 1944
LET ME TRY AGAIN
(Vasori Caraveli-Michel Jourdan-Paul Anka-Sammy Cahn)
Reprise Records
Arranged by Don Costa
Orchestra conducted by Gordon Jenkins
Recorded: June 21, 1973
LET ME TRY AGAIN
(Vasori Caraveli-Michel Jourdan-Paul Anka-Sammy Cahn)
Reprise Records
With Woody Herman and the Young Thundering Herd (Live recording)
Arranged by Don Costa
Orchestra conducted by Bill Miller
Recorded: October 13, 1974 (New York City)
LET US BREAK BREAD TOGETHER
(Traditional)
Reprise Records
With Bing Crosby and Fred Waring and his Pennsylvanians
Arranged by Roy Ringwald
Orchestra conducted by Fred Waring
Recorded: February 4, 1964
LET'S DO IT
(Cole Porter)
Capitol Records
With Shirley MacLaine
Arranged by Nelson Riddle
Recorded: September 22, 1959
LET'S FACE THE MUSIC AND DANCE
(Irving Berlin)
Reprise Records
Arranged by Johnny Mandel
Recorded: December 20, 1960
LET'S FACE THE MUSIC AND DANCE
(Irving Berlin)
Reprise Records
Arranged by Billy May
Recorded: September 19, 1979
LET'S FALL IN LOVE
(Harold Arlen-Ted Koehler)
Reprise Records
Arranged by Johnny Mandel
Recorded: December 19, 1960
LET'S GET AWAY FROM IT ALL
(Matt Dennis-Tom Adair)
Victor Records
With Tommy Dorsey and his Orchestra
Arranged by Sy Oliver
Featuring Connie Haines and The Pied Pipers
Recorded: February 17, 1941
LET'S GET AWAY FROM IT ALL
(Matt Dennis-Tom Adair)
Capitol Records
Arranged by Billy May
Recorded: October 1, 1957
LET'S TAKE AN OLD FASHIONED WALK
(Irving Berlin)
Columbia Pictures
With Doris Day and The Ken Lane Singers
Arranged by Axel Stordahl
Recorded: April 10, 1949
LIFE IS SO PECULIAR
(Johnny Burke-Jimmy Van Heusen)
Columbia Records
With Helen Carroll and The Swantones
Arranged by Percy Faith
Recorded: August 2, 1950
LIFE'S A TRIPPY THING
(Linda Laurie-Howard Greenfield)
Reprise Records
With Nancy Sinatra and vocal chorus
Arranged by Don Costa
Recorded: November 2, 1970
LIGHT A CANDLE IN THE CHAPEL
(Harry Pease-Ed Nelson-Duke Leonard)
Victor Records
With Tommy Dorsey and his Orchestra
Arranged by Axel Stordahl
Recorded: July 2, 1942
LIKE A SAD SONG
(John Denver)
Reprise Records
Arranged by Claus Ogerman
Orchestra conducted by Bill Miller
Recorded: September 27, 1976
LIKE SOMEONE IN LOVE
(Johnny Burke-Jimmy Van Heusen)
Capitol Records
Arranged by Nelson Riddle
Recorded: November 6, 1953
LILLY BELLE
(Dave Franklin-Irving Taylor)
Columbia Records
With The Charioteers
Arranged by Axel Stordahl
Recorded: May 16, 1945
LINDA
(Jack Lawrence-Ann Ronnel)
Reprise Records
Arranged by Nelson Riddle
Recorded: March 14, 1977
LITTLE GIRL BLUE
(Richard Rodgers-Lorenz Hart)
Capitol Records
Arranged by Nelson Riddle
Recorded: November 6, 1953
LITTLE GREEN APPLES
(Bobby Russell)
Reprise Records
Arranged by Don Costa
Orchestra conducted by Bill Miller
Recorded: November 13, 1968
LONDON BY NIGHT
(Carroll Coates)
Columbia Records
Arranged by Axel Stordahl
Recorded: September 21, 1950
LONDON BY NIGHT
(Carroll Coates)
Capitol Records
Arranged by Billy May
Recorded: October 3, 1957
LONDON BY NIGHT
(Carroll Coates)
Reprise Records
Arranged by Robert Farnon
Recorded: June 13, 1962
LONELY TOWN
(Leonard Bernstein-Betty Comden-Adolph Green)
Capitol Records
Arranged by Gordon Jenkins
Recorded: April 29, 1957
LONESOME MAN BLUES
(Oliver)
Film recording for: 'Meet Danny Wilson'
Universal International
Featuring George Fields, harmonica
Arranged by Joseph Gershenson
Recorded: June 21, 1951
LONESOME CITIES
(Rod McKuen)
Reprise Records
Arranged by Don Costa
Recorded: March 19, 1969
LONG AGO AND FAR AWAY
(Jerome Kern-Ira Gershwin)
V-Disc recording
Columbia Records
Arranged by Axel Stordahl
Recorded: February 9, 1944
LOOK TO YOUR HEART
(Sammy Cahn-Jimmy Van Heusen)
Capitol Records
With vocal chorus
Arranged by Nelson Riddle
Recorded: August 15, 1955
LOOKING AT THE WORLD THROUGH ROSE COLORED GLASSES
(J. Steiger-T. Malie)
Reprise Records
With Count Basie and his Orchestra
Arranged by Neal Hefti
Recorded: October 3, 1962
LOOKING FOR YESTERDAY
(Eddie DeLange-Jimmy Van Heusen)
Victor Records
With Tommy Dorsey and his Orchestra
Recorded: August 29, 1940
LOST IN THE STARS
(Maxwell Anderson-Kurt Weill)
Columbia Records
Arranged by Axel Stordahl
Recorded: August 8, 1946
LOST IN THE STARS
(Maxwell Anderson-Kurt Weill)
Reprise Records
Arranged by Nelson Riddle
Recorded: February 18, 1963
LOVE AND MARRIAGE
(Sammy Cahn-Jimmy Van Heusen)
Capitol Records
With band chorus
Arranged by Nelson Riddle
Recorded: August 15, 1955
LOVE AND MARRIAGE
(Sammy Cahn-Jimmy Van Heusen)
Reprise Records
Arranged by Nelson Riddle
Recorded: October 21, 1965
LOVE IS A MANY SPLENDORED THING
(Sammy Fain-Paul Francis Webster)
Reprise Records
Arranged by Nelson Riddle
Recorded: January 28, 1964
LOVE IS HERE TO STAY
(George Gershwin-Ira Gershwin)
Capitol Records
Arranged by Nelson Riddle
Recorded: October 17, 1955
LOVE IS JUST AROUND THE CORNER
(Leo Robin-Lewis Gensler)
Reprise Records
Arranged by Neal Hefti
Recorded: April 10, 1962
LOVE ISN'T JUST FOR THE YOUNG
(Miller-Kane)
Reprise Records
Arranged by Marty Paich
Recorded: July 31, 1963
LOVE LIES
(Carl Sigman-Ralph Freed-Joseph Meyer)
Victor Records
With Tommy Dorsey and his Orchestra
Recorded: July 17, 1940
LOVE LOCKED OUT
(Ray Noble-Max Kester)
Capitol Records
With The Hollywood String Quartet
Arranged by Nelson Riddle
Recorded: March 8, 1956
LOVE LOOKS SO WELL ON YOU
(Lew Spence-Marilyn Keith-Alan Bergman)
Capitol Records
Arranged by Nelson Riddle
Recorded: May 8, 1959
LOVE MAKES US WHATEVER WE WANT TO BE
(Sammy Cahn-Jule Styne)
Reprise Records
Arranged by Billy May
Recorded: August 17, 1982
LOVE ME
(Ned Washington-Victor Young)
Columbia Records
Arranged by Axel Stordahl
Recorded: March 27, 1951
LOVE ME AS I AM
(Frank Loesser-Louis Alter)
Victor Records
Arranged by Axel Stordahl
Recorded: May 28, 1941
LOVE ME TENDER
(Elvis Presley-Vera Matson)
Reprise Records
With vocal chorus
Arranged by Don Costa
Recorded: August 21, 1979
LOVE MEANS LOVE
(Arthur Lake-Carl Sigman)
Columbia Records
With Rosemary Clooney
Arranged by Axel Stordahl
Recorded: December 11, 1950
LOVE WALKED IN
(George Gershwin-Ira Gershwin)
Reprise Records
Arranged by Billy May
Recorded: May 18, 1961
LOVER
(Richard Rodgers-Lorenz Hart)
Columbia Records
Arranged by George Siravo
Recorded: April 14, 1950
LOVER
(Richard Rodgers-Lorenz Hart)
Capitol Records
Arranged by Heinie Beau
Orchestra conducted by Billy May
Recorded: March 22, 1961
LOVE'S BEEN GOOD TO ME
(Rod McKuen)
Reprise Records
Arranged by Don Costa
Recorded: March 20, 1969
LUCK BE A LADY
(Frank Loesser)
Reprise Records
Arranged by Billy May
Orchestra conducted by Morris Stoloff
Recorded: July 25, 1963
LUCK BE A LADY
(Frank Loesser)
Capitol Records
With Chrissie Hynde
Arranged by Billy May
Orchestra conducted by Patrick Williams
Recorded: July 9, 1990
LUNA ROSSA
(Vian-Kermit Goell-Vincenzo Decrescenzo)
Columbia Records
With The Norman Luboff Choir
Arranged by Axel Stordahl
Recorded: June 3, 1952
MACARTHUR PARK
(Jimmy Webb)
Reprise Records
Arranged by Don Costa
Recorded: August 20, 1979
MACK THE KNIFE
(Marc Blitzstein-Kurt Weill)
Qwest Records
Arranged by Frank Foster
Orchestra conducted by Quincy Jones
Recorded: April 16, 1984
MACK THE KNIFE
(Marc Blitzstein-Kurt Weill)
Reprise Records
Arranged by Frank Foster
Orchestra conducted by Quincy Jones
Recorded: October 30, 1986 (Vocal overdubbed over existing orchestra)
MACK THE KNIFE
(Marc Blitzstein-Kurt Weill)
Capitol Records
With Jimmy Buffet
Arranged by Frank Foster and Patrick Williams
Orchestra conducted by Patrick Williams
Recorded: May 17, 1994
MAD ABOUT YOU
(Ned Washington-Victor Young)
Columbia Records
Arranged by Jeff Alexander
Recorded: September 15, 1949
MAKIN' WHOOPEE
(Walter Donaldson-Gus Kahn)
Capitol Records
Arranged by Nelson Riddle
Recorded: January 16, 1956
MAMA WILL BARK
(Dick Manning)
Columbia Records
With Dagmar
Featuring Donald Bain, imitations
Arranged by Axel Stordahl
Recorded: May 10, 1951
MAM'SELLE
(Mack Gordon-Edmund Goulding)
Columbia Records
Arranged by Axel Stordahl
Recorded: March 11, 1947
MAM'SELLE
(Mack Gordon-Edmund Goulding)
Capitol Records
Arranged by Nelson Riddle
Recorded: March 3, 1960
MARIE
(Irving Berlin)
Victor Records
With Tommy Dorsey and his Orchestra and band chorus
Recorded: October 17, 1940 (Radio aircheck)
MAYBE YOU'LL BE THERE
(Rube Bloom-Sammy Gallop)
Capitol Records
Arranged by Gordon Jenkins
Recorded: May 1, 1957

ME AND MY SHADOW
(Al Jolson-Dave Cryer-Billy Rose)
Reprise Records
With Sammy Davis Jr.
Arranged by Billy May
Recorded: October 22, 1962
MEAN TO ME
(Roy Turk-Fred Ahlert)
Columbia Records
Arranged by Axel Stordahl
Recorded: October 31, 1947
MEDITATION
(Antonio Carlos Jobim-Ray Gilbert)
Reprise Records
With Antonio Carlos Jobim
Arranged by Claus Ogerman
Recorded: January 31, 1967
MEET ME AT THE COPA
(Axel Stordahl-Sammy Cahn)
Columbia Records
Arranged by George Siravo
Orchestra conducted by Axel Stordahl
Recorded: September 21, 1950
MELANCHOLY MOOD
(Vic Knight-Walter Schumann)
Columbia Records
With Harry James and his Orchestra
Arranged by Andy Gibson
Recorded: July 13, 1939
MELODY OF LOVE
(Harry Engleman-Tom Glazer)
Capitol Records
With Ray Anthony and his Orchestra
Arranged by Dick Reynolds
Recorded: December 13, 1954
MEMORIES OF YOU
(Eubie Blake-Andy Razaf)
Capitol Records
Arranged by Nelson Riddle
Recorded: January 9, 1956
MEMORIES OF YOU
(Eubie Blake-Andy Razaf)
Capitol Records
Arranged by Axel Stordahl
Recorded: September 11, 1961
MICHAEL AND PETER
(Bob Gaudio-Jake Holmes)
Reprise Records
Arranged by Charles Calello
Recorded: October 31, 1969
MIGHTY LAK' A ROSE
(Ethelbert Nevin-Frank Stanton)
Columbia Records
V-Disc recording
Arranged by Axel Stordahl
Recorded: July 8, 1944
MIGHTY LAK' A ROSE
(Ethelbert Nevin-Frank Stanton)
Columbia Records
Arranged by Axel Stordahl
Recorded: January 29, 1945
MIND IF I MAKE LOVE TO YOU?
(Cole Porter)
Capitol Records
Arranged by Nelson Riddle
MGM Studio Orchestra conducted by Johnny Green
Recorded: January 20, 1954
MISTER BOOZE
(Sammy Cahn-Jimmy Van Heusen)
Reprise Records
With Bing Crosby, Dean Martin, Sammy Davis Jr. and chorus
Arranged by Nelson Riddle
Recorded: April 10, 1964
MISTER BOOZE
(Sammy Cahn-Jimmy Van Heusen)
With Bing Crosby, Dean Martin, Sammy Davis Jr. and Chorus
Film recording for: 'Robin And The Seven Hoods'
Warner Bros.
Arranged by Nelson Riddle
Recorded: November 14, 1963
MISTLETOE AND HOLLY
(Dok Stanford-Hank Sanicola-Frank Sinatra)
Capitol Records
With The Ralph Brewster Singers
Arranged by Gordon Jenkins
Recorded: July 17, 1957
MISTY
(Erroll Garner-Johnny Burke)
Reprise Records
Arranged by Don Costa
Recorded: November 21, 1961
MOMENT TO MOMENT
(Henry Mancini-Johnny Burke)
Reprise Records
Arranged by Nelson Riddle
Recorded: October 21, 1965
MOMENTS IN THE MOONLIGHT
(Richard Himber-Irving Gordon-Al Kaufman)
Victor Records
With Tommy Dorsey and his Orchestra
Arranged by Paul Weston
Recorded: February 26, 1940
MONDAY MORNING QUARTERBACK
(Pamela Phillips-Don Costa)
Reprise Records
Arranged by Gordon Jenkins
Recorded: September 10, 1981
MONIQUE (Song from 'Kings Go Forth')
(Sammy Cahn-Elmer Bernstein)
Capitol Records
Arranged by Felix Slatkin
Recorded: May 29, 1958
MONTMART
(Cole Porter)
Capitol Records
With Maurice Chevalier and vocal chorus
Arranged by Nelson Riddle
Recorded: September 1, 1959
MOOD INDIGO
(Duke Ellington-Irving Mills-Barney Bigard)
Capitol Records
Arranged by Nelson Riddle
Recorded: February 16, 1955
MOODY RIVER
(Gary D. Bruce)
Reprise Records
With vocal chorus
Arranged by Don Costa
Orchestra conducted by Bill Miller
Recorded: November 13, 1968
MOON LOVE
(Mack David-Andre Kostelanetz)
Reprise Records
Arranged by Nelson Riddle
Recorded: November 29, 1965
MOON RIVER
(Henry Mancini-Johnny Mercer)
Reprise Records
Featuring Al Viola, guitar
Arranged by Nelson Riddle
Recorded: January 28, 1964
MOON SONG
(Sam Coslow-Arthur Johnston)
Reprise Records
Arranged by Nelson Riddle
Recorded: November 29, 1965
MOONLIGHT BAY
(Edward Madden-Percy Wenrich)
Film recording for: 'Ship Ahoy'
Metro-Goldwyn-Mayer
With Tommy Dorsey and his Orchestra
Featuring The Pied Pipers and vocal chorus
Arranged by Sy Oliver
Orchestra conducted by George Stoll
Recorded: December 29, 1941
MOONLIGHT BECOMES YOU
(Johnny Burke-Jimmy Van Heusen)
Reprise Records
Arranged by Nelson Riddle
Recorded: November 30, 1965
MOONLIGHT IN VERMONT
(Karl Suessdorf-John Blackburn)
Capitol Records
Arranged by Billy May
Recorded: October 3, 1957
MOONLIGHT IN VERMONT
(Karl Suessdorf-John Blackburn)
Reprise Records
With sextet accompaniment (Live recording)
Arranged by Neal Hefti and Billy May
Recorded: June 5, 1962 (Paris)
MOONLIGHT IN VERMONT
(Karl Suessdorf-John Blackburn)
Capitol Records
With Linda Ronstadt
Arranged by Patrick Williams
Recorded: October 12, 1993
MOONLIGHT MOOD
(Harold Adamson-Peter DeRose)
Reprise Records
Arranged by Nelson Riddle
Recorded: November 30, 1965
MOONLIGHT ON THE GANGES
(Sherman Myers-Chester Wallace)
Reprise Records
Featuring Emil Richards, percussion
Arranged by Billy May
Recorded: May 23, 1961
MOONLIGHT SERENADE
(Mitchell Parish-Glenn Miller)
Reprise Records
Arranged by Nelson Riddle
Recorded: November 29, 1965
MORE
(Riz Ortolani-N. Olivero-Ciorciolina-Norman Newell)
Reprise Records
With Count Basie and his Orchestra
Arranged by Quincy Jones
Recorded: June 12, 1964
MORE THAN YOU KNOW
(Billy Rose-Edward Eliscu-Vincent Youmans)
Reprise Records
With vocal chorus
Arranged by Billy May
Recorded: September 17, 1979
MR. SUCCESS
(Greines-Hank Sanicola-Frank Sinatra)
Capitol Records
Arranged by Nelson Hiddle
Recorded: September 11, 1958
MRS. ROBINSON
(Paul Simon)
Reprise Records
Arranged by Don Costa
Recorded: February 24, 1969
MY BABY JUST CARES FOR ME
(Gus Kahn-Walter Donaldson)
Reprise Records
Arranged by Nelson Riddle
Recorded: May 11, 1966
MY BLUE HEAVEN
(Walter Donaldson-George Whiting)
Columbia Records
Arranged by George Siravo
Recorded: April 24, 1950
MY BLUE HEAVEN
(Walter Donaldson-George Whiting)
Capitol Records
Featuring Plas Johnson, tenor saxophone
Arranged by Nelson Riddle
Recorded: August 23, 1960
MY BUDDY
(Walter Donaldson-Gus Kahn)
Columbia Records
With Harry James and his Orchestra
Arranged by Andy Gibson
Recorded: August 17, 1939
MY COUSIN LOUELLA
(Bernard Bierman-Jack Mannos)
Columbia Records
Arranged by John Guarnieri
Recorded: October 24, 1947
MY FOOLISH HEART
(Ned Washington-Victor Young)
Reprise Records
Arranged by Billy May
Recorded: June 6, 1988
MY FUNNY VALENTINE
(Richard Rodgers-Lorenz Hart)
Capitol Records
Arranged by Nelson Riddle
Recorded: November 5, 1953
MY FUNNY VALENTINE
(Richard Rodgers-Lorenz Hart)
Reprise Records
With sextet accompaniment (Live recording)
Arranged by Neal Hefti and Billy May
Recorded: June 5, 1962 (Paris)
MY FUNNY VALENTINE
(Richard Rodgers-Lorenz Hart)
Capitol Records
With Lorrie Morgan
Arranged by Patrick Williams
Recorded: October 14, 1993
MY GIRL
(Arthur Freed)
Columbia Records
Arranged by Axel Stordahl
Recorded: February 6, 1952
MY HEART STOOD STILL
(Richard Rodgers-Lorenz Hart)
Reprise Records
Arranged by Nelson Riddle
Recorded: February 18, 1963
MY KIND OF GIRL
(Leslie Bricusse)
Reprise Records
With Count Basie and his Orchestra
Arranged by Neal Hefti
Recorded: October 3, 1962
MY KIND OF TOWN
(Sammy Cahn-Jimmy Van Heusen)
Film recording for: 'Robin And The Seven Hoods'
Warner Bros.
With vocal chorus
Arranged by Nelson Riddle
Recorded: November 13, 1963
MY KIND OF TOWN
(Sammy Cahn-Jimmy Van Heusen)
Reprise Records
Arranged by Nelson Riddle
Recorded: April 8, 1964
MY KIND OF TOWN
(Sammy Cahn-Jimmy Van Heusen)
Reprise Records
With Count Basie and his Orchestra (Live recording)
Arranged by Quincy Jones and Billy Byers
Recorded: January 26-February 1, 1966 (Las Vegas)
MY KIND OF TOWN
(Sammy Cahn-Jimmy Van Heusen)
Reprise Records
With Woody Herman and the Young Thundering Herd (Live recording)
Arranged by Nelson Riddle
Orchestra conducted by Bill Miller
Recorded: October 13, 1974 (New York City)
MY KIND OF TOWN
(Sammy Cahn-Jimmy Van Heusen)
Capitol Records
With Frank Sinatra Jr.
Arranged by Nelson Riddle
Orchestra conducted by Patrick Williams
Recorded: July 9, 1993
MY LOVE FOR YOU
(Richard Heyman-Harry Jacobson)
Columbia Records
Arranged by Axel Stordahl
Recorded: January 9, 1947
MY MELANCHOLY BABY
(George Norton-Ernie Burnett)
Columbia Records
Arranged by Axel Stordahl
Recorded: January 29, 1945
MY ONE AND ONLY LOVE
(Guy Wood-Robert Mellin)
Capitol Records
Arranged by Nelson Riddle
Recorded: May 2, 1953
MY ROMANCE
(Richard Rodgers-Lorenz Hart)
V-Disc recording
Columbia Records
With Dinah Shore
Arranged and conducted by Axel Stordahl
Recorded: January 23, 1946
MY ROMANCE
(Richard Rodgers-Lorenz Hart)
Columbia Records
With Dinah Shore and vocal chorus
Arranged by Axel Stordahl
Recorded: April 25, 1947
MY SHAWL
(Stanley Adams-Xavier Cugat)
Columbia Records
Arranged by Xavier Cugat
Recorded: May 24, 1945
MY SHINING HOUR
(Johnny Mercer-Harold Arlen)
V-Disc recording
Columbia Records
Arranged by Axel Stordahl
Recorded: January 12, 1944
MY SHINING HOUR
(Johnny Mercer-Harold Arlen)
Reprise Records
With vocal chorus
Arranged by Billy May
Recorded: September 17, 1979
MY SWEET LADY
(John Denver)
Reprise Records
Arranged by Don Costa
Recorded: October 26, 1970
MY WAY
(Paul Anka-Claude Francois Ravaux-Gilles Thibault)
Reprise Records
Arranged by Don Costa
Recorded: December 30, 1968
MY WAY
(Paul Anka-Claude Francois Ravaux-Gilles Thibault)
Reprise Records
With Woody Herman and the Young Thundering Herd (Live recording)
Arranged by Don Costa
Orchestra conducted by Bill Miller
Recorded: October 13, 1974 (New York City)
MY WAY OF LIFE
(Burt Kaempfert-Herbert Rehbein-Carl Sigman)
Reprise Records
Arranged by Don Costa
Recorded: July 24, 1968
NAME IT AND IT'S YOURS
(Sammy Cahn-Jimmy Van Heusen)
Reprise Records
Arranged by Nelson Riddle
Recorded: November 22, 1961
NANCY
(Phil Silvers-Jimmy Van Heusen)
V-Disc recording
Columbia Records
Arranged by Axel Stordahl
Recorded: July 8, 1944
NANCY
(Phil Silvers-Jimmy Van Heusen)
Columbia Records
Arranged by Axel Stordahl
Recorded: December 3, 1944
NANCY
(Phil Silvers-Jimmy Van Heusen)
Columbia Records
Arranged by Axel Stordahl
Recorded: August 22, 1945
NANCY
(Phil Silvers-Jimmy Van Heusen)
Reprise Records
With sextet accompaniment (Live recording)
Arranged by Neal Hefti and Billy May
Recorded: June 5, 1962 (Paris)
NANCY
(Phil Silvers-Jimmy Van Heusen)
Reprise Records
Arranged by Nelson Riddle
Recorded: April 29, 1963
NANCY
(Phil Silvers-Jimmy Van Heusen)
Reprise Records
Arranged by Nelson Riddle
Recorded: March 9, 1977
NATURE BOY
(Eden Ahbez)
Columbia Records
With The Jeff Alexander Choir
Choral arrangement by Jeff Alexander
Recorded: April 10, 1948
NEIANI
(Axel Stordahl-Sy Oliver)
Victor Records
With Tommy Dorsey and his Orchestra
Featuring The Pied Pipers
Arranged by Axel Stordahl
Recorded: June 27, 1941
NEVERTHELESS
(Bert Kalmar-Harry Ruby)
Columbia Records
Featuring Billy Butterfield, trumpet
Arranged by George Siravo
Recorded: October 9, 1950
NEW YORK, NEW YORK
(Leonard Bernstein-Betty Comden-Adolph Green)
Film recording for: 'On The Town'
Metro-Goldwyn-Mayer
With Gene Kelly, Jules Munshin, Harry Stanton, Ralph Brewster, Charles Pavalato, Marvin Bailey and Bill Lee
Arranged by Saul Chaplin
Orchestra conducted by Lennie Hayton
Recorded: May 3, 1949
NEW YORK, NEW YORK
(Fred Ebb-John Kander)
Reprise Records
Arranged by Don Costa
Orchestra conducted by Vincent Falcone, Jr.
Recorded: September 19, 1979
NEW YORK, NEW YORK
(Fred Ebb-John Kander)
Capitol Records
With Tony Bennett
Arranged by Don Costa
Orchestra conducted by Patrick Williams
Recorded: July 6, 1993
NICE 'N EASY
(Lew Spence-Marilyn-Kieth-Alan Bergman)
Capitol Records
Arranged by Nelson Riddle
Recorded: April 13, 1960
NICE WORK IF YOU CAN GET IT
(George Gershwin-Ira Gershwin)
Capitol Records
Arranged by Nelson Riddle
Recorded: November 20, 1956
NICE WORK IF YOU CAN GET IT
(George Gershwin-Ira Gershwin)
Reprise Records
With Count Basie And His Orchestra
Arranged by Neal Hefti
Recorded: October 2, 1962
NIGHT
(Rod McKuen)
Reprise Records
Arranged by Don Costa
Recorded: March 21, 1969
NIGHT AFTER NIGHT
(Sammy Cahn-Paul Weston-Axel Stordahl)
Columbia Records
Arranged by Axel Stordahl
Recorded: March 3, 1949
NIGHT AND DAY
(Cole Porter)
Victor/Bluebird Records
Arranged by Axel Stordahl
Recorded: January 19, 1942
NIGHT AND DAY
(Cole Porter)
Film recording for: 'Reveille With Beverly'
Columbia Pictures
Arranged by Axel Stordahl and Morris Stoloff
Orchestra conducted by Morris Stoloff
Recorded: September 17, 1942
NIGHT AND DAY
(Cole Porter)
Columbia Records
Arranged by Axel Stordahl
Recorded: October 22, 1947
NIGHT AND DAY
(Cole Porter)
Capitol Records
Arranged by Nelson Riddle
Recorded: November 26, 1956
NIGHT AND DAY
(Cole Porter)
Reprise Records
Arranged by Don Costa
Recorded: November 22, 1961
NIGHT AND DAY
(Cole Porter)
Reprise Records

Featuring Al Viola, guitar (Live recording)
Solo guitar arrangement by Al Viola
Recorded: June 5, 1962 (Paris)

NIGHT AND DAY
(Cole Porter)
Reprise Records
Arranged by Joe Beck
Recorded: February 16, 1977

NO ONE EVER TELLS YOU
(Hub Atwood-Carroll Coates)
Capitol Records
Arranged by Nelson Riddle
Recorded: April 9, 1956

NO ORCHIDS FOR MY LADY
(Alan Stranks-Jack Strachey)
Columbia Records
Arranged by Axel Stordahl
Recorded: December 19, 1948

NOAH
(Joe Raposo)
Reprise Records
With vocal chorus
Arranged by Gordon Jenkins
Recorded: June 4, 1973

NOBODY WINS
(Kris Kristofferson)
Reprise Records
Arranged by Gordon Jenkins
Recorded: June 5, 1973

NONE BUT THE LONELY HEART
(Brandt)
V-Disc recording
Columbia Records
Arranged by Axel Stordahl
Recorded: January 31, 1945

NONE BUT THE LONELY HEART
(Brandt)
Columbia Records
Arranged by Axel Stordahl
Recorded: October 31, 1946

NONE BUT THE LONELY HEART
(Brandt)
Columbia Records
Arranged by Axel Stordahl
Recorded: October 26, 1947

NONE BUT THE LONELY HEART
(Brandt)
Capitol Records
Arranged by Gordon Jenkins
Recorded: March 24, 1959

NOT AS A STRANGER
(Jimmy Van Heusen-Buddy Kaye)
Capitol Records
Arranged by Nelson Riddle
Recorded: March 4, 1955

NOT SO LONG AGO
(Bickley Reichner-Ray Boland)
Victor Records
With Tommy Dorsey and his Orchestra
Arranged by Deane Kincaide
Recorded: November 11, 1940

NOTHING BUT THE BEST
(Rotella)
Reprise Records
Arranged by Neal Hefti
Recorded: February 27, 1962

NOTHING IN COMMON
(Sammy Cahn-Jimmy Van Heusen)
Capitol Records
With Keely Smith
Arranged by Billy May
Recorded: March 3, 1958

NOW IS THE HOUR
(Clement Scott-Maewa Kailau-Dorothy Stewart)
Reprise Records
Arranged by Robert Farnon
Recorded: June 14, 1962

O LITTLE TOWN OF BETHLEHEM
(Traditional)
Columbia Records
With The Ken Lane Singers
Arranged by Axel Stordahl
Recorded: December 28, 1947

O LITTLE TOWN OF BETHLEHEM
(Traditional)
Capitol Records
With The Ralph Brewster Singers
Arranged by Gordon Jenkins
Recorded: July 10, 1957

O'BRIEN TO RYAN TO GOLDBERG
(Roger Edens-Betty Comden-Adolph Green)
Film recording for: 'Take Me Out To The Ball Game'
Metro-Goldwyn-Mayer
With Gene Kelly and Jules Munshin
Arranged by Robert Tucker
Orchestra conducted by Adolph Deutsch
Recorded: July 23, 1948

OH HOW I MISS YOU TONIGHT
(Benny Davis-Joe Burke-Mark Fisher)
Reprise Records
Arranged by Gordon Jenkins
Recorded: January 17, 1962

OH! LOOK AT ME NOW
(John DeVries-Joe Bushkin)
Victor Records
With Tommy Dorsey and his Orchestra
Featuring Connie Haines and The Pied Pipers
Arranged by Sy Oliver
Recorded: January 6, 1941

OH! LOOK AT ME NOW
(John DeVries-Joe Bushkin)
Capitol Records
Arranged by Nelson Riddle
Recorded: November 26, 1956

OH WHAT A BEAUTIFUL MORNIN'
(Richard Rodgers-Oscar Hammerstein II)
Columbia Records
With The Bobby Tucker Singers
Choral arrangement by Alec Wilder
Recorded: August 5, 1943

OH, WHAT IT SEEMED TO BE
(George Weiss-Bennie Benjamin-Frankie Carle)
V-Disc recording
Columbia Records
Arranged by Axel Stordahl
Recorded: November 14, 1945

OH, WHAT IT SEEMED TO BE
(George Weiss-Bennie Benjamin-Frankie Carle)
Columbia Records
Arranged by Axel Stordahl
Recorded: November 30, 1945

OH, WHAT IT SEEMED TO BE
(George Weiss-Bennie Benjamin-Frankie Carle)
Reprise Records
Arranged by Nelson Riddle
Recorded: April 30, 1963

OH, YOU CRAZY MOON
(Johnny Burke-Jimmy Van Heusen)
Reprise Records
Arranged by Nelson Riddle
Recorded: November 30, 1965

OL' MACDONALD
(Lew Spence-Marilyn Keith-Alan Bergman)
Capitol Records
Arranged by Nelson Riddle
Recorded: September 1, 1960

OL' MAN RIVER
(Jerome Kern-Oscar Hammerstein II)
Columbia Records
Arranged by Axel Stordahl
Recorded: December 3, 1944

OL' MAN RIVER
(Jerome Kern-Oscar Hammerstein II)
V-Disc recording
Columbia Records
Arranged by Axel Stordahl
Recorded: April 14, 1945

OL' MAN RIVER
(Jerome Kern-Oscar Hammerstein II)
Film recording for: 'Till The Clouds Roll By'
Metro-Goldwyn-Mayer
Arranged by Kay Thompson
Orchestra conducted by Lennie Hayton
Recorded: March 18, 1946

OL' MAN RIVER
(Jerome Kern-Oscar Hammerstein II)
Reprise Records
Featuring Bill Miller, piano (Live recording)
Solo piano arrangement by Bill Miller
Recorded: June 5, 1962 (Paris)

OL' MAN RIVER
(Jerome Kern-Oscar Hammerstein II)
Reprise Records
Arranged by Nelson Riddle
Recorded: February 18, 1963

OLD DEVIL MOON
(Yip Harburg-Burton Lane)
Capitol Records
Arranged by Nelson Riddle
Recorded: January 16, 1956

OLD DEVIL MOON
(Yip Harburg-Burton Lane)
Reprise Records
Arranged by Nelson Riddle
Orchestra conducted by Morris Stoloff
Recorded: July 18, 1963

OLD SCHOOL TEACHER
(Robinson)
Columbia Records
Arranged by Mitch Miller
Recorded: November 15, 1945

ON A CLEAR DAY (You Can See Forever)
(Alan J. Lerner-Burton Lane)
Reprise Records
Arranged by Nelson Riddle
Recorded: May 16, 1966

ON A LITTLE STREET IN SINGAPORE
(Billy Hill-Peter DeRose)
Columbia Records
With Harry James and his Orchestra
Arranged by Andy Gibson
Recorded: October 13, 1939

ON THE ROAD TO MANDALAY
(Oley Speaks-Rudyard Kipling)
Capitol Records
Arranged by Billy May
Recorded: October 1, 1957

ON THE SUNNY SIDE OF THE STREET
(Dorothy Fields-Jimmy McHugh)
Capitol Records
Arranged by Heinie Beau
Orchestra conducted by Billy May
Recorded: March 20, 1961

ON THE TOWN
(Leonard Bernstein-Betty Comden-Adolph Green)
Film recording for: 'On The Town'
Metro-Goldwyn-Mayer
With Gene Kelly, Ann Miller, Vera Ellen, Betty Garrett,
Jules Munshin and Chorus
Arranged by Saul Chaplin
Orchestra conducted by Lennie Hayton
Recorded: March 23, 1949

ONCE I LOVED
(Antonio Carlos Jobim-Ray Gilbert-Vinicius DeMoraes)
Reprise Records
Arranged by Claus Ogerman
Recorded: February 1, 1967

ONCE IN A WHILE
(B. Green-M. Edwards)
Victor Records
With Tommy Dorsey and his Orchestra
Recorded: July 27, 1940 (Radio aircheck)

ONCE IN LOVE WITH AMY
(Frank Loesser)
Columbia Records
Featuring Henry Rowland, piano
Recorded: December 14, 1948 (Piano and vocal)

ONCE IN LOVE WITH AMY
(Frank Loesser)
Columbia Records
Arranged by Mitchell Ayres
Recorded: December 15, 1948 (Orchestra overdubbed)

(ONCE UPON A) MOONLIGHT NIGHT
(Sidney Clare-Irving Bibo)
Columbia Records
Arranged by Axel Stordahl
Recorded: August 22, 1946

ONCE UPON A TIME
(Lee Adams-Charles Strouse)
Reprise Records
Arranged by Gordon Jenkins
Recorded: April 14, 1965

ONE FINGER MELODY
(Al Hoffman-Kermit Goell-Fred Speilman)
Columbia Records
Arranged by Axel Stordahl
Recorded: September 18, 1950

ONE FOR MY BABY
(Harold Arlen-Johnny Mercer)
Columbia Records
Arranged by Axel Stordahl
Recorded: August 11, 1947

ONE FOR MY BABY
(Harold Arlen-Johnny Mercer)
Film recording for: 'Young At Heart'
Warner Bros.
Orchestra conducted by Ray Heindorf
Recorded: August 11, 1954

ONE FOR MY BABY
(Harold Arlen-Johnny Mercer)
Capitol Records
Featuring Bill Miller, piano
Recorded: June 24, 1958 (Rehearsal-piano & vocal only)

ONE FOR MY BABY
(Harold Arlen-Johnny Mercer)
Capitol Records
Featuring Bill Miller, piano
Arranged by Nelson Riddle
Recorded: June 26, 1958

ONE FOR MY BABY
(Harold Arlen-Johnny Mercer)
Reprise Records
Featuring Bill Miller, piano (Live recording)
Solo piano arrangement by Bill Miller
Recorded: June 5, 1962 (Paris)

ONE FOR MY BABY
(Harold Arlen-Johnny Mercer)
Reprise Records
With Count Basie And his Orchestra (Live recording)
Arranged by Quincy Jones and Billy Byers
Recorded: January 26-February 1, 1966 (Las Vegas)

ONE FOR MY BABY
(Harold Arlen-Johnny Mercer)
Capitol Records
Featuring Kenny G
Arranged by Patrick Williams
Recorded: July 1, 1993

ONE LOVE
(Leo Robin-David Rose)
Columbia Records
Arranged by Axel Stordahl
Recorded: February 3, 1946

ONE NOTE SAMBA
(Antonio Carlos Jobim-Newton Mendonca)
Reprise Records
With Antonio Carlos Jobim
Arranged by Eumir Deodato
Orchestra conducted by Morris Stoloff
Recorded: February 11, 1969

ONE RED ROSE
(Willard Moyle)
Victor Records
With Tommy Dorsey and his Orchestra
Recorded: March 27, 1941 (Radio aircheck)

ONLY FOREVER
(J. Burke-J. Monaco)
Victor Records
With Tommy Dorsey and his Orchestra
Recorded: October 17, 1940 (Radio aircheck)

ONLY ONE TO A CUSTOMER
(Jerry Leiber-Mike Stoller)
Reprise Records
Arranged by Billy May
Recorded: October 30, 1986

ONLY THE LONELY
(Sammy Cahn-Jimmy Van Heusen)
Capitol Records
Arranged by Nelson Riddle
Orchestra conducted by Felix Slatkins
Recorded: May 29, 1958

OUR LOVE AFFAIR
(Arthur Freed-Roger Edens)
Victor Records
With Tommy Dorsey and his Orchestra
Recorded: August 29, 1940

OUR TOWN
(Sammy Cahn-Jimmy Van Heusen)
Capitol Records
Arranged by Nelson Riddle
Recorded: August 15, 1955

OUT BEYOND THE WINDOW
(Rod McKuen)
Reprise Records
Arranged by Don Costa
Recorded: March 21, 1969

OVER THE RAINBOW
(Yip Harburg-Harold Arlen)
Columbia Records
With The Ken Lane Singers
Arranged by Axel Stordahl
Recorded: May 1, 1945

OVER THE RAINBOW
(Yip Harburg-Harold Arlen)
V-Disc recording
Columbia Records
Arranged by Axel Stordahl
Recorded: January 2, 1946

PALE MOON
(Jesse Glick-Frederick Knight Logan)
Victor Records
With Tommy Dorsey and his Orchestra
Recorded: August 19, 1941

PAPER DOLL
(Johnny Black)
Capitol Records
Arranged by Billy May
Recorded: March 22, 1961

PARADISE
(Nacio Herb Brown-Gordon Clifford)
Columbia Records
Arranged by Axel Stordahl
Recorded: December 7, 1945

PASS ME BY
(Cy Coleman-Carolyn Leigh)
Reprise Records
With vocal chorus
Arranged by Billy May
Recorded: October 3, 1964

PEACHTREE STREET
(Saunders-Mason-Frank Sinatra)
Columbia Records
With Rosemary Clooney
Arranged by George Siravo
Recorded: April 8, 1950

PEARL OF THE PERSIAN SEA
(Roger Edens-Betty Comden-Adolph Green)
Film recording for: 'On The Town'
Metro-Goldwyn-Mayer
With Gene Kelly and Jules Munshin
Arranged by Saul Chaplin
Orchestra conducted by Lennie Hayton
Recorded: March 24, 1949

PENNIES FROM HEAVEN
(Johnny Burke-Arthur Johnston)
Capitol Records
Arranged by Nelson Riddle
Recorded: January 10, 1956

PENNIES FROM HEAVEN
(Johnny Burke-Arthur Johnston)
Reprise Records
With Count Basie And his Orchestra
Arranged by Neal Hefti
Recorded: October 3, 1962

PEOPLE WILL SAY WE'RE IN LOVE
(Richard Rodgers-Oscar Hammerstein II)
Columbia Records
With The Bobby Tucker Singers
Choral arrangement by Alec Wilder
Recorded: June 22, 1943

PEOPLE WILL SAY WE'RE IN LOVE
(Richard Rodgers-Oscar Hammerstein II)
Columbia Records
With The Bobby Tucker Singers
Choral arrangement by Alec Wilder
Recorded: August 5, 1943

PICK YOURSELF UP
(Jerome Kern-Dorothy Fields)
Reprise Records
Arranged by Neal Hefti
Recorded: April 11, 1962

PLEASE BE KIND
(Sammy Cahn-Saul Chaplin)
Reprise Records
With Count Basie And his Orchestra
Arranged by Neal Hefti
Recorded: October 2, 1962

PLEASE DON'T TALK ABOUT ME WHEN I'M GONE
(Sammy Stept-Sidney Clare)
Reprise Records
Arranged by Billy May
Recorded: May 18, 1961

POCKETFUL OF MIRACLES
(Sammy Cahn-Jimmy Van Heusen)
Reprise Records
Arranged by Nelson Riddle
Recorded: November 22, 1961

POINCIANA
(Nat Simon-Buddy Bernier)
Columbia Records
Arranged by Axel Stordahl
Recorded: October 15, 1946

POINCIANA
(Nat Simon-Buddy Bernier)
Columbia Records
Arranged by Axel Stordahl
Recorded: October 29, 1947

POLKA DOTS AND MOONBEAMS
(Johnny Burke-Jimmy Van Heusen)
Victor Records
With Tommy Dorsey and his Orchestra
Arranged by Axel Stordahl
Recorded: March 4, 1940

POLKA DOTS AND MOONBEAMS
(Johnny Burke-Jimmy Van Heusen)
Reprise Records
Arranged by Sy Oliver
Recorded: May 2, 1961

POOR BUTTERFLY
(Raymond Hubbell-John L. Golden)
Reprise Records
With Duke Ellington And his Orchestra
Arranged by Billy May
Recorded: December 12, 1967

POOR YOU
(Yip Harburg-Burton Lane)
Film recording for: 'Ship Ahoy'
Metro-Goldwyn-Mayer
With Tommy Dorsey and his Orchestra,
Red Skelton and Virginia O'Brien
Arranged by Axel Stordahl
Orchestra conducted by George Stoll
Recorded: December 16, 1941

POOR YOU
(Yip Harburg-Burton Lane)
Victor Records
With Tommy Dorsey and his Orchestra
Arranged by Axel Stordahl
Recorded: February 19, 1942

PRETTY COLORS
(Al Giorgon-Chip Taylor)
Reprise Records
With vocal chorus
Arranged by Don Costa
Orchestra conducted by Bill Miller
Recorded: November 13, 1968

PRISONER OF LOVE
(Russ Columbo-Leo Robin-Clarence Gaskill)
Reprise Records
Arranged by Don Costa
Recorded: November 21, 1961

P.S. I LOVE YOU
(Gordon Jenkins-Johnny Mercer)
Capitol Records
With The Hollywood String Quartet
Arranged by Nelson Riddle
Recorded: March 8, 1956

PUT YOUR DREAMS AWAY
(Ruth Lowe-Stephen Weiss-Paul Mann)
V-Disc recording
Columbia Records
Arranged by Axel Stordahl

Recorded: May 24, 1944
PUT YOUR DREAMS AWAY
(Ruth Lowe-Stephen Weiss-Paul Mann)
Columbia Records
Arranged by Axel Stordahl
Recorded: May 1, 1945
PUT YOUR DREAMS AWAY
(Ruth Lowe-Stephen Weiss-Paul Mann)
Capitol Records
Arrranged by Nelson Riddle
Recorded: December 11, 1957
PUT YOUR DREAMS AWAY
(Ruth Lowe-Stephen Weiss-Paul Mann)
Reprise Records
Arranged by Nelson Riddle
Recorded: April 30, 1963
QUIET NIGHTS OF QUIET STARS
(Antonio Carlos Jobim-Gene Lees)
Reprise Records
With Antonio Carlos Jobim
Arranged by Claus Ogerman
Recorded: January 31, 1967
RAIN *(Falling From The Skies)*
(Robert Mellin-George Finlay)
Capitol Records
Arranged by Nelson Riddle
Recorded: December 9, 1953
RAIN IN MY HEART
(Teddy Randazzo-Vincent Pike)
Reprise Records
Arranged by Don Costa
Orchestra conducted by Bill Miller
Recorded: November 14, 1968
REACHING FOR THE MOON
(Irving Berlin)
Reprise Records
Arranged by Nelson Riddle
Recorded: November 29, 1965
REMEMBER
(Irving Berlin)
Reprise Records
Arranged by Gordon Jenkins
Recorded: January 16, 1962
REMEMBER ME IN YOUR DREAMS
(Morty Nevins-Hal David)
Columbia Records
With The Whippoorwills
Arranged by Axel Stordahl
Recorded: September 21, 1950
RING-A-DING-DING
(Sammy Cahn-Jimmy Van Heusen)
Reprise Records
Arranged by Johnny Mandel
Recorded: December 19, 1960
RIVER STAY 'WAY FROM MY DOOR
(Harry Woods-Mort Dixon)
Capitol Records
Arranged by Nelson Riddle
Recorded: April 13, 1960
ROSES OF PICARDY
(Haydn Wood-Fred Weatherly)
Reprise Records
Arranged by Robert Farnon
Recorded: June 13, 1962
SAME OLD SATURDAY NIGHT
(Reardon-Sammy Cahn)
Capitol Records
Arranged by Nelson Riddle
Recorded: July 29, 1955
SAME OLD SONG AND DANCE
(Sammy Cahn-Jimmy Van Heusen-Bobby Worth)
Capitol Records
Arranged by Billy May
Recorded: March 3, 1958
SAND AND SEA
(Gilbert Becaud-Mike Vidalin-Mack David)
Reprise Records
Arranged by Ernie Freeman
Recorded: November 18, 1966
SANTA CLAUS IS COMIN' TO TOWN
(Haven Gillespie-Fred Coots)
Columbia Records
Arranged by Axel Stordahl
Recorded: December 28, 1947
SANTA CLAUS IS COMIN' TO TOWN
(Haven Gillespie-Fred Coots)
A & M Records
With Cyndi Lauper
Arranged by Axel Stordahl
Additional instrumentation under the direction of Suzie Katayama
Frank Sinatra vocal recorded December 28, 1947
Cyndi Lauper vocal & additional instrumentation added 1992
SATISFY ME ONE MORE TIME
(Floyd Huddleston)
Reprise Records
Arranged by Don Costa
Recorded: May 21, 1974
SATURDAY NIGHT *(Is The Loneliest Night Of The Week)*
(Sammy Cahn-Jule Styne)
Special film recording for: 'All-Star Bond Rally'
20th Century Fox
With Harry James and his Orchestra
Arranged by George Siravo
Recorded: November 8, 1944
SATURDAY NIGHT *(Is The Loneliest Night Of The Week)*
(Sammy Cahn-Jule Styne)
Columbia Records
Arranged by George Siravo
Recorded: November 14, 1944
SATURDAY NIGHT *(Is The Loneliest Night Of The Week)*
(Sammy Cahn-Jule Styne)
Capitol Records
Arranged by Heinie Beau
Orchestra conducted by Billy May
Recorded: December 22, 1958
SAY HELLO
(Dick Behrke-Sammy Cahn)
Reprise Records
Arranged by Don Costa
Orchestra conducted by Vincent Falcone, Jr.
Recorded: July 21, 1981
SAY IT
(Frank Loesser-Jimmy McHugh)
Victor Records
With Tommy Dorsey and his Orchestra
Arranged by Axel Stordahl
Recorded: March 3, 1940
SECRET LOVE
(Sammy Fain-Paul Francis Webster)
Reprise Records
Arranged by Nelson Riddle
Recorded: January 28, 1964
SEND IN THE CLOWNS
(Stephen Sondheim)
Reprise Records
Arranged by Gordon Jenkins
Recorded: June 22, 1973
SEND IN THE CLOWNS
(Stephen Sondheim)
Reprise Records
Featuring Bill Miller, piano
Spoken introduction by Frank Sinatra
Recorded: February 5, 1976
SENORITA
(Edward Heyman-Nacio Herb Brown)
Film recording for: 'The Kissing Bandit'
Metro-Goldwyn-Mayer
With Kathryn Grayson and vocal chorus
Arranged by Leo Arnaud
Orchestra conducted by George Stoll
Recorded: June 28, 1947
SENORITA
(Edward Heyman-Nacio Herb Brown)
Columbia Records
Arranged by Axel Stordahl
Recorded: October 29, 1947
SENTIMENTAL BABY
(Lew Spence-Marilyn Keith-Alan Bergman)
Capitol Records
Arranged by Nelson Riddle
Recorded: September 1, 1960
SENTIMENTAL JOURNEY
(Lew Brown-Ben Homer-Bud Green)
Capitol Records
Arranged by Heinie Beau
Orchestra conducted by Billy May
Recorded: March 20, 1961
SEPTEMBER IN THE RAIN
(Harry Warren-Al Dubin)
Capitol Records
Arranged by Nelson Riddle
Recorded: August 31, 1960
SEPTEMBER OF MY YEARS
(Sammy Cahn-Jimmy Van Heusen)
Reprise Records
Arranged by Gordon Jenkins
Recorded: May 27, 1965
SEPTEMBER OF MY YEARS
(Sammy Cahn-Jimmy Van Heusen)
Reprise Records
With Count Basie and his Orchestra (Live recording)
Arranged by Quincy Jones and Billy Byers
Recorded: January 26-February 1, 1966 (Las Vegas)
SEPTEMBER SONG
(Kurt Weill-Maxwell Anderson)
Columbia Records
Arranged by Axel Stordahl
Recorded: July 30, 1946
SEPTEMBER SONG
(Kurt Weill-Maxwell Anderson)
Capitol Records
Arranged by Axel Stordahl
Recorded: September 11, 1961
SEPTEMBER SONG
(Kurt Weill-Maxwell Anderson)
Reprise Records
Arranged by Gordon Jenkins
Recorded: April 13, 1965
SERENADE IN BLUE
(Harry Warren-Mack Gordon)
Reprise Records
Arranged by Neal Hefti
Recorded: April 11, 1962
SHADOWS ON THE SAND
(Stanley Adams-Wilhelm Grosz)
Victor Records
Arranged by Fred Stulce
Recorded: September 17, 1940
SHAKE DOWN THE STARS
(Jimmy Van Heusen-Eddie DeLange)
Victor Records
With Tommy Dorsey and his Orchestra
Arranged by Paul Weston
Recorded: February 26, 1940
SHE SAYS
(Bob Gaudio-Jake Holmes)
Reprise Records
Arranged by Joseph Scott
With vocal chorus
Recorded: August 25, 1969
SHEILA
(Hayward-Frank Sinatra-Staver)
Columbia Records
With The Jeff Alexander Choir
Arranged by Axel Stordahl
Recorded: January 12, 1950
SHE'S FUNNY THAT WAY
(Neil Moret-Richard Whiting)
V-Disc recording
Columbia Records
Arranged by Axel Stordahl
Recorded: November 21, 1943
SHE'S FUNNY THAT WAY
(Neil Moret-Richard Whiting)
Columbia Records
Arranged by Axel Stordahl
Recorded: December 19, 1944
SHE'S FUNNY THAT WAY
(Neil Moret-Richard Whiting)
Film recording for: 'Meet Danny Wilson'
Universal International
Arranged by Joseph Gershenson
Recorded: June 13, 1951
SHE'S FUNNY THAT WAY
(Neil Moret-Richard Whiting)
Capitol Records
Arranged by Nelson Riddle
Recorded: March 2, 1960
SHOULD I?
(Nacio Herb Brown-Arthur Freed)
Columbia Records
Arranged by George Siravo
Recorded: April 14, 1950
SHOULD I?
(Nacio Herb Brown-Arthur Freed)
Capitol Records
Arranged by Nelson Riddle
Recorded: August 22, 1960
SIESTA
(Nacio Herb Brown-Earl Brent)
Film recording for: 'The Kissing Bandit'
Metro-Goldwyn-Mayer
Arranged by Leo Arnaud
Orchestra conducted by George Stoll
Recorded: May 27, 1947
SILENT NIGHT
(Franz Gruber-Joseph Mahr)
Special film recording for: Christmas Trailer
Metro-Goldwyn-Mayer
Arranged by Axel Stordahl
Recorded: August 17, 1945
SILENT NIGHT
(Franz Gruber-Joseph Mahr)
Columbia Records
With The Ken Lane Singers
Arranged by Axel Stordahl
Recorded: August 27, 1945
SILENT NIGHT
(Franz Gruber-Joseph Mahr)
Capitol Records
With The Ralph Brewster Singers
Arranged by Gordon Jenkins
Recorded: July 16, 1957
SILENT NIGHT
(Franz Gruber-Joseph Mahr)
Children's Records
Featuring Frank Sinatra, Jr., piano
Recorded: August 27, 1991
SINCE MARIE HAS LEFT PAREE
(Hy Glazer-Jerry Solomon)
Reprise Records
Arranged by Billy May
Recorded: July 17, 1964
SLEEP WARM
(Lew Spence-Marilyn Kieth-Alan Bergman)
Capitol Records
Arranged by Nelson Riddle
Recorded: September 11, 1958
SNOOTIE LITTLE CUTIE
(Bobby Troup)
Victor Records
With Tommy Dorsey and his Orchestra
Featuring Connie Haines and The Pied Pipers
Arranged by Sy Oliver
Recorded: February 19, 1942
SO FAR
(Richard Rodgers-Oscar Hammerstein II)
Columbia Records
Arranged by Axel Stordahl
Recorded: August 17, 1947
SO IN LOVE
(Cole Porter)
Reprise Records
With Keely Smith
Arranged by Nelson Riddle
Orchestra conducted by Morris Stoloff
Recorded: July 24, 1963
SO LONG, MY LOVE
(Sammy Cahn-Lew Spence)
Capitol Records
Arranged by Nelson Riddle
Recorded: March 14, 1957
SO THEY TELL ME
(Harold Mott-Jack Gale-Arthur Kent)
Columbia Records
Arranged by Axel Stordahl
Recorded: August 22, 1946
SOFTLY AS I LEAVE YOU
(Alfredo DeVita-Nick Calabrese-Hal Shaper)
Reprise Records
With vocal chorus
Arranged by Ernie Freeman
Recorded: July 17, 1964
SOLILOQUY
(Richard Rodgers-Oscar Hammerstein II)
Columbia Records
Arranged by Axel Stordahl
Recorded: April 7, 1946
SOLILOQUY
(Richard Rodgers-Oscar Hammerstein II)
Columbia Records
Arranged by Axel Stordahl
Recorded: May 28, 1946
SOLILOQUY
(Richard Rodgers-Oscar Hammerstein II)
Reprise Records
Arranged by Nelson Riddle
Recorded: February 21, 1963
SOME ENCHANTED EVENING
(Richard Rodgers-Oscar Hammerstein II)
Columbia Records
Arranged by Axel Stordahl
Recorded: February 28, 1949
SOME ENCHANTED EVENING
(Richard Rodgers-Oscar Hammerstein II)
Reprise Records
With Rosemary Clooney
Arranged by Nelson Riddle
Orchestra conducted by Morris Stoloff
Recorded: July 25, 1963
SOME ENCHANTED EVENING
(Richard Rodgers-Oscar Hammerstein II)
Reprise Records
Arranged by H.B. Barnum
Recorded: July 24, 1967
SOME OF YOUR SWEETNESS
(J. Clayborn-G. Clayborn)
Victor Records
With Tommy Dorsey and his Orchestra
Recorded: July 20, 1940 (Radio aircheck)
SOME OTHER TIME
(Sammy Cahn-Jule Styne)
Film recording for: 'Step Lively'
RKO Pictures
With Gloria DeHaven and vocal chorus
Arranged by Axel Stordahl
Orchestra conducted by Constantin Bakaleinikoff
Recorded: February 24-25, 1944
SOME OTHER TIME
(Sammy Cahn-Jule Styne)
V-Disc recording
Columbia Records
Arranged by Axel Stordahl
Recorded: May 17, 1944
SOME TRAVELING MUSIC
(Rod McKuen)
Reprise Records
Arranged by Don Costa
Recorded: March 21, 1969
SOMEONE TO LIGHT UP MY LIFE
(Antonio Carlos Jobim-Gene Lees-Vinicius DeMoraes)
Reprise Records
With Antonio Carlos Jobim
Arranged by Eumir Deodato
Orchestra by Morris Stoloff
Recorded: February 12, 1969
SOMEONE TO WATCH OVER ME
(George Gershwin-Ira Gershwin)
V-Disc recording
Columbia Records
Arranged by Axel Stordahl
Recorded: October 11, 1944
SOMEONE TO WATCH OVER ME
(George Gershwin-Ira Gershwin)
Columbia Records
Arranged by Axel Stordahl
Recorded: July 30, 1945
SOMEONE TO WATCH OVER ME
(George Gershwin-Ira Gershwin)
Film recording for: 'Young At Heart'
Warner Bros.
Arranged by Ray Heindorf
Recorded: July 12, 1954
SOMEONE TO WATCH OVER ME
(George Gershwin-Ira Gershwin)
Capitol Records
Arranged by Nelson Riddle
Recorded: September 23, 1954
SOMETHIN' STUPID
(C. Carson Parks)
Reprise Records
With Nancy Sinatra
Arranged by Billy Strange
Recorded: February 1, 1967
SOMETHING
(George Harrison)
Reprise Records
Arranged by Lennie Hayton
Recorded: October 28, 1970
SOMETHING
(George Harrison)
Reprise Records
Arranged by Nelson Riddle
Orchestra conducted by Vincent Falcone, Jr.
Recorded: December 3, 1979
SOMETHING OLD, SOMETHING NEW
(Ramez Idriss-George Tibbles)
Columbia Records
Arranged by Axel Stordahl
Recorded: February 24, 1946
SOMETHING WONDERFUL HAPPENS IN SUMMER
(Joe Bushkin-John DeVries)
Capitol Records
Arranged by Nelson Riddle
Recorded: May 20, 1957
SOMETHING'S GOTTA GIVE
(Johnny Mercer)
Capitol Records
Arranged by Billy May
Recorded: December 9, 1958
SOMEWHERE A VOICE IS CALLING
(Eileen Newton-Arthur Tate)
Victor Records
With Tommy Dorsey and his Orchestra
Arranged by Sy Oliver
Recorded: March 9, 1942
SOMEWHERE ALONG THE WAY
(Kurt Adams-Sammy Gallop)
Capitol Records
Arranged by Axel Stordahl
Recorded: September 12, 1961
SOMEWHERE IN THE NIGHT
(Mack Gordon-Josef Myrow)
Columbia Records
Arranged by Axel Stordahl
Recorded: May 28, 1946
SOMEWHERE IN YOUR HEART
(Russell Faith-Clarence Kehner)
Reprise Records
With vocal chorus
Arranged by Ernie Freeman
Recorded: November 10, 1964
SOMEWHERE MY LOVE
(Paul Francis Webster-Maurice Jarre)
Reprise Records
Arranged by Ernie Freeman
Recorded: November 17, 1966
SONG OF THE SABIA
(Chico Buarque de Hollanda-Antonio Carlos Jobim)
Reprise Records
With Antonio Carlos Jobim
Arranged by Eumir Deodato
Orchestra conducted by Morris Stoloff
Recorded: February 13, 1969
SONG SUNG BLUE
(Neil Diamond)
Reprise Records
With vocal chorus
Arranged by Don Costa
Recorded: August 22, 1979
SONG WITHOUT WORDS
(Gordon Jenkins)
Reprise Records
With The Los Angeles Philharmonic Symphony Orchestra and Chorus
Arranged by Gordon Jenkins
Recorded: December 17, 1979

SORRY
(Buddy Pepper-Richard Whiting)
Columbia Records
With The Modernaires
Arranged by Axel Stordahl
Recorded: November 8, 1949

SOUTH OF THE BORDER
(Jimmy Kennedy-Michael Carr)
Capitol Records
With band chorus
Arranged by Nelson Riddle
Recorded: April 30, 1953

SOUTH TO A WARMER PLACE
(Alec Wilder-Loonis McGlohon)
Reprise Records
Arranged by Gordon Jenkins
Recorded: July 21, 1981

S'POSIN'
(Andy Razaf-Paul Dennicker)
Columbia Records
Arranged by John Guarnieri
Recorded: October 24, 1947

S'POSIN'
(Andy Razaf-Paul Dennicker)
Capitol Records
Arranged by Nelson Riddle
Recorded: August 22, 1960

SPEAK LOW
(O. Nash-K. Weill)
V-Disc recording
Columbia Records
Arranged by Axel Stordahl
Recorded: December 5, 1943

SPRING IS HERE
(Richard Rodgers-Lorenz Hart)
Columbia Records
Arranged by Axel Stordahl
Recorded: October 31, 1947

SPRING IS HERE
(Richard Rodgers-Lorenz Hart)
Capitol Records
Arranged by Nelson Riddle
Orchestra conducted by Felix Slatkin
Recorded: May 29, 1958

STAR
(Sammy Cahn-Jimmy Van Heusen)
Reprise Records
Arranged by Nelson Riddle
Recorded: November 11, 1968

STARDUST
(Hoagy Carmichael-Mitchell Parish)
Victor Records
With Tommy Dorsey and his Orchestra
Featuring The Pied Pipers
Arranged by Sy Oliver
Recorded: November 11, 1940

STARDUST
(Hoagy Carmichael-Mitchell Parish)
Reprise Records
Arranged by Don Costa
Recorded: November 20, 1961

STARGAZER
(Neil Diamond)
Reprise Records
Featuring Sam Butera, saxophone
Arranged by Don Costa
Orchestra conducted by Bill Miller
Recorded: June 21, 1976

STARS FELL ON ALABAMA
(Frank Perkins-Mitchell Parish)
Capitol Records
Arranged by Nelson Riddle
Recorded: November 15, 1956

STARS IN YOUR EYES
(Gabriel Ruiz-Mort Green)
Columbia Records
Arranged by Xavier Cugat
Recorded: May 24, 1945

STAY WITH ME (Theme from 'The Cardinal')
(Jerome Moross-Carolyn Leigh)
Reprise Records
Arranged by Don Costa
Recorded: December 3, 1963

STELLA BY STARLIGHT
(Ned Washington-Victor Young)
Columbia Records
Arranged by Axel Stordahl
Recorded: March 11, 1947

STORMY WEATHER
(Harold Arlen-Ted Koehler)
Columbia Records
With The Ken Lane Singers
Featuring Yank Lawson, trumpet
Arranged by Axel Stordahl
Recorded: December 3, 1944

STORMY WEATHER
(Harold Arlen-Ted Koehler)
V-Disc recording
Columbia Records
With vocal chorus
Arranged by Axel Stordahl
Recorded: November 3, 1947

STORMY WEATHER
(Harold Arlen-Ted Koehler)
Capitol Records
Arranged by Gordon Jenkins
Recorded: March 24, 1959

STORMY WEATHER
(Harold Arlen-Ted Koehler)
Qwest Records
Arranged by Sam Nestico
Orchestra Conducted by Joe Parnello
Recorded: May 17, 1984

STRANGE MUSIC
(Robert Wright-George Forrest)
V-Disc recording
Columbia Records
Arranged by Axel Stordahl
Orchestra conducted by Raymond Paige
Recorded: October 23, 1944

STRANGE MUSIC
(Robert Wright-George Forrest)
Columbia Records
Arranged by Axel Stordahl
Recorded: October 15, 1946

STRANGE MUSIC
(Robert Wright-George Forrest)
Columbia Records
Arranged by Axel Stordahl
Recorded: October 22, 1947

STRANGERS IN THE NIGHT
(Bert Kaempfert-Charles Singleton-Eddie Snyder)
Reprise Records
Arranged by Ernie Freeman
Recorded: April 11, 1966

STREET OF DREAMS
(Victor Young-Sam Lewis)
Victor Records
With Tommy Dorsey and his Orchestra
Featuring The Pied Pipers
Arranged by Axel Stordahl
Recorded: May 18, 1942

STREET OF DREAMS
(Victor Young-Sam Lewis)
Reprise Records
With Count Basie and his Orchestra (Live recording)
Arranged by Quincy Jones and Billy Byers
Recorded: January 26-February 1, 1966
(Las Vegas)

STREET OF DREAMS
(Victor Young-Sam Lewis)
Reprise Records
Arranged by Billy May
Recorded: September 18, 1979

STRICTLY U.S.A.
(Roger Edens)
Film recording for: 'Take Me Out To The Ball Game'
Metro-Goldwyn-Mayer
With Gene Kelly, Jules Munshin, Esther Williams, Betty Garrett, Dick Lane, Tommy Dugan and Chorus
Arranged by Robert Tucker
Orchestra conducted by Adolph Deutsch
Recorded: September 8, 1948

STRICTLY U.S.A. (Finale)
(Roger Edens)
Film recording for: 'Take Me Out To The Ball Game'
Metro-Goldwyn-Mayer
With Gene Kelly, Esther Williams, Betty Garrett and The Judy Matson Vocalists and Chorus
Arranged by Robert Tucker
Orchestra conducted by Adolph Deutsch
Recorded: October 15, 1948

STROMBOLI
(Irving Taylor-Ken Lane)
Columbia Records
Arranged by Jeff Alexander
Recorded: September 15, 1949

STYLE
(Sammy Cahn-Jimmy Van Heusen)
Film recording for: 'Robin And The Seven Hoods'
Warner Bros.
With Bing Crosby and Dean Martin
Arranged by Nelson Riddle
Recorded: December 3, 1963

STYLE
(Sammy Cahn-Jimmy Van Heusen)
Reprise Records
With Bing Crosby and Dean Martin
Arranged by Nelson Riddle
Recorded: April 10, 1964

SUE ME
(Frank Loesser)
Film recording for: 'Guys And Dolls'
Samuel Goldwyn Production
With Vivian Blaine
Arranged by Nelson Riddle
Orchestra conducted by Jay Blackton
Recorded: March 9, 1955

SUMMER ME, WINTER ME
(Alan & Marilyn Bergman-Michel Legrand)
Reprise Records
Arranged by Don Costa
Recorded: August 20, 1979

SUMMER WIND
(Henry Mayer-Johnny Mercer)
Reprise Records
Arranged by Nelson Riddle
Recorded: May 16, 1966

SUMMER WIND
(Henry Mayer-Johnny Mercer)
Capitol Records
With Julio Iglesias
Arranged by Nelson Riddle
Orchestra conducted by Patrick Williams
Recorded: July 6, 1993

SUNDAY
(Ned Miller-Benny Krueger-Chester Conn-Jule Styne)
Capitol Records
Arranged by Nelson Riddle
Recorded: April 7, 1954

SUNDAY, MONDAY OR ALWAYS
(Johnny Burke-Jimmy Van Heusen)
Columbia Records
With The Bobby Tucker Singers
Choral arrangement by Alec Wilder
Recorded: June 7, 1943

SUNFLOWER
(Mack David)
Columbia Records
Arranged by Axel Stordahl
Recorded: December 6, 1948

SUNNY
(Bobby Hebb)
Reprise Records
With Duke Ellington And his Orchestra
Arranged by Billy May
Recorded: December 12, 1967

SUNRISE IN THE MORNING
(Paul Ryan)
Reprise Records
Arranged by Don Costa
Recorded: October 28, 1970

SUNSHINE CAKE
(Johnny Burke-Jimmy Van Heusen)
Columbia Records
With Paula Kelly
Arranged by Axel Stordahl
Recorded: November 8, 1949

SURE THING
(Johnny Burke-Jimmy Van Heusen)
Columbia Records
With The Modernaires
Arranged by Axel Stordahl
Recorded: November 8, 1949

SWEET CAROLINE
(Neil Diamond)
Reprise Records
Arranged by Don Costa
Recorded: May 8, 1974

SWEET LORRAINE
(Mitchell Parish-Cliff Burwell)
Columbia Records
With The Metronome All-Stars
Arranged by Sy Oliver
Recorded: December 17, 1946

SWEET LORRAINE
(Mitchell Parish-Cliff Burwell)
Reprise Records
Arranged by Nelson Riddle
Recorded: March 14, 1977

SWINGIN' DOWN THE LANE
(Isham Jones-Gus Kahn)
Capitol Records
Arranged by Nelson Riddle
Recorded: January 12, 1956

SWINGING ON A STAR
(Johnny Burke-Jimmy Van Heusen)
Reprise Records
Arranged by Nelson Riddle
Recorded: January 27, 1964

TAKE A CHANCE
(David Raskin-Dok Stanford)
Capitol Records
Arranged by Nelson Riddle
Recorded: December 8, 1953

TAKE ME
(Rube Bloom-Mack David)
Victor Records
With Tommy Dorsey and his Orchestra
Arranged by Axel Stordahl
Recorded: June 9, 1942

TAKE ME
(Rube Bloom-Mack David)
Reprise Records
Arranged by Sy Oliver
Recorded: May 1, 1961

TAKE ME OUT TO THE BALL GAME
(Alber von Tilzer-Jack Norworth)
Film recording for: 'Take Me Out To The Ball Game'
Metro-Goldwyn-Mayer
With Gene Kelly
Arranged by Robert Tucker
Orchestra conducted by Adolph Deutsch
Recorded: July 22, 1948

TAKE MY LOVE
(Jack Wolf-Joel Heron-Frank Sinatra)
Columbia Records
Arranged by Axel Stordahl
Recorded: November 16, 1950

TAKING A CHANCE ON LOVE
(Vernon Duke-John Latouche-Ted Fetter)
Capitol Records
Arranged by Nelson Riddle
Recorded: April 19, 1954

TALK TO ME
(Eddie Snyder-Rudy Vallee-Stanley Kahan)
Capitol Records
Arranged by Nelson Riddle
Recorded: May 14, 1959

TALK TO ME BABY
(Dolan-Johnny Mercer)
Reprise Records
Arranged by Don Costa
Recorded: December 3, 1963

TANGERINE
(Victor Schertzinger-Johnny Mercer)
Reprise Records
Arranged by Neal Hefti
Recorded: April 11, 1962

TEA FOR TWO
(Vincent Youmans-Irving Ceasar)
Columbia Records
With Dinah Shore
Arranged by Axel Stordahl
Recorded: April 25, 1947

TEACH ME TONIGHT
(Sammy Cahn-Gene De Paul)
Qwest Records
Arranged by Torrie Zito
Orchestra conducted by Quincy Jones
Recorded: April 17, 1984

TELL HER YOU LOVE HER
(Denison-Sol Parker-Halliday)
Capitol Records
Arranged by Nelson Riddle
Recorded: May 20, 1957

TELL HER YOU LOVE HER (Each Day)
(Gil Ward)
Reprise Records
With vocal chorus
Arranged by Ernie Freeman
Recorded: April 14, 1965

TELL ME AT MIDNIGHT
(Bickley Reichner-Ray Boland)
Victor Records
With Tommy Dorsey and his Orchestra
Recorded: August 29, 1940

TENNESSEE NEWSBOY
(Bob Manning-Percy Faith)
Arranged by Axel Stordahl
Recorded: June 3, 1952

THANKS FOR THE MEMORY
(Leo Robin-Ralph Rainger)
Reprise Records
Arranged by Gordon Jenkins
Recorded: July 20, 1981

THAT LUCKY OLD SUN
(Haven Gillespie-Beasley Smith)
Columbia Records
Arranged by Jeff Alexander
Recorded: September 15, 1949

THAT OLD BLACK MAGIC
(Johnny Mercer-Harold Arlen)
Columbia Records
Arranged by Axel Stordahl
Recorded: March 10, 1946

THAT OLD BLACK MAGIC
(Johnny Mercer-Harold Arlen)
Film recording for: 'Meet Danny Wilson'
Universal International
Arranged by Joseph Gershenson
Recorded: June 13, 1951

THAT OLD BLACK MAGIC
(Johnny Mercer-Harold Arlen)
Capitol Records
Arranged by Heinie Beau
Orchestra conducted by Billy May
Recorded: March 21, 1961

THAT OLD FEELING
(Lew Brown-Sammy Fain)
Columbia Records
Arranged by Axel Stordahl
Recorded: August 11, 1947

THAT OLD FEELING
(Lew Brown-Sammy Fain)
Capitol Records
Arranged by Nelson Riddle
Recorded: March 1, 1960

THAT'S ALL
(Bob Haynes-Alan Brandt)
Reprise Records
Arranged by Don Costa
Recorded: November 21, 1961

THAT'S HOW IT GOES
(L. Martin-M. Gentile)
Victor Records
With Tommy Dorsey and his Orchestra
Featuring Connie Haines and The Pied Pipers
Recorded: January 30, 1941 (Radio aircheck)

THAT'S HOW MUCH I LOVE YOU
Columbia Records
With The Page Cavanaugh Trio
Arranged by Page Cavanaugh
Recorded: December 15, 1946

THAT'S LIFE
(Dean Kay-Kelly Gordon)
Reprise Records
With vocal chorus
Arranged by Ernie Freeman
Recorded: October 18, 1966

THAT'S WHAT GOD LOOKS LIKE TO ME
(Stan Irwin-Lan O'Kun)
Reprise Records
With vocal chorus
Arranged by Don Costa
Recorded: August 21, 1979

THE BEAUTIFUL STRANGERS
(Rod McKuen)
Reprise Records
Arranged by Don Costa
Recorded: March 20, 1969

THE BELLS OF CHRISTMAS (Greensleaves)
(Adapted by Sammy Cahn-Jimmy Van Heusen)
Reprise Records
With Nancy, Frank Jr. and Tina Sinatra
Arranged by Nelson Riddle
Recorded: August 12, 1968

THE BEST I EVER HAD
(Danny & Ruby Hice)
Reprise Records
Featuring Sam Butera, saxophone
Arranged by Billy May
Recorded: June 21, 1976

THE BEST IS YET TO COME
(Cy Coleman-Carolyn Leigh)
Reprise Records
With Count Basie and his Orchestra
Arranged by Quincy Jones
Recorded: June 9, 1964

THE BEST IS YET TO COME
(Cy Coleman-Carolyn Leigh)
Capitol Records
With Jon Secada
Arranged by Quincy Jones
Orchestra conducted by Patrick Williams
Recorded: October 11, 1993

THE BEST OF EVERYTHING
(Fred Ebb-John Kander)
Qwest Records
Arranged by Joe Parnello
Orchestra conducted by Quincy Jones
Recorded: April 16, 1984

THE BIRTH OF THE BLUES
(Buddy DeSylva-Lew Brown-Ray Henderson)
Columbia Records
Arranged by Heinie Beau
Orchestra conducted by Axel Stordahl
Recorded: June 3, 1952

THE BOYS NIGHT OUT
(Sammy Cahn-Jimmy Van Heusen)
Reprise Records
Arranged by Billy May
Recorded: March 6, 1962

THE BROOKLYN BRIDGE
(Sammy Cahn-Jule Styne)
Film recording for: 'It Happened In Brooklyn'
Metro-Goldwyn-Mayer
Arranged by Axel Stordahl
Orchestra conducted by Johnny Green
Recorded: June 6, 1946

THE BROOKLYN BRIDGE
(Sammy Cahn-Jule Styne)
Columbia Records
Arranged by Axel Stordahl
Recorded: October 31, 1946

THE CALL OF THE CANYON
(Billy Hill)
Victor Records
With Tommy Dorsey and his Orchestra
Recorded: July 17, 1940

THE CHARM OF YOU
(Sammy Cahn-Jule Styne)
Film recording for: 'Anchors Aweigh'
Metro-Goldwyn-Mayer
Arranged by Axel Stordahl
Orchestra conducted by George Stoll
Recorded: August 18, 1944

THE CHARM OF YOU
(Sammy Cahn-Jule Styne)
Columbia Records
Arranged by Axel Stordahl
Recorded: December 3, 1944

THE CHRISTMAS SONG
(Mel Torme-Bob Wells)
Capitol Records
With The Ralph Brewster Singers

Arranged by Gordon Jenkins
Recorded: July 17, 1957
THE CHRISTMAS WALTZ
(Sammy Cahn-Jule Styne)
Capitol Records
With vocal chorus
Arranged by Nelson Riddle
Recorded: August 23, 1954
THE CHRISTMAS WALTZ
(Sammy Cahn-Jule Styne)
Capitol Records
With The Ralph Brewster Singers
Arranged by Gordon Jenkins
Recorded: July 16, 1957
THE CHRISTMAS WALTZ
(Sammy Cahn-Jule Styne)
Reprise Records
Arranged by Nelson Riddle
Recorded: August 12, 1968
THE COFFEE SONG
(Bob Hilliard-Dick Miles)
Columbia Records
Arranged by Axel Stordahl
Recorded: July 24, 1946
THE COFFEE SONG
(Bob Hilliard-Dick Miles)
Reprise Records
Arranged by Johnny Mandel
Recorded: December 20, 1960
THE CONTINENTAL
(Herb Magidson-Con Conrad)
Columbia Records
Arranged by George Siravo
Recorded: April 24, 1950
THE CONTINENTAL
(Herb Magidson-Con Conrad)
Reprise Records
Arranged by Nelson Riddle
Recorded: January 27, 1964
THE CURSE OF AN ACHING HEART
(Henry Fink-Al Piantadosi)
Reprise Records
Arranged by Billy May
Recorded: May 18, 1961
THE DAYS OF WINE AND ROSES
(Henry Mancini-Johnny Mercer)
Reprise Records
Arranged by Nelson Riddle
Recorded: January 28, 1964
THE DUM DOT SONG
(Julian Kay)
Columbia Records
With The Pied Pipers
Arranged by Axel Stordahl
Recorded: November 7, 1946
THE END OF A LOVE AFFAIR
(Redding)
With The Hollywood String Quartet
Capitol Records
Arranged by Nelson Riddle
Recorded: April 5, 1956
THE FABLE OF THE ROSE
(Bickley Reichner-Josef Myrow)
Victor Records
With Tommy Dorsey and his Orchestra
Arranged by Axel Stordahl
Recorded: March 12, 1940
THE FIRST NOEL
(Traditional)
Capitol Records
With The Ralph Brewster Singers
Arranged by Gordon Jenkins
Recorded: July 16, 1957
THE FUTURE
(Gordon Jenkins)
Reprise Records
With the Los Angeles Philharmonic
Symphony Orchestra and Chorus
Arranged by Gordon Jenkins
Recorded: December 3, 1979
THE GAME IS OVER
(Nick Perito)
Reprise Records
Arranged by Don Costa
Recorded: November 2, 1970
THE GAL THAT GOT AWAY
(Harold Arlen-George Gershwin)
Capitol Records
Arranged by Nelson Riddle
Recorded: May 13, 1954
**THE GAL THAT GOT AWAY/ IT NEVER
ENTERED MY MIND** (Medley)
(Arlen-Gershwin/Rodgers-Hart)
Reprise Records
Arranged by Nelson Riddle
Orchestra conducted by Vincent Falcone, Jr.
Recorded: April 8, 1981

THE GIRL FROM IPANEMA
(Antonio Carlos Jobim-Gene Lees-Vincent
DeMoraes)
Reprise Records
With Antonio Carlos Jobim
Arranged by Claus Ogerman
Recorded: January 31, 1967
THE GIRL NEXT DOOR
(Hugh Martin-Ralph Blane)
Capitol Records
Arranged by Nelson Riddle
Recorded: November 6, 1953
THE GIRL NEXT DOOR
(Hugh Martin-Ralph Blane)
Reprise Records
Arranged by Gordon Jenkins
Recorded: January 16, 1962
THE GIRL THAT I MARRY
(Irving Berlin)
Columbia Records
Arranged by Axel Stordahl
Recorded: March 10, 1946
**THE GIRL WHO STOLE
THE EIFFEL TOWER**
Special film recording for: 'Paris When It
Sizzles'
Paramount Pictures
Arranged by Nelson Riddle
Recorded: March 13, 1963
THE GIRLS I NEVER KISSED
(Jerry Leiber-Mike Stoller)
Reprise Records
Arranged by Billy May
Recorded: October 30, 1986
THE GOOD LIFE
(Sacha Distel-Jack Reardon)
Reprise Records
With Count Basie and his Orchestra
Arranged by Quincy Jones
Recorded: June 10, 1964
THE GYPSY
(Billy Reid)
Reprise Records
Arranged by Robert Farnon
Recorded: June 13, 1962
THE HOUSE I LIVE IN
(Lewis Allen-Earl Robinson)
Film recording for: 'The House I Live In'
RKO Pictures
Arranged by Axel Stordahl
Recorded: May 8, 1945
THE HOUSE I LIVE IN
(Lewis Allen-Earl Robinson)
Columbia Records
Arranged by Axel Stordahl
Recorded: August 22, 1945
THE HOUSE I LIVE IN
(Lewis Allen-Earl Robinson)
Reprise Records
With Fred Waring and his Pennsylvanians
Arranged by Nelson Riddle
Orchestra conducted by Fred Waring
Recorded: January 2, 1964
THE HOUSE I LIVE IN
(Lewis Allen-Earl Robinson)
Reprise Records
With Woody Herman and the Young
Thundering Herd (Live recording)
Arranged by Nelson Riddle
Orchestra conducted by Bill Miller
Recorded: October 13, 1974
THE HOUSE I LIVE IN
(Lewis Allen-Earl Robinson)
Capitol Records
With Neil Diamond
Arranged by Don Costa
Orchestra conducted by Patrick Williams
Recorded: October 14, 1993
THE HUCKLEBUCK
(Roy Alfred-Andy Gibson)
Columbia Records
Featuring Herbie Haymer, saxophone
Arranged by Axel Stordahl
Recorded: April 10, 1949
THE HURT DOESN'T GO AWAY
(Joe Raposo)
Reprise Records
Arranged by Gordon Jenkins
Recorded: June 5, 1973
THE IMPATIENT YEARS
(Sammy Cahn-Jimmy Van Heusen)
Capitol Records
Arranged by Nelson Riddle
Recorded: August 15, 1955
THE IMPOSSIBLE DREAM
(Joe Darion-Mitch Leigh)
Reprise Records
Arranged by Ernie Freeman
Recorded: November 18, 1966
THE LADY IS A TRAMP
(Richard Rodgers-Lorenz Hart)
Capitol Records
Arranged by Nelson Riddle
Recorded: November, 26, 1956

THE LADY IS A TRAMP
(Richard Rodgers-Lorenz Hart)
Film recording for: 'Pal Joey'
Columbia Pictures
Arranged by Nelson Riddle
Orchestra conducted by Morris Stoloff
Recorded: May 23, 1957
THE LADY IS A TRAMP
(Richard Rodgers-Lorenz Hart)
Reprise Records
With sextet accompaniment (Live recordings)
Arranged by Neal Hefti and Billy May
Recorded: June 5, 1962
THE LADY IS A TRAMP
(Richard Rodgers-Lorenz Hart)
Reprise Records
With Woody Herman And The Young
Thundering Herd (Live recording)
Arranged by Billy Byers
Orchestra conducted by Bill Miller
Recorded: October 13, 1974 (New York City)
THE LADY IS A TRAMP
(Richard Rodgers-Lorenz Hart)
Capitol Records
With Luther Vandross
Arranged by Billy Byers
Orchestra conducted by Patrick Williams
Recorded: July 1, 1993
THE LAMPLIGHTER'S SERENADE
(Hoagy Carmichael-Paul Francis Webber)
Victor/Bluebird Records
Arranged by Axel Stordahl
Recorded: January 19, 1942
THE LAST CALL FOR LOVE
(Yip Harburg-Marjorie Cummings-
Burton Lane)
Film recording for: 'Ship Ahoy'
Metro-Goldwyn-Mayer
With Tommy Dorsey and his Orchestra
Featuring The Pied Pipers
Arranged by Axel Stordahl
Orchestra conducted by George Stoll
Recorded: December 16, 1941
THE LAST CALL FOR LOVE
(Yip Harburg-Marjorie Cummings-
Burton Lane)
Victor Records
With Tommy Dorsey and his Orchestra
Featuring The Pied Pipers
Arranged by Axel Stordahl
Recorded: February 19, 1942
THE LAST DANCE
(Sammy Cahn-Jimmy Van Heusen)
Capitol Records
Arranged by Heinie Beau
Orchestra conducted by Billy May
Recorded: December 23, 1958
THE LAST DANCE
(Sammy Cahn-Jimmy Van Heusen)
Reprise Records
Arranged by Nelson Riddle
Orchestra conducted by Felix Slatkin
Recorded: December 21, 1960
THE LITTLE DRUMMER BOY
(Katherine Davis-Henry Onorati-Harry
Simeone)
Reprise Records
With Fred Waring & His Pennsylvanians
Arranged by Jack Halloran
Orchestra conducted by Fred Waring
Recorded: June 16, 1964
THE LONESOME ROAD
(Nathaniel Shilkret-Gene Austin)
Capitol Records
Arranged by Nelson Riddle
Recorded: November 26, 1956
THE LOOK OF LOVE
(Sammy Cahn-Jimmy Van Heusen)
Reprise Records
Arranged by Nelson Riddle
Orchestra conducted by Neal Hefti
Recorded: August 27, 1962
THE LORD'S PRAYER
(A. H. Malotte)
Columbia Records
With The Jeff Alexander Chorus
Arranged by Jeff Alexander
Recorded: October 26, 1949 (Radio
aircheck)
THE MAN IN THE LOOKING GLASS
(Bart Howard)
Reprise Records
Arranged by Gordon Jenkins
Recorded: April 22, 1965
THE MOON GOT IN MY EYES
(Johnny Burke-Arthur Johnston)
Reprise Records
Arranged by Nelson Riddle
Recorded: November 29, 1965
THE MOON WAS YELLOW
(Edgar Leslie-Fred Ahlert)
Columbia Records
With The Ken Lane Singers
Arranged by Axel Stordahl
Recorded: August 27, 1945
THE MOON WAS YELLOW
(Edgar Leslie-Fred Ahlert)
Capitol Records
Arranged by Nelson Riddle
Recorded: December 29, 1958

THE MOON WAS YELLOW
(Edgar Leslie-Fred Ahlert)
Reprise Records
Arranged by Nelson Riddle
Recorded: November 30, 1965
**THE MOST BEAUTIFUL GIRL
IN THE WORLD**
(Richard Rodgers-Lorenz Hart)
Reprise Records
Arranged by Nelson Riddle
Recorded: May 11, 1966
THE MUSIC STOPPED
(Harold Adamson-Jimmy McHugh)
Film recording for: 'Higher And Higher'
RKO Pictures
Arranged by Axel Stordahl
Orchestra conducted by Constantin
Bakaleinikoff
Recorded: September 1, 1943
THE MUSIC STOPPED
(Harold Adamson-Jimmy McHugh)
Columbia Records
With The Bobby Tucker Singers
Choral arrangement by Alec Wilder
Recorded: November 3, 1943
THE MUSIC STOPPED
(Harold Adamson-Jimmy McHugh)
Columbia Records
With The Bobby Tucker Singers
Choral arrangement by Alec Wilder
Recorded: November 10, 1943
THE MUSIC STOPPED
(Harold Adamson-Jimmy McHugh)
V-Disc recording
Columbia Records
Arranged by Axel Stordahl
Recorded: November 14, 1943
THE MUSIC STOPPED
(Harold Adamson-Jimmy McHugh)
Columbia Records
Arranged by Axel Stordahl
Recorded: October 29, 1947
THE NEARNESS OF YOU
(Hoagy Carmichael-Ned Washington)
Columbia Records
Arranged by Axel Stordahl
Recorded: August 11, 1947
THE NEARNESS OF YOU
(Hoagy Carmichael-Ned Washington)
Capitol Records
Arranged by Nelson Riddle
Recorded: March 2, 1960
**THE NIGHT IS YOUNG AND YOU'RE
SO BEAUTIFUL**
(I. Kahal-B. Rose-D. Seusse)
V-Disc recording
Columbia Records
With Dinah Shore
Arranged by Axel Stordahl
Recorded: September 26, 1945
THE NIGHT WE CALLED IT A DAY
(Matt Dennis-Tom Adair)
Victor/Bluebird Records
Arranged by Axel Stordahl
Recorded: January 19, 1942
THE NIGHT WE CALLED IT A DAY
(Matt Dennis-Tom Adair)
Capitol Records
Arranged by Gordon Jenkins
Recorded: April 10, 1957
THE OLD MASTER PAINTER
(Haven Gillespie-Beasley Smith)
Columbia Records
With The Modernaires
Arranged by Axel Stordahl
Recorded: October 30, 1949
THE OLDEST ESTABLISHED
(Permanent Floating Crap Game In
New York)
(Frank Loesser)
Film recording for: 'Guys And Dolls'
Samuel Goldwyn Production
With Stubby Kaye, Johnny Silver and Chorus
Arranged by Nelson Riddle
Orchestra conducted by Jay Blackton
Recorded: March 1, 1955
THE OLDEST ESTABLISHED
(Permanent Floating Crap Game In
New York)
(Frank Loesser)
Reprise Records
With Bing Crosby and Dean Martin
Arranged by Billy May
Orchestra conducted by Morris Stoloff
Recorded: July 29, 1963
THE ONE I LOVE (Belongs To Somebody
Else)
(Gus Kahn-Isham Jones)
Victor Records
With Tommy Dorsey and his Orchestra
Featuring The Pied Pipers
Arranged by Sy Oliver
Recorded: June 27, 1940
THE ONE I LOVE (Belongs To Somebody
Else)
(Gus Kahn-Isham Jones)
Capitol Records
Arranged by Gordon Jenkins
Recorded: March 25, 1959
THE ONE I LOVE (Belongs To Somebody
Else)
(Gus Kahn-Isham Jones)

Reprise Records
With Sy Oliver
Arranged by Sy Oliver
Recorded: May 3, 1961
THE ONLY COUPLE ON THE FLOOR
(John Durrill)
Reprise Records
With vocal chorus
Arranged by Don Costa
Orchestra conducted by Bill Miller
Recorded: March 5, 1975
THE RIGHT GIRL FOR ME
(Betty Comden-Roger Edens-Adolph Green)
Film recording for: 'Take Me Out To The
Ball Game'
Metro-Goldwyn-Mayer
Arranged by Robert Tucker
Orchestra conducted by Adolph Deutsch
Recorded: August 12, 1948
THE RIGHT GIRL FOR ME
(Betty Comden-Roger Edens-Adolph Green)
Columbia Records
Arranged by Axel Stordahl
Recorded: March 3, 1949
THE SADDEST THING OF ALL
(Michel Legrand-Carl Sigman-Eddy Barclay)
Reprise Records
Arranged by Gordon Jenkins
Recorded: August 18, 1975
THE SEA SONG (By The Beautiful Sea)
(Arthur Schwartz-Howard Dietz)
Capitol Records
With vocal chorus
Arranged by Nelson Riddle
Recorded: April 2, 1954
THE SECOND TIME AROUND
(Sammy Cahn-Jimmy Van Heusen)
Reprise Records
Arranged by Nelson Riddle
Orchestra conducted by Felix Slatkin
Recorded: December 21, 1960
THE SECOND TIME AROUND
(Sammy Cahn-Jimmy Van Heusen)
Reprise Records
With sextet accompaniment (Live recording)
Arranged by Neal Hefti and Billy May
Recorded: June 5, 1962 (Paris)
THE SECOND TIME AROUND
(Sammy Cahn-Jimmy Van Heusen)
Reprise Records
Arranged by Nelson Riddle
Recorded: April 29, 1963
THE SHADOW OF THE MOON
(E. Brown-H. Kiessling)
Reprise Records
Arranged by Don Costa
Orchestra conducted by Sonny Burke
Recorded: March 25, 1965
THE SHADOW OF YOUR SMILE
(Johnny Mandel-Paul Francis Webster)
Reprise Records
With Count Basie and his Orchestra (Live
recording)
Arranged by Quincy Jones and Billy Byers
Recorded: January 26-February 1, 1966
(Las Vegas)
THE SINGLE MAN
(Rod McKuen)
Reprise Records
Arranged by Don Costa
Recorded: March 19, 1969
THE SKY FELL DOWN
(Edward Heyman-Louis Alter)
Victor Records
With Tommy Dorsey and his Orchestra
Arranged by Axel Stordahl
Recorded: February 1, 1940
THE SONG IS ENDED
(Irving Berlin)
Reprise Records
Arranged by Gordon Jenkins
Recorded: January 15, 1962
THE SONG IS YOU
(Jerome Kern-Oscar Hammerstein II)
Victor/Bluebird Records
Arranged by Axel Stordahl
Recorded: January 19, 1942
THE SONG IS YOU
(Jerome Kern-Oscar Hammerstein II)
Victor Records
With Tommy Dorsey and his Orchestra
Arranged by Axel Stordahl
Recorded: September 3, 1942 (Radio
aircheck)

THE SONG IS YOU
(Jerome Kern-Oscar Hammerstein II)
Columbia Records
Arranged by Axel Stordahl
Recorded: February 13, 1946
THE SONG IS YOU
(Jerome Kern-Oscar Hammerstein II)
Columbia Records
Arranged by Axel Stordahl
Recorded: October 26, 1947
THE SONG IS YOU
(Jerome Kern-Oscar Hammerstein II)
Capitol Records
Arranged by Billy May
Recorded: December 9, 1958
THE SONG IS YOU
(Jerome Kern-Oscar Hammerstein II)
Reprise Records
Arranged by Billy May
Recorded: September 18, 1979
THE SONG'S GOTTA COME FROM THE HEART
(Sammy Cahn-Jule Styne)
Film recording for: 'It Happened In Brooklyn'
Metro-Goldwyn-Mayer
Arranged by Axel Stordahl
Orchestra conducted by Johnny Green
Recorded: September 26, 1946
THE STARS WILL REMEMBER
(Don Pelusi-Leo Towers)
Columbia Records
Arranged by Axel Stordahl
Recorded: July 3, 1947
THE SUMMER KNOWS
(Alan & Marilyn Bergman-Michel Legrand)
Reprise Records
Arranged by Gordon Jenkins
Recorded: May 7, 1974
THE SUMMIT (Comedy routine)
Reprise Records
With Dean Martin and Sammy Davis, Jr.
(Live performance)
Recorded: September 6-8, 1963 (Las Vegas)
THE SUNSHINE OF YOUR SMILE
(Leonard Cooke-Lillian Ray)
Victor Records
With Tommy Dorsey and his Orchestra
Arranged by Sy Oliver
Recorded: September 26, 1941
THE TENDER TRAP *(Main Title)*
(Sammy Cahn-Jimmy Van Heusen)
Film recording for: 'The Tender Trap'
Metro-Goldwyn-Mayer
Featuring Bill Miller, piano
Arranged by Jeff Alexander
Recorded: July 15, 1955
THE TENDER TRAP *(End Title)*
(Sammy Cahn-Jimmy Van Heusen)
Film recording for: 'The Tender Trap'
Metro-Goldwyn-Mayer
With Debbie Reynolds, David Wayne, Celeste Holm and Johnny Green
Arranged by Jeff Alexander
Recorded: July 27, 1955
THE TENDER TRAP
(Sammy Cahn-Jimmy Van Heusen)
Capitol Records
Arranged by Nelson Riddle
Recorded: September 13, 1955
THE TENDER TRAP
(Sammy Cahn-Jimmy Van Heusen)
Reprise Records
With Count Basie and his Orchestra
Arranged by Neal Hefti
Recorded: October 3, 1962
THE THINGS I LOVE
(H. Barlow-L. Harris)
Victor Records
With Tommy Dorsey and his Orchestra
Recorded: June 12, 1941 (Radio aircheck)
THE THINGS WE DID LAST SUMMER
(Sammy Cahn-Jule Styne)
Columbia Records
Arranged by Axel Stordahl
Recorded: July 24, 1946
THE TRAIN
(Bob Gaudio-Jake Holmes)
Reprise Records
Arranged by Joseph Scott
Recorded: August 25, 1969
THE TWELVE DAYS OF CHRISTMAS
(Sammy Cahn-Jimmy Van Heusen)
Reprise Records
With Nancy, Frank Jr. and Tina Sinatra
Arranged by Nelson Riddle
Recorded: August 12, 1968
THE VERY THOUGHT OF YOU
(Ray Noble)
Reprise Records
Arranged by Robert Farnon
Recorded: June 12, 1962
THE WAY YOU LOOK TONIGHT
(Dorothy Fields-Jimmy McHugh)
V-Disc recording
Columbia Records
With The Bobby Tucker Singers
Arranged by Axel Stordahl
Probably recorded: November 14, 1943
THE WAY YOU LOOK TONIGHT
(Dorothy Fields-Jimmy McHugh)
Reprise Records
Arranged by Nelson Riddle
Recorded: January 27, 1964
THE WEDDING OF LILI MARLENE
(Tommie Connor-Michael Reine)
Columbia Records
Arranged by Morris Stoloff
Recorded: July 21, 1949
THE WORLD IS IN MY ARMS
(Yip Harburg-Burton Lane)
Victor Records
With Tommy Dorsey and his Orchestra
Recorded: July 17, 1940
THE WORLD WE KNEW *(Over and Over)*
(Burt Kaempfert-Herbert Rehbein-Carl Sigman)
Reprise Records
Arranged by Ernie Freeman
Orchestra conducted by Billy Strange
Recorded: June 29, 1967
THEN SUDDENLY LOVE
(Paul Vance-Roy Alfred)
Reprise Records
With vocal chorus
Arranged by Ernie Freeman
Recorded: July 17, 1964
THERE ARE SUCH THINGS
(Stanley Adams-Abel Baer-George Meyer)
Victor Records
With Tommy Dorsey and his Orchestra
Featuring The Pied Pipers
Arranged by Axel Stordahl
Recorded: July 1, 1942
THERE ARE SUCH THINGS
(Stanley Adams-Abel Baer-George Meyer)
Reprise Records
Arranged by Sy Oliver
Recorded: May 3, 1961
THERE BUT FOR YOU GO I
(Alan J. Lerner-Frederick Lowe)
Columbia Records
Arranged by Axel Stordahl
Recorded: March 31, 1947
THERE USED TO BE A BALLPARK
(Joe Raposo)
Reprise Records
Arranged by Gordon Jenkins
Recorded: June 22, 1973
THERE WILL NEVER BE ANOTHER YOU
(M. Gordon-H.Warden)
Capitol Records
Arranged by Axel Stordahl
Recorded: September 11, 1961
THERE'LL BE A HOT TIME IN THE TOWN OF BERLIN
(Joe Bushkin-Johnny DeVries)
V-Disc recording
Columbia Records
Arranged by Axel Stordahl
Recorded: October 17, 1943
THERE'LL BE A HOT TIME IN THE TOWN OF BERLIN
(Joe Bushkin-Johnny DeVries)
Special film recording for: 'The Shining Future'
Warner Bros.
Arranged by Axel Stordahl
Orchestra conducted by Leo Forbstein
Recorded: March 4, 1944
THERE'S A FLAW IN MY FLUE
(Johnny Burke-Jimmy Van Heusen)
Capitol Records
With The Hollywood String Quartet
Arranged by Nelson Riddle
Recorded: April 5, 1956
THERE'S A SMALL HOTEL
(Richard Rodgers-Lorenz Hart)
Film recording for: 'Pal Joey'
Columbia Pictures
Arranged by Nelson Riddle
Orchestra conducted by Morris Stoloff
Recorded: June 14, 1957
THERE'S A SMALL HOTEL
(Richard Rodgers-Lorenz Hart)
Capitol Records
Arranged by Nelson Riddle
Recorded: August 13, 1957
THERE'S NO BUSINESS LIKE SHOW BUSINESS
(Irving Berlin)
Columbia Records
With vocal chorus
Arranged by Axel Stordahl
Recorded: August 22, 1946
THERE'S NO YOU
(Hal Hopper-Tom Adair)
Columbia Records
Arranged by Axel Stordahl
Recorded: October 11, 1944
THERE'S NO YOU
(Hal Hopper-Tom Adair)
Columbia Records
Arranged by Axel Stordahl
Recorded: November 14, 1944
THERE'S NO YOU
(Hal Hopper-Tom Adair)
Capitol Records
Arranged by Gordon Jenkins
Recorded: April 10, 1957
THERE'S SOMETHING MISSING
(Dave Dryer-Gilbert Wolf)
Columbia Records
Arranged by George Siravo
Recorded: January 16, 1951
THESE FOOLISH THINGS
(Jack Strachey-Harry Link-Holt Marvell)
Columbia Records
Arranged by Axel Stordahl
Recorded: July 30, 1945
THESE FOOLISH THINGS
(Jack Strachey-Harry Link-Holt Marvell)
Capitol Records
Arranged by Axel Stordahl
Recorded: September 12, 1961
THEY ALL LAUGHED
(George Gershwin-Ira Gershwin)
Reprise Records
Arranged by Billy May
Recorded: September 18, 1979
THEY CAME TO CORDURA
(Sammy Cahn-Jimmy Van Heusen)
Capitol Records
Arranged by Nelson Riddle
Recorded: December 29, 1958
THEY CAN'T TAKE THAT AWAY FROM ME
(George Gershwin-Ira Gershwin)
Capitol Records
Arranged by Nelson Riddle
Recorded: November 5, 1953
THEY CAN'T TAKE THAT AWAY FROM ME
(George Gershwin-Ira Gershwin)
Reprise Records
Arranged by Neal Hefti
Recorded: April 10, 1962
THEY CAN'T TAKE THAT AWAY FROM ME
(George Gershwin-Ira Gershwin)
Reprise Records
With sextet accompaniment (Live recording)
Arranged by Neal Hefti and Billy May
Recorded: June 5, 1962 (Paris)
THEY CAN'T TAKE THAT AWAY FROM ME
(George Gershwin-Ira Gershwin)
Capitol Records
With Natalie Cole
Arranged by Patrick Williams
Recorded: July 1, 1993
THEY SAY IT'S WONDERFUL
(Irving Berlin)
Columbia Records
Arranged by Axel Stordahl
Recorded: March 10, 1946
THEY SAY IT'S WONDERFUL
(Irving Berlin)
Columbia Records
Arranged and conducted by Axel Stordahl
Recorded: April 24, 1945
THIS HAPPY MADNESS
(Antonio Carlos Jobim-Gene Lees-Vinicius DeMoraes)
Reprise Records
With Antonio Carlos Jobim
Arranged by Eumir Deodato
Orchestra conducted by Morris Stoloff
Recorded: February 13, 1969
THIS IS ALL I ASK
(Gordon Jenkins)
Reprise Records
Arranged by Gordon Jenkins
Recorded: April 22, 1965
THIS IS MY LOVE
(Jim Harbert)
Reprise Records
Arranged by Gordon Jenkins
Recorded: July 24, 1967
THIS IS MY SONG
(Charles Chaplin)
Reprise Records
Arranged by Ernie Freeman
Recorded: July 24, 1967
THIS IS THE BEGINNING OF THE END
(Mack Gordon)
Victor Records
With Tommy Dorsey and his Orchestra
Recorded: March 12, 1940
THIS IS THE NIGHT
(Red Evans-Lewis Berlin)
Columbia Records
Arranged by Axel Stordahl
Recorded: July 24, 1946
THIS LOVE OF MINE
(Sol Parker-Hank Sanicola-Frank Sinatra)
Victor Records
With Tommy Dorsey and his Orcehstra
Arranged by Axel Stordahl
Recorded: May 28, 1941
THIS LOVE OF MINE
(Sol Parker-Hank Sanicola-Frank Sinatra)
Capitol Records
Arranged by Nelson Riddle
Recorded: February 17, 1955
THIS NEARLY WAS MINE
(Richard Rodgers-Oscar Hammerstein II)
Reprise Records
Arranged by Nelson Riddle
Recorded: February 19, 1963
THIS TOWN
(Lee Hazelwood)
Reprise Records
Arranged by Billy Strange
Recorded: July 24, 1967
THIS WAS MY LOVE
(Jim Harbert)
Capitol Records
Arranged by Nelson Riddle
Recorded: May 14, 1959
THREE COINS IN THE FOUNTAIN
(Sammy Cahn-Jule Styne)
Capitol Records
Arranged by Nelson Riddle
Recorded: March 1, 1954
THREE COINS IN THE FOUNTAIN
(Main Title)
(Sammy Cahn-Jule Styne)
Film recording for: 'Three Coins In The Fountain'
20th Century Fox
Arranged by Victor Young
Recorded: March 31, 1954
THREE COINS IN THE FOUNTAIN
(Sammy Cahn-Jule Styne)
Reprise Records
Arranged by Nelson Riddle
Recorded: January 27, 1964
TIE A YELLOW RIBBON ROUND THE OLD OAK TREE
(Larry Brown-Irwin Levine)
Reprise Records
Arranged by Don Costa
Recorded: May 21, 1974
TIME AFTER TIME
(Sammy Cahn-Jule Styne)
Film recording for: 'It Happened In Brooklyn'
Metro-Goldwyn-Mayer
Arranged by Axel Stordahl
Orchestra conducted by Johnny Green
Recorded: September 17, 1946
TIME AFTER TIME
(Sammy Cahn-Jule Styne)
Columbia Records
Arranged by Axel Stordahl
Recorded: October 24, 1946
TIME AFTER TIME
(Sammy Cahn-Jule Styne)
Capitol Records
Arranged by Nelson Riddle
Recorded: November 25, 1957
TINA
(Sammy Cahn-Jimmy Van Heusen)
Reprise Records
Arranged by Nelson Riddle
Orchestra conducted by Felix Slatkin
Recorded: December 21, 1960
TO LOVE A CHILD
(Joe Raposo-Hal David)
Reprise Records
Featuring Nikka Costa and vocal chorus
Arranged by Don Costa
Orchestra conducted by Vincent Falcone, Jr.
Recorded: December 5, 1981
TO LOVE AND BE LOVED
(Sammy Cahn-Jimmy Van Heusen)
Capitol Records
Arranged by Nelson Riddle
Recorded: October 15, 1958
TOGETHER
(Buddy DeSylva-Lew Brown-Ray Henderson)
Reprise Records
Arranged by Gordon Jenkins
Recorded: January 16, 1962
TONIGHT WE LOVE
(Adapted from Tchaikovsky)
Film recording for: 'Anchors Aweigh'
Metro-Goldwyn-Mayer
Orchestra conducted by George Stoll
Recorded: March 2, 1945
TOO CLOSE FOR COMFORT
(Jerry Bock-Larry Holofcener-George Weiss)
Capitol Records
Arranged by Heinie Beau
Orchestra conducted by Billy May
Recorded: December 23, 1958
TOO MARVELOUS FOR WORDS
(Richard Whiting-Johnny Mercer)
Capitol Records
Arranged by Nelson Riddle
Recorded: January 16, 1956
TOO MARVELOUS FOR WORDS
(Richard Whiting-Johnny Mercer)
Reprise Records
With sextet accompaniment (Live recording)
Arranged by Neal Hefti and Billy May
Recorded: June 5, 1962 (Paris)
TOO ROMANTIC
(Johnny Burke-James Monaco)
Victor Records
With Tommy Dorsey and his Orchestra
Arranged by Paul Weston
Recorded: February 1, 1940
TRADE WINDS
(Cliff Friend-Charlie Tobias)
Victor Records
With Tommy Dorsey and his Orchestra
Recorded: June 27, 1940
TRISTE
(Antonio Carlos Jobim)
Reprise Records
With Antonio Carlos Jobim
Arranged by Eumir Deodato
Orchestra conducted by Morris Stoloff
Recorded: February 13, 1969
TRY A LITTLE TENDERNESS
(Harry Woods-Jimmy Campbell-Reg Conolly)
Columbia Records
Arranged by Axel Stordahl
Recorded: December 7, 1945
TRY A LITTLE TENDERNESS
(Harry Woods-Jimmy Campbell-Reg Conolly)
Capitol Records
Arranged by Nelson Riddle
Recorded: March 1, 1960
TWIN SOLILOQUIES *(Wonder How It Feels)*
(Richard Rodgers-Oscar Hammerstein II)
With Keely Smith
Arranged by Nelson Riddle
Orchestra conducted by Morris Stoloff
Recorded: July 24, 1963
TWO HEARTS ARE BETTER THAN ONE
(Johnny Mercer-Jerome Kern)
Columbia Records
Arranged by Axel Stordahl
Recorded: February 3, 1946
TWO HEARTS, TWO KISSES
(Henry Stone-Otis Williams)
Capitol Records
With The Nuggets
Arranged by Dave Cavanaugh
Recorded: March 7, 1955
TWO IN LOVE
(Meredith Willson)
Victor Records
With Tommy Dorsey and his Orchestra
Recorded: August 19, 1941
UNTIL THE REAL THING COMES ALONG
(Sammy Cahn-Saul Chaplin)
Qwest Records
Arranged by Sam Nestico
Orchestra conducted by Quincy Jones
Recorded: April 13, 1984
VIOLETS FOR YOUR FURS
(Matt Dennis-Tom Adair)
Victor Records
With Tommy Dorsey and his Orchestra
Arranged by Heinie Beau
Recorded: August 19, 1941
VIOLETS FOR YOUR FURS
(Matt Dennis-Tom Adair)
Victor Records
Arranged by Heinie Beau
Recorded: September 26, 1941
VIOLETS FOR YOUR FURS
(Matt Dennis-Tom Adair)
Capitol Records
Arranged by George Siravo
Orchestra conducted by Nelson Riddle
Recorded: November 5, 1953
WAIT FOR ME *(Johnny Concho Theme)*
(Nelson Riddle-Dok Stanford)
Capitol Records
With vocal chorus
Arranged by Nelson Riddle
Recorded: April 5, 1956
WAIT TILL YOU SEE HER
(Richard Rodgers-Lorenz Hart)
Capitol Records
With The Hollywood String Quartet
Arranged by Nelson Riddle
Recorded: April 4, 1956
WALK AWAY
(Paul Anka-Sammy Cahn)
Reprise Records
Arranged by Gordon Jenkins
Recorded: June 22, 1973

WALKIN' IN THE SUNSHINE
(Bob Merrill)
Columbia Records
Arranged by George Siravo or Heinie Beau
Orchestra conducted by Axel Stordahl
Recorded: January 7, 1952

WANDERING
(Gayle Caldwell)
Reprise Records
Arranged by Don Costa
Orchestra conducted by Bill Miller
Recorded: November 14, 1968

WAS THE LAST TIME I SAW YOU
(The Last Time)
(E. Osser-M. Goetschius)
V-Disc recording
Columbia Records
Arranged by Axel Stordahl
Recorded: November 7, 1945

WATCH WHAT HAPPENS
(Norman Gimbel-Michel Legrand)
Reprise Records
Arranged by Don Costa
Recorded: February 24, 1969

WATERTOWN
(Bob Gaudio-Jake Holmes)
Reprise Records
Arranged by Charles Calello
Recorded: August 26, 1969

WAVE
(Antonio Carlos Jobim)
Reprise Records
With Antonio Carlos Jobim
Arranged by Eumir Deodato
Orchestra conducted by Morris Stoloff
Recorded: February 11, 1969

WE HATE TO LEAVE
((Sammy Cahn-Jule Styne)
Film recording for: 'Anchors Aweigh'
Metro-Goldwyn-Mayer
With Gene Kelly
Arranged by Axel Stordahl
Orchestra conducted by George Stoll
Recorded: June 13, 1944

WE JUST COULDN'T SAY GOODBYE
(Harry Woods)
Columbia Records
Arranged by John Guarnieri
Recorded: October 24, 1947

WE KISS IN A SHADOW
(Richard Rodgers-Oscar Hammerstein II)
Columbia Records
Arranged by Axel Stordahl
Recorded: March 2, 1951

WE OPEN IN VENICE
(Cole Porter)
Reprise Records
With Dean Martin and Sammy Davis, Jr.
Arranged by Billy May
Orchestra conducted by Morris Stoloff
Recorded: July 10, 1963

WE THREE
(Dick Robertson-Nelson Cogane-Sammy Mysels)
Victor Records
With Tommy Dorsey and his Orchestra
Arranged by Sy Oliver
Recorded: August 29, 1940

WE WISH YOU THE MERRIEST
(Les Brown)
Reprise Records
With Bing Crosby and Fred Waring and his Pennsylvanians
Arranged by Jack Halloran and Harry Betts
Orchestra Conducted by Fred Waring
Recorded: June 19, 1964

WEEP THEY WILL
(Carl Fischer-Bill Carey)
Capitol Records
Arranged by Nelson Riddle
Recorded: October 17, 1955

WELL DID YOU EVAH?
(Cole Porter)
Capitol Records
With Bing Crosby
Arranged by Skip Martin
Orchestra conducted by Johnny Green
Recorded: January 17, 1956

WE'LL BE TOGETHER AGAIN
(Frankie Laine-Carl Fischer)
Capitol Records
Arranged by Nelson Riddle
Recorded: January 16, 1956

WE'LL GATHER LILACS
(Ivor Novello)
Reprise Records
Arranged by Robert Farnon
Recorded: June 14, 1962

WE'LL MEET AGAIN
(Hughie Charles-Ross Parker)
Reprise Records
Arranged by Robert Farnon
Recorded: June 14, 1962, London

WHAT A FUNNY GIRL *(You Used To Be)*
(Bob Gaudio-Jake Holmes)
Reprise Records
Arranged by Charles Calello
Recorded: August 27, 1969

WHAT ARE YOU DOING THE REST OF YOUR LIFE?
(Alan & Marilyn Bergman-Michel Legrand)
Reprise Records
Arranged by Don Costa
Recorded: May 21, 1974

WHAT DO I CARE FOR A DAME?
(Richard Rodgers-Lorenz Hart)
Capitol Records
With vocal chorus
Arranged by Nelson Riddle
Orchestra conducted by Morris Stoloff
Recorded: September 25, 1957

WHAT IS THIS THING CALLED LOVE?
(Cole Porter)
Capitol Records
Arranged by Nelson Riddle
Recorded: February 16, 1955

WHAT MAKES THE SUNSET?
(Sammy Cahn-Jule Styne)
Film recording for: 'Anchors Aweigh'
Metro-Goldwyn-Mayer
Arranged by Axel Stordahl
Orchestra conducted by George Stoll
Recorded: June 30, 1944

WHAT MAKES THE SUNSET?
(Sammy Cahn-Jule Styne)
Columbia Records
Arranged by Axel Stordahl
Recorded: December 1, 1944

WHAT NOW MY LOVE?
(Gilbert Becaud-Carl Sigman)
Reprise Records
With vocal chorus
Arranged by Ernie Freeman
Recorded: November 17, 1966

WHAT NOW MY LOVE?
(Gilbert Becaud-Carl Sigman)
Capitol Records
With Aretha Franklin
Arranged by Don Costa
Orchestra conducted by Patrick Williams
Recorded: July 6, 1993

WHAT TIME DOES THE NEXT MIRACLE LEAVE?
(Gordon Jenkins)
Reprise Records
With the Los Angeles Philharmonic Symphony Orchestra and chorus
Arranged by Gordon Jenkins
Recorded: December 18, 1979

WHATEVER HAPPENED TO CHRISTMAS?
(Jim Webb)
Reprise Records
With vocal chorus
Arranged by Don Costa
Recorded: July 24, 1968

WHAT'LL I DO?
(Irving Berlin)
Columbia Records
Arranged by Axel Stordahl
Recorded: October 29, 1947

WHAT'LL I DO?
(Irving Berlin)
Reprise Records
Arranged by Gordon Jenkins
Recorded: January 17, 1962

WHAT'S NEW?
(Bob Haggart-Johnny Burke)
Capitol Records
Arranged by Nelson Riddle
Recorded: June 24, 1958

WHAT'S NOW IS NOW
(Bob Gaudio-Jake Holmes)
Reprise Records
Arranged by Joseph Scott
Recorded: August 26, 1969

WHAT'S WRONG WITH ME?
(Nacio Herb Brown-Edward Heyman)
Film recording for: 'The Kissing Bandit'
Metro-Goldwyn-Mayer
Arranged by Leo Arnaud
Orchestra conducted by George Stoll
Recorded: February 26, 1948

WHEN DAYLIGHT DAWNS
(Bea Huberdo)
Victor Records
With Tommy Dorsey and his Orchestra
Recorded: January 30, 1941 (Radio aircheck)

WHEN I LOST YOU
(Irving Berlin)
Reprise Records
Arranged by Gordon Jenkins
Recorded: January 15, 1962

WHEN I STOP LOVING YOU
(Cates-Copland-Greene)
Capitol Records
With vocal chorus
Arranged by Nelson Riddle
Recorded: August 23, 1954

WHEN I TAKE MY SUGAR TO TEA
(Sammy Fain-Irving Kahal-Pierre Norman)
Reprise Records
Arranged by Johnny Mandel
Recorded: December 21, 1960

WHEN I'M NOT NEAR THE GIRL I LOVE
(Yip Harburg-Burton Lane)
Reprise Records
Arranged by Nelson Riddle
Orchestra conducted by Morris Stoloff
Recorded: July 18, 1963

WHEN IS SOMETIME?
(Johnny Burke-Jimmy Van Heusen)
Columbia Records
Arranged by Axel Stordahl
Recorded: December 30, 1947

WHEN NO ONE CARES
(Sammy Cahn-Jimmy Van Heusen)
Capitol Records
Arranged by Gordon Jenkins
Orchestra conducted by Nelson Riddle
Recorded: May 14, 1959

WHEN SLEEPY STARS BEGIN TO FALL
(Sibyl Allen)
Victor Records
With Tommy Dorsey and his Orchestra
Recorded: February 27, 1941 (Radio aircheck)

WHEN SOMEBODY LOVES YOU
(Smith-Greenfield-Keller)
Reprise Records
With vocal chorus
Arranged by Ernie Freeman
Recorded: April 14, 1965

WHEN THE SUN GOES DOWN
(Walter O'Kieffe-Orton)
Columbia Records
With The Modernaires
Arranged by Axel Stordahl
Recorded: February 23, 1950

WHEN THE WIND WAS GREEN
(Don Hunt)
Reprise Records
Arranged by Gordon Jenkins
Recorded: April 14, 1965

WHEN THE WORLD WAS YOUNG
(Phillippe Gerard-Johnny Mercer)
Capitol Records
Arranged by Axel Stordahl
Recorded: September 11, 1961

WHEN YOU AWAKE
(Henry Nemo)
Victor Records
With Tommy Dorsey and his Orchestra
Arranged by Deane Kincaide
Recorded: September 9, 1940

WHEN YOU AWAKE
(Henry Nemo)
Columbia Records
Arranged by Axel Stordahl
Recorded: November 5, 1947

WHEN YOUR LOVER HAS GONE
(Einar A. Swan)
Columbia Records
Arranged by Axel Stordahl
Recorded: December 19, 1944

WHEN YOUR LOVER HAS GONE
(Einar A. Swan)
Capitol Records
Arranged by Nelson Riddle
Recorded: February 17, 1955

WHEN YOU'RE SMILING
(Larry Shay-Mark Fisher-Joe Goodwin)
Columbia Records
Arranged by George Siravo
Recorded: April 24, 1950

WHEN YOU'RE SMILING
(Larry Shay-Mark Fisher-Joe Goodwin)
Film recording for: 'Meet Danny Wilson'
Universal International
Arranged by Joseph Gershenson
Recorded: June 13, 1951

WHEN YOU'RE SMILING
(Larry Shay-Mark Fisher-Joe Goodwin)
Capitol Records
Arranged by Nelson Riddle
Recorded: August 22, 1960

WHERE ARE YOU?
(Jimmy McHugh-Harold Adamson)
Capitol Records
Arranged by Gordon Jenkins
Recorded: May 1, 1957

WHERE DO YOU GO?
(Alec Wilder)
Capitol Records
Arranged by Gordon Jenkins
Recorded: March 26, 1959

WHERE DO YOU KEEP YOUR HEART?
(Al Stillman-Fred Ahlert)
Victor Records
With Tommy Dorsey and his Orchestra
Recorded: May 23, 1940

WHERE DOES LOVE BEGIN?
(Sammy Cahn-Jule Styne)
Film recording for: 'Step Lively'
RKO Pictures
With Anne Jeffreys
Arranged by Axel Stordahl
Orchestra conducted by Constantin Bakaleinikoff
Recorded: February 21, 1944

WHERE DOES LOVE BEGIN? *(Finale)*
(Sammy Cahn-Jule Styne)
Film recording for: 'Step Lively'
RKO Pictures
Arranged by Ken Darby
With George Murphy, Gloria DeHaven and Chorus
Orchestra conducted by Constantin Bakaleinikoff
Recorded: February 25, 1944

WHERE IS MY BESS?
(George Gershwin-Ira Gershwin-Dubois Heyward)
V-Disc recording
Columbia Records
Arranged by Axel Stordahl
Recorded: January 16, 1946

WHERE IS MY BESS?
(George Gershwin-Ira Gershwin-Dubois Heyward)
Columbia Records
Arranged by Axel Stordahl
Recorded: February 24, 1946

WHERE IS THE ONE?
(Alec Wilder-Edwin Finkel)
Columbia Records
Arranged by Axel Stordahl
Recorded: December 30, 1947

WHERE IS THE ONE?
(Alec Wilder-Edwin Finkel)
Capitol Records
Arranged by Gordon Jenkins
Recorded: April 10, 1957

WHERE OR WHEN
(Richard Rodgers-Lorenz Hart)
Columbia Records
With The Ken Lane Singers
Arranged by Axel Stordahl
Recorded: January 29, 1945

WHERE OR WHEN
(Richard Rodgers-Lorenz Hart)
Capitol Records
Featuring Bill Miller, piano
Arranged by Nelson Riddle
Recorded: September 11, 1958

WHERE OR WHEN
(Richard Rodgers-Lorenz Hart)
Reprise Records
With Count Basie and his Orchestra (Live recording)
Arranged by Quincy Jones and Billy Byers
Recorded: January 26-February 1, 1966 (Las Vegas)

WHERE OR WHEN
(Richard Rodgers-Lorenz Hart)
Capitol Records
With Steve Lawrence and Eydie Gorme
Arranged by Billy Byers
Orchestra conducted by Patrick Williams
Recorded: October 14, 1993

WHILE THE ANGELUS WAS RINGING
(Dick Manning-Jean Willard)
Columbia Records
Arranged by Axel Stordahl
Recorded: December 19, 1948

WHISPERING
(John Schonberger-Richard Coburn-Vincent Rose)
Victor Records
With Tommy Dorsey and his Orchestra
Featuring The Pied Pipers
Arranged by Fred Stulce
Recorded: June 13, 1940

WHITE CHRISTMAS
(Irving Berlin)
Columbia Records
With The Bobby Tucker Singers
Arranged by Axel Stordahl
Recorded: November 14, 1944

WHITE CHRISTMAS
(Irving Berlin)
Columbia Records
Arranged by Axel Stordahl
Recorded: December 28, 1947

WHITE CHRISTMAS
(Irving Berlin)
Capitol Records
With vocal chorus
Arranged by Nelson Riddle
Recorded: August 23, 1954

WHO
(O. Harbach-O. Hammerstein II-J. Kern)
Victor Records
With Tommy Dorsey and his Orchestra
Recording date unknown (1940-1942)
Radio aircheck

WHO TOLD YOU I CARED?
(Richard Whiting-Bert Reisfeld)
Columbia Records
With Harry James and his Orchestra
Arranged by Andy Gibson
Recorded: October 13, 1939

WHO WANTS TO BE A MILLIONAIRE?
(Cole Porter)
Capitol Records
With Celeste Holm
Arranged by Conrad Salinger
Orchestra conducted by Johnny Green
Recorded: January 20, 1956

WHOSE BABY ARE YOU
(Sammy Cahn-Jule Styne)
Film recording for: 'It Happened In Brooklyn'
Metro-Goldwyn-Mayer
Arranged by Axel Stordahl
Orchestra conducted by Johnny Green
Recorded: July 18, 1946

WHY CAN'T YOU BEHAVE?
(Cole Porter)
Columbia Records
With The Phil Moore Four
Arranged by Phil Moore
Recorded: December 15, 1948

WHY REMIND ME?
(Wilner-Doris Tauber)
Columbia Records
With the Modernaires
Arranged by Axel Stordahl
Recorded: October 30, 1949

WHY SHOULD I CRY OVER YOU?
(Miller-Conn)
Capitol Records
Arranged by Nelson Riddle
Recorded: December 8, 1953

WHY SHOULDN'T I?
(Cole Porter)
Columbia Records
Arranged by Axel Stordahl
Recorded: December 7, 1945

WHY SHOULDN'T IT HAPPEN TO US?
(Mann Holiner-Alberta Nichols)
Columbia Records
Arranged by Axel Stordahl
Recorded: October 15, 1946

WHY TRY TO CHANGE ME NOW?
(Cy Coleman-Joseph McCarthy)
Columbia Records
Arranged by Percy Faith
Recorded: September 17, 1952

WHY TRY TO CHANGE ME NOW?
(Cy Coleman-Joseph McCarthy)
Capitol Records
Arranged by Gordon Jenkins
Recorded: March 24, 1959

WHY WAS I BORN?
(Jerome Kern-Oscar Hammerstein II)
Columbia Records
Arranged by Axel Stordahl
Recorded: December 28, 1947

WILLOW WEEP FOR ME
(Ann Ronnell)
Capitol Records
Arranged by Nelson Riddle
Orchestra conducted by Felix Slatkin
Recorded: May 29, 1958

WINCHESTER CATHEDRAL
(Geoff Stevens)
Reprise Records
Arranged by Ernie Freeman
Recorded: November 17, 1966

WINNERS
(Joe Raposo)
Reprise Records
Arranged by Don Costa
Orchestra conducted by Gordon Jenkins
Recorded: June 21, 1973

WINTER WONDERLAND
(R. Smith-F. Bernard)
Columbia Records
With The Jeff Alexander Chorus
Arranged by Jeff Alexander
Recorded: October 26, 1949 (Radio aircheck)

WITCHCRAFT
(Cy Coleman-Carolyn Leigh)
Capitol Records
Arranged by Nelson Riddle
Recorded: May 20, 1957

WITCHCRAFT
(Cy Coleman-Carolyn Leigh)
Reprise Records
Arranged by Nelson Riddle
Recorded: April 30, 1963

WITCHCRAFT
(Cy Coleman-Carolyn Leigh)
Capitol Records
With Anita Baker
Arranged by Nelson Riddle
Orchestra conducted by Patrick Williams
Recorded: July 9, 1993

WITH EVERY BREATH I TAKE
(Leo Robin-Ralph Rainger)
Capitol Records
With The Hollywood String Quartet
Arranged by Nelson Riddle
Recorded: April 5, 1956

WITHOUT A SONG
(Vincent Youmans-Billy Rose-Edward Eliscu)
Victor Records
With Tommy Dorsey and his Orchestra
Arranged by Sy Oliver
Recorded: January 20, 1941

WITHOUT A SONG
(Vincent Youmans-Billy Rose-Edward Eliscu)
V-Disc recording
Columbia Records
Arranged by Axel Stordahl
Recorded: October 24, 1945

WITHOUT A SONG
(Vincent Youmans-Billy Rose-Edward Eliscu)
Reprise Records
Arranged by Sy Oliver
Recorded: May 2, 1961

WITHOUT A SONG
(Vincent Youmans-Billy Rose-Edward Eliscu)
Reprise Records
With sextet accompaniment (Live recording)
Arranged by Neal Hefti and Billy May
Recorded: June 5, 1962 (Paris)

WIVES AND LOVERS
(Burt Bacharach-Hal David)
Reprise Records
With Count Basie and his Orchestra
Arranged by Quincy Jones
Recorded: June 12, 1964

WORLD WAR NONE
(Gordon Jenkins)
Reprise Records
With The Los Angeles Philharmonic
Symphony Orchestra
Arranged by Gordon Jenkins
Recorded: December 18, 1979

WRAP YOUR TROUBLES IN DREAMS
(Ted Kohler-Billy Moll-Harry Barris)
Capitol Records
Arranged by Nelson Riddle
Recorded: April 7, 1954

YA BETTER STOP
(MacIntyre-Ferre)
Capitol Records
Arranged by Nelson Riddle
Recorded: December 8, 1953

YEARNING
(B. Davis-J. Burke)
Victor Records
With Tommy Dorsey and his Orchestra
with band chorus
Recorded: November 7, 1940 (Radio aircheck)

YELLOW DAYS
(Alvaro Carillo-Alan Bernstein)
Reprise Records
With Duke Ellington and his Orchestra
Arranged by Billy May
Recorded: December 11, 1967

YES INDEED
(Sy Oliver)
Capitol Records
Arranged by Billy May
Recorded: March 21, 1961

YES INDEEDY
(Roger Edens-Betty Comden-Adolph Green)
Film recording for: 'Take Me Out To The Ball Game'
Metro-Goldwyn-Mayer
With Gene Kelly, Jules Munshin and Chorus
Arranged by Robert Tucker
Orchestra conducted by Adolph Deutsch
Recorded: July 22, 1948

YES SIR, THAT'S MY BABY
(Gus Kahn-Walter Donaldson)
Reprise Records
Arranged by Nelson Riddle
Recorded: May 11, 1966

YESTERDAY
(John Lennon-Paul McCartney)
Reprise Records
Arranged by Don Costa
Recorded: February 20, 1969

YESTERDAYS
(Jerome Kern-Otto Harbach)
Reprise Records
Arranged by Don Costa
Recorded: November 20, 1961

YOU AND I
(Meredith Wilson)
Victor Records
With Tommy Dorsey and his Orchestra
Arranged by Sy Oliver
Recorded: June 27, 1941

YOU AND ME (We Wanted It All)
(Carol Bayer-Sager-Peter Allen)
Reprise Records
Arranged by Don Costa
Recorded: August 20, 1979

YOU AND THE NIGHT AND THE MUSIC
(Arthur Schwartz-Howard Dietz)
Reprise Records
Arranged by Johnny Mandel
Recorded: December 21, 1960

YOU ARE THE SUNSHINE OF MY LIFE
(Stevie Wonder)
Reprise Records
Arranged by Don Costa
Recorded: May 24, 1974

YOU ARE THE SUNSHINE OF MY LIFE
(Stevie Wonder)
Reprise Records
With Woody Herman and the Young Thundering Herd (Live recording)
Arranged by Don Costa
Orchestra conducted by Bill Miller
Recorded: October 13, 1974 (New York City)

YOU ARE THERE
(Harry Suckman-Paul Francis Webster)
Reprise Records
Arranged by Gordon Jenkins
Recorded: June 29, 1967

YOU ARE TOO BEAUTIFUL
(Richard Rodgers-Lorenz Hart)
Columbia Records
Arranged by Axel Stordahl
Recorded: August 22, 1945

YOU ARE TOO BEAUTIFUL
(Richard Rodgers-Lorenz Hart)
V-Disc recording
Columbia Records
Arranged by Axel Stordahl
Recorded: April 24, 1946

YOU BROUGHT A NEW KIND OF LOVE TO ME
(Sammy Fain-Irving Kahal-Pierre Norman)
V-Disc recording
Columbia Records
Arranged by Axel Stordahl
Recorded: October 3, 1945

YOU BROUGHT A NEW KIND OF LOVE TO ME
(Sammy Fain-Irving Kahal-Pierre Norman)
Capitol Records
Arranged by Nelson Riddle
Recorded: January 9, 1956

YOU BROUGHT A NEW KIND OF LOVE TO ME
(Sammy Fain-Irving Kahal-Pierre Norman)
Reprise Records
Arranged by Nelson Riddle
Recorded: February 21, 1963

YOU CAN TAKE MY WORD FOR IT BABY
(Ticker Freeman-Irving Taylor)
Columbia Records
With the Page Cavanaugh Trio
Arranged by Page Cavanaugh
Recorded: December 15, 1946

YOU DON'T REMIND ME
(Cole Porter)
Columbia Records
Arranged by Axel Stordahl
Recorded: November 16, 1950

YOU DO SOMETHING TO ME
(Cole Porter)
Columbia Records
Arranged by George Siravo
Recorded: April 14, 1950

YOU DO SOMETHING TO ME
(Cole Porter)
Columbia Records
Arranged by Nelson Riddle
Recorded: August 22, 1960

YOU FORGOT ALL THE WORDS
(Bernie Wayne-E.H. Jay)
Capitol Records
Arranged by Nelson Riddle
Recorded: October 17, 1955

YOU GO TO MY HEAD
(Fred Coots-Haven Gillespie)
Columbia Records
Arranged by Axel Stordahl
Recorded: July 30, 1945

YOU GO TO MY HEAD
(Fred Coots-Haven Gillespie)
Capitol Records
Arranged by Nelson Riddle
Recorded: March 1, 1960

YOU GOT THE BEST OF ME
(Joy Font)
Victor Records
With Tommy Dorsey and his Orchestra
Featuring Connie Haines and The Pied Pipers
Recorded: January 16, 1941 (Radio aircheck)

YOU LUCKY PEOPLE YOU
(Johnny Burke-Jimmy Van Heusen)
Victor Records
With Tommy Dorsey and his Orchestra
Arranged by Sy Oliver
Recorded: January 15, 1941

YOU MAKE ME FEEL SO YOUNG
(Josef Myrow-Mack Gordon)
Capitol Records
Arranged by Nelson Riddle
Recorded: January 9, 1956

YOU MAKE ME FEEL SO YOUNG
(Josef Myrow-Mack Gordon)
Reprise Records
With Count Basie and his Orchestra (Live recording)
Arranged by Quincy Jones and Billy Byers
Recorded: January 26-February 1, 1966 (Las Vegas)

YOU MAKE ME FEEL SO YOUNG
(Josef Myrow-Mack Gordon)
Capitol Records
With Charles Aznavour
Arranged by Quincy Jones
Orchestra conducted by Patrick Williams
Recorded: July 6, 1993

YOU MIGHT HAVE BELONGED TO ANOTHER
(Pat West-Lucille Harmon)
Victor Records
With Tommy Dorsey and his Orchestra
Featuring Connie Haines and The Pied Pipers
Arranged by Axel Stordahl
Recorded: January 6, 1941

YOU, MY LOVE
(Jimmy Van Heusen-Harry Gordon)
Film recording for: 'Young At Heart'
Warner Bros.
Arranged by Ray Heindorf
Recorded: July 13-14, 1954

YOU, MY LOVE
(Jimmy Van Heusen-Harry Gordon)
Film recording for: 'Young At Heart'
Warner Bros.
With Doris Day
Arranged by Ray Heindorf
Recorded: August 25, 1954

YOU, MY LOVE
(Jimmy Van Heusen-Harry Gordon)
Capitol Records
Arranged by Nelson Riddle
Recorded: September 23, 1954

YOU NEVER HAD IT SO GOOD
(Sammy Cahn-Jimmy Van Heusen)
Reprise Records
With Bing Crosby and Fred Waring and his Pennsylvanians
Arranged by Jack Halloran
Orchestra conducted by Fred Waring
Recorded: February 4, 1964

YOU TURNED MY WORLD AROUND
(Bert Kaempfert-Rehbein-Carnes-Ellington)
Reprise Records
Arranged by Don Costa
Recorded: May 8, 1974

YOU WILL BE MY MUSIC
(Joe Raposo)
Reprise Records
Arranged by Gordon Jenkins
Recorded: June 4, 1973

YOU'D BE SO EASY TO LOVE
(Cole Porter)
Reprise Records
Arranged by Johnny Mandel
Recorded: December 20, 1960

YOU'D BE SO NICE TO COME HOME TO
(Cole Porter)
Capitol Records
Arranged by Nelson Riddle
Recorded: November 28, 1956

YOU'LL ALWAYS BE THE ONE I LOVE
(Al Freeman-Sunny Skylar)
Capitol Records
Arranged by Nelson Riddle
Recorded: December 11, 1957

YOU'LL GET YOURS
(Jimmy Van Heusen-Dok Stanford)
Capitol Records
Arranged by Nelson Riddle
Recorded: September 13, 1955

YOU'LL KNOW WHEN IT HAPPENS
(Carmen Lombardo-John Loeb)
Columbia Records
Arranged by Axel Stordahl
Recorded: July 24, 1946

YOU'LL NEVER KNOW
(Mack Gordon-Harry Warren)
Columbia Records
With The Bobby Tucker Singers
Choral arrangement by Alec Wilder
Recorded: June 7, 1943

YOU'LL NEVER WALK ALONE
(Richard Rodgers-Oscar Hammerstein II)
Columbia Records
With The Ken Lane Singers
Arranged by Axel Stordahl
Recorded: May 1, 1945

YOU'LL NEVER WALK ALONE
(Richard Rodgers-Oscar Hammerstein II)
Reprise Records
Arranged by Nelson Riddle
Recorded: February 19, 1963

YOUNG AT HEART
(Johnny Richards-Carolyn Leigh)
Capitol Records
Arranged by Nelson Riddle
Recorded: December 9, 1953

YOUNG AT HEART (Opening and Finale)
(Johnny Richards-Carolyn Leigh)
Film recording for: 'Young At Heart'
Warner Bros.
Arranged by Nelson Riddle
Orchestra conducted by Ray Heindorf
Recorded: July 13-14, 1954

YOUNG AT HEART
(Johnny Richards-Carolyn Leigh)
Reprise Records
Arranged by Nelson Riddle
Recorded: April 29, 1963

YOUNGER THAN SPRINGTIME
(Richard Rodgers-Oscar Hammerstein II)
Reprise Records
Arranged by Billy Strange
Recorded: September 20, 1967

YOUR LOVE FOR ME
(Ross Parker)
Capitol Records
Arranged by Nelson Riddle
Recorded: December 3, 1956

YOU'RE A LUCKY FELLOW MR. SMITH
(Raye-Prince-Black)
Reprise Records
With Fred Waring and His Pennsylvanians
Arranged by Jack Halloran
Orchestra conducted by Fred Waring
Recorded: January 2, 1964

YOU'RE A SWEETHEART
(Harold Adamson-Jimmy McHugh)
Film recording for: 'Meet Danny Wilson'
Universal International
Featuring Ken Lane, piano
Arranged by Joseph Gershenson
Recorded: June 13, 1951

YOU'RE AWFUL
(Roger Edens-Betty Comden-Adolph Green)
Film recording for: 'On The Town'
Metro-Goldwyn-Mayer
With Betty Garrett
Arranged by Saul Chaplin
Orchestra conducted by Lennie Hayton
Recorded: March 24, 1949

YOU'RE BREAKING MY HEART ALL OVER AGAIN
(J. Cavanaugh-J.Redmond-A. Altman)
Victor Records
With Tommy Dorsey and his Orchestra
Arranged by Deane Kincaide
Recorded: September 17, 1940

YOU'RE CHEATIN' YOURSELF (If You're Cheatin' On Me)
(Al Hoffman-Dick Manning)
Capitol Records
Arranged by Nelson Riddle
Recorded: May 20, 1957

YOU'RE DRIVING ME CRAZY
(Walter Donaldson)
Reprise Records
Arranged by Nelson Riddle
Recorded: May 11, 1966

YOU'RE GETTING TO BE A HABIT WITH ME
(Harry Warren-Al Dubin)
Capitol Records
Arranged by Nelson Riddle
Recorded: January 10, 1956

YOU'RE GONNA HEAR FROM ME
(Andre & Dory Previn)
Reprise Records
Arranged by Ernie Freeman
Recorded: November 18, 1966

YOU'RE LONELY AND I'M LONELY
(Irving Berlin)
Victor Records
With The Dorsey Sentimentalists
Arranged by Axel Stordahl
Recorded: April 23, 1940

YOU'RE MY GIRL
(Sammy Cahn-Jule Styne)
Columbia Records
Arranged by Axel Stordahl
Recorded: October 19, 1947

YOU'RE NOBODY 'TIL SOMEBODY LOVES YOU
(L. Stock-R. Morgan-James Cavanaugh)
Reprise Records
Arranged by Billy May
Recorded: May 23, 1961

YOU'RE NOBODY 'TIL SOMEBODY LOVES YOU
(L. Stock-R. Morgan-James Cavanaugh)
Reprise Records
With sextet accompaniment (Live recording)
Arranged by Neal Hefti and Billy May
Recorded: June 5, 1962 (Paris)

YOU'RE ON YOUR OWN
(Harold Adamson-Jimmy McHugh)
Film recording for: 'Higher And Higher'
RKO Pictures
With Dooley Wilson, Mel Torme, Marcy McGuire, Michelle Morgan,
Victor Borge and Cast
Arranged by Gene Rose and Axel Stordahl
Orchestra conducted by Constantin Bakaleinikoff
Recorded: August 24, 1943

YOU'RE PART OF MY HEART
(Virginia Sloane)
Victor Records
With Tommy Dorsey and his Orchestra
Featuring Connie Haines and The Pied Pipers
Recorded: January 2, 1941 (Radio aircheck)

YOU'RE SENSATIONAL
(Cole Porter)
Capitol Records
Arranged by Nelson Riddle
Orchestra conducted by Johnny Green
Recorded: January 20, 1956

YOU'RE SENSATIONAL
(Cole Porter)
Capitol Records
Arranged by Nelson Riddle
Recorded: April 5, 1956

YOU'RE SO RIGHT (For What's Wrong In My Life)
(Teddy Randazzo-Vincent Pike)
Reprise Records
Arranged by Gordon Jenkins
Recorded: August 20, 1973

YOU'RE STEPPING ON MY TOES
(Robert Terry)
Victor Records
With Tommy Dorsey and his Orchestra
Featuring The Pied Pipers
Recorded: January 9, 1941 (Radio aircheck)

YOU'RE THE ONE
(Ned Washington-Victor Young)
Columbia Records
Featuring Stan Freeman, piano
Arranged by Axel Stordahl
Recorded: January 16, 1951

YOU'VE GOT A HOLD ON ME
(Frederick Lowe-Alan J. Lerner)
V-Disc recording
Columbia Records
Arranged by Axel Stordahl
Recorded: November 21, 1943

YOURS IS MY HEART ALONE
(Franz Lehar-Smith-Graham)
Victor Records
With Tommy Dorsey and his Orchestra
Arranged by Axel Stordahl
Recorded: April 10, 1940

ZING WENT THE STRINGS OF MY HEART
(James Hanley)
Reprise Records
Arranged by Johnny Mandel
Recorded: December 21, 1960

Index

CREDITS